Leisure and Recreation *for* Vocational A level

formerly Advanced GNVQ

Tony Outhart,
Lindsey Taylor, Ray Barker
And Neil Procter

Series Editor: Tony Outhart

Published by HarperCollins*Publishers* Limited
77-85 Fulham Palace Road,
Hammersmith
London
W6 8JB

www.**Collins**Education.com
On-line support for schools and colleges

First published 2000
Reprinted 2001 (twice)

ISBN 00 00 329110 3

British Cataloguing in Publication Data.
A cataloguing record for this publication is available from the British Library.

Series commissioned by Charis Evans
Series designed by DSM Partnership
Layouts and typesetting by Martin Harris Creative Media
Edited by Jack Messenger
Cover designed by Patricia Briggs
Cover picture by The Image Bank
Picture research by Thelma Gilbert
Illustrations and cartoons by Barking Dog Art
Index by Julie Rimington
Project managed by Kay Wright and Sue Chapple
Production by Emma Lloyd-Jones
Printed and bound by Scotprint

Contents

Acknowledgements

The authors would like to thank everybody involved in supporting them during the writing and production of this book.In particular, the authors wish to thank Mintel for access to their online leisure reports.

The authors and Publisher would like to thank the following for permission to reproduce photographs and other material:

Collections: Neil Calladine (p. 3);
Nigel Hawkins (p. 50);
Robin Weaver (p. 60);
Allsport: p. 226;
Mike Hewitt (pp. 145, 229);
Ross Kinnaird (p.148);
Clive Mason (p. 173);
Stu Forster (pp. 187, 203);
Mark Thompson (pp.192, 397);
Ross Kinnaird (p. 205);
Billy Stickland (p. 207);
Shaun Botterill (pp. 207, 219);
Gary M Prior (p. 208);
Stephen Munday (p.209);
Al Bello (p. 222);
Clive Brunskill (p. 228);
Simon Bruty (p. 229)
Brewers Fayre: p. 360
British Olympic Association: p. 187
British Sports Trust/Central Council of
Physical Recreation:
Butlins: pp. 16, 338
Center Parcs: p.17
Gena Davies (p. 119);
Brian Shuel (p. 126); Graham Burns (p. 165)
Empics Ltd: John Marsh (p. 411);
Steve Mitchell (p. 234)
English Federation of Disability Sport: p.187
English Heritage: p. 35
Football Association: p. 215
Helen Evans: p. 293
Holmes Place: pp. 163, 322
Mirror Group Newspapers: p. 210
National Trust Photographic Library/
Chris King: p. 315
P & O Cruises : p. 330
Premier League: p. 216
Photodisc: p88,
REX Features: p. 298
Robert Harding Picture Library: pp. 135, 136, 245;
Jon Gardey (p.178): Robert Francis (p. 264)
Sally & Richard Greenhill: Sally Greenhill (pp. 67, 233); Richard Greenhill: (p.264)
Sport England: p. 34
Sport Scotland: p. 34
Sports Council for Wales: p. 34
Tony Stone Images: pp.102;
Paul Kenward (pp. 89,165)
UK Sport: p. 34
V&A Museum: p. 294
Welcome Host: p. 318
Zoom/Allsport: p. 173, 183p,

Every effort has been made to contact copyright holders, but if any any have been inadvertently overlooked, the publisher will be pleased to make the necessary arrangements at the first opportunity.

Introduction

Vocational A levels

A **Vocational A level** is a qualification of the same standard as a traditional A level but with a different focus. It used to be called an Advanced GNVQ, which stands for **General National Vocational Qualification**.

The Vocational A level qualification relates to the world of work and employment. In contrast to **GCSEs** and traditional **A levels**, which are based on knowledge and understanding of academic subjects, Vocational A levels relate to the ways in which people earn their living in leisure and recreation, in travel and tourism, in hospitality and catering, and in many other areas of work.

Vocational A levels introduce you to a general area of work rather than to a particular job. You may have heard of NVQs (**National Vocational Qualifications**). These relate to the skills you need to undertake particular jobs. A Vocational A level, on the other hand, covers a broad area of work and is designed for people who are usually studying full-time at school or college, and usually aged between 16 and 19.

How will I study?

If you have achieved an Intermediate GNVQ, you should already have a good idea of what it is like to study a Vocational A level. However, if you have taken GCSEs, you will find that studying for a Vocational A level is different in several ways from GCSE work, and from studying for traditional A levels.

First, as a Vocational A level student, you will take more responsibility for your own learning, for planning your work, for making your own investigations, and for keeping proper records of what you have done. Your tutor will play an important part in teaching you some of what you need to know and in helping you to plan your work, to keep to your plan and to respond to problems and setbacks. However, in the end you have to take responsibility for your programme of study, just as you will have to take responsibility for your work when you are employed in the future.

Secondly, much of your learning will be acquired through carrying out your own enquiries and investigations, often in connection with assignments agreed with your tutor. These investigations can involve a wide range of tasks and activities, drawing on several different sources of information. For example, you may:

- do research in libraries and resource centres
- visit work places and talk to people currently working in the leisure and recreation industry
- learn from visits by local employers and business people
- carry out surveys of peopleís activities, preferences and opinions
- study company brochures and gather information from press and television reports
- study particular examples of people, places and firms that relate to your work
- learn from work experience with a local employer (if this can be arranged).

Overall, you will be actively investigating the real world of work and presenting your findings in various ways, including giving talks and presentations. All these activities develop skills which are essential in the world of work.

Thirdly, two-thirds of your work will be assessed through assignments that you complete during the course, which you will assemble in a portfolio. Only one third will be assessed through tests.

The structure of the course

The structure of the Vocational A level in leisure and recreation is quite simple. There are twelve units in the full award. Six are **compulsory units**; every student takes them. Each of the compulsory units is covered in this textbook. Six are **optional units**. Each awarding body has produced its own set of optional units and you will probably choose which of these you will study. These optional units are not covered in this book, although you will find the information contained in the compulsory units a useful foundation for your optional unit work.

All units are the same size. To gain the full award you have to take all twelve units and your overall result is worked out by adding up the results you get on each unit. Since the new A levels have six units, your twelve-unit Vocational A level is worth two traditional A levels. You may be able to take a six unit Vocational A level award that is equivalent to one A level.

Course specifications

Your tutor will give you a copy of the specifications for the units you will need in your course and will go through them with you. All units have the same basic characteristics. They are addressed directly to you, the student. They have three sections:

- **about this unit** - this briefly describes what the unit covers
- **what you need to learn** - this clearly states the knowledge, understanding and skills you need to complete the unit
- **assessment evidence** - this sets out the evidence you need to produce for the unit, including what you need to produce to get higher grades, and the tasks you will be set in the units which are assessed through tests.

The unit specifications are designed to let you know exactly what skills and knowledge you have to demonstrate; if you demonstrate them, you achieve the qualification.

What are key skills?

There are six **key skills units**.

- communication
- application of number
- information technology
- working with others
- improving own learning and performance
- problem solving.

The first three key skills -communication, application of number, and information technology - make up the Key Skills Qualification, which is available to every student or trainee, whatever course they are following. To achieve the Key Skills Qualification, you have to pass these three units at any level. You can pass each one at a different level and still achieve the qualification. Most Vocational A level students will aim for Level 3 in these key skills.

How will I be assessed?

Four of your six compulsory units are assessed through a **portfolio of evidence** that you will compile. This is assessed by your tutors. The other two compulsory units -for health and safety and marketing - will be assessed by a test that is set and marked by the awarding body.

The portfolio is the heart of your course. Everything in it should be your own work and it must meet all the requirements set out in the **assessment evidence** sections of the unit specifications. It has to be carefully planned, organised and maintained, and it must have an index so that you can show how everything in it relates to the evidence requirements.

Evidence can take several forms. Much of it will be your own written work. However, some evidence will be provided by your tutor or some other person (maybe an employer) who has witnessed you taking part in a discussion, or dealing with a customer, or making a presentation. Your tutor, or other witness to your work, needs to provide a written statement that you have reached the required standard.

Your portfolio of evidence may contain video or audio recordings of role plays, work experience and research activities. It may also include letters, photographs, computer printouts and graphics, sketches and plans. All this evidence must be carefully recorded and indexed.

You need to build up a separate portfolio for your key skills evidence.

Grading

Vocational levels are **graded A to E**, exactly like traditional A levels. You will be given a grade for each unit. These grades will then be combined to give your overall grade for the whole qualification. When you have completed the course successfully, you will be awarded a Vocational A level certificate from your awarding body. This will list all the units you have completed, with grades, and will also specify your grade for the whole qualification.

How this book is organised

The content, structure and features of *Vocational A level for Leisure and Recreation* are designed to help you to get the most out of your course. The content directly matches all the underpinning knowledge that you will need to complete the compulsory units. The units in this book are organised into sections that make them easier to follow. Each section is packed with information, case studies and activities to help you learn in an active and stimulating way. You can identify each section within a unit by looking at the top right hand corner of every right hand page.

The special features include **activities case studies** and **webstracts** that will help you to develop your understanding of what you have been reading and to apply it to your own experience and studies. A webstract is a case study that is based upon information gathered from the internet. All special features are indicated by distinct icons and banners.

You will be able to complete many of the activities in class, sometimes by working with other people. Some activities will require you to make enquiries or investigations outside the classroom. Some activities will ask you to analyse case studies, documents, and figures that you will find in this book. Whatever the type of activity, you will be given clear instructions on what to do.

Each section within a unit ends with a feature called **build your learning**. This lists the key words and phrases that you have covered. **Key words and phrases** are also highlighted in orange where they first appear in the section, and are fully referenced in the index at the back of the book.

As you complete each section within the unit, there is an **end of section activity**. These are usually bigger than the activities and case studies that appear throughout the preceding section and can include some useful opportunities for you to generate evidence for your portfolio assignments.

Portfolio assessments

You will find portfolio assessments for each of the four compulsory units that are not externally assessed on pages 454 to 460 at the back of the book. These are based on the assessment criteria that you are required to meet in order to pass your Vocational A level. You are also given tips and suggestions on where to find information that will help you complete these assessments. Check with your teacher before starting any assessment work that will contribute to your portfolio of evidence.

There is no portfolio assessment for Unit 2, Safe working practices, and Unit 4, Marketing in leisure and recreation, as these will be externally assessed by the awarding body.

Resource directory

The resource directory provides you with useful information that will help you complete your assessment portfolio and also prepare for the externally set tests. You are provided with a list of key sources of information and data on the leisure and recreation industry.

There is a massive amount of information about leisure and recreation available on the internet. This section also provides you with a mini-directory of useful internet websites, listed in alphabetical order, to further help you with your research.

Good luck with your course!

Author biographies

Tony Outhart was formerly Curriculum Manager for Hospitality and Leisure at York College and has been involved in leading GNVQ Leisure and Tourism programmes since their introduction. Tony is part-time FEFC inspector and has worked for QCA, Edexcel and FEDA in the development of the 2000 curriculum. Since 2000, he has been a freelance education and training consultant. He has been a professional footballer and a director of a children's activity company. Tony is Series Editor for Collins GNVQ Leisure and Tourism.

Lindsey Taylor is a Senior Lecturer in Leisure, Tourism and Sport and GNVQ Co-ordinator at Yorkshire Coast College. She has worked in marketing consultancy within the leisure and tourism industry and as a personnel and training manager for Forte Hotels.

Ray Barker is a Senior Lecturer in Leisure and Tourism at University College Scarborough. He has worked as an outdoor activity and events manager and an independent consultant organising personal and staff development courses. Ray has also been a lecturer in sport and recreation.

Neil Procter is a lecturer in Leisure and Recreation Management at York College. He has an MSc in Sports Management and has extensive experience of teaching on a wide range of Sport and Leisure programmes.

Preview

Leisure and recreation affect everyone's lives. This unit provides a general understanding of the dynamic UK leisure and recreation industry, which is one of the fastest-growing industries in the UK.

You will investigate the key factors that have contributed to the rapid growth of the industry since the 1960s and research the structure and scale of today's UK leisure and recreation industry. You will learn that the industry is made up of many public, private and voluntary organisations that interact to supply an enormous range of products and services.

You will also investigate the wide-ranging career opportunities available in leisure and recreation, so that you can identify possible employment opportunities that match your aspirations, skills and abilities.

This is an important unit because it lays the foundation for study in many other units of the Vocational 'A' Level in Leisure and Recreation. In particular, there are links with the more detailed discussion in Unit 3 of the sports industry (see page 144).

1

Investigating Leisure and Recreation

Contents

Introduction to leisure and recreation

Definitions of leisure and recreation

Leisure can be defined as the time that an individual sets aside for activities or pastimes outside work or other necessities such as sleeping. Using this definition, the term 'leisure' can be applied to the entire range of activities that individuals undertake in their free time. **Recreation**, on the other hand, refers to the type of activities undertaken for enjoyment or relaxation during a person's leisure time.

There are many available definitions of leisure and recreation. For example, the Collins English Dictionary provides the following definitions:

leisure a time or opportunity for ease, relaxation, etc.

recreation refreshment of health or spirits by relaxation and enjoyment

How much leisure time do we have?

The conventional view is that leisure is something that people have at the end of the working day, at the weekends, in paid or unpaid holidays, and in the years of retirement. This view is true for that proportion of the population who are in full-time employment and full-time retirement thereafter. However, it is not applicable to an increasing proportion of the UK population; for example, those who take early retirement, the unemployed and those in part-time or temporary employment. For these groups the amount of leisure time may be significantly higher than for those in full-time employment.

It is important to understand that the range of leisure-time activities is enormous. We can divide the total time available to us in a day, week, year or, indeed, our whole lifetime, into three broad categories:

- **essential activities**, including sleep, personal care and hygiene, eating, basic household and family care
- **work**, including travel time to, from and for work
- **free time** or **leisure time**, which comprises the time not required for the activities in the other two categories.

In these three broad categories, free time is the time left over after the demands of essential activities and any work commitments. Figure 1.1 shows the percentage of time spent by the UK population in essential activities, work and leisure. In 1996, it was estimated that the UK population spent 30.6 per cent of its year, and almost half its waking hours, in leisure. The data also indicate that the time available for leisure increased only marginally between 1971 and 1996.

Figure 1.1: The uses of time in the UK

Division of total time of UK population (%)	1971	1996
Essential activities*		
Sleep	35.0	35.0
Other (personal care, hygiene, eating, home care)	26.0	26.0
All essentials	61.0	61.0
Paid work and travel to work	9.8	8.4
Free time (leisure time)	29.2	30.6
Total all time in year	100.00	100.00

* The absence of change in the overall amount of estimated time allocated to essential activities masks significant changes for different types of activity and for different groups within the population, such as the unemployed and early retired.

Given the large amount of free time available for leisure activities and the vast range of things people can choose to do in it, we can begin to appreciate the scale and diversity of the UK leisure and recreation industry. That industry comprises an enormous range of providers, facilities, products, services and events. All have one thing in common: they aim to satisfy consumer needs and expectations for leisure-time experiences, activities and pastimes.

ACTIVITY

Defining leisure

Read the following definition of leisure:

the opportunity available to an individual, after completing the immediate necessities of life, when he or she has the freedom to choose and take part in activities or experiences which are expected to be personally satisfying.

What do you think are the key phrases in this definition? Make a list of the activities which you think could be classed as 'immediate necessities of life' and 'activities or experiences which are expected to be personally satisfying'. Compare your list with someone else's in your group.

Types of leisure activity

The list of things that people do in their free time is almost endless. Each individual decides his or her own leisure needs, so leisure activities vary according to personal preferences. What one person may enjoy, another may loathe! Many factors influence people's leisure needs and choice of activities, including their age, sex, family circumstances, where they live, their friends, income, job, traditions, culture and religion. It is because there is such a variety of preferences and types of customer that the leisure and recreation industry has to provide such a broad range of activities, products and services.

There are two main distinctions between the various types of leisure and recreation activity. The first distinction concerns the level of activity required and the second involves classifying activities as taking place either in the home or away from the home. Thus, leisure and recreation activities can be:

- **active** (e.g. playing sport, walking) or **passive** (e.g. reading, watching television);
- **home-based** (e.g. listening to music in the home) or **away from home** (e.g. going to the pub, going to the cinema).

Figures 1.12 and 1.13 on page 23 shows examples of home-based and away-from-home leisure activities. It shows that home-based activities such as watching television and reading are by far the most popular types of leisure activity. It also forecasts the future popularity of activities, with little change anticipated by 2003 in the pattern of many activities that were popular in the 1980s and 1990s. However, the popularity of activities such as listening to CDs, gardening, knitting, doing the pools and open-air outings appears to have changed, according to this research. There is a wide range of factors that can influence the popularity of a leisure activity, such as changing consumer needs and expectations, socio-economic conditions and developments in technology. Changing trends and fashions are a characteristic feature of the leisure industry, which is why the industry is continually evolving. Later in this unit we will investigate the main factors that have influenced the development of the leisure industry.

Leisure products

Before looking at the leisure and recreation industry in detail, we need to understand what is meant by the term leisure product and the difference between products (or goods) and services.

Leisure **products** can be **goods** or **services** or a combination of both. Goods are things which can be seen, touched and perhaps taken away. They are objects, such as souvenirs, exercise bikes or computer games. Services cannot be seen or touched; rather, they are skills or information provided by trained people, such as sports coaches, concert organisers and caterers. These intangible services are much harder to describe because they cannot be bought and consumed, or taken away, by the purchaser or user.

Many leisure products and services are provided in **facilities**. In a leisure and recreation context this refers to the equipment, buildings, structures or features that provide opportunities for leisure usage. A leisure and recreation facility may be a building with specialised equipment, such as a cinema, a leisure centre or a heritage centre. It might, on the other hand, be a natural feature of the landscape, such as a lake which provides the opportunity for fishing, or a mountain suitable for climbing or skiing.

There are also many events in the leisure and recreation industry. You may be involved in planning and running an event of your own as part of Unit 6. An **event** refers to activities with significant and specific requirements for planning, resources and evaluation. An event can include the provision of a product or a service.

The buyers and/or users of leisure products and services are **customers**. Customers may be individuals, groups or businesses. You will learn about the different types of customer in Unit 5 (page 335). The quality of the leisure product or service is usually based on the skills, knowledge and attitude of the people who provide them: these people are referred to as **providers**. Consequently, the quality of the customer's experience may vary depending on who provides the product or service, how they do it and whether it satisfies customer needs and wants.

Taking all these terms together, we can say, for example, that a football club (**the provider**) offers its supporters (**the customers**) a seat (**a service**) at a match (**an event**) in a stadium (**a facility**) and sells them a souvenir programme (**a good**).

Distribution of leisure

Figure 1.2 shows how the total distribution of free time varies for certain groups in the UK population. Over the period 1971 to 1996 it is clear that the distribution of this free time, based on age and employment status, has changed significantly. However, although the estimated amount of free time for all people in the UK increased by 10 per cent between 1971 and 1996, to 143 billion hours, this increase was not consistent across all groups. For example, children's free time was reduced by 15 per cent, while for adults it increased by 18 per cent. This change in the distribution of free time is due to a range of demographic and socio-economic factors, such as:

- a 15 per cent decline in the number of children under 16 years of age
- a 25 per cent rise in the number of people aged 65 and over
- 3 million (-24 per cent) fewer men in full-time employment
- 3 million more women (+34 per cent) in paid employment.

We will investigate how socio-economic factors have influenced the development of the leisure and recreation industry since the 1960s in the next section (see pages 10-18).

Figure 1.2: Distribution of leisure time

Leisure time in the UK for:	1971 billion hours	1971 % distribution	1996 billion hours	1996 % distribution	1971-96 % change
Children (under 16 years)	**33**	**23**	**28**	**18**	**-15**
Adults (16+)	**110**	**77**	**129**	**82**	**+18**
Of whom:					
Full-time paid employees	43	30	38	24	-11
Part-time paid employees	8	6	15	10	+93
Self-employed, forces, training, etc.	6	4	9	6	+56
Registered unemployed	3	2	8	5	+2
'Unoccupied' under 60/65	22	15	23	14	+4
Retired 60/65 and over	28	20	36	23	+26
Total adults in paid employment	**57**	**40**	**62**	**40**	**+11**
Total adults not in paid employment	**53**	**37**	**67**	**42**	**+25**
For all people in UK	**143**	**100**	**157**	**100**	**+10**

Source: LIRC *Leisure Forecasts*

BUILD YOUR LEARNING

Keywords and phrases

You should know the meaning of the words and phrases listed below. If you are unsure about any of them, go back through the last three pages to refresh your understanding.

- Leisure
- Recreation
- Essential activities
- Work
- Free time
- Leisure time
- Active
- Passive
- Home-based leisure
- Away-from-home leisure
- Products
- Services
- Goods
- Facility
- Event
- Customer
- Provider

End of section activity

1 Work out the total amount of time over the last seven days you spent in:

- essential activities such as sleeping, personal care and hygiene, eating, basic household and family care
- working (including your time at school/college or at a part-time job)
- free time or leisure time (i.e. the time not required for the other two categories).

Compare your findings with those of others in the group. Identify the average amount of time spent on essential activities, work and leisure over the last seven days.

2 Copy the table below and estimate the amount of time spent during the week on each free-time activity for each category of person.

You may be able to base your survey on people you know, such as friends or relatives. When you have gathered your information, discuss your findings with other group members and identify the most popular leisure-time activities associated with each category of person surveyed.

Free time use categories	Yourself	Retired person aged 50+	Mother with young child	Boy or girl aged 10-12	Single man or woman aged 25-34
Television/radio					
Visiting friends					
Reading					
Talking, socialising and telephoning friends					
Eating and drinking out					
Walks and other recreation					
Doing nothing					
Sports participation					
Religious, political and other meetings					
Concerts, cinema and sports spectating					
Other free time activities (except sleeping)					
All free time					

Development of the UK leisure and recreation industry

Since the 1960s the UK leisure and recreation industry has experienced huge growth in consumer spending and product development. There are many different factors that have combined to produce this increase. This section will investigate how **socio-economic and technological developments**, together with **changing consumer needs**, have led to the rapid growth of the leisure and recreation industry since the 1960s. It is important to realise, however, that leisure activities existed long before this time. Indeed, many of our present-day leisure activities can be traced back to ancient times, particularly those which have a competitive element to them. Athletics, horse racing and archery were a part of military training in many early civilisations.

To take part in leisure activities in the 1990s we need time, money, access to transport and an awareness of the range of activities available. The factors that have stimulated the growth of the UK leisure and recreation industry, and will most likely continue to do so, are all interrelated. In this section we will consider seven **interrelated factors** that have combined to stimulate this demand:

- increase in leisure time for many individuals
- increase in disposable income
- improved mobility
- demographic changes
- changing fashions and trends
- technological developments
- government legislation.

We will need to investigate each of these factors in order to understand the main reasons for the development of the leisure and recreation industry since the 1960s.

Time available for leisure activities

Time is an essential ingredient of all forms of leisure and recreation activity. Many people assume that the industry's growth since the 1960s has been underpinned primarily by an expansion in the

Figure 1.3 Time and money for leisure 1971-96

% change over period	1971-81 (10 years)	1981-91 (10 years)	1991-6 (5 years)	1971-96 (25 years)
LEISURE TIME				
Total leisure hours in the UK	+6	+2	+2	+10
Leisure hours, average per person	+5	nil	nil	+5
LEISURE SPENDING (at constant prices)				
Total spending on leisure goods and services	+26	+33	+18	+98
Leisure spending per person	+25	+30	+16	+89

Source: BTA/ETC *Insights*, January 1998

Figure 1.4: Trends in paid working time 1971-96

FULL-TIME WORKERS	1971	1981	1991	1996	2001*
Weekly hours of work	42.0	40.3	40.0	40.2	39.7
Paid holiday days	16.7	22.8	24.2	24.6	25.1
Public holiday days	6.0	9.0	8.0	8.0	8.0
Annual hours of work per worker	1,999	1,844	1,829	1,832	1,807
KEY LABOUR-FORCE STATISTICS					
% of labour force employed as part-time workers	15.5	20.9	25.3	27.9	30
Numbers in employment (millions)	24.7	24.5	26.3	25.9	27.1
Numbers registered unemployed (millions)	0.7	2.4	2.2	2.1	1.2

* 2001 figures are forecasts Source: *Leisure Forecasts*

amount of free time that people have available for leisure. However, a detailed investigation of what has been happening to the nation's leisure time shows that this assumption cannot be justified. Figure 1.3 shows that over the 25-year period to 1996, total leisure time in the UK rose by only 10 per cent. Although leisure spending per person increased by 89 per cent over the same period, the average amount of leisure time per person in the UK rose by only 5 per cent. Leisure time per person has grown at an average rate of just 0.2 per cent a year since 1971, despite huge increases in consumer spending on leisure.

The amount of leisure time available to the majority of people in the UK increased steadily up to the early 1970s, but has levelled off since then. It is estimated that by the early 1970s, 29 per cent of the year was spent at leisure by the UK population (see Figure 1.1, page 4). By the end of the century the average amount of leisure time available in the year had only increased marginally from the 1970s total. The main reasons why leisure time increased up to the 1970s were increasing amounts of paid annual holiday entitlement, and a gradual reduction in the weekly working hours for the majority of workers. Since the 1970s other factors have had a greater influence on the availability of time for leisure pursuits, such as:

- **Flexible work patterns** and/or shift work for many workers
- Widespread use of labour-saving devices in the home
- Increasing numbers of unemployed and retired in the population

Distribution of free time

The most significant changes in the distribution of free time in the UK since the early 1970s arise from shifts in the **population age structure** and in the extent to which different elements of the population participate in **paid employment**, rather than changes in average weekly working hours and holidays. Figure 1.2 (page 6) and Figure 1.4 show trends in the distribution of available leisure time based on age and employment, and in paid working time between 1971 and 1996.

Figure 1.2 indicates that 42 per cent of all free time is now in the hands of adults who spend none of their time in paid employment. This group includes not only those past the normal age of retirement, but also the unemployed and those under the retirement age who are defined as 'unoccupied'. This latter term covers the growing number of early retired (under 60/65 years) and full-time home and family carers. As the proportion of part-time paid employees, retired, early retired and unemployed has increased since the 1970s, so has the demand for leisure time activities from these groups.

In Figure 1.4 we can see that the average working week for full-time workers has reduced by only 5 per cent to 40.2 hours. There has been no significant increase in leisure time available to those in full-time employment since 1971, and this is not forecast to change much between 1996 and 2001. However, the percentage of part-time workers within the UK labour force will have doubled to 30 per cent by 2001, according to research forecasts. The trend towards more flexible, part-time employment since the 1970s has meant that increasing numbers of the workforce have had more free time in which to pursue leisure activities.

ACTIVITY

Distribution of free time

1 Figure 1.2 (page 6) summarises how available free time is now divided between different groups of the UK population and the way in which this changed between 1971 and 1996. Explain why you think each of the following groups listed in Figure 1.2 experienced an increase or decrease in the percentage distribution of the total leisure time available between 1971 and 1996:

- Children (under 16)
- Adults 16+ in full-time paid employment
- Adults 16+ in part-time paid employment
- Adults 16+ in self-employment
- 'Unoccupied' under 60/65
- 60/65 and over, retired

2 In small groups, discuss what you think are the main factors determining how much free time you have.

Levels of disposable income

The main factor behind the development of the leisure and recreation industry since the 1960s is the major rise in affluence in the UK and other Western countries. As standards of living have risen, free time has been used in a much more 'money-intensive' way than it was in the past. For example, consumer spending has increased significantly on 'free-time' activities such as eating out, days out, holidays and sports.

Household disposable income

The amount of money people have to spend on leisure activities depends on the amount of money left over after they have paid for items of immediate necessity such as food, household bills, rent or mortgage. The remaining money is referred to as **personal disposable income** or **household disposable income**. Overall, the trend in the UK has been for personal and household disposable incomes to rise in recent years (although for some, such as the unemployed, it has fallen). This trend has led to an enormous increase in consumer spending on leisure activities. Figure 1.3 (page 8) shows that average leisure spending per person increased by 89 per cent between 1971 and 1996. Figure 1.5 shows that between 1971 and 1997 UK household disposable income per head nearly doubled in real terms.

Household expenditure on leisure

Government research shown in Figure 1.6 estimates that the average UK household spends £51.60 per week on leisure goods and services out of a total average expenditure of £313.70. This represents 16 per cent of their weekly budget. The proportion of average weekly expenditure devoted to leisure is second only to that for food (18 per cent) and on a par with housing and motoring/fares.

The level of disposable income and spending on leisure items varies from household to household and region to region within the UK. People who live on low incomes such as pensioners, the unemployed and single parents, may be prevented from taking part in leisure activities. To cater for the leisure needs of low-income groups, local authorities in particular developed a range of initiatives from the 1970s in order to provide subsidised or free leisure services for these groups.

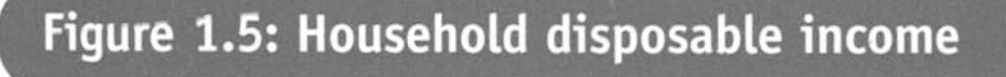

Figure 1.5: Household disposable income

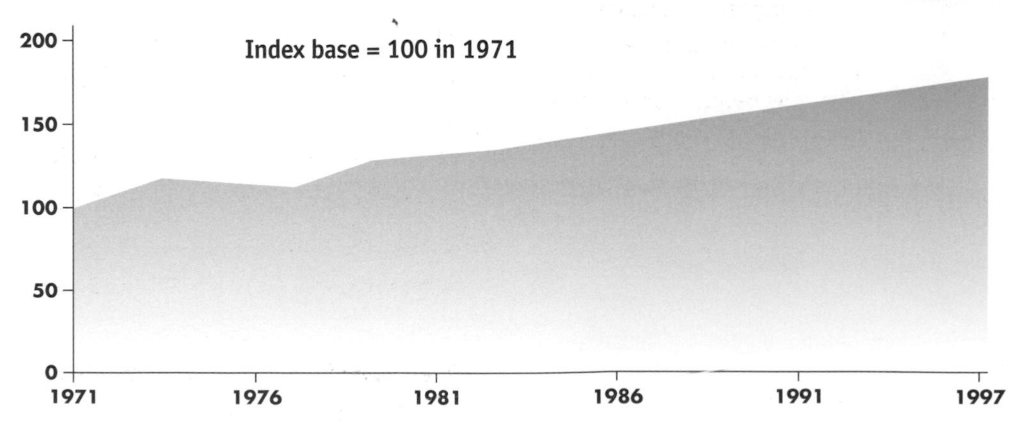

Source: *Social Trends* 29, 1999

Figure 1.6: UK household expenditure (one week) by commodity and service, 1995-8

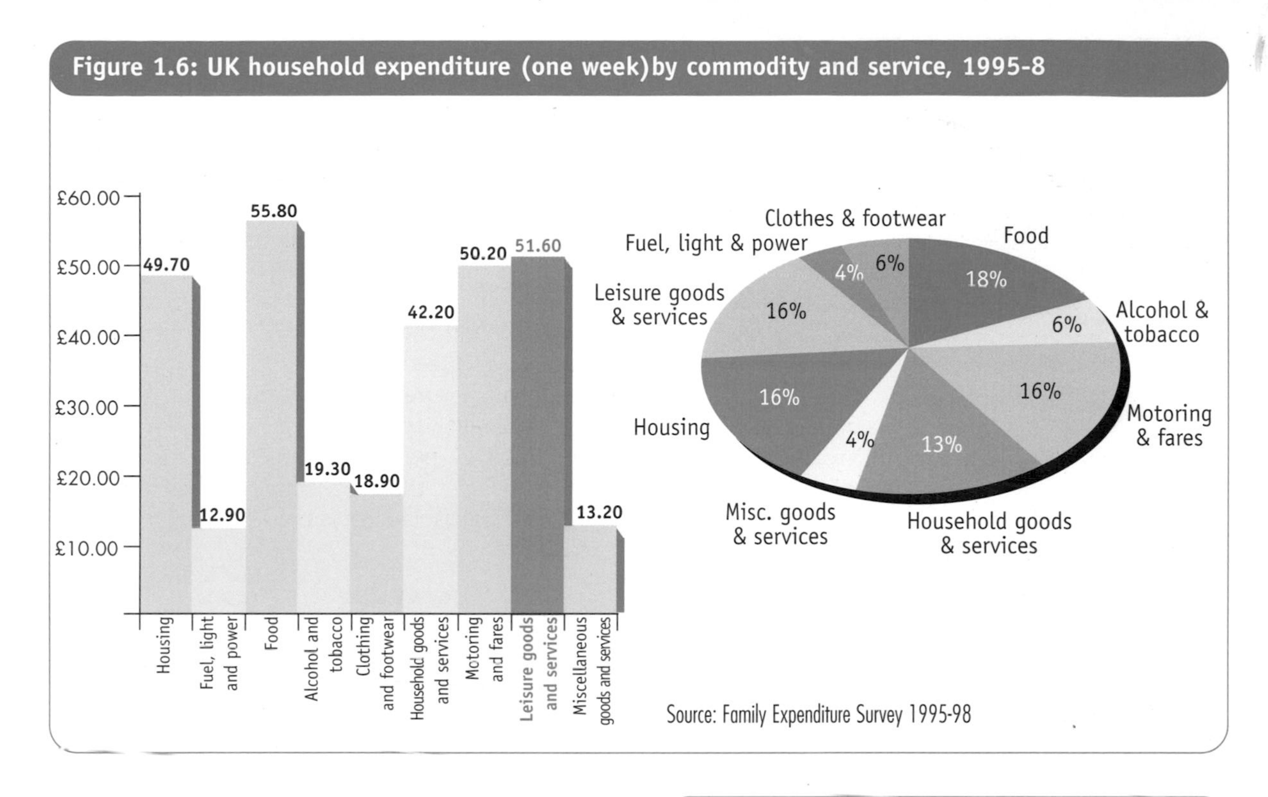

Source: Family Expenditure Survey 1995-98

Consumer spending on leisure

Figure 1.3 (page 8) shows a major rise in **consumer spending** on leisure since the 1970s. Between 1971 and 1996 total spending on leisure goods increased by 98 per cent, while leisure spending per person increased by 89 per cent. It is predicted that by 2003 consumer spending in the UK on home-based and away-from-home leisure will total £179 billion, representing 25.8 per cent of all consumer spending. If we consider that total consumer expenditure on leisure was £108 billion in 1993, it is clear that the UK leisure industry continued to expand rapidly throughout the 1990s.

Figure 1.7 shows the predicted increase in consumer spending on selected leisure activities between 1993 and 2003. The largest percentage increases are predicted for holidays overseas and gambling. It is also forecast that leisure spending on away-from-home activities will increase by 69 per cent over this period, compared to an increase of 57 per cent for home-based leisure activities.

Figure 1.7: Consumer spending value (£ billion)

Activity	1993	2003	Forecast % increase
Reading	5.34	6.65	25
Home entertainment	10.85	18.06	66
House and garden	7.57	13.07	73
Hobbies and pastimes	5.79	8.76	51
Total home-based leisure	**29.55**	**46.53**	**57**
Eating and drinking	22.25	39.54	78
Local entertainment	2.95	5.05	71
Gambling	3.45	7.45	116
Active sport	4.40	6.67	52
Holidays in the UK and sightseeing	7.34	10.88	48
Holidays overseas	13.65	29.23	114
Total away-from-home leisure	**78.43**	**132.59**	**69**
Total all leisure	**107.99**	**179.12**	**66**

Source: LIRC, Leisure Forecasts 1999-2003

ACTIVITY

Consumer spending on leisure

1 Estimate the percentage of the weekly budget spent on leisure within a selected household. You may find it easiest to base your research on the household that you live in yourself. As a starting point, you will need to estimate the total weekly expenditure on selected leisure items. You could use the items shown in Figure 1.6 (page 11) and add others if appropriate. When you have done this you will need to calculate the approximate total household weekly income in order to obtain the percentage of the weekly budget spent on leisure items, as shown below:

$$\frac{\text{Total weekly expenditure on leisure items}}{\text{Total weekly household income}} \times 100 = \text{\% of budget spent on leisure items}$$

2 Using the figures provided in Figure 1.7 that show predicted consumer spending in 2003 compared to 1993, produce the following charts.

- A bar chart showing 1993 and 2003 values of consumer spending for each leisure activity listed.
- Two pie charts showing the proportion of total home-based and away-from-home leisure consumer spending for 1993 and 2003.
- One pie chart showing the proportion of consumer spending in 2003 for each leisure activity.

Improved mobility

The UK population has benefited from **improved mobility** since the 1960s due to advances in **transport technology**. Most people now have access to efficient transport networks which have made leisure and recreation facilities, products, services and events much more readily accessible. However, the greatest single transport factor promoting increased demand for leisure products and services is the significant increase in car ownership since the 1970s. Since many leisure facilities, services and events rely on attracting customers from a wide area in order to be viable, the level of **car ownership** is an important influence on the numbers of people using and attending them.

There was a five-fold increase in the number of private cars on UK roads between 1951 and 1970, and around a ten-fold increase between 1951 and the mid-1990s. It is now estimated that there are over 20 million privately owned cars in the UK, with over 70 per cent of all households in the UK having access to at least one car (see Figure 1.8). In addition, 20 per cent of UK households now own two cars or more, which means that even if one householder uses a car to go to work, it is still possible for other adult members of the household to use their second car to access leisure services. Increasing car ownership has been a major factor in the rising popularity of visits to leisure facilities, events and 'days-out' visitor attractions, such as theme parks, museums, stately homes, country parks and sports stadia.

Figure 1.8: Trends in car ownership, 1970-2003

Year	% of households owning a car
1970	52
1975	57
1980	60
1985	63
1990	67
1995	72
2000	73
2003	76

Sources: 1970-90 data CSO Family Spending; 1990-2000 data, Mintel; 2003 figure forecast by LIRC, *Leisure Forecasts*, 1999-2003

The improvement in transport networks and increasing car ownership have been major factors in opening access to the countryside for leisure activities. Until the mid-1960s, recreational use of the countryside in Britain was still fairly limited in scale. However, the numbers visiting the countryside for leisure purposes increased significantly after the 1960s, and it is now estimated that over three-quarters of the UK population visit the countryside on at least one occasion per year. National park areas such as the Lake District, Snowdonia and Dartmoor now attract millions of visitors every year.

Demographic changes

Demographic factors concerning the size, age structure and distribution of the population have influenced the development of the leisure and recreation industry. In general, people have tended to lead healthier, fitter lives since the 1970s. This trend, combined with improving levels of healthcare, has meant that **life expectancy** has continued to increase, as highlighted in Figure 1.9. Thus, there are increasing numbers of retired people with large amounts of free time in which to pursue leisure activities. This is why many leisure organisations provide specific products and services to this large market, sometimes referred to as the 'grey market'. Another notable demographic trend in the UK since the 1970s has been the falling **birth rate**. Consequently, while the population has increased due to longer life expectancy, the proportion of children in the UK population has decreased, as also shown in Figure 1.9.

Impact of age distribution on leisure

The **age distribution** within the UK population can affect demand for certain types of leisure product or service. For example, the ageing population has been generally considered beneficial to attendances at museums, art galleries, historic buildings and gardens. Government forecasts for the period 1994–2002 show that the UK population will grow by 2 per cent. Within this total, there are some quite significant differences in the rates of growth, and some key age groups are set to decline in number. Among the child population, the number of children aged four and under is set to contract, and to a lesser extent so is the number of children aged between five and nine. This sort of trend is not particularly positive for leisure organisations which derive a high proportion of their business from young children, such as theme parks like Legoland Windsor, zoos and wildlife parks. Numbers of 10–14 year-olds are set to grow by 4 per cent, which will benefit theme parks with a slightly older age positioning, such as Alton Towers and Thorpe Park. Also, after a long period of decline, the numbers of 15–24 year-olds will grow by almost 4 per cent between 1994 and 2002, which is good news for the leisure business generally and attractions like theme parks particularly. The trend of decline which affected the 15–24 year-old age group in the first half of the 1980s has now been transferred to the 25–34 year-old age range. Many of these consumers have babies or young children, so leisure organisations targeting young families will undoubtedly find their target market shrinking in the next five years.

The numbers of consumers aged 35-44 years, who would typically have slightly older children, are forecast to boom between 1994 and 2002, growing by 18 per cent. This trend is positive for the many leisure organisations that target more mature families (many theme parks fall into this category). Finally, the number of 55-64 year olds is set to grow by 11 per cent, faster than any other age group within the total population. Such a trend must be regarded as positive for organisations appealing to older consumers, since this age group is often relatively affluent, in that many of them are still working, but their children have left home and they have paid off their mortgage. After strong growth in the late 1980s and throughout the 1990s, the number of over-65s is still forecast to grow, but by the reduced rate of 0.3 per cent. The case study overleaf shows how one market research organisation, Mintel, thinks demographics will affect selected leisure markets between 1998 and 2002.

Figure 1.9: UK Population by selected age-groups

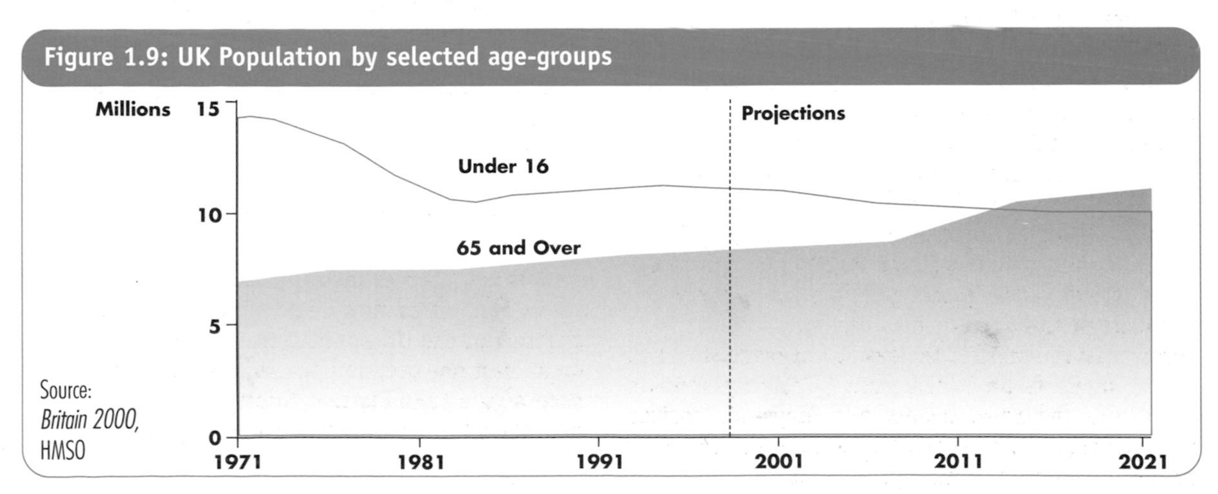

Source: *Britain 2000*, HMSO

CASE STUDY

Impact of changing demographics on selected leisure markets, 1998 - 2002

This case study has been adapted from several Mintel research reports and provides us with some further examples of how changing demographics are forecast to influence the development of selected leisure markets.

Figure 1.10: Trends in the age structure of the UK population, 1998 and 2002

Age	1998-9		2002		% change
	000	%	000	%	1998-2002
0-4	3677	6.2	3562	6.0	-3.1
5-9	3905	6.6	3718	6.2	-4.8
10-14	3795	6.4	3945	6.6	+4.0
15-19	3685	6.2	3767	6.3	+2.2
20-24	3510	5.9	3684	6.2	+5.0
25-34	9154	15.5	8130	13.6	-11.2
35-44	8492	14.4	9257	15.5	+9.0
45-54	7755	13.1	7726	13.0	-0.4
55-64	5871	9.9	6530	11.0	+11.2
65+	9241	15.6	9268	15.6	+0.3
Total	**59085**	**100.00**	**59587**	**100.00**	**+0.8**

Data may not equal totals due to rounding Source: Mintel

Theme parks

Fluctuations in the demographic spread of the UK population are a contributing factor to the long-term health of the theme park industry. Since families with children aged under 15, along with young adults aged 15-24, have been shown by Mintel's consumer research to be the main target audience for theme parks, the numbers of such sectors in the population are obviously of relevance. Between 1998 and 2002 the number of 0-9 year old children is expected to fall significantly, suggesting that operators such as Legoland which target this age group may have to increase their offer of attractions aimed at a slightly older age range in order to continue to flourish.

However, there is good news for theme park operators overall, as other key target groups are set to rise as a proportion of the population during the same period. The number of children in the 10-14 age range will rise by 4 per cent, while the number of 15-19 year olds will grow by 2.2 per cent. In addition, the next few years will see the proportion of 20-24 year olds in the UK jump by 5 per cent - clearly grounds for optimism among operators which offer a good range of so-called 'white knuckle' rides and other more sophisticated high-tech offerings (such as those incorporating video and computer game-based entertainment) which appeal to this age group.

Over the same five years the number of 35-44 year olds - those most likely to have a family with young children - will increase by a staggering 9 per cent. There is little doubt that this core target group, which has grown up with theme parks such as Alton Towers and Chessington, is likely to continue to look favourably upon such leisure offerings and to want to incorporate visits to them as part of their overall leisure experience.

Children's play areas

Population changes, particularly those affecting the number of children in the population, have a significant bearing on the market for children's play areas. Between 1994 and 2002 the number of pre-school children is expected to fall by 8 per cent, while the number of 5-9 year olds is predicted to drop by almost 3 per cent. Since the majority of children's play areas tend to target these age groups, this is obviously not an encouraging factor. However, during the same period the proportion of youngsters aged 10-14 is expected to rise by 8 per cent, suggesting that operators would do well to include this (often neglected) age range when planning facilities, activities and promotions. Some of the larger pub-based operators have been deliberately targeting older children by installing Sony Playstations and interactive video games which can be installed alongside the traditional slides, soft play areas and scramble nets, which tend to appeal mainly to under-11s.

▼ Theme parks are affected by changing demographics

ACTIVITY

Demographic changes

The case study shows examples of how demographic changes between 1994 and 2002 are forecast to influence selected leisure markets. Select five other leisure and recreation facilities, products or services, and for each one describe how you think they have been influenced by demographic changes in the 1990s. You may need to obtain data on the UK population and its age distribution to complete this activity. Some of this information is contained in this book. You might also find it useful to obtain data from publications such as *Social Trends* and the *Annual Abstract of Statistics,* both of which can usually be obtained from libraries, or from the internet.

Try www.ons.gov.uk

Changing fashions and trends

Consumer needs and expectations of leisure products and services are continually changing. We are now members of a healthier, fitter and more prosperous society that is constantly seeking new leisure experiences - and the more experiences that are provided, the greater our needs and expectations become.

The effect of **changing fashions and trends** since the 1960s on the UK leisure and recreation industry is clearly evident if we consider the development of selected leisure activities. These include the:

- development of many city or town-centre football stadia into modern, purpose-built all-seater stadia
- decline of some town and city-centre shopping areas and the development of huge multi-leisure parks that include a range of retail and leisure facilities
- development of traditional cinemas with one large screen into multiplex cinemas with several screens, a restaurant, a bar and other facilities on one site
- increasing popularity of health and fitness activities such as step aerobics and keep-fit, as people become more aware of the health benefits of regular exercise
- fluctuating popularity of individual and team sports such as football, cricket, snooker, darts, squash and running
- increasing popularity of home-based leisure activities due to home entertainment systems, digital television, computers and the internet
- development of new hi-tech holiday centres from the traditional holiday camps of the 1950s and 1960s.

The following case study shows examples of how selected leisure facilities and activities have been affected by changing consumer expectations and fashions in the 1980s and 1990s, and how the industry has responded to these changes.

▼ The Butlins holiday camps of the 1960s have been transformed

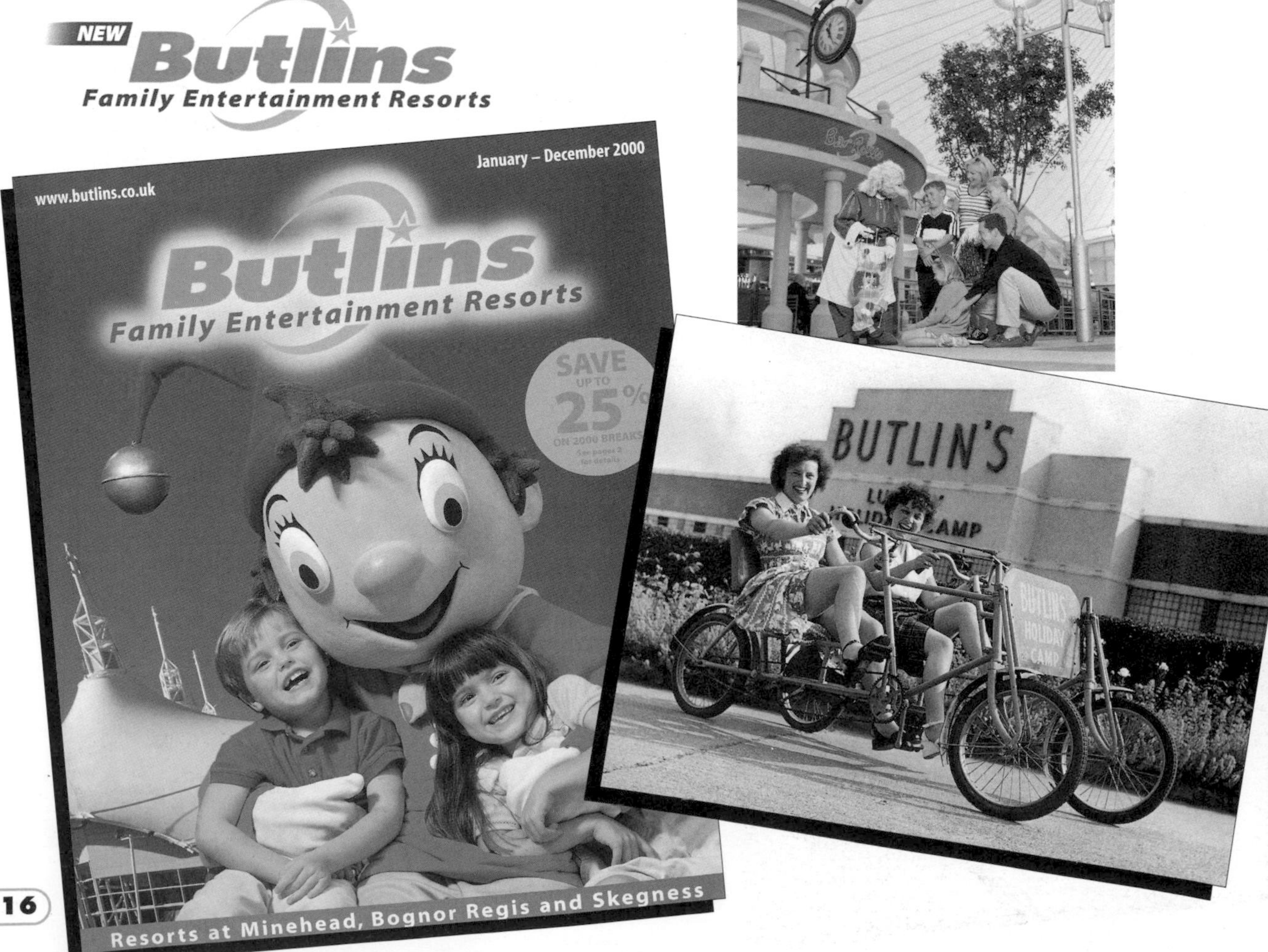

CASE STUDY

The impact of changing fashions

The demise of the traditional UK holiday camp

The popular early-1980s television sitcom Hi-de-Hi adversely affected attendance levels at traditional UK holiday camps such as Butlins and Pontins. It portrayed holiday camps as amateurish and downmarket, thus mocking the holiday-camp tradition that had been so popular in the 1950s and 1960s. As a means of fighting back against their decline in market share, these places invested considerable amounts of money during the 1980s and 1990s to improve their image and to meet changing consumer needs and expectations. Facilities were updated and standards improved, the range of amusements and activities was increased and the entertainment was revitalised. The accommodation arrangements were also adjusted to be more flexible, increase product appeal and cater for the growing market for short breaks. New holiday themes and styles included activity holidays, educational breaks, adult-only breaks and no-children holidays. Special arrangements have also been introduced for single parents and pensioners.

The traditional format of swimming pool, mini-golf, bars, discos and night-time entertainment still forms the basis for many of the new breed of holiday centres such as Centre Parcs and Oasis. However, modern holiday centres now include a wider range of sporting and leisure activities, such as indoor fun pools with flumes, sauna and solarium, snooker, outings, horse riding, fishing trips, sailing, sub-aqua and golf, to name just a few. Greater variety in catering facilities has also increased the appeal of holiday centres.

The establishment of the Center Parcs holiday village format in the UK in 1987 introduced a new concept and one which has appealed to groups that have traditionally stayed away from British holiday centres. The holiday village is typically sited in natural woodland and is designed to complement the ecology of the local environment. The range of leisure activities available emphasises a healthy lifestyle. Accommodation is self-catering, although good-quality restaurants and brasseries exist on site to tempt the holidaymaker.

Investment in upgrading and extending the range of options and offerings by the holiday centres has been a positive move and has been instrumental in transforming the downmarket image of these businesses. Market researchers Mintel estimate that spending on holiday-centre breaks has grown from £405 million in 1990 to £750 million in 1996. These estimates relate to the booking price only and exclude extra goods and services purchased at the holiday centre.

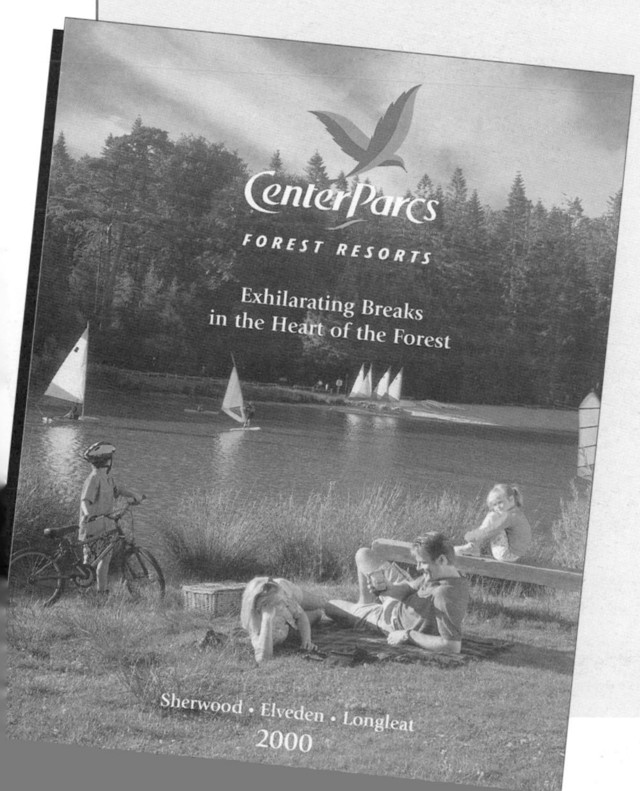

CenterParcs
FOREST RESORTS
Exhilarating Breaks
in the Heart of the Forest
Sherwood · Elveden · Longleat
2000

Sport and changing fashions

Participation in sport increased steadily from the 1960s onwards to the late 1980s. Since the early 1990s evidence suggests most sports are either levelling off or declining in popularity. The fundamental change in the consumer sports market over the last twenty years has been the shift from sports with elements of competition or individual prowess to activities whose primary goals are fitness and health.

This does not mean that all team or individual sports have necessarily lost out to hi-tech gyms or aerobics sessions. The teenagers and young adults, mainly male, who have always dominated these sports continue to play them, but the underlying social trend has been towards men and women of all ages playing more sport or keeping fit, and this has changed the character of both participation and provision.

Fitness/health-motivated sport

Jogging was the first of the major fitness trends to catch on with the public. At its peak in the late 1970s, its most important contribution to market value was the inspiration it gave to the early growth of sports clothing companies such as Nike and Reebok, and a plethora of marathons and fun runs throughout the UK. For most people, running is based on jogging for fitness rather than competitive athletics. In the 1970s and 1980s squash also became a major fitness-motivated sport. Jogging and squash were predominantly male; aerobics classes arrived to satisfy women's demand for a safe, preferably social, indoor fitness activity. The frivolous elements of aerobics and dance classes eventually gave way to more serious fitness training for women (including yoga), initially in classes (e.g. Step Reebok) and ultimately in hi-tech gyms by the late 1980s. The 1990s produced other important trends in the health and fitness market in response to changing consumer needs and expectations, such as;

- installation of well-equipped gyms in most public leisure centres, accompanied by the necessary employment of qualified trainers to supervise the use of equipment;
- a boom in development of private fitness clubs, first by independent clubs but subsequently through investment by hotel groups, leisure conglomerates and brewers (e.g. Stakis, Granada, Kunick/Relaxion, Virgin);
- an expanded market for home fitness equipment.

Development of multi-leisure parks

Consumer enthusiasm for the concept of grouping together complementary leisure facilities on a large site offering ample car parking is reflected in the strength of admissions currently enjoyed by operators situated on these sites. There was something of a boom in the building of multi-leisure complexes, or leisure parks as they are often known, during the late 1980s and early 1990s, but this has now slowed due to a more restrictive planning environment, which has virtually halted development of out-of-town sites.

The general shift towards 'one-stop' shopping in many sectors of consumer lifestyle, such as the retail sector, has become apparent in the leisure sector. Increasingly, consumers wish to be able to drive to one location where they can enjoy a range of leisure activities. This option appeals particularly to families as, for example, it is more convenient than having to drive to a cinema, see a film, then put the children back in the car and drive to a restaurant somewhere else. In addition, young people brought up in a convenience-oriented society also enjoy the benefits of watching a film or playing amusement machines or tenpin bowling, having a drink and then a meal, all in one location.

ACTIVITY

Changing fashions

1 The case study provides examples that illustrate how the leisure and recreation industry has developed to meet changing consumer needs, expectations and fashions. Read through them and then answer the following questions:

- Why did the holiday camp concept become so popular in the 1950s and 1960s?
- What were the key factors that contributed to the decline of these camps in the 1980s?
- What types of product development and innovation were introduced by the holiday centre operators throughout the 1990s in order to satisfy changing consumer needs and expectations?
- Why has personal fitness and individual sport become so popular over the last twenty years?
- Why do you think that participation in team sports remains so popular despite increasing competition from individual sports?
- Why did multi-leisure parks become so popular with consumers in the 1990s?

2 Identify five leisure and recreation activities, products or services (other than those provided in the case studies) and for each one describe how it has been influenced by changing consumer needs, expectations and fashions over the past twenty years. For example, you may look at the popularity of sporting activities such as football, athletics, rugby, hockey and tennis. Alternatively, you could consider the development of leisure facilities such as health and fitness clubs, sports centres, bingo halls, nightclubs and tenpin bowling centres.

You may be able to use this information for your end of portfolio assessment on page 454.

Technological developments

The two major technological innovations that have shaped people's leisure activities since the 1960s are the car and television. The impact of widespread car ownership on the industry has been covered already (see page 12). Any investigation into leisure time activity within the UK will undoubtedly reveal that watching television has been and continues to be the most popular leisure activity. With the advent of satellite, cable and digital television the range of home-based leisure opportunities will be extended in the future, as consumers replace their existing televisions with new digital equipment and new services are introduced.

Developments in technology have created new opportunities for both home-based and away-from-home leisure activities. For example, advances in micro-electronics since the 1980s have led to a whole range of consumer electronic leisure goods that have increased demand for home-based leisure, such as:

- the Sony Walkman
- CD players
- VCRs
- personal computers
- camcorders
- Sony Playstations.

Technology has also provided opportunities for away-from-home leisure operators such as theme parks and museums to create exciting leisure experiences for their customers. Over the next 25 years technology will deliver new ways of using leisure time. Many believe that the internet and interactive television will be the major technological influences on the leisure industry in the next few decades. The following case study is just one view of what the leisure market could be like in the 21st century. Many of the industry developments suggested in the case study will be directly influenced by developing technology.

ACTIVITY

Leisure in the future

1 The case study overleaf provides just one view of how the leisure market will develop in the future. Working in small groups, describe the types of leisure activities that you think will be popular in 20,50 and 100 years' time.

2 What influence do you think developments in technology will have over the next 20 years on the leisure activities that you identified?

▲ Technological innovations are extending home-based leisure opportunities

CASE STUDY

The changing face of leisure

Is this the future of leisure?

Cosmic Travel, McDonald's at Buckingham Palace, and floor-to-ceiling TV screens in your living room.

AT THE BEGINNING of the 20th century, 'leisure' comprised music halls, dance halls, public houses, restaurants, museums and magnificent exhibitions. Great stadia were about to be built for football, cricket and rugby, and of course there were majestic hotels for the millions of visitors to Britain from its widespread empire.

Whereas today the leisure community is without class barriers, in 1899 overlapping of the classes occurred only occasionally, with the masses concentrating their interest in football, public houses and dance halls. Working hours were unsocial, long and ill-paid, with limited disposable income for the majority and proportionately short leisure and entertainment time.

The new millennium signals the juxtaposition of these factors. The greatest momentum of interest in leisure has been gained in the last decade, with nearly a tenth of the working population currently employed in leisure-related industries, and with greater dynamic growth to come.

Technology

All operators will have to satisfy the concerns of a sophisticated public in respect of transport, security, environmental issues, the need for variety and ever more interesting technological improvements. No doubt the influence of IT on working location and hours will mean that more leisure time is available in the daytime and early evening.

The IT revolution will probably be the biggest competition for the leisure market. The advances in virtual reality, the internet, home computers and communications have been astounding in the last decade, but can you imagine how those approaching the last millennium would have considered this wonderworld of technology?

What will the next ten years bring, let alone the next hundred? Perhaps we will see virtual reality tenpin bowling, where you can compete with your friends in your front room while they are hundreds of miles away. In 2035, will the Mirabelle tele-transport four courses for you and your guests on a Saturday night to your semi-detached in Bromley, à la Star Trek?

Fast approaching is the competition from interactive and digital television and home screen improvements, including the possibility of whole-wall screens being commonplace in the home within 20 years. With most leisure development depending upon the almost unique density of the UK's population (commonly over 500,000 people within a 20-minute drive time), what happens if the fundamental plank of demand - the need to leave the home at all - is removed?

Fly me to the moon?

So, in 2099 what will our successors be saying about our own leisure activities? My prophecy is that the greatest leisure activity will be travel, worldwide and possibly cosmically, and health, fitness and nutrition will be of great importance. Leisure will employ 20 per cent of the UK population.

Adapted from an article in *Leisure Management*, August 1999, by David Coffer.

Central and local government

Central and local government has influenced the development of the UK leisure and recreation industry, particularly since the 1970s. In 1960 there was only one purpose-built indoor public sports facility in the UK; now there are over 2,500. Until the 1970s public sector leisure provision was largely confined to swimming baths, museums, art galleries, parks and gardens. The philosophy behind this provision was one of education and health rather than recreation.

Following local government reorganisation in 1974, the provision of public sector sport and recreation facilities became widespread. At this time many councils created specific departments that could co-ordinate and manage the provision of leisure and recreation facilities, services and events in their areas.

Since the 1960s a wide range of **government legislation** and initiatives has also directly influenced the development of the UK leisure and recreation industry. Some of the most important of these are highlighted in Figure 1.11. Legislation that relates to health, safety and security is also covered in Unit 2 (pages 99-120).

Compulsory competitive tendering

The Local Government Act 1988 (Competition in Sport and Leisure Facilities Order) was one of the most important pieces of government legislation influencing the provision of public sector leisure and tourism facilities and services. This legislation introduced a process known as **compulsory competitive tendering** (CCT). The general aim was to develop services with greater value for money through the improved management of facilities (see also Unit 3, page 189).

Best value

In 2000, CCT was replaced with '**Best Value**', which requires local authorities to provide efficient and effective services for the communities they serve. The new scheme sets targets based on national benchmarks, against which performance is measured, in order to assess the quality and efficiency of services provided. The government requires councils to review all of their services over a five-year period, and their performance will be inspected and monitored by external auditors (see also Unit 3, page 191).

Figure 1.11: Key government legislation and initiatives

- **1964** Public Museums and Libraries Act
- **1968** National Parks and Access to the Countryside Act
- **1969** Development of Tourism Act and formation of national/regional tourist boards
- **1972** Local Government Act
- **1972** Sports Council established by Royal Charter
- **1974** Local government reorganisation in England
- **1974** Health and Safety at Work Act
- **1975** Safety at Sports Grounds Act
- **1981** Wildlife and Countryside Act
- **1984** Data Protection Act
- **1987** Fire Safety and Safety of Places of Sport Act
- **1988** Local Government Act and introduction of Compulsory Competitive Tendering
- **1989** Children's Act
- **1990** Food Safety Act
- **1992** Department of National Heritage formed
- **1992** EU directives on health and safety introduced in the UK
- **1994** Disability Discrimination Act
- **1995** First National Lottery draw
- **1997** UK Sports Council and English Sports Council replace existing Sports Council
- **1998** Department of Culture, Media and Sport replaces Department of National Heritage
- **1999** Sport England replaces English Sports Council
- **2000** Duty of 'Best Value' replaces compulsory competitive tendering, following Local Government Act, 1999

ACTIVITY

Government legislation

Figure 1.11 highlights some of the key government legislation since the 1960s that has influenced the development of the leisure and recreation industry. Select three pieces of legislation and explain how you think each of them has influenced the development of the industry.

Provide suitable examples to support your explanation.

Future developments: short-term factors and forecasts

Investigating the key factors that have influenced the development of the leisure and recreation industry to the present day is a relatively straightforward process given the vast amount of information and data available. However, forecasting how it will develop is a much more complex issue. For example, it is difficult to predict how people will spend their leisure time in the future, when we don't know what technology will be possible or available to us. It is likely that the range of factors identified at the start of this section (see page 8) which have influenced the industry since the 1960s will continue to influence it in the short to medium term.

The Leisure Industries Research Centre (LIRC) forecasts that until 2003 the home and away-from-home leisure markets will grow at similar rates, based on the volume of consumer spending, as shown in Figures 1.12 and 1.13.

Home-based leisure markets

Figure 1.12 shows LIRC's predictions for the growth in home leisure market sectors between 1998 and 2003. Expenditure in television shows the highest rate of growth, with a 32 per cent increase in the volume of expenditure forecast between 1998 and 2003. Audio equipment is second with a growth rate of just over 30 per cent and expenditure in gardening is third with a growth rate just below 30 per cent.

The digital revolution is driving the high long-term growth rate in the television and audio sectors. Increasingly over the next few years consumers will replace their existing televisions with new digital equipment. This change will lead to further increased expenditure on the wider choice of subscription channels available in digital.

The strong growth in gardening expenditure may reflect a reaction to technology's increasing role in our lives. Perhaps surprisingly, Figure 1.12 shows that the video market will not benefit from the new technology, with virtually no growth in expenditure in the forecast period. This is partly due to uncertainty about whether the future for videos will be Near Video on Demand (NVOD), Digital Versatile Disc-Video (DVD-V), or even Electronic Digital Delivery (EDD). Consumers are likely to hedge their bets and avoid investing in the 'wrong' system by putting off major new expenditure on hardware or by renting.

Figure 1.12 also shows that newspapers are the only home leisure market to show decline in the volume of expenditure over the forecast period. This is mainly due to the increasing influence of the internet.

Away-from-home leisure markets

Figure 1.13 shows the distribution of the growth predicted by LIRC in away-from-home leisure expenditure among the various market sectors between 1998 and 2003. Dining out and expenditure on wine is forecast for strong growth, at just below 20 per cent. This is caused by the steady growth in personal disposable incomes over the period. Other alcohol markets, however, show a decline in the volume of expenditure, with spirits showing the highest rate of decline, at over 8 per cent between 1998 and 2003. Gambling also shows much slower growth (at around 3 per cent) than any other away-from-home leisure sectors.

When forecasting future leisure trends it is important to consider a range of information sources. The case study on pages 24-25 provides a summary of research undertaken by Mintel as part of its 1999 report, *The Leisure Business*.

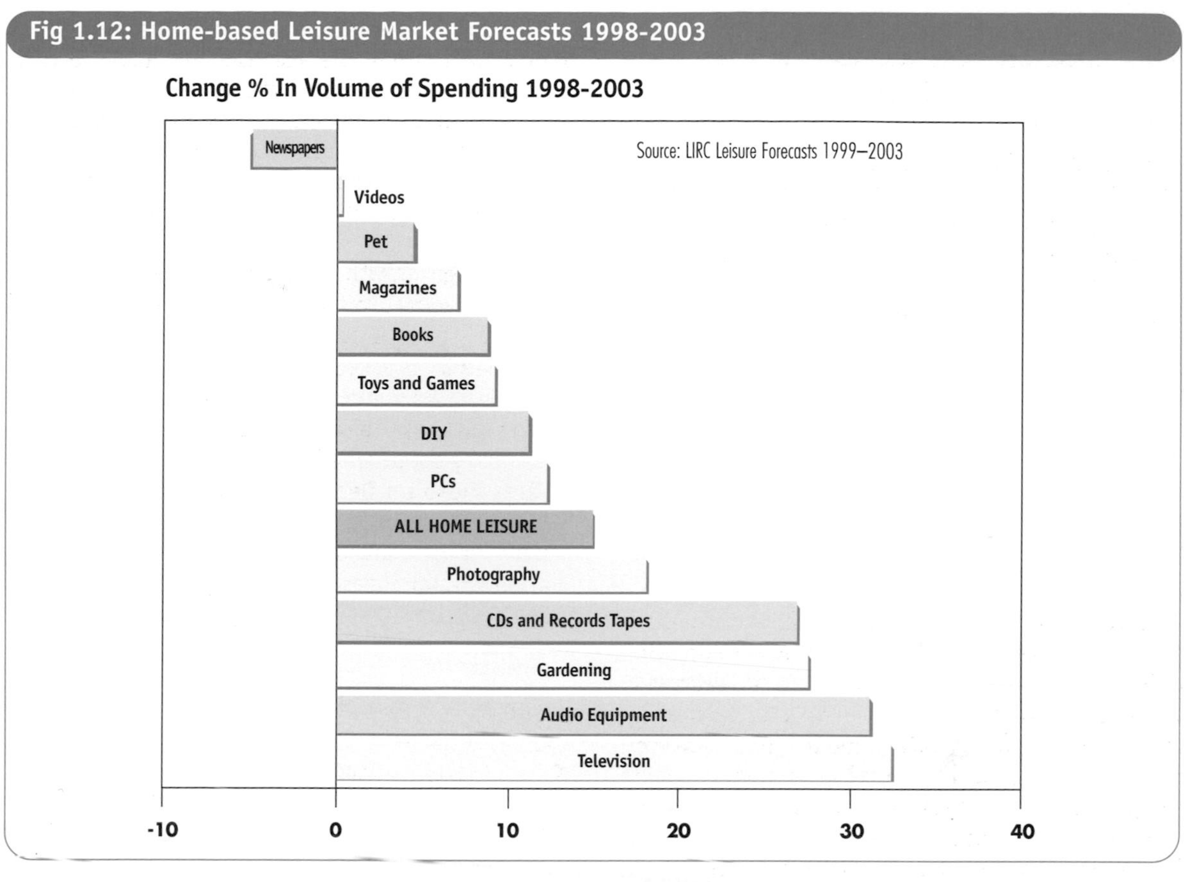

Fig 1.12: Home-based Leisure Market Forecasts 1998-2003

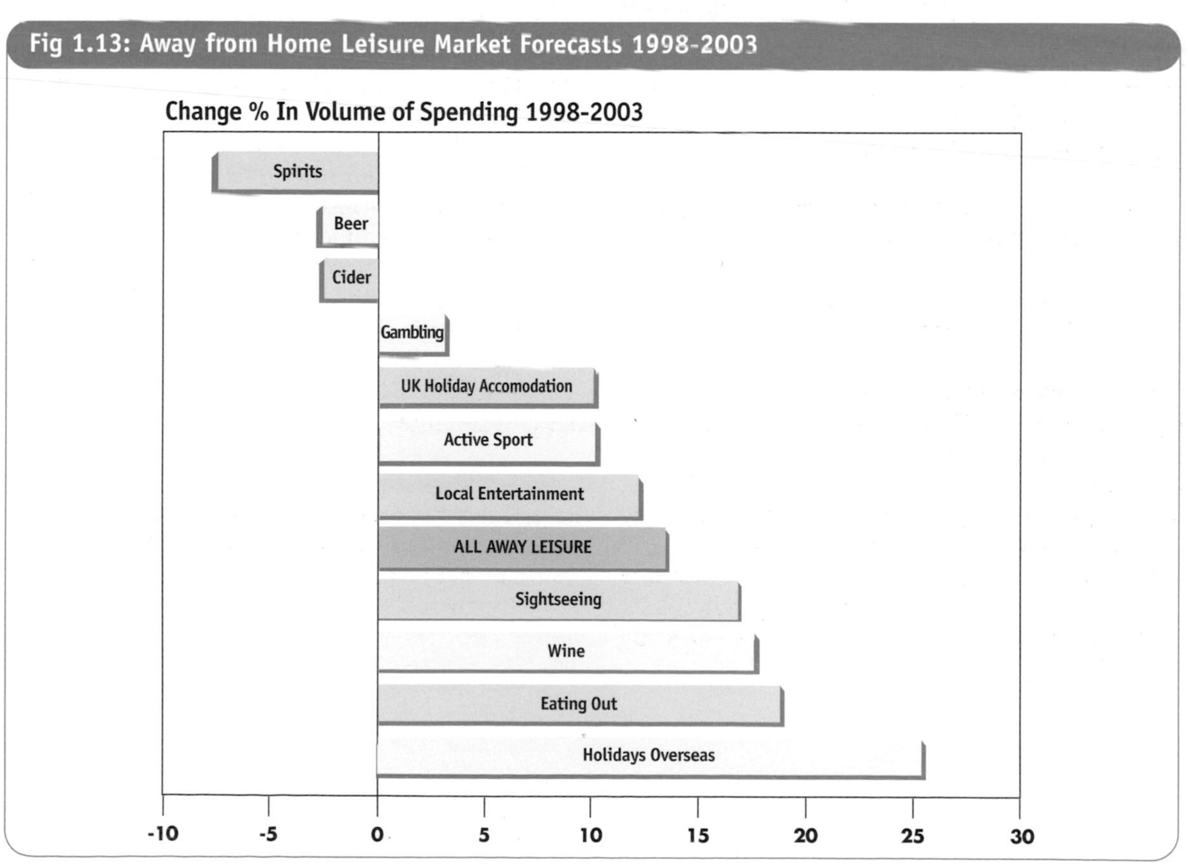

Fig 1.13: Away from Home Leisure Market Forecasts 1998-2003

CASE STUDY

Mintel research on the leisure business, 1999-2003

The future: general trends

Anecdotal evidence, supported by Mintel's consumer research, suggests that consumers increasingly have less time to devote to leisure activities but more money to spend on them, i.e. a 'cash-rich, time-poor' generation. Mintel's research in 1999 found that 51 per cent of adults claimed to have less leisure time than they did five years ago, but 44 per cent said they had more money to spend on leisure than they did five years ago. Clearly, the challenge is for operators to respond to this trend by offering consumers a rewarding experience during the limited time they have available, while at the same time maximising their financial returns.

General trends which will shape the leisure business in the years to come include:

- **the growing influence of women**
- **a greater acceptance of the needs of families**
- **the ageing population**
- **the growth in the number of students**
- **changes in the age structure of the population**
- **the increasing preparedness of consumers to travel long distances to visit leisure venues.**

As more and more women work, their spending power and influence is growing. There is greater recognition within the industry that perhaps the influence of women has tended to be ignored or understated and that opportunities have been missed because outlets were not sufficiently 'female-friendly'. Similarly, the family market has traditionally been one which has been poorly served by some sectors of the business, while others which rely on this type of customer for their core business are far more adept at catering for their requirements. The family pub, featuring dining facilities combined with indoor and outdoor play areas, is one concept which has helped maintain the viability of many pubs in the face of a steady decline in sales of their core products - alcoholic beverages and beer in particular.

The economic wealth of the over-50s is another market which leisure companies are all trying to tap into. This age range comprises an extremely disparate grouping of consumers. Some will still be working, some will have paid off their mortgages, others will have retired and will either be living off a state pension supplemented by their own pension or a state pension alone. Clearly, each of these different groups will have different levels of spending power and different priorities when it comes to leisure venues and activities.

Other changes in the age structure of the population will also have their effect. Outlets targeting younger consumers will be encouraged by the projected growth during the next five years in the numbers of 15-24 year olds, but discouraged by the knowledge that numbers of 25-34 year olds are set to decline by more than a tenth. However, the numbers of 35-44 year olds are also set to increase, so it seems that outlets whose customer base is made up primarily of 25-34 year olds will have to readjust their targeting to appeal to older or younger consumers.

Pubs and bars

Pubs and bars will be influenced by all the factors already outlined. Indeed, the changes which are taking place in this sector typify the challenges faced by the industry as a whole. During the past decade, the pubs and bars sector has changed almost beyond recognition, with the emergence of clearly defined offers such as those targeting families, students and the grey market, as well as the adoption of branding as an alternative to simply having the name of the brewer on the pub sign.

Restaurants and fast food

People are eating out more and more, but they want informality. Often the decision to eat out is taken on impulse and customers do not want to have to bother with reservations. They want the quality of a 'proper' restaurant but the informality of fast food. The widespread availability of fast food has continued to result in an expansion of this market and there is no reason why this should not continue. Further changes to traditional working patterns will continue to erode traditional meal-times, which can only be to the benefit of fast-food operators.

Nightclubs and discotheques

One area where there is likely to be considerable change during the next five years is nightclubs. Major companies with a presence in this area have suffered badly at the hands of entrepreneurial bar operators and, more recently, other major companies that have moved into the late-night bars sector. The main reason for this is that a large part of their business has been taken away due to the relaxation in attitudes of the licensing authorities in recent years, which has seen a number of late-night bars opening almost as late as clubs are allowed to. As one nightclub operator put it:

What nightclubs must focus on now is to concentrate on what makes them different from bars. That is, people want the experience of dancing with other people on the floor. Nightclubs have got to remember that is what their Unique Selling Point is.

One likely boost for the industry is the introduction of Sunday opening, previously prohibited by a law originally drafted in the eighteenth century. Operators see this as a valuable opportunity to increase their business, with one speculating that it could lead to a 5-10 per cent growth in turnover. Since bars can already open on Sundays, this will assist nightclubs and discotheques to compete on equal terms.

Bars have obviously got their Sunday licences anyway, but as far as the nightclub business is concerned it will bring quite a good, substantial, incremental revenue, so that is good potential for the future. (Nightclub operator)

Health and fitness

Health and fitness is probably the most frequently mentioned area of growth in the leisure business, so much so that multi-sector leisure businesses such as Vardon (now Cannons) and First Leisure have off-loaded their other businesses in order to focus solely on this sector. Even the renowned entrepreneur Richard Branson has decided that this is an area where Virgin Group should be involved.

The past few years have seen a tremendous 'rush for growth' among the major players in the industry, which has resulted in a number of acquisitions and a huge increase in the number of new clubs being developed and opened. The major question for the industry, having expanded so rapidly, is how to prolong the growth and maintain their existing business in the face of stiffening competition. One major multi-sector operator said:

Health and fitness has got a way to go. There is mileage in it yet. People who are in it are settling down in that market but there is still business to be got there.

ACTIVITY

The next five years

Based on the LIRC and Mintel research discussed above, summarise the key factors that you think will affect the development of the leisure industry over the next five years. You may also find it useful to refer to the journal article in the case study on page 20. In your summary include examples of leisure activities, products, services and facilities that will be affected by these factors.

Long-term factors and forecasts

It is more difficult to predict longer-term trends that will affect the leisure and recreation industry. Bill Martin and Sandra Mason of Leisure Consultants suggest that there are two contrasting scenarios ('conventional success' and 'transformed growth') that they believe will influence the development of the industry in the next 25 years. **Conventional success** represents a view in which the next 25 years develop in a way very similar to the recent past. The main trends established since the 1980s will continue, with well-maintained economic growth and little reduction in working time. In contrast, **transformed growth** describes a future in which there is still good economic growth, but also significant rethinking about lifestyle priorities. This would involve a new emphasis on the quality of life and the contribution that free time can make to it, with significant shifts in how free time is used. The implications of these two contrasting scenarios for leisure are summarised in Figure 1.14.

Figure 1.14: Leisure under two scenarios

CONVENTIONAL SUCCESS	TRANSFORMED GROWTH
Work remains prime political and personal priority	Rethinking of priority given to paid work
	More stress on quality as well as quantity of life
All growth in leisure spending	Rise in leisure time as well as spending
Working time falls very little	Total working hours fall significantly
Unemployment falls, more part-time working and early retirement	Unemployment stays low, with greater flexibility in working year/life (e.g. sabbaticals)
Further widening of inequalities in people's money/time	Trend to more even distribution in money and time
Conventional working hours broadly maintained with time stress for workers	Workers act to obtain better balance between work/family/personal time
Free time essentially a period for rest and entertainment - leisure as a reward after work	Free time as opportunity to develop and learn
	More time spent in home/neighbourhood using IT
Pressure for higher quality/money-intensive free-time activities	Interest in more time-intensive stretching/satisfying use of free time

Source: Adapted from Leisure Consultants, Transforming the Future: Rethinking Free Time and Work

Conventional success or transformed growth?

Whether the actual future lies more with conventional success or transformed growth is impossible to say. Martin and Mason believe that over the next couple of decades the UK will be pushed in the direction of transformed growth. Emerging social and environmental problems and the impact of new technologies make them doubt whether continuing conventional success can be sustained.

Transformed growth would not mean the disappearance of growth in leisure markets. Figure 1.15 shows the expected rate of expansion in consumer spending on free time over a 25-year period from 1996 to 2021 compared with what might be anticipated if the world of conventional success were to be maintained. The overall rate of growth in leisure spending under transformed growth is 78 per cent, although this is notably less than that likely under the conventional success alternative. Expansion in certain away-from-home markets like eating out, alcohol, gambling and holidays overseas would be notably slower in a transformed world.

These differences reflect the underlying shifts in free-time priorities likely to be seen in a world of transformed growth. These include more interest in 'demanding' forms of free time, like learning, exercising, helping and experiencing, rather than using free time just for rest and entertainment. Free time will gradually be seen more as an opportunity to develop oneself and to do something, rather just as a reward for having worked. For example, instead of themed catering outlets and family entertainment centres, people will be looking for new types of sports, health and learning facilities. The different implications for each of the main leisure markets are highlighted in Figure 1.16.

Figure 1.15: Alternative views of leisure markets 1996-2021

Consumer spending on free time (% change in volume)	1996-2021 conventional success	1996-2021 transformed growth
Reading	-14	-22
Home entertainment	+254	+234
House and garden	+134	+159
Hobbies and pastimes	+100	+69
Free time at home	+161	+153
Eating out	+143	+56
Alcoholic drink	+58	+24
Local entertainment	+56	+57
Gambling	+50	+23
Sport	+142	+156
Sightseeing	+146	+124
UK holiday accommodation	+128	+129
Holiday overseas	+227	+157
Free time away	+123	+74
All free time*	**+135**	**+99**
All consumer spending	**+95**	**+78**

* Narrow definition

Source: Leisure Consultants, *Transforming the Future: Rethinking Free Time and Work*

Figure 1.16: Changes expected within key leisure markets

Market	Examples of emphasis under conventional success	Examples of emphasis under transformed growth
Reading	Glossy magazines	Educational books
Home entertainment	Multi-channel television	Computers, CD-Roms, internet
House and garden	Garden leisure	Exercise and study rooms
Hobbies and pastimes	Video games, collecting	Crafts, study courses
Eating out	Fashionable restaurants, takeaway	Facilities linked to other activities
Alcoholic drink	New mixed drinks	Real beer, good-quality wine
Local entertainment	Visiting stars and groups, major spectator sports	Local productions and sports events, local relays of events
Gambling	Casinos, bingo	Local raffles
Sport	Status clubs (golf, tennis, health clubs, etc.)	Walking and keep fit, team games
Sightseeing	Major theme parks	Local museums and visitor centres

Source: Leisure Consultants, *Transforming the Future: Rethinking Free Time and Work*

In the future, people will choose to spend more of their free time either at or near their homes, making greater use of the new modes of electronic communications such as the internet and interactive television. This is likely to lead to the creation of networks of new neighbourhood leisure centres in place of the multi-operator leisure projects of recent years. An important feature will be the development of virtual leisure experiences, bringing relays of performances and events of all kinds, and virtual travel, into the home.

Barring major, unforeseeable disasters, the continued development of the leisure and recreation industry in both the short and long term appears assured. It will be the changes in social attitudes about how leisure time is used, the amount of personal disposable income available and technological developments that will influence the direction of the industry in the future.

▲ Keeping fit, a significant leisure activity

BUILD YOUR LEARNING

Keywords and phrases

You should know the meaning of the words and phrases listed below. If you are unsure about any of them, go back through the last 20 pages to refresh your understanding.

- Socio-economic developments
- Technological developments
- Changing consumer needs
- Interrelated factors
- Amount of free time
- Population age structure
- Paid employment
- Personal disposable income
- Household disposable income
- Consumer spending
- Improved mobility
- Transport technology
- Car ownership
- Demographic factors
- Life expectancy
- Birth rate
- Age distribution
- Consumer needs/expectations
- Changing fashions and trends
- Government legislation
- Compulsory Competitive Tendering (CCT)
- Best Value
- Conventional success
- Transformed growth

End of section activity

1 Using suitable examples and data, explain clearly the key factors that have promoted the rapid development of the UK leisure and recreation industry since the 1960s. You should include:

- increase in leisure time available for many individuals
- increase in disposable income
- improved mobility
- demographic changes
- changing fashions and trends
- technological developments
- government legislation.

2 The following list provides some examples of important milestones in the development of the UK leisure and recreation industry between 1960 and 2000 (excluding government legislation). Make a list of your own that shows the important milestones in the development of the UK leisure and recreation industry from the 1960s to the present day. For example, you might include the first National Lottery draw, which was held in 1995. You may also find it useful to include some of the government legislation listed in Figure 1.11 (page 21).

Important milestones in the development of the UK leisure and recreation industry might include:

1960	First motorway restaurant opens (Newport Pagnell, M1)
1962	First legal casino in the UK opens in Brighton
1972	Sports Council established by Royal Charter. First video game invented
1977	First municipal lottery (Chester-le-Street, Co. Durham)
1978	Walkman developed by Sony
1983	CD player first introduced in Great Britain
1992	Department of National Heritage formed
2000	Opening of the Millennium Dome

3 Summarise the key factors that you think will affect the short-term and long-term development of the industry. Support your views with appropriate information, data and examples. You may find it useful to read through the case studies on pages 20 and 24 before completing this task.

Scale and significance of the UK leisure and recreation industry

LEISURE AND RECREATION in the UK is a multi-billion pound industry which has a major impact on the country's economy in terms of consumer spending and employment. However, because the industry is so diverse and fragmented, it is often difficult to assess its exact contribution to the national economy.

Several organisations produce statistics on the numbers employed in various sectors of industry and the contribution they make to the national economy. Perhaps the best-known sources of data are government statistics published by the Office for National Statistics, such as Social Trends and the Annual Abstract of Statistics. Other sources of information include the national and regional tourist boards, the sports councils and professional bodies such as the Institute of Leisure and Amenity Management (ILAM).

The scale and significance of the industry nationally is best explained by means of an analysis of these four areas:

- breakdown of **consumer spending** in the UK on leisure and recreation products and services
- **employment statistics;**
- **participation trends** in popular leisure and recreation activities;
- **cultural and social significance** of leisure and recreation.

Consumer spending

The leisure and recreation industry is a major source of income for the UK economy, with the value of consumer spending currently estimated at around £147 billion per year. This level of spending is likely to increase as consumer demand for leisure goods and services continues to rise.

Government research indicates that between 1995 and 1998 households in the UK on average spent 16 per cent of their weekly budget on leisure goods and services (see Figure 1.6, page 11). Further research

Figure 1.17: Consumer spending forecast on selected goods and services, 1999

Leisure activity	Consumer spending value (£ billion)	Consumer spending volume (£ billion)
Reading	5.93	5.10
Home entertainment	15.78	16.77
House and garden	10.68	9.91
Hobbies and pastimes	7.41	6.94
Total home-based leisure	39.80	38.71
Eating out	31.07	27.74
Alcoholic drink	30.08	26.59
Local entertainment	4.04	3.48
Gambling	6.48	5.79
Active sport	5.68	5.13
Holidays in the UK and sightseeing	9.20	8.27
Holidays overseas	21.54	22.68
Total away-from-home leisure	108.10	99.67
Total all leisure	147.90	138.39

Source: LIRC, *Leisure Forecasts 1999-2003*

by the Leisure Industries Research Centre (LIRC), shown in Figure 1.17, forecast that the combined UK leisure, recreation, travel and tourism industries would generate over £138 billion in consumer spending in 1999. LIRC estimates that the actual value of this consumer spending to the UK economy is just over £147 billion.

Although the LIRC forecasts provide a useful overview, it is important to note that a high proportion of this spending arises from 'holidays overseas', which cannot be classified as part of the UK leisure and recreation industry. However, research undertaken by Mintel provides more specific details about consumer spending within the UK in three broad away-from-home leisure markets: leisure catering, leisure activities and leisure accommodation/tourism. Mintel's research findings are summarised in Figure 1.18. Mintel describes these three key leisure markets as significant areas of consumer expenditure, worth an estimated £60.3 billion in 1999.

Tax revenues

The leisure and recreation industry also contributes to the national economy via central and local government taxation, including corporation tax and value added tax (VAT). Leisure and recreation organisations contribute to local government finances through the payment of business rates. For example, in 1995 the Sports Council estimated that sport attracted £9.75 billion in consumer spending and contributed £3.6 billion in taxation.

Numbers employed nationally

It is estimated that the leisure and recreation industry and related industries employ around 1.7 million people in the UK. This accounts for approximately 12 per cent of the total UK labour force (1995 figures, from the Department for Education and Employment). The industries are therefore regarded as major providers of employment opportunities, with around 50,000 new jobs created every year.

Because the leisure and related tourism industries are so diverse it is often difficult to obtain an accurate breakdown of numbers employed. Figure 1.19 shows employment in selected leisure and tourism-related industries in 1998. The figures should only be used as guidelines, as they exclude some of the components which make up the leisure and recreation industry, such as commercial sport.

Figure 1.18: Consumer spending volume forecast on selected leisure markets, 1999 (£m)

Leisure catering	**36,488**
Fast food/takeaways	5,060
Restaurants	4,505
Pubs and bars (catering)	4,590
Pubs and bars (beverages)	15,428
Pubs and bars (other)	3,680
Wine bars	470
Roadside catering	460
In-store catering	1,035
Other catering	1,260
Leisure activities	**11,394**
Cinema	798
Theatre	310
Tenpin bowling	210
Nightclubs and discotheques	2,101
Gambling	6,750
Health and fitness	1,225
Leisure accommodation/tourism	**12,370**
Other holidays at home	4,650
Hotels (leisure only)	3,100
Short breaks	2,900
Days out	1,720
The leisure business	**60,252**

Source: Mintel, *The Leisure Business 1999*

ACTIVITY

Consumer spending

Figures 1.17 and 1.18 show the volume of consumer spending in selected leisure activities/markets.

Draw pie charts that show the proportion of

- consumer spending (volume) for home and away-from-home activities;
- consumer spending (volume) for the three key leisure markets (catering, activities and accommodation/tourism).

Figure 1.19 Employment in leisure and tourism-related industries in Great Britain (as of June 1998)

	Thousands (not seasonally adjusted)
Hotels and other tourist accommodation	318.7
Restaurants, cafés, etc.	356.0
Bars, pubs, clubs	364.1
Travel agents, tour operators	83.5
Libraries, museums, culture	77.0
Sport and other recreation	291.7
Estimated self-employment in leisure and tourism industry	194.0
Total employees/self-employed in leisure-related industries	**1,685.1**

Source: Office for National Statistics, *Annual Abstracts of Statistics 1999*

Voluntary work

The employment figures in Figure 1.19 do not include the vast numbers of people who work in the leisure and recreation industry on a voluntary basis. If the combined economic value, in terms of total hours worked, was taken into account, it is probable that the industry would be the largest employer in the UK. (See also Unit 3, page 169.)

ACTIVITY

Employment in leisure-related industries

1 Obtain up-to-date information on the numbers employed in various parts of the leisure and recreation industry. You will find the quarterly *Employment Gazette* and the *Annual Abstracts of Statistics* useful starting points for your research. These are available at your school, college or local library.

2 Imagine you have been asked to give a talk to a group of 14-16 year olds about job opportunities within the leisure and recreation industry. From the national employment data you have gathered, produce a handout which presents your data in a format suitable for your intended audience. This may include use of graphs, tables or charts. You may be able to use this information as evidence for the portfolio assignment for this unit (see page 454).

Participation trends in popular leisure activities

Figure 1.20 shows participation rates for selected home-based and away-from-home leisure activities since 1986, based on the percentage of UK adults who took part in the activity in the four weeks prior to the survey. Home-based leisure activities such as socialising with friends and relatives, and watching television are by far the most popular leisure activities. Going out for a drink or meal is the most popular leisure activity outside the home for adults.

Figure 1.20: Participation trends

Adults taking part in leisure activities (%) (most popular quarter)	**1986**	**1998**	**2003 (forecast)**
Reading books	59	(67)	(69)
Watching television	99	(99)	(100)
Listening to radio	87	(89)	(89)
Listening to records and tapes	69	(82)	(84)
DIY	42	(44)	(44)
Gardening	57	(64)	(66)
Needlework/knitting	29	(23)	(20)
Hobbies, etc.	8	(8)	(9)
Amateur music or drama	4	(5)	(5)
Games of skill	18	(19)	(19)
Going out for meal	53	(55)	(57)
Going out for drink	59	(57)	(57)
Visits to cinema	13	(15)	(16)
Visits to live arts	7	(7)*	(7)*
Visits to all entertainments	21	(22)	(22)
Museums and galleries	12	(13)*	(14)*
Historic buildings	14	(15)*	(15)*
All places of interest	24	(26)	(27)
Watching football	5	(5)	(5)
All spectator sport	13	(13)	(14)
Dancing	11	(12)	(12)
Betting	5	(17)	(15)
Doing pools	20	(17)	(15)
Going to bingo	9	(9)	(9)
All active outdoor sport	55	(58)*	(59)*
All active indoor sport	38	(40)*	(42)*
Open-air outings	25	(32)	(35)
Social activities with friends/relatives	94	(96)	(96)
Leisure classes	3	(4)	(4)

* Indicates change in survey method or definition from earlier years. Figures are derived from the General Household Survey and show the percentage of adults who took part in activity in the four weeks prior to interview in each period. 'Most popular quarter' is that with highest participation rate.

Cultural and social significance of leisure and recreation

The UK leisure and recreation industry has a significant impact on our lives and on society in general. Local communities benefit from the provision of public, private and voluntary sector leisure and recreation facilities and services, ranging from libraries and museums to pubs and sports facilities. The traditional British pub, parish hall or community centre is still the focal point of many communities in the UK. Furthermore, regeneration schemes have led to improvements and increased investment in many deprived or neglected areas. Cities such as London, Glasgow, Liverpool, Leeds, Birmingham and Hull have undertaken urban regeneration schemes which have included investment in leisure and recreation facilities to improve the quality of life for both residents and visitors.

There are also many examples of community sport and recreation schemes in the UK where the overall aim is to improve the standard of living for local residents. Indeed, sports provision is often seen as a method of developing community spirit and improving people's quality of life.

BUILD YOUR LEARNING

Keywords and phrases

You should know the meaning of the words and phrases listed below. If you are unsure about any of them, go back through the last four pages to refresh your understanding.

- Consumer spending
- Employment statistics
- Participation trends
- Cultural significance
- Social significance

End of section activity

Describe fully the scale of the leisure and recreation industry and explain its economic and social importance to the UK. You should consider the following key areas:

- the breakdown of consumer spending in the UK on leisure and recreation products and services;
- employment statistics;
- participation trends in popular leisure and recreation activities;
- the cultural and social significance of leisure and recreation.

Support your findings with relevant accurate data.

Structure of the UK leisure and recreation industry

We can divide leisure and recreation organisations into two groups: those which are publicly owned and those which are privately owned. We can further divide the latter into privately-owned organisations operating on a commercial basis (the private sector) and private groups operated largely by volunteers (the voluntary sector):

- **Public sector** organisations are largely funded by central or local government, which also influence their strategies and policies. They include local authorities which provide facilities such as leisure centres, arts centres and museums.
- **Private sector** enterprises are, directly or indirectly, in private ownership and are in business to make a profit. Examples of facilities include theme parks, cinemas and health and fitness clubs.
- **Voluntary sector** organisations are managed and operated by volunteers. They are often non-profit making or charitable. Examples of facilities include local sports clubs, youth clubs and associations, and conservation groups.

You will need to be able to identify the range of public, private and voluntary sector organisations in each component of the industry, and also evaluate their key characteristics to illustrate differences in:

- **business objectives**
- **funding or revenue generation**
- stakeholder or shareholder expectations.

The public sector

Public sector services are provided for the public and collectively paid for by the government. Their operation is ultimately accountable to elected bodies, including local councils and Parliament. The public sector regards the provision of leisure services as a social service to the community rather than as a profit-making venture. Consequently, local authorities usually provide subsidised, or in some cases free, services for the communities they serve. In so doing, they cater for the needs of groups such as school children, young mothers, the unemployed, the disabled and the elderly.

Public sector provision can be at one of two levels: national government or local government. The latter includes county councils, metropolitan councils, unitary authorities and district councils.

Central government

Historically, national government has seldom been a direct provider of leisure facilities in the UK. Its main task is to make the laws which govern their provision and provide assistance to a wide range of organisations representing the leisure and recreation industry. The government has four main functions:

- planning and control: setting the boundaries for leisure provision to ensure that development of the industry is in line with government policies
- marketing: promoting the benefits of leisure activities
- financial provision: providing funding through distribution of government monies
- co-ordination: ensuring that the activities carried out by different government organisations and departments do not conflict.

Most of these functions are carried out through the Department of Culture, Media and Sport.

Department for Culture, Media and Sport

The Department of Culture, Media and Sport (DCMS) is the central UK government department responsible for government policy on:

- the arts
- sports and recreation
- the National Lottery
- libraries, museums and galleries
- broadcasting and film
- the built heritage
- the royal estates, parks and palaces
- tourism.

Figure 1.21: Expenditure by the Department of Culture , Media and Sport (£ millions)

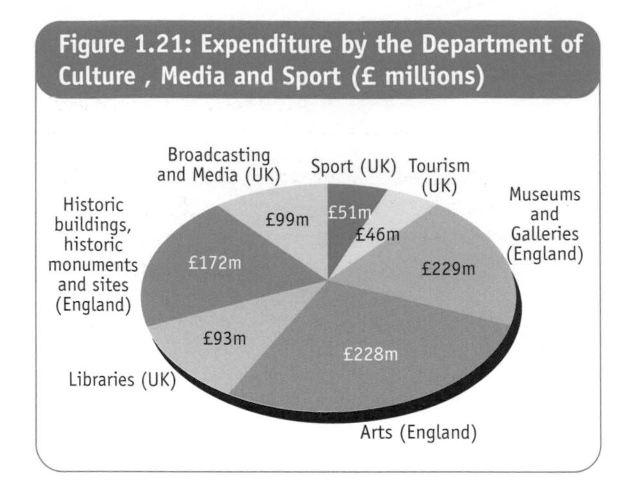

ACTIVITY

National Lottery Funding

The National Lottery funds a large number of projects. These range from major national developments such as the refurbishment of the Royal National Opera House, to small community projects such as the funding of a local swimming pool or theatre group. Look through past copies of trade journals or national newspapers and find examples of how the National Lottery has helped finance leisure and recreation projects. You will find the journals *Leisure Management* and *Leisure Opportunities* particularly useful sources of information.

Forecast departmental expenditure in 1999/2000 (excluding National Lottery grants) was £989 million. The main beneficiaries of this expenditure are shown in Figure 1.21.

Sports councils

Sports councils play an important role in the development of sport and physical recreation. Government responsibilities in sport and recreation are largely channelled through five sports councils:

- the UK Sports Council, operating as UK Sport
- the English Sports Council, operating as Sport England
- the Sports Council for Wales
- the Scottish Sports Council, operating as Sport Scotland
- the Sports Council for Northern Ireland.

SPORT ENGLAND

sportscotland

widening opportunities • developing potential • achieving excellence

All the sports councils distribute government and lottery funds. UK Sport focuses on elite athletes, while the home country sports councils are more concerned with the development of sport at community level. This involves promoting participation by all sections of the community, giving support and guidance to facility providers, and supporting the development of talented sportsmen and women, including people with disabilities. The home country sports councils also manage the thirteen national sports centres, including:

- Bisham Abbey, Berkshire (main sports: tennis, football, hockey, weightlifting, squash, rugby union and golf)
- Crystal Palace, London (main sports: athletics, swimming and sports injury centre)
- Lilleshall, Shropshire (main sports: football, hockey, gymnastics and archery)
- National Watersports Centre, Holme Pierrepont, Nottinghamshire
- National Mountain Centre, Plas y Brenin, North Wales
- Glenmore Lodge, Aviemore (mountaineering, ski-ing and kayaking)
- Inverclyde in Largs (gymnastics, golf and sports medicine)
- Scottish National Watersports Centre, Cumbrae, Firth of Clyde
- Tolleymore Mountain Centre, County Down, Northern Ireland.

The role of the sports councils is also covered in Unit 3 (pages 183).

Arts councils

The independent arts councils of England, Scotland, Wales and Northern Ireland are the main channels for the distribution of government grants and lottery funding to the visual, performing and community arts. The arts councils give financial assistance and advice not only to the major performing arts organisations, but also to small touring theatres and local arts groups. They provide funds for promoting education and public access to, and participation in, performing and visual arts.

English Heritage

English Heritage is the national body created by Parliament in 1984 charged with the protection of the historic environment and with promoting understanding and enjoyment of it. English Heritage is the government's official adviser in England on all matters concerning heritage conservation. This includes buildings, monuments, gardens, archeological remains and even landscapes. The webstract below lists their principal aims and their sources of income for 1998-9.

ACTIVITY

Public sector objectives

Find out information about a sports council, arts council or other major public sector organisation in the UK. You may need to visit a library or use the internet to obtain this information. Produce notes that explain the organisation's aims and objectives and the activities it undertakes to achieve them. You should also identify its main sources of funding or income.

ENGLISH HERITAGE

No one does **more** for England's heritage

English Heritage

English Heritage's principal aims are to:

- secure the conservation of England's historic sites, monuments, buildings and areas;
- promote people's access to, and enjoyment of, this shared heritage;
- raise the understanding and awareness of the heritage and thereby increase commitment to its protection.

English Heritage is financed by the DCMS and also raises money through its marketing activities. In 1998-9 it received £103.9 million in grant aid from the government. It raised a further £28.3 million from a range of sources, as shown in Figure 1.22.

Figure 1.22 Breakdown of non-government grant aid income 1998-9 (£ m)

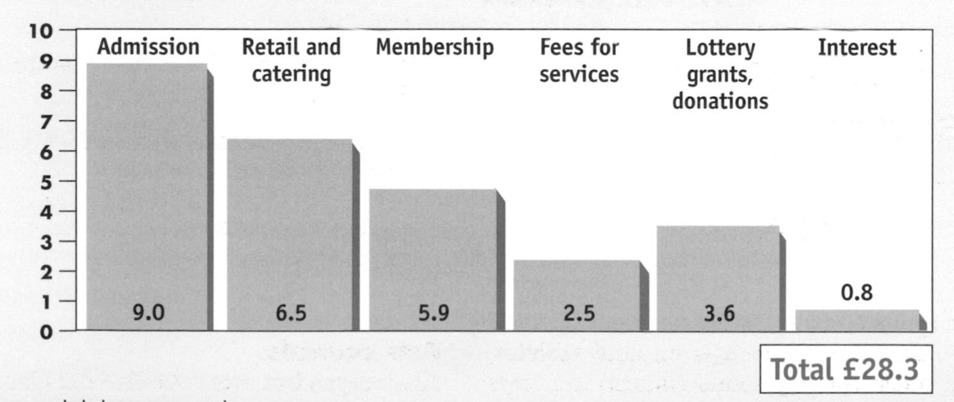

Source: www.english-heritage.org.uk

Local authorities

Local authorities are by far the largest providers of local public leisure facilities and services. Most provide a wide range of facilities, which normally include museums, art galleries, theatres, swimming pools and leisure centres, youth and community centres, parks and open spaces, playing fields and sports centres, public halls and conference centres, and tourist information centres. They also usually provide catering services at their facilities.

Most local authority leisure and recreation services are subsidised by local taxes. The two main sources of income are the council tax, which is paid by householders, and business rates, which are paid by commercial organisations. Both of these taxes are paid directly to local authorities. Local authorities may also generate income by charging for the facilities, products and services they provide. Charging for admission is the most common form of revenue. Public sector organisations sometimes make profits but do not have profitability as their main objective.

Local authorities have a legal duty to provide some leisure amenities such as libraries, but generally the provision of leisure and recreation facilities is discretionary: the council does not have to provide them. Because of this the amount spent on leisure, recreation, the arts and tourism varies from one local authority to another, depending upon the council's aims, objectives and priorities. The following Webstract gives an example of the leisure services provided by a local authority in Merseyside, Knowsley Metropolitan Borough Council.

ACTIVITY

Local authority facilities

1. Make a list of the range of leisure facilities, activities and services provided by a local authority of your choice. You may find it useful to select an authority near you, or obtain information from the internet.

2. Find out about the mission and objectives of your chosen authority in relation to the provision of community leisure services.

3. Find out how the local authority fund its leisure provision.

WEBSTRACT

Knowsley Leisure and Community Services

The mission statement of the Leisure and Community Services Department is:

To provide relevant, affordable, accessible leisure services to the people of Knowsley and to contribute to the Council's other strategic objectives of economic development, education and health so as to improve the quality of life in the Borough.

Services include:

Arts and Museum Services
- Touring Arts
- Arts in Schools
- Visual Art
- Performing Arts
- Festivals and Events
- Prescot Museum
- Educational Services

Special Events
- Community events
- Local events
- Regional events
- National and International events

Library Service
- Recreational Reading
- Educational Support
- Independent Learning for adults
- Information Technology
- Library Facilities
- Local History

Community and Youth Service
- Development
- Community Facilities
- Playwork Children 5-11 year olds
- Youth Work Provision

Parks and Countryside Service
- Country Parks and Urban Parks
- Public Open Space
- Estate Management
- Playgrounds
- Playing Fields
- Allotments

Sports and Leisure Management
- Leisure Centres
- Sports Development
- Bowring Park Golf Course
- Walks in Knowsley
- Duke of Edinburgh, Mayors Award and Citizenship Award

Source: www.knowsley.gov.uk

The private sector

The private sector is made up of a variety of commercial operators owned by individuals or companies, whose main aim is to generate profits from the services and products which they provide for their customers. The main activities of the private sector in the leisure and recreation industry take place in:

- retail sales
- catering and accommodation
- entertainment
- home-based leisure
- health and fitness.

Many private sector leisure organisations such as Rank, Ladbroke and Virgin are household names and make a major contribution to the wealth of the United Kingdom.

Leisure and recreation facilities commonly provided by the private sector include golf courses, theme parks, health and fitness clubs, nightclubs, restaurants and pubs. In general, private sector companies are unlikely to get involved in the non-profit making areas of the leisure and recreation industry.

Figure 1.23 lists the UK's major leisure operators and shows the main areas of the industry in which they are involved. The case study on page 38 provides more information about one of these major operators, Whitbread plc.

Figure 1.23: Major UK leisure companies and their operations

	Allied Domecq	Allied Leisure	Bass	First Leisure	Granada	Greenalls	Hilton Group	Rank Group	Scottish & Newcastle	Stanley Leisure	Whitbread
Leisure catering											
Fast food/Takeaways	x	x			x						x
Restaurants			x		x			x	x		x
Pub catering	x					x		x	x		x
Pubs/bars (excl. catering)	x	x	x	x		x		x	x		x
Wine bars											
Roadside catering					x						
In-store catering					x						
Other catering									x		x
Leisure activities											
Cinema								x			
Theatre											
Tenpin bowling		x	x	x				x			x
Nightclubs/discos	x	x		x				x	x		
Bingo								x			
Betting							x			x	
Football pools							x				
Casinos							x	x		x	
Amusement machines						x					
Health and fitness				x		x	x				x
Snooker/pool bars		x						x			
Leisure accommodation											
Holidays at home			x	x	x	x	x	x	x		x
Hotels (leisure only)			x		x	x	x	x	x		x
Short breaks			x		x	x	x		x		x
Days out											

Source: Mintel, *The Leisure Business 1999*

CASE STUDY

Whitbread plc

For many years, Whitbread has been the standard to which other private sector leisure businesses in the UK aspire and it continues to lead the way in terms of its financial performance, new product and site development and the areas in which it has targeted its investment. In 1999, the company made an operating profit of £418 million, a rise of 3 per cent on the previous year. Its main leisure divisions and their contribution to the company's profits in 1999 are shown in Figure 1.24.

Figure 1.25 shows the major branded leisure businesses of Whitbread. In total, there are around 1,600 managed pubs within the Inns division, about 700 of which are unbranded community local pubs. In addition, it has some 1,730 tenanted/leased pubs within its Pub Partnerships division.

Figure 1.24: Divisional analysis of Whitbread plc, by operating profit,* 1999

	1999 (£	% m)	% change 1998-9
Beer	51.6	12	+16
Other drinks	19.0	4	-25
Pub Partnerships	57.3	13	-7
Inns	179.1	41	+4
Restaurants	62.7	14	-10
Hotels	48.0	11	+31
Sports, health and fitness	21.3	5	+12
Sub-total	439.0	100	+2
Central services	-16.8		
Share Ownership Scheme Allocation to Whitbread	3.7		
Total	**418.5**	**+3**	

* Includes profit from joint ventures and associates
Source: Company Annual Reports and Accounts/Mintel

Figure 1.25: Major UK leisure businesses of Whitbread plc, July 1999

Business /brand name	Sector	Outlets
Brewers Fayre	Pubs/bars	378
Pizza Hut*	Restaurants	286**
Beefeater	Restaurants	256
Travel Inn	Hotels	207
Hogshead	Pubs/bars	149
Costa Coffee	Coffee shops	134
Café Rouge	Restaurants	108
Bella Pasta	Restaurants	71
Wayside Inn	Pubs/bars	66
Family Inn	Pubs/bars	43
Beer Engine	Pubs/bars	33
Tut 'n' Shive	Pubs/bars	29
T.G.I. Friday's	Restaurants	29
David Lloyd Leisure	Health and fitness	28
Marriott Hotels	Hotels	26
Dome	Restaurants	18
Hotshots	Pubs/bars	15
Pitchers	Pubs/bars	15
Mamma Amalfi	Restaurants	11
Kiln and Kettle	Pubs/bars	10
O'Hagans /J. J. Murphy	Pubs/bars	10
Courtyard by Marriott	Hotels	10
Curzons The Gym	Health and fitness	8
Peppers	Pubs/bars	6

* 50/50 joint venture with Tricon
** plus 113 delivery units
Source: Mintel

ACTIVITY

Private sector leisure operators

Most reference libraries keep copies of the annual reports of some major private sector companies such as Whitbread. These contain information about the companies' financial performance and usually give short commentaries on their business objectives and operations.

1 Obtain a copy of the annual report of a private sector company with leisure interests and prepare a short summary which includes details about its:

- range of business operations
- financial performance
- mission statement and business objectives
- financial returns to its shareholders.

You may also find it useful to check if your chosen company provides information on the internet.

2 Look at the share price section in any broadsheet national newspaper, such as *The Times*, the *Daily Telegraph* or the *Guardian*. Find and make a list of the companies that appear under the heading 'leisure'. In groups, discuss the types of organisations listed and what products and services they provide. Which components of the leisure and recreation industry are best represented?

The voluntary sector

Across the UK many thousands of voluntary organisations exist, ranging from national bodies to small local groups. It is estimated that there are more than 200 national voluntary leisure groups, with a combined membership of over 8 million people. These include:

- youth and community groups
- sports clubs and associations
- conservation and heritage groups
- touring groups
- social clubs
- arts associations.

If we add to these the thousands of small local clubs and other groups that can be found throughout the UK, it becomes clear that the voluntary sector is a major provider of leisure opportunities. Many volunteers are involved in work that improves the quality of life in their local communities, or give their time to help organise events or groups in areas such as sport, heritage, the environment and the arts.

Most amateur sport in the UK, for example, is managed by local voluntary clubs and associations which are supported by their members, local businesses and members of the community. In the field of art and entertainment, there are thousands of arts clubs and societies which are run by volunteers and which receive support from the Arts Council through its regional offices. Access to the countryside for recreation is promoted through voluntary organisations like the National Trust, the Ramblers Association and Youth Hostel Association which have been established for more than a century. In the countryside, environmental protection is promoted by organisations which provide many volunteers who give up their time to restore the natural environment. And in the field of visitor attractions, museums and art galleries frequently rely upon volunteers to act as guides, while many smaller tourist attractions are run entirely on a voluntary basis.

One of the most important features of voluntary sector organisations is their ability to influence decision-makers. Larger organisations, such as the National Trust, the Central Council for Physical Recreation (CCPR) and the Ramblers Association are able to influence, pressurise and lobby national and local government. For example, the CCPR has been involved in a long-standing campaign to prevent the sale of school playing fields

Funding in the voluntary sector

The voluntary sector is funded in a number of different ways. Large organisations like the National Trust, for example, may operate along similar lines to private sector organisations and run commercial operations but, like all voluntary sector organisations, it also relies heavily on a range of other funding sources, including:

- subscriptions from members, donations, gifts and legacies
- grants from central and local government
- sponsorship and fundraising events
- earnings from commercial activities and investments.

Usually, if a voluntary sector organisation makes a profit as a result of its activities it will either return this to its members in the form of lower prices, or re-invest to improve the service it offers them.

Many voluntary organisations have charitable status. This gives them some financial advantages which may include rate and VAT relief, and relief from income tax on investments, bank deposits and covenants.

Voluntary sector organisations which register as charities have to satisfy certain conditions. Their objectives must be charitable, non-profit making, and for the advancement of education or for other purposes beneficial to the community.

WEBSTRACT

The National Trust

The National Trust for Places of Historic Interest or Natural Beauty is a charity which holds countryside and buildings in England, Wales and Northern Ireland for the benefit of everyone.

THE NATIONAL TRUST

The Trust is independent of government: it depends on the generosity of those who give it properties and the money to maintain them, on more than 2.5 million subscribing members and on its friends and supporters everywhere. The Trust accepts grants from statutory bodies in the same way that other owners of historic properties and other charities may accept them when eligible. It is 'national' in the sense that it works on behalf of the nation.

The Trust employs around 3,000 salaried staff, and over 4,000 seasonal staff, and relies on the support of over 38,000 volunteers.

Figure 1.26 The National Trust income and other receipts 1996-7 %

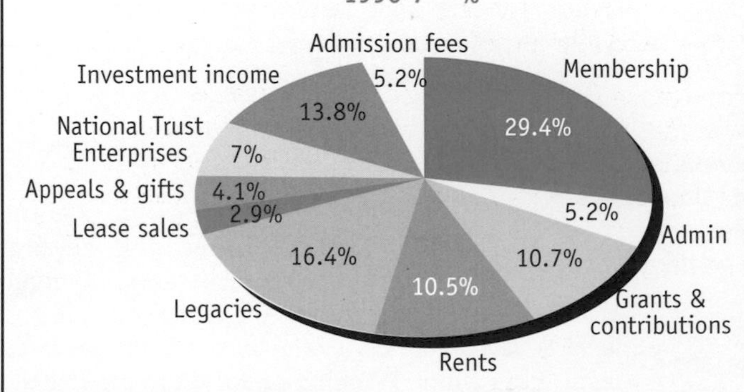

Total income: £166.2 million March 1996-February 1997
Source: www.nationaltrust.org.uk

Today the Trust is the country's largest private landowner. It protects and opens to the public 165 historic houses, 19 castles, 49 industrial monuments and mills, 48 churches and chapels, 9 prehistoric and Roman properties, 12 farms, 165 gardens and 76 landscape/deer parks. It also protects some 271,000 hectares of countryside and 575 miles of coastline.

National Trust members are admitted free on production of their membership cards to properties which the public pays to visit (although they may be charged for special events and for additional attractions which are not an integral part of a property).

ACTIVITY

Voluntary Organisations

Give examples of the following types of voluntary organisations in an area of your choice:

- a uniformed group which provides recreational opportunities for teenagers;
- a youth organisation affiliated to a religious group;
- a conservation group;
- a sports group or association;
- an art or drama group;
- a registered charitable organisation.

Compare your findings with those of others in your group. Using these findings, compile a list of all the voluntary organisations in your area. For each organisation identify which industry component it belongs to. Select one organisation from your list and identify its mission and objectives, and how it is funded.

Partnerships between the sectors

Although the public, private and voluntary sectors have differing objectives they have become increasingly interdependent in recent years, the principle being that joint ventures between two or more sectors can lead to outcomes which could not otherwise result. There are many examples of such joint ventures, such as contracting, dual use, joint provision and co-operative ventures.

Dual use and **joint provision** are both types of shared provision. Dual use has been defined as 'the longer-term regular use on an organised basis of facilities, particularly those financed from public funds, by the general public, either as members of groups or clubs or as individuals, for whom the facility was not primarily intended'. The most common form of dual use is where schools and the public use the same leisure facilities. This may involve a school allowing use of its sports hall or swimming pool by the public outside school hours and during holiday periods. This type of provision usually involves liaison between the local education authority, the local authority and local voluntary organisations.

If leisure facilities are shared between the school and the public during the day, and used by the public at all other times, then this is referred to as joint provision. Joint provision facilities are usually funded primarily by local authorities, with assistance from local education authorities.

Dual use and joint provision schemes are not confined to partnerships within the public sector. Many large private sector organisations provide leisure facilities for their employees, and they often have agreements with public and voluntary sector organisations to encourage multiple use of their facilities.

BUILD YOUR LEARNING

Keywords and phrases

You should know the meaning of the words and phrases listed below. If you are unsure about any of them, go back through the last nine pages to refresh your understanding.

- **Private sector**
- **Public sector**
- **Voluntary sector**
- **Business objectives**
- **Funding or revenue generation**
- **Dual use/joint provision**

End of section activity

Obtain issues of *Leisure Management* and/or *Leisure Opportunities* (they should be available in your school, college or local libraries). Find examples of leisure developments involving partnerships between organisations from the different sectors. For each example, make brief notes on the organisations involved and give a description of the development.

Components of the UK leisure and recreation industry

Key components

The UK leisure and recreation industry is extremely diverse and offers a vast range of facilities, products and services. Because of this diversity it is useful to group the most significant areas of activity into the six **key components** shown in Figure 1.27. These components are interrelated. For example, a public park may provide opportunities for sports and physical recreation, entertainment and countryside recreation. Similarly, a leisure centre will provide facilities and activities from several industry components, such as sport and recreation (e.g. badminton), entertainment (e.g. children's parties) and catering (e.g. a café). It is also important to remember that the industry is closely linked to the travel and tourism industry. For example, tourists use products and services from the leisure industry when they eat out, visit places of entertainment, visit attractions and attend sports events. All of these components have one main feature in common: they provide opportunities for people to spend their leisure time.

In the rest of this section we will investigate the main types of organisation, facilities, products and services within each of these components.

Figure 1.27: Key components of the UK leisure and recreation industry

Industry components and sectors

1 Study this list of well-known UK leisure and recreation facilities and complete the table as indicated.

Facility/area	Industry component	Location	Sector
Stonehenge	*Heritage*	*Salisbury Plain*	*Private*
Norfolk Broads	*Countryside recreation*	*Norfolk*	*Public*
Madame Tussauds	*Arts and entertainment*	*London*	*Private*
St Paul's Cathedral			
Tower of London			
Edinburgh Castle			
Royal National Theatre			
Wembley Stadium			
Giant's Causeway			
Hadrian's Wall			
Bisham Abbey			
Plas-y-Brenin National Mountain Centre			
Twickenham			
National Science Museum			
National Railway Museum			
St Andrew's Golf Course			
Silverstone			
Alton Towers			
Chessington World of Adventures			

2 Compile another table like the one above which identifies the main away-from-home leisure and recreation facilities in your own locality. You should include a minimum of three facilities for each component (except home-based) within the leisure and recreation industry.

3 Locate each of the local facilities you have identified on a map of your area and compile a key to their exact locations.

Arts and Entertainments

This component of the leisure and recreation industry covers a very broad range of activities, from pubs and social clubs to museums and art galleries. When thinking of arts and entertainment, it is useful to distinguish between those activities which occur in the home and those which take place in public. This section will concentrate on activities that take place away from the home, as home-based leisure is considered later (page 62).

Figure 1.28 provides an indication of the range of arts and entertainment facilities in the UK, and the sectors that run them.

Cinema

The popularity of the cinema reached its peak in 1946, when 1,600 million tickets were sold. By 1984 this number had fallen to only 53 million, due largely to the development of television. However, since the mid-1980s there has been an increase in attendances, with 145 million visits to UK cinemas in 1999. One of the main reasons for this growth has been the development of large multi-screen cinemas (sometimes known as multiplexes) which can cater for a wider range of customer tastes. There were eleven multiplexes in the UK in 1988 and over 100 by 1995. Figure 1.29 shows the major operators in the UK cinema market in 1998.

Figure 1.28: Examples of arts and entertainment facilities

Facility	Sectors	Examples
Cinema	Private	Virgin Cinemas, UCI
Theatres and concert halls	Private, public	London Palladium, Barbican Centre
Museums and art galleries	Private, public and voluntary	Madame Tussauds, British Museum
Pubs and clubs	Mainly private	Yates Wine Lodge, Mecca bingo halls
Theme and leisure parks	Private	Alton Towers, Legoland Windsor
Libraries	Mainly public	Local authorities, county councils

Figure 1.29: Leading operators in the UK cinema market, 1998

Operator trading name	Sites	Screens	Screens per site
Odeon	76	414	5
ABC	73	213	3
UCI	31	285	9
Virgin	31	240	8
Warner Bros	18	164	9
Showcase	15	196	13
Apollo	14	57	4

Source: Mintel, *UK Cinema Market* 1998

Maximising audiences is vital for the film industry. Large-budget films currently cost around £45-60 million to make, and over half of all films lose money. On the other hand, successful films such as *The Full Monty* and *Four Weddings and a Funeral* can make huge profits from box office takings worldwide. Because of the amount of money that has to be invested, and the high risk involved, this part of the leisure and recreation industry is dominated by the private sector.

Theatres and concert halls

Theatres, concert halls and other facilities for live performance range from temporary venues and those adapted for 'one-off' events (such as an outdoor stage or school hall) to national venues with resident companies, such as the Barbican Centre, which is home for half the year to the Royal Shakespeare Company. The voluntary sector is well represented in this area, with numerous amateur music and drama groups, operatic societies and other groups of performing clubs and societies. However, most of the well-known venues are in the private sector. Major theatres such as the London Palladium and concert venues such as Wembley and Earl's Court are owned by private companies.

Theatres and other venues for live performance are often heavily subsidised by the public sector. The main national companies – the Royal National Theatre on London's South Bank, the Royal Shakespeare Company and the Royal Opera and

ACTIVITY

Seventy years of movies we'll never forget ... and some we wish we could

Study the following list of twenty films, half of which represented the top ten profitable films, and half of which represented the top ten flops between 1963 and 1998. When you have decided on each category, attempt to rank them in order of most profitable and biggest flops. To help get you started the first film has been given for each category. (The answer to this activity is given on page 461.)

Titanic 1998
The Avengers 1998
Full Monty 1997
Men in Black 1997
The Lost World: Jurassic Park 1997
Independence Day 1996
Waterworld 1995
The Lion King 1995
Toy Story 1995
Four Weddings and a Funeral 1994
Last Action Hero 1993
Jurassic Park 1993
Hudson Hawk 1991
Ghost 1990
The Bonfire of the Vanities 1990
Ishtar 1987
Raise the Titanic 1980
Heaven's Gate 1980
Revolution 1980
Cleopatra 1963

Rank	Top ten hits	Profit (£ m)	Rank	Top ten flops	Loss (£ m)
1	Titanic	68	1	Waterworld	70
2			2		
3			3		
4			4		
5			5		
6			6		
7			7		
8			8		
9			9		
10			10		

Ballet, Covent Garden – all receive funding from the Arts Council of England. The Arts Council also supports many regional and local organisations including dance, opera and theatre companies. These organisations usually supplement this funding with donations and sponsorship, often from private sector organisations.

Most of the larger theatres and concert venues are located in major cities. The greatest concentration of theatres is in London's West End, where there are 51 private and public theatres. The Society of London Theatre estimates that in 1998 West End theatres attracted a total of 11.9 million attendances from over 16,000 performances, generating receipts of £257.9 million. There are around 500 theatres outside London in the UK, many of which are owned by public sector organisations. There are also many theatrical and entertainment festivals, ranging from small local festivals to internationally known events such as the Edinburgh Festival.

Museums more popular than live socce

New research by MORI on behalf of the Museums and Galleries Commission (MGC) and the Campaign for Museums shows that the popularity of museums is growing, and has overtaken theatre-going and sports events.

The survey shows that in 12 months 35 per cent of British adults had been to a museum or art gallery, compared with 33 per cent going to a zoo or wildlife park, 32 per cent to a stately home and 30 per cent to performances of drama, opera or ballet. Only 26 per cent went to live sporting events, and theme parks, seen as main competition for museums, attracted only 28 per cent. And the traditional reason fo putting people off museums that they 'don't make peopl feel welcome', has all bu disappeared. Only 1 in 100 sai they were intimidated by museums.

Loyd Grossman, chairman o the Campaign for Museums and MGC commissioner, said: 'This research proves a key message of the Campaign for Museums – that this country's museums and galleries are exciting and popular places to visit. I believe that more and more people will learn that the United Kingdom has museums for everyone.'

Source: *Campaign for Museums*, 7 June 1999

Museums and art galleries

Millions of people visit museums and art galleries in the UK every year for a variety of recreational, educational and cultural reasons. Museums are run by organisations in the public, private and voluntary sectors, although the principal ones are mainly publicly owned. Facilities range from large national museums, such as the British Museum and the National Gallery, to important regional and local collections and small local museums run by volunteers. Recent research by MORI shows that the popularity of museums is growing, as shown in the article above.

The Museums Association defines a **museum** as 'an institution which collects, preserves, exhibits and interprets material evidence and associated information for the public benefit'. This definition encompasses general municipal museums and those which specialise, for example, in social history, natural history, transport, science, military artefacts, past industrial processes and agriculture. The Campaign for Museums has developed the '24 Hour Museum', which provides extensive information about museums on the internet. Its web site includes a museum finder, with museum collections placed in a number of categories. These categories give some idea of the different types of collections that museums provide:

- Archeology
- Art and Design
- Transport
- Maritime
- Personalities
- Weapons and War
- Natural History
- Science and Technology
- Social History
- National Collections
- Costume
- Archives
- World Cultures
- Coins and Medals
- Music

ACTIVITY

Museum facilities

If you have access to the internet go to the 24 Hour Museum site (www.24hourmuseum.org.uk).

Conduct a detailed search for information on museums in a chosen locality. Find out information about facilities and complete the table below. An example is provided to help get you started.

If you do not have access to the internet, then gather the information from visitor guides or by visiting the museums.

Museum	Sector	Facilities available	Collection details
British Museum	*Public*	*Shop, library, catering, disabled access, baby rooms*	*Archeology, archives, world cultures, weapons and war, costume, coins and medals, art and design, social history*

The English Tourism Council (formerly English Tourist Board) lists about 950 museums in the United Kingdom, each attracting at least 5,000 visitors a year. There are fourteen national collections in England which are funded by the public sector. The most popular of these collections are shown in Figure 1.30.

In Scotland the national collections are held by the National Museums of Scotland and the National Galleries of Scotland, which attracted 632,000 and 842,000 visitors respectively in 1998-9. The National Museum of Wales, in Cardiff, and the National Museums and Galleries of Northern Ireland, also provide national collections.

London is the major centre for museums of all kinds, with 47 public museums and galleries attracting 50,000 or more visits a year. London also contains eight of the twelve most popular national museums in England in terms of visitor numbers, as shown in Figure 1.30.

Outside the capital, the largest museums are located in major cities, such as the Glasgow Art Gallery and Museum and the Royal Armouries in Leeds, which attracted over 1 million and 400,000 visitors respectively in 1998-9.

Figure 1.30: Visits to national museums and galleries in England: attendance in 1998-9 (millions)

British Museum	5.5
National Gallery	4.8
Tate Gallery	3.0
National Museum of Science and Industry*	2.2
Natural History Museum	1.9
Victoria and Albert Museum	1.5
Imperial War Museum	1.4
National Portrait Gallery	1.2
National Museums and Galleries on Merseyside	0.7
National Maritime Museum	0.5
Royal Armouries	0.4
Wallace Collection	0.2

* NMSI also has two regional museums: National Railway Museum, York and the National Museum of Photography, Film and Television, Bradford.

Source: Department of Culture, Media and Sport.

Pubs and clubs

Public houses and social clubs are an important part of British life. The local pub or social club is a central feature of many communities and provides valued leisure and recreational opportunities for customers. A wide variety of social clubs and associations has evolved to cater for the needs of all types of people, including working men's clubs and institutes, ex-armed forces associations and political clubs. National chains of privately owned social clubs, such as those of Mecca Leisure and the Rank Organisation, provide bingo and other entertainments, as well as nightclubs and discos. Figure 1.31 provides some key facts about the importance of the UK pub trade.

Libraries

The public library system covers the whole of the UK, from large libraries in towns and cities to small branch and mobile libraries in less densely populated areas. There are currently 4,227 libraries and 663 mobile public libraries in the UK, and these attracted 303 million visits in 1999. Most funding for the library service comes from the public sector, as shown in Figure 1.32. Libraries play an important part in leisure and in recent years they have diversified to offer records, cassettes, compact discs and videos. The library service is generally regarded as an essential element of public sector provision, although funding cutbacks in the last decade have often meant fewer new titles and a reduced level of service. However, from 2001 the government has decided to implement new regulations that will raise standards of library provision in the UK, as shown in the article below.

Theme and leisure parks

The phrase **theme park** describes an action packed, family-centred leisure and entertainment complex. Parks often include high-technology versions of traditional funfair rides and roller coasters (sometimes referred to as white-knuckle rides), as well as amusement arcades, adventure playgrounds, computer simulations and laser games. They often have a variety of sports facilities, heritage activities, zoos and wildlife areas. The top ten theme/leisure parks and piers in the UK are shown in Figure 1.33.

Figure 1.31: The bar facts

- There are 61,000 pubs in the United Kingdom.
- They employ more than 600,000 people.
- Eight out of ten people who go to a pub once a week regard themselves as happy.
- Pubs raise £60 million a year for good causes.
- Two in five adults in England and Wales eat in a pub at least once a month.
- Pubs are the top choice for eating out, serving 25 million meals a week.
- Pub grub is now a £4.8 billion-a-year market.
- More than 36,700,000 barrels of beer are drunk in pubs each year.
- Britons spend more than £15 million a year on beer.
- The busiest day of the year is Mother's Day followed by St Valentine's Day.
- The trade is worth £22 billion a year, growing by 10 per cent each year.
- More than £12 million a week is spent refurbishing and extending pubs.
- The average pub injects at least £64,000 a year into the local economy before business taxes.

Source: *Financial Mail on Sunday*, 12 April 1998

Figure 1.32: How libraries are funded

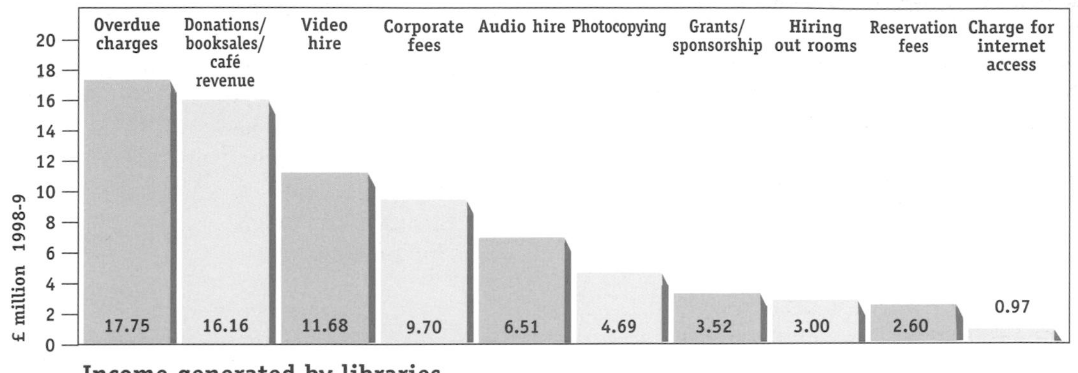

Total	76.58
Government funding	743.24
Libraries total income	**819.82**

New Chapter for Public Libraries

The only aspect of the public library service that has not diminished during the past ten years is the number of members.

At the end of the 1980s, 33.1 million people, representing 58 per cent of the population, held library cards. Last year there were 34.4 million members, equal to the same proportion of the population. But records kept by the Library and Information Statistics Unit (LISU) at Loughborough University show a sad decline in the national library service. Since 1989, 445 branches have closed, along with 39 mobile units. The total stock of library books has been reduced by nearly 18 million and there are 29 per cent fewer librarians.

In the early 1980s, when local government spending cuts began paring down library budgets, there was no co-ordinated opposition. Then in 1984 the Library Campaign was launched. For the past 15 years it has waged gentle but determined opposition to spending cuts in the service. The government has promised to set minimum standards for the service, which local authorities will be obliged to meet. The guidelines will cover the amount of new books to be bought each year, the location of libraries, opening hours and the provision of professional staff.

'This policy is along the right lines', says Jill Wight, a director of the Library Campaign. 'Local government has a statutory obligation to provide library services but they can be monitored only if formal standards are set.'

Source: *Financial Mail on Sunday*, February 20, 2000

Figure 1.33: Top ten theme/leisure parks and piers, 1998 visits

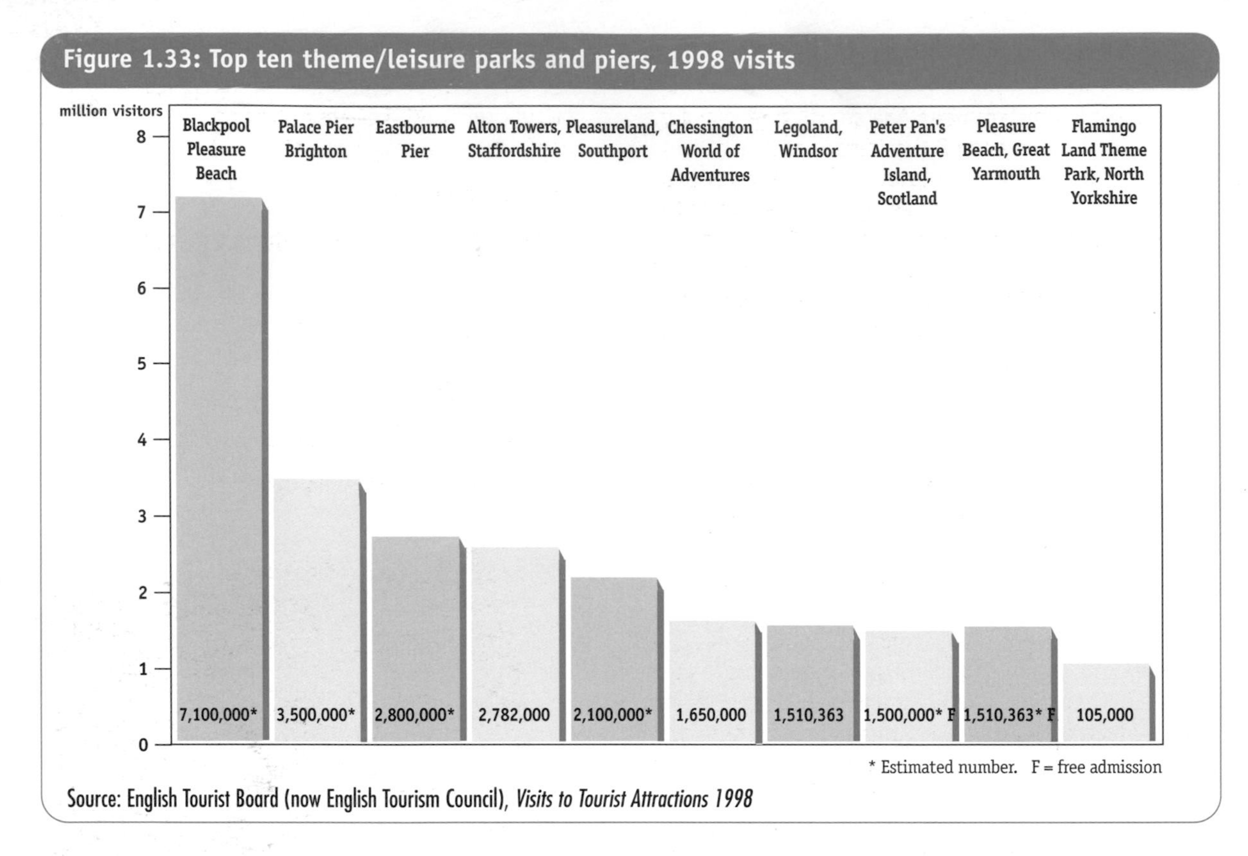

Source: English Tourist Board (now English Tourism Council), *Visits to Tourist Attractions 1998*

UK theme and leisure parks attracted over 37 million visitors in 1998. Theme parks usually charge a daily admission fee, covering the cost of all rides and entertainments. Alton Towers is the largest admission-charging theme park in the UK, attracting over 2.7 million visitors in 1998.

Some theme and leisure parks do not charge admission fees, so it is possible to estimate only the total number of visitors each year. It is estimated that 7.1 million people visited Blackpool Pleasure Beach in 1998.

Theme and leisure parks are big business, attracting huge numbers of visitors. This has involved major financial investment, running into millions of pounds. For example, the Pepsi Max Big One roller coaster at Blackpool Pleasure Beach cost £12 million, while the Nemesis ride at Alton Towers cost £10 million. Legoland, near Windsor, is the most recent theme park to be built at a cost of £85 million. It has 17 rides, 21 attractions and 5 live shows. In 1998 over 1.6 million people visited Legoland Windsor. Most theme parks are run by private sector organisations.

ACTIVITY

Arts and entertainment

In small groups, brainstorm examples of arts and entertainments facilities and activities available in your area. You may find it useful to look at the 'What's On' or entertainment section of your local newspaper. From your brainstorming session, compile an A-to-Z list of arts and entertainment facilities and activities available in your area. This could range from amusement arcades to zoos.

▲ Legoland

Sports and physical recreation

Like arts and entertainment, the **sports and physical recreation** component of the leisure and recreation industry covers a very broad range of facilities, events, products, services and activities. We will investigate the sports industry in detail as part of Unit 3. This section provides an overview of this industry component. Figure 1.34 highlights some of the main sport and recreation facilities and activities in the UK, and the sectors that run them.

Participating in sport and physical recreation activities

There is an enormous range of sport and physical recreation activities available to individuals and groups. Figure 3.18 on page 171 lists the most popular sports and physical recreation activities in the UK. Growing interest in healthy lifestyles and the link with fitness and exercise have been a major influence on sports participation since the 1980s. Among the many facilities used for sport and physical activities are sports centres, leisure centres, ice rinks, squash courts and fitness centres. There are also specially constructed outdoor facilities such as athletics tracks, golf courses, natural and artificial playing pitches and sports stadia. Natural resources such as rivers, lakes (and reservoirs), beaches, hills, mountains and caves provide suitable sites for a range of sports and physical activities.

Swimming pools

Most recreational swimming takes place in indoor pools which are nearly all provided by the public sector. In 1998, it was estimated that there were about 1,400 public indoor swimming pools in the United Kingdom and a further 3,500 pools in schools. These are mainly conventional 25-metre pools. However, in recent years a number of new-style leisure pools with flumes, chutes and wave machines, islands and water rapids have been developed. The private sector is also involved in swimming provision, usually via pools in hotels or health and fitness clubs.

Sports centres

In 1960 there was only one purpose-built public sports facility in Britain; now there are over 2,500. Like swimming provision, this area is dominated by the public sector, including local authorities and schools. Sports centres vary in size, facilities and the range of services they offer. They usually contain a main sports hall with changing and reception facilities. Sometimes there are also specialist facilities available such as squash courts, weights rooms, a climbing wall and social areas, including cafés, bars and function rooms. A sports centre will provide a range of products and services, some of which will be more obvious than others. For example, a sports centre might provide

- sports activities
- lessons and classes for different groups of people
- functions, such as parties, wedding receptions, etc.
- food and drink
- special rates for members and/or groups
- purchase and hire of equipment.

▲ Swimming pools offer a wide range of activities

Figure 1.34: Main facilities/activities in sport and recreation

Facility/activity	Sector	Examples
Sports/leisure centres	Mainly public, some private and voluntary	Local authority sports centres, national sports centres (all public), YMCA centres (voluntary)
Swimming pools	Mainly public, some private	Local authority pools, pools in hotels
Health and fitness centres	Public and private	Local authority centres, David Lloyd Leisure, Courtneys Leisure Clubs, hotel leisure clubs
Sports participation	Public, private and voluntary	Football, hockey, golf, tennis, rugby, athletics
Sports coaching and development	Public, private and voluntary	Local authority schemes, national governing body coaching programmes, local sports clubs
Sports spectating	Mainly private and public, some voluntary	Football, horse racing, motor racing, cricket, rugby
Sports retail goods	Private	Nike, Adidas, Reebok, Olympus Sports, JJB Sports
Sports gambling	Private	Ladbrokes, William Hill, Coral

Health and fitness centres

Growing awareness of the health benefits of an active lifestyle has created a demand for health and fitness products and services. These products and services are often provided at private health and fitness centres which contain weights rooms and equipment such as exercise bikes, treadmills and rowing machines, designed to improve heart and lung (cardiovascular) fitness (see also Unit 3, pages 162-164). Some also provide swimming pools, saunas, jacuzzis, steam rooms and other health-related services such as massage, aromatherapy and beauty therapy. It is estimated that there are now around 2,200 private health and fitness clubs in the UK.

Many of the larger hotel chains, including Forte and Thistle Hotels, have also developed health and fitness suites as part of the services provided free to guests. Specialist 'health farms' and country clubs have also come into being to cater for the needs of

Figure 1.35: Sources of income generation for private sector UK health and fitness

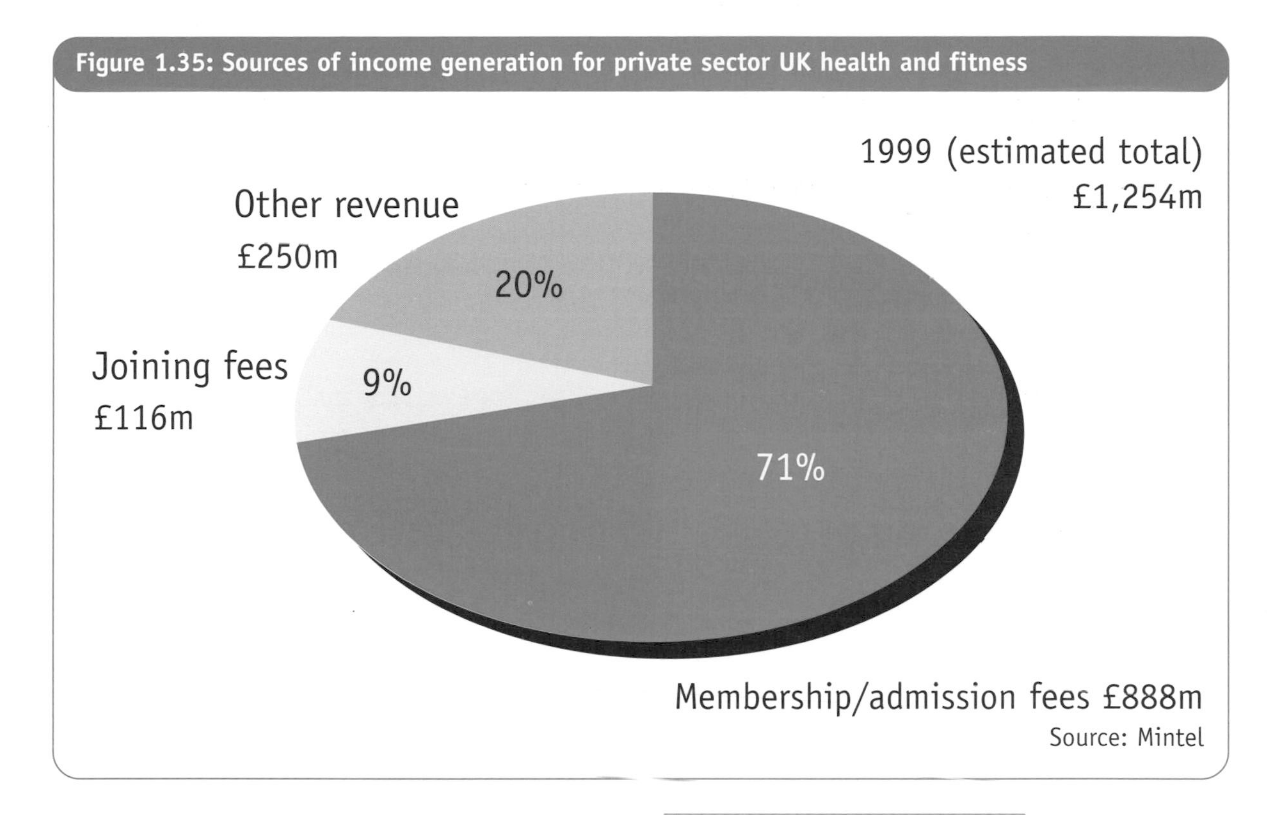

Source: Mintel

an increasingly health-conscious society.

Membership revenue, whether from monthly, annual or joining fees, represents the vast majority of the turnover of the average health and fitness club. The largest proportion of this is in the form of membership fees, which are usually paid either monthly or annually. These are estimated to have represented 70 per cent of the total in 1999, as Figure 1.35 demonstrates.

Fitness First and Whitbread are the largest operators of dedicated health and fitness clubs in the UK, while Granada and Hilton Group continue to vie for the position of largest operator of hotel-based UK health and fitness clubs. In terms of revenue and profit, the number of members is a far more important indicator than the number of clubs operated. By this measure, Whitbread is the clear market leader. With its purchase of the Racquets & Healthtrack group and the opening of several new David Lloyd clubs towards the end of 1999, it has broken through the 200,000-member barrier for the first time.

Four other companies – Cannons, Holmes Place, Esporta and Fitness First – have 100,000 members or more but no operator is close to rivalling the size and scale of Whitbread's operations as shown in Figure 1.36.

▼ Kensington Sports Centre - a local authority sports facility

Figure 1.36 Leading operators of UK health and fitness clubs, December 1999

Company	Members
Whitbread plc	205,676
Cannons Group plc	130,000
Holmes Place plc	109,700
Esporta plc	103,000
Fitness First plc	100,000
Hilton Group plc	88,000
Kunick plc/The Leisure Connection	71,000
Granada Group plc	64,600
Greenalls Group plc	61,000
DC Leisure Group	54,600
Pulse Fitness plc	38,000
LA Fitness plc	32,000
Lady in Leisure Group plc	30,000

Source: Mintel report, *Health and Fitness Clubs*, 1999

ACTIVITY

Health and fitness clubs

Make a list of the facilities and activities provided at a health and fitness facility in your locality. You may need to visit the facility, or obtain details of its programme to complete this activity. You may also be able to use the internet to obtain this information.

Local sports clubs and associations

There are estimated to be 150,000 voluntary sports clubs in Britain affiliated to the 400 or so national governing bodies of sport. If you look in the sports section of any local newspaper, or the Yellow Pages, you will find many examples of these sports clubs.

Sometimes a community forms a 'sports association' that provides a range of activities. For example, a typical village sports association might provide facilities for football, cricket, hockey, tennis and bowls. Many will also provide social facilities, such as a bar, function room and meeting room. As the vast majority of these clubs and associations operate on a 'not-for-profit' basis, they are classified as voluntary sector organisations.

ACTIVITY

Sports clubs and associations

Obtain a copy of the Yellow Pages for a locality of your choice and find the section on sports clubs and associations. Make a list of the sports clubs and associations in the locality. You will probably find that there are too many listed in the directory, in which case limit your list to a specific locality within the region.

Select one of the clubs or associations from your list and find out more information about it. You may need to visit the organisation, or interview someone who is a member. You need to find out:

- the club's aims and objectives
- what sports and physical recreation activities it provides
- who it provides them for
- what facilities it has (include social facilities as well as sports facilities)
- how it generates income to pay for the facilities and activities it provides
- who runs the club.

Playing pitches

It is impossible to obtain an accurate estimate of the total number of playing pitches. The English Sports Council calculates that there are 70,000 pitches in England alone. Football accounts for about half of all pitch provision and cricket one quarter. The remainder are mainly rugby and hockey pitches. In addition to this provision, there are now around 300 artificial grass pitches in England.

Figure 1.37: Distribution of sport facilities, UK

	England	Scotland	Wales	Total
Indoor bowls	300	50	15	365
Ice rinks	40	34	2	76
Athletics tracks	412	49	24	485
18-hole golf courses	1,270	385	121	1,776
Dry ski-slopes				99

ACTIVITY

Spectator facilities

1 Match each well-known facility in the table with the spectator sport it caters for. Some facilities may provide a venue for more than one sport. (The answers are on page 461.)

Facility	Spectator sport
1 Lords	A Rugby union
2 Vicarage Road	B Horse racing
3 The Crucible	C Motor racing
4 Murrayfield	D Football
5 Epsom	E Football and rugby union
6 Silverstone	F Snooker
7 Wimbledon	G Cricket
8 Wentworth	H Rowing
9 Aintree	I Football and rugby league
10 Henley	J Tennis
11 Elland Road	K Golf
12 Stadium of Light	L Horse racing

2 Select one of the venues listed and identify the range of facilities, products and services it offers its customers. Alternatively, you could investigate a sports spectator facility in your area with which you are familiar.

Sports spectating

Popular national sports such as football, rugby league, rugby union, cricket, golf, motor racing and horse racing can draw large crowds of spectators. In recent years many facilities have been redeveloped to provide better services for both participants and spectators. Indeed, sports stadia are now often multi-purpose leisure facilities. Old Trafford, for example, home of Manchester United Football Club, is not only a venue for football matches but has also hosted rugby league matches and pop concerts. The stadium has been developed by increasing its capacity, improving parking facilities and making it an all-seater facility, with a range of spectator services from family enclosures to executive boxes costing several thousand pounds per game. The club also offers guided tours of the stadium, has a football museum and operates as a venue for conferences, exhibitions and private functions such as weddings and parties.

Sports retail

The popularity of sporting and physical recreational activities has created a huge consumer demand for a wide range of sports clothing and equipment (see also Unit 3, pages 147-150). In 1998 consumers spent an estimated £3,500 million on sportswear and equipment and manufacturers such as Nike, Adidas, Puma and Reebok have all become household names. Chains of sports retailers such as JJB Sports and Sports Division, with 449 outlets between them in 1999, have emerged alongside the many independent sports shops, to ensure that sports retail outlets are commonplace in the high street. Sports manufacturers and retailers are all private sector organisations, as they aim to make a profit.

▲ An example of one of many sports brands

Heritage sites and attractions

The English Tourism Council (formerly English Tourist Board) defines a **visitor (tourist) attraction** as:

> *a permanently established excursion destination, a primary purpose of which is to allow public access for entertainment, interest or education, rather than being a primary retail outlet or venue for sporting, theatrical or film performances. It must be open to the public, without prior booking, for published periods each year, and should be capable of attracting day visitors or tourists as well as local residents.*

Obviously, this definition encompasses a much broader range of visitor attractions than just heritage. Some of the other types of attraction, such as theme parks and museums, have been covered already within the arts and entertainment industry component. Visitor attractions can be classified in a variety of ways, such as

- those which charge an admission fee, such as Madame Tussauds, or those which allow free entry, such as Westminster Cathedral
- natural attractions, such as the Lake District, or built attractions, such as the Royal Armouries.

Visitor attractions are a vital component of the UK leisure industry. The English Tourism Council (ETC) estimated that visits to all categories of visitor attraction in England totalled 396 million in 1998. Heritage attractions such as Madame Tussauds that are run by private sector organisations aim to make a profit, but those run by charities, such as the National Trust, or by the public sector, are often heavily subsidised. (See also p.284.)

Heritage attractions range from centuries-old historic sites, such as Stonehenge and Skara Brae, to the latest technology-enhanced attractions, such as the Earth Gallery Experience at the National History Museum in London. The cultural significance of what is deemed to be 'heritage' is far reaching and consists of:

- historic buildings, e.g. Windsor Castle
- historic cities and towns, e.g. Bath, York
- places with historic, literary and cultural associations, e.g. Elgar and Malvern, Dickens and Rochester
- cultural collections, e.g. Royal Armouries
- historic landscapes, e.g. historic parks and gardens
- industrial heritage, e.g. Ironbridge
- local traditions and cultures, e.g. morris dancing
- pageantry, e.g. the Changing of the Guard.

Visiting our heritage is one of the key components of the UK leisure industry. It is estimated that UK heritage attractions attracted over 50 million visitors in 1998. Some of the most popular heritage attractions are listed in Figures 1.38 and 1.39.

Historic buildings and sites

There are around 450,000 listed historic buildings and sites in the United Kingdom. They include:

- stately homes, palaces and manors, e.g. Blenheim Palace, Castle Howard
- castles and forts, e.g. Edinburgh, Caernarfon, Dover
- cathedrals, churches and abbeys, e.g. Westminster Abbey, Coventry Cathedral, Rievaulx Abbey
- monuments and ruins, e.g. Hadrian's Wall, Glastonbury Tor
- battlefields, e.g. Naseby, Towton
- historic ships, e.g. Cutty Sark, HMS Victory, HMS Belfast.

Many historic buildings and sites are owned and run by religious organisations, including Westminster Abbey and York Minster, both of which attract more than 2 million visitors every year.

Local authorities, the National Trust and English Heritage are also involved in preserving and maintaining historic buildings for the public to visit, while the five historic palaces – the Tower of London, Hampton Court, Kensington Palace, Kew Palace and the Banqueting House, Whitehall – are run by the government agency, Historic Royal Palaces.

Approximately a third of the historic properties in the UK open to the public are owned and managed by the private or voluntary sector. This includes the properties owned by the National Trust. Figures 1.38 and 1.39 show the most visited historic houses and monuments, cathedrals and churches in the UK in 1998.

Figure 1.38: Top ten UK historic houses and monuments 1999

Historic house/monument	Visits
1 Tower of London	2,422,181
2 Windsor Castle	1,280,000
3 Edinburgh Castle	1,219,720
4 Roman Baths and Pump Room, Bath	918,867
5 Stonehenge, Wiltshire	838,880
6 Warwick Castle	793,000
7 Hampton Court Palace, London	699,218
8 Leeds Castle, Kent	569,505
9 Shakespeare's birthplace, Stratford-upon-Avon	510,150
10 Chatsworth House, Derbyshire	422,816

Source: English Tourist Board, *Visits to Tourist Attractions 1999*

Figure 1.39: Top ten UK cathedrals and churches 1998

Cathedral/church	Visits
1 Westminster Abbey	3,000,000
2 York Minster	2,000,000
3 Canterbury Cathedral	1,500,000
4 St Paul's Cathedral, London	1,095,299
5 Chester Cathedral	1,000,000
6 Salisbury Cathedral	800,000
7 Norwich Cathedral	540,000
8 St Martins in the Fields, London	500,000
9 Truro Cathedral	500,000
10 Durham Cathedral	466,559

Source: English Tourist Board, *Visits to Tourist Attractions 1998*

Heritage experience attractions

Heritage experience attractions such as the Jorvik Viking Centre in York are a relatively new group of attractions. They offer a simulated experience through technology-based techniques such as interactive displays, rides, animation, sounds and even smells. Such attractions are expensive to develop and build, so many are run by the private sector and an admission fee is charged. The Natural History Museum's Earth Gallery Experience attraction cost £12 million and enables visitors to 'descend' into a volcano to witness a lava flow while a platform rocks in a mock earthquake.

ACTIVITY

Heritage sites and attractions

1 Obtain a touring map of an area of your choice and identify the main heritage sites and visitor attractions. Include both natural and purpose-built attractions and find out whether they charge an admission fee or offer free entry to visitors.

2 Select one of the attractions you have identified and find out who owns and runs it, and how they are funded.

Heritage sites which are visited by large numbers of people are likely to provide additional facilities and services, such as

- retail and souvenir outlets
- cafés
- restaurants
- guide services.

▲ The Jorvik Viking Centre and an associated exhibition

Catering

Hospitality, **catering** and accommodation is an industry in its own right, but one which is closely linked to the leisure and recreation industry. Many leisure and recreation facilities and events include some form of catering. Examples include:

- sports centres – bars, cafés, meeting rooms
- cinemas – bars, snack and confectionery shops
- theme parks – restaurants, bars, accommodation
- swimming pools – vending machines, cafés
- sports stadia – conference and reception facilities, restaurants
- social clubs – bars, restaurants, reception facilities.

In 1998, there were around 44,500 restaurants, cafés and takeaway food shops in the UK, with a combined turnover of £13.5 billion. All sectors of the industry are involved in providing some form of catering services. However, it is the private sector that dominates provision, both on a local and national scale. Figure 1.40 shows the largest UK restaurant chains.

Figure 1.40: Top UK restaurant chains 1998 (excluding fast food restaurant chains)

Restaurant chain	Number of sites in UK
1 Pizza Hut	273
2 Beefeater	253
3 Pizza Express	177
4 Pierre Victoire	108
5 Café Rouge	102
6 Deep Pan Pizza	89
7 Bella Pasta	78
8 Caffe Uno	46
9 Garfunkels	43

Source: *The Leisure Industry Report 1998*, October 1998

Catering facilities

The enormous number of catering facilities within the UK provide a wide range of food and beverage products and services. The list of catering establishments serving food and drink is seemingly endless, from expensive, à la carte restaurants, to self-service cafeterias, burger bars, pizza houses and takeaways.

Both the restaurant and take-away markets have continued to grow in the UK, as shown in Figure 1.41 and the article below. This growth is partly due to the increasing popularity of ethnic restaurants and takeaways in the UK, although pub meals still accounted for the largest proportion of consumer expenditure in 1997. The article also illustrates how the catering industry is responding to changing consumer needs and expectations.

A taste for the exotic

Eastern cuisine accounts for almost a quarter of spending in restaurants and takeaways. With Britons spending £32 million every week on Indian food, it could be argued that curry is now as much a national dish as fish and chips.

Despite their substantial share of the market, Chinese and Indian restaurateurs should not be complacent. Other cooking styles such as Thai and Japanese are growing at a faster rate, with an increase in spending of 38 per cent over the past four years, compared with 12.5 per cent for Indian restaurants and 8 per cent for Chinese.

Travel to far-flung destinations has led to greater demand for more adventurous eating-out among the more affluent. Interest in Southeast Asian cuisine is increasing, reflected by the good performance of such restaurants and the recent appearance in supermarkets of ingredients such as lemongrass and Thai fish sauce.

We may yet find coriander in our Cornish pasties and lime leaves on our Yorkshire pudding.

Source: *Mail on Sunday*

Figure 1.41: The restaurant and takeaway market

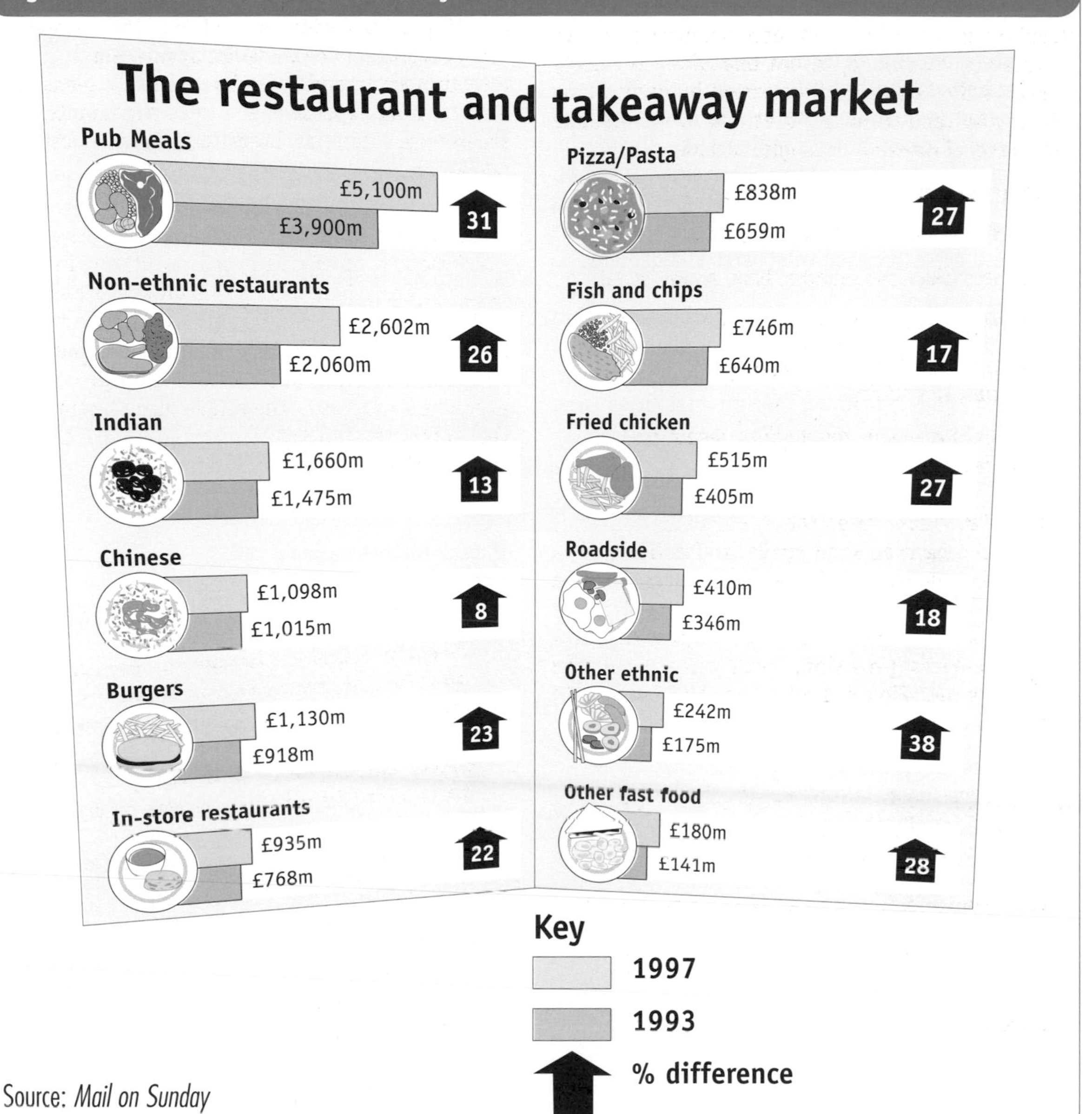

Source: *Mail on Sunday*

ACTIVITY

Catering facilities

Give examples of catering facilities for each of the categories listed in Figure 1.41 in a locality of your choice. You may find it useful to refer to a copy of the Yellow Pages or a local newspaper.

Countryside recreation

The term **countryside recreation** covers a broad range of leisure and recreational activities which can be classified as land-based (e.g. walking, potholing), water-based (e.g. sailing, water-skiing) or air-based (e.g. hang-gliding, hot-air ballooning). Obviously, many leisure activities in the countryside are sports, or require particular physical effort, but there are many other activities which need not be, for example those associated with parks and gardens.

All sectors of the industry are represented within this component. For example, in a national park area the following organisations will be involved in managing and providing leisure facilities and services:

- Public sector: Parks Authority, Local Authority, Countryside Agency, Forestry Commission.
- Private sector: accommodation and catering providers, shops, pubs, farmers and attractions.
- Voluntary sector: recreation and conservation groups such as the Ramblers Association and the National Trust.

Countryside parks

Perhaps the best known areas of the countryside providing recreational opportunities are the national parks, which were initially created by an Act of Parliament in 1949. There are twelve national parks in England and Wales, and three in Scotland (known as regional parks). The Act describes them as 'areas of great natural beauty giving opportunity for open air recreation, established so that natural beauty can be preserved and enhanced, so that the enjoyment of the scenery by the public can be promoted'.

The countryside provides significant opportunities for millions of people to enjoy a variety of leisure pastimes and activities, including outings, drives, picnics, walks and visits to parks, monuments and historic properties. For many, the countryside is a place to enjoy the scenery, the wildlife and the tranquillity.

The Countryside Commission estimates that around 10 million people visit the national parks each year. In addition to the national parks there are other designated areas of the countryside which provide recreational opportunities. These include:

- areas of outstanding natural beauty, e.g. Kent Downs, North Pennines
- heritage coasts, e.g. southwest coast, Norfolk coast
- national trails and long-distance paths, e.g. Cleveland Way, Thames Path
- world heritage sites, e.g. Hadrian's Wall and Giant's Causeway
- country parks, e.g. Strathclyde Park, Motherwell, Crawfordsburn Park, Belfast.

▼ Peak District National Park

Figure 1.42: National Parks.

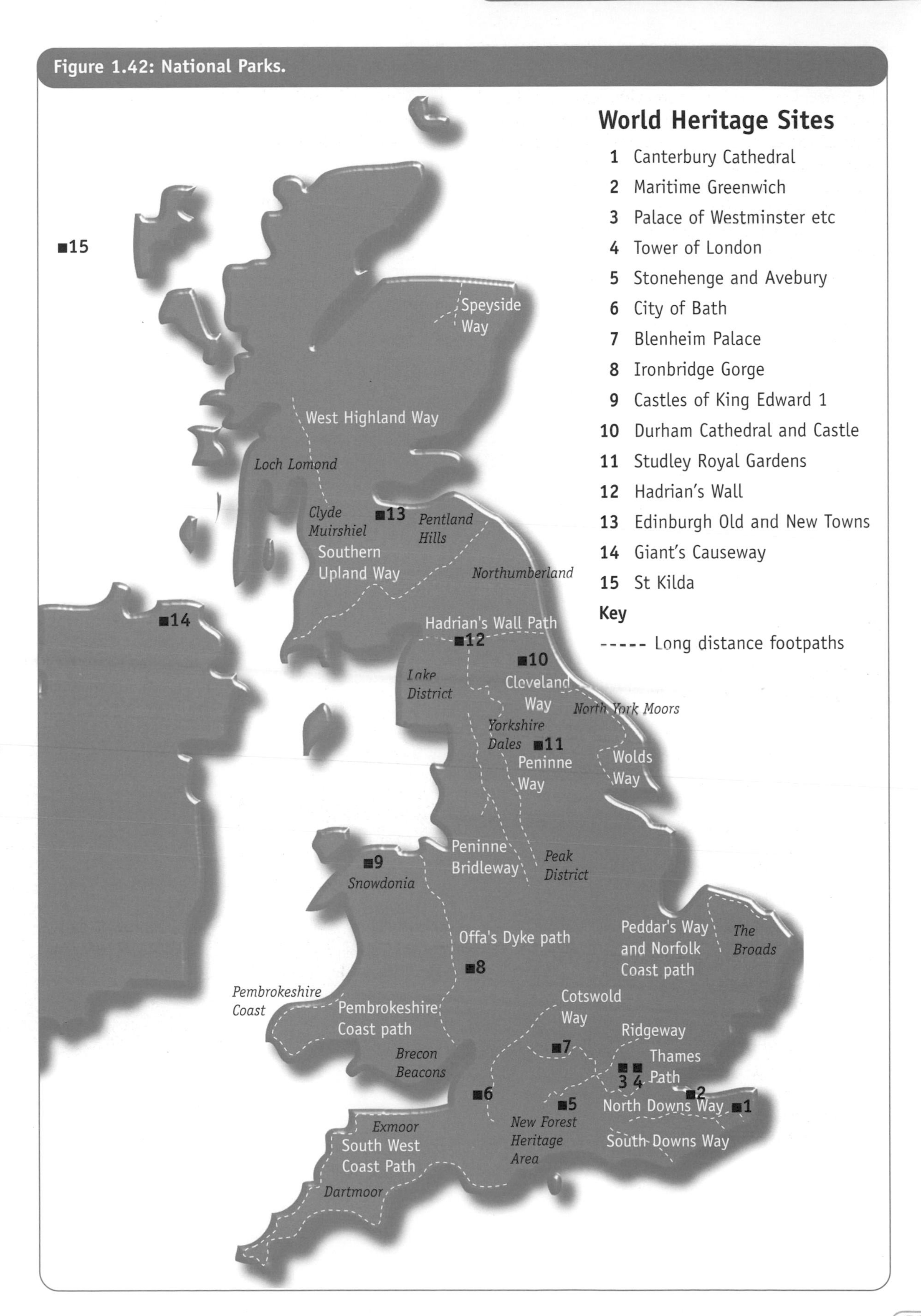

Urban parks, gardens and amenities

Provision of land for common recreational use dates back to the Middle Ages. The loss of these 'commons', due to their enclosure by local landlords mainly in the first half of the nineteenth century, led to parliament making specific provision for open spaces and playgrounds (although not until 1926). It was, however, with the creation of local town and city councils a hundred years ago that public gardens and parks were created in any number, and today most local authorities have a parks department.

Many areas have urban parks, gardens and allotments in addition to the more recent development of amenities such as children's play areas, walking trails and cycleways. Some of the best-known urban parks include Hyde Park, Regent's Park and St James's Park in London; Kelvingrove Park in Glasgow; Sefton Park in Liverpool; and Sophia Gardens in Cardiff. London also contains two of the most visited gardens in the United Kingdom: Kew Gardens and Hampton Court.

Outdoor pursuits

There are over a thousand centres in the UK which specialise in providing outdoor adventure holidays. For example, Skern Lodge is an outdoor activities centre near Bideford, Devon. It provides visitors with a range of services, including accommodation, meals, transport and instruction in a wide range of outdoor activities, such as canoeing, sailing, raft-building, archery, climbing, horse riding and abseiling. It also has a swimming pool, assault course, games field, bar and recreation lounge.

ACTIVITY

Countryside recreation

Select an area of countryside used for recreational purposes and complete the following tasks:

1 Make a list of the types of recreational activity that take place, and the facilities/services available in your chosen area.

2 Identify the organisations involved in providing these activities and facilities, and name the sector in which they operate.

Home-based leisure

The term **home-based leisure** covers a wide range of activities. LIRC identifies the following main types of home-based leisure markets, based on the volume of UK consumer spending:

- video
- pets
- magazines
- books
- toys and games
- DIY
- PCs
- photography
- CDs, records and tapes
- gardening
- audio equipment
- television

Figure 1.12 (page 23) shows that spending on home leisure will continue to expand, with some areas such as audio equipment and television seeing growth in consumer spending of over 30 per cent between 1998 and 2003. The vast majority of households in the UK now have television, radio and music systems.

In 1998, digital television was launched and the internet continues to expand, providing opportunities for both business and leisure usage. The digital revolution will increase spending on new television products and services, as well as on computers, but video may suffer from this competition. Demand for DIY and gardening products will remain buoyant, but some traditional activities such as reading books and newspapers are forecast to decline.

ACTIVITY

Home-based leisure suppliers

For each of the home-based leisure markets listed in Figure 1.12, identify at least one organisation that provides this activity, service or product. For example, Amstrad supply PCs.

Figure 1.43: Home-based leisure in the UK: key facts and forecasts in 2000

- 31.9 million adults read books, spending over £1.9 billion.
- 96,000 new books published.
- 39 million adults read newspapers, spending over £2.5 billion.
- Average daily newspaper circulation of 13.5 million.
- 31.8 million adults read magazines, spending £1.5 billion.
- 100 per cent of households with a television set, 98 per cent with a colour television, 59 per cent with a second colour set and 42 per cent with cable or satellite television.
- Consumer spending on television of £7.2 billion.
- Around 400 television channels are forecast to be available to consumers by 2013, including terrestrial television, 'Pay per view' and 'On-demand' services.
- 92 per cent of all households have a video (owned or rented), spending over £2.9 billion on equipment, rentals and video cassettes.
- 42.1 million adults listen to radio, and 39 million listen to CDs and tapes.
- 84 per cent of households own CD players.
- 203 million CDs and 95 million singles sold in the UK.
- 32 per cent of households have a PC and 36 per cent have video games, with consumer spending of £3.1 billion.
- 20.9 million adults do DIY, accounting for 69 per cent of all households.
- Consumer spending on DIY of £7.8 billion.
- 30.7 million adults involved in gardening, spending over £3.1 billion.
- 88 per cent of households own a camera and 23 per cent own a camcorder.
- Consumer spending on toys and games of £2.1 billion.

Source: LIRC *Leisure Forecasts 1999-2003*

The industry catering for the home-based leisure market is huge and is dominated by the private sector. LIRC estimates that the volume of UK consumer spending on home-based leisure activities is around £40 billion (see Figure 1.7, page 11).

Figure 1.43 provides some key facts and forecasts about the UK home-based leisure market in 2000.

The internet

As the internet becomes more widely used, shopping for leisure on the internet is likely to increase spending on home-based leisure up to and beyond 2002. The main areas of leisure purchasing by UK internet users are currently books (e.g. amazon.com) CDs (e.g. hmv.co.uk) and travel tickets and holidays (e.g. www.lastminute.com). By 1999 it was estimated that 6.2 million UK households had access to the internet (Mintel, 1999).

Take-up is further encouraged by the introduction of entirely free internet service provision from the likes of Freeserve and Tesco. Internet access is also possible through cable television channels and digital television services.

As the internet becomes more established as a source of interactive leisure activity, its influence on the market will become significant. It already offers endless opportunities for information retrieval, online shopping, software downloads, e-mail and so on. It will become an increasingly popular resource for gaming, gambling and music-listening leisure activities.

In-home interactive media

The market for in-home interactive media hardware and services includes computer hardware, computer software and non-terrestrial broadcasting, as well as the internet. The beginning of interactive in-home entertainment came with programmed games software played through cassette-driven hardware, which constituted a closed environment.

Now interaction is with a limitless number of sources outside the home via the modem and the digital communications link. This considerable change means it is no longer necessary to visit a retail outlet in order to buy a computer game or hire a video, as it is now possible to gain immediate access at home.

In-home interactive media is a sector with enormous potential, although with options for technology advancing all the time and little research, its exact level is not easy to determine. What is clear, however, is that interactivity offers a revolutionary challenge to the way in which such things as leisure, shopping, banking and communication are conducted.

The greater variety of activities available through the internet, and digital broadcasting, and which can be chosen at will, is likely to have an effect upon more passive forms of entertainment such as conventional scheduled television. If consumers have the ability to watch what they want, when they want, they might be less inclined to sit down to an evening's viewing planned by someone else.

The ability to access a video on demand or download a computer game via a digital delivery system removes the need to buy or hire from the high street or mail order. This is likely to create considerable repercussions for the retail trade and the video rental trade.

The same is true of shopping via the internet. Whether buying a book, a CD or computer software, it increases the role of direct selling and is likely to have a negative effect upon conventional forms of retailing. It will also affect the nature of the product. Software, in particular, may cease to have a physical presence if downloaded directly to the hard-drive and this will have an impact on the manufacturers of video tape, CD-Roms and DVD-Roms.

There has been a great deal of debate about the advantages offered by digital television. Its most important technical features are as follows:

- better pictures with no interference
- CD-quality sound
- access to e-mail and the internet
- opportunities for interactive television (including home banking, shopping, etc.)
- wide-screen television
- more channels (capacity for a virtually unlimited number)
- pay-TV options
- improved teletext service
- electronic programme guides.

The technical possibilities offered by digital television appear to match those of the PC, perhaps with the exception of computing functions. It can provide internet access and gaming possibilities, as well as audio-visual and interactive services. In many households the absence of a computer will be far outweighed by these advantages.

BUILD YOUR LEARNING

End of section activity

Summarise the present structure and key components of the UK leisure and recreation industry, giving suitable examples. You should cover the following sectors and key industry components:

- **Sectors:** public
  private
  voluntary.
- **Key components:**
  arts and entertainments
  sports and physical recreation
  heritage attractions
  catering
  countryside recreation
  home-based leisure.

For each component you should explain the range of facilities, events, products and services within it, and the range of public, private and voluntary sector organisations that provide them.

Keywords and phrases

You should know the meaning of the words and phrases listed below. If you are unsure about any of them, go back through the last 23 pages to refresh your understanding.

- **Key components**
- **Arts and entertainments**
- **Museum**
- **Theme park**
- **Sports and physical recreation**
- **Heritage attractions**
- **Visitor attraction**
- **Catering**
- **Countryside recreation**
- **Home-based leisure**

Working in the leisure and recreation industry

AS WE HAVE SEEN, the leisure and recreation industry is very wide-ranging and consists of a great variety of enterprises of different sizes. Leisure is one of Britain's biggest growth industries. Few industries can match it for the range of employment opportunities it offers people of all ages.

The list of job opportunities for people with the right skills, knowledge and personal qualities is vast. In this section we will investigate:

- the range of employment opportunities
- the nature of employment
- personal and technical skills and qualities required by employers
- how to find jobs in leisure and recreation.

Part of the assessment for this unit requires you to select a job from the leisure and recreation industry that best matches your own aspirations, skills and abilities. To do this you will need to be able to answer such questions as:

- what are my strengths, weaknesses and interests?
- what sectors of the industry are available to me?
- what job opportunities exist?
- what personal and technical skills are required to do my chosen job?
- how can I prepare myself to pursue my career progression aims?

Range of employment opportunities in leisure and recreation

Employment opportunities range from jobs for people leaving school with GCSEs, Vocational 'A' levels or even no qualifications at all, to careers for degree graduates. The vast range of jobs reflects the breadth and diversity of the key industry components. This section cannot provide an exhaustive list of all types of employment opportunity within each of these components. Instead, we will investigate some of the most common employment opportunities across the industry.

To give some idea of the opportunities available, look at Figure 1.44, which lists a selection of jobs from each component of the leisure and recreation industry. It is important to remember that some jobs, such as facility management, sales and marketing will be available across all sectors, while others are more specific to that particular industry component.

▲ The range of jobs within the industry is diverse, as are the opportunities for on the job training.

Figure 1.44: Examples of jobs within industry components

Arts and entertainments
Performers/Presenters
Theatre/Concert Hall Manager/
Assistant Manager
Box Office Manager/Assistant
Museums Officer/Warden/Assistant
Visitor Services Assistant/Manager
Education Officer
Barmaid/Barman
Publican

Sport and physical recreation
Health and Fitness Instructor
Outdoor Pursuits/Education Instructor
Physical Education Teacher
Professional Sportsperson
Sports Administrator
Sports Centre Manager
Leisure Facility Manager/Assistant/
Duty Manager
Sports Development Officer
Sports Medicine/Physiotherapist
Sports Coach
Swimming Pool Attendant/
Lifeguard/Manager
Sales Assistant/Sports Retail

Catering
Head Chef/Sous Chef/Commis Chef
Waiter/Waitress
Head Waiter/Waitress
Restaurant Manager
Pub Manager
Fast Food Floor Manager
Barman/Barmaid
Conference and Banqueting
Manager/Assistant

Heritage attractions
Education Officer
Facility Manager/Assistant Manager
Customer Services Manager/
Assistant Manager
Guide
Marketing/PR Manager/Assistant
Conservator
Archeologist

Countryside recreation
Gardener
Groundsperson
Countryside Warden/Ranger
Park Ranger/Assistant
Conservator
Outdoor Pursuits Instructor/Leader
Gamekeeper
Countryside Recreation Officer/Manager
Education Officer

Home-based
Sales assistant (e.g. music shop, hi-fi supplier, etc.)
Shop Manager/Assistant Manager
Food and beverage sales (takeaway)

Nature of employment

Because the leisure and recreation industry is regarded as a 'people industry', vast numbers of jobs involve dealing with customers in person. Consequently there are many more jobs at a basic level or operative level than there are in management. If you are a school or college leaver starting out on your career, your first job will probably be at the operative level. The following list gives some typical examples:

- Waiter or waitress
- Leisure assistant
- Fitness instructor
- Lifeguard
- Sports coach
- Rides attendant
- Box office cashier

Progression opportunities

The leisure and recreation industry offers good promotion prospects. Many people progress from basic jobs to supervisory and higher management positions. Some examples of career progression are shown in Figure 1.45.

For some people, promotion from operative to supervisory and management levels can be relatively quick, although competition for jobs at all levels is often intense. Another feature of work in the leisure and recreation industry is the potential for changing career paths. For instance, if you work for an employer who owns a range of facilities, such as hotels, pubs, restaurants and leisure facilities, it may be possible to move from one to another. Even if this is not the case, there are numerous opportunities to diversify into different areas of the industry.

Seasonality

A particular feature of the UK's leisure and recreation industry is the vast number of **full-time** and **part-time seasonal** jobs that it provides. For example, employment opportunities in leisure are drastically reduced outside the peak school summer holiday months of July and August.

Conditions of service

Shift work including evenings and weekends is normal. Even in higher-level posts it is common to find that evening and weekend work forms an integral part of the job. Therefore working in the leisure industry means being prepared to work **unsocial hours**, often on a regular basis.

ACTIVITY

Working unsocial hours

1 List ten jobs in the leisure and recreation industry that you think involve working unsocial hours. For each one explain why you think the hours worked are unsocial.

2 In small groups discuss how you think employers could compensate their employees for working unsocial hours.

Figure 1.45: Examples of progression in the leisure industry

Operative →	Supervisory →	Management
Leisure assistant →	Duty manager →	Sports centre manager
Waiter/waitress →	Head waiter/waitress →	Restaurant manager
Lifeguard/attendant →	Duty manager →	Swimming pool manager
Ride attendant →	Ride manager →	Head of operations
Trainee golf professional →	Assistant golf professional →	Golf professional

ACTIVITY

Personal qualities

1 Look at Figure 1.44 on page 67, which illustrates the range of jobs available in the main components of the leisure and recreation industry. In small groups discuss the most common skills and abilities that you think employers look for.

2 Make a list of the leisure and recreation jobs that are currently available in a selected locality. You will find it useful to look at your local paper and perhaps visit the local job centre. From your investigation identify the most common types of job available within the leisure and recreation industry. Select one of the jobs from your list and describe working conditions, qualifications required and skills and personal qualities required to do the job.

People industry

As already mentioned, the leisure industry is often described as a 'people industry'. What does this mean? It simply means that in most jobs in the leisure industry employees will have a great deal of contact with other people, often the customers. Thus an ability to enjoy meeting and relating to a wide range of people from many walks of like is essential. Similarly, good communication skills, both written and oral, are important.

Personal qualities

Employers look for enthusiasm, commitment and self-motivation in job applicants. Workers will be expected to remain cheerful and enthusiastic, even at the end of a long shift. Thus having and maintaining a keen interest in the job is essential. The following case study shows the personal qualities that one leisure operator seeks when recruiting staff.

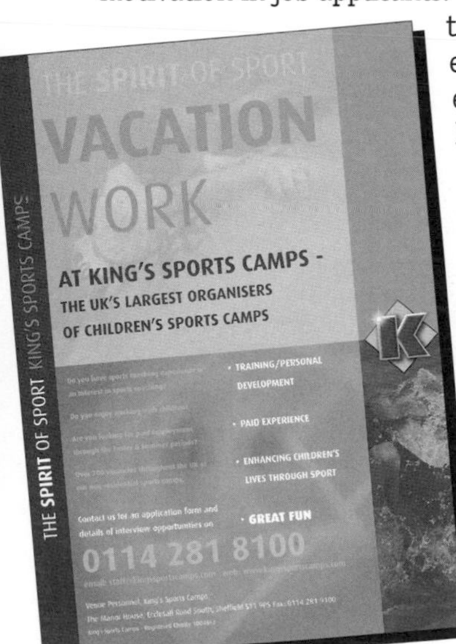

▲ Job opportunities may be seasonal

CASE STUDY

White Rose Line

The White Rose Line is a small leisure operator based in York that runs riverboat tours along the River Ouse. It provides the following specification to anyone seeking full-time or part-time employment with the company.

White Rose Line: person specification
When recruiting new staff to join our team, we are very interested in your personal qualities and your attitude to working with our customers. The following list of indicators helps us to decide who will fit into our team.

You will have a positive attitude to work, which means:

- you will be happy to be here;
- you will be smiling and cheerful;
- you will show an interest in your job;
- you will see solutions to challenges, not problems;
- you will be happy to laugh at your own mistakes;
- you will not let personal problems get in the way of work.

Our customers are very important to our continued success. You will need to be:

- proactively helpful to customers;
- happy to talk to customers;
- interested in customers - ask them questions;
- thoughtful about how you can make a difference to customers' enjoyment.

While at work you will be flexible, happy to:

- perform other duties;
- understand the interdependency between differing roles;
- work different shifts;
- show tolerance to customers and colleagues.

Your work ethic should mean:

- starting work on time and getting on with your work;
- managing your own time;
- understanding why the work is important;
- understanding that customers are the reason we have jobs.

During your time at White Rose Line you will want to:

- show the ability to learn new things and ways of working;
- think actions through and consider the effects on the customer;
- recognise that you can learn from others.

We will be happy to spend as much time as necessary training you in the technical skills that you may require to do your job. However, we want to employ people who have the right attitude from the start and who will contribute to our success during their time with White Rose Line.

ACTIVITY

Qualities, skill and knowledge

Study the following list of comments from people working in the industry who were asked, 'What are the most important personal qualities, skills and knowledge requirements for your job?'

1 'I must understand how to motivate people and this means finding exactly the right approach for each individual. The most important skills are the ability to communicate (sometimes in foreign languages), teach others and inspire confidence. I have to be physically fit as the job is very demanding.'

2 'I need business acumen and flair to develop new ideas and increase use of the facility. It is important to be able to handle people, both employees and customers. Good communication skills are important with staff and customers. Numeracy and information technology skills are needed in order to cope with the financial and management information aspects of the job. Finally, there is a high level of responsibility as I am accountable for the day-to-day running of the facility and for the health and safety of visitors and staff.'

3 'I have to be confident and outgoing whilst at work. It is important to get on well with people. Also important are organisational ability, business skills, competence in financial matters and knowledge of a range of skills such as cookery, food and beverage service and hygiene. At peak times the work is hectic and the ability to work under pressure is vital.'

4 'Good customer service, communication and numeracy skills are essential for my job. I deal with customers face to face so I need to be enthusiastic at all times.'

5 'Good customer service and communication skills are essential, combined with bags of enthusiasm. I need to know everything about the facility so that I can answer any questions from visitors.'

These comments were made by people employed as a:

- hotel manager
- tour guide
- skiing instructor
- fast-food restaurant manager
- barperson.

Try to match each description with the job. In small groups, discuss what knowledge and skill requirements are common to all of these jobs. Record the main requirements in a table like the one top right.

Personal and technical skills and qualities required by employers

The personal and technical skills and qualities required by employers vary from job to job. However, while it is true that technical skills will vary according to the exact nature of the job, many of the personal skills required by employers are common across the industry.

The following list gives an indication of the personal skills most commonly sought by employers in the leisure and recreation industry.

- Good communication skills
- Customer service
- Common sense
- Good spoken and written English
- Literacy and numeracy
- Outgoing personality
- Sense of humour
- Enthusiasm and flexible approach
- Flexibility
- Stamina and good health
- Organisational skills
- Experience of dealing with the general public, e.g. ex-forces, charity work, working in shops and fast-food outlets
- Ability to work well in a team
- Smart appearance
- Ability to 'think on your feet'

Description	Job role	Qualities/knowledge/skills required
1		
2		
3		
4		
5		

Job descriptions and person specifications

Usually employers outline the personal and technical skills required to do the job in a **job description** and **person specification**. The job description describes the duties and responsibilities involved in a particular job. A person specification outlines the skills, knowledge and characteristics that are required to carry out the job.

It is important that you understand the structure and content of a job description and person specification so that you can make appropriate choices for your own career progression.

The details included in a job description vary, but generally the following should always appear:

- The job title, e.g. waitress, lifeguard, fitness instructor.
- The reporting structure. This should include to whom the job-holder reports and whether anyone reports to them. For example, the head waiter reports to the restaurant manager. The waiting staff, cashier and trainees report to the head waiter.

Job responsibilities are often categorised into main responsibilities and occasional responsibilities. The main job responsibilities are those carried out on a regular basis; occasional ones are those that may only sometimes be part of the job.

The areas of responsibility in a job description, such as the one shown in Figure 1.46, often specify outcomes rather than responsibilities. In other words, it specifies what the job holder is expected to do. For example, the responsibility for delivering customer service may be expressed as 'to offer customers relevant information and assistance to meet their needs'.

Figure 1.46: Job description for ACTION SPORT TEAM CO-ORDINATOR, YORK LEISURE SERVICES

Reporting structure
The job holder will be accountable to the Head of Community Recreation via the Sports Development Officer.

Reporting to the job holder
The job holder will have a supervisory management responsibility for a small team of sports leaders and creche workers.

Overall purpose of the job
To co-ordinate the City Council's mobile Community Sports and Recreation initiative Action Sport on a day-to-day basis. To take a lead role in the development, promotion, management and implementation of this work, and to supervise a team of workers in the overall co-ordination of this programme.

Job activities
1 To co-ordinate the setting-up, organising and supervising of a varied programme of sport and recreational activities.
2 To co-ordinate and supervise a small mobile team of Community Sports leaders.
3 To take the lead role in the smooth and successful running of the sports sessions.
4 To co-ordinate the initiation and planning of new Action Sport plans and ventures.
5 To take the lead role in the planning of all Action Sport activities.
6 To liaise with officers of the Leisure Services Department, in particular the Sports Development Officer.
7 To co-ordinate and organise the Action Sport projects publicity and maintain a high profile for this work in the city.
8 To be responsible for all Action Sport administration staff time sheets, holiday and sickness returns and other necessary administration procedures.
9 To be responsible for all Action Sport money, including petty cash, all session income and the safe receipting and banking of this income.
10 To liaise with the Council's DLO to co-ordinate the regular maintenance and upkeep of three project vehicles.
11 To carry out necessary project visits to ensure a high standard of service is provided by the Action Sport team.
12 To ensure that a high standard of safety in terms of equipment, vehicles and, where appropriate, buildings is maintained at all times.
13 To be aware of all emergency procedures and the Health and Safety at Work Act relating to the various Action Sport sites.
14 Any other tasks, commensurate with the grade of the post, as the Director of Leisure Services shall from time to time determine.

A person specification involves identifying the specific skills and characteristics needed to fulfil the job description. It may include sections on some or all of the following:

- personal attributes
- personal qualities
- personal achievements
- vocational qualifications
- academic qualifications
- competence.

Usually a job interview will cover each area identified on the person specification in order to distinguish the most suitable candidate from those of equal standing in other respects. Sometimes organisations indicate which skills and personal attributes are essential and which are merely desirable.

Personal attributes are personal characteristics. For example, a person working in the travel industry deals with many people and needs good communication skills. A resort representative needs to be confident, friendly and assertive, as well as having good communication skills.

Personal qualities are similar to attributes, but whereas attributes relate to personality, qualities refer to the way in which that person behaves. Many reference forms ask for specific details about the applicant such as whether he or she is hardworking, reliable, honest, a good timekeeper, easy to work with and well-presented. These are all examples of personal qualities often required by employers.

Personal achievements can relate to both work experience and activities outside work. Work achievements might include the types of jobs held, the length of service in each or the nature of duties and experience. Other personal achievements include interests, hobbies or activities that may reflect the ability to perform a job competently.

For example, an assistant working for Camp America will be required to work well as a member of a team. On the person specification under 'personal achievements' it may say: 'Provide clear evidence of having worked successfully as a team member on a number of occasions'. One applicant may satisfy this by explaining how he or she has had several holiday jobs in children's activity centres. Another applicant could satisfy this if he or she had been involved in organising a voluntary youth club.

Vocational qualifications are based on a particular type of job and are intended to lead to employment: they include NVQs and Vocational A levels. Academic qualifications are those based on theoretical subjects and include GCSEs and 'A' levels.

Competence relates to the job skills required. For example, taxi drivers in London have to acquire 'the knowledge' before they are able to operate a black cab service. This means that they must show familiarity with all routes and locations within the city. For example, a fitness instructor needs to be competent in computer literacy and fitness testing.

Sources of information about jobs in leisure and recreation

There are many sources of information to help you make the right decisions. Here are some of the main providers of careers guidance and information for jobs in leisure and recreation.

Careers service

Your school or college should have someone responsible for providing careers education and guidance who can help you. Alternatively, local careers services have extensive libraries and

computer databases which provide information on most types of jobs. Careers service offices also display vacancies for employers and, in some cases, will arrange interviews for you. Addresses of local careers service offices are listed in the telephone directory.

Libraries

There are numerous books and other publications on jobs and careers. Your local library is likely to contain a selection dealing with the leisure and recreation and tourism industries, together with information on how to apply for jobs. Titles to request include the *Handbook of Jobs in Leisure and Tourism*, published annually by Hobsons and the *Working in Series*, published by the Careers and Occupational Information Centre.

Jobcentres

Jobcentres display details about vacancies sent to them by employers. Staff can also advise you about job opportunities in your area and on education and training schemes. Jobcentres are listed in the telephone directory under Employment Services.

Employment agencies

Many employers choose to place vacancies with private employment agencies rather than advertise in local newspapers or jobcentres. Some employment agencies specialise in particular areas of the travel and tourism industries, such as catering and accommodation. Employment agencies in your locality will be listed in the Yellow Pages.

Professional associations

If you are a member of a professional body, such as the Institute of Leisure and Amenity Management (ILAM), you will be able to obtain information about careers and job vacancies through their publications.

Talking to people already doing the job

Talking to people already employed in your chosen area can be an effective way of finding out about jobs and career opportunities. You may be able to do this as part of a work placement. Ask them how they got started and what skills and qualifications are required for a particular job. Many schools and colleges arrange visits to local travel and tourism facilities to find out how they operate and what sorts of jobs are available. Many careers books contain accounts from people working in the industry that also provide a useful insight into what a particular job is like. Three examples of such accounts are provided in the following case study.

▼ Information about job vacancies is available through professional associations

CASE STUDY

Job Profiles

Job title
LOCAL AUTHORITY ACTION SPORT DEVELOPMENT OFFICER

Qualifications
HND in Leisure Studies, GNVQ Advanced Leisure and Recreation

Short Course Qualifications
RSA Exercise to Music, CSLA, Short Tennis Coaching, Fitness Training Coach, First Aid Certificate

Experience and relevant background
Temporary post with Garden Festival, Wales; Duty Officer in Leisure Centre; genuine interest in sport and working with people

Brief description of the job
Organise, develop and promote Community Sports Development programme throughout the Borough; liaison with Education Authority, Youth and Community organisations, sports clubs and other voluntary agencies; develop national initiatives at a local level to promote participation; assist in the organisation and promotion of annual events programme.

Main likes about the job
Variety; meeting a lot of new people; satisfaction of creating successful networks; challenging post requiring self-motivation

Less attractive features of the job
Shift work and weekend work; difficulty of pursuing own sporting interests because of work commitments

Job title
TRAINEE ASSISTANT GOLF PROFESSIONAL

Qualifications
GNVQ Intermediate in Leisure and Tourism; GCSEs in English and Maths (both essential requirements for PGA registration); English Golf Union Registered Handicap 5.6

Experience and relevant background
Weekend job in Golf Club Pro's Shop (experience gained in sales and equipment repairs); Saturday job in golf retail shop as equipment adviser

Brief description of the job
30 hours per week working in Professional's shop advising members and selling equipment; 15 hours per week of training with PGA Professional and the Retail Manager; training includes repairs, the golf swing, product knowledge, computer operation and accounts

Things liked about the job
Being able to play golf in working hours; repairing golf clubs; selling equipment; the training programme set up by the PGA

Less attractive features of the job
The working hours in the summer; the wages of an assistant professional.

Job title
ARTS ADMINISTRATOR
(based at a local authority arts theatre group)

Qualifications
GNVQ Advanced in Leisure and Recreation, CLAIT

Experience and relevant background
One-year traineeship on Employment Training with a touring theatre company; part-time bar work at an arts theatre and other temporary assignments

Brief description of the job
Responsible for staffing, banking, payment of artists; catering - stock control, buying, bar work; Health and Safety at work; front-of-house operations; administering courses; answering enquiries from the public; providing help and advice to work experience students.

Things liked about the job
Variety of work, working in a team, helping customers, seeing productions.

Less attractive features of the job
Long hours, evening and weekend work, low pay initially.

Contacting employers

Many of the larger employers in the leisure and recreation industries provide information about job opportunities, the skills and qualifications required, and how to apply. Virgin, McDonald's, Thorpe Park and Jarvis Hotels are four examples of companies that provide careers advice to people wishing to work in the industry.

The following case study about Virgin Our Price provides a good example of the sort of information you can obtain from an employer.

ACTIVITY

Finding out about a job

Interview someone who is currently working in the leisure and recreation industry about their job. Try to obtain information about:

- how they got started and how long they have worked in the industry;
- what qualifications are required to do the job;
- what skills and qualities are required to do the job;
- working conditions;
- what they like (or dislike) about the job.

CASE STUDY

Virgin Our Price

'A Career with the Stars' Have you got what it takes?

Who we are

Following three years of continued expansion, Virgin Our Price now has over 300 stores throughout the UK and Ireland and has long been established as one of the leading entertainment retailers in the world.

Our success comes as a direct result of recruiting people who strive to meet high standards of customer service, and who have a passion for the products we sell.

Recruitment decisions within the business are based purely on the grounds of a candidate's relevant skills and experience, which is supported by our diversity policy. We therefore need people who can bring with them some customer service experience, preferably in a retail environment, and who are willing to learn more about the entertainment retail industry.

Our success

Virgin Our Price employees have the unique opportunity to join one of the country's most dynamic, responsive and high-profile retailers. As an employee within this organisation you will be encouraged to learn and will have access to development opportunities throughout your career with us.

As an organisation we take pride in valuing each individual's contribution and in return for their commitment offer a competitive salary and benefits package.

A variety of roles

The majority of new employees to the business will be applying for positions as Customer Service Assistants. However, there is a variety of roles available to prospective employees including Stockroom Assistants and Administration Assistants, who ensure that the whole store operation runs smoothly behind the scenes. Of course, if you come to us with previous relevant retail experience then you will join us at the most appropriate position available. This means that with the right level of experience you can come in to the business at junior, supervisory or management level.

Training

On joining the business you will have the opportunity to work within a comprehensive retail training framework. The framework offers ongoing training and will enable you to not only learn and develop according to your present role, but will also encourage you to develop and learn more about other roles, which in turn encourages multi-skilling within the store environment.

Once in a managerial position, you will then be able to move on to the management training framework which will continue to support your learning and development in your store management role. The emphasis at this stage is with each employee taking the initiative and responsibility for driving their own development and working with the business to facilitate their learning.

What next? Still think you could cut a career with the stars?

If you think you've got what it takes to be a commercially aware retailer with Virgin Our Price the sky's the limit if you have the drive and commitment to succeed.

In the first instance, please apply to the Our Price or Virgin Megastore of your choice.

Adur District Council Leisure and Direct Services Department
Adur Leisure DSO invites applications from suitably qualified and experienced leisure personnel to undertake the following role:

DUTY OFFICER
Salary Scale 2/3 £11,085-£12,663 (pay award pending)
Based at one of the three sites in the Adur District - Lancing Manor Leisure Centre, Southwick Leisure Centre or Wadur's Community Pool - the successful candidate will be required to assist in the management, operation and development of the Council's leisure facilities. Suitable candidates will be able to demonstrate leadership skills, flexibility and a knowledge of both wet and dry facility operations. Relevant leisure-based qualifications and previous experience will also be a distinct advantage.

A National Pool Lifeguard Qualification, First Aid Certificate and ideally a Pool Plant Operator's Certificate are required for this position. The above posts are based on 37 hours and 39 hours per week respectively, and as you would expect are subject to unsocial hours, shift work and Bank Holidays on a rota basis. In return, we offer a competitive salary and the opportunity to enhance your career prospects with a well motivated organisation. Applications are welcome from people with disabilities and job sharers. Childcare subsidy is payable in appropriate cases. These posts involve access to children and therefore the successful candidates' applications will be subject to satisfactory police checks.

Application forms and job descriptions are available from the Human Resources Division, Civic Centre, Ham Road, Shoreham-by-Sea, West Sussex BN43 6PR. Telephone: 01273 263118 (answerphone)
Closing date: Wednesday 8 March 2000

Source: www.leisureopportunities.co.uk

Using the internet

There are now several excellent sites on the internet that provide information about career opportunities and job vacancies within the leisure and recreation industry. Three of the most popular ones are:

www.careercompass.co.uk

www.ilam.co.uk

www.leisureopportunities.co.uk

Some employers also have recruitment sections on their web sites (e.g. Thorpe Park at www.thorpepark.co.uk). The Duty Officer post at Adur above was advertised on the internet.

Indentifying a suitable job in the industry

Your starting point is to decide what are your personal aims and interests and then identify jobs and career paths which suit them. This will involve doing some research to find out about jobs, qualifications, prospects and employers. When identifying suitable job roles you should consider the range of criteria listed opposite.

Am I being realistic?

Most employers expect prospective employees to be ambitious, but you must also be realistic in terms of the level at which you will enter the industry. As we have seen, for most people this is initially at the operative level. It is best to discuss your plans with a careers adviser.

What are my circumstances?

You must take into account your personal circumstances when you are considering jobs. How far are you prepared to travel to find employment? Is your age an important factor? Some employers specify that you must be willing to work anywhere in the country, and some jobs have minimum age requirements (for example, bar staff and lifeguards must be 18 or over). If you are a 16 or 17-year-old school leaver, the range of full-time job opportunities in the industry will be limited, unless you are on a training scheme sponsored by an employer.

What are my interests?

Consider your current interests when looking for suitable jobs. This may involve an evaluation of your leisure pastimes and activities. For example, if you are interested in fitness you may consider working as a fitness instructor in a health and fitness club.

What qualifications, skills and experience are required?

It is important to obtain advice on the qualifications, skills and experience required for your chosen job. A useful starting point is to list the relevant qualifications, skills and experience you have already, identify what others you are in the process of obtaining, and, finally, list any others you think you will need to obtain. This may involve undertaking more training and work experience at your local school, college or other training provider before you are ready to seek employment. You must also consider the type of person required by prospective employers and ask yourself the question, 'Do I have the personal qualities that they are looking for?'

What opportunities are available?

You must also consider what opportunities are available for gaining employment. For instance, if you live in a popular tourist area you may be able to identify a number of opportunities in the travel and tourism industry within your locality. Alternatively, you may need to look outside your locality for suitable employment opportunities. Make sure you keep up to date with current developments by looking in newspapers, magazines and journals, as they can be a useful source of information on employers and potential job opportunities.

ACTIVITY

Selecting a job

Select at least one job from within the leisure and recreation industry that you think is suitable based on your personal aims, interests and abilities. In small groups, discuss why you have selected the particular job. You will find this exercise useful when undertaking the end of section activity on page 79.

Training and qualifications

In the past, employers in the leisure and recreation industry had a relaxed attitude towards qualifications. In many cases, the ability to do the job efficiently and the right mix of personal qualities were considered more important than an academic or vocational qualification. However, because of increased competition for jobs, and the need for higher standards in areas such as health and safety and customer service, many employers now value qualifications and training.

Gaining skills and experience

Skills and experience are not the same thing, but they are often grouped together. Your skills are the particular abilities you have to do things well. In most cases, you will acquire your skills through education and training, but you can also develop skills through experience and through learning from others at work.

Some of the skills you need to succeed in the industry are specific (for example, the skill of delivering a football coaching session, or making a fitness assessment), but many others are generic skills that can apply with any job. For example, the ability to supervise a group of people can be developed in many different contexts, including at school or college. Encouraging people to work together as a team in seeking to achieve a shared goal is something you may have done in a sporting context, or even in organising a party. You may have experience of organising a day out for a group of friends or, more simply, of getting a group of people from one place to another. All this experience will have helped you develop skills which you will be able to use in your work.

Most employers will expect you to work hard, show commitment and work effectively in teams. They will also expect you to have a number of personal qualities which enhance your ability to deal with customers in a variety of situations. As many jobs in leisure and recreation involve working unsocial hours, including shift work, you will often have to work evenings and weekends.

The range of specific vocational knowledge and skill requirements obviously varies from job to job. However, as a general rule, staff working in the leisure and recreation industry need to be:

- cheerful and enthusiastic, focusing on solutions rather than problems
- polite and patient
- well-organised and able to take responsibility
- able to work in teams
- good listeners and clear, fluent talkers
- smart in appearance
- numerate and literate.

Some of these personal qualities and skills can be developed through training and experience, but others are closely related to the personality of the individual concerned. For example, someone who is extremely shy is unlikely to make a successful tour guide. What is important is to know one's strengths and weaknesses and to choose a job which is in harmony with them.

Part-time work?

We have identified a range of qualifications and training opportunities which will help you gain employment in the industry. In addition to gaining qualifications at your local school, college or training provider, you may be able to acquire useful skills and experience from part-time or voluntary work.

Due to the seasonal nature of the industry there are many opportunities for temporary and part-time employment. If there is no way of finding part-time or temporary paid work you may be able to find voluntary work in order to learn about the job and make useful contacts. Moreover, in undertaking voluntary work you will have gained experience and shown commitment to the industry.

If you already have a job in the leisure and recreation industry your employer may provide you with on-the-job training. For example, staff who have face-to-face contact with customers may receive some form of on-the-job training, to develop their skills in a variety of situations. Some employers also encourage their employees to undertake qualifications and training programmes at local colleges and training providers through day or block release.

Whatever your chosen career path and personal circumstances, the acquisition of qualifications, skills and experience will be of vital importance. Remember to seek advice before committing yourself to a particular training course or job; careful career planning at this stage could enable you to establish a successful career in your chosen field.

BUILD YOUR LEARNING

Keywords and phrases

You should know the meaning of the words and phrases listed below. If you are unsure about any of them, go back through the last 13 pages to refresh your understanding.

- Full-time
- Part-time
- Seasonal
- Unsocial hours
- Job description
- Person specification
- Personal attributes
- Personal qualities
- Personal achievements
- Vocational qualifications
- Competence

End of section activity

1 Summarise the range of employment opportunities available within the leisure and recreation industry. You should cover the most common employment opportunities for each industry component.

2 Find out about the types of jobs available in one of the following facilities:

- Swimming pool
- Museum
- Cinema
- Library
- Sports centre
- Heritage attraction
- Nightclub
- Professional football club
- Theatre
- Fast-food restaurant

You may find it useful to visit the facility, or write to the organisation that runs it to obtain information about the range of jobs. For larger organisations it may be possible to obtain information from the internet.

3 Select one job from the leisure and recreation industry that best matches your own aspirations, skills and abilities. Gather information about the job, such as a job description and person specification, so that you can describe how the job is suitable for you. If possible, interview someone who has personal knowledge of the job and what it involves.

Pursuing a career in leisure and recreation

Competition for many jobs in the leisure and recreation industry is intense. It is important, therefore, to understand how to present personal information to prospective employers in order to increase your chances. This section will give you some useful tips on applying for jobs, and how to produce a Curriculum Vitae (CV), as well as how to prepare yourself for interview.

Applying for jobs

When you hear of a job, or see one advertised in a newspaper, you usually have to write or telephone for further details. Writing the letter or making the telephone call is the first chance you have of impressing the employer, so it is important to get it right. Always apply for a job as soon as possible; it shows that you are genuinely interested.

When you have received more information, the next stage is to write a letter of application, complete the employer's printed application form, or send a copy of your CV. The quality of your letter or form, both in terms of content and presentation, will often determine whether you obtain an interview. Always make sure that your application is with the employer before the closing date, as most will not consider late entries.

Writing letters of application

A **letter of application** should give all the relevant information in a logical sequence and without rambling. There are four stages in writing the letter.

1 State what job is being applied for, and where it was advertised.
2 Give brief details about qualifications and experience.
3 Explain why the job is suitable.
4 Show enthusiasm.

The content of the letter is very important, but equally important is the way in which it is presented, for that creates the first impression that an organisation has of an applicant. Figure 1.47 provides one example of how to layout a letter to a prospective employer.

A positive first impression can be achieved by following these guidelines:

- Make sure you write the letter in the correct format with your address, the date and the full address of the employer. Write to a named person if you have been given this information.
- Always write neatly and clearly. It is a good idea to make a practice copy first. Better still, word process your letter.
- Use plain, unlined white or cream paper and blue or black ink. Envelopes should match the colour of the paper. If you find it difficult to write straight on unlined paper, use bold lines under the paper to guide you.
- Always use a first class stamp on the envelope.
- Check spelling, or get someone else to check it if you are not certain.
- Letters to 'Dear Sir' or 'Dear Madam' end 'Yours faithfully'; letters to a named person ('Dear Mr Johnson') end 'Yours sincerely'.
- Make your signature clear and print your name underneath.
- Always say what job you are writing about, using a reference code if one is given in the job advert, and where you saw the advert. This is particularly important if a firm has several vacancies at the same time.
- Keep a copy of your letter, so that you can refer to it if you get an interview.
- If you include the names of people who will give you a reference, make sure you ask their permission first.
- Write the 'right' letter. If you are responding to a job advert, follow the instructions given. For example, do not include personal details if the advert requests you to write for further details or write for an application form. However, if you are asked to 'apply in writing' you should give details about yourself and state clearly why you are applying for the job. Look at the example of an application to Pulse Fitness Club, which requests the applicant to 'apply in writing'.

Even if no suitable job vacancy is advertised, it is still worthwhile writing to a company to enquire if there will be any job opportunities in the near future. With this type of letter, too, you will need to include details about yourself (or provide a CV) and identify areas of work in which you are interested.

PULSE FITNESS CLUB

Wanted:

Trainee Fitness Instructor

Energetic, enthusiastic young person to train as a fitness instructor with this local health and fitness club. You will provide advice and guidance to club members about their exercise programmes and maintain the exercise equipment. You will be required to work shifts, including evening and weekend work.

Attractive starting salary for the right applicant and a two-year on-the-job or college day release training programme leading to a nationally recognised qualification in Health and Fitness.

Apply in writing to: Mr Plant, Manager,

Pulse Fitness, High Street, Anytown, AL5 9PQ

1

5 Southfields Road,
Anytown, AL6 7DD

11 September 2000

2

Mr Plant
Manager
Pulse Fitness
High Street
Anytown
AL5 9PQ

Dear Mr Plant

3

Trainee Fitness Instructor

4

I would like to apply for the post of Trainee Fitness Instructor, as advertised in the Anytown Evening News on 5 September 2000.

5 6

I am 18 and left Anytown College this June after completing a Vocational A Level in Leisure and Recreation, gaining a C grade. During the two-year full-time course, I studeied a range of leisure and related subjects, including customer service, marketing, organising events and health and safety, as well as developing skills in information technology, communication and numeracy.

7

I would really like to work at Pulse Fitness because it is a well-established local facility. I am also keen to gain further vocational qualifications and would welcome the opportunity to work towards NVQs in Sport and Recreation during the training programme.

8

Since leaving college, I have worked at Shades Fitness Centre as a part-time instructor at weekends and in the evenings. During my course, I completed a three-week placement at Elstree Sports Centre in Bambry. I thoroughly enjoyed this experience and found it very useful to observe experienced sports coaches and to assist in the recreation programme.

9

I am a friendly, outgoing person who enjoys meeting people. My personal interests include hockey, football, eating out and keep-fit. I am a member of Emperors Health and Fitness Centre and regularly attend step classes. If you wish to obtain references, please contact:

10

Mr R Deacon
Vocational Co ordinator
Anytown College
Anytown
AD8 6DL

Mrs J Rose
Manager
Shades Fitness Centre
London Road
Anytown
AL5 7PQ

I am available to come for interview at any time.
Yours sincerely

Jane Cook 11

Key

1. Do not forget your address and the date.
2. Make sure you reply to the named person (if given) and correct address.
3. Say what job you are applying for.
4. Say where you saw the advert.
5. Give your age.
6. List your qualifications (you may also wish to include your GCSEs).
7. Say why you you want the job.
8. Give details about any relevant skills and experience you have. Remember to include details of previous jobs or work placements.
9. Give brief details, including information about your main interests.
10. Give two references, remembering to ask their permission first.
11. Make sure you finish the letter in the correct manner ('yours sincerely' in this example), and print your name clearly below the signature.

ACTIVITY

Letter of application

Imagine that you wish to apply for the Trainee Fitness Instructor job in the advert on page 81. For this exercise assume that you meet the minimum age criterion for your chosen job and that you have been asked to apply in writing. Write an appropriate letter of application.

Filling in application forms

Many organisations send applicants an **application form**. This ensures that the organisation receives all the necessary information in a format that is easy to evaluate. This is important for jobs that require much specific information, for example sports coach or outdoor pursuits instructor. Not all application forms need be as detailed, but most will include spaces to list:

- personal details
- qualifications
- employment history
- hobbies and interests
- referees (people who are willing to make a statement about the applicant's character, particularly in regard to the applicant's employment potential).

Here are some useful tips to help you fill in job application forms.

- Photocopy the form and complete the copy before filling in the original.
- Read through the whole form before you start to fill it in, and make sure to put all the information in the correct places and try to answer all the questions.
- Always use dark ink, preferably black on the final copy, as the firm may wish to photocopy the form.
- Write clearly and neatly and check your spelling.
- Keep a copy of the form so that you can refer to it if you get an interview.
- Obtain permission from the people you are nominating as referees.
- Write a brief covering letter, to send with the completed form. If the application form does not ask you to give reasons why you are applying for the job, or to outline why you feel you are suitable, then it is a good idea to make the covering letter longer to include these points.

ACTIVITY

Completing an application form

Copy and complete the application form on the opposite page.

Producing a CV

CV' stands for **Curriculum Vitae**, which literally means 'the course of one's life'. A CV (sometimes called a résumé) is a concise document which outlines the relevant facts about yourself and your experience to a prospective employer. Unlike filling in an application form, writing a CV offers you the chance to present information about yourself in the way you feel highlights your strengths and particular experience to good advantage.

When do you need a CV?

- In response to an advertised vacancy, when the employer has asked for a CV to be included with your application.
- For sending speculatively to an organisation in which you would be keen to work.
- To use as a personal reference, to help you complete application forms.

What should be included?

While there are different opinions as to exactly what details a CV should contain, it is advisable to include the following information.

- **Personal details:** name, address, telephone number and date of birth are essential. Details of nationality, marital status and children may be included if you choose.
- **Your skills and employment experience.** These are the most important aspect of your CV. Remember to include skills you have developed through any unpaid work, such as voluntary work or work placements, as well as any paid employment. People often overlook the

experience they have developed through non-paid activities. List your employment experience in reverse chronological order.

- **Education and qualifications**: names of schools from secondary level (and colleges, etc. if applicable) with dates attended. List all qualifications gained with dates, by subject and level. Remember to include any job-related or other qualifications done at work, through day release, evening class or professionally. List these details in reverse chronological order.
- **Additional information.** Include information about particular skills you have, e.g. fluency in languages, first aid qualifications, driving licence or membership of any organisations, or clubs.
- **Interests.** If you choose to mention this, list a few genuine interests and don't forget any voluntary activities and involvement with local organisations, e.g. sports clubs, playgroups, etc.
- **Referees**: not essential, but names and addresses of two referees could be included. As you may wish to use different referees for different purposes it may be easier to leave these out, but leave a space to insert them as necessary.

Application for Employment

Strictly Confidential

Position for which you are applying? ....

Where did you learn of the vacancy? ....

PERSONAL DETAILS

Surname .... Mr/Mrs/Miss/Ms (delete as applicable) Telephone ....

First name (s) .... Date of birth ....

Address .... Age ....

.... Nationality ....

.... Marital status ....

....

FULL AND PART-TIME EDUCATION (Please continue on a separate sheet if necessary.)

School, College, University	From	To	Qualifications obtained
....	....	....	....
....	....	....	....
....	....	....	....
....	....	....	....
....	....	....	....
....	....	....	....
....	....	....	....
....	....	....	....
....	....	....	....

PRESENT AND PREVIOUS EMPLOYMENT
(Please continue on a separate sheet if necessary.)

Name and address of employer	From	To	Job title, duties and responsibities
....	....	....	....
....	....	....	....
....	....	....	....
....	....	....	....
....	....	....	....
....	....	....	....
....	....	....	....

How to present your CV

There are many different ways of laying out your CV. The style you use and the order in which you present your information is up to you. The important thing is to decide on the way of presenting the information that suits you best. With the very latest word-processing packages, it is possible to produce CVs that look very professional.

A good starting point is to write a rough 'factual draft' first. List all your jobs, skills, training and qualifications. From this list, identify the most important skills and experience you have in relation to the kind of work you are looking for. It is these you need to highlight on your CV.

Use the limited space wisely. Ask yourself: 'What do I need to communicate to the employer and why? What is the most important information about myself?' If you are not sure whether to include something, ask yourself: 'Is it relevant? Is it positive?'

Employers start to form a picture of you as soon as they begin to read the CV, so aim to make a good impression at the earliest stage. Decide what are the most important facts you wish the employer to know about you and put that information where it will catch their attention. One way of doing this is to include a short 'profile' statement at the beginning of your CV which summarises 'you' in terms of your skills, experience and attributes. The rest of the CV can expand on this. Remember:

- Your CV is an advertising document for yourself.
- Make sure you don't overlook you skills and experience.
- Use your CV to make the most of yourself.

Layout and content of your CV

There are no strict rules about the layout of your CV, but it should be neat, logical and pleasing to the eye. Above all it should be easy for the employer to find a particular piece of information quickly. This is usually achieved by using bold headings. There are several acceptable layouts for producing a CV. Whichever you choose, here are some general points to guide you.

- A CV should usually be presented on one or two sheets (no more) of A4 paper, preferably typed.
- Continually update your CV to take into account changes in your circumstances, such as a change of address or a newly gained qualification.
- Enhance the presentation by using clear, bold headings neatly arranged.
- Obtain several good copies of your CV so that you can use it in approaching other employers.
- Always write a covering letter with your CV to explain your reasons for applying for the particular job and outlining why you think you are suitable.
- If possible, produce your CV on a computer word-processing package so you can amend details easily. Using a computer should also enhance the quality of presentation, particularly if you can use a good laser printer.
- Always check spelling and grammar.

The CV below provides an example of a layout, presentation style and range of content which would be suitable for sending to prospective employers. Before you send your CV, make sure someone checks it for you. Teachers and careers advisers will usually give you advice and help.

Covering letter

You should always send a covering letter with a CV. This letter needs to be short and to the point, explaining why you are sending the CV. If it is in response to an advertised job, you could draw the employer's attention to the skills and experience you have that are particularly relevant to the post. Take care not to repeat exactly what is in your CV. If you have sent the letter speculatively, you could say that you will follow up the enquiry with a telephone call.

ACTIVITY

Profile statement

1 Compile a short 'profile' statement suitable for insertion at the beginning Sarah Mill's CV that summarises her in terms of her skills, experience and attributes. Imagine that she intends to send out this CV speculatively to private sector tennis centres in an attempt to obtain full-time employment as an Assistant/trainee Tennis Coach.

2 Write a suitable covering letter for Sarah's CV.

CURRICULUM VITAE

Name: Sarah Mills
Address: 17 West Park Avenue, Bisham, Woldshire WD1 7PQ
Date of Birth: 20 May 1982

Bisham College of Further Education 1997-2000
Advanced Level (2000) Leisure and Recreation, Grade – Distinction
GNVQ Intermediate Level (1998) Leisure and Tourism, Grade – Merit

Bisham Comprehensive School 1992-7
GCSEs (1997)
English Language B
Geography C
History D
French D
Mathematics D
Biology E

EMPLOYMENT EXPERIENCE

1999-Present
Banton's Sports retail outlet, part-time sales assistant, Saturdays and Sundays. Duties include advising customers, handling sales, stocktaking and using electronic cash register.

1999
Member of the team that ran the College's fashion show. The show was very successful and raised £250 for charity. My role was to co-ordinate the fundraising activities and ensure the project met its financial targets.

1998
College work placement (four weeks) at Rudston Mining Museum. I was involved in taking bookings and escorting groups on guided tours. During the placement I completed a project about the museum's marketing mix and made recommendations on how to increase visitor numbers.

1996
School work experience project: completed three weeks' full-time work experience at Freedom travel agency. Duties included assisting with customer enquiries and bookings.

INTERESTS

Wide variety of sports, including tennis, swimming and keep-fit. I have represented Woldshire County Tennis Association at under-15 and under-19 levels and am currently the Bisham under-19 district champion. I am also interested in tennis coaching and have gained the Lawn Tennis Association (LTA) Leader's Coaching Award. Outside of sport, my main interests include travel and music.

OTHER QUALIFICATIONS/AWARDS

Clean driving licence; St John's Ambulance First Aid Certificate; LTA Leader's Coaching Award; Community Sports Leader's Award.

REFEREES

Mrs S Jameson
Head of Leisure and Recreation
Bisham College of Further Education
Bisham
WI0 7LD

Mr J Tate
Head Coach
Woldshire Tennis Centre
17 Parkland Centre
Rudston

Interview skills

When you are invited for an interview, there are some useful things to remember. These are often called **interview skills.**

Before the interview

- Think positively: you have already done well to get this far!
- Think carefully about why you want the job, and why you believe you are the best person to do it.
- Be prepared for anything. Interviews can vary tremendously, from a very formal interview with several interviewers and a written test, to a more casual approach.
- Organise yourself. Make sure you know where the company is, where the interview is to be held and how you are going to get there.
- Learn as much about the company as you can and, if possible, find out more about the type of work for which you are applying.
- Dress smartly. All employers will appreciate your having made an effort to look good.

During the interview

- Project a positive image, smile and look interested.
- Avoid simple 'yes' and 'no' answers: they stop conversation. When you answer each question give as much relevant information as you can.
- Tell the truth. Untruths often come to light either during or after the interview.
- When you have a chance to ask questions, ask one that shows enthusiasm for the job. Your last question could be about clarifying pay and conditions.

ACTIVITY

Interview questions

In groups, role-play the following interview questions. The interviewees should consider exactly what is being asked and give an answer that satisfies the question.

'Why do you want to work in the leisure and recreation industry?'

'What job would you like to be doing in five years' time?'

'Which aspect of your education and/or previous work experience has been of most benefit to you?'

'What would you say are your main strengths?'

'What do you consider to be your main weaknesses?'

'How do you think you could overcome your main weaknesses?'

'If you could choose anything, what would your ideal job be, and why would you choose it?'

'What do you think constitutes a good work team?'

'What role do you usually play when working in a team?'

BUILD YOUR LEARNING

End of section activity

1 Using the guidelines provided in this section put together your own CV in a format suitable for sending to a prospective employer. Your CV should highlight the skills and abilities that are important for the type of leisure and recreation job that you selected in the activity on page 82.

2 Write a covering letter to accompany your CV.

Keywords and phrases

You should know the meaning of the words and phrases listed below. If you are unsure about any of them, go back through the last seven pages to refresh your understanding.

- Letter of application
- Application forms
- Curriculum Vitae (CV)
- Interview skills

Preview

All organisations, whether large or small, must take action to ensure the safety and security of everyone on their premises - staff, customers and suppliers. Ensuring the health, safety and security of leisure and recreation users, customers, participants and staff is both a legal requirement and essential commercial sense. In this unit you will learn how organisations manage these issues, which laws or regulations they have to comply with, how they assess the risks associated with their activities or premises, and what measures they take to eliminate and reduce those risks.

We will begin by looking at the benefits that effective health and safety measures can bring to many aspects of an organisation's operations, such as greater appeal for families or good public image, and then go on to highlight the possible consequences of not having effective measures in place, such as fines or even prosecution.

The next section identifies the key legislation, regulations and codes of practice that leisure and recreation organisations must follow. You are not required to know the precise details of all the laws, but you must be aware of their nature and purpose, how they are applied, and where to obtain further information or advice about them.

The later sections of the unit will show how organisations go about assessing those health, safety and security risks which may apply to their activities, facilities and equipment.

Health, safety and security is such an important topic that it is covered in other units of your programme, such as Unit 5 (in terms of the need to keep customers and their belongings safe at all times) and Unit 6 (which describes how every project or event must conform to health and safety requirements).

This unit will be assessed by an externally - set case study or test.

2

Safe working practices

Contents

Working within the law

Organisations in the leisure and recreation industry have to comply with health, safety and security requirements in order to **work within the law**. In this case the law means European Directives or United Kingdom Acts of Parliament or local authority regulations. Ensuring safe working practices means complying with **statutory regulations** (which cannot be ignored) and **voluntary codes** (which are advisable, though not compulsory, to follow). Consequently, creating 'safe working environments' and 'working within the law' go hand in hand.

These requirements cannot be ignored by any leisure or recreation operator, whether they run a small private gym, a large all-seater stadium, a jet-ski business or a video hire shop. Obviously the policies and procedures they all use to ensure health, safety and security vary depending upon their facilities, services, staff, working environment and customers. What is clear is that an effective health, safety and security policy is essential throughout the industry, since all organisations have a **duty of care**, i.e. a duty to take all reasonable measures to ensure people will be safe.

In this country the **Health and Safety Executive (HSE)** is the main body which ensures organisations implement the laws that are laid down. **Local authorities** and **sports governing bodies** or **associations** also play important roles in controlling the safe working practices of the organisations in their particular area of the leisure and recreation industry.

Getting hurt at work is not a pleasant subject to think about. The reality is that 300 people a year lose their lives at work in Britain. In addition around 158,000 non-fatal injuries are reported each year and an estimated 2.2 million suffer from ill-health caused or made worse by work.
Health and Safety Executive,1998

The leisure and recreation industry, by its very nature, involves people in a range of potentially dangerous activities, through competitive sport, mass popular events or adventure activities. Increasingly every year cases are reported of injuries and even fatal accidents.

Figure 2.1 lists several of the most common injuries. Can you add any more from your experience? Figure 2.2 shows which sports cause the most sports injuries and deaths in the UK.

Figure 2.1: Common injuries

RUGBY produces the most number of spinal injuries: in the late 1990s this was 20 per cent of the total.

FOOTBALL puts a great deal of pressure on lower limbs: 13 per cent of injuries are to the shins.

RUNNING produces tears, strains, pulls, impact and friction injuries.

CYCLING: The biggest danger of cycling is falling off at speed or in rough terrain.

BOXING: being punched hard is the equivalent of a thump with a 4.5 kilo hammer.

Figure 2.2: The most dangerous sports

Top ten sports causing the most injuries	Top five sports causing deaths
1 Football	1 Unsupervised swimming
2 Rugby	2 Horse riding
3 Cricket	3 Air sports
4 Netball	4 Motor sports
5 Riding	5 Mountaineering
6 Swimming	
7 Gymnastics	
8 Skiing	
9 Hockey	
10 Martial arts	

Source: Society of Public Health

Users of leisure facilities and participants in their activities are prone to accidents. It is therefore vital that the organisations that run them have appropriate policies and procedures in place and suitably qualified staff. Many other activities take place away from premises where supervision or help is not at hand; consequently it is essential to observe safe practices. Throughout this unit we will look at how these policies, procedures and practices are applied.

The **Department of Trade and Industry** via their **Consumer Safety Unit** has identified a range of leisure and recreation locations where accidents and injuries most often occur. These include:

Hotels	Bars and pubs
Crèches	Restaurants and cafés
Playgrounds	Cinemas and theatres
Sports halls	Camp and caravan sites
Swimming pools	Parks and countryside
Stables	Waterside areas
Golf courses	Aboard vessels
Fairgrounds	Discos
Outdoor sports areas	Social centres

Further data from the Consumer Safety Unit shows why it is so important to follow safe working practices in the leisure and recreation industry. In 1995, the numbers of reported accidents were:

- Outdoor sports areas: 235,000
- Playgrounds: 122,000
- Indoor sports facilities: 82,000
- Parks: 72,000,
- Indoor sports areas: 62,000
- Countryside areas: 58,000

The following case study illustrates why safe working practices must be followed.

ACTIVITY

Where do accidents happen?

Which of the following age groups do you think run the greatest risk of accident or injury in the locations shown on the left?

Age ranges: 0-4, 5-14, 15-24, 25-44, 45-59,60-74, 75+

For example, 0-4s are more likely than other age groups to have accidents in crèches and parks.

CASE STUDY

Fatal accident

£35,000 Fine imposed!

Fines totalling £35,000 have been imposed after a boy drowned while a group of 47 Hounslow school children were on a trip to an activity centre in Buckinghamshire, in June 1996. The school failed to check the centre's staff's qualifications, and the Scouts did not inform the school that there were no lifeguards on site.

Two cases were heard at Aylesbury crown court under the Health and Safety at Work Act, for failure to ensure the public's safety. In the first case brought by the Health and Safety Executive (HSE), the London Borough of Hounslow was fined £25,000 and ordered to pay £2,765 costs. In the second case brought by Chiltern District Council, the Greater London Middlesex West County Scout Council was fined £10,000, with £7,000 costs.

In his summary of prosecution the barrister said: 'There should have been an absolute minimum of two qualified lifeguards. In fact there were none. The requirement for lifeguards is elementary and well recognised. It is set out in the joint HSE/Sports Council publication *Safety in Swimming Pools*. The fact and circumstances of the boy's death show all too vividly the wisdom of this guidance.'

The HSE's prosecuting inspector said: 'The tragedy highlighted two important lessons for the organisations involved: they should provide schools with clear guidance on planning and running activities and should have processes in place to check this had been followed.'

Chiltern District Council issued a statement warning associations like the Scouts to consider the health and safety not only of its members, volunteers and employees, but also that of visitors to their sites. It is not enough to assume visiting organisations will act safely, nor is insurance cover a substitute for the proper control of risks.

Source: from a report in the Health and Safety journal of January 1998

Benefits of following safe working practices

There are many benefits arising from effective health, safety and security practices, including those for:

- an organisation (e.g. meeting legal obligations, reducing numbers of accidents, enhancing reputation)
- facilities (e.g. clean, safe activity and changing areas)
- events (e.g. effective crowd control and parking)
- staff (e.g. safer place to work, better working conditions)
- customers (e.g. safe environment, good standard of customer service)
- the environment (e.g. limiting damage by people, vehicles or dangerous substances).

Organisations

Since all organisations, whether they operate in the public, private or voluntary sector, have to apply safe working practices by law, failure to do so can have very serious consequences. Inadequate health, safety and security procedures may cause accidents, and as a result cause the operator to experience a dramatic loss of custom or even go out of business. **Prosecution** and expensive **compensation** claims may result, which in the worst cases might lead to large fines, bankruptcy or even imprisonment. The case study below illustrates the reasons why both statutory regulations and voluntary codes need to be followed.

ACTIVITY

Vistastar Leisure

What impact do you think the prosecution of Vistastar Leisure had in terms of:

- the image and reputation of the organisation?
- its staff?
- its customers?
- its business viability?
- its health and safety policy and procedures?
- its insurance premium?

CASE STUDY

Vistastar Leisure

Council prosecutes health club

Vistastar Leisure was last month fined £2,500 and ordered to pay £700 in costs for operating a franchise of Gold's Gym without a licence from the Council.

On a spot-check visit in January, officers from Barking and Dagenham Council found the club didn't have a licence and had a number of life-threatening hazards, including live electrical sockets, wires hanging off the walls and blocked fire escapes. A follow-up visit the next day showed the facilities were still in use.

The chairperson of the Health and Consumer Services Committee said: 'This case should act as a deterrent to other businesses who fail to apply for a licence. These premises were an accident waiting to happen and the swift action of the council has possibly prevented a tragedy.'

Gold's Gym now holds a licence, having carried out the required work. However, it took them a further three months to meet the health and safety standards laid down.

Source: Leisure Opportunities magazine, September 1999

Organisations with effective health, safety and security procedures may create benefits for themselves by:

- attracting lower insurance premiums
- having fewer accidents or injuries to staff or customers
- having a good image with the public
- passing inspections.

Staff working in organisations with good health, safety and security will often produce better work and services, and generally feel safer. For example, attention to the security aspects of an organisation may well reduce theft and fraud.

▲ Examples of health and safety manuals

It is also a requirement to have all of these procedures written down in a **health and safety manual**, so that anyone can consult it for guidance and up-to-date information. This is of particular benefit for new members of staff.

Many larger leisure and recreation organisations have a designated **safety officer** whose responsibility it is to check and update the processes in operation and ensure that staff know and follow the correct procedures. Most organisations also develop a system for implementing and checking their arrangements regularly.

Facilities

The safety and security of all types of leisure and recreation facilities are of great importance for a number of reasons. For example:

- theft is reduced
- customers are protected while on the premises
- fraud can be detected
- bad behaviour can be quickly dealt with
- access and egress can be controlled
- dangerous areas, such as building sites and so on, can be cordoned off.

It is also important that premises are protected (safe and secure) when they are closed, to prevent theft, damage and accidents.

Projects or events

Working within the law and meeting the needs of participants, customers and staff for an event (a one-off activity) or a short project held over a number of days/weeks often represents a health and safety challenge. This is because there is very little about an event or project that is routine. For example, the organisers of a canoe slalom, a charity fun run, a swimming gala and a hot-air balloon race will all have varying health and safety aspects to consider. This will involve identifying hazards and assessing risks so as to put in place appropriate health and safety procedures. Such health, safety and security procedures are discussed in Unit 6.

Staff

Members of staff are required by law and the organisation for which they work to have a good awareness of health, safety and security in their workplace. Leisure operators usually have an **induction** and ongoing health and safety **training programme** for staff to follow. This should contain details of what to do in certain circumstances, such as evacuations, using equipment safely and reporting accidents. This benefits staff in a number of ways:

- Safer workplace environment. In the case of a busy restaurant kitchen, for example, with lots of hot surfaces and appliances, it is very reassuring for staff to know that everything has been checked and everyone is well trained.
- Better working conditions. For example, staff working during a busy exhibition may rest in a comfortable lounge area, away from the hustle and bustle of the hall.
- Increased awareness of likely dangers. For example, when all the lifeguards around a busy swimming pool with flumes, waves and currents are thoroughly trained in all aspects of water safety management they will have greater awareness of their role and needs.
- Higher staff morale, and reduced absence due to work-related illness or injury.

Working within the law also means observing, for example, **Equal Opportunities** and **Maternity rights**. Policies avoiding **sex and disability discrimination** also apply to staff welfare. Disability issues will be covered later on page 108.

Customers

Customer safety, especially in dangerous leisure and recreation activities such as white-water rafting, car racing or contact sports involving large crowds, is of paramount concern. Ensuring customer safety may involve a great deal of equipment and a high level of staff training. In general, for leisure and recreation activities there are two main aims for an organisation:

- To create and maintain a safe environment: you can judge an organisation's performance in terms of safety by checking its accident records.
- To provide good standards of customer service: you can assess how effective an organisation is in terms of its standards of service by checking the numbers and frequency of customer complaints.

Any organisation that fails to create a safe environment for customers and staff will very soon find that its image and reputation suffers. Staff turnover will probably be high and customers will just not come back! For commercial reasons alone, therefore, it is vital that organisations follow safe working practices.

The environment

The need to maintain and sustain both our natural environment and our built environment also involves health, safety and security. Outdoor leisure and recreation activities can erode and damage the countryside, while the lives of people who dwell in towns where major sports events are held can be disrupted by traffic congestion, noise and pollution. For these reasons there are a number of laws and standards designed to protect the environment set out in the **Environmental Protection Act 1990**.

Organisations that work hard to minimise environmental hazards can enhance their public image, create good community relations and avoid 'bad press' and the costs of expensive clean-up campaigns. The **Environment Agency** (the governmental body charged with monitoring and protecting our environment) frequently takes action against organisations that do not work within the law.

ACTIVITY

Causes of hazards

The following list provides examples of environmental health and safety hazards. For each hazard suggest two possible causes arising from leisure and recreation activities. An example is given to get you started.

- **noise** *from a nightclub or motocross event*
- **litter**
- **chemical spillage**
- **exhaust fumes**
- **erosion/ destruction of countryside**

Ensuring safe and secure working conditions

All managers, owners and staff in leisure and recreation facilities have a duty to provide a safe and secure environment for staff and visitors (whether paying customers or not). This means:

- Regular inspections of all aspects of the facility or location.
- Ongoing staff training.
- Adhering to legislation and codes of practice.
- Seeking advice from expert safety organisations.
- Allocating adequate financial resources to ensure health and safety.
- Making provision for people with special needs who may work at or visit the facility.

It is important to remember that creating safe working environments in an ever-changing leisure and recreation industry is a continual process. Everyone in an organisation must be committed to this process: managers need to ensure that adequate resources and time are provided, while all staff need to be vigilant about reporting hazards and following safety procedures.

There are plenty of examples of disasters caused by 'short cuts' and lack of investment in safety equipment and training. Two very good examples of the constant need to review and check safety procedures and installations are described below.

In August 1999 all land-based equipment dependent on satellite navigation systems (global positioning devices) used by many people in the leisure and recreation industry for work and play - including yachting enthusiasts, hikers, pilots, balloonists and so on - had to be reset manually after an automatic systems failure. Potentially, this was a huge hazard in the air, on the ground and on water. Fortunately, a great deal of advance notice was given and users were able to cope.

Similarly, when the year 2000 arrived, equipment that incorporated microchip technology was potentially at risk if its memory system was unable to cope with the change of date. Massive publicity was undertaken to alert people to the hazards of what became known as the millennium bug. It was feared that the country could grind to a halt if this problem was not solved. Some of the possible consequences for the leisure and recreation industry were:

- Computers, accounting and budgeting, invoicing and ordering, payroll and stock control systems failing.
- Electronically stored records becoming invalid, phones and faxes going off, production and delivery systems stopping.
- Building entry systems shutting down, security and fire controls failing, air conditioning and heating going off.

Due to extensive preparation and planning very few health, safety and security problems actually occurred as a result of the millennium bug. However, these types of problem can also happen if there is no emergency back-up system in case of power failure. The maxim for leisure facilities is: 'Be ready!'

Importance of ensuring health, safety and security

The absence of effective health, safety and security measures can result in life-threatening accidents. The costs to organisations that fail to implement safe working practices can be very high indeed. These costs include:

- Manslaughter charges and imprisonment.
- Court cases leading to bankruptcy.
- Fines ranging from £20,000 upwards for severe cases.
- Bad publicity destroying a company's image.
- Poor standards causing loss of major customers.
- Temporary or permanent closure of premises.
- Compulsory improvement notices issued with limited time scales.
- Clean-up costs for environmental accidents.

In addition, HSE information suggests that the financial costs could represent as much as:

- 37 per cent reduction in profit, due to poorer quality services
- 5 per cent increase in operating costs, to put things right
- 36 times the insurance premium costs, to settle claims.

Avoiding the cost of accidents by having effective and safe working practices is therefore of considerable importance for leisure and recreation organisations. Changes in society in general have increased the need for safe working practices. We now live in an era where there is greater public awareness about negligence and who is responsible. Customers may sue leisure operators if they fail to follow the proper health, safety or security procedures. Ever-increasing legislation only adds to the importance of preventing accidents, injury and prosecution by taking simple, basic precautions to ensure properly planned, safe working practices.

Funfairs are often unjustly criticised for their standards of safety. Contrary to popular belief, they are in fact heavily regulated, as the following case study shows.

ACTIVITY

Breaches in health and safety

1. Find four different examples from the leisure and recreation industry where health and safety rules or regulations have been broken. You may like to use current articles in newspapers, recreation magazines and leisure journals, or back issues of such publications in your library. Sources might include *Leisure Opportunities, Leisure Week, Leisure Management/Manager, Health and Safety,* Royal Society for the Prevention of Accidents magazines, or health and safety web sites such as the HSE's.

2. What happened to the organisation and the people involved?

3. Suggest what could have been done to prevent each occurrence. Present each case on a one-page summary sheet for discussion and evaluation in your group.

CASE STUDY

Funfair checks means thrills with few spills

A common-held view is that fairground equipment is carelessly thrown together by tinkers who scavenge scrap metal when they have finished fleecing the punters on the hoop-la stall! But the truth about travelling fairs is that they are part of a highly regulated business with stringent safety checks, huge public liability insurance and strict membership rules.

Showmen - they are not travellers - operate rides at 250 annual fairs and must belong to the Showmen's Guild of Great Britain. This polices the conduct of 4,700 members and looks after their interests. The Guild requires all equipment to be tested annually by independent engineers for electrical or mechanical faults, and every two years for metal fatigue. Accident statistics show that fairgrounds are safer than playgrounds.

Insurance broker Yates and Son, specialists in fairground insurance, comment 'that travelling showmen are more likely to spot wear or tear on machinery because they dismantle the equipment regularly'. Showmen must carry standard public liability insurance of £1 million and an additional cover of £9 million from the Guild.

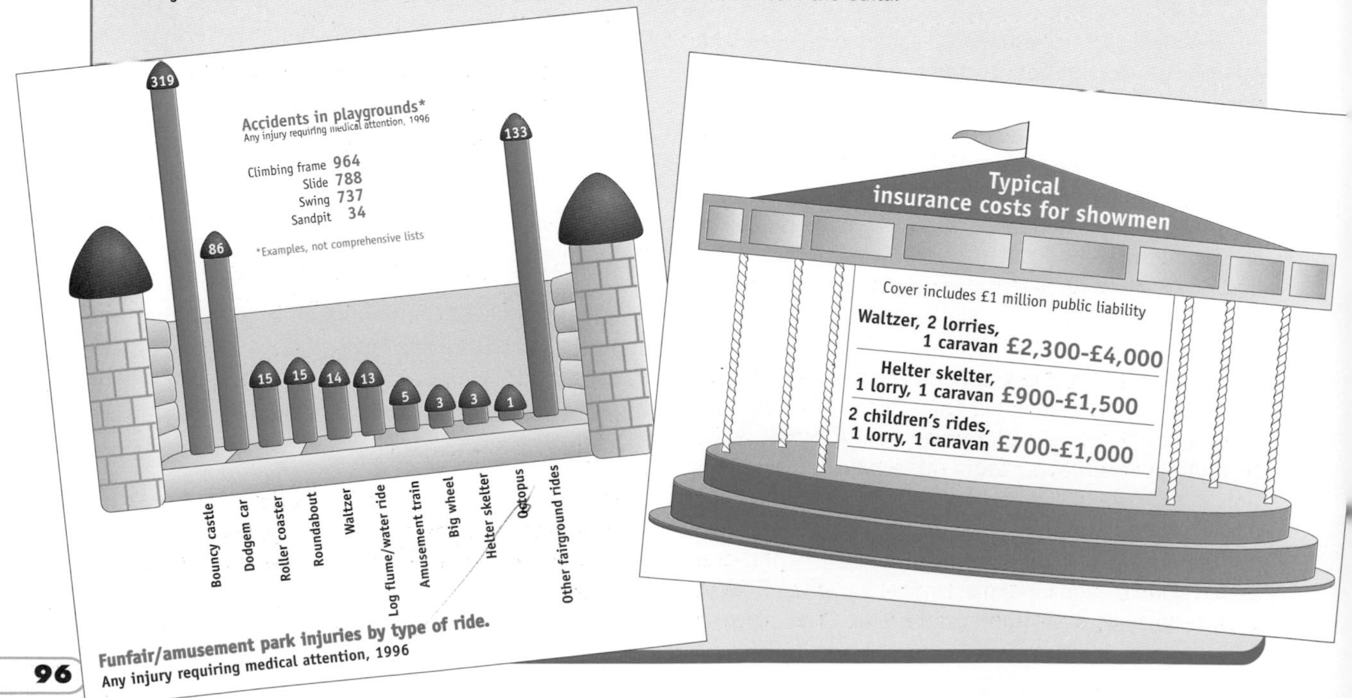

Funfair/amusement park injuries by type of ride.
Any injury requiring medical attention, 1996

Health and safety policies

All leisure and recreation organisations who employ five or more people are required by law to have a **written statement** describing their **health and safety policies and procedures**. Such statements are specific to each organisation and represent a basic action plan on health and safety which all employees should read, understand and follow. For various reasons it makes sense for employers to have an effective policy and to keep it up to date.

- By introducing a formal written policy the employer emphasises the importance of health and safety to employees.
- The incidence of accident, injury and illness in the workplace can be reduced if all employees are aware of safe working procedures.

The written statement (which has to be revised regularly) must:

- state the general policy on health and safety
- specify the arrangements for carrying out the policy
- be brought to the notice of all employees
- be revised whenever necessary, with the revisions brought to the attention of staff.

The policy should state in simple terms the general aims for health and safety and stress the need for co-operation and good communications. It is also usual to mention the consequences of neglecting duties and responsibilities.

Within large organisations in the leisure and recreation industry many health and safety duties will be delegated to managers and supervisors; in a smaller organisation the owner may have to be responsible for everything. Whatever their size, the starting point for most organisations is to analyse all their activities and then outline how they should be covered by a health and safety policy. Some larger organisations have a safety committee to carry out this task.

Once the policy has been written it is best to give a copy to every member of staff for study and reference. Some staff training may have to be undertaken to familiarise people with procedures; this should then be a continuing process. Revisions need to be made to the policy as soon as there is a change in the law or procedures, and the operation of the policy and procedures should be monitored and reviewed if found ineffective. The Fitness Industry guidelines shown in Figure 2.3 show their advice to operators about the probable contents of a safety policy statement.

▲ Fitness suite

Figure 2.3: Fitness Industry guidelines

Health and safety

- Have at least one fully stocked first-aid kit.
- Have at least one member of staff on site at all times who holds a current First Aid Certificate from a recognized body, which includes pulmonary resuscitation.
- Have a written emergency action procedure in accordance with the law.
- Display clear rules for the safe use of pool, spa, sunbed and steam.

Programming

- Offer a standardised health history questionnaire to all new club members before they begin using any of the club's athletic or fitness equipment/facilities.
- Request clearance for members with an identified risk factor or condition.
- Review each member's exercise programme regularly and modify if necessary.
- Instruct all members on safe exercise practice and safe use of equipment.

Staffing

- Employ staff who have appropriate qualifications for their responsibilities.
- Ensure that your staff are fully conversant with the club's health and safety emergency procedures.

Facility management

- Have a system of regular checks, and maintenance agreements with suppliers, to ensure the safe operation of all equipment and services.

Help in writing the statement can be obtained from the HSE, a trade/professional organisation appropriate to the type of facility or activity, or the environmental health department of a local authority. The actual format is up to the organisation: some produce a summary version with a more detailed parent copy held centrally. The HSE recommends the following checklist of points when compiling a health and safety policy document:

- show commitment in what you say
- state who is responsible for implementation and review
- have it signed and dated
- take all views into account
- does everyone accept their duties?
- emphasise co-operation and consultation
- describe the duties clearly and fully for (1) recording and investigating accidents; (2) fire safety; (3) first aid; (4) inspections; (5) training; (6) checking and monitoring.

Keywords and phrases

You should know the meaning of the words and phrases listed below. If you are unsure about any of them, go back through the last nine pages to refresh your understanding.

- **Work within the law**
- **Statutory regulations**
- **Voluntary codes**
- **Duty of care**
- **Health and Safety Executive (HSE)**
- **Local authorities**
- **Sports governing bodies and associations**
- **Department of Trade and Industry**
- **Consumer Safety Unit**
- **Prosecution**
- **Compensation**
- **Health and safety manual**
- **Safety officer**
- **Induction and training programme**
- **Equal Opportunities**
- **Maternity rights**
- **Sex and disability discrimination**
- **Environment Agency**
- **Environmental Protection Act 1990**
- **Written statement of health and safety policies and procedures**

BUILD YOUR LEARNING

End of section activity

Obtain a copy of a health and safety policy statement or staff safety handbook for two local leisure or recreation organisations or facilities. Working in small groups, discuss whether your chosen organisations or facilities implement an appropriate range of measures (statutory and voluntary) to ensure the health and safety of staff and customers. The following checklist will help you, as it shows some of the most common areas covered by an organisation's written health and safety policies and operating procedures.

- Person(s) responsible for health and safety in the organisation.
- Personal responsibilities of staff with regard to health and safety.
- Emergency procedures.
- Cleaning and maintenance schedules.
- Room environment conditions (heat, light, space).
- Staff facilities.
- Lifting, carrying and storage of materials.
- Fire precautions and equipment.
- First aid equipment and training.
- Budget allocation for health and safety activities.

Health and safety laws and regulations (employers and employees)

In this section we will look at examples of the statutory (compulsory) laws, regulations and voluntary codes and guidelines which apply to organisations and employees within the leisure and recreation industry. Figure 2.4 shows the main European Regulations and UK Acts of Parliament that affect the leisure and recreation industry.

You are not expected to know the precise details of all the relevant legislation, but you must be aware of the key intentions (main purposes) and requirements of the most important laws affecting the industry under the headings:

- Employees' and employers' responsibilities.
- Special groups and areas.

Before we investigate individual legislation, it is useful to consider how all the regulations and codes relate to each other. Figure 2.5 shows the different **tiers of legislation**, where we can see the source and level of importance of each type of regulation and guidance issued.

Figure 2.5: Tiers of legislation

European Regulations and Directives apply to all EU countries

United Kingdom Acts of parliament are statutary: they must be followed in the UK

Local authority laws and regulations apply to that area only

Codes of practice and guidelines are voluntary: they are advisable to follow in the UK

Figure 2.4 Key health and safety legislation and regulations

European health and safety regulations/employer/employee responsibilities

- Management of Health and Safety at Work 1992
- Workplace Regulations 1992
- Manual Handling Operations Regulations 1992
- Provision and Use of Work Equipment 1992
- Personal Protective Equipment 1992
- Display Screen Equipment 1992

UK legislation employer/employee responsibilities

- Health and Safety at Work Act 1974
- Occupiers Liability Act 1984
- Control of Substances Hazardous to Health 1994
- Working Time Regulations 1998
- First Aid Regulations 1981
- Reporting of Injuries, Diseases and Dangerous Occurrences 1995

Health and Safety Laws and Regulations, specific groups and areas

- Disability Discrimination Act 1995
- Children's Act 1989
- Data Protection Act 1984
- Food Safety Act 1990
- Safety at Sports Grounds Act 1975
- Fire Safety, and Safety of Places of Sport Act 1987
- Licensing and Gambling Laws
- Adventure Activities Regulations 1996
- Trades Description Act 1968
- Consumer Protection Act 1987
- Sale of Goods Act 1979

European health and safety regulations

Since 1992 **European regulations** have in some cases superseded some **UK Acts of parliament** in terms of importance. Most British health and safety regulations now have their origins in European Union Directives. A group of six EU regulations (often referred to as 'the 6-pack') have particular significance for people working in the leisure and recreation industry.

Management of Health and Safety at Work Regulations 1992

These regulations clarify what actions must be taken by employers in order to comply with their duties. They stress the prevention of accidents by means of compulsory risk assessments on the part of employers. **Risk assessments** involve assessing the health and safety risks present in the workplace. (Risk assessment is covered in more detail on pages 121-130.) The assessments undertaken by employers should cover all situations which could present a danger to staff, visitors or users. In a leisure and recreation context this could be anything from children running on slippery changing-room floors, to obstructions in passageways for wheel-chair users.

Workplace (Health, Safety and Welfare) Regulations 1992

This specifies which aspects of the workplace and its facilities apply for risk assessment purposes. All facilities in the leisure and recreation industry, whatever their nature, have to be checked. Figure 2.6 provides specific examples.

ACTIVITY

Workplace regulations

For each of the workplace regulations listed in Figure 2.6 identify an area within a leisure or recreation facility, or a facility itself, for which this could be an important issue and say why you think this could be so. For example, the toilet area should include a suitable toilet for people with disabilities.

Figure 2.6: Workplace regulations summary

Maintenance	Equipment, devices and systems must be regularly maintained and in good repair
Ventilation	Enclosed areas must be ventilated with clean, fresh air
Temperature	A reasonable temperature must be maintained throughout the building
Lighting	Lighting must be suitable, sufficient and have an emergency power supply
Cleanliness	Workplaces and furnishings must be clean with no waste accumulating
Space	Floor area, height, personal space and toilet provision must be adequate
Workstations	Must be appropriate and equipped with a suitable seat
Floors	Must be suitable to prevent slipping, tripping and free from obstructions
Falls	Measures must be taken to prevent objects or people falling
Windows	Must be transparent or translucent, be of a safe material and marked
Traffic	Safe circulation must be ensured for people and vehicles
Doors	Must be properly constructed and meet required specifications
Escalators	Must operate smoothly and have visible emergency stop controls
Toilets	Clean conveniences must be provided in accessible places
Washing	Sufficient and suitable facilities must be provided in accessible places
Water	Supplies of clean water with drinking cups clearly marked are needed
Clothing	Adequate storage, any special clothes and changing facilities are required
Staff rooms	Arrangement of rooms must protect non-smokers and those eating.

Manual Handling Operations Regulations 1992

These regulations deal predomimantly with the lifting and loading of objects at work. Employers have a responsibility to reduce the amount of physical effort required by staff and the risk of injury. Employees must follow any established systems, use correctly any equipment supplied for lifting or loading, and take care that no one else can be injured by their activities.

If employees and employers co-operate about such things, then solutions to problems should be found easily. Figure 2.7 provides some examples of good practice.

Figure 2.7: Examples of good practice for manual handling

- Change the layout: e.g. lower shelf displays.
- Cut carrying distances: position heavy or frequently lifted material close to the storeroom.
- Avoid repetitive work: mechanise or automate where possible, or break-up routines.
- Make loads lighter or easier to carry: supply trolleys.
- Improve lighting: light-up darker corners such as cupboards.
- Provide training: e.g. in the use of new technology.

Provision and Use of Work Equipment Regulations 1992

The primary objective of PUWER (as these regulations are often known) is to ensure the provision of safe work equipment and its proper use. Here are some examples of the type of equipment within the scope of PUWER which we might find in the leisure and recreation industry:

- Check-out machine/photo-electric devices
- Lawnmower
- Computer
- Overhead projector/video
- Ladder/mobile access platform
- Maintenance tools such as saws, drills, etc.

Employees and employers are covered by these regulations that are designed to prevent improper use and encourage correct use of equipment. In the leisure and recreation industry, organisations will be involved in:

- checking that equipment supplied or used by operatives is suitable for the job
- providing training and instructions in the use of equipment
- ensuring that all equipment is properly maintained and guards are in place
- ensuring temperatures, gauges and other controls are clearly displayed
- making certain that all equipment is secure and well lit.

For example, employees working with mechanical equipment in a theme park or a funfair will be affected by these regulations.

Personal Protective Equipment at Work Regulations 1992

'PPE' covers the following types of personal protective clothing found in the leisure and recreation industry:

- Aprons/gloves
- Adverse-weather or high-visibility clothing
- Protective footwear/headwear/eyewear
- Lifejackets/safety harnesses
- Respirators and breathing apparatus

Items such as clothing supplied as a uniform or for food-hygiene purposes are not subject to these regulations. Likewise, the regulations do not require all professional sports people to use shin guards or head protection, for example. However, they do require canoe instructors to wear lifejackets, stable staff to wear riding helmets and climbers to wear climbing helmets. The regulations also apply to the wearing of crash helmets when using quad bikes, for example.

Many additional considerations apply to the equipment used in the leisure and recreation industry because it is so diverse. Such factors include:

- physical effort and duration of the activity;
- requirements for visibility and communication;
- ease of cleaning;
- range of sizes/quality/newness.

As with other regulations, training and information on the use of the PPE also needs to be given. Maintenance, defects or modifications all need to be observed as part of a regular inspection programme for all personal protective equipment.

ACTIVITY

Personal Protective Equipment

Here is a list of leisure and recreation activities for which we would expect staff to be wearing PPE. Which type of PPE would you expect to find in each case?

Activity	PPE
A caving instructor	
Jet-ski riders	
Football stewards	
A team of lighting riggers erecting a gantry for a rock concert	
A gardener spraying weedkiller	

Health and Safety (Display Screen Equipment) Regulations 1992

Badly organised display screen equipment or visual display units (VDUs) and workstations can lead to discomfort and further health problems, disorders or stress. Some common problems include aching hands, arms and neck (repetitive strain injuries); temporary eye-strain and headaches; fatigue. People in the leisure and recreation industry working with VDUs can use the checklist in Figure 2.8 to make sure they are working in a safe environment.

Figure 2.8: VDU health and safety checklist

- Is the display-screen image clear?
- Is the keyboard comfortable?
- Does my furniture fit with the workstation and meet my needs comfortably?
- Is the environment around my workstation free from obstruction and well-lit?
- Do I suffer from any repetitive strain injuries (aches, pains and disorders)?
- Is the VDU affecting my eyesight?

▲ People wearing examples of PPE

These types of questions are important for staff using computer-based booking systems or word processors with graphics or spread-sheet applications on a regular basis. Employers in the leisure and recreation industry also have a checklist (Figure 2.9) to follow to help them decide whether they comply with regulations or not.

Figure 2.9 Regulation checklist

Analyse workstations – the seating, type of job, any special needs – then assess and reduce any risks.	❑ workstations ❑ the seating ❑ type of job ❑ any special needs
Ensure workstations have good features, for example adjustable chairs and suitable lighting.	❑ adjustable chairs ❑ suitable lighting
Plan work so there are breaks or changes of activity: frequent short breaks are better than fewer long breaks.	❑ breaks
Provide eye tests if requested by staff and provide regular check-ups.	❑ eye tests ❑ regular check-ups
Provide training and information for staff on how best to avoid health problems.	❑ training ❑ information

UK legislation: Health and Safety at Work Act 1974

The law relating specifically to health and safety in the UK is predominantly based on the **Health and Safety at Work Act 1974** (often shortened to HASAWA). Employers must comply with this Act, which applies to all workers in all types of work. If they do not, they may be prosecuted.

Key sections of the 1974 Act can be summarised as follows:

- Section 2, states that employers have a general duty to provide for the health, safety and welfare of those they employ. This section also requires employers to consult employees about health and safety arrangements and prepare a written health and safety policy statement.
- Section 3 obliges employers to make sure that their operations do not put non-employees (such as visitors and contractors) at risk. For example, this means ensuring that precautions and warnings are in place to advise and protect customers while a team of decorators are on the premises repainting the walls.
- Section 6 specifies that adequate information about any work-related hazards and the precautions needed to contain them must be made available. An example of this is the use and storage of swimming-pool cleaning and filtration chemicals.
- Section 7 places a duty on employees to take reasonable care to ensure their own health and safety at work and that of any other people who might be affected by their actions, particularly by following the correct operating proceedures.

HASAWA also uses the words 'as far as is reasonably practicable' in relation to employers' duties with regard to the health and safety of employees. In other words, employers have a duty to provide reasonable safety protection for their workforce within certain limits of money, time and effort.

Occupiers Liability Act 1984

The **Occupiers Liability Act 1984** is an important piece of legislation because it imposes a 'duty of care' on those in control of premises to ensure that visitors are 'reasonably safe' in the premises for the purposes for which they were invited or allowed by the occupier. Organisations must therefore ensure that their premises are suitable for all visitors. In a people orientated industry, nearly all leisure or recreation organisations come under the auspices of this Act, for the industry depends on visitors for survival.

There are many examples of tragedies which could have been avoided if a better duty of care had been exercised, especially at large sports or entertainment events. In many cases if negligence can be proved then action can be taken to sue for damages or imprisonment, as happened with the Hillsborough Football Stadium disaster and the Lyme Bay canoeing tragedy.

Control of Substances Hazardous to Health Regulations 1994

This regulation - better-known as **COSHH** - requires employers to control exposure to hazardous substances to prevent ill-health, so that both employees and others who may be exposed are protected. In the leisure and recreation industry these substances could include:

- paints when redecoration is underway
- cleaning agents when toilets, kitchens or changing rooms are being cleaned
- fumes from special effects in visitor centres
- smoke from bonfires or fireworks
- dust around a dirt track used by bikes or cars
- chemicals used to clean swimming pools.

The detrimental effects of hazardous substances can include:

- skin irritation or burns
- asthmatic attacks
- loss of consciousness
- bacterial infection.

Failure to follow COSHH requirements could result in falling productivity, the possibility of closure or prosecution and compensation claims. COSHH is best seen as a useful tool for managers when checking for potential hazards, as it sets out seven basic steps for employers and employees to follow (see Figure 2.10).

Working Time Regulations 1998

The **Working Time Regulations** which came into force in 1998 have made an impact on many workers and employers in the leisure and recreation industry. Some staff in the industry are specifically not included, however, such as those who are engaged in rail, road, air and waterway transport or emergency services.

The aim of the regulations is to ensure that staff are not required to work unduly long hours. As workers in the UK have traditionally worked longer hours than those elsewhere in Europe, the regulations also aim to bring the UK into line with regulations in other EU countries. Research suggests that working consistently long hours can have an adverse effect on health and well-being, so there is an underlying health and safety aim here too.

Figure 2.10: COSHH procedures

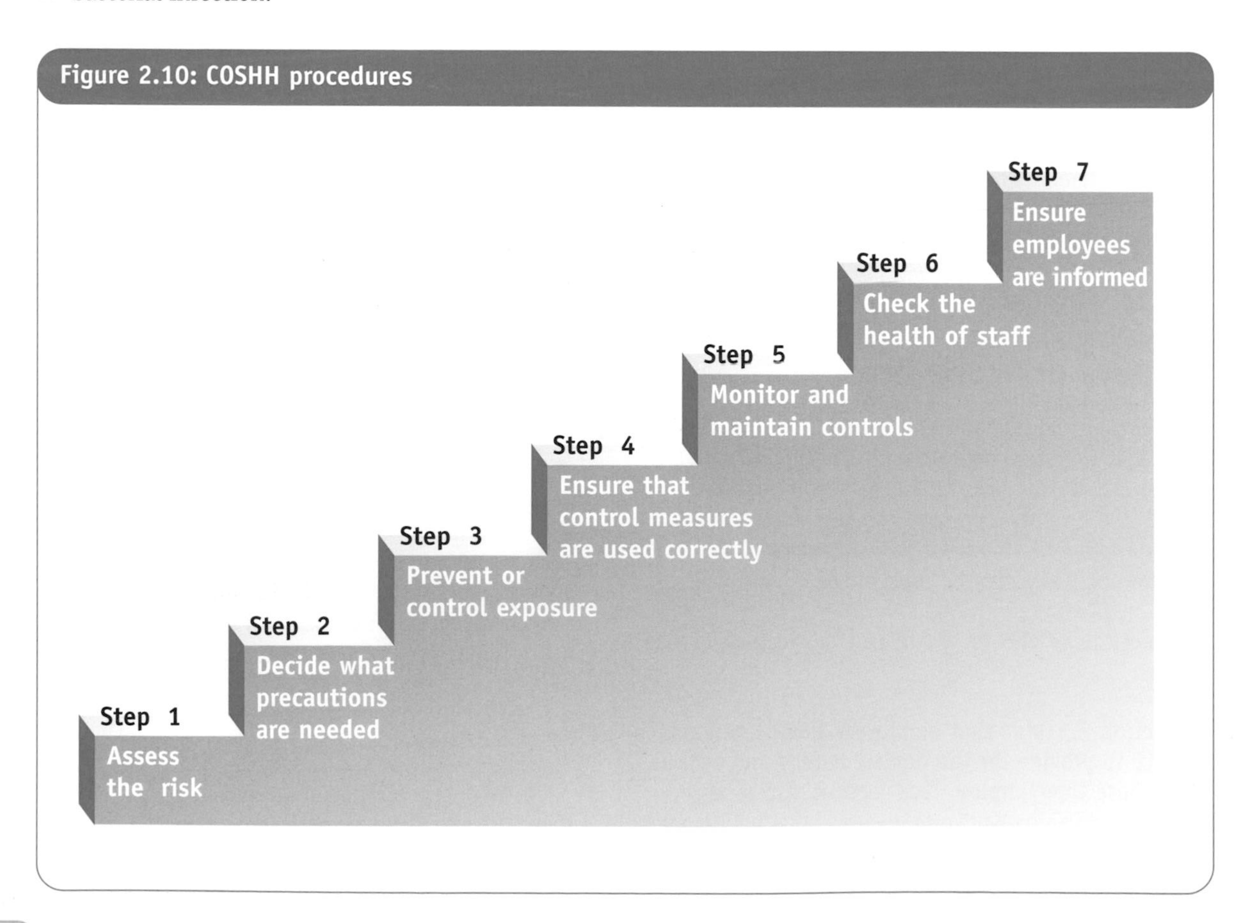
Step 1
Assess the risk
Step 2
Decide what precautions are needed
Step 3
Prevent or control exposure
Step 4
Ensure that control measures are used correctly
Step 5
Monitor and maintain controls
Step 6
Check the health of staff
Step 7
Ensure employees are informed

The regulations limit the maximum amount of working time and regulate the way working time is organised, as shown in Figure 2.11.

Figure 2.11: Working time regulations

- An average weekly working time limit of 48 hours
- An average daily working time limit of 8 hours
- Health assessments for night workers
- Weekly rest periods
- Daily rest periods
- Rest breaks at work
- Paid annual leave

The regulations also contain specific provisions applicable to 16-18 year olds - so if you have a part-time job, some of them may apply to you. Workers can also opt out of the arrangements if they wish, so there is a certain amount of flexibility built into the regulations to cover the many ways and places in which people work.

Health and Safety (First Aid) Regulations 1981

The chances are that if someone is injured at work, the first person on the scene who can help will be a trained first-aider. The regulations require organisations to provide 'adequate and appropriate personnel' for this purpose and support them with facilities and equipment to enable first aid to be given. What is adequate and appropriate will depend on the circumstances, but the minimum that staff and customers should expect is:

- a suitably stocked first-aid kit
- a qualified first-aid person.

These should be available at all times. There is no standard list of items for a first-aid kit, as the necessary contents depends on the special risks which might exist in the building or at the facility. However, as a guide the HSE recommends the minimum stock of items shown in Figure 2.12.

No tablets or medicines are to be kept in a first-aid kit in case young children gain access, or someone should use the wrong combination or more than the prescribed dose.

Figure 2.12: Minimum first aid items

20 individually-wrapped sterile adhesive dressings

2 sterile eye-pads

4 individually-wrapped triangular bandages (sterile preferred)

6 safety pins

6 medium-sized, individually-wrapped unmedicated wound dressings

2 large sterile individually-wrapped unmedicated wound dressings

1 pair of disposable gloves

As already noted, an organisation should have an 'appointed first-aid person', preferably someone who is trained in first aid meeting with HSE approval and able to take control and look after first-aid equipment. In addition, qualified first-aiders will be needed to cover the site during all working hours. All staff, visitors and customers need to be made aware of first-aid arrangements throughout the facility.

There are a number of other Regulations which may have a bearing on safe working conditions in leisure and recreation facilities. We shall look at two of these: Electricity at Work and RIDDOR.

Electricity at Work Regulations 1989

Each year about 1,000 accidents at work involving electric shocks or burns are reported to the HSE. Many of these are fatal accidents, but even non-fatal shocks can cause severe or permanent damage.

The most common causes of electric shocks at work are faulty equipment and staff falling into appliances – contact with live parts above 230 volts (normal mains voltage) will shock, burn or kill. Electrically started fires are the next most dangerous sources of injury, especially if flammable or explosive substances are involved. One example of where these types of risk are greatest are special-event road crews who set-up outdoor concert stages with light and sound cables, especially if the weather is wet. In an everyday context, staff working in a building which is being refurbished or is cluttered with electrical appliances, overloaded sockets and extension cables may well be more at risk.

Perhaps the people most vulnerable to electrical dangers are found in home-based leisure and recreation. An enthusiastic DIY person, for example, who thinks they know what they are doing and improvises a connection or installation in the home or garden, or uses a new power tool without checking the instructions, puts themselves at risk.

The Electricity at Work Regulations advise that all installations should be properly maintained and meet suitable standards. Other precautions include:

- only having qualified staff to carry out electrical repairs
- ensuring cut-off devices are installed and are clearly visible
- using correct connectors and couplings
- built-in devices to detect faults automatically.

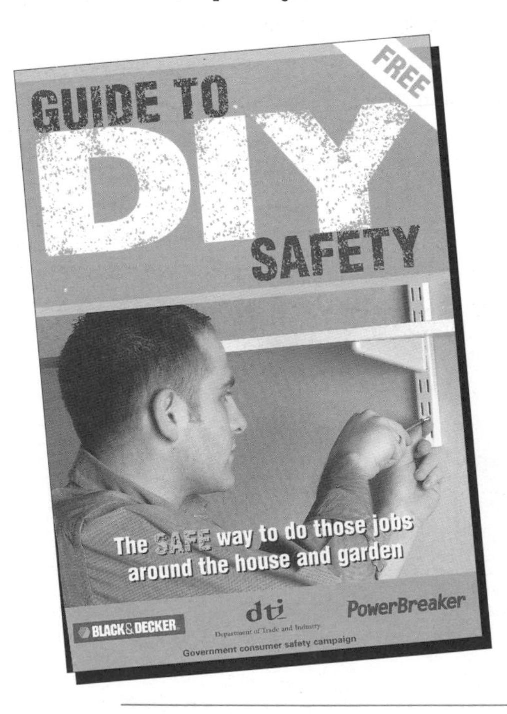

▲ Safety guidelines are freely available

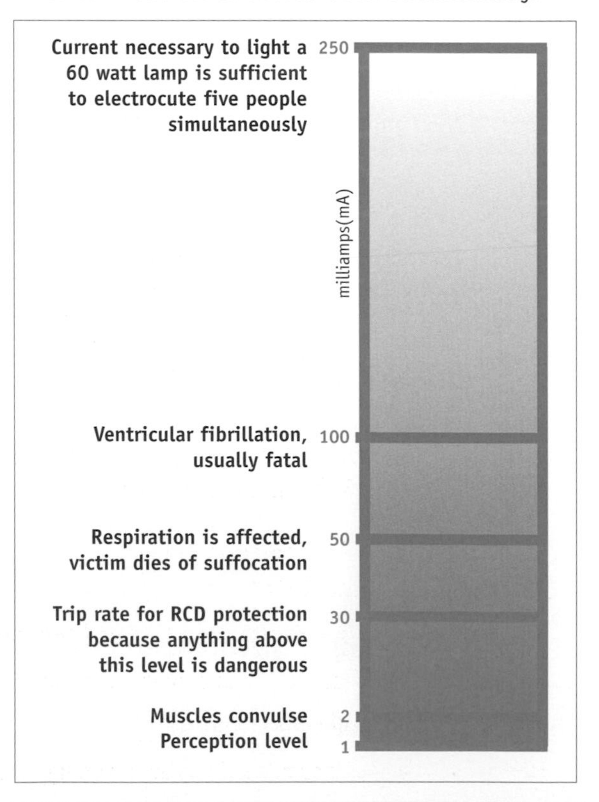

▲ HSE guidelines on electrical safety for entertainers

The following case studies give examples of people at risk in the leisure and recreation industry.

CASE STUDY

Use of electrical equipment

One category of people in the leisure and recreation industry especially at risk are entertainers who use electrical equipment for their acts. Even a very small electric current flowing through your body can kill you; a shock from a 40-watt light bulb, for example, can cause pain, paralysis of chest muscles and after only a few seconds upset the heart beat, possibly leading to death. The most common problems arise through:

- wrong connections
- damaged cable
- faulty equipment
- overheating
- lack of technical knowledge.

ACTIVITY

Use of electrical equipment

As a group, brainstorm as many different examples as you can of entertainers who use electrical equipment. Give an example of the types of safety check your group would recommend for each act.

Electrical safety is just one of the factors that have to be considered by leisure and recreation event organisers. If, for example, you plan to use any electrical systems for your project in Unit 6, ensure that you obtain the correct technical advice about setting it up and operating it safely, as highlighted in the following case study.

CASE STUDY

Using audio-visual equipment

Setting up an event, big or small, indoors or out, can be a daunting-enough task, with arrangements for staging, catering and entertaining. Two vital ingredients which are easily overlooked are lighting and sound.

The difficulty with audio-visual (AV) systems is that they are highly technical and without expertise in the field it can be difficult to establish what equipment is required for the desired effect. Also, costs can be enormous, so advice on the most cost-effective way to equip your event is vital. For these reasons, the vast majority of AV equipment is hired, not bought, and a good AV company hiring the equipment to you will offer advice on how to achieve the best results and use it safely.

Be sure that your supplier has the capacity to provide you with what you want and when you want it. A good reputation, adequate insurance and membership of an approved organisation should also demonstrate safety is top of the agenda. Before identifying what resources you are going to need, consider the following questions:

- What effect do you want?
- What size is your venue?
- What are your time-scales for set-up and testing?
- Are there any restrictions to consider such as local residents, noise pollution, laws and regulations?
- What is your budget?

Finally, involve your insurers early in the planning process so that they can advise.

Source: article by Clive Dickin in *Leisure Manager*, August 1998

Reporting of Injuries, Diseases and Dangerous Occurrences Regulations 1995

Reporting accidents and ill-health is a legal requirement according to this Act (RIDDOR). Organisations need to keep a record going back three years which shows the following information:

- Nature and date of reporting.
- Date/time and place of the event.
- Personal records of those involved (kept on file/log or disc).
- A brief description of the nature of the event.

In the main, such records are used for insurance purposes, helping to review procedures and tracking down sources of problems. Figure 2.13 shows some typical examples in the three categories of RIDDOR - injuries, diseases and dangerous occurrences - which might apply to the leisure and recreation industry.

Most good operators take precautions to ensure safe practices. For example, Fitness for Industry, an organisation that runs numerous corporate fitness centres, including those for Texaco Ltd, McDonald's and the BBC, believe that all accidents and injuries should be reported regardless of the situation or liability. Each case will have its own characteristics or specific elements and needs to have the details recorded. It is much safer to report everything, follow RIDDOR guidelines and leave the decision on whether it needs following up to the health and safety authorities (Environmental Health Officers).

ACTIVITY

RIDDOR incidents

For each of the entries in the RIDDOR incidents table shown in Figure 2.13, identify a possible situation where each could occur in a leisure and recreation environment.

Health and safety laws and regulations (specific groups and areas)

Within the range of Directives, Acts and Regulations which apply to the leisure and recreation industry, there are a number which have particular relevance for people working either with specific groups or within areas which require special legislation. Some of these are discussed in the following sections.

Disability Discrimination Act 1995 (DDA)

In terms of this Act, 'disability' means 'a physical or mental impairment, which has a substantial and long-term adverse effect on a person's ability to carry out normal day-to-day activities'. The Act came about through public pressure to persuade operators and businesses to remove the barriers facing people with disabilities.

The leisure industry is a major provider of goods, facilities and services attractive to people with disabilities, so this legislation is particularly

Figure 2.13: Examples of incidents reported under RIDDOR

Injuries	Diseases	Dangers
Major fractures	Poisoning	Collapse of structures
Amputation	Contagious skin conditions	Explosion
Dislocation	Lung diseases	Equipment touching power lines
Loss of sight	Infections, e.g. hepatitis	Accidental demolition
Burns/shocks	Vibration syndrome	Release of chemicals
Hypothermia	Muscle disorders	Scaffolding collapse
Unconsciousness		Burst water mains

important. For example, facilities such as leisure centres, museums and art galleries have to be accessible to those with restricted mobility or in wheelchairs.

Public transport providers have been encouraged to adapt their vehicles and facilities to make it easier for people with disabilities to use their services, for example by fitting low access steps to buses. The Act also applies to employment rights. It is now against the law to discriminate against current or prospective employees with disabilities without a justifiable cause.

In the long term, service providers in the leisure industry will be expected to make reasonable changes to policies, practices and procedures to make it possible for people with disabilities to work in or use their facilities.

ACTIVITY

Access for disabled customers

Leading facilities in the UK have made the following kinds of changes to enhance disabled access. Can you think of five more examples?

- Installation of lifts
- Free access to those escorting a person with disabilities
- Braille signs
- Designated parking
- Special training for front-of-house staff
- Low-level signs and counters
- Guide dogs and hearing dogs welcomed
- Picture images and large print

Children's Act 1989

The **Children's Act** is of major importance to the leisure and recreation industry because so many of the industry's products and services are aimed at young people. The Act places particular responsibilities on those with substantial access to children, such as sports coaches and leaders, teachers and swimming instructors. People must obtain clearance from the police (who check their records) to prove their suitability before they can work with children. Under the Children's Act, organisations that provide play services have to be registered and at least half their staff must be properly qualified.

More detailed child protection guidance extends into sports contexts because of the abuse which has come to light in recent years. Child abuse in sport and other leisure activities can take four forms and organisations need to plan carefully so that these are prevented or eliminated. They are:

- Physical abuse: hitting, shaking, squeezing, burning, biting, drugs.
- Sexual abuse: adult fondling or sexual contact, pornographic material.
- Emotional abuse: persistent lack of affection; shouting, threatening, taunting.
- Neglect: failing to meet basic needs, or exposure to danger and injury.

In line with Home Office guidelines, the Institute for Leisure and Amenity Management (ILAM) recommends that the welfare of children is safeguarded. In its document entitled *Safe from Harm*, leisure and recreation organisations that have children on their premises, or that provide activities for children, are advised to devise a policy to create safe working practices for children. Recommendations include:

- Planning work to minimise situations where abuse could occur.
- Having a system whereby children can talk to an independent responsible person.
- Involving all staff in any procedures and training them to supervise or protect children.
- Checking references and staff records thoroughly.
- Issuing guidelines on how to deal with the disclosure or discovery of child abuse.

These guidelines also received the endorsement of the UK Sports Council at the time, who stated that 'there is a collective responsibility on the part of all individuals and organisations involved in the provision of sport to ensure that all children and young people have a safe, enjoyable and rewarding sporting experience'.

CASE STUDY

Child protection procedures in swimming

In 1996 the main swimming bodies forming the Amateur Swimming Federation of Great Britain, in conjunction with the National Coaching Foundation (NCF) and the National Society for the Prevention of Cruelty to Children (NSPCC), came together to create a blueprint for how child safety and welfare could best be looked after in swimming. They wholeheartedly adopted the principles outlined as good practice earlier and turned those into a plan covering the following features for others to follow:

- Put welfare first.
- Watch for different types of abuse, in various situations.
- Exercise good listening skills.
- Take action with poor practice or abuse.
- Ensure confidentiality and accurate records.
- Involve social services or the police early.
- Keep records of recruitment, references and personal details.

In a further effort to ensure the health and safety of children at play, new European standards for outdoor play areas were adopted in the UK in 1999. These standards cover outdoor playground equipment and playground surfacing and are designed to help the UK to harmonise with other EU countries. The standards are endorsed by several important and knowledgeable safety organisations in the leisure and recreation industry, such as the Royal Society for the Prevention of Accidents (RoSPA), the National Playing Fields Association (NPFA) and the Association of Play Industries (API).

A Guide to the
New European
Playground Equipment
and Surfacing Standards
API
RoSPA
The Royal Society for the Prevention of Accidents

◄ RoSPA leaflet

Data Protection Act 1984

This Act gives customers the right to know if personal data is held about them on computer, for example a membership database for a gym, or personnel files. The main aim is to ensure that personal details held electronically are not passed to a third party without permission. It forbids organisations or individuals to hold personal data about a person unless they are registered with the data protection registrar. Failure to register is an offence and is punishable by a fine. There is no upper limit to these fines, so it is imperative that organisations register and conform to the requirements of the Act. The Act gives individuals the right to:

- gain access to the information held about them and change it if it is incorrect
- make claims for improper use or inaccurate information, such as circulating personal information of a confidential nature (e.g. about medical conditions)
- check that the information is only used for the purpose specified and not shared with other parties.

Organisations must also ensure that only necessary and relevant information is held about their staff. In other words, data such as expired disciplinary notices should not be retained. Organisations must keep the information secure so that unauthorised access is not possible.

ACTIVITY

Data protection

Undoubtedly there are a great many benefits from being able to store and access information electronically. Make a list of these benefits and then list possible difficulties or aspects open to misuse.

Food Safety Act 1990

Many organisations provide food and beverages as part of their leisure and recreation service. This Act was a significant step forward in consumer protection. It aims to:

- ensure that food produced is safe to eat (not contaminated or unfit)
- ensure that food is not misleadingly presented (contents)
- strengthen legal powers and penalties (closure, improvement notices or fines)
- comply with European regulations (EU directives)
- keep pace with technological change (e.g. genetic modifications).

The Act applies to all premises and covers a whole range of issues about food, including:

- preparation and processing
- sources and storage
- wrappings and transport
- ingredients and handling;
- animal products distribution
- manufacturing and packaging
- slimming aids
- drink and water.

All leisure and recreation organisations involved in preparing and serving food must set safety priorities to prevent accidents to staff. Preventative effort should be concentrated in areas which have caused the most accidents in the past. For example:

- Production areas: over 90 per cent of major and minor injuries which keep people off work for more than three days happen in production.
- General activities: two-thirds of major injuries and those causing absences exceeding three days are caused by poor handling, maintenance and cleaning techniques.

The Act requires all permanent food producers and retailers to register and to train their staff in food hygiene practices. Additionally, the Act is supported by many other specific pieces of food legislation, such as regulations on labelling, hygiene, importing and premises. Figure 2.14 provides a sample extract from food hygiene regulations.

Figure 2.14: Extract from food hygiene regulations

Schedule I, Chapter II	Equipment and Facilities	Actions
Specific requirements in rooms where foodstuffs are prepared, treated or processed (excluding dining areas and those premises specified in Chapter III).		
II. 1: Rooms where food is actually prepared, treated or processed.	**Floors, walls, ceilings and surfaces (which come into contact with food) must be adequately maintained, easy to clean and where necessary disinfect.**	Keep all surfaces, fixtures and fittings hygenic, to prevent contamination of food.
II.2: Cleaning and disinfecting of tools, utensils and equipment.	Provide adequate facilities, including hot and cold water, for cleaning and where necessary disinfecting tools and equipment.	**Clean and disinfect tools and equipment so as to ensure food safety.**
II.3: Washing of tools	**Where appropriate provide adequate facilities for washing food. Supply with hot and/or cold water as required.**	Wash food properly where necessary.

Safety at Sports Grounds Act 1975

Spectators are vital to many sporting events; not only do they provide 'atmosphere' but also important income for the organisation hosting the event. This Act imposes duties upon the occupiers of a recreational stadium to 'ensure the safety of spectators as much as is reasonably possible'.

Although the Act is primarily aimed at football stadia, it applies to any place where sports or competitive activities take place. A stadium with a capacity of more than 10,000 requires a safety certificate.

Safety certificates issued under the Act are of two different types:

- The more common general certificate covers specific activities at a particular ground, for an indefinite period.
- The special certificate is issued for a single event or a short series of events. This certificate also applies, for example, when a rock concert is staged at a sports stadium.

In most cases, local authorities receive and process certificate applications under the Act. Failure to comply or co-operate with a local authority ruling may lead to fines or closure.

Factors to be considered in connection with 'reasonable safety' for a stadium to include:

- maximum number of spectators
- grouping of spectators
- number of entrances and exits
- records of attendance and maintenance
- existing provision of barriers
- seating arrangements.

The cost of any measure required is entirely the responsibility of the owners or operators of a stadium. The following case study on Anfield provides a working insight into the safety demands placed upon a stadium manager.

CASE STUDY

The role of the Stadium Manager for Liverpool Football Club

The role of the Stadium Manager for Liverpool Football Club includes responsibility for running the whole of the stadium, including the training of all the full-time and part-time staff concerned with safety.

The Safety Certificate Holder is responsible for the pre-planning and the match-day arrangements for any certified event at the stadium. As developments take place at a ground it is important for this person to also be involved to help design-in safety features at the start of building work. New stands have been springing up around the country as clubs modernize and expand, especially northern clubs such as Manchester United and Leeds United hoping to be selected as grounds for England's hosting of future European or World Cups.

Having an all-seat stadium gives tremendous advantages over the old terraces, which suffered from crushing and overcrowding, for it means a strong control system is in place, with one person/one ticket/one seat and much less movement of people. There is no overcrowding and behaviour is better when people have a seat and you can pick up trouble-makers on camera very easily.

The recruitment and training of staff is more professionally done, plus the ratio of staff and stewards present is properly calculated and includes paramedics and first-aiders. The most important new room from a health, safety and security point of view in a new stadium is the control room, from where instant communication can flow out around the ground from its vantage point in the stadium.

Source: Leisure Manager, October 1997

The list of contents of Leeds United's Health and Safety Policy shows how comprehensive such a policy has to be to cover all the needs of such a large club:

LEEDS UTD FOOTBALL CLUB HEALTH AND SAFETY POLICY

CONTENTS:

- **Risk Assessment**
- **Hazard Reporting**
- **Monitoring**
- **The Personal Protective Equipment at Work Regulations**
- **The Noise at Work Regulations**
- **VDUs and Associated Equipment**
- **Manual Handling**
- **COSHH**
- **The Electricity at Work Regulations**
- **Food Safety**
- **Legionellosis**
- **Safety Advice and Information**
- **Training and Induction**

Fire Safety, and Safety of Places of Sport Act 1987

This Act amended the Fire Precautions Act of 1971. As a consequence of a number of serious accidents over the years involving large football crowds, the safety of spectators became of great importance under the Safety of Sports Grounds Act of 1975. The most important provision of this Act is the requirement of a safety certificate for any permanent stand which provides covered accommodation for 500 or more spectators at any type of sports ground. Unfortunately, this legislation was unable to prevent the Hillsborough Stadium tragedy in 1989.

The Taylor report which followed it recommended the more stringent application of the provisions in the Safety of Sports Grounds Act of 1975 and particularly that Premiership and Football League clubs should have all-seater stadia. All clubs were meant to comply by 1999; however, this was amended to prevent smaller clubs going bankrupt and the government introduced tax relief to help with ground redevelopment. The Football Licensing Authority was established to review the safety certificates issued and to inspect the clubs. Many clubs, such as Derby, Sunderland and Middlesborough, decided to build new stadia rather than convert old ones in line with the new legislation. Others, such as Manchester United and Newcastle United, have upgraded their grounds.

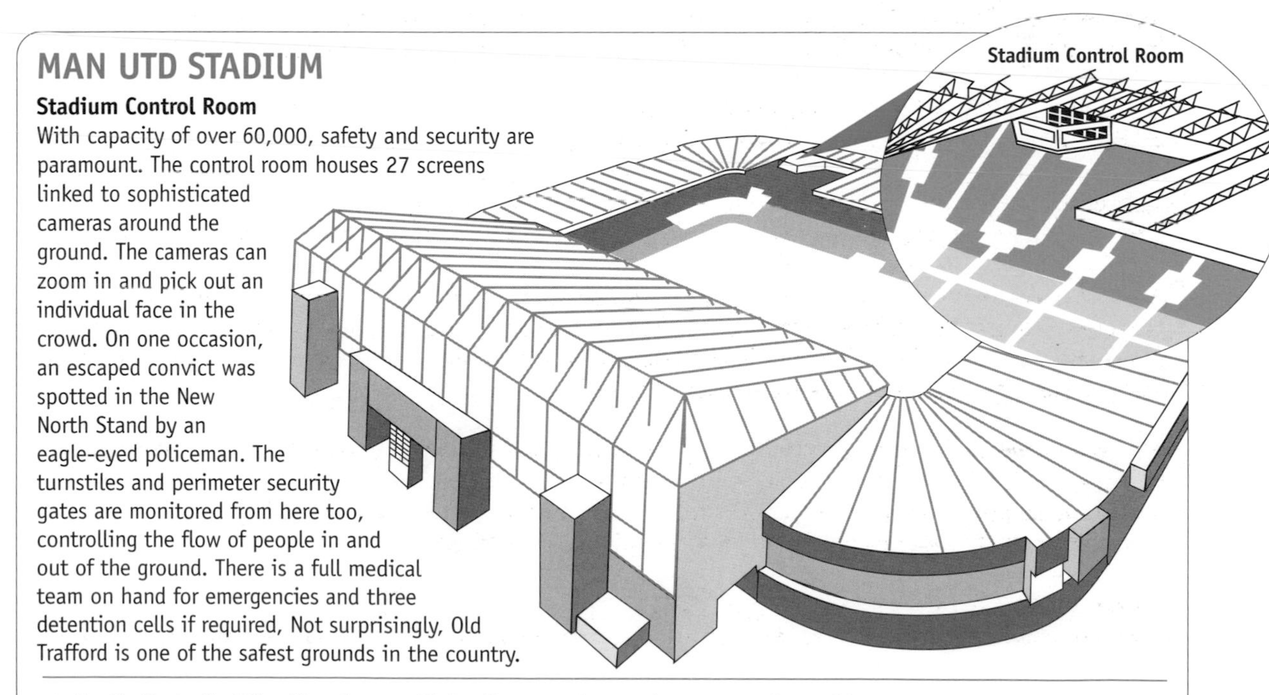

MAN UTD STADIUM
Stadium Control Room
With capacity of over 60,000, safety and security are paramount. The control room houses 27 screens linked to sophisticated cameras around the ground. The cameras can zoom in and pick out an individual face in the crowd. On one occasion, an escaped convict was spotted in the New North Stand by an eagle-eyed policeman. The turnstiles and perimeter security gates are monitored from here too, controlling the flow of people in and out of the ground. There is a full medical team on hand for emergencies and three detention cells if required, Not surprisingly, Old Trafford is one of the safest grounds in the country.
Stadium Control Room

▲ Football stadia Like Manchester United's ground, now have a number of important safety features.

One of the main requirements of the Fire Safety Act of 1971 is that any organisation providing entertainment, recreation or club facilities where there are more than twenty people on the ground floor, or more than ten above ground-floor level, must apply for a fire certificate from the local fire authority. Hotels and other accommodation must also obtain a fire certificate if they sleep more than six guests. To obtain a fire certificate, an organisation must:

- keep all means of escape clear from obstruction
- have regular fire drills
- provide fire safety training for employees
- keep records on fire safety
- set maximum occupancy numbers.

In 1999, new regulations about fire safety were introduced, as shown below.

FIRE SAFETY NEWS UPDATE

The Fire Precautions (workplace) regulations

1997 have been amended and the new regulations will come into force on 1 December 1999.

This change in Fire Safety Law could affect your business.

The main amendments are:-

1. All workplaces are now required to have a Fire Risk Assessment. This includes those remises previously exempt from the original regulations because they had been issued with or have applied for a Fire Certificate under the Fire Precautions Act 1971 eg Hotels, Large Shops and Offices, factories, etc.

2. The amended regulations make it a criminal offence for employers who fail to comply with the regulations.

▲ New fire safety regulations

Licensing and Gambling laws

These laws are frequently updated to keep pace with changes in the leisure and recreation industry. **Licences** are legal permits, such as those for alcohol consumption and fishing, putting up posters in public places, or entertainment purposes. Licensing laws are probably among the oldest types of law with which operators must comply in the leisure and recreation industry. There are several different kinds which may apply.

- On licence: issued to a named person to allow consumption of alcohol on the premises, for example, a pub, wine bar or club.
- Off licence: issued to a named person to permit sale of alcohol, for example from a shop or supermarket, for home consumption.
- A table licence: issued to premises that normally provide meals and wish also to serve liquor to supplement meals; for example, a small guest house or restaurant.
- A residential licence: issued to hotels, for example, so that residents can enjoy a drink without having to go out.
- An occasional licence: issued to event promoters for various functions, such as dances, dinners, fetes and galas. For this licence the police need a 24-hour notice to check arrangements.

All licences are of a limited duration, which means that the Justices granting the licences can keep a regular check on applicants for any unsafe or illegal practices which may have occurred since the last application. Opening hours are also controlled and inspections can take place to ensure premises are fit for their purpose before a licence is granted or renewed. Licensees can be convicted for numerous offences: serving under-age drinkers; serving beyond opening times; serving from unlicensed premises. Fines and imprisonment are the sanctions for most offences, but occasionally the licence itself is taken away.

Gambling refers to games, activities or machines which allow people as part of their leisure or recreation time to engage in transactions in which money is won or lost on the happening of an event, the outcome of which is uncertain. Common examples are the National Lottery, a horse race or sports match. Regulations also exist specifically for bingo, gaming machines, clubs, private lotteries and casinos. If you plan to raise funds through your project for Unit 6 you may need to have a licence to sell tickets or hold a raffle.

ACTIVITY

Running a lottery or raffle

Check with your local authority or police station to identify what the regulations would be if your class or group wished to operate a fundraising lottery or raffle in your school or college. List the key points in order to assess the feasibility and conditions of this proposal.

Adventure Activities Licensing Regulations 1996

After the tragic Lyme Bay canoeing accident of 1993, in which several young people lost their lives, the government brought in legislation designed to control the operation of outdoor activity centres. The Activity Centres (Young Person's Safety) Act 1995, required commercial providers of climbing, watersports, trekking (on foot/horse/cycle) and caving activities in remote or isolated areas (for young people under 18 years) to undergo inspection of their safety management systems and become registered as being licensed.

In 1996 the **Adventure Activities Licensing Authority (AALA)** was formed and regulations were produced to govern safety aspects of outdoor pursuits. At present, the licensing and inspection is carried out by Tourism Quality Services Ltd on behalf of the Health and Safety Executive.

Once a licence has been issued it lasts for three years before re-inspection is required, except in the case of large multi-activity centres employing temporary, seasonal staff, which are inspected annually. The example of East Barnby Outdoor Centre, owned by North Yorkshire Local Education Authority, shows how great care is taken to prepare for safety responsibilities.

The **Department for Education and Employment (DfEE)** has also issued a comprehensive set of guidelines for use on educational visits. These cover responsibilities for visits, planning visits, supervision and preparing pupils.

Les Brettle, Director of the Centre, issues a ten-page document that specifies health and safety standards. These include the following:

- The centre's aim to deliver a high-quality, safe residential experience.
- A policy of equality of access for all, so that all kinds of visitors can be accommodated safely.
- The appointment of staff educated to degree level and highly qualified, all of whom are checked on recruitment and reviewed annually.
- Operating according to Department of Education guidelines, safety guidelines for educational visits and outdoor activities, and sports governing body standards.
- The director, staff, teachers and leaders are all expected to maintain health and safety requirements during a group's stay, round the clock.
- Emergency actions are specified for various contingencies, including fire (smoke alarms are fitted throughout the buildings) trekking, sea and river activities.
- A doctor is always on call for the centre.
- Stringent transport rules are adhered to when transferring groups.
- Insurance arrangements for staff and students are in place.
- Pre-course forms ask for relevant personal details of each participant so that special dietary, medical or non-swimmer information can be logged.
- Parental consent forms are supplied as well as kit lists

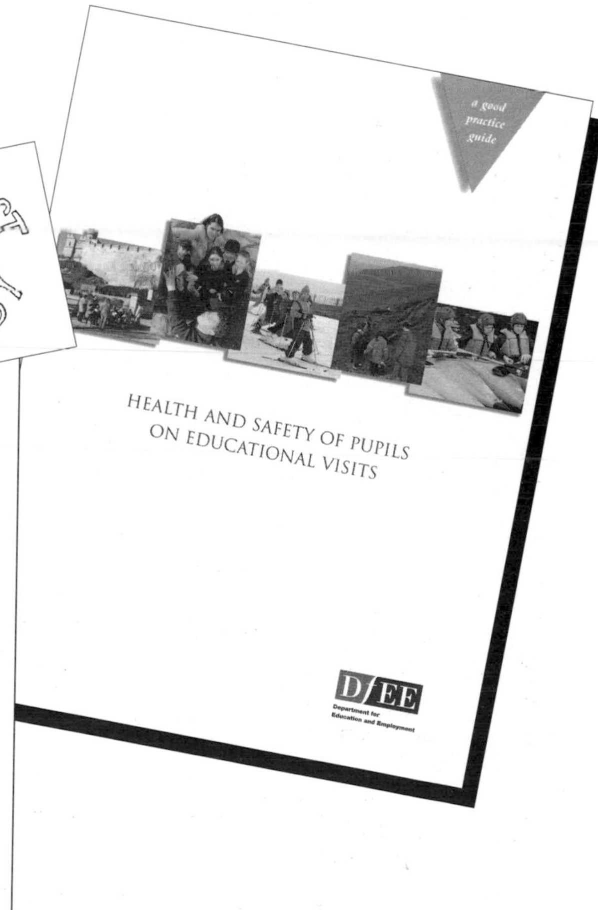

▲ Department for Education and Employment document on guidelines for educational visits

ACTIVITY

Residential visits

Your school or college may well have organised trips or residential visits. Carry out some research to identify what guidelines and procedures staff have to follow in order to gain permission and prepare for the safety aspects of such visits.

Trades Description Act 1968

This Act is designed to protect consumers against false descriptions by organisations that sell or provide goods and services. For example, if music retailers advertised CDs as originals when they were really only cheap copies, they would be liable to prosecution under this Act.

Consumer Protection Act 1987

This Act was put in place to prevent customers from being misled accidentally or deliberately by organisations providing products or services; for example, if a hire company advertised a bouncy castle as suitable for up to twenty children when in fact the manufacturer's recommendation was a maximum of ten, or if a glossy brochure described new facilities as complying with safety standards when in fact they do not. Under the terms of this Act such dangerous examples would be an offence. It is therefore important that leisure and recreation organisations check that their publicity material is factual. The best practitioners will have a customer charter and quality checks to help ensure that the products and services which are described or sold by staff are accurate, relevant and comply with recommended standards.

Sale of Goods Act 1979

This Act protects consumers from the sale of falsely labelled goods; for example, fake 'designer' labels. It also helps prevent goods being sold which are not suitable or are unsafe for the job for which they are advertised, such as unsafe children's toys or DIY tools and equipment.

Many complaints about consumer issues are dealt with by the **Office of Fair Trading**, a government agency set up to ensure fair competition between businesses and the protection of consumer interests.

Enforcement agencies

Most health and safety legislation in the workplace is enforced by the **Health and Safety Executive (HSE)** and local authority environmental health departments. The HSE is made up of a number of inspectorates which cover mines, quarries, factories, nuclear installations, agriculture, railway safety, explosives and health and safety on offshore installations.

In general, shops, offices and warehouses, plus some leisure centres and places of entertainment, are covered by **local authority environmental health officers**.

Powers of enforcement

There are three powers available to the **enforcement agencies.**

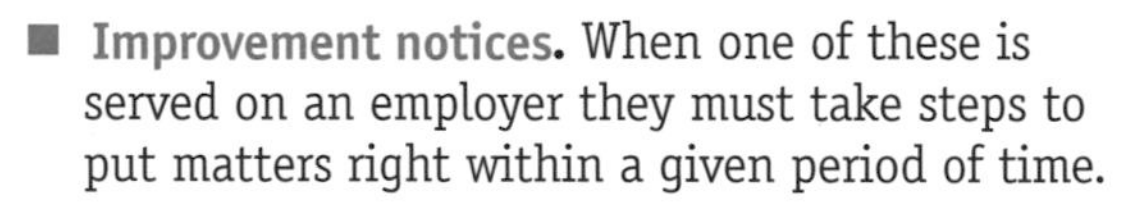

- **Improvement notices.** When one of these is served on an employer they must take steps to put matters right within a given period of time.
- **Prohibition notices.** Such a notice can be issued if an employer fails to comply with an improvement notice. A prohibition notice has the effect of halting the operation which produces the risk. An immediate prohibition notice may be issued by inspectors if they think the operation in question presents a risk of immediate danger to the public or to workers. Inspectors also have the power to issue deferred prohibition notices. Appeals against both improvement and prohibition notices have to be made to an industrial tribunal. Such appeals can result in a 'stay of execution' as regards an improvement notice. A prohibition notice, on the other hand, must be implemented immediately if the inspector thinks that there is an imminent risk of serious personal injury.
- **Fines and imprisonment.** Failure to comply with improvement and prohibition notices is an offence. The penalties for such offences are a maximum fine of £20,000 if the case is brought before a lower court, and imprisonment of up to two years or an unlimited fine if the case is brought before a higher court.

Voluntary codes of practice

In some cases **voluntary codes of practice** are introduced by governing bodies of sport or national organisations concerned with safety. These are practices and procedures which, although they are not enforced by law, are recommended ways of operating safely.

Water safety codes

One of the best-known safety codes is the Royal

'Have Fun - Stay Safe'

1 Spot the dangers: avoid slippery banks.
2 Take safety advice: choose a beach or pool where there are lifeguards.
3 Don't go alone: go with a friend and tell your parents where you are going.
4 Learn how to help: stay calm, but shout for help, reach out with a stick or pole to the person.
5 Call 999 or 112 to ask for help.

Other organisations which produce codes include the Environment Agency (EA), which focuses on the correct and safe use of rivers by canoeists. Their slogan for the code is 'Have fun, have a care'.

The Royal Yachting Association (RYA), concerned with watersports such as sailing, windsurfing, power boating and pleasure craft, has a series of guidance notes for inspectors of watersports centres. These notes cover general aspects of safety and also provide guidance on appropriate clothing, safety craft and personal kit, with an additional section on the EU standards required of lifejackets and buoyancy aids. A small extract from the section on safety craft is provided in the case study on page 118.

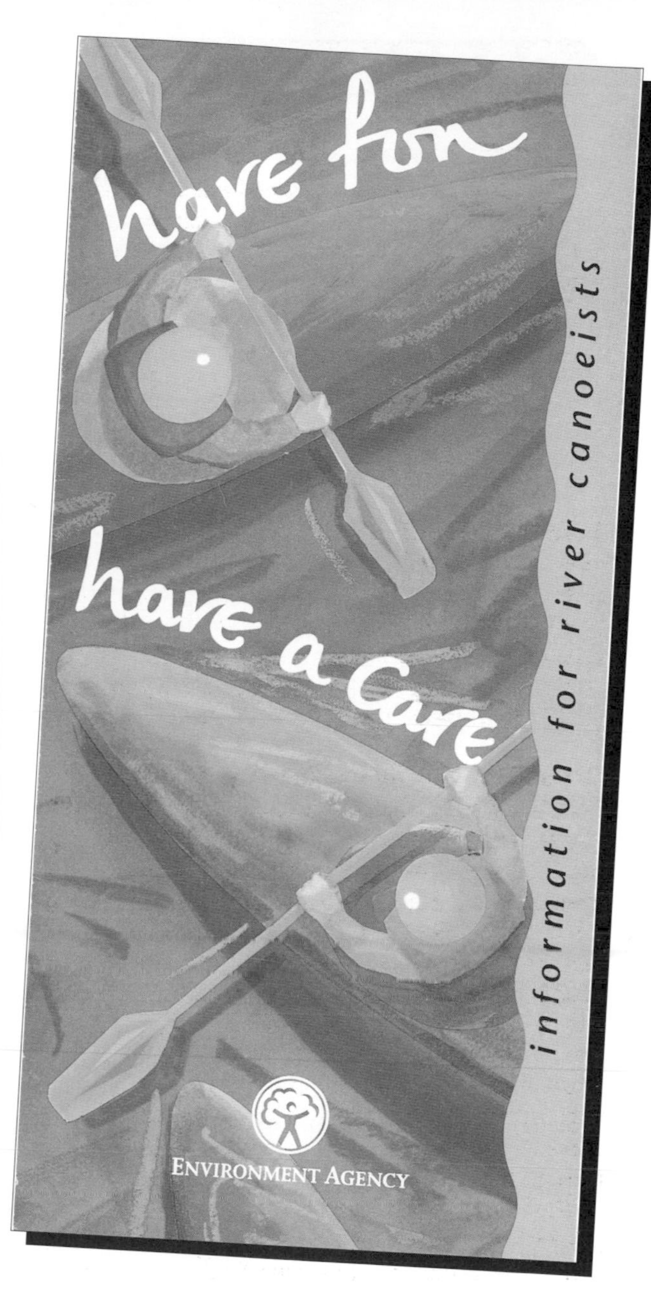

▲ Environment Agency leaflet

CASE STUDY

Water safety

Sufficient safety boats must be available to provide separate cover for all courses in progress at any one time. It is not acceptable to expect the instructors teaching basic skills courses to also provide safety cover for large groups on open water. For more advanced courses the safety boat may be manned by a safety boat driver holding the Safety Boat Certificate, together with the instructors leading the session. RYA courses, or any other tuition at a recognised centre, must comply with the following safety boat requirements:

Activity	Safety boat ratio
Windsurfing	**12 : 1**
Dinghies	**Up to 6 : 1 safety boat** **6-15 : 2 safety boats** **15 + : 3 safety boats**
Keelboats	**Radio contact with a rescue boat or shore base, or a buddy system if one boat can tow another**
Personal water craft vessel	**These should not go out solo, but always have a buddy on the water at the same time**

Safety boats must be suitably manned and equipped for the type of activity being covered, the prevailing conditions and area, and distance from the shore. Details of the equipment must be given in the health and safety manual. For centres operating at sea the minimum is:

- paddles or oars;
- bucket or bailer;
- bridle secured to towing eyes;
- towline;
- spare starter cord and tool kit;
- survival bag or thermal protection aid;
- first-aid kit in a water-tight container;
- anchor suitable for the craft;
- chain and warp line of suitable length;
- flare pack.

The boats themselves need to be properly maintained/have kill cords/fuel tanks secured/carry VHF radios.

Figure 2.15: English Ski Council Skiway Code

Skiers must:

- **Behave responsibly and ensure their equipment is safe.**
- **Adapt their speed to suit terrain, snow and weather conditions and other skiers.**
- **Allow freedom of movement to others ahead.**
- **Leave enough space for unexpected manoeuvres when overtaking.**
- **Look up and down a ski run (piste) before joining it.**
- **Only stop at the side of a piste and avoid stopping at narrow parts.**
- **Try to avoid walking on the piste.**
- **Observe all signs on the piste, especially warning ones.**
- **Assist at an accident if possible.**
- **Provide details, if a witness at an accident.**

This summary of the skiway code, issued by the English Ski Council, is based on the International Ski Federation rules

Examples of land-based activity codes of practice

The English Ski Council (ESC) focuses on the rules for safe skiing on all kinds of slopes and also how they expect instructors or coaches to act. This forms the basis of their 'skiway code', as shown in Figure 2.15.

Brecon Beacons National Park has issued guidelines for walkers called 'On the Hills'.

▲ Brecon Beacons National Park

ACTIVITY

Codes of practice

Choose any sport that has a code of practice for participators and/or coaches, and complete the following tasks:

1 Identify the governing body or national organisation for the sport.

2 Contact them to ask if they could send you a copy of their code of practice.

3 Compare the codes of practice you have received with others in your group, to assess the most effective. For the organisations that do not have a code of practice, make recommendations as to what they could include, based on the examples your group has discussed.

Figure 2.16: Brecon Beacons National Park code of practice

Many hills in the National park exceed 450m (1500ft) in height, with some almost 900m (3000ft). They offer challenging and very rewarding opportunities to walkers, but they must be treated with respect. The most important safety factor when introducing groups of young people to mountain and moorland areas is good leadership (with skills in navigation and knowledge of First Aid)

Brecon Beacons National Park

- **carry spare clothes**
- **pack a torch and whistle**
- **leave a route card**
- **stay together**
- **check the weather**

On the hills

SUMMIT

BUILD YOUR LEARNING

Keywords and phrases

You should know the meaning of the words and phrases listed below. If you are unsure about any of them, go back through the last 21 pages to refresh your understanding.

- Tiers of legislation
- European Regulations/Directives
- UK Acts of Parliament
- Management of Health and Safety at Work Act 1992
- Risk assessment
- Workplace Regulations 1992
- Provision and Use of Work Equipment 1992
- Manual Handling Regulations 1992
- Provision and Use of Work Equipment 1992
- Personal Protective Equipment 1992
- Display Screen Equipment Regulations 1992
- Health and Safety at Work Act 1974 (HASAWA)
- Occupiers Liability Act
- Control of Substances Hazardous to Health Regulations 1994 (COSHH)
- Working Time Regulations 1998
- Health and Safety (First Aid) Regulations 1981
- Electricity at Work Regulations 1989
- Reporting of Injuries and Dangerous Diseases or Occurrences 1995 (RIDDOR)
- Disability Discrimination Act 1995 (DDA)
- Children's Act 1989
- Data Protection Act 1984
- Food Safety Act 1990
- Safety at Sports Grounds Act 1975
- Fire Safety and Safety of Places of Sport 1987
- Licences
- Adventure Activities Licensing Authority (AALA)
- Consumer Protection Act 1987
- Trades Description Act 1968
- Sale of Goods Act 1979
- Office of Fair Trading
- Health and Safety Executive (HSE)
- Local authority environmental health officers
- Enforcement agencies
- Improvement notices
- Prohibition notices
- Voluntary codes of practice

End of section activity

Investigate two leisure and recreation facilities/organisations to assess:

1 How they comply with relevant legislation and regulations and codes of practice.

2 How this ensures a 'safe working environment' for staff, visitors and other users.

3 Their effectiveness in meeting health, security and safety needs.

Report on your findings and draw some conclusions and/or make some recommendations based on your analysis.

You may need to visit the organisation/facility to complete this activity.

Identifying hazards and assessing risk

HEALTH AND SAFETY LAW in the United Kingdom and other European Union countries is now based on the principle of risk assessment. The onus is on employers to assess health, safety and security risks and hazards, then take measures to eliminate or control them.

Hazards are anything that can cause us harm in our everyday lives, such as chemical spillage, fumes, walking across a busy street, fire or eating undercooked food. **Risks** are the chance, or level of probability, however great or small, that someone will be harmed by a hazard. The chance of a hazard harming us is obviously increased if we do not identify the hazard and take suitable measures to protect ourselves, such as wearing seat belts in motor vehicles, using protective clothing, or washing our hands after using the lavatory. **Health and safety measures** are precautions that we take to reduce the chance of accidents occurring, or to minimise the harm that an accident can cause; for example, having swimming pool lifeguards on duty at public sessions, checking that safety equipment is in good working order, or ensuring that food is correctly prepared and stored. The degree to which an organisation is exposed to hazards will depend on a range of factors, such as its scale of operation, number of locations and nature of its activities.

In Unit 6 you will need to use these definitions when identifying hazards and risks associated with running a leisure and recreation project.

Risk assessment

The generally accepted definition of **risk assessment** is that it involves making

> 'reasoned judgements about the risks and extent of these risks to people's health, safety and security, based on the application of information which leads to decisions on how risks should be managed'

Besides carrying out a risk assessment, employers must also:

- make arrangements for implementing the health and safety measures identified as necessary by the risk assessment
- appoint competent people to help them implement the arrangements
- set up emergency procedures
- provide clear information and training for employees
- work together with other employers sharing the same workplace.

The risk assessment process

The managers of all facilities, services and events, in conjunction with staff, must carry out risk assessments. These should be conducted in order to comply with the Health and Safety Executive's guidelines. An assessment of risk is a careful examination of what could cause harm to people, in order to decide whether enough precautions have been taken to prevent harm. The aim is to protect employees and the general public. Figure 2.17 shows the **five steps to risk assessment.**

Figure 2.17: Five steps to risk assessment

Step 1
List the significant hazards you can identify

Step 2
List the groups of people who are at risk from the hazards

Step 3
List existing measures and evaluate whether they are adequate; if they are not adequate, identify what action is needed

Step 4
Propose measures to reduce risks to an acceptable level and record these

Step 5
Review your assessment as required and monitor implementation

As we have seen already (page 97), most organisations keep a health and safety manual, so some of the evidence for risk assessment will be recorded there. The remainder may be found in policy documents, company rules and instruction manuals - as long as it is all easy to locate.

Identifying hazards

Health and safety hazards in the leisure and recreation industry are anything that can inflict harm or cause an accident to staff, customers or participants. **Identifying hazards** can be a complex task for organisations in the leisure and recreation industry, especially those with a diverse operation. The following categories are quite comprehensive (but not exhaustive) and give a fair indication of what managers and staff have to look out for when checking their workplace.

- Slipping/tripping hazards, e.g. torn carpets, leaky roofs, obstructions in the organisation's administration offices.
- Fire hazards, e.g. piles of flammable waste or materials kept in boxes under stairs, or faulty wiring of electrical appliances.
- Chemical hazards, e.g. lack of secure or appropriate storage for cleaning fluids or paints in a maintenance area.
- Machinery, e.g. lack of protective guards, poorly trained staff or mechanical breakdown.
- Working at a height, e.g. ascending ladders to conduct repairs, or using scaffolding while redecorating.
- Pressure systems, e.g. hydraulic pistons on rides or steam boilers in the heating plant.
- Vehicles, e.g. golf carts, small fork-lifts used for unloading deliveries.
- Electricity, e.g. hazards from wrongly wired plugs, or circuits overloaded by additional appliances at a concert.
- Dust, e.g. hazards could be created through redecoration, or demolition for an extension, or the discovery of unsafe asbestos on the premises.
- Fumes, e.g. those generated by vehicles in confined spaces or exhaust gases given off from generators or poorly maintained heaters.
- Manual handling, e.g. hazards occur frequently with loading and unloading duties.
- Noise, e.g. from music in a club, machines producing leisure products, vehicles passing by constantly.
- Poor lighting, e.g. under-powered or the wrong type for the job.
- Poor ventilation, e.g. windows that don't open, vents that are painted over or closed, fans and extractors that need repairs.
- Hand tools, e.g. the suitability for the job of those tools used by maintenance staff, or whether staff are trained in the safe use of such things as floor polishers and power tools.
- Display screen equipment, e.g. frequency and duration of use can cause hazards, as can the design of workstations.
- Falling objects, e.g. in store rooms especially, or where overhead work takes place, as in a theatre.
- Windows and doors: these should be made of safety glass in many cases and sign-posted if they are emergency escapes.
- Clothing and headgear, e.g. to protect staff in kitchens or from overhead obstacles or dirty materials.
- Adverse weather, e.g. causing transport problems, such as the flooding in April 2000 of Murrayfield and Silverstone.

The variety of facilities and locations in the leisure and recreation industry means that each sector will have its own particular hazards. For example, a theme park will differ greatly from a swimming pool, a playground from a cinema, an outdoor location from a leisure centre. Additionally, the complexity of hazards will depend on a number of factors including:

- Scale of operation: in other words, the size of facility and how many sites are involved.
- Actual location(s): an outdoor activity centre, for example, may have crags for climbing, a river for canoeing, a lake for rafting, caves for exploring, etc. The height of the crags, the speed of the water and the depth of the caves will all affect how dangerous they are.
- Numbers, ages and experience of participants.
- Such things as equipment, weather and materials in use all have a bearing on the likelihood of hazards arising.

ACTIVITY

Identifying hazards

Look at the picture and make a list of all those things that you consider to be a potential hazard. You should be able to find ten.

Deciding who might be harmed and how

Deciding who might be harmed might seem an easy task: staff and customers immediately spring to mind. However, it is more effective to split these two categories down further into different types, for example:

- children
- teenagers
- adults
- over-50s
- individuals or groups with special requirements;
- people with disabilities.

This type of analysis helps to anticipate how different groups might get hurt and what are the best measures to reduce hazards for each of them.

Don't forget such groups as:

- young workers, trainees and new and expectant mothers, who may be at particular risk
- cleaners, visitors, contractors and maintenance workers, who may not be in the workplace all the time.

Evaluating risks arising from hazards

The process of **evaluating risks** arising from hazards is probably the most problematic for leisure and recreation organisations, especially those smaller organisations that usually have no health and safety expert on their staff. Evaluation is best done by assessing the likelihood (**probability**) of hazards occuring and also how harmful they could be (their **severity**).

Probability

In order to measure the likelihood of a hazard occurring, we have to know how many times the hazard has been a problem in the past. We can do this by looking at statistics published by the Health and Safety Executive, the Department of Trade and Industry and industry advisory committees. We can also:

- consult other centre managers or event organisers;
- visit the local council's department of environmental health or building control;
- carry out research in a library;
- contact a governing body;
- seek advice from the police, fire, rescue and other emergency services.

The probability of a hazard occurring depends on whether it is a current hazard (in other words, if it exists already, such as a broken piece of equipment), or whether it is a potential hazard (such as possible plumbing leaks or electrical faults) and therefore may not occur at all. Hazards identified as current obviously increase the probability of an accident occurring, so it is important that some sort of evaluation scale is devised to grade the relative probability (chance) of a hazard causing an accident.

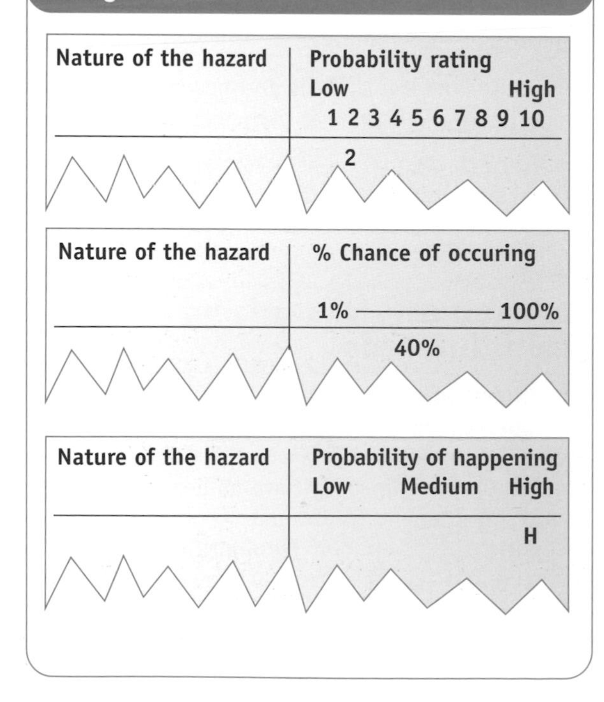

Nature of the hazard
Probability rating
Low High
1 2 3 4 5 6 7 8 9 10
2
Nature of the hazard
% Chance of occuring
1% 100%
40%
Nature of the hazard
Probability of happening
Low Medium High
H

Figure 2.18: Some examples of probability ratings for hazards

Some suggested scales are shown in Figure 2.18.

Severity

The second factor which must be considered is the severity of harm the hazard could cause. There are many examples of accidents and injuries which cause varying degrees of harm, from cuts and bruises to broken limbs and even loss of life. Again, a scale must be created to register the severity of the accidents that may occur, perhaps using 'minor', 'medium' and 'major' ratings.

An example of minor severity is a child tripping over in a temporary car park and grazing his or her hands. This requires minor first-aid treatment, and staff need to be trained and equipped correctly. Although it has a minor rating, it has a high probability factor if many children are present at an event or facility and the temporary car park is on rough ground, for example at a local agricultural show.

An example of a medium-severity hazard is breaking a piece of equipment that requires immediate repair. Staff will have to cope with the disruption while the repair is carried out. Quite often a chain of incidents can increase in severity from minor, to medium, to major, if quick action is not taken. Training will help staff to distinguish between major hazards that may be life-threatening or cause serious injury requiring professional assistance, and minor ones which can probably be dealt with by staff themselves.

Collisions and capsizes at sea are examples of a major-severity hazard with life-threatening consequences. Yachts or dinghies capsizing at sea while taking part in a regatta, or collisions between merchant vessels, ferries and cruise liners happen infrequently, but can result in the loss of many lives. Like the skippers of these vessels, managers must try to cover the most severe hazards by suitably equipping their facilities and making sure that staff know and practise the procedures required should an accident occur.

As part of the project you will run in Unit 6, you may have to carry out a detailed evaluation of hazards and risks. In general, these can be grouped as follows:

- Main activities: the content of the event.
- Supporting activities, such as catering, cleaning, deliveries, equipment handling.
- Customers: spectators and participants.
- Staff, including volunteers, temporary and permanent staff, team members.

Figures 2.19 and 2.20 illustrate how a college has arranged its **risk level indicators** and **risk control plan** with the criteria it regards as important, together with the required actions and timescales.

Figure 2.19: Simple Risk Level Indicator

Probability (Low → High)	Severity scales (Low → High): Slightly harmful	Harmful	Extremely harmful
Highly unlikely	Trivial Risk	Tolerable Risk	Moderate Risk
Unlikely	Tolerable Risk	Moderate Risk	Substantial Risk
Likely	Moderate Risk	Substantial Risk	Intolerable Risk

The relationship between combinations of probability and severity.

Figure 2.20: Simple Risk Based Control Plan

Risk level	Action and Timescale
Trivial	No action is required and no documentary records need to be kept.
Tolerable	No additional controls are required. Consideration may be given to a more cost-effective solution or improvement that imposes no additional cost burden. Monitoring is required to ensure that the controls are maintained.
Moderate	Efforts should be made to reduce the risk, but the costs of prevention should be carefully measured and limited. Risk reduction measures should be implemented within a defined period of time. Where the moderat risk is associated with extremely harmful consequences, further assessment may be necessary to establish more precisely the likelihood of harm as a basis for determining the need for improved control measures.
Substantial	Work should not be started until the risk has been reduced. Considerable resources may have to be allocated to reduce the risk. Where the risk involves work in progress, urgent action should be taken.
Intolerable	Work should not be started or continued until the risk has been reduced. If it is not possible to reduce risk even with unlimited resources, work has to remain prohibited.

ACTIVITY

Increased probability of accidents

Certain factors can increase the probability and severity of accidents. Two examples of such factors are given below. Can you add five more examples and estimate how much they would increase the hazard's impact? You can use the scales or ratings shown in Figures 2.18. and 2.19

- Crowd reactions could cause a pitch invasion, with a significant increase in hazards.
- Equipment working at full capacity may break down,with a significant increase in hazards.

CASE STUDY

Fireworks safety

We can illustrate how to structure a risk assessment and identify key hazards in order to carry out an impact evaluation, by considering an organised fireworks display. This example, drawn from an article in *Leisure Manager*, recommends that nine aspects of the event should be evaluated.

- **Personnel.** Are the organisers themselves going to set off the fireworks or will a professional fireworks display operator be employed? Evaluation of the size of the display and the audience, along with the expertise of the organisers, will dictate the decision. If the organisers decide not to employ specialist personnel (perhaps because the numbers are small and someone has good previous experience), they are responsible for checking that the fireworks comply with the British Standard for fireworks: BS 7114. They should not risk using other types of firework, which may be dangerous. The HSE also recommends that organisers should buy only full display kits with good instructions, rather than individual fireworks, as these need to be arranged and set off by specialist personnel.

- **Display plan.** The detail of the display plan is the key to covering all eventualities. The HSE recommends that an overall display leader be elected who will co-ordinate all activities. As part of the plan, team members can then have responsibility for various aspects, such as ordering, storing and setting off the fireworks; liaison with the local fire brigade, St John's Ambulance and police; and arranging site facilities and any parking and crowd safety required.

- **Location or site.** The display site must provide enough space to accommodate both fireworks and spectators, which should be well apart from each other. It must also allow any falling debris to be clear of buildings, cars and people. Access to and exit from the site needs to be free-flowing, with routes kept clear for emergency vehicles at all times.

- **Crowd control.** This can be evaluated according to the nature of the crowd; for example, whether it is composed of children, adults, families or people with disabilities. The level of excitement likely to be generated must be evaluated. For example, young children may be scared, or adults may have consumed too much alcohol. In the latter case, organisers may decide that police or stewards are required. If this is decided, then the logistics of clearly identifying the stewards, marking out crowd areas and providing effective communication methods have to be built into the plan.

- **Environmental and community impacts.** Neighbouring land or property owners may be affected by the display and will need to be informed. An evaluation of the locality identifying the people, any livestock, hospitals or old people's homes that may be affected is a necessity. If the site is near the sea, the coastguard needs to be informed, as fireworks are very similar to distress flares. Similarly, if a display is near an aerodrome, the airport authority needs to be notified at least a week in advance. Event organisers can contact the Civil Aviation Authority (CAA) for guidance.

- **Storage of the display fireworks** (prior to the display). Fireworks (or any flammable materials) need to be stored in a cool, dry, secure place, preferably in a metal container and in a building that can be locked. If a bonfire is constructed, check its strength and stability and ensure that an even burn will take place by lighting it with paper and firelighters at three points. Check the contents to ensure that rubbish such as foam-filled furniture, aerosols, tins of paint and pressurized gas containers will not fill the air with toxic fumes or explode.

- **Contingency planning.** Effective contingency plans have to be made to cover emergencies and disruptions. Suitable equipment must be available so that emergency procedures can swing into action quickly, via an effective communication system between organisers, stewards and the emergency services.

- **Firing arrangements.** The firing instructions should be clearly displayed and able to be read in the dark. If the fireworks are to be set off electrically, then the correct leads should be attached and under no circumstances should any attempt to convert a non-electrical type of firework be made. Check whether provision for fireworks which do not go off has been made; for example, a safety time before they may be touched and a bucket of water to place them in afterwards.

- **Post-event hazards.** Hazards may linger after the event, with spent fireworks or a smouldering bonfire and spectator debris around the site. A clear-up and clean-up campaign needs to be prepared, with suitable extinguishing equipment and rubbish collection. If fireworks have not gone off these should not be burned, but should be soaked and stored safely until disposal advice has been received from the manufacturer.

You can apply the type of evaluation used in the firework display case study to any type of recreation facility or event management, either by examining each aspect in detail or by following a flow chart of activities from the start to the finish of the event. It is important to record on a chart your findings about each aspect as the evaluation proceeds. Appropriate proposals and measures can then be mapped out, to ensure that the hazards and risks identified are eliminated completely or reduced to achieve an acceptable level of risk.

Propose measures to eliminate or reduce risks

The main aim of any proposals or measures is to take action to reduce the risk presented by any hazard. The familiar adage 'prevention is better than cure' is certainly true in this context. As mentioned previously the best-prepared leisure and recreation operators produce safety manuals which contain procedures for staff to follow to reduce the risk of a hazard or to deal with emergencies.

Risk reduction

It is important to adopt a systematic approach in order to evaluate each of the risks identified. The scale of action (measures) required to reduce these risks to acceptable levels will be determined by the probability of the hazard occurring and its degree of severity should it occur. Many other factors and variables might complicate the measures proposed, however, and these also have to be taken into account by the organisation. They include:

- numbers of customers or participants;
- skill and knowledge of staff;
- availability of resources;
- budget restrictions;
- quality of equipment.

A careful systematic approach is needed to identify these variables and to allow organisations to propose suitable risk-reducing measures. The HSE guidelines suggest that the following important questions are asked.

- Which hazards are 'significant' and is the risk high, low or medium?
- Can I eliminate the hazard?
- If not, how can I control the risks so that harm is unlikely?

Figure 2.21: Hazard checklist

Hazards	Proposals
Disposal of waste	Provide clearly marked bins and containers
Food contamination	Ensure facilities and equipment are clean
Activities	Provide approved protection gear
Equipment	All electrical appliances checked by qualified engineer
Environment	Organised litter pick

Evaluation may even show that a particular aspect of a facility has too high a risk and may need to be changed if its 'significance' cannot be reduced to an acceptable level. The HSE states that assessments need to be 'suitable' and 'sufficient' for the type of hazard. Managers can refer to a range of documents for guidance in deciding the measures to be taken, such as manuals, health and safety policies, company rules, manufacturers' instructions and advice from local health and safety officers.

For every significant hazard found, a realistic measure has to be proposed which reduces the hazard significantly. Risks can often be reduced by adopting relatively simple measures, such as fencing around an open area, posting suitable warning signs, using plastic glasses or undertaking first-aid training. Figure 2.21 shows a checklist with selected examples that could be used to match proposals to hazards in order to maintain health and safety.

Emergency actions

Measures proposed to deal with emergencies should be made to the highest recommended standards and must cover a very diverse range of emergencies, such as fire, collapse of structures, flooding, chemical spills, explosions, electrocution and vehicle collisions. Proposals should:

- anticipate emergencies and suggest measures to deal with them and identify any training needs;
- inform each team member what to do in advance, how to raise the alarm, where safety equipment is and how to use it properly;
- explain how to make the area safe in the event of an accident, how to administer first aid and where to get help;
- explain how to report an accident: recording details is compulsory under RIDDOR (see page 108);
- be realistic in terms of the resources and time available.

In addition, **emergency actions** should take account of the following factors.

- Staff members' skills and abilities. Someone who is not trained or competent in a safety procedure cannot take effective action. A trained person may not be available immediately at the scene of the emergency. Sufficient numbers of appropriately qualified staff must therefore be on hand. Proposals for emergency actions also need to be backed up by effective communications to make them realistic.
- Finance within the centre's budget. Any measures proposed must be cost-effective and within a reasonable budget. If this is not possible, then a change of activity or more funding might be needed to ensure that the measure proposed both meets acceptable safety standards and is affordable.
- Time to train and practise emergency procedures. It is unlikely that a staff team will attain any more than a basic level of competence in dealing with emergencies and even this takes time to attain. A facility may therefore need to have professional support or back-up.
- Materials and equipment. Protective clothing or equipment may be required, so staff need to pay attention to any instructions provided for their use.

Record the findings

For ease of reference it is best to have all records of risk assessments kept centrally or in one reference document or file. There is no legal requirement to do this, but it saves looking through various manuals, planning documents and rule books. Each section of a leisure or recreation facility should hold its own copies for ease of reference. If rules change, the person appointed as safety officer can relay the details to staff and prepare sections for inclusion in the department's records. Figure 2.22 provides an example of a proforma for recording hazards.

A number of software packages now exist for organising and recording health and safety information or risk assessments. For example, Enviro

Plus V, like other similar software, holds information on

- work areas
- employees
- equipment
- processes
- hazardous substances and situations.

Because the information is stored electronically it is easy to update.

Review and revision of the risk assessment

It is good practice for organisations to review their assessments to make sure that their precautions are still working effectively. Usually an organisation reviews its risk assessment on an ongoing basis. In particular, if new hazards emerge, if the level of risk increases, or the law changes amendments will need to be made to the organisation's health and safety procedures.

Figure 2.22: Hazard recording sheet

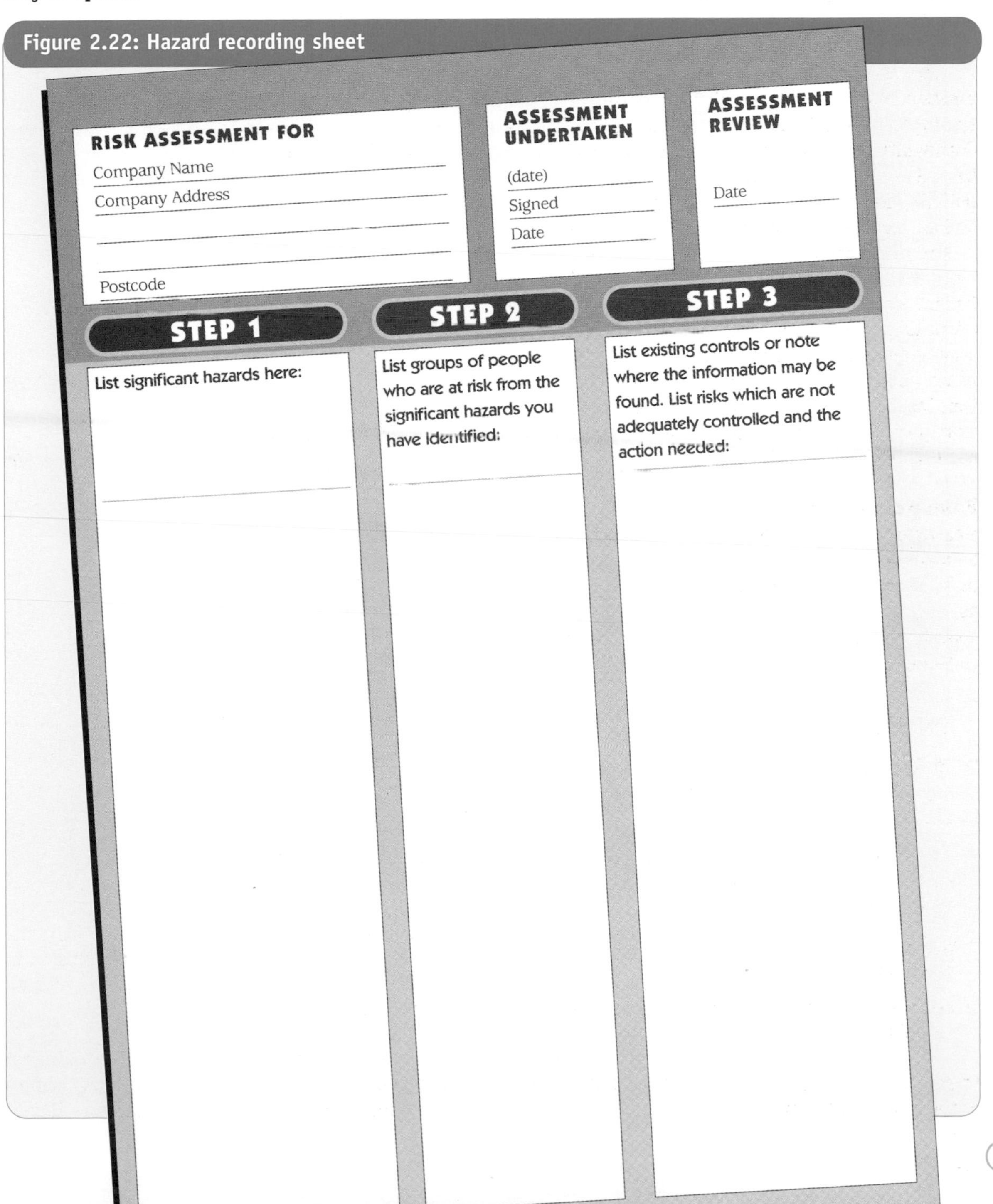

RISK ASSESSMENT FOR

Company Name

Company Address

Postcode

ASSESSMENT UNDERTAKEN

(date)

Signed

Date

ASSESSMENT REVIEW

Date

STEP 1

List significant hazards here:

STEP 2

List groups of people who are at risk from the significant hazards you have identified:

STEP 3

List existing controls or note where the information may be found. List risks which are not adequately controlled and the action needed:

BUILD YOUR LEARNING

End of section activity

1 Select a leisure and recreation facility in your area and carry out a full risk assessment to identify key hazards.

2 Identify an event in your area, preferably one which you can attend, and carry out a similar risk assessment to identify key hazards.

3 Based on your analysis of the risk assessments, suggest relevant and realistic measures or make recommendations that could be adopted to minimize the risks you identified for the facility and the event.

4 You can use the partial sample proforma in Figure 2.22, but you will need to create steps 4 and 5 yourselves to complete the chart, ready to record your findings and recommendations.

Keywords and phrases

You should know the meaning of the words and phrases listed below. If you are unsure about any of them, go back through the last nine pages to refresh your understanding.

- **Hazards**
- **Risk**
- **Risk assessment**
- **Health and safety measures**
- **Five steps to risk assessment**
- **Identifying hazards**
- **Deciding who might be harmed**
- **Evaluating the risks**
- **Probability**
- **Severity**
- **Risk level indicators and risk control plan**
- **Emergency actions**

Security measures in the leisure and recreation industry

Security measures vary depending on the organisation and may include use of elaborate entry systems, **closed-circuit television cameras** (CCTV) and the deployment of specialist security personnel. The need for security measures stems from the need to ensure that staff, customers, goods and possessions are safe on the premises. Larger attractions will have a security team with different areas of responsibility, as we can see in the Alton Towers case study.

The security aspects of one-off activities or events, such as a football match or grand prix race, can be complicated due to the nature and location of the event and the large numbers of people attending. As with health and safety, the starting point for facility managers and event organisers is to identify and evaluate the security hazards for the building or location. Once this is done it is possible to consider the measures necessary to ensure security for customers, staff and other site users.

The hazards which need to be identified depend on the scale of the operation, location and the sector in which the organisation operates. The range of security hazards associated with a small local sports centre, for example, is far smaller than that associated with the running of a major event such as the Wimbledon Tennis Championships. Major events such as Wimbledon could include the following security threats:

- Violence against spectators, players, VIPs or staff (e.g. crowd violence between English and French football fans during the 1998 World Cup Finals).
- Theft of information, cash, stock, equipment or property (e.g. paintings stolen from an art gallery in York in 1999).
- Fraud – the sale of fake tickets, for instance (e.g. the distribution of some match tickets for the England v Scotland Euro 2000 qualifying game in 1999).
- Terrorism and sabotage – bombs and protest break-ins, for instance (e.g. the cancelling of the Grand National at Aintree due to a bomb scare).
- Damage, either accidental, deliberate or criminal (e.g. abandonment of a Headingley Cricket Test Match due to protesters digging-up the wicket).

CASE STUDY

Security at Alton Towers

The Alton Towers security department consists of:

- Head of Security plus six permanent day staff and four permanent night staff.
- Ten part-time staff are also employed.

Supporting the security team are eight part-time administrators. Altogether they look after:
500 acres of land
34 catering units
5 restaurants
29 shops
80 rides
7 arcades

The main responsibilities of the security team are:
1 Movement and control of traffic
2 Co-ordination of any evacuations required
3 Prevention of loss or damage
4 To assist the police when necessary
5 To ensure the safety and well being of everyone.

They need to have an awareness of making arrests, when to apply caution and how to take statements, and the following Acts:

- Theft Act 1968/78
- Offences Against Persons 1861
- Criminal Damage 1971

Above all they need to be smart and tidy, self-disciplined, fit, know the principles of good communication and teamwork and be able to apply common sense under pressure. Honesty and integrity are paramount.

3.2.2 BOMB ALARM PROCEDURE

UPON RECEIVING A TELEPHONED BOMB THREAT:

- do not panic
- obtain as much information as possible by using the bomb alarm call check list
- be friendly
- inform **THE GROUND SAFETY OFFICER** immediately.

ACTION TO BE TAKEN:

- sound any bomb alarm warning system if fitted
- dial **'999'** and give the operator the telephone number of the company and ask for the **POLICE**
- when the Police reply, say distinctly:

  We have a telephoned bomb threat at

  Derby County Football Club,
  Pride Park Stadium,
  Derby,
  Derbyshire,
  DE24 8XL

- do not replace the receiver until the address has been repeated and correctly acknowledged
- vacate the premises by the nearest Fire Exit after collecting your coats and any bags you may have, and assemble at the designated assembly point, indicated below:

CAR PARK

EMPLOYEES UPON HEARING THE BOMB ALARM OR LEARNING OF A BOMB SCARE:

- check for any suspicious objects within your work area
- if you find one **DO NOT TOUCH OR MOVE IT IN ANY WAY**
- report your findings to **your supervisor**
- vacate the premises by the nearest Fire Exit after collecting any coat or bag you may have, and assemble at the designated assembly point.

BOMB

▲ A typical bomb alarm procedure

ACTIVITY

Handling security threats

As a group, brainstorm other real-life examples of security incidents in each of the categories listed on page 131. You may need to look at past newspaper reports for details.

Violence

The possibility of **violence** is something that event organisers, facility managers and security officers have to consider on a regular basis. If we take the example of a Premiership football club playing in a packed stadium, the frequency and likelihood of a security problem is quite high. This is why football clubs must have specific procedures for dealing with security incidents, as we will see in some of the examples in this section.

There are many other examples of violent incidents at events or on special occasions, such as the stabbing of the tennis player Monica Seles during a tournament, while injuries or intimidation of players and officials after a match is common. Egg or paint thrown at unpopular politicians at opening ceremonies for new facilities is not unknown either.

Violence, which is often alcohol-related, can be aimed at participants, spectators, staff or even passers-by, and may take the form of verbal abuse, threats or physical assault. The risk of violence must, of course, be minimised by security teams. Football clubs such as Manchester United, Arsenal and Derby County, for example, work hard to identify all the security hazards associated with violence, both inside and outside the stadium, in order to implement the most effective strategies to ensure public safety and security.

Much of this type of security is carried out through video surveillance in conjunction with the police, with dossier evidence compiled against habitual offenders so that they can be readily identified and arrested. The following case study on Leeds United Football Club highlights the club's commitment to combatting bad behaviour and hooliganism.

CASE STUDY

Leeds United FC

Leeds United has many approaches to combat bad behaviour and hooliganism, ranging from the purely practical (cameras, stewards, etc.) to the purely moral (appealing to people's sense of responsibility). Our aim is to attract a full cross-section of supporters – families, old and young, ethnic mixes, etc. – and to demonstrate to them that not only are they perfectly safe, but Elland Road has first-class facilities, and is an excellent place to spend your time. Below are some of our methods:

- The average number of staff on duty on match day is 489.
- This includes stewards, first-aiders, turnstile operators, car-parking staff.
- Average match costs are £15,900 per game.
- Police inside the ground number between 18 and 60; the number is swelled by those on duty around the ground and approach roads.
- Supporters are segregated inside and outside the stadium.
- Up to 400 stewards staff the gangways and passages and have to pass an NVQ in crowd control before they are employed.
- Specialist security guards are employed for particularly sensitive areas such as the players' tunnel and entrance and corporate hospitality areas.
- Stewards travel to away games to protect supporters there too.
- Home games are all-ticket.
- There are 24 CCTV cameras inside the stadium covering private rooms, car parks, approach roads and seating areas. The cameras can focus on something as small as a 10p piece up to half a mile away.
- There are two police cells beneath the stadium which are available every match!
- A public relations section promotes good behaviour and liaises with special needs groups.
- A safety officer controls the operation on match day via a two-way radio system.
- Sixteen cleaners are constantly working to clear litter during and after the game.
- Four paramedics, a mobile hospital and two ambulances are on hand for first-team games.

Situations which may need to be dealt with in a leisure facility can include arguments, disputes and physical violence. These can sometimes be quelled by a common-sense approach, but security procedures and systems should be instigated at the first sign of escalation. Staff must be able to call in trained help, such as stewards, security guards or the police. Staff dealing with the public, for example outside a pub or club, are in a particularly vulnerable position, for they are usually in the front line until help arrives.

CASE STUDY

Training for door supervisors

In an article entitled 'Safe Exit' Kath Seward, Deputy Editor of *Leisure Opportunities*, describes some recent changes within the Rank Organisation about door supervisors. Rank has introduced a pilot scheme in conjunction with the police and a leisure security firm by starting a register for people working as door supervisors. This has become necessary as there are now more people doing this job than working in the coal or steel industries. Rank are keen to get rid of the image of 'bouncers' who are 7 feet tall and have a shaven head! Rank takes a tough line on recruitment, making several checks on suitability.

The main feature of the scheme is that all supervisors will have to pass a two-day course which covers:

- conflict management
- drugs awareness
- customer care
- first aid
- licensing issues
- fire safety.

Following completion of the course, they are issued with a non-transferable badge, an ID number and photograph, and put on the national register. A three-monthly check will be made to ensure they have not committed any offences. The database and list of supervisors may go onto the internet.

Under the Health and Safety at Work Act 1974, organisers or employers have a duty to make working conditions as safe as possible for their staff. Managers or security officers for a leisure facility therefore have a duty to consider how they can reduce the possibility of staff being abused, threatened or assaulted, and to identify, reduce or eliminate the possibility of violent incidents disrupting the event.

There are a number of courses that door security people can go on to learn appropriate techniques to keep situations under control, before violence breaks out as shown in the case study on the left.

The article below by Melanie Swift in *Leisuremoves* magazine highlights the threat of violence facing those who work in the industry.

'Road rage, supermarket rage, aeroplane rage – intolerance and anger seem to be spilling over everywhere. There have been reports of hotel rage and swimming-pool lane rage. But dealing with aggression is no laughing matter, especially if you're just trying to do your job. Just ask the three attendants at York City Art Gallery who were tied-up by masked, armed thieves at 5 p.m. on 22 January 1999, while 20 pictures worth almost £1 million were taken from the walls around them. Luckily no one was injured, and while this is an extreme example which no amount of training could have prevented from happening, it highlights the very real threats facing those who work in the industry.'

ACTIVITY

Instances of violent acts

Using recent copies of a local or national newspaper identify three examples of violence at a match, an event or leisure facility which involved stewards or the police taking action. Discuss what punishment you think would be appropriate for the culprits and what could have been done to reduce or eliminate the problem in the first place.

Theft

Several types of **theft** can occur at an event or from premises where leisure or recreation activities take place.

Information can be stolen in a number of ways. For example, personal details (such as addresses and telephone numbers) about clients or participants may be copied from entry forms. Unscrupulous operators may sell their membership database to others such as marketing companies, who will then send advertising or sales mail to people on the list. The Data Protection Act identifies the need to protect personal information about clients from theft or nuisance.

Cash or the equivalent can be taken in the form of money, cheque books or credit cards. Customers' belongings are most vulnerable when they are left unattended and where there is no provision for locking valuables or money away safely. Pickpockets operate most effectively in a crowd, where there is a lot of distracting hustle and bustle and physical contact. Leisure managers must make adequate provision for cash security within their premises, both for the sake of their staff and their profits, as the case study below describes.

▲ Pickpocket threat

CASE STUDY

Handling cash

All necessary precautions should be taken where cash is available on site, whether at the cash register, being moved to and from the bank or being moved from the cash register to the office.

If a leisure facility has an outlet such as a retail store, snack bar or restaurant on site, then cash protection starts before the facility is even open. When the cash float is made up for the till before commencement of trading, this must be carried out with the facility closed and locked before customers enter the premises. On a busy site it is likely that cash will build up in the till. This should be avoided. It is only necessary to keep sufficient money in the till for the cashier to give change for up to a £50 note. Most companies now remove all surplus notes and place them in a counter cache which is permanently bolted underneath or beside the cash till. By removing surplus cash you remove two temptations: a cash snatch at the till and the temptation for an employee to borrow money from the till.

When the day's trading is finished it is essential to have secure cashing up procedures. Make sure that all doors are locked, including the back door, and that all customers have left the premises. Cashing up should take place out of sight of passers-by, preferably in an office or stock room.

While cash is on the premises it is at risk; the sooner it is off the premises the better. Many companies now are using equipment such as friction note counters and coin sorters to speed up cashing-up processes. This increases security by getting the money counted and off the premises quickly; can save money by allowing for a reduction in the number of staff in the cash office; and makes you money - the sooner the money is in the bank the quicker it can earn interest for you.

Operators of leisure sites may be taking cash at many points throughout the site. The movement of cash throughout the area must be carried out securely, preferably using a secure cash-carrying case.

Source: Frank Pegg, *Leisure Manager*, June 1999

ACTIVITY

Handling cash

Compile a one-page checklist you could use to circulate to reception staff in a leisure centre to remind them of the most secure way to handle and store cash.

Another problem for leisure centres is the secure movement of cash to and from the bank. A cash in transit (CIT) vehicle means that there should be little trouble, although violent raids on cash-in-transit staff, vehicles and depots are on the increase. Customers using CIT vehicles can assist in reducing the risks by having a safe and secure area where the CIT vehicle can enter and leave.

Using a private vehicle and carrying cash on foot means choosing the right person for this responsible job: new employees and temporary or casual staff should not be used. Leisure and recreation facility managers should devise a cash protection programme to cover all aspects of risk for their premises.

Stock can also be stolen by casual staff, part-time staff, full-time staff, or customers. Shoplifting is a very common crime today, as the layout of many leisure retail outlets is open-plan, making it easy for customers to view and choose goods, but of course tempting to those who cannot afford to buy them.

Equipment can be removed by bogus workers, staff, organised gangs or anyone with access to premises. Organised gangs will identify in advance what they want to steal and pinpoint the best time to remove it. They may use sophisticated equipment and elaborate plans to carry out the theft depending on the value or the volume of goods to be stolen. Computers, televisions and videos are common choices. Smash-and-grab or ram raids may be undertaken to enter premises for valuable items.

Personal property is at risk if doors are not locked, bags are left lying around and valuables are left visible. Shoppers are especially at risk in a busy mall, as their attention is drawn to shop windows and not to their handbags and wallets. Experienced car thieves can break into most models in seconds, so anything left in clear view inside the car can be gone in minutes. Company property can be stolen if it is not secured by some means, such as chains or steel cable. Many organisations carefully bar-code or secretly mark or put an electronic trace on their possessions so that they can be identified if stolen.

Electronic theft is a fairly new concept, but with the increasing use of mobile phones and the internet to buy leisure products and use banking services, sophisticated operators are able to tap into communication systems and transfer goods or credit to themselves.

Whenever customers' personal possessions are collected for safety or security reasons, it is the organisation's duty to ensure that there are appropriate storage facilities. For example, in swimming pools customers are provided with lockers in which to store their personal belongings while swimming.

In outlets where cash transactions are made, the presence of security guards deters pickpockets and store thieves. Retail outlets also extensively 'tag' their goods as well, so that sensors at the exits can detect goods that are not paid for, either deliberately or accidentally.

Today, much of the anti-theft security of leisure and recreation facilities is tackled at the design stage and can involve huge investments in elaborate security systems. Many organisations use some or all of the following security devices to ensure that theft is minimised and to make possible the controlled movement of people and equipment:

- Special lighting
- Intruder alarms
- Bars, shutters and screens
- CCTV
- Access and door-locking controls
- Turnstiles and barriers
- Swipe-card systems

▲ Security cameras

ACTIVITY

Security measures

Look at the list of security measures given on page 136. For each category, give three examples of leisure or recreation operators that you know of who use them to prevent theft.

Fraud

Fraud is classed with a variety of illegal acts called criminal deception. It includes such things as the passing of forged cheques, the use of stolen credit cards or counterfeit money, using fake tickets or goods, and pretending to be someone else. Ticket fraud is a common problem for event organisers in the leisure and recreation industries. Such fraud can be attempted from inside or outside the organisation. Internal ticket fraud consists of:

- fraudulent behaviour of staff
- theft of tickets for resale by staff
- free entry allowed by staff
- discrepancies in vouchers or ticket sales from entry booths.

External ticket fraud can include:

- counterfeiting of tickets
- alteration of tickets, signatures or photos
- fraudulent re-entries or re-use of tickets
- transfer of season tickets or memberships.

Large-scale sports events are a particular target for this type of deception, as tickets are at a premium and in short supply. Fraud of this nature can run into many thousands of pounds and lead to serious crowd disorder when fans realise they cannot gain entry to an event. On a smaller scale, a less scrupulous gate operator may let friends and family into a ground for free, thereby depriving the club of valuable income. There will always be similar temptations when cash is paid to gain admittance, so staff need to be recruited carefully and some form of accounting for ticket money strictly applied.

Sabotage

Sabotage is deliberate damage designed to prevent a match, for example, from being held or continuing. In the leisure and recreation industry sabotage could comprise damage to property, equipment or facilities by protesters, hooligans, angry crowds or even political extremists and terrorists. Sabotage is carried out for a variety reasons, by a range of groups. In the recent past these have included the following:

- Animal rights activists protesting against fox hunting or horse racing.
- People with a grudge, perhaps over dismissal, may damage a company's equipment.
- Crowds may invade the playing area to prevent their team losing.
- Political activists may stage a demonstration in the middle of an event to gain publicity.
- Terrorists may attempt to sabotage an event with bomb or death threats against VIPs, spectators, passers-by or performers.
- Protesters against a building development may occupy part of a site to prevent further construction.

Ticket racket

Wembley officials have launched a drive to combat the misuse of match tickets following the England v Scotland Euro 2000 playoff, when around 3,500 tickets are believed to have reached the 'pirate' hospitality market. Although tickets sold via the Wembley box office were limited to four per person, it seems a number of companies obtained quantities of tickets which were illegally sold on.

'What we found was extraordinary', says Wembley's safety officer, Noel Jeffs. 'Unlicensed venues selling alcohol, meals cooked in transit vans in car parks and prices ranging from £299 to £1,015 per head for virtually the same thing.'

In the future the stadium authorities will be working closely with the Football Association, the Metropolitan Police and Trading Standards Officers to combat the problem.

Source: Sports Management, February 2000

▲ Ticket fraud is common at high-profile sports events

Most of these examples would require considerable resources to identify and prevent. Even with extensive and sophisticated security measures in place it still may not be possible to eliminate the risk of some kind of sabotage. The element of surprise is always on the side of the saboteurs or protesters.

Accidental or deliberate damage

Accidental damage is the security hazard most likely to occur at a leisure or recreation event or facility. Quite simply, the more activities there are and the more people there are involved, the greater is the probability of accidental damage. Staff or customers may drop equipment or misuse it, and people may be unfamiliar with how things operate or the surroundings in which they are working. Staff working in the industry have to try to anticipate where this type of damage is most likely to occur and either have someone on hand to ensure it doesn't happen, or propose measures such as clear instructions and warnings to help minimise it. Most organisations will make sure that their insurance covers accidental or deliberate damage and any injuries to participants or spectators for activities they undertake.

Deliberate damage caused by vandals, for example, which often poses a real danger, is costly and time-consuming to rectify. Graffiti and broken doors and windows are the most common forms of damage, but if a leisure event or facility is not secure then vandals may gain access and destroy equipment, materials and other resources. For example, a leisure operator running a bonfire and fireworks display has to take measures to minimize the risk of vandals setting fire to the bonfire before the event.

Modern materials are often designed to be vandal-proof or easily replaced to help reduce the impact of vandalism. However, it may detract from the look of a facility if robust materials have to be used and it may also mean an additional design cost at the building stage. The POP museum in Sheffield actually ran some trials with hordes of school children on their premises to see what and how things on display would survive. Many had to be redesigned, as they were damaged either deliberately or by accident.

ACTIVITY

Prevention of damage

Visit a leisure or recreation facility in your locality and identify features which have been designed to be robust, vandal-proof, hard-wearing or cheap to replace if damaged.

Evaluating security hazards

An evaluation of identified security hazards must be undertaken to complete a risk assessment. The criteria and process for this are similar to those employed in the evaluation of health and safety hazards (see pages 127-129). Security hazards for all aspects of a facility can be evaluated in terms of:

- how likely they are to occur (probability)
- the type of likely loss
- the level (severity) of likely loss.

These three criteria will help managers and staff to decide which hazards pose the greatest threat and which counter-measures should be taken. The hazards identified are given ratings of probability and severity to assess their nature. The tables in Figures 2.18 - 2.22 can be used when you carry out the evaluation of each security hazard. As with health and safety hazards, by allocating a rating to each aspect (low, medium or high, or using a scale of 0-10) you can evaluate which risks warrant the most attention, so as to eliminate or reduce the security hazard.

Once a risk assessment is completed, specific advice and guidance and the necessary measures are put in place to ensure security is as good as it can be. The following case study shows how leisure and recreation operators can implement risk assessment procedures.

CASE STUDY

Risk management in action

Risk analysis is all about identifying threats, assessing the potential impacts to business associated with each type of threat and looking at how well we are defended against those threats to see where reductions in impact can be best achieved. This process can be applied to all types of risk, including the risks that we face with regard to crime.

Attributes of risk, including impact and vulnerability, can be measured using a simple three-point scale (Low, Medium, High). Criticality assessment is the process used to combine impact and vulnerability ratings [similar to the probability and severity ratings on page 124] into a single risk category to prioritise areas of concern which require remedial attention.

Once priorities have been identified, the next step is to plan the actions to deal with high-risk categories. These will be plans to increase security and control, and to reduce vulnerability. Such controls might include: additional outside lighting around a building; better physical security locks on doors and windows; CCTV cameras to monitor and record activity in certain areas; visitor procedures to eliminate casual entry; awareness campaigns for staff and customers to sensitize them to certain risks; and management review procedures after significant incidents.

The last part of the process is monitoring success. After we have completed the project, we ask certain questions to assess the effectiveness of the risk management programme. These include:

- Have lower impacts and fewer incidents occurred?
- Have the installations given value for money?
- Are areas still vulnerable or under threat?
- Which installations have had the best benefit?

Source: John Sherwood, *Leisure Manager*, June 1998

Security hazards will of course vary greatly from facility to facility and at different times, so assessment will vary as well. Some sort of system has to be devised to predict when the most dangerous periods are likely to be, for example:

- If a queue builds up people may become impatient and may be abusive to staff.
- At peak times (e.g. sale days) in a shop, goods may be more likely to be stolen.
- Big matches attract ticket touts selling forgeries.
- Certain football matches attract 'away fans' with a reputation for causing trouble.
- Periods of time when valuable equipment is left unattended.
- Overnight is an especially dangerous time for any leisure facility.
- Areas away from the main facility are at high risk.

ACTIVITY

High security risks

Can you think of other occasions when the leisure facilities listed below have high security risks?

- Theatre or cinema
- Marina
- Race course
- Caravan park
- Retail outlet
- Art gallery

Activities requiring security coverage

Sports events with large opening or closing ceremonies are usually evaluated as high-risk security factors. High-risk security factors can comprise the people, premises or equipment required for activities. They might consist of a key piece of equipment such as a computer or a sound system, or a single facility, building or outdoor location.

Such aspects rate highly in any evaluation as key factors needing protection, for without them the event might not be able to take place. Aspects with a lower rating might need a different type of coverage in order to minimise them as security risks.

Supporting activities for a sport or recreation event may also require security measures. These could include:

- car-park stewarding and surveillance
- secure storage of supplies (for example, catering or souvenirs)
- secure storage of promotional materials or equipment.

Each situation will have a unique combination of activities requiring security coverage. The measures taken to ensure security should be based on the impact any loss or incident would have on the overall facility or plan.

Customers and staff security

The customers using a facility may be a diverse range of people. All types of customers are important to a leisure facility, so staff will have to ensure the security of everyone involved. In addition, organisers and staff must not forget to consider their own security. Some staff may be in vulnerable positions or have hazardous responsibilities, such as collecting money, controlling access, dealing with complaints, co-ordinating activities or looking after VIPs.

The role of each member of staff should be evaluated for likely security hazards, such as:

- violence
- theft
- fraudulent acts
- exposure to sabotage
- dealing with damage or vandalism.

The best preparation is to have good communications between staff and professional support on hand should it be required. Training should also be undertaken to practise security procedures agreed by the staff team or advised by the authorities, so that the time between any incident and response is minimal.

Measures to ensure security

Measures to ensure security can be divided into two categories: risk reduction and emergency action.

Risk reduction

The main priority of any proposed security measures should be to eliminate or reduce risk to a minimum. Figure 2.23 shows just a few examples of risk reduction measures used in the leisure and recreation industries.

Figure 2.23: Risk reduction measures

Hazards	Measures
Cars in car park	CCTV
Trophies in display cabinet	Alarms fitted to glass
Pilfering of stock	Stock room coded entry system
Threats to staff	Glass screens
Unauthorised entry	Swipe cards

The following case study about access control gives an insight into the importance of combining a secure environment with a friendly atmosphere in a leisure and recreation facility.

CASE STUDY

Health and fitness security systems

It is a fine balancing act to be performed when implementing any security system in a health and fitness facility. After all, no one wants to go to a gym that resembles Colditz. Equally, many gym operators are now moving away from automatic doors and turnstiles, making sure that users are greeted by a real person, helping to promote the feeling of belonging to a gym rather than just attending.

Access control modules can link the main databases of a facility to most turnstiles, doors or car-park barriers. By doing this the centre operators can decide not only who has access to certain parts of the facility, but at what times of the day. This is particularly useful when operating peak and off-peak memberships: if a member upgrades, they do not need to be issued with another card as the system handles everything. The system has proved effective in busy leisure centres where a turnstile allows users with pre-booked activities to by-pass reception while still capturing the demographic information vital to operators.

One of the most unusual installations Microcache have been involved with is at the Hyatt Carlton Hotel in central London. To gain access to the Peak Health and Fitness Club, members use the same lift as the hotel guests. A card reader has been installed that links into the lift controls, allowing only members of the club to select the floor where the club is situated. The hotel also has a swimming pool and the same access control system is used to stop unauthorized use.

A secondary advantage of installing access control is that all users are forced to swipe in, ensuring accurate usage statistics are collated. Several sites have also installed turnstiles on the exits, both to record the time spent in the gym and to ensure that off-peak members do not stay in the gym well into the peak hours.

It is equally important that the security system implemented does not put the users at risk. Fail-safe systems should be installed so that if there is a power-cut the doors and turnstiles will open. It is also recommended that any security system be linked into the building's fire alarm system.

Source: Keith Emery of Microcache, *Leisure Manager*, June 1999

ACTIVITY

Effective security systems

List the benefits to staff and customers of having an effective security system in place.

Emergency action

Emergency action must be devised and rehearsed for any potential security hazard. Such action may be necessary to deal with:

- evacuation on land or water (e.g. from ferries)
- violence
- fire
- theft
- unauthorised entry
- vandalism.

If a facility is properly equipped the first warning of a security hazard staff receive is often an alarm. Alarms of many types are available, including:

- Personal alarms for staff – pagers, attack buttons and radio-based mobiles.
- Fire alarms and smoke detectors – individual and multi-zone versions.
- Intruder alarms – infra-red beams, pressure pads, lights and circuit breakers.
- Surveillance equipment – CCTV, pinhole cameras.
- Detection equipment – electronic monitoring gates, metal detectors.

Any measures a manager or member of staff proposes should be based on advice from the emergency services. The fire and rescue, police, ambulance and coastguard services can all provide advice to event organisers on appropriate emergency action.

Familiarisation training is essential, so that everyone knows exactly what to do at the first sign of trouble. This type of procedure needs communicating to customers as well, so that they become part of the communication chain in case of emergency, especially where they are at risk.

Measures to ensure security must cover every aspect of an emergency, relate exactly to what is needed and be carried out by the people present. Account must be taken of important factors before an emergency occurs, such as the:

- skills and abilities of people involved, either as organisers, helpers or participants
- financial resources available
- time available to train staff and rehearse procedures
- materials or equipment required.

Proposals will be unrealistic if they do not take these constraints into account. The measures proposed should ensure the security of every aspect of the risk assessment above the trivial level. A checklist/action system is probably the best way of ensuring all of these aspects are adequately investigated and covered.

After any emergency the effectiveness of these proposals and of their implementation by the staff or event team can be referred to on the plan and used as a basis for evaluation. From this, new proposals or recommendations can be made if the measures are found to be insufficient or inadequate.

Programme organisers and facility managers in the leisure and recreation industry adopt a wide range of measures to cover security risks. The Alfred McAlpine Stadium in Huddersfield, for example, was the world's first stadium to be equipped with a computerised system and closed-circuit television with an alarm interface, external detectors, remote access and barrier control, an integrated public address system and surveillance 24 hours a day.

The security measures for most facilities will probably not include such high-tech systems as these. Whatever the security measures adopted, the important thing for each team member to remember is to stick to the agreed measures and not to indulge in any heroics. If there is any sort of trouble, they should quickly get help.

FIRE SAFETY INSTRUCTIONS
for
DERBY COUNTY FOOTBALL CLUB

FIRE ALARM

The fire alarm system is:

A CONTINUOUS VOICE ANNOUNCEMENT OPERATED BY BREAK GLASS CALL POINTS

IF YOU DISCOVER A FIRE:

1. Operate the nearest fire alarm.
2. Immediately vacate the premises by the nearest available exit and proceed to the assembly point indicated below.

DO NOT RE-ENTER THE BUILDING TO COLLECT PERSONAL BELONGINGS.

If it is SAFE to do so tackle the fire with the nearest appropriate fire extinguisher. Always ensure there is a safe exit route before attempting to extinguish any fire.

WHEN INFORMED OF A FIRE:

1. Immediately vacate the premises by the nearest available exit.
2. Proceed to the assembly point indicated and await roll call.

ASSEMBLY POINT:

CAR PARK

DO NOT RE-ENTER THE BUILDING UNTIL TOLD TO DO SO BY MANAGEMENT, UNDER INSTRUCTION BY THE SENIOR FIRE OFFICER

8 June 1998 DC LL2.7a

▲ Fire safety instructions at Derby County Football Club

BUILD YOUR LEARNING

End of section activity

1. Identify a local leisure or recreation facility or event and seek permission to undertake a security risk assessment for the facility. You may be able to combine this with a health and safety risk assessment. Of course, you will not be an expert, but by using the guidance provided here and perhaps by interviewing organisers, managers and security experts, you should be able to build up a very good risk assessment profile of your chosen facility or event.

2. Discuss your findings with a colleague and evaluate whether you think the proposed measures are effective enough. Where you think that some alternative or improved measures could be applied make recommendations which could be used. You can use the pro formas and suggestions given in Figures 2.18 - 2.22 to assist your research.

Keywords and phrases

You should know the meaning of the words and phrases listed below. If you are unsure about any of them, go back through the last 12 pages to refresh your understanding.

- **Security measures**
- **Closed circuit television cameras**
- **Violence**
- **Theft**
- **Fraud**
- **Sabotage**
- **Accidental damage**

Preview

Unit 3 builds on the work completed in Unit 1 by focusing on one aspect of leisure and recreation: the sports industry.

Sport is big business. The industry has a complex structure, a large turnover and an impact on many people's lives, either as participants or spectators. In this unit we will investigate the nature of the sports industry, its scale, its contribution to the UK economy, and some of the current trends in sport. You will learn about the structure and organisation of the industry and how it is funded. The unit also explores the relationship between sport and the mass media, including the influence of the media on the development of sport. The 'Sport files' at the end of the unit illustrate the significance and development of two popular sports, football and tennis.

Unit 3 also links closely with many of the sports-related optional units that you may study, such as Sports Coaching, Sports Leadership and Sports Development.

This unit is assessed by the portfolio assessment on pages 456-457.

3

The sports industry

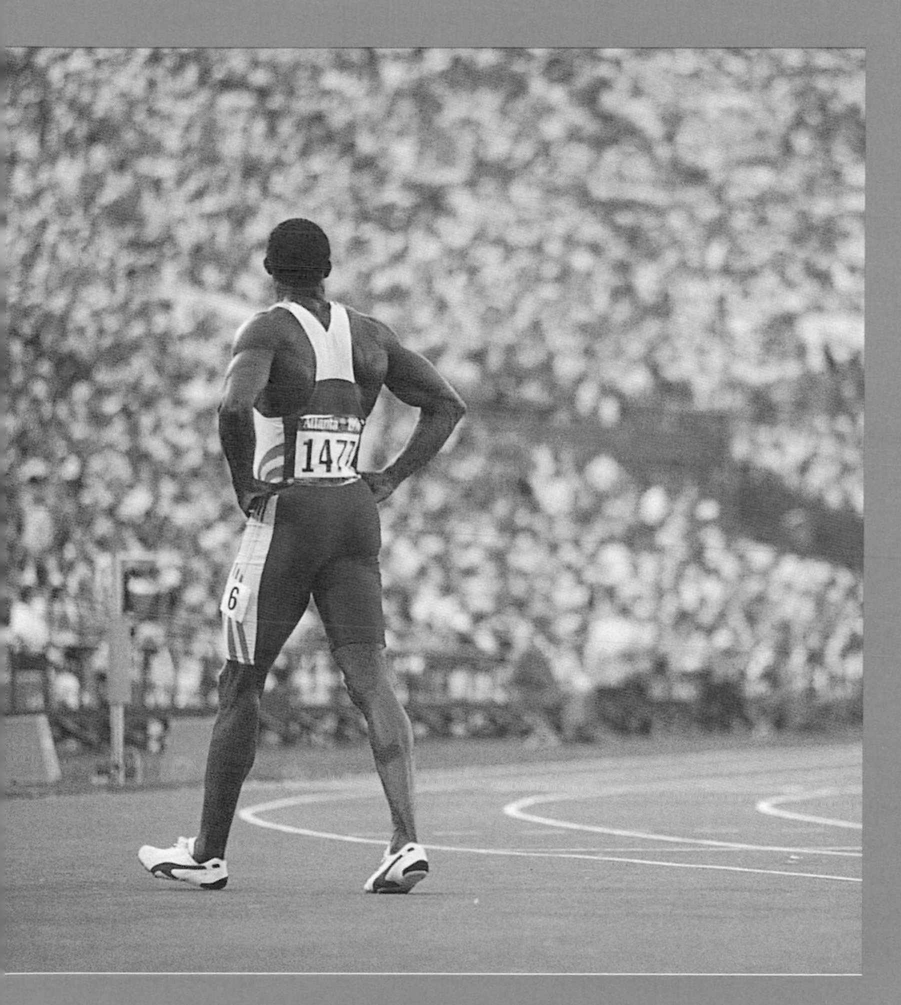

Contents

The nature of the sports industry

Definitions

Collins English Dictionary defines **sport** as follows:

> *An individual or group activity pursued for exercise or pleasure, often involving the testing of physical capabilities and taking the form of a competitive game such as football, tennis, etc.*

From this definition we can see that sport involves:

- some form of physical activity
- an element of competition

Other characteristics of sport are:

- activities determined by rules, regulations or laws
- activities with a distinct goal or outcome
- activities that involve some form of organisation, such as a pitch, area, track or court.

Reasons vary as to why people become involved in sport:

- for leisure and recreational purposes
- to earn a living
- to organise, officiate, coach or develop sports
- for improved personal health and fitness
- for socialising purposes
- to watch or support an individual, team or country.

Often people involve themselves in sport for a combination of such reasons. In Unit 1, the sports and physical recreation industry was described as containing a very broad range of providers, facilities, events, products, services and activities.

Sport is a big business with a complex structure, a large turnover, and an impact on many people's lives. To understand the nature of the sports industry we need to be aware that it contains various components:

- sporting goods (e.g. high street sports retailers, equipment and clothing manufacturers)
- sports coaching;
- facility provision, maintenance and management (e.g. sports and leisure centres, stadia, race tracks)
- sports development (e.g. local authority sports development officers, governing body sports development initiatives)
- sports tourism (e.g. packages for fans attending sporting events such as the Olympics or World Cups)
- professional sport (e.g. players, coaches, managers, agents)
- sports-related gambling (e.g. on horse racing, greyhound racing, football matches)
- sports medicine (e.g. physiotherapists, sports injury clinics)
- health and fitness (e.g. health clubs, GP referral schemes, personal fitness trainers)
- outdoor and adventure activities (e.g. climbing, cycling, mountain biking, skiing, kayaking).

In this section we will look at each of these key components.

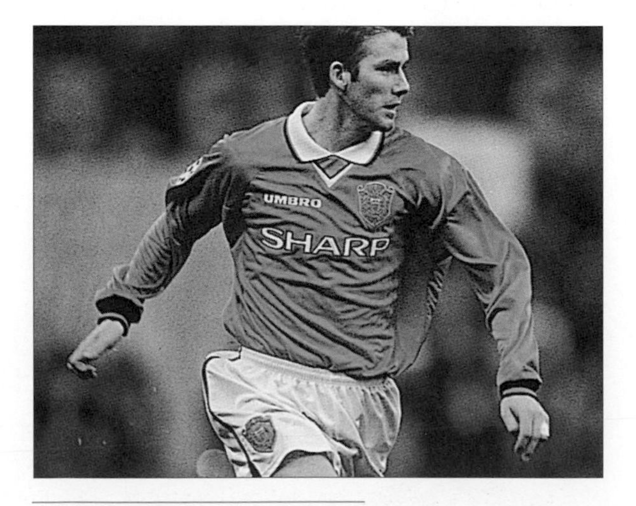

▲ Sports retail is big business

Sports goods

Consumer expenditure on sporting goods can be broken down into several categories, such as equipment, footwear, clothing, accessories and fashion. Market researchers Mintel estimate that UK consumers spent £3,470 million on **sports goods** in 1998 (see Figure 3.1). Growth rates in consumer spending were very high between 1993 and 1998. In real terms, the market has continued to grow each year thanks to relatively low price inflation. Between 1992 and 1998, on this measure, the 'real market' for sports goods expanded by 40 per cent. Taking an even broader view (final column of Figure 3.1), sports goods represent 0.65 per cent of total consumer spending, which came to £506 billion in 1997.

Nature of the sports goods market

Although it is now virtually impossible to distinguish between 'fashion and function' in sportswear sales, the sports goods market can be broadly segmented into two categories: **clothing/footwear** and **equipment**. The latter falls entirely into the category of function, and the former is split between **leisurewear** and **performance products**.

While clothing and footwear can be amalgamated, it is conventional to keep them separate, producing the three-way split in sales shown in Figure 3.2.

Figure 3.1: The UK market for sports goods, 1992-1998

	£ m	Index	% annual change	£ m at 1992 prices	Index	% annual change	% total consumer spending
1992	2,348	100	-6.2	2,348	100	–	0.61
1993	2,506	107	+6.7	2,483	106	+5.7	0.62
1994	2,695	115	+7.5	2,663	113	+7.2	0.63
1995	2,820	120	+4.6	2,800	118	+4.5	0.63
1996	3,065	131	+8.7	2,782	129	+9.0	0.65
1997	3,275	140	+6.8	3,033	136	+5.1	0.65
1998	3,470	148	+6.0	3,278	140	+2.8	0.65

Source: Mintel *Sports Industry Report 1999*

Figure 3.2: Product sectors of the consumer sports goods market, 1998

1998	£ m	%
Clothing	**1,800**	**52**
Footwear	**1,050**	**30**
Equipment	**620**	**18**
Total	3,470	100

Data may not equal totals due to rounding

Source: Mintel *Sports Industry Report 1999*

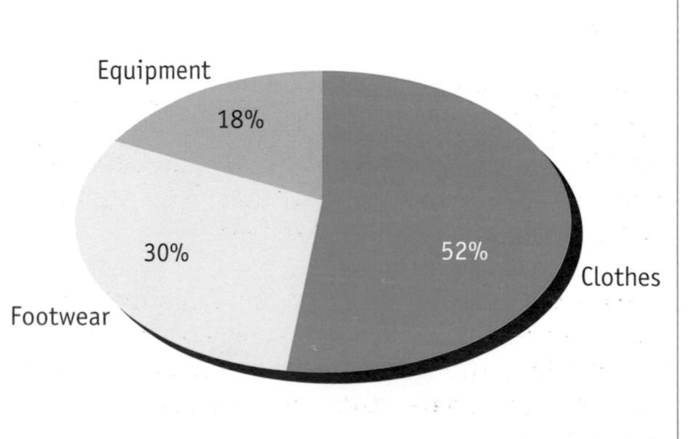

Fashion trends mean that clothing has a dominant share of the market. Yet fashion has not been the only contributor to clothing's rising market share. The 'big brands' phenomenon crossed over from footwear to clothing in the mid-1990s, so that it became desirable to be seen wearing branded clothing as well as shoes and boots. Whereas consumers once spent large sums on premium-priced trainers or boots but wore cheaper, unbranded T-shirts and tops, they now pay the same premium price for manufacturers' branded clothing.

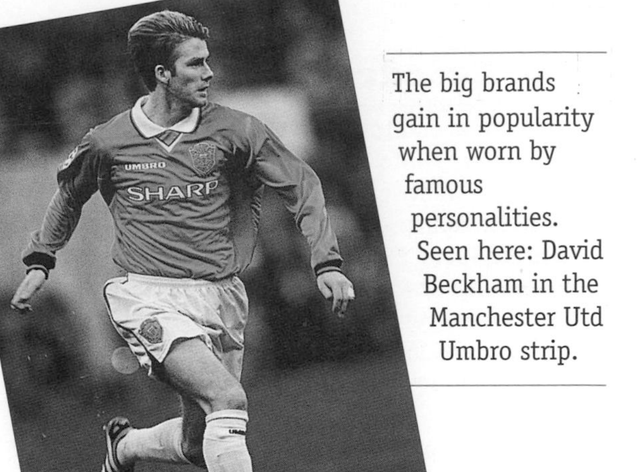

The big brands gain in popularity when worn by famous personalities. Seen here: David Beckham in the Manchester Utd Umbro strip.

Leading manufacturers and brands

Figure 3.3 lists the companies whose **brand names** currently dominate the supply of sports goods. All of the companies listed have achieved annual sales within the UK (excluding exports) worth at least £20 million at retail prices.

Figure 3.3: Leading sports goods manufacturers

Companies	Origin	Brand(s)	Principal product ranges and main sports
Adidas	Germany	Adidas	Clothing, footwear, equipment. Football, rugby, tennis, athletics
Dunlop Slazenger	UK	Various*	Equipment. Golf, racket, cricket, hockey
Hi-Tec Sports	UK	Hi-Tec	Footwear. Fitness, running, racket, outdoor
Mizuno	Japan	Mizuno	Equipment, footwear. Golf, football, rugby
Nike	US	Nike	Footwear, clothing. Running, football, fitness, tennis
Pentland Group	UK	Various**	Footwear (sport and general), sports and leisurewear. Swimming, football, US football
Puma	Germany	Puma	Footwear, clothing. Football, fitness, athletics. Distribution by Dunlop Slazenger
Reebok	US	Reebok	Footwear, clothing. Fitness, running, football, tennis, outdoor
Russell Athletic	US	Russell	Clothing. American sports, tracksuits, athletic fleeces, athletics
Spalding Sports	US	Spalding	Equipment. Golf, American sports
Umbro	UK	Umbro	Football clothing and footwear
Wilson Sporting Goods	US	Wilson	Equipment. Golf, racket, American sports. Part of Amer Group, Finland, but US origin

* Dunlop, Slazenger, Carlton, Puma (agency)
** Main brands represented (some owned, some agency): Speedo, Mitre, Ellesse, Pony, Reusch, Lacoste, Berghaus
Source: Mintel

CASE STUDY

Adidas

Adidas is Europe's largest sports goods manufacturer. In the 1970s, it was the pioneer of the modern sports shoe market, creating the original football trainer in addition to producing football boots, running shoes, athletic equipment and tracksuits. During the 1980s its market leadership was quickly eroded by Nike and Reebok, which were quicker to detect the sports-as-fashion trend and also benefited from the sports boom in the US, where Adidas had limited market penetration. Even in its core market for training and running shoes, Adidas' market share was down to 10 per cent by the end of the 1980s.

Efforts to reorganise and refocus the Adidas empire started to pay off in the early 1990s. In the UK, notable gains in market share were made in football, the original Adidas heartland into which Nike and Reebok had started to diversify, and successful ranges of tennis shoes and bags were launched. Adidas also currently supplies football kit to many famous teams around Europe.

The company built on the heritage of its 'three stripes' logo and found that young sports participants, along with fashion-conscious sportswear purchasers, had retained awareness of Adidas brand values. An 'Earn Them' campaign related to the three stripes was created to emphasise the brand's commitment to serious sport, almost hinting that non-sportsmen and women should not really be wearing the Adidas product. However, this campaign did not deter the fashion demand, which received a considerable boost through 1996 and 1997 when a number of pop celebrities opted to wear Adidas – without any official endorsement – for their stage shows and promotional photographs. By the end of 1997, Adidas was firmly established as the UK's leading sports clothing brand, overtaking its arch rivals Reebok and Nike. In footwear, recent concepts from Adidas include 'Feet You Wear' and 'Response Feet You Wear', which mimic the shape of the foot.

Sports goods and fashion

The sports boom started in footwear and the giants of the original 'trainers' market moved adeptly into clothing ranges. Adidas, Reebok and Nike are the leaders in a sports clothing and footwear market where brand names are highly marketable.

Sportswear is now fashionable as leisurewear, producing extra demand for sports clothing and footwear that would not have existed if the market were restricted to active users. It is estimated that only 10 per cent of purchased sports shoes are used exclusively for sport. This fashion trend meant that clothing increased its share of the sports goods market to 52 per cent by 1998.

According to a Mintel sports industry report, the UK market for outdoor goods for walking and climbing grew by some 59 per cent between 1992 and 1998 to £623 million. This was part of a fashion trend towards the 'outdoor look' which began to emerge in the late 1980s and became a mainstream trend in the early 1990s.

Sports retail

Sports retailing involves many diverse outlets, including leisure goods and department stores, mail order and fashion multiples as well as sports specialists. While many sports shops can still be categorised as independents (often in buying groups such as Intersport), the multiple groups have increased their dominance of the market. In 1998 £200 million worth of sportswear was bought via the major multiples as compared to £160 million worth via independents. The biggest development of 1998 was the acquisition of Sports Division by JJB Sport, giving the chain outright leadership of the sports goods multiple retailing sector.

Sports brands survey

Undertake a survey within your group to find out about the types of sports clothing, footwear and equipment people buy. First of all, ask each member of the group to list any sports goods (for leisurewear or participation in sport) they have purchased in the last 12 months. Ask them to name the brand, purpose and place of purchase of each item and its approximate cost. You could use the following table as a guide to how to record the information.

Description of goods	Name of brand	Main purpose of purchase: leisurewear or participation	Approximate cost (£)	Place of purchase
Basketball boots	*Nike*	*Leisurewear*	*£85.00*	*Mail order*

When you have finished the survey, work with the rest of the group to complete the following tasks:

- Calculate the average amount spent on sports goods per person over the 12-month period.
- Calculate the percentage of spending on each of the three key categories of sports goods: clothing, footwear and equipment. You may wish to present this information as a pie chart.
- Calculate the percentage of spending on sports goods purchased primarily for leisurewear and purchased primarily for sports participation.
- For each of the three sports goods categories identified (clothing, footwear and equipment), list the three most popular items and the three most popular brands. You can base your selections either on the most frequently listed items and brands, or on the total value of purchases for each item.
- Calculate the percentage of spending on sports goods purchased from the following outlets: independent specialist sports shops, major sports retail chains, department stores, general clothing/footwear outlets or mail order. You may also wish to include an 'others' category if some places of purchase are none of the above. Your findings could be presented as a pie chart.

Future forecasts

Some of the major features of the sports goods market in the next few years will hinge on the following trends:

- A general rise in the awareness of the need to keep fit.
- Outdoor lifestyles and relaxation of dress codes, with informality stimulating the acceptance of sportswear for everyday use.
- The advance of football generally, particularly club-related products such as replica kits.
- Media coverage of sports, especially satellite (and eventually multi-channel) television.
- Technological developments in fabrics, footwear and equipment.
- The growth in the female market.

Sports coaching

In its broadest context **sports coaching** is about helping people to be better sports performers at all levels. Coaches set exercises, practices and tasks to facilitate the acquisition of skills and plan programmes to produce improvements in performance. However, coaching is not just about improving performance. Coaches also need to recognise the overall welfare and development of the performer. This involves attending to some of their social, emotional, physical and moral needs. The National Coaching Foundation (NCF) uses the following definition of sports coaching:

> *The organised provision of assistance to an individual performer or group of performers in order to help them develop and improve in their chosen sport.*

Sports coaches work at all levels, from teaching youngsters basic skills and techniques to preparing individuals or teams for major international competitions. At grassroots level many coaches operate on a voluntary or part-time basis. Their work focuses on developing sport by teaching people the basic skills and techniques they require to take part. At a higher level, most coaches work on a full-time salaried basis, although such opportunities are fairly limited compared to the number of coaches at the grassroots level. There is a wide variety of organisations involved in providing sports coaching in the UK, including:

- schools, colleges and universities
- local authorities
- governing bodies of sport
- the National Coaching Foundation
- sports councils
- private sector clubs and organisations
- voluntary sector clubs and associations.

Sports coaching in the UK has gained in significance over recent years due to a number of factors.

Coach education

In the past, the lack of a national structure for sports coaching qualifications and programmes was a limiting factor in the recognition accorded by both employees and the public to the importance of coaching. The National Training Organisation for Sport, Recreaton and Allied Occupations (SPRITO), in conjunction with other key organisations such as the National Coaching Foundation (NCF) and governing bodies of sport, has set out a national framework of qualifications and levels, as shown in Figure 3.4. By 1998 there were qualifications matched to national standards in 36 sports. However, despite this progress there is still much work to be done in order to achieve a national framework adopted by all sports governing bodies.

Figure 3.4: National coaching framework

Level	What should a coach be able to do?	How governing bodies might describe a coach
Level 5	Coaches having significant and repeated success at the highest level of the world stage. Competent to assume full responsibility for the organisation, management and delivery of all elements of a world-class performer's (or team's) preparation for competitive international success.	National Coach/Staff Coach
Level 4	Coaches with substantial and proven practical coaching experience at club and representative level. Competent to take full responsibility for the management of every aspect of a performer's (team's) preparation for competition at an international level.	Regional Coach/Mentor Coach/Advanced Coach
Level 3	Coaches competent to plan, coach and evaluate an annual coaching programme for committed club level and representative performers competing at county, regional and/or national levels.	Club Coach/Senior Coach
Level 2	Coaches competent to plan, coach and evaluate a series of sessions for recreational participants and those competing in local leagues.	Coach/Instructor/Teacher
Level 1	Competent to assist more experienced coaches and lead sessions of safe, fun, recreational sport.	Assistant Coach/Leader

The NCF works closely with sports governing bodies, local authorities, and higher and further education institutions. Supported by the sports councils, it provides a comprehensive range of services for coaches in all sports. Since 1983 the NCF has provided educational and development opportunities for 115,000 coaches. In 1998, 15,000 coaches and 12,000 school teachers participated in NCF coach education programmes. The webstract below provides an insight into the work of the NCF.

WEBSTRACT

National Coaching Foundation

The National Coaching Foundation (NCF) is proud of helping the UK to win.

The NCF is based in Leeds with regional offices within Sport England's ten Regional Training Units for Sport and the Coaching Units of Northern Ireland, Wales and SportScotland. It has an annual turnover of approximately £3.4 million. Its main sources of funding in 1998/99 were grant aid from UK Sport and Sport England (72.7 per cent), earned income (22.2 per cent) and subscriptions (5.1 per cent).

Our vision:

The National Coaching Foundation will work to improve the quality of coaching in sport in the UK and continue to earn the respect of our sporting communities by enabling the education and continuous development of coaches at all levels.

Our web site:

Visit www.ncf.org.uk for regularly updated information on NCF products, courses, staff, news and views and much more. This is the coaches' web site allowing you to e-mail the NCF, or contact coaches worldwide on our Coaches' Forum – an interactive bulletin board. The NCF wants to hear from you.

Our Motto:

Better coaching ...

Better Sport

ACTIVITY

Coach education programmes

Find out information about the coach education programme for a sport of your choice. You may find it useful to contact the governing body responsible for your chosen sport – most provide information about coaching programmes on their web sites. You can obtain useful links to some governing-body web sites from the NCF or Sport England web sites: www.ncf.org.uk and www.english.sports.gov.uk.

If you can obtain sufficient information, draw a chart that shows the names of the various qualifications and their levels.

Facilities for sport

In Unit 1 (pages 51-5) the main types of indoor and outdoor sports facilities were described. The following list also shows some of the most common types of **sports facilities** that can be found throughout the UK:

- Gymnasiums
- Halls
- Playing pitches
- Swimming pools
- Golf courses
- Health and fitness centres
- Outdoor centres
- Visitor attractions
- Community centres
- Dry ski slopes
- Ice rinks
- Outdoor activity centres
- Sports, recreation and leisure centres
- Sports stadia/grounds
- Watersports centres
- Snooker halls
- Tenpin bowling halls
- Sports clubs
- Sports grounds

Most communities in the UK have access to a range of sports facilities operated by the public, private and voluntary sectors. There are around 3,300 local authority sports centres in the UK, about a quarter of which are solely swimming pools.

Figure 3.5 gives the breakdown between the various types of local authority provision.

The following case study shows the results of research undertaken by Mintel into venues for sports participation. It highlights the fact that the local authority leisure centre is the most popular venue for sport, followed by private clubs and the home.

Figure 3.5: The UK market for local authority leisure centres and swimming pools by type of site, 1998

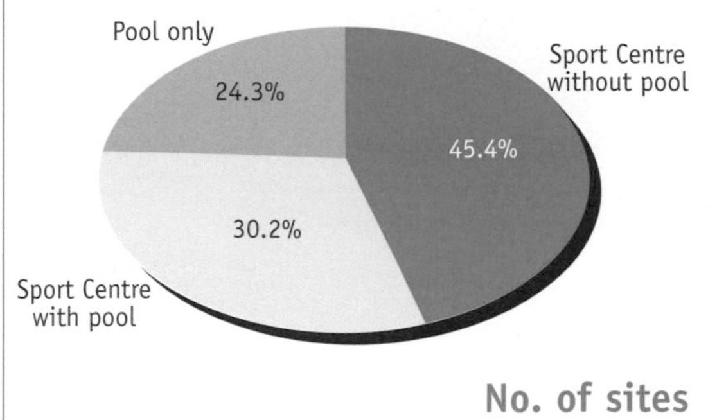

	No. of sites
Sports centre, no pool	**1,483**
Sports centre with pool	**975**
Pool only	**807**
Total	**3,265**

*** Data may not total 100 due to rounding**

Source: *Online Leisure UK Diary & Yearbook*

CASE STUDY

Popular venues for sport

Mintel research into where people go to play sport
The local authority centre is the most popular venue for sport. A half of the sample had used a local authority centre in the year up to March 1998. Nevertheless, a third of respondents had used a private club, while almost a quarter of the sample had taken part in sport within their own home, confirming the increasing trend towards sport for exercise rather than competition. Usage of one type of venue is not exclusive. Even those who have paid to join a private club still use other places for sport, with the significant difference being that they are less likely to use a local authority sports centre.

Where do people go to do sport?
Those respondents who participated in sport regularly were also asked: 'In which of these places have you participated in sport in the last 12 months?' The results are shown in the table opposite.

Activities undertaken at home are likely to be done alone, using such props as exercise bicycles or aerobics videos, and are a long way from the traditional competitive sports. It was evident from the response that sports participants use more than one type of venue.

Location of sports participation, March 1998

Base: 1,126 adults who participate in sport regularly	%
Local authority sports centre	50
Private club	32
Home	24
Local park	23
School/college/university	17
Local authority sports ground	12
Place of employment	8
Elsewhere	31
Don't know	1

Source: BMRB/Mintel

ACTIVITY

Sports facilities

Select a sport and list the facilities available to its participants in an area of your choice. You should consider facilities run by public, private and voluntary organisations. For your chosen sport, identify the most popular venue(s) for participants, and give reasons why you think it is so popular.

Sports development

Sports development is about ensuring that the pathways and structures are in place to enable people to:

- learn basic skills
- participate in sports of their choice
- develop their competence and performance
- reach high levels of excellence.

Sport England has devised a model for sports development, known as the **Sports Development Continuum** (see Figure 3.6). The continuum identifies the pathways for participants as they move through different stages. Foundation level is about ensuring sport is introduced to primary school children in a way that enables them to acquire basic movement skills, in a safe and enjoyable environment. Providing sporting opportunities at the participation level encourages active participation and a healthy lifestyle, combined with highlighting the social benefits of taking part in sport. The performance level represents a more structured involvement in sport, including coaching and competitive opportunities to improve playing standards. The last stage, 'excellence', represents the pinnacle of excellence, where sportsmen and women perform at the highest levels. There are many sports development programmes and initiatives in the UK aimed at developing each of these levels, some of which will be outlined in this section.

This pyramidal model of sports development is widely accepted, although it is also recognised that individual development in sport does not flow smoothly from a broad base at foundation level to a pinnacle of excellence.

Figure 3.6: The Sports Development Continuum

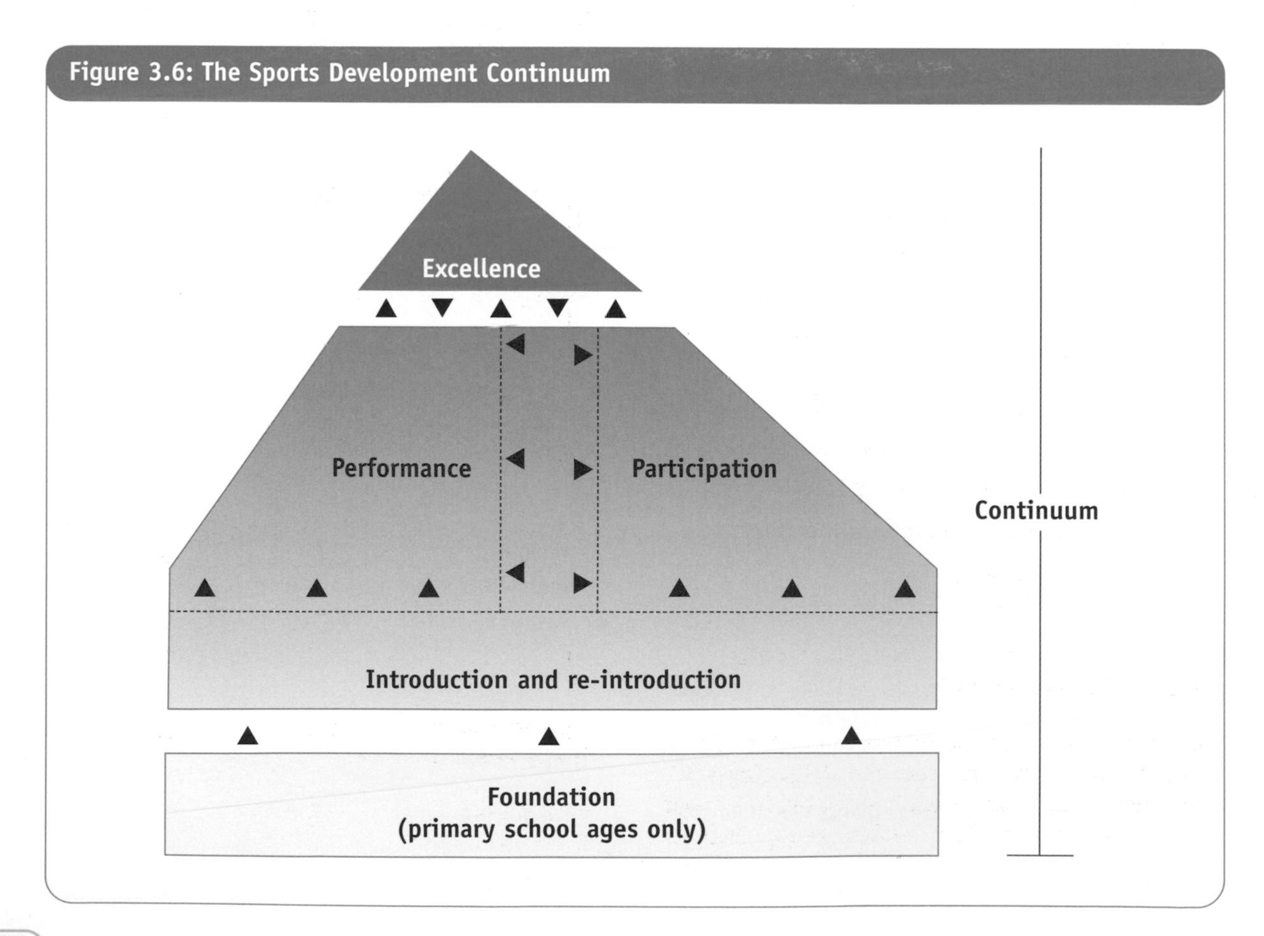

Sports Development Officers

Administrators, coaches, teachers, instructors, parents and other volunteers all contribute crucially to the development of sport in Britain, from basic learning and enjoyment to international excellence. The emergence of people with specific responsibility for enabling individuals and organisations to take part in sport started with the Central Council for Physical Recreation in the late 1930s. This was continued with the Sports Council's programmes to appoint National Development Officers to some governing bodies, often with grant aid, from the 1960s onwards. Their local counterparts developed as sport leaders. Teams were supported through the Action Sport programme, by the Sports Council's National Demonstration Projects and through projects supported by regional grants. By 1988–9 the Sports Council was grant-aiding some 180 Sports Development Office (SDO) posts in local authorities and 40 with governing bodies and national voluntary organisations with sports interests. It was also supporting training and professional-experience workshops in every one of its ten regions.

With the passage of time and in response to major national strategies for sport, such as Sport in the Community: The Next 10 Years (1982), Into the 90s (1987), and Coaching Matters (1991), the following specialisms in sports development have arisen:

- Generalist SDOs: serving a wide area, a number of sports and several target groups.
- Community SDOs: serving local communities/housing estates.
- Target group SDOs: serving young people, or other specific groups such as the unemployed, ethnic minorities and women.
- Sport-specific development officers.
- Officers seeking to extend access to sites or facilities, sometimes community use of schools.
- Officers seeking to promote health and fitness.
- Officers managing sports development and working on strategies.
- Officers working in other ways, e.g. through organising special events.

The different forms of sports development involve a wide range of day-to-day tasks and skills. Figure 3.7 shows those tasks which were highlighted in a major survey of the work of SDOs, undertaken by Michael Collins at the Institute of Sport and Recreation Planning and Management, Loughborough University, in 1995.

Figure 3.7: Tasks and skills in local sports development

Task or skill	% chosen	% ranked as 1st most important task
Creating networks	84	28
Marketing and publicity	74	8
Working with target groups	74	30
Finding/training coaches, leaders	73	10
Advice and research	68	10
Developing sports policy and strategy	67	17
Finding new facilities	66	3
Collecting/collating information	66	5
Monitoring, evaluation	66	4
Controlling sports development budget	65	2
Opening up school, other facilities	64	6
Working with specific sports	60	17
Sponsorship, fundraising	54	2
Supervising sports development staff	49	2
Training sports development staff	38	1

Sports development programmes

The following lists show a selection of previous and current well-known sports development programmes in the UK. The webstract then briefly describes one current sports development programme.

Previous initiatives include:

- **Sport for All (1972–7)**
- **Sport for All 'Disabled People' (1980–1)**
- **50+ All to Play For (1983–4)**
- **Ever Thought of Sport? 'Young People' (1985–6)**
- **What's Your Sport? (1987–8)**
- **Year of Sport (1991)**

Current initiatives include:

- **National Junior Sports Programme, including BT TOP Play and BT TOP Sport**
- **Sportsmark**
- **Challenge Funding**
- **Coaching for Teachers**
- **More People: Active Schools**
- **More People: Active Communities**
- **More People: Active Sports**
- **More Medals: World Class Programme**

ACTIVITY

Sports development programmes

Find out about a local or national sports development programme and answer the following questions:

- Who is the programme aimed at?
- What sports are included in the programme?
- What organisation(s) run it and what are their objectives?
- How is the programme funded?

More people: Active Schools and Active Communities

Active Schools and Active Communities contribute to the Sports Development Continuum by introducing more young people to sport. Active Schools is designed to offer schools and teachers the training and resources required to give pupils the best possible physical education. BT TOP Play and BT TOP Sport were launched in 1996 and are an integral part of the National Junior Sport Programme, which has been developed in conjunction with the Youth Sport Trust. TOP Play is aimed at those teaching core physical skills and generic sports to children aged 4–9 years old. BT TOP Sport is targeted at teachers introducing sport-specific activities to children aged 7–11 years old. Both programmes provide equipment, activity resources and training.

In addition, Active Schools incorporates a number of other initiatives. Sportsmark and Sportsmark Gold are quality awards that can be attained by those schools offering the very best in physical education provision. Coaching for Teachers offers primary and secondary school teachers the opportunity to improve their skills by gaining recognised governing body coaching qualifications. And finally, Sporting Ambassadors is a programme that introduces young people to some of the country's most successful sports stars.

Active Communities looks at the contribution that local communities can make towards sports participation. This programme contains a number of elements such as training opportunities for community sports leaders to deliver the community version of TOP Play and TOP Sport in a variety of community locations, and the employment of more Sports Development Officers.

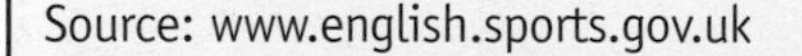

Source: www.english.sports.gov.uk

Sports tourism

Sports tourism is now more popular and economically important than ever before, due to the following factors:

- A greater desire to travel, coupled with rising disposable incomes.
- Lower air fares and easier travel, especially long-haul flights.
- Greater interest in a growing number of sports.
- More information on and awareness of international sports fixtures, especially via the internet and global sports broadcasts.
- The growing popularity of short-break, activity and special-interest holidays.
- Improved marketing by the sports and tourism industries.

There are many sporting events in the UK that attract large numbers of spectators, both from abroad and within the UK. For example, the three-day Cheltenham horse racing festival in March attracts over 60,000 spectators each day, with many of these travelling from Ireland.

▼ The Cheltenham festival attracts thousands of tourists to the area

The British Tourist Authority (BTA) has recognised the huge potential for sports tourism by launching a sports tourism initiative in the year 2000. This involves working in partnership with the Department of Culture, Media and Sport, UK Sport and other sports bodies, sport sponsors, and travel and tourism organisations. The partnership will integrate, strengthen and capitalise on Britain's many top-quality sporting attractions. In developing its Sport Tourism Strategy, the BTA aims to maximise the potential of sport for inbound tourism to Britain. It has identified five strategic objectives:

- To position sports as an integral part of the British tourism product alongside heritage, culture, lifestyle and the countryside.
- To raise awareness within the sports industry of the economic benefit and potential of foreign visitors.
- To contribute to the winning of major international sporting events.
- To position the BTA as the leading agency of an integrated approach to the development of sports tourism.
- To complement the sports strategies of the Department of Culture, Media and Sport, the Scottish Parliament and the Welsh Assembly.

The case study on page 158 highlights key aspects of the BTA initiative.

CASE STUDY

A sporting chance for Britain

A sporting chance for Britain

Visitors come to Britain for sport. And they come in their millions – to watch, to play, to visit famous sporting venues and to enjoy a wide variety of leisure and recreational activities.

A sporting destination: what does Britain offer?

Few countries can offer as many top-quality, top-name sports as Britain. World-famous sporting events include the FA Cup Final, the British Grand Prix, the Grand National and Wimbledon. There's also Six Nations Rugby, the Derby, the British Open Golf, test and county cricket and Premiership football – to name a few. Having hosted the Cricket World Cup and Rugby World Cup in 1999, and with the new National Stadium planned at Wembley, Britain has the world-class facilities and long-held expertise to host and bid for other prestigious sporting events, assisted by the Lottery Sports Funded World Class Events Programme. Confirmed events include the Rugby League World Cup 2000, the UCI World Track Cycling Championship 2000 and the XVII Commonwealth Games 2002, with bids underway for the IAAF World Athletics Championship and the FIFA World Cup in 2006.

Britain's sport tourism trails include famous venues such as Wembley, Old Trafford, The Oval, Lord's, Headingley, Murrayfield, Twickenham, St Andrew's, Ascot and Wimbledon. The new Millennium Stadium in Cardiff, Hampden's Field of Dreams, Belfast's Odyssey and other impressive sports facilities are part of Britain's £5 billion millennium programmes – the biggest of its kind in the world

From the London Marathon to sports summer schools, there's plenty of scope to participate in leisure, recreational and adventure sports, including golf, fishing, horse riding, gliding and canoeing. Visitors can soar above the Chiltern Hills, climb in Snowdonia National Park, walk the West Highland Way, explore the new national cycle network. ... and enjoy and indulge in as much fast-paced or slow-paced sport as they like. Great sports-themed activities include sports museums and sports-appreciation halls of fame, together with sports exhibitions, festivals, congresses, conferences, attractions and themed restaurants.

So what next?

By working together, we can stay several steps ahead of the competition. Sports tourism in Britain has a tremendous future – but only if we seize the opportunity. So let's make it happen together. There's strength in numbers and the race – with very strong international competition – has already started. We need to ensure that Britain stays ahead of the game.

Source: BTA leaflet *Sporting Chance for Britain*

ACTIVITY

Sports tourism

Find out information about sports or sporting events in the UK that you think attract foreign tourists. For each event/sport, identify the main benefits of 'sports tourists' to the sport/event and to the economy of the area in which it takes place.

Professional sport

Throughout the country, thousands of people take part in sport as amateurs. At the same time, there is a small group of **professional sportsmen and women** who earn their living by playing sport. Those who achieve the standard of excellence needed to become professional sportsmen and women are relatively few in number, and they face intense competition in the struggle to reach the very top.

Overall, there are around 415,000 people employed in the sports industry, but less than 5 per cent of them are professional players.

Source: Working in Sport and Fitness, COIC/DfEE

In between these two extremes are many people who obtain help in playing sport or receive rewards for playing sport. This group includes part-time professionals, who are paid for playing but still earn a living outside sport.

ACTIVITY

Wealthiest sportsmen in the UK

Figure 3.8 relates to the wealth of the UK's top ten sporting celebrities in 1998, but is presented in no particular order

1 Rearrange the names on the list by placing them in order of wealth, from first to tenth.
2 Estimate the value of each person's wealth in 1998.
3 Who do you think would be in the current list of the ten wealthiest UK sports celebrities?
4 Why do you think the list is continually changing?
5 Why do you think there are no women on the list?

Answers to questions 1 and 2 are provided on page 461.

Professionals are paid to compete in sport. The more successful they are, the more money they earn. They usually train full time and devote themselves to their sport. They sign contracts and must take part in competitions. There are a limited number of sports in Britain where professional players can earn a living. Most of these are male dominated. Only in tennis, golf and athletics do women professionals have a high profile, and even in these sports their rewards for success are much less than for men. Figure 3.8 shows the ten wealthiest sportspeople in the UK in 1998. They are all male, and the list is dominated by high-profile sports that attract mass-media coverage and huge sponsorship, such as football, golf and motor racing. The relationship between sport and the mass media is covered in detail later in this unit (see page 194). Sports that have a high media profile and are attractive to both spectators and sponsors are the ones that tend to have 'professional sportspeople':

- football
- horse racing
- motor racing
- tennis
- golf
- rugby league and rugby union
- athletics
- snooker
- boxing
- cricket
- cycling
- basketball
- ice hockey

Figure 3.8: Wealthiest sportsmen in the UK

Name	Sport	Worth 1998 (£ m)
Nigel Mansell	Motor racing	
Paul Gascoigne	Football	
Colin Montgomerie	Golf	
Damon Hill	Motor racing	
Linford Christie	Athletics	
Nick Faldo	Golf	
Lennox Lewis	Boxing	
Naseem Hammed	Boxing	
Ian Woosnam	Golf	
Alan Shearer	Football	

Sports-related gambling

Gross expenditure in the UK on all forms of gambling, including the National Lottery, is estimated at approximately £40 billion a year. The main markets for gambling in the UK are:

- National Lottery
- Casinos
- Bingo
- Football pools
- Sports races, matches and events
- Gaming machines

In this section we will only investigate **sports-related gambling**.

Figure 3.9: Off-course sports gambling, by type of sport

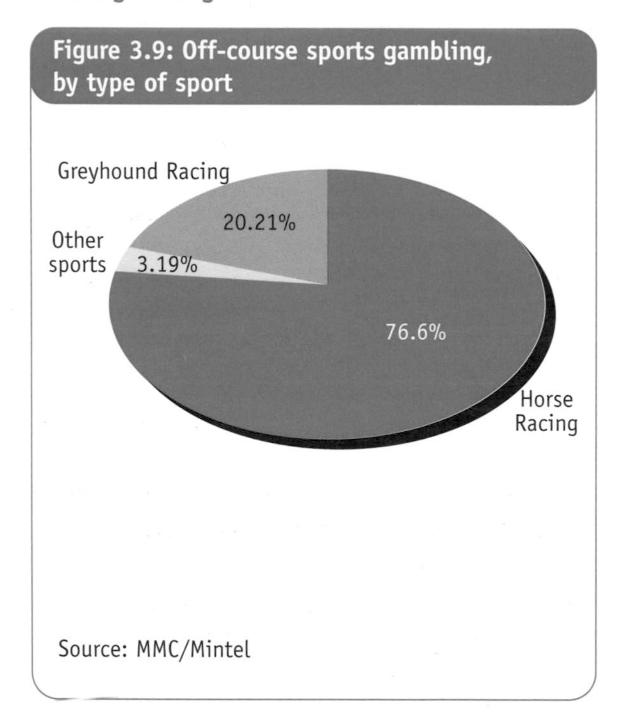

Source: MMC/Mintel

Sports betting

The sports gambling/betting market in the UK developed out of the passion for horse racing, one of the earliest popular sports in the UK. It could be argued that horse racing was one of the first leisure mass markets to attract support from all strata of society. The 'Sport of Kings' attracted interest from all levels of eighteenth- and nineteenth-century society. The aristocracy competed for prize money and the social prestige that came from owning a champion thoroughbred, and the working classes used it as an excuse for enjoyment. Horse racing is still very important: in 1998 it accounted for 72 per cent of total sports bets placed in the UK. Although this share has been declining in recent years (whereas gambling on football matches has increased), the sport of horse racing and the bookmaking industry are still strongly interdependent. Figure 3.9 shows the proportion of money staked by type of sport in 1998.

Bets may be placed with on-course bookmakers at racecourses and greyhound tracks, or off-course through around 9,000 licensed betting offices in the UK. In addition, telephone and internet betting has grown steadily. Figure 3.10 shows that in terms of turnover, five major operators have a combined market share of 68 per cent, with all of the independents (the 'others' column) accounting for a total of 32 per cent. In terms of branches, the 'Big Five' are less dominant, indicating that on a per branch basis their outlets are bigger and hence more profitable. Mintel estimates that in 1998 a further £700 million was spent on sports gambling on the course.

Figure 3.10: Market shares in off-course sports betting at licensed bookmakers, 1997/8

	No. of outlets	Share %	Turnover (£m)	%	Average turnover per outlet (£)
Ladbroke	1,904	21	1,577	26	828,256
William Hill	1,515	17	1,360	22	897,690
Coral	833	9	765	12	918,367
Stanley	475	5	380	6	800,000
Tote	214	2	130	2	607,477
Others	4,042	45	1,978	32	489,362
Total	**8,983**	**100**	**6,190**	**100**	**689,079**

Source: MMC/Mintel

Betting on soccer has been the most dynamic growth area for bookmakers in recent years, with events such as the World Cup and European Championships now regarded as major betting events. However, Figure 3.11 shows that the amount staked on the football pools has declined since 1995 due to the introduction of the National Lottery. There are now just three pools companies left in existence: Littlewoods, Vernons (currently owned by Ladbrokes) and Zetters.

Figure 3.11: Football pools: stakes and winnings, 1990/1 -1997/8

	Total stakes £ m	Index	Total winnings £ m	Index	Winnings as a % of stake
1990/1	772.5	94	214.8	100	27.8
1994/5	823.0	100	215.2	100	26.2
1995/6	555.9	68	128.5	60	23.1
1996/7	427.5	52	112.6	52	26.3
1997/8	319.4	39	81.2	38	25.4

'Years' relate to football seasons, i.e. 1 August–31 July

Source: PPA/Mintel

Sports medicine

As people have become more aware of the health benefits associated with participation in active sports, the demand for **sports medicine** services and products to 'maintain' levels of fitness and performance has grown. In addition, sportsmen and women operating at the higher levels have realised the need for effective (and safe) sports medicine in order to compete. Higher-level performers in particular can now be helped by specialist sports physiotherapists, sports injury and rehabilitation clinics, sports psychologists and sports dieticians.

The National Sports Medicine Institute (NSMI), funded by UK Sport and Sport England, is responsible for the co-ordination of sports medicine services. Based at the medical college of St Bartholomew's Hospital, London, its facilities include a physiology laboratory, library and information centre.

In Scotland a network of 26 accredited sports medicine centres provides specialist help with sports injuries. Wales has 11 sports medicine centres, accredited by the NSMI, which are linked closely with the UK Sports Institute network in Wales. The Northern Ireland Sports Medicine Centres is a partnership between the Sports Council for Northern Ireland and a local healthcare trust.

Other groups involved in sports medicine include the following:

- Association of Chartered Physiotherapists in Sports Medicine (ACPSM). A group of chartered physiotherapists with a specialist interest and/or qualification in sports medicine.
- British Association of Sport and Exercise Sciences (BASES). A representative body of nearly 2,000 people working in the field of sports science.
- British Association of Sports Medicine (BASM). A medical body which promotes education in sports medicine.
- British Chiropractic Sports Council (BCSC). The BCSC represents chiropractors with a specialist interest in sports medicine.
- British Orthopaedic Sports Trauma Association (BOSTA). A medical body of orthopaedic and surgical specialists which hosts a number of meetings throughout the UK.
- Osteopathic Sports Care Association (OSCA). The representative body for osteopaths with a specialist interest in sports medicine.
- Society of Sports Therapists. A professional body for sports therapists, which also provides validated educational qualifications.
- Academy of Sports Therapy. The AST offers specialized training courses in sports therapy along with seminars accredited by Middlesex University.

Drug misuse

Drug misuse has become an important issue in today's sport. Although the use of illegal performance-enhancing substances by athletes appears to be quite low, there have been some high-profile cases that have tarnished the reputation of the sports concerned. Perhaps the most famous incident was the disqualification of the Olympic 100 metres champion, Ben Johnson, following a positive drugs test.

In this country, UK Sport is the body responsible for preventing doping and it has a commitment to drug-free sport and ethical sporting practices. It co-ordinates a drugs testing programme and conducts a comprehensive education programme aimed at changing attitudes to drug misuse.

In 1998–9, the drugs testing programme involved nearly 60 national governing bodies and 22 international sporting federations from 38 sports. A total of 5,147 tests were conducted - 3,141 in competition and 2,006 out of competition - and 98.5 per cent were negative. UK Sport provides a Drug Information Line to allow athletes to check whether a licensed medication is permitted or banned under their governing body's regulations, and issues a comprehensive guide on drugs and sport competitors and officials. The UK is at the forefront of work to establish a new international anti-doping agency.

Health and fitness

Health and fitness is a term covering a variety of activities, such as exercise to music, aqua exercise, weight training and circuit training. Exercise England is the national governing body in England for exercise and fitness, and aims to promote a positive approach to sport and health. The Keep Fit Association (KFA), which has 1,500 teachers and a membership of 12,000, promotes fitness through movement, exercise and dance for people of all ages.

General Practitioners (GPs) also have a vested interest in promoting health and fitness to their patients, which is why many GPs are now involved in GP referral schemes, whereby they recommend a particular health and fitness programme as part of a patient's prescription.

ACTIVITY

Drug misuse in sport

Select a high-profile sport, such as football, cricket, tennis, swimming or athletics, and find out information about the governing body's policy and procedures on drug misuse by sportsmen and women.

If you can, find examples of athletes that have been caught out taking illegal substances to enhance performance. What happened to them as a result, and what impact do you think it has had on the sport?

Health and fitness clubs

Since the 1980s, health and fitness has become an important sector of the sports industry. Mintel estimates that there are just over 2.4 million members of private health and fitness clubs in the UK, representing 5.1 per cent of the adult population. These club members spend an average of £514 per year. Figure 3.12 shows that membership of private health and fitness clubs in the UK has increased by 49 per cent in just five years between 1994 and 1999. The growth in this sector is even more impressive if one considers that these figures do not include membership at publicly owned facilities such as sports centres and swimming pools, or casual usage of health and fitness clubs by non-members.

Facilities in health and fitness clubs

Figure 3.13 shows the most common facilities offered by health and fitness clubs. Not surprisingly, the most common facility found in health and fitness clubs is a fitness room. Sky/cable/satellite television is also found in almost 85 per cent of sites, reflecting the fact that it is often used to relieve the tedium of exercise. Aerobics/fitness studios, one of the most popular facilities for women to use in a health club, are found in almost 84 per cent of clubs. A sauna is the most popular of the 'passive' facilities (more than eight out of ten clubs have one), and a similar proportion of clubs have air conditioning. Over three quarters of clubs now feature a café/bar, a growing area for some clubs and viewed as a necessity even if it does not always produce a profit. A solarium is the most popular beauty-orientated facility, while over two thirds of clubs offer some form of physiotherapy/massage treatment. Slightly more than half the clubs have a crèche, as a significant proportion of their members have children.

Figure 3.12: Key health and fitness club member statistics, 1994-9

(million)	Members	Index	Members as % of adult pop.	Av. spend per member (£)	Index
1994	1.64	100	3.5	423	100
1995	1.70	104	3.6	452	107
1996	1.81	110	3.8	472	112
1997	1.98	121	4.2	481	114
1998	2.16	132	4.5	502	119
1999	2.44	149	5.1	514	122

Source: Mintel

Figure 3.13: Facilities offered by health and fitness clubs, November 1999

	%
Fitness room	99.4
Sky/cable/satellite TV	84.6
Aerobics/fitness studio	83.7
Free weights	82.8
Sauna	81.2
Air conditioning	80.6
Café/bar	76.8
Solaria	75.2
Physiotherapy/massage	66.8
Adult swimming pool	61.8
Steam room	60.8
Beauty salon	60.2
Crèche	50.8
Spa pool/whirlpool	50.5
'Pro' shop selling clothing, etc.	42.0
Squash courts	36.7
Children's play area	32.0
Children's swimming pool	25.4
Outdoor tennis courts	23.8
Restaurant	19.4
Women-only gym	16.0
Beginners' gym	11.0
Indoor tennis courts	9.7
Children's gym	6.3
Nursery	3.8
Don't know/not stated	0.3

Base: 319 clubs

Source: FIA/Mintel, Health Clubs Survey

Income generation

Membership revenue, whether from monthly, annual or joining fees, represents the vast majority of the turnover of the average health and fitness club. The largest proportion of this is in the form of membership fees, which are usually paid either monthly or annually and are estimated to have represented 71 per cent of the total in 1999, as Figure 3.14 demonstrates.

Other revenue has shown the strongest growth of all, with an increasing number of clubs deriving more revenue from activities such as health and beauty treatments, as well as the café/bar/restaurant area.

▲ In the fitness room

Figure 3.14: The UK market for health and fitness clubs in 1994 and 1999

	1994 £ m	%	1999 (estimated) £ m	%	% change 1994–9
Membership admission fees	513	74	888	71	+73.2
Joining fees	**62**	**9**	**116**	**9**	**+88.4**
Other revenue (e.g.beauty, sunbeds, bar, shop, etc.)	118	17	250	20	+126.9
Total	**692**	**100**	**1,254**	**100**	**+83.7**
Totals may not equal 100 due to rounding					

Source: Mintel

CASE STUDY

David Lloyd clubs

As of 1 December 1999, there were 39 David Lloyd sites, excluding the newly acquired Racquets & Healthtrack outlets, with a total of 124,800 members. The company is continuing to follow a rapid development programme in order to maintain its prominent position in the market-place.

Facilities at David Lloyd clubs typically include tennis courts, a swimming pool, dance studios, a gym, café-bar/restaurant area, nursery and crèche. The most popular of these are the tennis facilities, the gym and the swimming pool. The average club has a membership of around 3,900, with membership fees representing around 70 per cent of total club turnover.

The social side of being a David Lloyd member is given great emphasis and viewed by the company as almost as important as using the facilities. Consequently, the bar/restaurant is regarded as a focal point of the club. On average, the social side, including the bar/restaurant, accounts for around 20 per cent of club revenues. A typical site will incorporate a 40–50 seater restaurant, a bar, a coffee area, large lounge with television screen and an adjacent children's play area.

Source: David Lloyd Leisure/Mintel

Outdoor and adventure activities

The market for outdoor activities in the countryside was covered in Unit 1 (see page 00). The broad range of **outdoor and adventure activities** in the countryside can be split into three main categories:

Outdoor activities or pursuits do not just take place in remote rural areas. Some activities take place in urban venues such as climbing walls and dry ski slopes.

Land-based activities such as:

- Walking
- Rambling
- Climbing
- Mountain biking
- Orienteering
- Pony trekking
- Shooting
- Cycling

Water-based activities such as:

- Water skiing
- Canoeing
- Kayaking
- Power boating
- Sailing
- Scuba diving

Air-based activities such as:

- Ballooning
- Hang gliding
- Gliding

▲ Walking in Scotland is a popular activity

BUILD YOUR LEARNING

Keywords and phrases

You should know the meaning of the words and phrases listed below. If you are unsure about any of them, go back through the last 20 pages to refresh your understanding.

- **Sport**
- **Sports goods**
- **Leisurewear products**
- **Performance products**
- **Sports clothing**
- **Sports footwear**
- **Sports equipment**
- **Sports retailing**
- **Sports coaching**
- **Brand names**
- **Sports facilities**
- **Sports development**
- **Sports Development Continuum**
- **Sports tourism**
- **Professional sportsmen/women**
- **Sports-related gambling/betting**
- **Sports medicine**
- **Drug misuse**
- **Health and fitness**
- **Outdoor and adventure activities**

End of section activity

Undertake some research about a popular sport that interests you and write a short article suitable for a magazine or newspaper that covers the following areas:

- Sports goods and suppliers for participants in the sport.
- The governing body's coaching framework/programmes.
- Examples of well-known facilities where the sport is played.
- Examples of sports development initiatives.
- Examples of major events, competitions and matches that attract tourists.
- Details of people involved on a professional basis (i.e. players, coaches, managers, agents).
- Details of any licensed gambling related to the sport.
- Impact of sports medicine on the sport.
- Details of any health and fitness benefits associated with taking part in the sport.

The scale of sport, its contribution to the UK economy and key trends

A large proportion of the UK population takes part in or watches sport; this, in turn, generates considerable economic activity. This section illustrates the scale of sport, its contribution to the UK economy and how the industry is influenced by trends and changing fashions. We will investigate:

- The economic contribution that sport makes in terms of consumer spending by the UK population.
- The number of people working in sport (paid and voluntary).
- The number of people who participate in sport.
- Trends in sport.

Consumer spending

According to the Leisure Industries Research Centre (LIRC), overall **consumer expenditure on sport** grew by 30 per cent between 1985 and 1995 (see Figure 3.15),with the strongest growth in subscription charges and fees for participation sports, and expenditure on sports clothing and footwear. These three items all doubled in volume over the period. Overall growth in consumer expenditure on sport was greater than growth in total consumer expenditure, so that sport accounted for a higher share of total consumer expenditure in 1995 than it did in 1985 (2.33 per cent in 1995 compared to 2.01 per cent in 1985).

These figures, however, may underestimate the real economic significance of sport, for they do not take into account the economic importance of sports events, sports tourism and the voluntary sector in sport. Consumer expenditure statistics do not reflect expenditure on sports events, particularly when those events generate an international audience.

For instance, Euro '96 attracted 280,000 visiting foreign spectators and media to the UK. These visitors spent around £120 million in the eight host cities and surrounding regions, yet none of this is included in conventional estimates of the economic value of sport.

Figure 3.15: Increase in consumer expediture on selected sport-related goods and services (constant prices) 1985-1995

	1985 (£ m)	1995 (£ m)	% increase 1985–1995
Participant sports			
Subscription and fees	627.82	1,348.63	115
Clothing sales	459.83	943.66	105
Footwear sales	306.55	629.11	105
Travel	290.47	317.85	9
Gambling			
Football pools	375.91	424.74	13
Horse racing	1,267,72	1,542.09	22
Other consumer expenditure on sport			
	2,027.25	1,776.84	-13
Total	**5,365.56**	**6,982.93**	**30**

Source: LIRC

Latest research by LIRC indicates that sport's economic significance to the UK economy is increasing, as reported in the following press article. In the future the biggest single change to the economic importance of sport is likely to be the rise in the sale of television rights for sports events. Many deals have already been completed (such as £670 million from BSkyB for Premier League football matches for the period 1997–2001), so we already know there will be substantial increases in the revenues of professional sports clubs. It is estimated that the arrival of digital television could add another £2.5 billion a year. There can be little doubt that sport is now big business, and it looks like it will become even bigger in the future.

Sport worth £11 billion thanks to couch potatoes

British consumers now spend almost twice as much a year on sport as they do going on holiday within this country. But the news does not necessarily indicate a healthier society: armchair followers are to thank for the rise in spending, and the biggest area of increased expenditure is pay-television subscriptions.

The analysis was carried out for Sport England, formerly the Sports Council, and details for England alone show an annual spend of over £11 billion, an increase of over 17 per cent since 1995. It also reveals an increase in employment in sport of more than 20,000 over the same period. The study was undertaken by the Leisure Industry Research Centre at Sheffield University, which found increased spending reflected in all areas of sport except football pools, where income has dropped 40 per cent due to competition from the National Lottery.

The biggest rises were seen in television rental, and cable and satellite subscriptions related to sport, which went up almost 100 per cent – reflecting the increasing share of the television sports market taken by BSkyB.

'Sport is very sexy at the moment. It's sexy in terms of being cool and in terms of the whole growth in health and fitness activity,' said Professor Chris Gratton, who heads the Sheffield department. He used the example of football, which in the past ten years has been transformed from an industry in long-term decline to a business with a tremendous image and global impact. But even in the area of participation sports he sees a 'radical change' over this period. 'Sport has gone from something driven by government grants and voluntary effort into a major industry,' he said.

Spending on equipment and services is double what it was 15 to 20 years ago. While participation in team sports such as football and rugby is static, the growth has been in relatively high-cost areas like gym membership and clothing. The study shows that spending on sports clothing rose by more than 18 per cent to £1.4 million, while subscriptions and fees over the 1995–8 period rose by 21 per cent to nearly £2.1 million.

Trevor Brooking, CBE, chairman of Sport England, said: 'More people are joining clubs, which suggests that we're getting more people into sport. The value of sport to the individual, the community and the country continues to grow.'

Source: Independent, February 2000

Employment in sport

There is a wide range of jobs available in the sports industry throughout the public, private and voluntary sectors. According to LIRC, **employment in sport** was 415,000 in 1995, compared to 324,470 in 1985. It accounted for 1.61 per cent of total employment in the UK in 1995, compared to 1.52 per cent of total employment in 1985.

The economic significance of sport is further increased if we consider the **value of voluntary work** in the sports industry. Only the market activities of the voluntary sector are included in statistics on consumer spending and employment, with no allowance for the potential value of volunteer labour. This time has been estimated to be worth just over £1.5 billion, which alone would contribute a further 15 per cent to the economic resources associated with sport (see Figure 3.16). Of the many different types of organisation providing volunteers for sport, it is clearly sports clubs and governing bodies that are the bedrock of voluntary inputs and value. They provide over 90 per cent of the total estimated hours and value.

Figure 3.17 shows the value of volunteer labour in the top ten sports. Given that bowls is predominantly a game played by older people, it's not surprising to see this top of the list, as a high proportion of its players are retired with time to devote to voluntary work.

Figure 3.16: The value of volunteers in UK sport

Types of sports volunteer	Number of volunteer hours per year	Value of volunteer hours at £8.31 per hour (£m)
Governing bodies and sports clubs in 93 sports	169,554,902	1,409.0
14 international events in UK	277,680	2.3
Sport for people with disabilities	3,162,744	26.3
Schools	2,576,972	21.4
Youth organisations	11,617,709	96.5
Totals	**187,190,007**	**1,555,5**

Source: LIRC, *Valuing Volunteers in UK Sport*

Figure 3.17: Top ten sports in terms of the value of volunteer labour

Sport	UK total volunteers	Number of volunteer hours per year	Value at £8.31 per hour (£m)
Bowls	223,863	33,130,704	275.5
Football	235,477	27,450,306	228.1
Cricket	98,549	15,356,640	127.6
Hockey	33,769	7,826,488	65.0
Rugby union	72,138	7,314,142	60.8
Golf	36,621	4,911,314	40.8
Tennis	51,051	4,267,387	35.4
Angling	21,429	4,246,080	35.2
Athletics	22,774	3,797,472	31.5
Squash	23,105	2,897,755	24.1

Source: LIRC, *Valuing Volunteers in UK Sport*

Participation in sport and physical activities

It is impossible to provide participation data for every sport and physical recreation activity: the list would be enormous! The main source of information about **participation rates in sport and physical activities** is the General Household Survey (GHS) carried out by the Office for National Statistics. Figure 3.18 opposite was taken from the 1996 GHS. It shows that in 1996, 81.4 per cent of adults in Britain took part in at least one sport or physical activity during the 12 months leading up to the survey.

Looking at more regular participation, 63.6 per cent of adults had participated in some form of sport or physical activity during the four weeks before interview. Men were more likely to have participated in a sport or physical activity than women, with 70.9 per cent of men and 57.5 per cent of women having taken part in at least one activity in the four weeks prior to interview. The most popular activity for both men and women was walking, defined as a walk or hike of two miles or more, in which over two-thirds of adults (68.2 per cent) had participated in the past 12 months.

Membership of sports clubs

Sports club membership statistics are another useful indicator of sports participation. It is estimated that there are 150,000 sports clubs covering a range of sporting and recreational activities.

The top ten sports in terms of club membership in 1995 are listed in Figure 3.19.

ACTIVITY

Sports participation

Using the data from the GHS survey in Figure 3.18, complete the following tasks:

1 List the top five sports/activities (excluding walking) for the following categories:

- men in the four weeks prior to interview;
- women in the four weeks prior to interview;
- men and women in the four weeks prior to interview;
- men and women in the twelve months prior to interview.

2 Suggest reasons for the popularity of sports in each category, and differences in the popularity of activities between males and females. Why do you think it is that individual activities dominate each of your lists?

3 List the top five team sports for the following categories:

- men in the four weeks prior to interview;
- women in the four weeks prior to interview.

4 Suggest reasons for any differences in the popularity of team sports between males and females.

5 This research was undertaken in 1996. Suggest five activities from the list that you think will have since changed in popularity (increased or decreased) and give reasons for your selections.

Figure 3.19: Sports club membership and number of clubs

Sport	Members	Number of clubs
1 Football	1,650,000	46,150
2 Billiards/snooker	1,500,000	4,500
3 Golf	1,217,000	6,650
4 Squash	465,000	1,600
5 Bowls	435,000	11,000
6 Sailing	450,000	1,650
7 Angling	392,000	1,750
8 Rugby union	284,000	3,250
9 Lawn tennis	275,000	2,800
10 Swimming	288,000	1,950

Source: Individual sports organisations; Keynote, *UK Sports Market; 1996 Market Review*

Figure 3.18: Participation in sport in Great Britain, 1996

	Male and female – previous 4 weeks %	Male - previous 4 weeks %	Female – previous 4 weeks %	Male and female - previous 12 months %
At least one activity	63.6	71	58	81.4
Walking	44.5	49.0	40.8	68.2
Any swimming	14.8	12.7	16.5	39.6
Swimming: indoor	12.8	10.6	14.6	35.1
Swimming: outdoor	2.9	3.0	2.9	14.9
Keep fit/yoga	12.3	6.8	16.9	20.7
Snooker/pool/billiards	11.3	19.6	4.3	19.2
Cycling	11.0	14.8	7.8	21.4
Weight training	5.6	8.7	2.9	9.8
Any soccer	4.8	10.0	0.4	8.5
Soccer: outdoor	3.8	7.8	0.3	6.9
Soccer: indoor	2.1	4.5	0.1	4.8
Golf	4.7	8.3	1.6	11.0
Running (jogging, etc.)	4.5	7.2	2.3	8.0
Darts*	–	–	–	8.6
Tenpin bowling/skittles	3.4	3.9	2.9	15.5
Badminton	2.4	2.8	2.0	7.0
Tennis	2.0	2.4	1.7	7.1
Any bowls	1.9	2.5	1.3	4.6
Carpet bowls	1.1	1.4	0.9	3.0
Lawn bowls	0.9	1.3	0.5	2.8
Fishing	1.7	3.4	0.3	5.3
Table tennis	1.5	2.3	0.9	5.3
Squash	1.3	2.2	0.5	4.1
Weight lifting	1.3	2.1	0.6	2.6
Horse riding	1.0	0.4	1.5	3.0
Cricket	0.9	1.7	0.1	3.3
Shooting	0.8	1.6	0.1	2.8
Self-defence	0.7	1.2	0.3	1.7
Climbing	0.7	1.1	0.3	2.5
Basketball	0.7	1.2	0.2	2.0
Rugby	0.6	1.2	0.0	1.3
Ice skating	0.6	0.4	0.7	3.2
Netball	0.5	0.1	0.8	1.4
Sailing	0.4	0.6	0.2	2.3
Motor sports	0.4	0.8	0.1	1.6
Canoeing	0.4	0.5	0.3	1.6
Hockey	0.3	0.4	0.3	1.1
Skiing	0.3	0.5	0.2	2.6
Athletics (track and field)	0.2	0.3	0.1	1.2
Gymnastics	0.2	0.2	0.1	0.7
Windsurfing	0.2	0.3	0.1	1.1

* In 1996 respondents were asked about darts only in relation to the last 12 months and not the last 4 weeks.

All persons aged 16+

Source: General Household Survey, *Participation in Sport in Great Britain, 1996*

Social benefits of sport

In addition to the direct and indirect economic effects of sport, as captured in national income statistics and employment data, there are some important **social benefits** resulting from participation in sports:

- improvements in health and fitness;
- reductions in anti-social behaviour;
- positive contribution to the quality of life;
- inward investment attracted to the local and regional economy as a result of investment in sports infrastructure.

Sport offers the opportunity to millions of adults to maintain and improve their health and foster camaraderie. Every week across Britain hundreds of thousands of people go out to support, or play for, their local side. Every town, every village, every school draws some part of its spirit and identity from the performance of its sporting teams and individuals.

Sport also provides a ladder of fulfilment and success to youngsters. It offers positive role models. It provides a context of discipline, self-awareness and self-satisfaction to many who might be tempted to selfishness or even petty crime. For every individual it offers the experience of working with others and achieving goals that seemed beyond reach.

Trends in sport

The sports industry is continually changing and developing. Anyone involved in the industry needs to understand why **trends in sport** occur, and how they influence the development of the industry. For example, the sports industry needs to react to such trends as:

- sporting activities with increasing participation (e.g. health and fitness)
- sporting activities with decreasing participation (e.g. squash)
- the changing expectations of participants and spectators (e.g. soccer players' pay, seating and ancillary facilities at sports stadia)
- changing markets for sporting activities (e.g. the 'ageing population' and improved health has resulted in more retired people staying active for longer)
- technological developments (e.g. fabrics and materials used in the construction of sports equipment, and improvements in design)
- the **influence of fashion** on sport (e.g. the wearing of trainers and fleece jackets as leisurewear rather than for sports performance).

Trends in participation

Participation in sport increased steadily from the 1960s onwards through to the late 1980s. Since the early 1990s, evidence suggests that adult participation in most sports is either levelling off or declining. Although busier consumer (and worker) lifestyles may be responsible, it is also believed that the shift towards fitness and away from competitive sport has been the main cause. In other words, it may be that fewer people are finding time to commit themselves to teams, clubs and games generally, but are using more of their leisure time to keep fit in a less organised way. This might involve swimming, walking, joining indoor fitness groups, and above all using gyms and home fitness equipment.

Participation in sport by women has been another major factor. In the past, men dominated sport and fitness and approached it in a typically masculine way, valuing competition, team effort, personal achievement and punishing routines. Women have brought a different approach, emphasising individual enjoyment but within the socially structured environment of a private club, an aerobics class or leisure centre.

Research undertaken by the British Market Research Bureau (BMRB) shows a significant decline in sports participation from 1994 to 1998 (see Figure 3.20). From a list of 33 activities, people were asked which they had taken part in during the previous year. Though many consumers are concerned about health and fitness, there is little evidence that they are taking more part in sport. Only ten sports showed an increase in interest, with cycling and climbing showing the biggest gains. Dramatic falls were seen in racket sports and traditional team sports such as hockey and cricket. These trends are possibly caused by the hectic lifestyles that became a hallmark of the 1990s.

Figure 3.20: Percentage change in sports participation, 1994-8

The winners*	%
Cycling	+19
Climbing	+13
Running/training	+12
Trout fishing	+10
Football	+1.9
Golf	+1.3

The losers*	%
Squash	-31
Skiing	-28
Walking/rambling	-25
Table tennis	-21
Clay/target shooting	-21
Badminton	-19
Tennis	-17
Swimming	-17
Hockey	-17
Cricket	-17
Snooker	-14
Sailing	-11

* Examples not an inclusive list. Survey respondents were asked if they had participated in given sports one or more times in the preceding year.

Source BMRB/*Mail on Sunday*

Technological developments

Developing technology has made a tremendous contribution to the sports industry. For example, new technology has provided active sports participants with superior 'performance' sports products, including thermal materials for outdoor pursuits, superior synthetic materials for golf clubs, tennis rackets and football boots, and footballs which respond to 'bending and dipping'.

In footwear, the demand for specialised running shoes and trainers, such as Nike's Air concept, allowed the big sports footwear firms to distance their products from the numerous cheaper models on the market. In some cases, the new-technology products have turned out be equally attractive to fashion buyers (e.g. fleece materials, gas-filled footwear). Products like Lycra and Gore-Tex are becoming familiar as consumer fashion brands to the general public, despite the fact that their original purpose was for sports performance.

New technologies allow today's athletes to perform at incredibly high standards and achieve feats that at one time were considered impossible. Yet despite the benefits of state of the art equipment, facilities, training techniques and the new knowledge about nutrition and rehabilitation, sport, in some instances, has actually suffered as a result of science.

Technological advances and sports performance

No sport is immune to the advance of technology. Much of the huge sums of money that sport generates is ploughed back into research on equipment, training, nutrition – anything that can result in that extra centimetre or millisecond to improve performance. The following article from sports coaching magazine FHS provides examples of the influence of technology on sports performance, and raises some concerns about its use.

▲ New technology has revolutionised some sports.

Has technology improved sport?

Equipment

Technological leaps in the development of equipment seem to have no bounds. The Atlanta Summer Olympics showcased numerous examples of the latest innovations. Michael Johnson's unique 3.4 ounce shoes were specially designed by Nike. The rowers pulled newly designed oars with hatchet shaped blades that move more water with each stroke. The softball players hit more home runs with a bat made from a new ultra-light metal alloy. In the Winter Olympics at Nagano, racers skied on smart skis equipped with sensors to measure vibrations from the shifting terrain, which caused the skis to stiffen and relax accordingly and so increased control at high speeds. Craig Taylor, a world-class triathlete, uses special training shoes that are personalised for heel strike and degree of pronation or supination. He also uses an aerodynamic lightweight bike with aero wheels and a hydrophobic wetsuit.

Rehabilitation

Perhaps the greatest technological advances have been in the field of sports medicine. Shortwave machines emit electromagnetic energy, increasing the temperature of the targeted area. Ultrasound can relieve pain and stimulate the repair of soft tissue injuries by producing heat. Laser therapy decreases pain and inflammation, increases vascularisation, speeds up collagen synthesis and provides control of micro-organisms.

The real price of technology

As with all technological advances, there is a price to pay. In sport, it's not in ozone depletion or global warming, but in the potential damage to the athletes and the destruction of the nature and the spirit of sport.

The human body should not be expected to perform like a machine. When scientists use quantitative information, such as joint angles and pressure points to design the optimal equipment, human factors can be overlooked. Humans, unlike machines, have tendons, cartilage, muscles, fat, a limited supply of energy, human anxiety and emotion, all of which can affect performance.

Strings on tennis rackets are now so powerful they can cause players to get shoulder and elbow strain. Boxing gloves designed to reduce cuts have led to more serious blunt-blow injuries. Wind-resistant material of downhill ski suits is so slippery that the skier will slide treacherously after a crash.

Drugs

Since the 1950s, anabolic steroids have been in common use to improve performance. The side effects of these drugs include overly aggressive behaviour, depression, sterility in males, masculinisation and premature ossification of bones in women. Prolonged use can lead to heart disease and liver damage. As with technology, these drugs can cause a vicious cycle among athletes – they feel they must use these drugs to stay competitive.

Tradition

Pierre de Coubertin may have wanted athletes to aspire to being faster, higher, stronger, but he was very wary of using science to build athletes. Rintala points out that if performance depends so much on technology, perhaps the real competitors are the equipment manufacturers and the athletes merely their means of competition. World records have less meaning – they are now broken at almost every meet, sometimes by calculable amounts, so that the feat can be repeated again and again. New media technology has seen rule changes which alter the very nature of sport: the 20-second rule and 3-point basket in basketball, the sudden-death play-off in golf, goal-line camera technology in football. Traditional sports are in decline as big-time sport goes global. Technology is at the root of all the changes.

So where to now?

Technology in sport can provide numerous benefits, yet athletes – perhaps even sport itself – may be at risk if technological advances are allowed to continue unchecked. It is the responsibility of coaches, as the guardians of sport, to proceed cautiously and weigh the consequences of technological advances. We cannot afford to get caught up in a technology race with no thought for the consequences. Athletes will always be the losers.

Source: adapted from an article by Emily Root, Andrea Domonkos, Miriam Granek and Matthew Hustler, McMaster University, Canada, in FHS, no. 2, December 1998

BUILD YOUR LEARNING

End of section activity

Undertake some research about a popular sport that interests you and write a short article suitable for a magazine or newspaper that covers the following areas:

- The economic contribution that the sport makes in terms of consumer spending by the UK population.
- The number of people working in the sport (paid and voluntary).
- The number of people who participate in the sport.

Also consider key trends in the development of the sport, including:

- increasing/decreasing participation rates;
- changing expectations of participants or spectators;
- emerging or declining markets (participants and/or spectators);
- influence of technological developments;
- influence of fashion.

You may like to choose the same sport that you selected for the end of section activity on page 166.

Keywords and phrases

You should know the meaning of the words and phrases listed below. If you are unsure about any of them, go back through the last 8 pages to refresh your understanding.

- **Consumer expenditure on sport**
- **Employment in sport**
- **Value of voluntary work**
- **Participation rates in sport and physical recreation**
- **Sports club membership**
- **Social benefits**
- **Trends in sport**
- **Influence of fashion**
- **Developing technology**

Organisation and funding of sport

Many sports would not survive without sound managerial and administrative support, nor could they continue without the financial assistance received from a variety of sources. This section focuses on the organisation and funding of sport, the key elements of which are shown in Figure 3.21.

Major sources of funding

Each sport has developed its own unique funding profile. In spite of the variations, however, the **major sources of funding** are:

- grant aid
- sponsorship
- charges for activities
- membership fees
- charges for spectating
- merchandising
- fees for media coverage (see pages 194-211).

Grant aid

A number of government and non-governmental agencies offer **grant aid**. The most significant recent development in this area has been the introduction of the National Lottery in 1994, which identified sport as one of its 'good causes'. As the Lottery Sports Fund is very closely linked to other national sports initiatives, we will consider its impact later. In the meantime, let us look at two other important sources of grant aid for sport.

Figure 3.21: Organisation and funding of sport

The Foundation for Sport and the Arts (FSA) offers grant aid to sport and the arts using money from the football pools. Initially these grants were targeted at building new sports facilities, but more recently money has been released to support the on-going running costs of a variety of sports projects.

Sports Aid is a charitable organisation that offers grants to talented young people, both nationally and regionally, to assist with their sporting development. To qualify for a national grant individuals must be a member of a national squad and not already in receipt of a similar National Lottery award. To be considered for a regional grant, an applicant must have top-six national standing and/or be in a national squad.

Sponsorship

Sponsorship is a business arrangement whereby an organisation offers money or goods in kind to a sports organisation in return for promotional and publicity opportunities. Sports sponsorship has grown significantly over recent years, with the market increasing from £36 million in 1970 to £626 million in 1999 at current prices.

This growth prompted the formation of a new body, the Institute of Sports Sponsorship (ISS) in 1985. The main role of the ISS has been to represent the interests of both sponsors and different sports, so that both parties gain maximum benefit from sponsorship arrangements. The ISS currently boasts a host of well-known sponsors such as Mars and BT as part of its membership.

One of the ISS's most significant achievements was to persuade the government to create a pound for pound matching scheme for sport. In 1992 Sportsmatch was formed, along with a government commitment to match every pound spent on the sponsorship of grassroots sport with a pound of government money.

In line with European legislation that took effect in 1998, most sports were required to renounce any tobacco sponsorship by July 2003, or in exceptional cases by July 2006. For some sports like motor racing, darts and snooker this legislation has posed a serious threat to their financial well-being. In response, organisations like the ISS and other interested parties have set about the task of identifying potential new sponsors for these sports.

Sports sign-up to drop tobacco sponsorship

The Sports Minister today welcomed the news that seven sports have sought help to quit using tobacco sponsorship. Rugby league, darts, snooker, clay pigeon shooting, pool, angling and ice hockey have all agreed to work with the government to find replacement sponsorship. A series of meetings with each sport will begin in the New Year.

Source: DCMS press release, 10 December 1998

ACTIVITY

Sports sponsorship

A number of sports attract sponsorship from high-profile companies. Can you think of any such examples for the following sports?

Cricket	*Cornhill, National Westminster Bank, Benson & Hedges*
Football	
Golf	
Tennis	
Hockey	
Rugby League	
Snooker	
Formula One motor racing	

Charges for activities (entry fees and memberships)

Many sports activities require some form of financial concession in order to participate. In most cases charges are usually made by way of an entrance fee or membership scheme. For private sector providers like fitness centres, **entry charges and membership fees** are usually set at a level that maximises revenue from customers. Figure 3.14 on page 164 showed how entry fees and membership income was a vital component of the total income of such facilities. Public sector facilities like swimming pools, on the other hand, must be equally aware of their social responsibilities. This usually means that prices are deliberately kept low in order to attract user groups on low incomes, although even here the trend is towards higher entrance fees.

Charges for spectating

The price of sports spectating is largely a matter of supply and demand, with popular sports like football, tennis and golf usually able to assert their market advantage by charging higher prices. Over recent years a new commercialism has seen the cost of spectating rise significantly in a number of high-profile sports. For example, the cost for a family (two adults and two children) attending a Premiership football match is likely to be in the region of £100 for the tickets alone. It remains to be seen whether developments in media technology (such as pay-per-view television) will encourage more supporters to stay at home in the future.

Merchandising activities

Increased commercialism has resulted in many sports organisations developing **merchandising** activities. For private sector organisations like professional football clubs, it is commonplace to find commercial departments hard at work producing replica kits and other souvenirs. However, even public sector organisations like the Sports Council are now having to generate an increased proportion of their income through merchandising activities, such as the sale of publications.

▲ Sports events can attract huge crowds.

Manchester United FC: sources of income

The following table gives a breakdown of the main income sources for Manchester United FC plc over a two-year period.

Income source	1999 (£ m)	1998 (£ m)
Gate receipts and programme sales	41,908,000	29,778,000
Television	22,503,000	16,203,000
Sponsorship, royalties and advertising	17,488,000	11,771,000
Conference and catering	7,189,000	6,046,000
Merchandising and other	21,586,000	24,077,000
Total	**110,674,000**	**87,875,000**

1 Calculate the value of the merchandising income as a percentage of total income for both years.
2 Explain why merchandising income may have been less in 1999 than 1998.
3 Display the income sources for 1998 and 1999 as two separate pie charts.

Organisation and funding of sport at international level

Figure 3.22 provides an overview of the relationship between key international sports organisations. We will begin by looking at International Sports Federations and then go on to examine the organisation and funding of the Olympic movement.

International Sports Federations

International Sports Federations (ISFs) are responsible for the administration and development of their sport at an international level. A selection of these federations is provided in Figure 3.23. A key part of their work involves establishing playing and eligibility rules, organising major events and competitions, and selecting referees, judges, umpires and other officials.

Figure 3.23: Selection of International Sports Federations

IAAF International Amateur Athletic Federation
FISA International Rowing Federation
IBF The International Badminton Federation
FIBA International Basketball Federation
AIBA International Amateur Boxing Association
ICF International Canoe Federation
UCI International Cycling Union
FEI International Equestrian Federation
FIFA Federation Internationale de Football Association

Source: International Sports Federations. www.olympic.org/ioc/e/org/if/list-all-e.html

Figure 3.22: Organisation of the Olympic movement

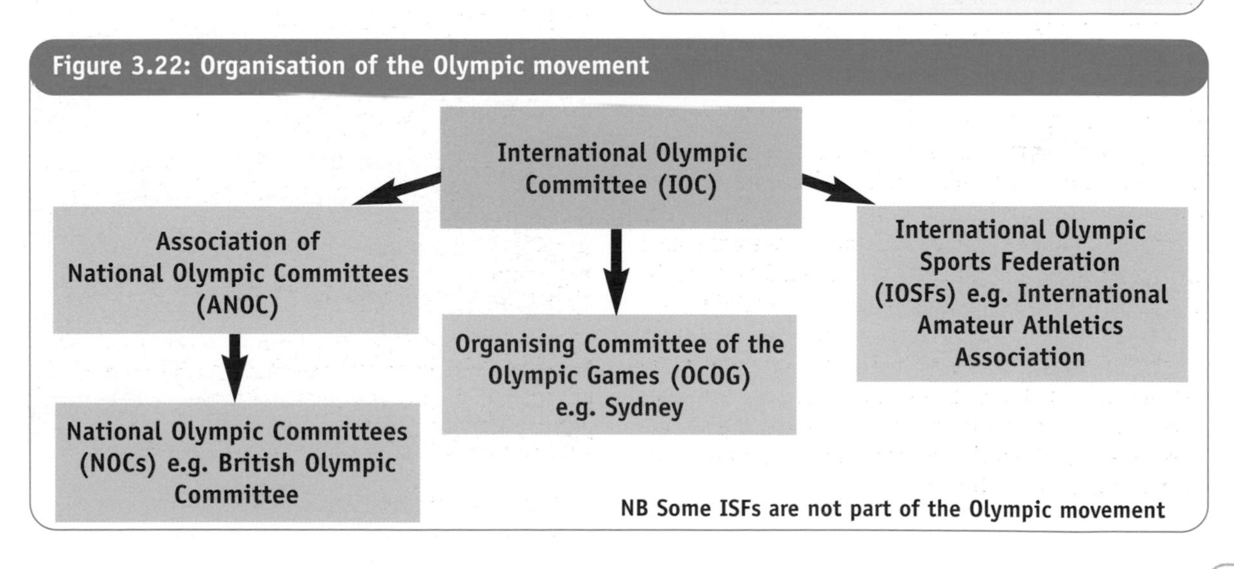

The Olympic movement

The **International Olympic Committee (IOC)** is the organisation responsible for promoting and regulating the Olympic Games. Both the summer and winter Olympic Games are held every four years, although since 1994 they have been staggered and are now held two years apart from each other. The IOC is an international non-governmental, non-profit organisation that owns all rights to the Olympic symbols, flag, motto, anthem and the games themselves. Although the IOC is the main international Olympic organisation, there are a number of other organisations that play an important role in the Olympic movement.

The Association of National Olympic Committees (ANOC) is a body which brings together all the National Olympic Committees (NOCs) from around the world and facilitates the exchange of information between NOCs and the IOC. Each country has its own NOC, which is charged with the responsibility for selecting and preparing athletes for the Olympics as well as raising the funds necessary for this operation. In the UK these responsibilities are undertaken by the British Olympic Association (BOA).

Although the IOC is responsible for selecting the location of the Olympic Games, it is the host nation that is charged with the responsibility for organising them. The country hosting the games forms the organising Committee of the Olympic Games (OCOG). In view of the financial difficulties encountered by some host nations, like Montreal Canada in 1976, the commercial success of the 1984 Los Angeles Olympics has provided the blueprint for the funding of all recent games. IOC revenue for the Olympic quadrennium 1997–2000 is set to top $3.5 billion, most of which will be generated by the sale of global television rights and sponsorship. Figure 3.24 shows the value and growth of television income since the 1984 games.

ACTIVITY

Olympic Games TV revenues

Figure 3.24 shows the value of television revenue for all summer and winter Olympic Games since 1984.

1 Describe the main trends in television revenue for the summer and winter games.

2 Why do you think that the summer games receive more in television revenue than the winter games?

3 If the total income for Sydney 2000 is $3.5 million, what is television income as a percentage of total income?

Figure 3.24: The value of television revenue for summer and winter Olympic Games since 1984

Summer Games	$ m	Winter Games	$ m
1984 Los Angeles	287	1984 Sarajevo	103
1988 Seoul	403	1988 Calgary	325
1992 Barcelona	636	1992 Albertville	292
1996 Atlanta	895	1994 Lillehammer	353
2000 Sydney	1,318*	1998 Nagano	513
2004 Athens	1,482*	2002 Salt Lake City	748*
2008 ?	1,697*	2006 Turin	832*

* Rights fees negotiated to date
Source: www.olympic.org

In 1985 the IOC introduced The Olympic Partners (TOP) in a bid to attract additional revenue. This means that global brands like Coca-Cola, Pepsi and McDonald's are invited to compete with one another for the right to sponsor the games. In return the successful company is afforded a range of benefits including the use of all Olympic imagery on their products and preferential access to Olympic broadcast advertising.

All income generated from television, sponsorship and other sources is payable to the IOC, but is then distributed throughout the Olympic movement. Although the IOC retains a small share, the majority of this income is divided between the NOCs, the OCOGs and the International Olympic Sports Federations (IOSFs) (See Figure 3.25).

Organisation and funding of sport at national level

The organisation and administration of sport in the UK has traditionally been dependent on the enthusiasm and goodwill of volunteers. In more recent times, however, the government has sought to play a more influential role in the organisation of sport, culminating in a range of new developments designed to have an impact at both national and local level. In this section, we will trace some of the key national developments in sports organisation, beginning with the role of **central government**.

Figure 3.25: Olympic revenue distribution

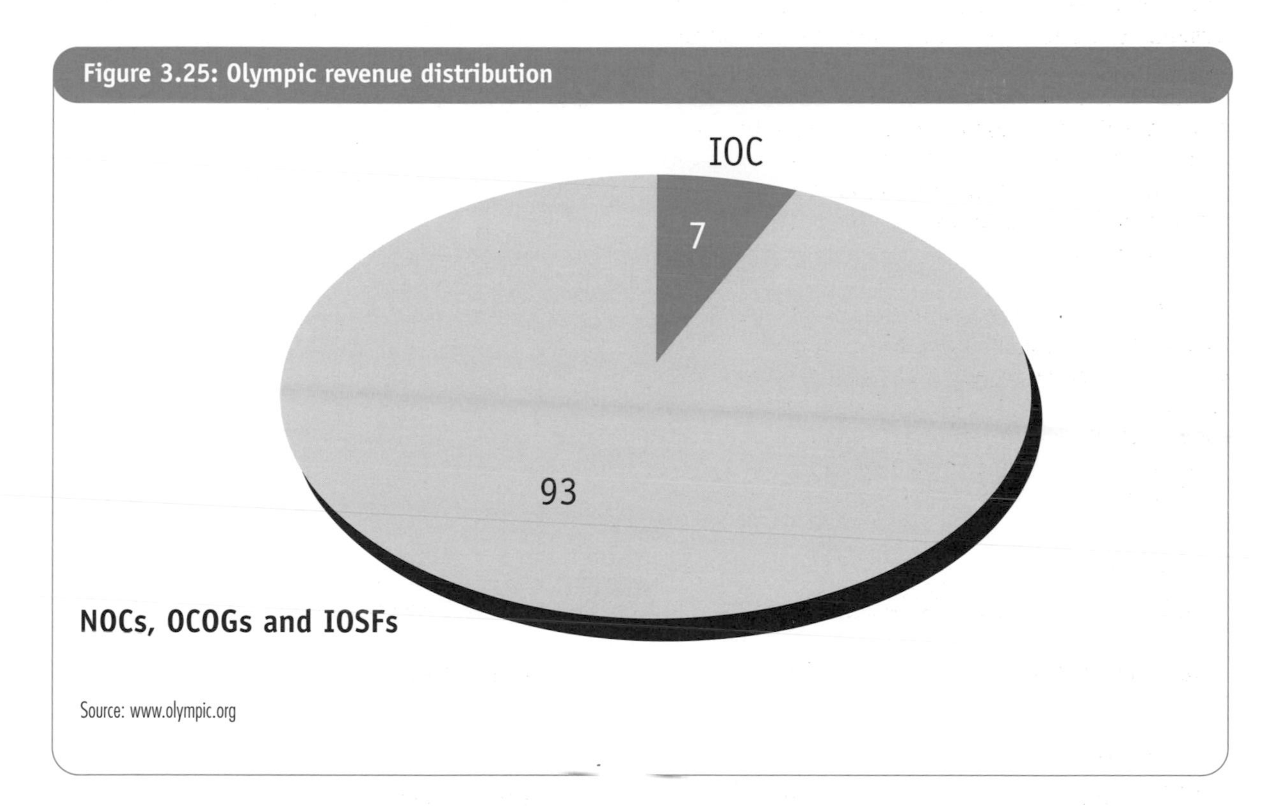

Source: www.olympic.org

Central government

Figure 3.26 highlights the central government departments with a responsibility for sport.

In 1992, John Major's Conservative government created the Department of National Heritage (DNH) in a bid to give cultural activities like sport a higher profile at national level. Following the election of a Labour government in 1997, the department was immediately renamed the **Department of Culture, Media and Sport (DCMS)** in order to give people a better understanding of its full range of work (see also Unit 1, pages 33–4).

The DCMS aims to promote wider participation in sport and support the development of sporting excellence. In order to achieve these objectives the department funds **UK Sport** and **Sport England** (also known as the UK Sports Council and the English Sports Council). This relationship has been further strengthened by the creation of a 'Sports Cabinet' under the chairmanship of the Culture Secretary, whose remit is to work alongside UK Sport. The department is also currently committed to attracting key international events to the UK, such as a future Olympic Games and the Football World Cup.

The Department of the Environment, Transport and Regions (DETR) is a large government department with a variety of functions. One of its main roles is to part-fund the workings of local government, whose links with sport include the provision of sports services and facilities, as well as physical education in schools. DETR also has a responsibility for the Single Regeneration Budget (SRB), which aims to stimulate the regeneration of economically deprived areas. Sports projects may benefit from this fund if it can be shown that they contribute to the economic life of a community.

Figure 3.26: The relationship of government to sport

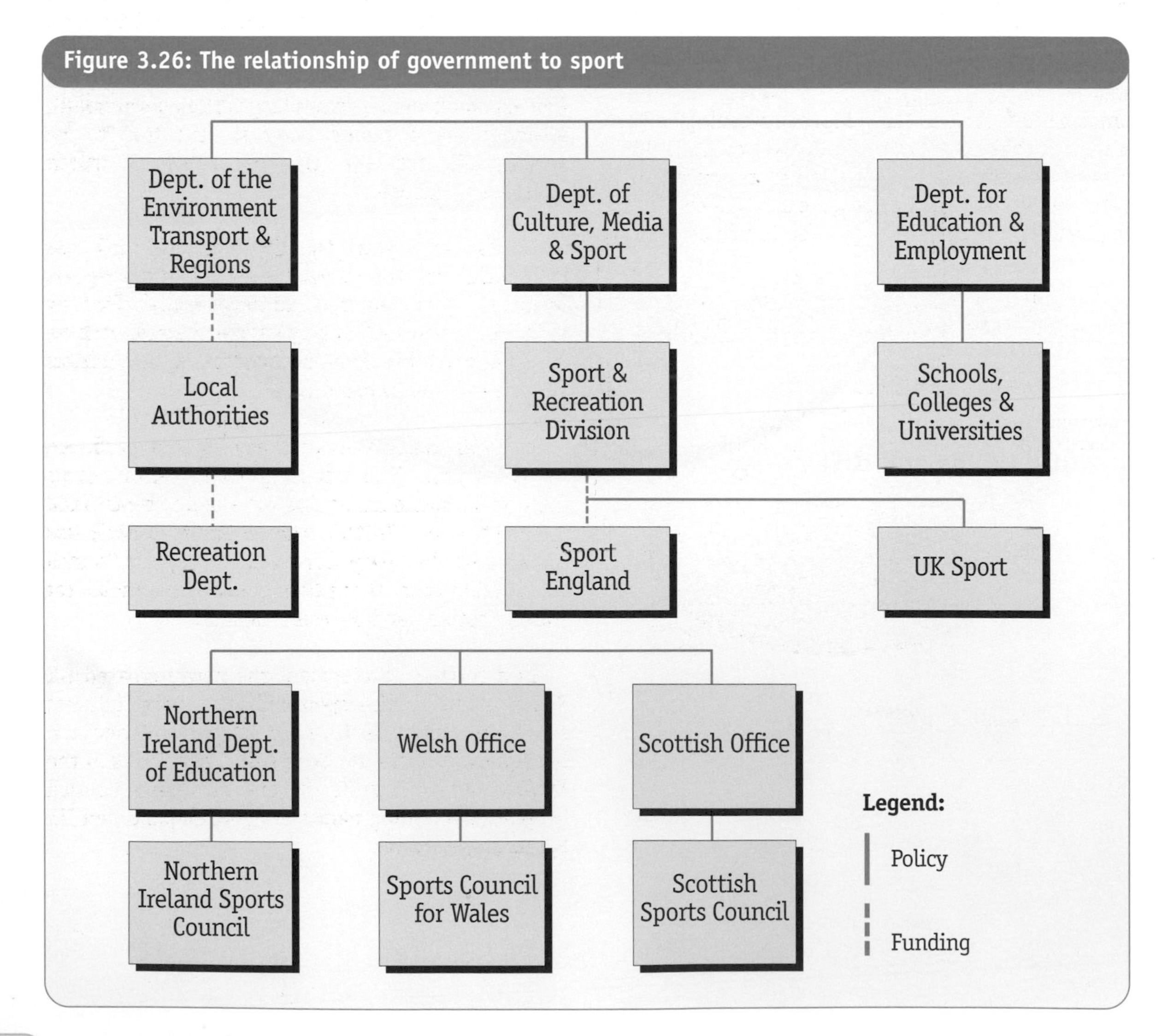

The main connection between the Department for Education and Employment and sport comes from the place of physical education in the National Curriculum. We will look more closely at physical education in schools later. At this point it is important to note that the Department for Education and Employment has a policy role to play in helping to decide the content of what children should study in schools.

The Central Council of Physical Recreation

The **CCPR** was formed in 1944, replacing the former Central Council of Recreative Physical Training (CCRPT). Although it is a voluntary body, the CCPR continues to attract most of its income from Sport England. Figure 3.27 gives a breakdown of the CCPR's main sources of annual income, which currently stands at nearly £1 million.

The original role of the CCPR was to use sport to address problems of unemployment and ill-health, as well as provide a forum for a variety of sports organisations such as the national governing bodies. Although the emergence of the Sports Council in 1972 created something of an overlap in responsibilities between the two organisations, the CCPR has continued to provide an independent voice for its members.

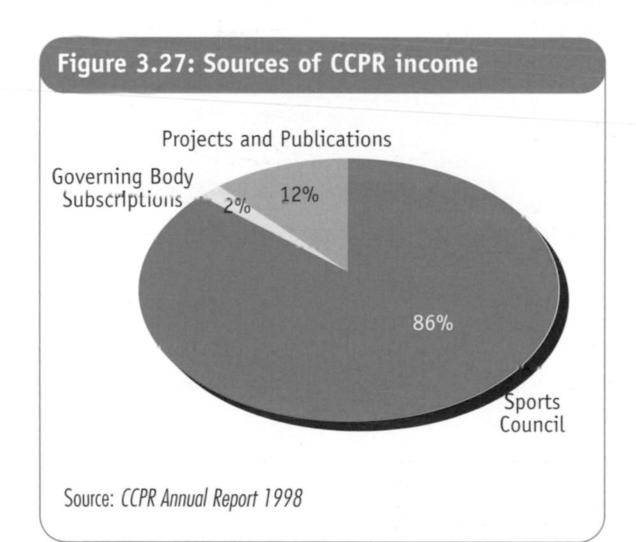

Figure 3.27: Sources of CCPR income

Source: *CCPR Annual Report 1998*

British Sports Trust

The British Sports Trust is a subsidiary of the CCPR and is responsible for the development of Sports Leader Awards, which aim to teach young people the skills required to become sports leaders in their community. There are currently four awards available to young people, plus a range of training opportunities for those who wish to deliver the awards. The awards are:

- Junior Sports Leader
- Community Sports Leader (CSLA)
- Higher Sports Leader
- Basic Expedition Leader.

The sports councils

By the 1950s it was obvious that sport had assumed a much greater importance in society than at any time before, but it was not until 1972 that the new GB Sports Council was given an independent status by way of a Royal Charter. This meant that the Sports Council could work at arm's length from government, although as a public body it still had to be accountable for the way in which it spent government money.

In its early years the GB Sports Council was influential in the development of more sports facilities. By the early 1980s tough targets for new swimming pools had already been surpassed, with an even more ambitious target for indoor sports centres well on the way to being met.

In 1995 the Conservative government produced its policy paper 'Sport: Raising the Game'. One of its main recommendations was for a more streamlined sports structure. In 1997 the GB Sports Council was replaced by the newly formed English Sports Council to sit alongside the existing sports councils for Wales, Scotland and Northern Ireland.

In a further development the newly created UK Sports Council took responsibility for sporting issues at the UK level, such as doping control and the headquarters of the UK Sports Institute. In 1999 the English Sports Council and the UK Sports Council adopted the trading names of Sport England and UK Sport, respectively.

Sport England

Sport England is accountable to parliament through DCMS. Its members are appointed by the Secretary of State for Culture, Media and Sport and its work is funded jointly by central government and the National Lottery. In 1999 Sport England received £45 million from DCMS, while UK Sport was awarded £13 million. Additional funds from the Lottery currently benefit sport by about £200 million a year.

The main objective of Sport England is to work in partnership with the public, voluntary and private sectors in order to fulfil three strategic aims. These aims are best understood through the Sport England slogan: 'More People, More Places and More Medals'. In order to achieve these aims Sport England has developed a number of initiatives that form part of four main programmes, namely Active Schools, Active Communities, Active Sports and World Class (see Figure 3.28). As most of these initiatives are delivered alongside other partners such as local authorities, governing bodies and schools, you will find more details in the section on sports development on pages 154-156.

The UK Sports Institute (UKSI)

The aim of UKSI is to provide elite athletes with the facilities and support services needed to succeed at the highest levels. The initial idea was to create a British Academy of Sport along the same lines as the Australian Institute of Sport in Canberra. However, after listening to athletes and coaches, UKSI will now consist of one central site supported by a range of network and satellite centres (see Figure 3.29). The main purpose of UKSI headquarters is to provide expert advice and training to athletes, coaches and network-centre staff on a range of sports science and medicine services.

Figure 3.28: Sport England's big picture of sports programmes

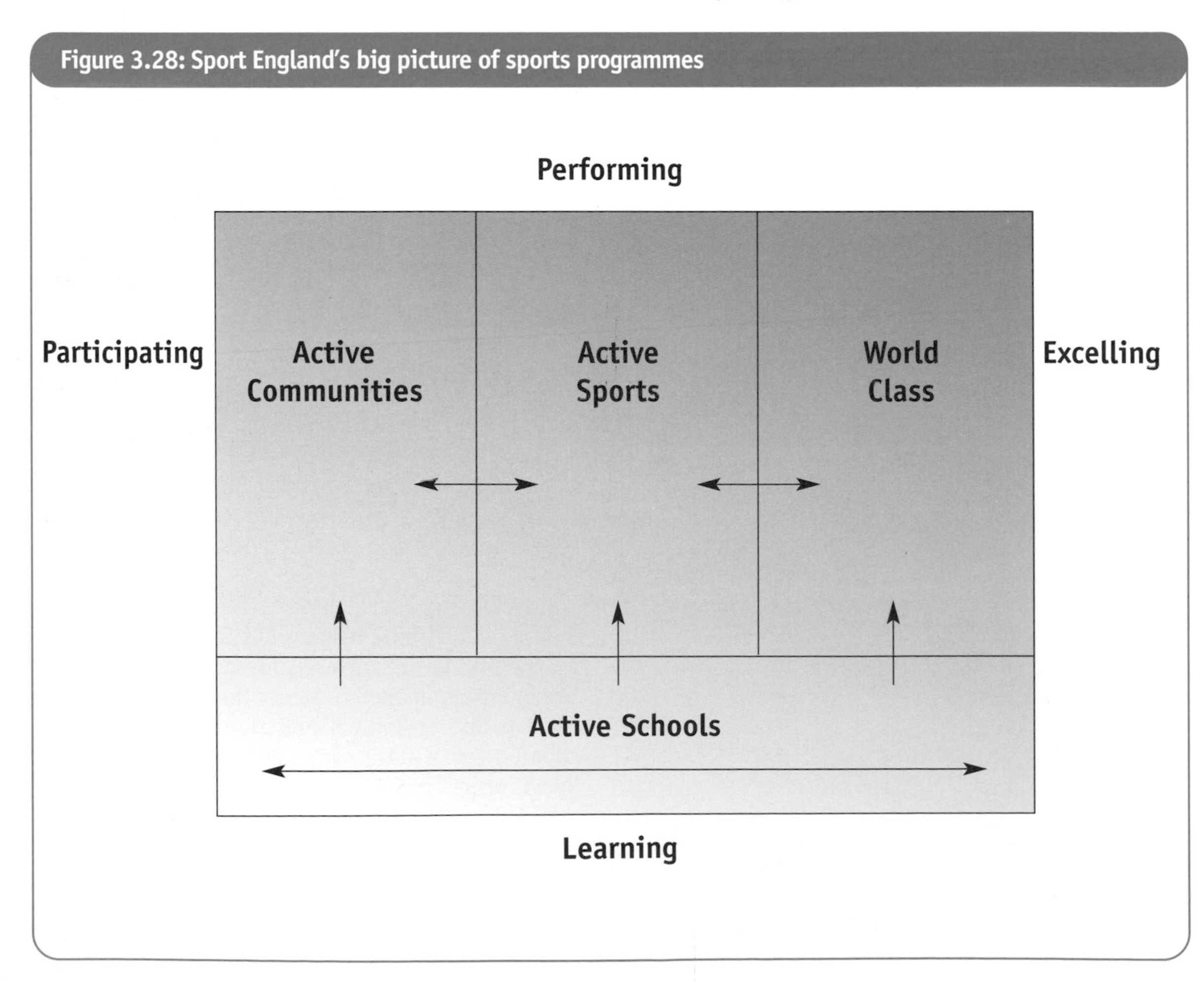

Figure 3.29: UKSI centres

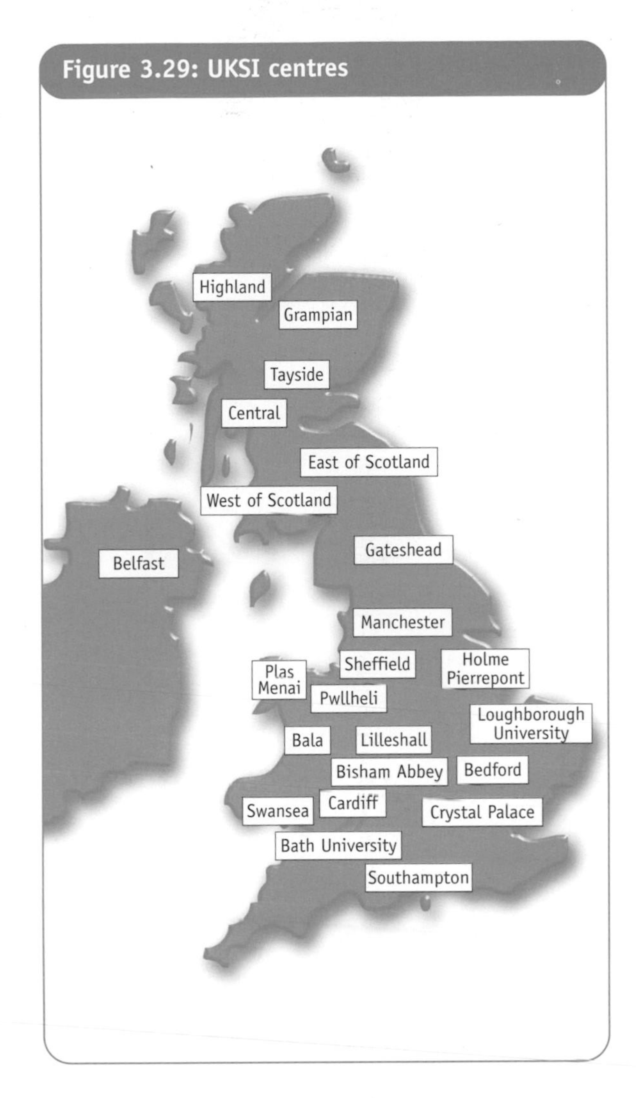

Figure 3.30: The division of Lottery money between good causes

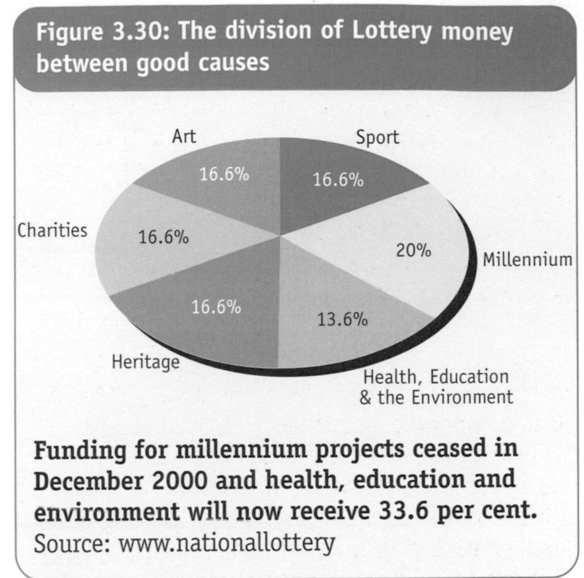

Funding for millennium projects ceased in December 2000 and health, education and environment will now receive 33.6 per cent.
Source: www.nationallottery

The National Lottery and Lottery Sports Fund

In 1993 the National Lottery Act paved the way for the UK's first **National Lottery.** Although the Lottery is regulated by central government, a commercial consortium called Camelot was awarded a seven-year licence to run the Lottery in May 1994.

Out of every pound spent on the Lottery, nearly 28 pence is divided between six good causes which include arts, sports, charities, heritage, celebrating the millennium and a new health, education and environment cause.

Figure 3.30 shows the way in which the money is currently divided.

Although the level of donations is dependent on Lottery ticket sales, it can be estimated that sport will continue to benefit from the Lottery by about £200 million a year until 2002 and beyond. One of the main requirements of the National Lottery Reform Bill 1998 was for a more planned approach to Lottery funding. In response to this legislation, Sport England unveiled a new structure for Lottery sports funding in 1999 (Figure 3.31).

It can be seen that Lottery money for sport is divided into two core funds, namely the Community Projects Fund and the World Class Fund. The main aim of the Community Projects Fund is to increase levels of sports participation.

The World Class Fund, delivered in partnership with UK Sport, is geared more toward sporting excellence and the achievement of international sporting success. As part of this programme funds have already been allocated to meet the training needs of elite performers, as well as for the development of the United Kingdom Sports Institute and other specialist sports facilities.

Figure 3.31: Diagram of Lottery awards structure

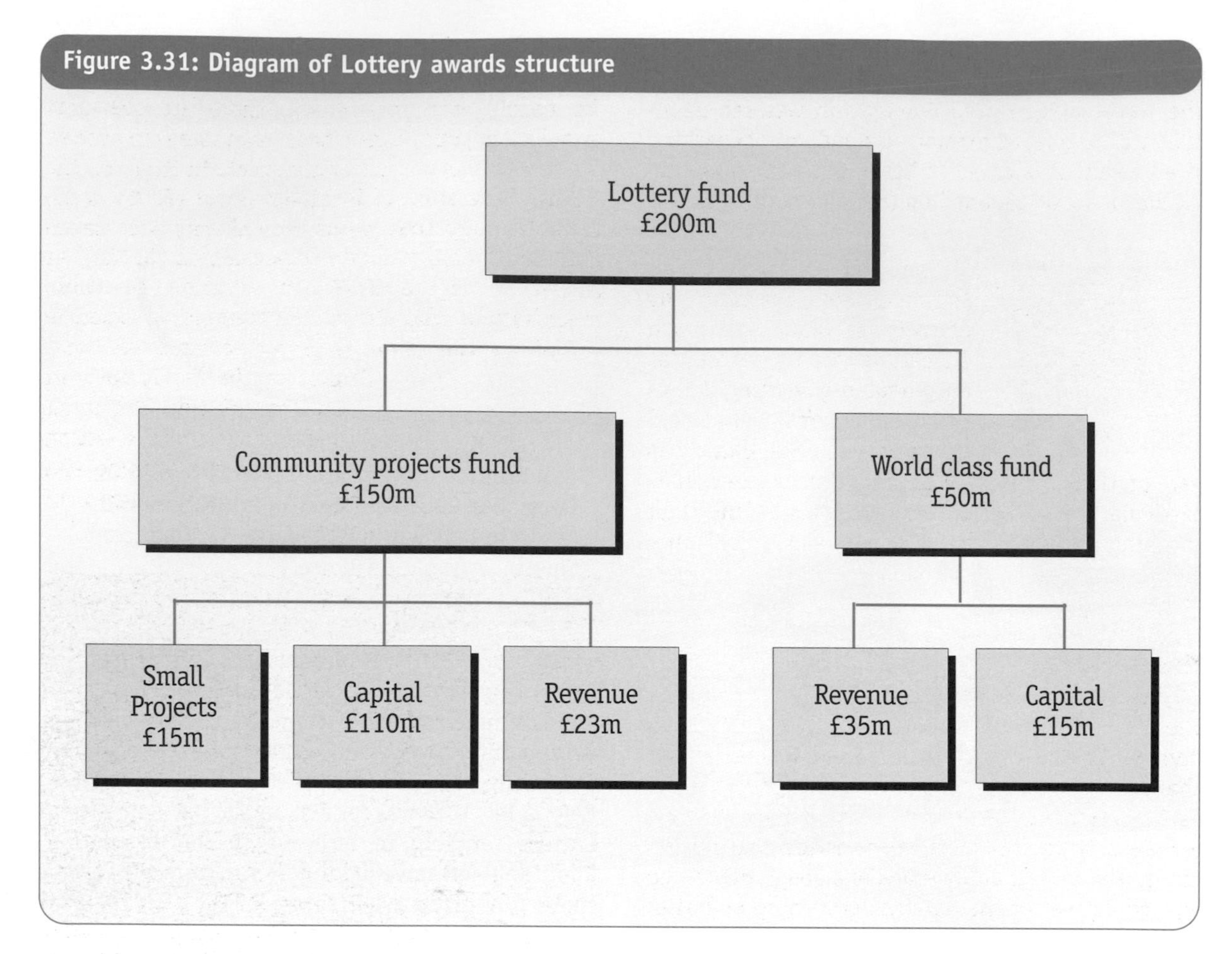

A key part of Sport England's work is to ensure that the allocation of Lottery money delivers the maximum possible benefits for sport. Under its revised structure for Lottery funding, the government and Sport England believe it is now in a better position to achieve this objective, even if some decisions remain controversial.

This latter point was recently illustrated by the decision to allocate Lottery funds for the redevelopment of Wembley Stadium. The original intention of the project was to build a stadium that could accommodate both football and athletics, but the government was criticised when the Football Association produced plans for a football stadium only.

ACTIVITY

National Lottery funding

Since it began in 1994 the Lottery has provided additional money for six good causes:

- Sport
- The arts
- Charities
- Heritage
- Projects to celebrate the millennium
- One-off health, education and environment projects

1 Discuss whether sport should benefit from the Lottery and how important it is compared with the other good causes.

2 Find examples of local and national sports projects funded by the Lottery.

The National Coaching Foundation (NCF)

The **National Coaching Foundation** was set up in 1984 with the remit to improve standards of coaching at all levels. It is based in Leeds and has an annual income of about £3.4 million (see also page 150).

The NCF aims to raise standards of coaching by offering a range of coach education courses, as well as encouraging governing bodies to implement National Occupational Standards as part of their own coaching award structures. It is particularly keen for governing bodies to link their coaching awards to the standards shown in Figure 3.4, page 151.

The British Olympic Association (BOA)

The **British Olympic Association** is the National Olympic Committee (NOC) for Great Britain and is charged with the responsibility for organising the participation of the British Team in the Olympic Games, setting standards for selection and raising funds. The BOA is an independent body comprising representatives of the national governing bodies of Olympic sports.

In 1980 the authority of the BOA was challenged by the Conservative government, which instructed the BOA not to send a team to the Moscow Games in protest over the Soviet invasion of Afghanistan. Having evaluated the situation, the BOA asserted its independence by rejecting the government's demands and a Team was sent.

The BOA is entirely funded through sponsorship, a Nationwide Judiciary Appeal and donations from the private sector and general public.

In between Olympic Games the BOA makes vital contributions to the preparation of competitors. Its British Olympic Medical Centre at Northwick Park Hospital has been developed to offer athletes a range of medical services, while national governing bodies receive specialist sports science assistance in areas such as psychology, biomechanics and nutrition.

Disability sports organisations

Although all sports providers have a responsibility for people with disabilities, there are specialist disability organisations whose main role is to oversee the development of disability sport. In England, the English Federation of Disability Sport (EFDS) is the umbrella body that works very closely with seven National Disability Sports Organisations (NDSOs), as shown in Figure 3.32. In addition to these organisations the British Paralympic Association (BPA) has the remit to enter teams from Great Britain in the Paralympics or other World Games. This remit also extends to squad selection and meeting the training and preparation requirements of competitors.

▲ Tanni Grey wins a gold medal for Great Britain in the 1998 European Championships

Figure 3.32: Structure of sport for people with a disablilty

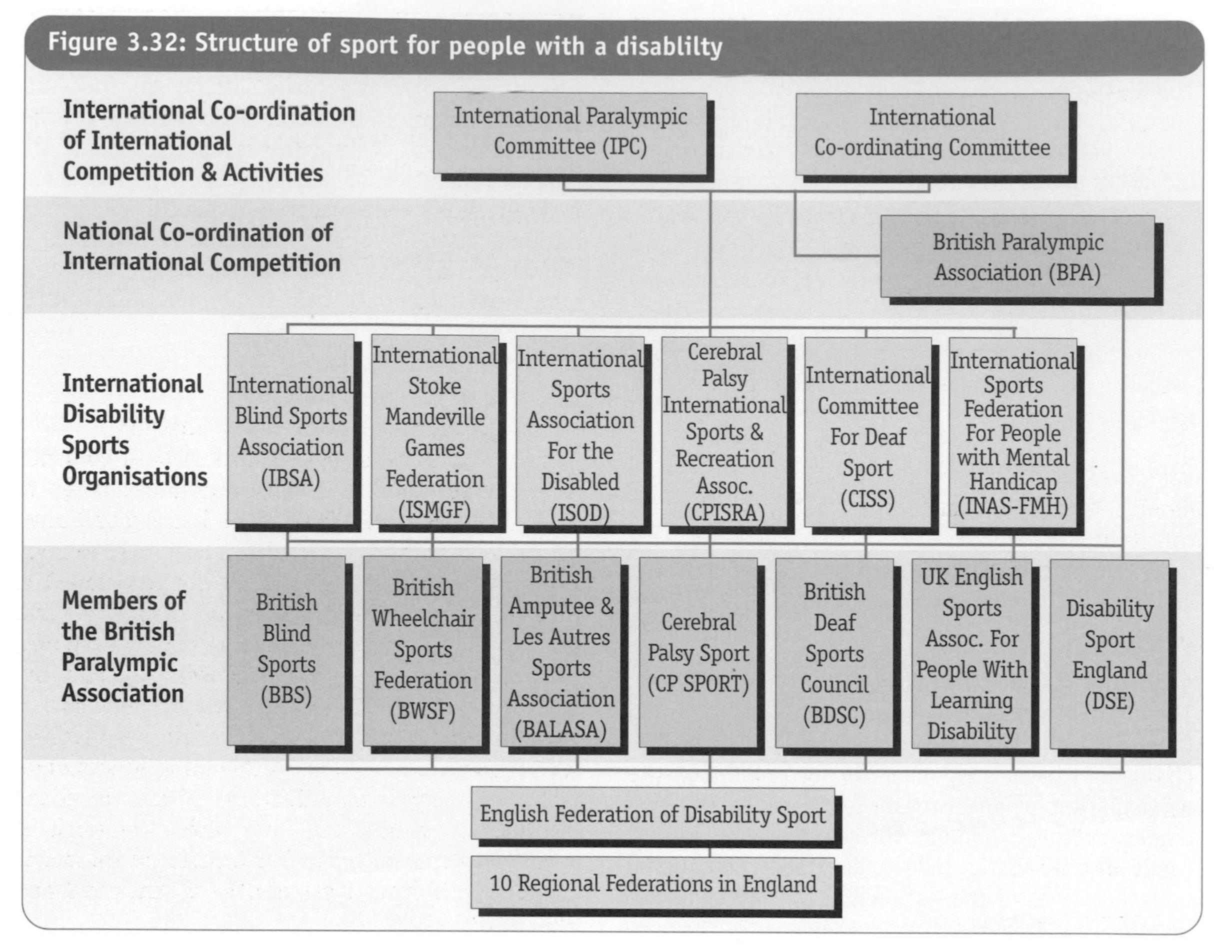

National governing bodies of sports

Many **national governing bodies** of sports (NGBs) such as the Football Association (FA) and the Lawn Tennis Association (LTA) have their origins in the development of modern sport towards the end of the nineteenth century. There are currently more than 400 independent governing bodies, some of which are organised on a home country basis, while others are constituted for the entirety of the UK or Great Britain.

All governing bodies share a number of common duties:

- framing and amending the rules
- implementing disciplinary procedures
- organising national competitions and events
- developing coaching award structures
- selecting and training national squads.

ACTIVITY

Sports governing bodies

Listed below are the initials of some of the best-known governing bodies for sport in the UK. Can you identify the name of the governing body that each set of initials represents?

RFU	Rugby Football Union	AAA
FA		ASA
LTA		BAE
RFL		BJA
AENA		EHA
EBBA		EVA
ETTA		PGA
SRA		RLSS
RYA		WPBSA
ABA		
BCU		
ARA		

For most governing bodies common sources of income include:

- grant aid
- affiliation fees from sports clubs or individual members
- commercial revenue (e.g. sponsorship, television, coaching courses, merchandising)
- tournaments and events.

Due to their relatively low public profile, sports like netball and hockey find it difficult to generate funding. As a consequence, some sports have become reliant on grant aid from Sport England. In return for this funding Sport England requires all governing bodies to produce development plans from the grassroots to the highest competitive levels which include provision for participants with disabilities. Figure 3.33 shows the income profile for the All England Netball Association (AENA).

Figure 3.33: All England Netball Association (AENA) income profile 1998

Income source	£
English Sports Council – Lottery grants	697,844
English Sports Council grants – normal activities	310,790
Contribution from regions – RDOs	11,411
Sponsorship income	5,000
Further Education Funding Council grant	7,996
Members' subscriptions	460,973
Members' insurance	21,381
Sale of publications, goods, etc.	231,164
Members' activities fees	88,214
International matches	97,974
Telephone compensation	1,000
Total	**1,933,747**

Source: AENA Annual Report 1998

The organisation and funding of regional and local sport

There are four main categories to consider at regional and local levels:

- Local government/ local authorities
- Physical education in schools
- Private sector
- Voluntary sector

Local government/local authorities

Local authorities, sometimes called local councils, have the responsibility to co-ordinate a range of public services such as education, housing and town planning. Traditionally, local authorities have been involved in two broad areas of sports provision. The first relates to the direct provision of facilities and other areas to play sport, such as swimming pools, sports centres, tennis courts, bowling greens and playing pitches. The second type of provision is often referred to as outreach work and has involved sports development officers attempting to stimulate levels of sports participation within localised neighbourhood settings. Very often the work of sports development teams has focused on the needs of groups like young people, the unemployed and the elderly.

Due to the social nature of provision most council services require a financial subsidy to survive. A subsidy represents the difference between the cost of providing a service and the amount recovered from paying customers. This difference is made up largely from central government grant aid and local taxation such as council tax and business rates.

Very often the work of council employees is co-ordinated within specialist departments such as leisure services departments. Figure 3.34 overleaf outlines a simple local authority structure.

The Local Government Act 1988 (Competition in Sport and Leisure Facilities Order) required local authorities to invite bids from the private sector for the management of some local authority sports facilities. This process was known as compulsory competitive tendering (CCT) and the overall aim was to develop more cost-effective services through the improved management of facilities (see also Unit 1, page 21).

Figure 3.35: A simple local authority structure

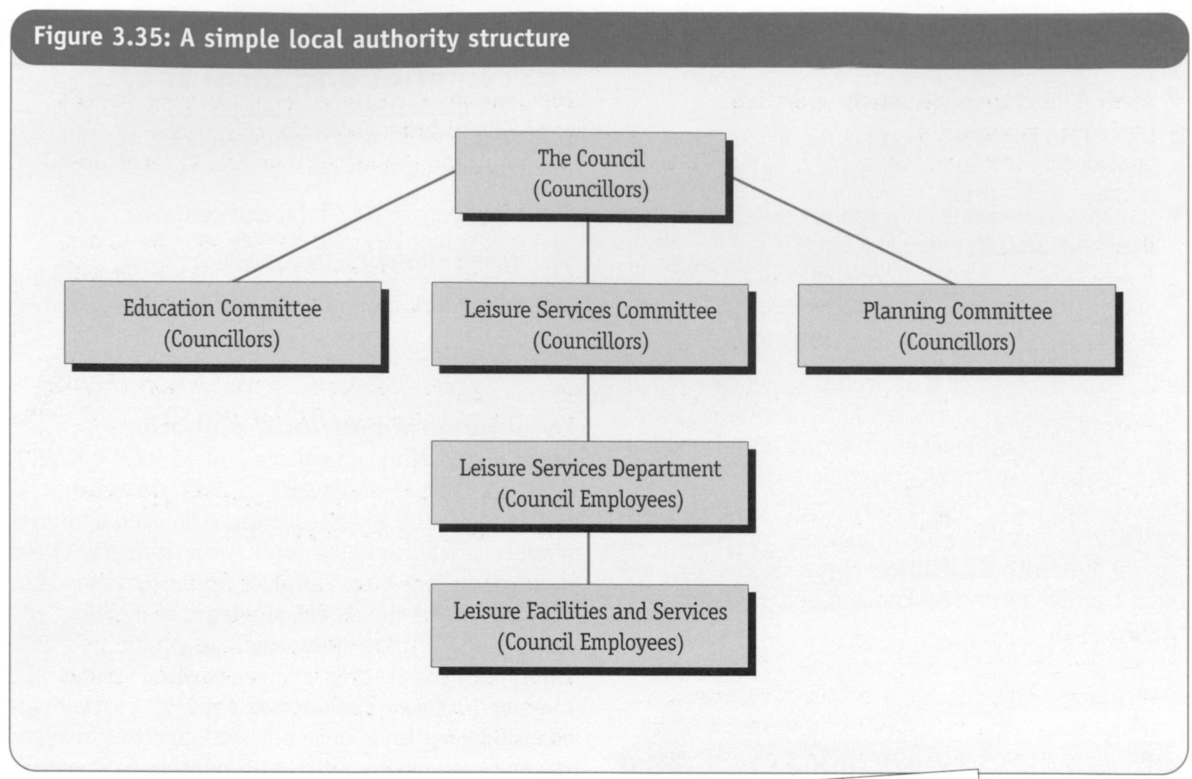

As a consequence of the 1999 Local Government Act, CCT was replaced by a new initiative called **Best Value**. Under Best Value the cost of providing a service remains important, but not at the expense of service quality and effectiveness.

Local authority leisure services departments are now being urged to consult more widely with members of the community in order to establish which services are really needed. They are also required to draw up detailed leisure plans which identify the strengths and weaknesses of leisure provision within the community as well as clarifying objectives and strategies for future developments.

Part of the problem with CCT was that a number of local authorities were unclear about what they were trying to achieve. This made it very difficult to write service specifications that protected social objectives like quality of life and equal access. Some of the important terms surrounding the development of Best Value are defined in Figure 3.35.

Under Best Value it is thought that local authorities will be seen more as enablers rather than direct providers. The result could be that more local sports services are delivered by a combination of public, private and voluntary partnerships.

▲ Local authority leisure centres can offer a range of opportunities

Figure 3.35: ILAM glossary of terms for Best Value

Audit Commission nationally specified performance indicators
Specified by the Audit Commission to facilitate national comparisons.

Benchmarking
A benchmark is a point of reference or standard against which things are measured. Benchmarking is a comparative exercise and, as such, staff undertaking a benchmarking exercise in councils will have to source information on performance and costs of organisations which provide a similar service, or perform particular functions that are similar to their own. Benchmarking is therefore about identifying, adopting and then adapting best practices to help continuously improve service performance.

Best Value
Best Value for these purposes is described as securing continuous improvement in the exercise of all functions undertaken by the authority, whether statutory or not, having regard to a combination of economy, efficiency and effectiveness.

Challenge
To challenge the need for a service to be delivered at all.

Compare
To compare the levels of service being provided against the best available, both inside and outside the public sector.

Competition
To ensure that services are competitive, in the sense that they bear comparison with the best, and that competition, in whatever form, has been properly employed to bring about the continuous improvements in services that Best Value requires.

Consult
To consult their local community, in order to give them a real voice in determining the quality and type of services which they use and pay for.

Economy
Obtaining given services, supplies or work of given quantity and quality and at lowest cost.

Effectiveness
The extent to which inputs secure the ultimate purpose of given services or work.

National performance indicators for services specified by ministers. Public interest, national priority or big-spending areas; targets to be included in local performance plans. Will include some national targets for quality and cost/efficiency.

Performance plans
Local performance plans depending on the country: annual performance plans made by English and Scottish local authorities as part of Best Value, quoting the performance indicators to be used.

Reviews
Best Value reviews – the reviews of their own functions to be made by Best Value authorities in England and Wales, referred to as performance reviews or fundamental performance reviews.

Source: Extract from ILAM fact sheet

Physical education in schools

As part of the Education Reform Act (1988) all primary and secondary schools have a legal duty to deliver physical education as part of the National Curriculum. In 1992 the then Department for Education and Science published the first National Curriculum specifications for PE, which clarified the broad areas of physical activity that children would need to undertake.

These areas incorporated:

- games
- swimming
- gymnastics
- athletics
- outdoor and adventurous activities
- dance.

In 1995 the Department for Education published a revised version of the National Curriculum document for PE which maintained the same breadth of activities, but hinted at a more prominent role for competitive team games.

ACTIVITY

School PE lessons

Think back to the time you spent at primary and secondary school.

1 How much time did you spend on PE in a typical week at primary school? Was it more or less than 2 hours?

2 Make a list of all the physical activities you did in PE lessons.

3 Do you think that schools should provide a range of different physical activities or just concentrate on a few?

4 Why do you think that secondary schools have more qualified PE staff than primary schools?

5 Did you or any of your friends not enjoy PE at school? What were the main reasons for this?

Private sector

The private sector is made up of a variety of commercial operators owned by individuals or companies, whose main aim is to generate profits from the services and products which they provide for their customers. The private sector's involvement with sport relates primarily to sponsorship, (see also page 177), the provision of facilities for participation, the sports goods market and professional sport.

In terms of facility provision, the private sector is most closely associated with health and fitness activities and sports such as football, golf, motor racing and horse racing.

▲ Private sector sponsorship in Formula 1 motor racing

Traditionally, football clubs have always been owned by a mixture of family interests and local business communities. This has changed recently with a number of clubs seeking to maximise new commercial opportunities by issuing shares on the Stock Exchange and becoming public limited companies. Consequently, a growing number of clubs have responsibilities to shareholders as well as supporters, which can create conflicts of interest. An example of this arose in 1999 when an official group of Manchester United supporters applied pressure on the government to block a bid by Rupert Murdoch's BSkyB Corporation to take over the club.

Voluntary sector

Voluntary organisations at all levels have historically formed the backbone of sport and recreation in the UK. At a national level, organisations like the CCPR and governing bodies have been very prominent, but it is at the local level where voluntary groups exert their main influence. Voluntary leisure organisations come in a variety of forms, as we saw in Unit 1 (pages 39–41), but in terms of sport, voluntary activity is primarily organised through local clubs.

Local sports clubs are self-sufficient, which means they usually obtain funding from a variety of sources, such as:

- members' subscriptions
- match fees, donations
- fundraising activities
- sponsorship
- grant aid.

BUILD YOUR LEARNING

End of section activity

1 Select a sport and briefly describe its organisation at all levels: international, national, regional and local.

2 Explain how your chosen sport is funded and how commercialisation has affected it. Support your findings with relevant information. You could use the sport you selected for the end of section activities on pages 166 and 175.

Keywords and phrases

You should know the meaning of the words and phrases listed below. If you are unsure about any of them, go back through the last 17 pages to refresh your understanding.

- **Major sources of funding**
- **Grant aid**
- **Sponsorship**
- **Entry charges and membership fees**
- **Merchandising**
- **International Sports Federations**
- **International Olympic Committee**
- **Central government**
- **Department of Culture, Media and Sport**
- **Sport England and UK Sport**
- **Central Council for Physical Recreation (CCPR)**
- **National Lottery**
- **National Coaching Foundation**
- **British Olympic Association**
- **National governing bodies of sport**
- **Local authorities**
- **Best Value**
- **Voluntary organisations**

Sport and the mass media

The relationship between sport and the mass media is very close and has been the subject of intense debate. As most people experience sport via the media rather than actively participating or spectating at events, it is important to understand the nature of the mass media's relationship with sport. We will now investigate:

- The scope and development of the mass media.
- The importance of sport for the mass media.
- How mass media influence sport.

The mass media

The mass media play a pivotal role in the functioning of all modern societies. As part of this section we will trace the history and development of the **mass media** and especially their relationship with sport. In particular we will look at developments in print (newspapers, magazines and books), radio and television (terrestrial, cable and satellite).

Newspapers, magazines and books

The influence of the print media can be traced to the middle of the nineteenth century. At that time the success of the *Sporting Life*, a sports newspaper, forced other newspapers to include sports sections for their readers.

Since then, the national press and regional and local **newspapers** have given considerable space to sports coverage. Sport also provides the subject matter for numerous books and specialist magazines.

ACTIVITY

Sports publications

Sports publications can be found in abundance on the shelves of bookstores, newsagents and supermarkets.

1 Name five famous sportspeople who have published their autobiography.

2 Name a specialist sports magazine for each of five different sports, e.g. tennis has *Ace* magazine.

▼ Sports magazines

Radio

The main breakthrough for **radio** came between 1926 and 1939, when the number of radio licences rose from 2 million to 8 million and the number of households with access to a radio reached 71 per cent. At this time the BBC was the sole broadcaster and used its influence to broadcast sporting events that it thought were of national significance. Nowadays the BBC still plays a leading role in sports broadcasting, most notably through its 5 Live channel, though the emergence of the commercial station Talk Sport is currently threatening to challenge that.

Television

Of all the media, it is **television** that has exerted the biggest influence on the development of modern sport. The BBC began broadcasting a limited black and white service during the 1940s. By the time commercial television arrived in the 1950s, football was already being used as a way of encouraging more people to hire or purchase television sets. Since then, television ownership has continued to grow, so that nearly all households in the UK now have access to at least one set.

For sport, one of the most influential developments in recent times was the 1984 Cable and Broadcasting Act, which cleared the way for subscription television in the form of cable and satellite. Before this legislation, sport could only be viewed on free-to-air terrestrial channels like the BBC or ITV. Following the merger of Sky TV with British Satellite Broadcasting (BSB) in 1991, Sky Sports was launched as the country's first subscription sports channel. In its first year Sky Sports showed more than 7,000 hours of sport, significantly more than all the terrestrial channels combined. In 1996 it screened Frank Bruno's defence of his World Heavyweight title as its first 'pay-per-view' event, which required viewers to pay a special one-off fee in addition to their yearly subscription. More recently, the introduction of digital television has enabled Sky Sports to introduce the concept of interactive television, which provides subscribers with extra services such as match statistics and action replays at the touch of a button.

Sky Sports

Sky Sports Extra brings a totally new perspective to watching soccer on television. Once it was a passive pastime with no choices for the viewer. Now you can use a range of features to see the game – and much more. Enhanced programming on Sky Sports Extra will mean that while watching the match live, you can also select:

- An alternative view of the match.
- The highlights of the match so far.
- Detailed match facts and statistics about teams and their players.
- A replay of the live match coverage.

While satellite and cable viewing has increased significantly since its inception in 1989, it should be noted that free-to-air terrestrial channels still dominate the market for television audiences. Figure 3.36 shows the current share of television viewing of free-to-air terrestrial channels and cable and satellite stations.

Figure 3.36: Annual percentage shares of viewing (individuals) (1990-8)

Year	BBC 1	BBC 2	ITV	CH 4	CH 5	Cable/satellite
1990	37%	10%	44%	9%	–	–
1991	34%	10%	42%	10%	–	4%
1992	34%	10%	41%	10%	–	5%
1993	33%	10%	40%	11%	–	6%
1994	32%	11%	39%	11%	–	7%
1995	32%	11%	37%	11%	–	9%
1996	33%	11%	35%	11%	–	10%
1997	31%	11%	33%	11%	2%	12%
1998	30%	11%	32%	10%	4%	13%

Source: BARB (www.barb.co.uk)

Developing media technology

A feature of modern media technology is the speed of new developments and the range of innovations now under consideration. For example, the article on the right shows how hardware manufacturers like Ericsson and Vodafone are already preparing for the day when mobile internet devices will be used to broadcast sport.

Handheld mobile internet

For every new piece of hardware or technology you need some equally impressive content to make people buy it. In Rupert Murdoch's case sport, particularly football, was the reason to buy it.

Now the battleground has moved out of the living room. Hand-held mobile internet devices that allow people to keep in touch with news, sports results and friends are the great hope of hardware companies.

Electronics manufacturer Ericsson predicted yesterday that there will be 600 million mobile internet devices in use worldwide by 2002. The hardware may have changed in ten years but the rule remains the same. Content, especially football, sells.

Yesterday's deal between Vodafone, the world's largest mobile phone company, and Manchester United, the world's richest football club, will allow fans to watch clips of goals on their handsets in three seasons' time. Soon after that United games could be broadcast live.

Source: *Guardian*, 12 February 2000

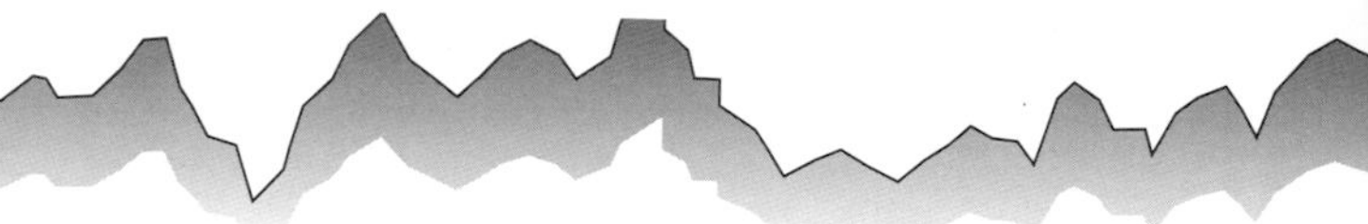

The importance of sport for the mass media

There can be little doubt that the mass media view sport as a key weapon in the battle for viewers, listeners and readers. More recently, sport has become such a great source of revenue that the media are prepared to pay ever increasing sums of money to secure the broadcasting rights to key sports events. Figure 3.37 identifies the key factors that shape the media's interest in sport.

Audience size

For newspapers and commercial television companies like ITV and Sky there is a strong relationship between readership or **audience size** and turnover. Publicly funded broadcasting organisations like the BBC are equally concerned about audience size, though more as an indicator of its own quality and value for money than as a source of profit. What is significant in all instances is the role that some sports play in securing large audiences. With sports like football and horse racing, media coverage simply caters for a demand that has always been present. For other sports, however, the picture is somewhat different. Back in the 1960s, for example, snooker was a minority sport with limited media exposure, but by the late 1970s and early 1980s greater coverage had elevated its status to one of the nation's most popular sports. One of the main reasons for this was the advent of colour television, which enabled viewers to follow games much more easily.

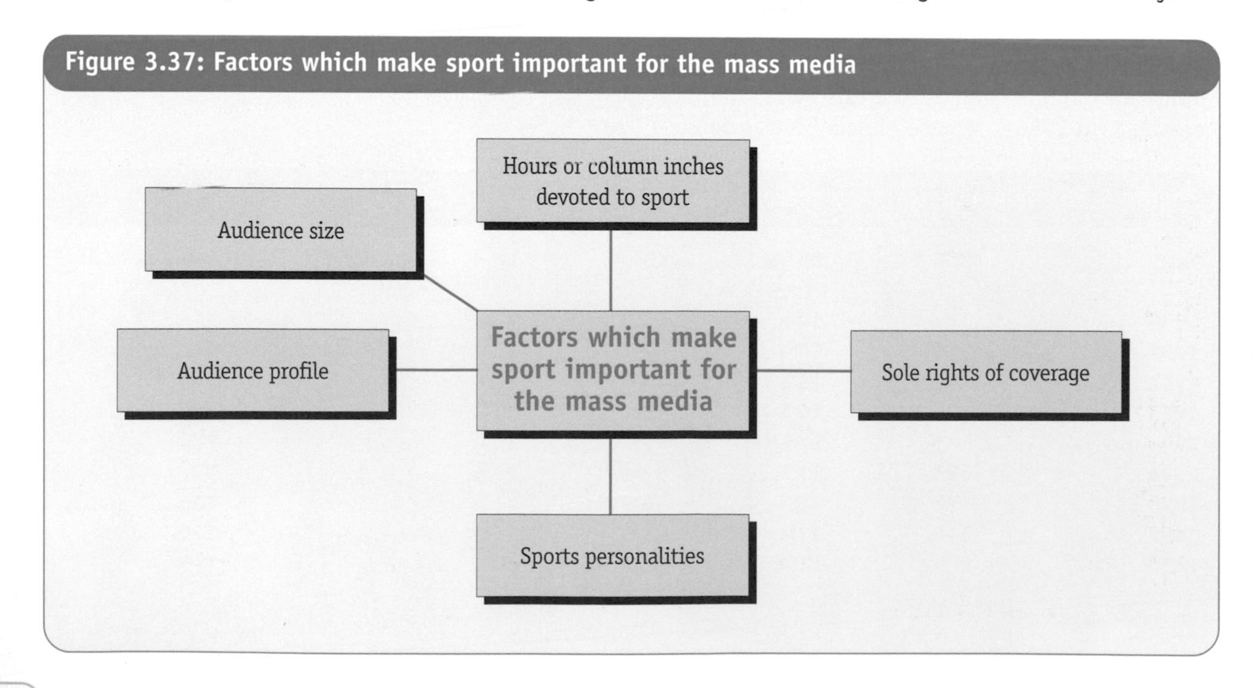

Figure 3.37: Factors which make sport important for the mass media

Mass media and sport

Do you think that sports coverage influences a person's decision to buy a particular newspaper, or are other factors more important? Explain your views using suitable examples.

Audience size plays a vital role in the media's decisions to cover certain sports. Identify any instances of the following:

1 Sports that have a ready-made television audience (e.g. football).

2 Sports which have grown in popularity due to television coverage, (e.g. snooker).

3 Sports which are considered to be 'media unfriendly',(e.g. squash, which has been forced to make a number of adaptations at key tournaments in order to improve the visibility of the ball on television).

Not surprisingly free-to-air terrestrial channels like the BBC and ITV attract the largest audiences for a variety of programmes, including sport. Figure 3.38 shows the audience figures for some of the most popular sporting events televised by the BBC.

Figure 3.38: Audience (millions) of major sporting events 1990-99 (BBC only)

Sporting event	1990	1991	1992	1993	1994	1995	1996	1997	1998	1999
Grand National	10.3	16.8	11.6	16.5	16.7	11.9	11.2	12.0	11.4	10.1
FA Cup Final	11.2	14.9	13.4	10.9	11.8	11.4	13.3	11.1	ITV	ITV
Commonwealth Games	–	–	–	–	3.0	–	–	–	2.4	–
Olympic Games	–	–	4.0	–	–	–	2.3	–	–	–
Football World Cup	10.3	–	–	–	6.3	–	–	–	8.5	–
Wimbledon Women's	7.2	7.0	4.9	7.1	8.1	6.8	5.9	5.1	4.2	5.1
Wimbledon Men's	7.8	8.1	10.9	7.6	6.2	7.9	7.2	5.4	6.0	7.0
World Snooker Final	7.6	6.7	8.9	4.9	8.1	4.3	4.1	4.6	5.4	6.0
London Marathon	5.3	5.1	4.8	5.6	4.2	3.4	4.1	4.1	3.9	3.2
University Boat Race	5.4	5.5	9.7	7.1	5.7	7.0	6.5	6.2	5.2	5.7
British Open Golf4.8	3.5	4.3	4.4	2.8	4.1	4.0	3.6	3.5	4.6	

Source: *BBC Audience Information 2000*

Due to the expense incurred by the viewer it is not surprising that fewer people watch subscription channels than free-to-air terrestrial channels. Typical weekly viewing figures for the most popular sports programmes shown on Sky are shown in Figure 3.39.

For Sky Sports the financial benefits of increased profit, despite smaller audiences than terrestrial television, makes sound commercial sense. However, some people fear that a lack of television exposure for some sports could pose a threat to their long-term existence. This is the focus of the following article.

Who will lead the way

Outside of football, the biggest sporting audience last year was for the Grand National followed by the Brazilian Formula One Grand Prix, the World Athletics Championships, the Wimbledon men's final and the Rugby World Cup (England v New Zealand). In 13th place was the world snooker final and in 16th was the Open at Carnoustie. Note that cricket, in the year of the World Cup, failed to register in the top 20, and that boxing, in the year when Lennox Lewis twice beat Evander Holyfield (sort of), did not come close. Boxing did not come close, of course, because the fights were shown on pay-television. But boxing's problem is that, by retreating so far into the domain of pay-television, it may end up losing much of its market.

This is why Mark Lewis-Francis – currently an aspiring 17 year old – has more chance than Naseem Hammed of being sports personality of the next decade. Lewis-Francis is the World Youth Games 100 metres champion and is already the eighth fastest man in Britain. What really stands in his favour, though, is that his sport delivers big audiences to terrestrial television, this nurtures the advertisers and, more importantly, the fans that boxing risks losing. Despite all the problems that athletics faces with drugs, this nevertheless appears to secure its future.

Source: Sunday Telegraph, 2 January 2000

Hours and column space devoted to sport

The importance of sport for the media can be readily established by analysing the amount of programming time devoted to sport on television and radio, as well as the amount of space given to sports coverage in the press.

Sport has always figured prominently in television schedules and the trend is for even greater coverage. Figure 3.40 provides evidence from recent Mintel research that shows television sports coverage increased by 44.8 per cent between 1996 and 1998. Equally important, however, is that the cable/satellite market share of 85.5 per cent of all sports coverage is only available to a third of UK homes with either satellite or cable.

Figure 3.39: Selected audience figures for most popular programmes on Sky Sports during a typical week in 1999

Programme	Channel	Audience size (millions)
FA Cup Special Live	Sky Sports 2	1.03
Monday Night Football	Sky Sports 1	0.95
Darts Live	Sky Sports 2	0.38
Test Cricket Live (Mon 0800)	Sky Sports 2	0.25
WWF Raw	Sky Sports 3	0.24
Big Fight (Tues 2200)	Sky Sports 3	0.06
NFL	Sky Sports 3	0.04

Source: BARB

Figure 3.40: Time devoted to sport on television 1996-8

	Total 1996 hours devoted to sport	1996 % of all sports coverage	Total 1998 hours devoted to sport	1998 % of all sports coverage	% change 1996–8
BBC 1	868	4.2	720	2.4	-17.1
BBC 2	881	4.2	1,028	3.4	+16.7
ITV	299	1.4	528	1.8	+76.6
CH 4	694	3.3	803	2.7	+15.7
CH 5	n/a	n/a	1,290	4.3	n/a
Total free-to-air terrestrial television	**2,742**	**13.2**	**4,369**	**14.5**	**+59.3**
Sky	11,738	56.5	19,418	64.5	+65.4
Eurosport	6,304	30.3	6,307	21.0	
Total cable/satellite	**18,042**	**86.8**	**25,752**	**85.5**	**+42.6**
Total all channels	**20,784**	**100.0**	**30,094**	**100.0**	**+44.8**

Source: Mintel, *Spectator Sports Report 1999*

Obviously, not all sports receive the same amount of television coverage. The decision as to what to cover has always been a reflection of the level of public interest in particular sports.

Figure 3.41 shows the time devoted to specific sports on television. Not surprisingly the popularity of football means that it dominates overall sports coverage on all channels. With the possible exception of horse racing there are few other differences between the sporting priorities of free-to-air terrestrial channels and cable and satellite providers.

With respect to mass-circulation newspapers, the sports section has always played a vital role in helping sustain market position. In the early days nearly all coverage centred around match reports and individual performances, but more recently the public's appetite for newsworthy stories about the private lives of sporting celebrities has created a new genre in sports journalism.

We will look at the way in which some sports people become media personalities later (page 203).

Figure 3.41: Sports coverage on free-to-air terrestrial television and cable and satellite

	Total minutes	%
Free-to-air terrestrial television		
Football	24,989	16.5%
Horse racing	22,032	14.5%
General sports	17,573	11.6%
Cricket	15,571	10.3%
Tennis	12,369	8.1%
Snooker	12,773	8.4%
Motor sports	8,859	5.8%
Golf	6,753	4.4%
Athletics	6,520	4.3%
American football	4,193	2.8%
Rugby union	3,882	2.6%
Sky and Eurosport		
Football	234,705	17.7%
Golf	136,175	10.3%
General sports	134,755	10.2%
Tennis	84,535	6.4%
Motor sports	83,550	6.3%
Cricket	80,015	6.0%
Rugby union	47,125	3.6%
Rugby league	44,075	3.3%
Wrestling	37,890	2.9%
Boxing	37,110	2.8%
Motor cycling	36,005	2.7%

Source: Mintel, *Sports Betting Report 1998*

ACTIVITY

Press sports coverage

The table below relates to research that was carried out some years ago. As a way of updating these findings you will need to select copies of two of the newspapers listed in the table so you can undertake your own research.

Percentage of space devoted to sport in tabloid newspapers

Newspaper	%
Daily Star	22%
Sun	20%
Mirror	17%
Daily Express	16%
Daily Mail	14%

Source: Hargreaves, *Sport Power and Culture*

1 Calculate the percentage space that each of your selected newspapers currently devotes to sport.

2 How do your findings compare with some of those in the table above? If there are any differences suggest reasons why this might be the case.

Audience profile

In order to maximise the size of an audience it is vital that sports coverage represents the interests of a particular type of reader, listener or viewer. In marketing terminology this is often referred to as market segmentation (see Unit 4, page 266) and is based on the idea that different products are tailored to meet the needs of different user groups. Marketing personnel now employ very sophisticated techniques to identify specific customer groups, which often begin with the use of demographic information such as age, gender and social class. In Figures 3.42 and 3.43, for example, it is clear that the working-class profile of *News of the World* readers is very different to the more middle-class profile of *Sunday Times* readers. It therefore makes commercial sense for the *News of the World* to devote more space to sports with a stronger working-class appeal like football, rugby league and horse racing, while the *Sunday Times* is likely to cover sports like rugby union, cricket and football.

Similarly, Sky Sports has commissioned extensive research into its football audience profile. The results indicate that viewers tend to be younger affluent males who fit into one of the three categories in Figure 3.44 (see also page 219). Consequently Sky has attempted to satisfy the needs of its main football audience by providing innovations such as new camera angles and in-depth statistical analysis at the touch of a button.

Figure 3.42: Social class profile of News of the World readers

Social class grouping		News of the World readership profile %
A	Upper middle class	1%
B	**Middle class**	**6%**
C1	Lower middle class	24%
C2	**Skilled working class**	**29%**
D	Manual workers	27%
E	**Those at lowest level of subsistence**	**13%**

Source: *News International*

Figure 3.43: Social class profile of Sunday Times readers

Social class grouping		Sunday Times readership profile %
A	Upper middle class	12%
B	**Middle class**	**45%**
C1	Lower middle class	30%
C2	**Skilled working class**	**7%**
D	Manual workers	4%
E	**Those at lowest level of subsistence**	**4%**

Source: *News International*

Figure 3.44: Typology of Sky Sports football viewers

The commentator	**Wants to analyse and needs to be informed. They love to learn and discuss the game with others.**
The manager	**Knows their football and wants to be in control of what they watch and how they see it.**
The player	**Is fixated by the match. Devoted to one team. Once the match kicks off the blinkers are on.**

ACTIVITY

Audience profiles

The media are usually well aware of the characteristics of people who watch sport. Very often these characteristics are based on demographic information like age, gender and social class which are likely to vary across different sports. For example, the audience profile of Formula One spectators has recently been identified as 57 per cent ABC1 males. How might you describe the demographic profiles of people who watch the following sports?

- Football: *mainly male, aged 15–40, predominantly upper working class but becoming more middle class*
- Golf
- Rugby league
- Netball
- Rugby union
- Greyhound racing
- Tennis

Figure 3.45: A history of television deals for the rights to cover football in the UK

1938	FA Cup Final shown live for first time
1964	First ever Match Of The Day on BBC 2
1979	BBC/ITV joint contract for League football: £9.2 million over four years
1983	BBC/ITV joint contract for League football: 10 games Friday night matches on BBC (5) Sunday afternoon matches on ITV (5) £5.2 million over two years
1986	BBC/ITV joint contract for League football: 14 games: £6.2 million over two years
1988	ITV: £44 million over four years for League and Littlewoods Cup – 21 live matches BSB/BBC: Five-year deal for FA Cup and England internationals Sky TV: Live coverage of ZDS Cup and Autoglass Trophy
1992	Sky: exclusive live rights to 60 games from FA Premier League BBC: Match Of The Day returns with Premier League highlights ITV: Four-year deal for live coverage of League and Coca-Cola Cup CH 4: Italian Serie A live
1996	Sky: exclusive live rights to 60 games from FA Premier League: £670 million BBC: four-year deal for FA Premier League highlights: £73 million
2000	Sky: £1.1 billion for 3 years premiership football live rights NTL Cable TV: £3.28 million for 3 years pay per view rights for premiership football ITV: £183 million for 3 years rights of premiership football highlights

Source: BSkyB

Sole rights of coverage

Perhaps the main controversy surrounding televised sport is the issue of television rights. For many years people became accustomed to watching major sporting events on free-to-air terrestrial television channels like the BBC, but the introduction of subscription channels like Sky has forced both the television companies and sports governing bodies to rethink their priorities. The main difference is that subscription channels are now prepared to offer some governing bodies like the Football Association vast sums of money in return for **sole rights of coverage**. Consequently, the pressure on terrestrial channels to match the bids of Sky has been so great that a number of key sporting events have since been lost.

Figure 3.45 details the history of television football rights deals and the article on page 202 explains the decision of the Restrictive Practices Court to uphold the way in which the Premier League sells its television rights.

Ball lands in court of sports bodies': Premier League Annual Report

Two fundamental matters were considered by the Restrictive Practices Court last month when it found in favour of the FA Premier League (and its 30 past and present members), BSkyB and the BBC, upholding the way the Premier League sells its television rights. Sports bodies take note.

The fundamental matters considered by the court were the sale of TV rights to FA Carling Premiership matches on a collective basis by the Premier League, and their sale on an exclusive basis, so as to give a broadcaster the right to select which matches to televise.

The court upheld collective selling, concluding that the rule preventing the clubs from selling TV rights individually was not against the public interest. It also upheld the exclusivity granted to BSkyB and the BBC in their previous agreements, which ended in 1996–97, and in their agreements that expire in 2001.

The court decided that the limit on the number of matches televised live (60 out of 380) was not in place to maximise price because a broadcaster would pay more for a larger number of matches. Similarly, the Premier League could not be regarded in the same way as a normal industrial cartel because the 'Premier League itself produces a product towards the production of which all the clubs contribute'.

The court also decided that pay-TV broadcasters differentiate their programme offerings by having exclusive rights in sporting events. Here, exclusivity was found to encourage competition between broadcasters. Other sporting bodies wishing to sell their TV rights on a collective and/or exclusive basis will have to point to pro-competitive benefits if required to justify their arrangements. Benefits highlighted in the Premier League case included investment by clubs in stadia, facilities and players, which is of substantial benefit to the public. A reduction in TV income would reduce this benefit substantially and make it more difficult for clubs to compete in a world market for the best players.

Collective licensing enables the Premier League to sell TV rights as part of a product that the broadcaster and the viewer both want: the Premier League Championship as a whole, i.e. to select the matches that tell the story.

Source: Denton Hall in FA Premier League Annual Report 1998/99

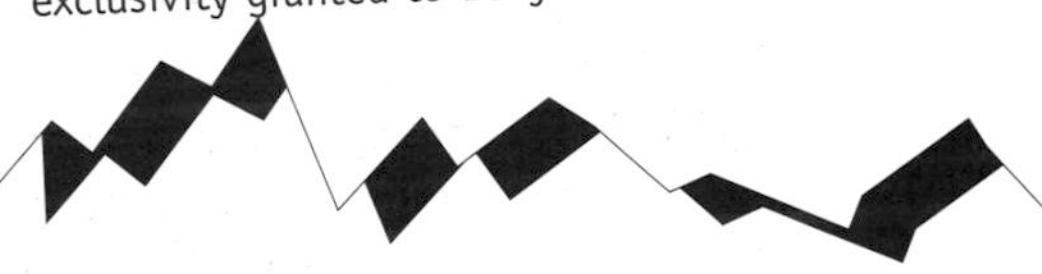

While some sports have gained enormous financial benefits from these arrangements, there are concerns that the majority of sports fans who do not have access to cable and satellite television have been treated unfairly. In response to these concerns the government has made some attempt to look after the interests of non-Sky subscribers by protecting a number of sporting events as part of the 1996 Broadcasting Act (Figure 3.46).

Figure 3.46: List of protected sports events under Part IV of the Broadcasting Act 1996

Group A (full live coverage protected)	Group B (secondary coverage protected)
Olympic Games	Cricket Test Matches played in England
Football World Cup	Non-final play in the Wimbledon Tournament
European Football Championship Finals	All other matches in the Rugby World Cup Finals
FA Cup Final	Five Nations rugby matches involving home countries
Scottish FA Cup Final (in Scotland)	Commonwealth Games
Grand National	World Athletics Championships
The Derby	Cricket World Cup: final, semi-finals and matches involving home nations' teams
Wimbledon Tennis Finals	Ryder Cup
Rugby League Challenge Cup Final	Open Golf Championship
Rugby World Cup Final	

Source: *DCMS*

Live coverage of Group A events is protected for transmission on free-to-air terrestrial television including the BBC, the ITV network and Channel 4. It is important to note that the protection of Group A events does not guarantee coverage on one of these channels. It guarantees only that the rights to live coverage will be offered to these channels on fair and reasonable terms. As it reaches only 70 per cent of the population, Channel 5 is not classed as part of this group. With regard to a subscription channel like Sky, exclusive live coverage of Group B events is permitted provided that adequate arrangements are made for delayed coverage or highlights on a free-to-air, terrestrial channel.

Sports personalities

A feature of the media's involvement in sport is the way in which some sports people are able to achieve celebrity status both on and off the field of play. For international stars like Tiger Woods, Michael Jordan and Ronaldo their sporting ability combined with huge personal earnings make them the subject of much media attention. The same can be said of home-grown celebrities like David Beckham, whose exploits off the field tend to command the same level of media attention as his performances on it.

While most famous sports people generally welcome the attention of the media, there have been cases when the media have been accused of using a sportsperson's fame for their own financial gain. One such example occurred when a Sunday newspaper tried to uncover a drugs scandal involving the then England rugby union captain Lawrence Dallaglio. As a consequence the player was suspended and his international career placed in jeopardy, despite his claims that the newspaper used improper methods to secure its story. In response the newspaper maintained that it was acting in the public interest by exposing the illegal and immoral behaviour of a sporting role model.

▲ David Beckham and Victoria Adams

First the sting, now the Stradey treatment for Lawrence Dallaglio

Lawrence Dallaglio will be in Llanelli this afternoon, at Stradey Park where the old ground is cold and muddy and the steaming terraces are loud and threatening. As the captain of Wasps, the only unbeaten English club in the European Cup and the bright young London team aiming to ruin Llanelli's dream of qualifying for the quarter-finals, Dallaglio will be singled out by the Scarlet choir. He will also warrant special attention for, apart from being the best player on either side of the seething park, his is the most famous face in English rugby. If his renown is still rooted in the driving and ferocious quality of his rugby, the notorious saga of last summer forced upon him that dark and hunted kind of celebrity which is the very opposite of stardom.

Late on the Saturday night of May 22 the News of the World hit the streets with an outrageous front-page screamer: 'England Rugby Captain Exposed As Drug Dealer'. The newspaper insisted that 'pin-up Dallaglio, 27, a father of two young children' and 'a 6ft 4in sporting legend' had astonished its reporters with his brazen candour. They wrapped Dallaglio's 'confessions' around the first five pages of that saucy edition. The allegations were so wild and breathless that it was hard to recognise the England captain who had made such a different impression with his scrupulous and diplomatic determination to avoid controversy on the back pages. But the damage was as deep as it was instant.

Source: Guardian, 15 January 2000

ACTIVITY

Press coverage

Read the extract on page 203 from a press article about the former England rugby union captain Lawrence Dallaglio.

1 Do you think the press has a duty to uncover the immoral behaviour of sportspeople if it thinks it has strong evidence to support its claims?

2 Should the press have to adhere to certain ethical standards before it publishes stories about sportspeople?

3 Can you think of any instances where the press has been justified in revealing personal details about a sports performer?

4 Can you think of any instances where the press should not have published details about a particular sports performer?

How mass media influence sport

The debate surrounding the **influence of the mass media on sport** has continued for many years, but with the introduction of new media forms such as satellite, cable and digital television that debate has intensified. Those who favour media involvement in sport point to benefits such as increased revenues for sports governing bodies, the exposure of sports to wider audiences, as well as the promotion of healthy forms of competition. Others, however, view the media as having distorted sport, either for their own financial gain or as a means of social control. This section analyses a variety of interrelated themes that have emerged in the debate:

- funding
- media presentation of sport
- rules of the game
- event programming
- the effects on sports participation
- the conduct of players and supporters.

Funding

The **financial rewards** that stem from the media's involvement in sport are now a key feature of the way sport is organised in a global market-place. For terrestrial channels, the justification for securing television rights to sport is to gain an advantage in the battle for viewers. Sport is seen as attractive in the ratings battle because it has the capacity to attract large numbers of viewers, sometimes on a worldwide scale. For subscription channels like Sky the importance of securing high-profile sporting events lies in the fact that most income is generated from direct-to-home subscribers. The total turnover split for BSkyB is presented in Figure 3.47.

Figure 3.47: Sky turnover split

Direct-to-home subscribers	67%
Cable subscribers	16%
Advertising	14%
Other	3%

Source: BSkyB

This tends to the advantage of some sports like football, tennis, motor racing and cricket which, due to their worldwide appeal, have benefited from the sale of television rights and the lucrative sponsorship deals that have followed. This was clearly the case for the English Cricket Board (ECB) when it was selected to organise the 1999 Cricket World Cup. The extract below shows how the ECB was able to use global television exposure as an incentive for sponsors to commit further money toward the event.

> ***England hosted the 1999 Cricket World Cup, involving 12 countries. Around 476,800 spectators watched the matches, and the worldwide television audience was estimated at 2 billion. This level of television exposure helped the English Cricket Board attract four official sponsors: Emirates Airlines, National Westminster Bank, Pepsi and Vodafone.***
>
> Source: adapted from *Sport and Active Recreation*

Sports such as judo, netball and hockey, on the other hand, suffer intrinsic commercial disadvantages in that they fail to attract significant public interest, which in turn reduces their media appeal and their value to potential sponsors. Consequently, a number of sports have become reliant on funding from other sources, such as grant aid from Sport England and the Lottery Sports Fund. Figure 3.48 compares the very different income profiles of tennis and hockey.

▲ Hockey is at a commercial disadvantage

ACTIVITY

Income profiles: tennis and hockey

Figure 3.48 outlines the income profile of the national governing bodies for tennis and hockey.

1 What are the main sources of income for the Lawn Tennis Association?

2 What are the main sources of income for the English Hockey Association?

3 Why do you think that tennis is able to generate more income than hockey from competitions and events?

4 Suggest reasons why tennis has more lucrative sponsorship deals than hockey.

5 Why do you think that the Lawn Tennis Association does not receive a Sports Council grant?

Figure 3.48: Income profiles of the Lawn Tennis Association and the English Hockey Association

INCOME SOURCE	£
LAWN TENNIS ASSOCIATION	
Wimbledon Championships	30,223,000
Other tournaments and events	6,311,000
Sponsorship and commercial	1,870,000
Subscriptions/affiliations	897,000
Investments	2,013,000
Total	**41,314,000**
ENGLISH HOCKEY ASSOCIATION	
Competitions	321,113
Sponsorship and commercial	85,503
Affiliation fees and memberships	883,885
English Sports Council grant	94,336
Lottery World Class Performance grant	2,201,779
Total	**3,586,616**

Sources: *LTA Annual Report* and *EHA Annual Report*

Media presentation of sport

It is commonly believed that the media simply report sport in an objective and unbiased manner. This view appears to be confirmed by the fact that sport occupies its own space on television and at the back of newspapers, thus creating the impression that it has nothing to do with issues of power or politics.

What should not be overlooked, however, is the power of the media to select which sports are worthy of coverage and the manner in which they are presented and interpreted. Although the media cover a variety of sports, there is a clear tendency (certainly among mass-circulation newspapers) to focus on sports with a large, predominantly working-class following such as football and horse racing.

Attempting to satisfy demand by focusing on sports with a mass appeal is an obvious strategy employed by the media. There is, however, another way that the media seek to maintain their audience, which is more to do with presenting sport as an entertaining spectacle.

The aim of this strategy is usually to provide the viewer or reader with a familiar format and one they readily understand. Examples of this can be found in the type of language used in match reports and other sports stories, which often has more in common with war and the battlefield. It is not uncommon for opponents to be 'crushed', 'destroyed' and 'humiliated', while players are frequently 'blasted' by their critics for poor performances and other misdemeanours.

Beckham Back in Demand

Stopping just short of sticking up a Lord Kitchener 'Your Country Needs You' poster outside David Beckham's hotel room, Kevin Keegan yesterday declared that the midfielder dropped by Manchester United on Sunday would not only start for England tomorrow but would be given the playmaking role. So Beckham remains the centre of attention on and off the field.

His spat with Alex Ferguson originated from his decision to stay at home and tend his ailing son rather than attend training on Friday. Keegan refused to be drawn into this obvious tension within the corridors of England's biggest club. 'Like the other United players, Beckham is dedicated to his profession but, clearly, a problem exists in balancing his passion for United while being married to a strong-willed pop star who wants to live closer to London.'

Asked whether sport and showbiz can mix, Keegan said: 'A lot of people think they are the same thing now! Beckham has to live under slightly different pressures to some of the other players. I know what it is like not to be able to go down a street. But I am not saying that my life is as hectic as David's because football has changed so much.'

We're Sick to the Beck Teeth

Manchester United's players are backing Sir Alex Ferguson over his dressing down of David Beckham. I can reveal that Beckham's treble winning team mates have become fed up with the golden boy's antics. There is little sympathy for the England star over his axing from Sunday's critical win at Leeds. Nor for that matter, is there any dressing room disquiet over Ferguson's decision to blast Beckham in front of other senior players on the training ground last Saturday.

The United stars have become irritated by Beckham's tendency to take Ferguson's patience to the limit. When the 24-year-old player missed training last Friday it was the SECOND TIME in SEVEN DAYS. That did not impress his team mates

Examples of sports reporting are provided in the two extracts on this page. Both deal with the same story but are taken from different newspapers.

The entertainment values that underpin much sports coverage are often evident in the media's fascination with peripheral events. Important boxing matches, for example, are rarely complete without extensive coverage of the pre-match hype that typically surrounds the weigh-in and press conferences. Similarly, football matches are painstakingly analysed by presenters and pundits selected not only for their expert sporting knowledge, but also their ability to entertain the viewers.

Although this style of presentation is not practised by all sections of the media, there can be little doubt that it has been highly effective in attracting and sustaining a mass sporting audience.

Sources: *Daily Telegraph*, 22 February 2000; *Daily Star*, 22 February 2000

ACTIVITY

Media presentation

The two extracts opposite are from press articles taken from different newspapers, but are based on the same events.

1 Which article do you think appeared in the *Daily Telegraph* and which in the *Daily Star*?

2 Comment on the style of presentation in each article.

3 Discuss whether you think the articles are aimed at different types of reader.

4 Collect your own examples of how different newspapers report the same story in different ways.

Rules of the game

All sports are controlled by their respective international and national governing bodies, an important part of whose role involves the formulation and amendment of the rules of the game. Although the media cannot directly influence the way in which a sport is governed, there have been instances when the media have exerted pressure on sports governing bodies to amend the rules to suit their needs. The main reason for such action is to win larger audiences by making sport more 'media friendly'.

▲ Linford Christie was disqualified from the Olympics in 1996 for two false starts

Instances of **media pressure to change the rules** are many and varied. In athletics, for example, the International Amateur Athletics Federation (IAAF) has made radical proposals to reduce the number of false starts which consistently affect major sprint races, and thus to speed up the action for television. One of the proposals under consideration is to disqualify any athlete that causes a false start without giving them a second chance.

In tennis there is constant debate about whether new racket technology and developments in sport science have combined to make the game less of a spectacle, while cricketers have had to become more accustomed to playing the game in its one-day format so as to ensure faster scoring rates and exciting climaxes to games. Although developments of this nature may alarm the traditionalists, they are clearly designed to win new audiences by enhancing the entertainment value of sport.

Another way in which the media can influence the rules is when media technology is used to assist sport officials. Positive examples of this include the use of slow motion replays in cricket matches to help adjudicate close run-out decisions and the use of video evidence in football to highlight serious foul play not spotted by the referee.

On the negative side some people believe that the use of media technology threatens the very nature of the game. Football, for example, has always prided itself on being a fast-flowing sport with few interruptions, but proposals for the use of media technology to help referees make decisions have raised concerns that the game will become fragmented by lengthy delays while officials scrutinise the evidence.

▲ Close run-out decisions in cricket are now decided following video replays

ACTIVITY

Rule changes

The press article on the right shows how the International Amateur Athletics Federation is currently contemplating a rule change that will make the sport more media friendly.

Can you think of any other sports where rule changes have been made primarily to suit the needs of television?

Try to think of three different examples.

Days of repeated false starts numbered as IAAF gets radical

Automatic disqualification proposed for sprinters who jump the gun

False starts, which have blighted so many big sprint races down the years, may soon be a thing of the past if a radical proposal from the International Amateur Athletics Federation is accepted. Under pressure from television companies, who complain that too many false starts throw their schedules out of synch and turn viewers off, the world governing body is investigating scrapping the current system of allowing each runner two chances before being disqualified. 'Sometimes you have four or five (false starts)', said Istvan Gyulai, the IAAF secretary. 'It is controversial, takes time and is quite boring.'

Source: Guardian, 27 February 2000

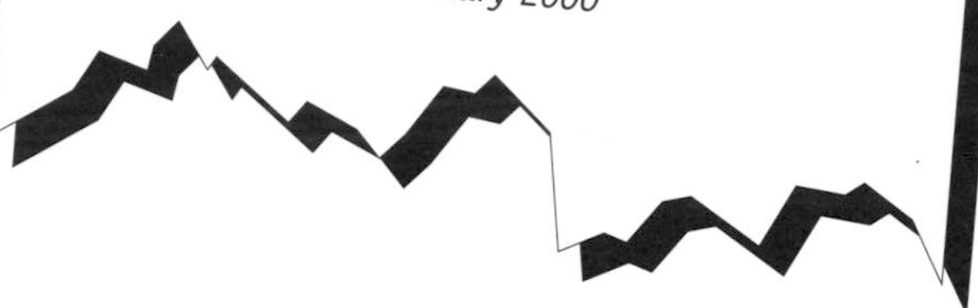

Event programming

Competition among television companies to screen major sporting events has created a vital revenue stream for some sports governing bodies through the sale of broadcasting rights. There can be little doubt that a limited number of sports have gained enormous financial benefits from such arrangements, but some have questioned whether governing bodies have had to make unacceptable concessions in return. One area of concern has been the scheduling of key sports events. For television, this means **programming key sports events** at times that are more likely to attract peak viewing figures. It is not difficult to identify sports where traditional arrangements have been affected by the influence of television. At the 1999 World Athletics Championships in Seville, for example, marathon runners were forced to run in unsuitably hot conditions during the middle of the day rather than early in the morning, in anticipation of a larger television audience. For some this provides clear evidence that television companies are responding to viewers' wishes for greater flexibility. For others there is a fear that traditional sporting arrangements are being compromised.

▲ Marathon runner Abel Anton after winning in Seville

Similarly the press article below provides a good example of how the needs of the mass media are influencing the scheduling of one of the biggest sporting events in the world.

Dispute with FIFA

Japanese organisers are heading for a dispute with FIFA over kick-off times at the 2002 World Cup. Japan are proposing three separate kick-off times but say FIFA want them adjusted to serve the European television market. The Japanese, who are eight hours ahead of most of Europe, want games to kick off at 4am, 6.30am and a final slot no later than 1.30pm European time. Senior Japanese official Yasuhiko Endo said: 'FIFA say this is too early because of European TV but it would be impossible for us to hold games later than that'

Source: *Daily Telegraph* 29 March 2000

ACTIVITY

TV influence on scheduling

Many sports have had to amend their schedules to suit the needs of television. We have highlighted an example in athletics. Can you think of three others?

Effects on sports participation

Media coverage of sport can be a highly effective way of **reaching new audiences**, bringing with it a number of potential benefits. One benefit is the effect that media coverage can have on levels of sports participation. Although reliable evidence is hard to come by, it is safe to assume that recent increases in the number of young people playing tennis are largely down to the exploits of Tim Henman and Greg Rusedski, both of whom have occupied positions in the world top ten rankings.

Similarly, levels of hockey participation were given a boost by the gold-medal performance of the British team at the 1988 Seoul Olympics, as were the numbers of young people wishing to play football following the success of England at the 1990 World Cup in Italy.

Not all sports, however, have benefited in this way. A number of minority sports such as canoeing, judo and archery still find it difficult to attract media coverage, even though British participants often excel on the international stage. In this respect the policy of Channel 4 to feature minority sports such as basketball and cycling has so far been the exception rather than the rule.

ACTIVITY

TV influence on participation

It is often claimed that television coverage of sport leads to more people taking part. Can you think of three occasions when this might have happened?

The conduct of players and supporters

In contrast to its early development, professional sport is now a highly organised and highly commercialised form of entertainment. As a consequence, the pressure to win has become so great that the line between fair play and misbehaviour is more blurred than it once was.

In this respect, golf has always prided itself on the behaviour of its players and supporters, but events at the 1999 Ryder Cup cast serious doubts on the direction in which the game was heading. On an exhilarating final day the American team came from a long way behind to defeat their European rivals. Following the event no one disputed the quality of the American team's play, but serious questions were asked about the biased antics of some elements of the crowd and the lack of golf etiquette shown by a number of American players. For many commentators the events of the 1999 Ryder Cup could be traced to a previous match between the teams at Kiawah Island in 1991, which the American media notoriously billed the 'War on the Shore!'

▲ Justin Leonard (USA) is mobbed after holing a huge putt on the 17th green in the 1999 Ryder Cup.

A similar theme emerges when developments in media technology are considered. Recent innovations now mean that the spectator is made aware of almost everything that is said and done by sports participants. In this respect the argument for media technology is that offenders, be they players or supporters, can be singled out and punished accordingly. The argument against media technology is that it sensationalises the misbehaviour of participants and sets a bad example to younger performers and spectators.

ACTIVITY

Media presentation of sport

As part of the build-up to England's semi-final match with Germany in the 1996 European Football Championships, a British tabloid newspaper made derogatory remarks about the German team using references from the Second World War.

Do you think that this type of media presentation has any great effect on:

- the behaviour of supporters before, during and after the match?
- the behaviour of players on the field of play?

Explain your views.

England played Germany again in Euro 2000. Compare the newspaper coverage of that match with the Euro '96 match.

DAILY Mirror

Monday, June 24, 1996 PEARCE IN OUR TIME 30p

66 96

ACHTUNG! SURRENDER

For you Fritz, ze Euro 96 Championship is over

CUT OUT AND STICK IN YOUR WINDOW

Mirror declares football war on Germany

BY THE EDITOR

I AM writing to you from the Editor's office at Canary Wharf, London.

Last night the Daily Mirror's ambassador in Berlin handed the German Government a final note stating that, unless we heard from them by 11 o'clock that they were prepared at once to withdraw their football team from Wembley, a state of soccer war would exist between us.

I have to tell you now that no such undertaking has been received, and that consequently we are at soccer war with Germany.

Home

It is with a heavy heart we therefore print this public declaration of hostilities and urge every loyal subject to cut it out and place it in a prominent place in their home, office or car.

We desired a peaceful and honourable settlement but the German manager Herr Vogts would not have it.

Having over-run defenceless Russia, the Czech Republic and Croatia, he has evidently made up his mind to attack England at the semi-finals on Wednesday.

His actions show that there is no chance that this man will ever give up his practice of using force, long balls and quick breaks to achieve his ends. He must be stopped.

Safe

The situation in which no team could feel their goalmouth safe has become intolerable.

The Mirror therefore, in fulfilment of our obligations, is going to the aid of our loyal forces, who are so bravely resisting this unprovoked assault in their determination to liberate the European Championship trophy.

You can imagine what a bitter blow it is to me that all my long struggle to win peace

Turn to Page 6

▼ *The Mirror* newspaper front page headline and story about England v Germany in Euro '96

BUILD YOUR LEARNING

Keywords and phrases

You should know the meaning of the words and phrases listed below. If you are unsure about any of them, go back through the last 17 pages to refresh your understanding.

- **Mass media**
- **Radio**
- **Newspapers**
- **Television – terrestrial, cable, satellite, video**
- **Audience size**
- **Audience profile**
- **Sole rights of coverage**
- **Influence of the mass media on sport**
- **Financial rewards**
- **Media pressure to change rules**
- **Programming key sports events**
- **Reaching new audiences**

End of section activity

Select two sports of your choice and complete the following tasks.

1 Describe the mass-media coverage of each sport and explain how the mass media benefit from this coverage.

2 Describe ways in which the mass media have influenced the development of the sports and the people who play them.

3 Compare the ways in which the mass media have influenced your selected sports.

You may find it useful to select the same sports as in earlier activities on pages 166, 175 and 193.

Sport file: football

The development of football

Trends in football spectating reveal some important factors that link the game with developments in the sports industry as a whole. Figure 3.49 shows how professional football attendances reached their peak in 1948–9 at 41 million, but then declined to around 16 million in 1985.

Although in this period there was also a general growth in personal disposable income, it was clear that people now had a greater variety of leisure options from which to choose. With developments in television, the threat of football hooliganism and the notoriously poor standard of facilities at most football grounds, it is hardly surprising that fewer people wished to spend money watching live football.

Since 1986 a number of factors have been influential in the game's revival, although two in particular are worthy of further consideration (see Figure 3.50). First, the Hillsborough disaster in 1989 prompted Lord Justice Taylor to make a series of recommendations about standards of ground safety. Following the publication of his report all clubs set about the task of modernising their stadia so as to make them safer and easier to use. For some clubs this meant developing stadia in new locations that provided better access for supporters. Second, the introduction of the Premier League in 1992 forced the football authorities to follow the lead of the leisure industry as a whole by embracing the idea of marketing more actively. In this respect the introduction of talented foreign players like Dennis Bergkamp and David Ginola has been instrumental in creating a new exciting product that fans want to see.

Figure 3.49 Football league attendances (millions) 1947-85

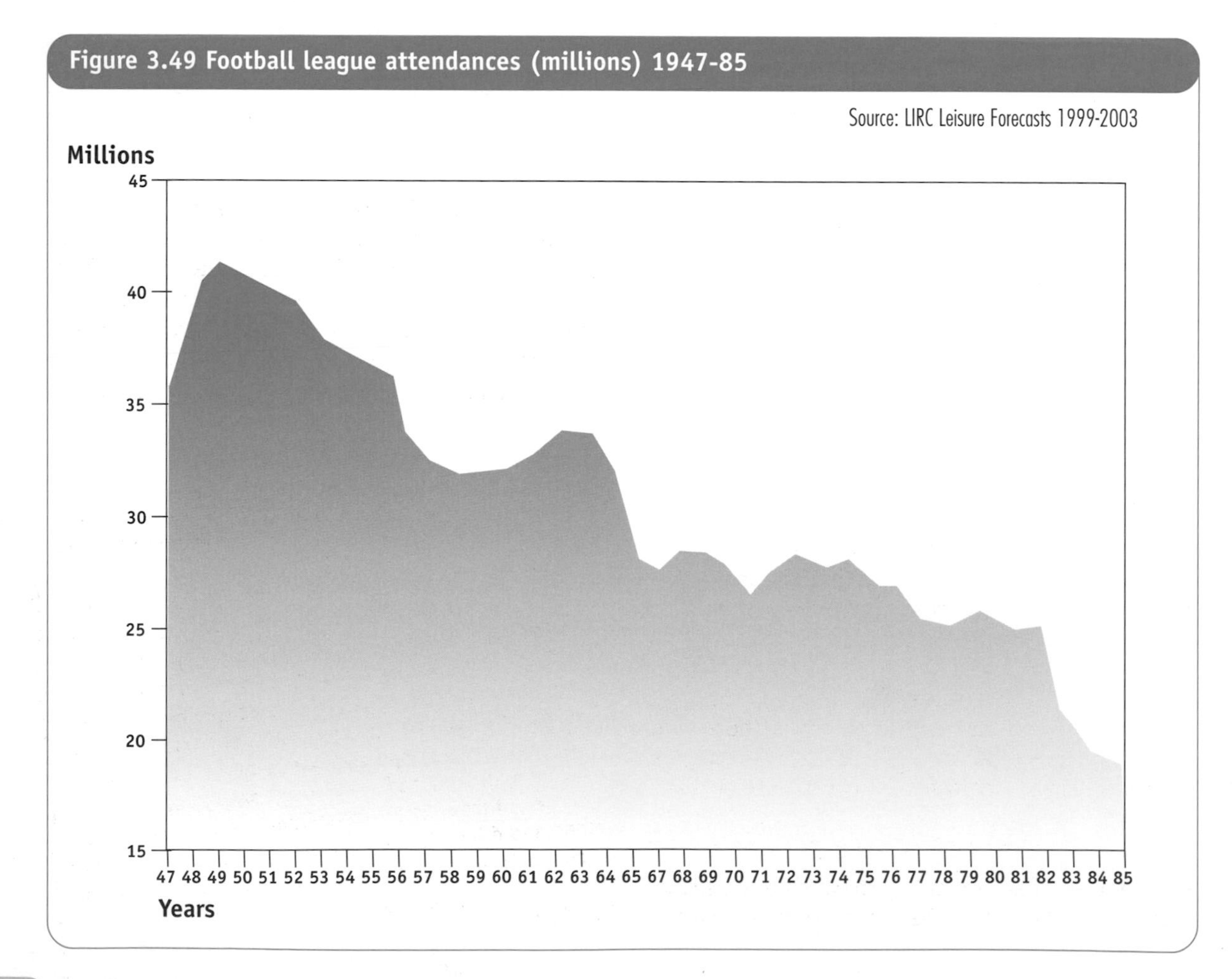

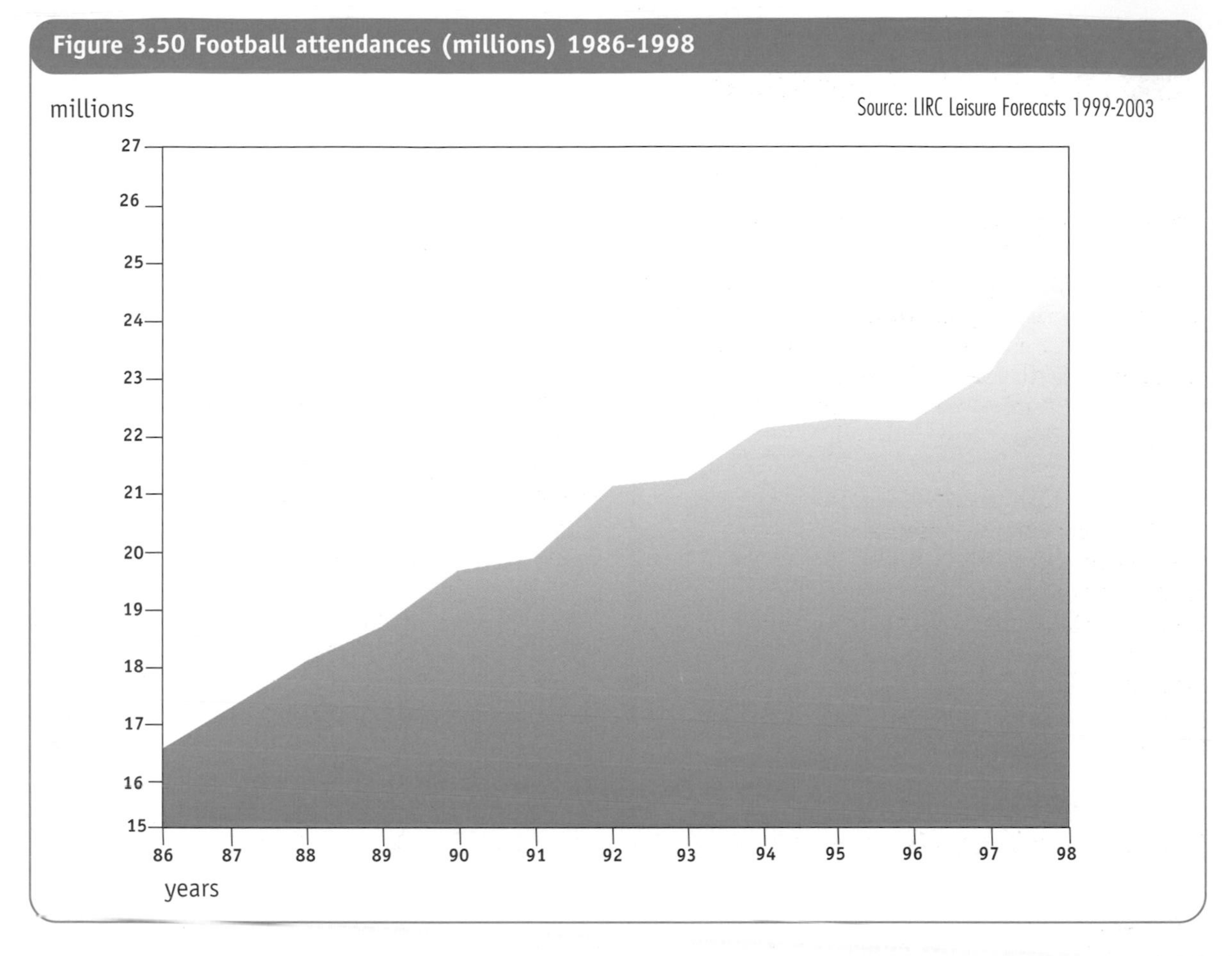

Figure 3.50 Football attendances (millions) 1986-1998

Scale and economic significance of football

Football continues to attract massive worldwide interest, both from participants and spectators. In this case study we will analyse the main factors that contribute to the scale and economic importance of the game.

Participation

According to the General Household Survey 1996, football is the sixth most popular participant sport in the UK, with 5 per cent of adults claiming to have played at least once in the four weeks prior to interview. In terms of team sports football is easily the most popular sporting activity, with its nearest rival, cricket, some way behind. The major interest in football, however, emanates from those who watch the game, rather than those who play it. Further research undertaken by Mintel reveals that:

- 35 per cent of all adults are interested in football
- 6 per cent of all adults pay to watch live football, making it the top 'at the event' spectator sport.

Economic significance of football

The economic significance of football has recently become an important subject of discussion for those academics and policy-makers who wish to measure the game's influence on spending patterns and employment opportunities. For example, Euro '96 made a significant economic contribution to each of the host cities that staged matches.

The economic impact of Euro '96

In total over 280,000 visiting spectators and media came to the UK to attend Euro '96 matches, spending approximately £120 million in the eight host cities and surrounding regions. These visitors generated over 900,000 bed-nights in hotels, guest houses and camp sites, and created over 4,000 full-time-equivalent job years. The average spectator attended 1.24 matches, staying in each respective host city for an average of 1.05 nights and had an average daily expenditure of £77.00. Of total visitor expenditure, 35 per cent went on food and drink, 21 per cent on accommodation, 14 per cent on travel within the host cities and 12 per cent on souvenirs and shopping.
Source: LIRC

In a similar study the Football Research Unit at Liverpool University undertook research designed to evaluate the economic impact generated by the city's two professional league clubs. The research provides clear evidence of the positive economic impact that both Liverpool FC and Everton FC make on the local Liverpool economy.

The football business and the Merseyside economy

About 3,000 full-time jobs in the local economy are dependent on the football industry, plus the 1,400 part-time jobs of those working for the clubs on match days. For every £1 spent by the two clubs combined, 31 pence remains within the local Liverpool economy: around 78 per cent of those questioned noted a significant increase in weekend takings on a match day. Merseyside hotels have a higher than average occupancy rate during the football season. Nearly 750,000 visitors come to the city for football-related reasons.

Source: Football Research Unit, Liverpool University

One of the problems in measuring the true economic value of sport is that much economic activity takes place in the voluntary sector. This is a problem because volunteers usually offer their services free of charge, which makes conventional economic measurements such as the monetary value of labour meaningless. As part of its research into the size and scope of the voluntary sector the Sports Council solved this problem by applying an average-wage rate of £8.31 per hour to the work of various sports volunteers. From this research it was demonstrated that football volunteers contribute the equivalent of £228 million to the national economy, making it the second most valuable sport behind bowls. (See also Figure 3.17, page 169.)

The organisation of football

International level

Internationally, football is organised by the Federation Internationale de Football Association (FIFA), the game's international governing body. FIFA was founded in France in 1904 and initially comprised seven member countries. England joined soon after in 1905 and was quickly followed by the Associations for Scotland, Wales and Ireland. As the international custodian of football, FIFA has a number of key responsibilities which include making and amending the rules of the game and organising the World Cup once every four years.

National level

In England football is controlled by the Football Association (FA), which was founded in 1863. Similar bodies exist for the game in Scotland, Wales and Northern Ireland.

Some of the chief responsibilities of the FA are to oversee the development of England's national teams at all levels, and to organise a range of competitions including the FA Cup. In 1992 the FA formed a subsidiary company with sole responsibility for a Premier League made up of 20 clubs. A further 72 full-time clubs participate in three main divisions run by the Football League.

In Scotland 10 clubs play in the Scottish Premier League with a further 30 clubs playing in three divisions of the Scottish Football League. The National League of Wales contains 20 semi-professional clubs, while another 16 semi-professional sides from Northern Ireland compete in the Irish Football League.

The overall development of the game from grassroots to the highest level is currently in the hands of the FA's Technical Director, who made a number of recommendations in the FA's strategy document, *A Charter for Quality*. These included the establishment of centres of excellence for coaching and developing youngsters, and a reduction in 11-a-side football for very young players.

Regional and local levels

In England the FA delegates a significant proportion of its work to the County Football Associations, who in turn receive more than £1.2 million towards implementing key FA initiatives such as coaching and education programmes. In 1996 the FA restructured its coaching awards programme to suit better the needs of coaches, teachers and medical staff at all levels of football. Changes to the programme are outlined in Figure 3.51.

At local and regional levels the game appears to be stronger than ever, with more than 42,000 clubs affiliated to their regional or district associations. Some of this football is organised along semi-professional lines, but most of it takes place in a voluntary setting.

Figure 3.51: Changes in the FA coaching course structure

Levels	Old courses/awards	New FA course/awards	New UEFA awards
5	–	FA Coaching Diploma	UEFA 'Pro' Coaching Award
4	FA Advanced Coaching Licence	FA Advanced Coaching Licence Youth/Senior	UEFA 'A' Coaching Award
3	FA Preparatory Course /FA Intermediate Award	FA Coaching Licence	UEFA 'B' Coaching Award
2	FA Preliminary Award	FA Coaching Certificate	–
1	Football Leaders Award	FA Junior Team	–
FA Teachers Certificate	FA Teaching Certificate	Managers' Award	–

Source: *FA, Coaching and Education Scheme 1996*

The funding of football

The Football Association (FA)

As the national governing body for football the FA has an important financial responsibility for the game. Its current income stands in the region of £70 million and is derived from four main sources, as shown in Figure 3.52.

Figure 3.52: FA sources of income

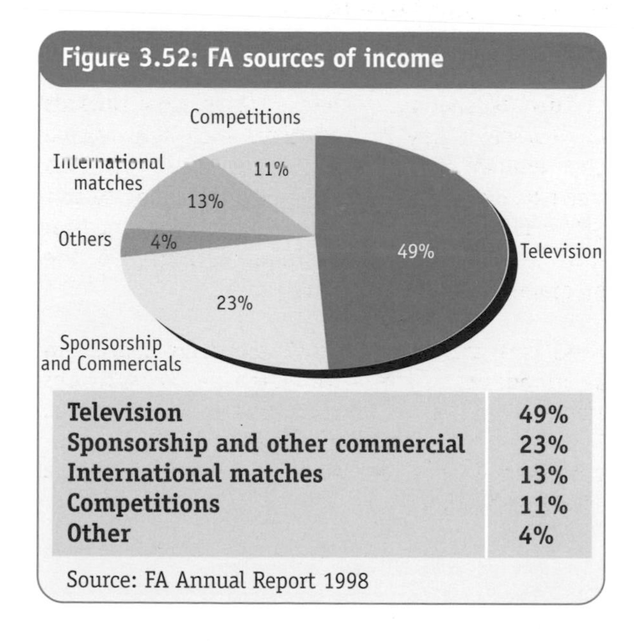

Television	49%
Sponsorship and other commercial	23%
International matches	13%
Competitions	11%
Other	4%

Source: FA Annual Report 1998

The FA has been able to use its major properties, namely the England team and the FA Cup, to generate television income through its domestic contract with BSkyB and the BBC. It has also recently initiated a new four-year sponsorship programme under the title of Football Associates. This is based around a family of ten sponsors that includes AXA, Nationwide, Coca-Cola and Carlsberg.

The FA Premier League

The massive interest which surrounds the professional game is clearly reflected in the annual turnover of the FA Premier League, which now exceeds £200 million. Most of this income is generated through the television deal agreed by the Premier League, BSkyB and the BBC. A breakdown of this income is shown in Figure 3.53.

Since the inception of the Premier League in 1992 some clubs have reaped unprecedented financial benefits, largely through the redistribution of television moneys, but also through additional funding for professional centres of excellence and stadium redevelopment.

The system for distributing television money to clubs from the BSkyB Premiership deal is as follows:

- 50% is distributed equally between the clubs.
- 25% is for the number of television appearances (facility fee).
- 25% is based on a club's final league position (merit award).

Figure 3.55 opposite shows how television money was distributed to each Premier League club in the 1998/99 season.

Professional clubs

All full-time professional football clubs are now run on a highly commercial basis, although not all clubs can command the same level of financial resources. Commercialism has always been part of football, but following the formation of the Premier League in 1992 two different financial tiers have emerged to split the game. Due to its worldwide appeal, membership of the Premier League brings with it a range of commercial opportunities that simply cannot be realised in the leagues below. These include significant shares in television revenue, interest from high-profile sponsors, increased season ticket and gate receipts, and greater merchandising opportunities. These trends are perfectly illustrated by Manchester United, reputedly the richest football club in the world. The income profile of Manchester United for 1998 and 1999 can be seen on page 179.

Figure 3.53: FA Premier League sources of income

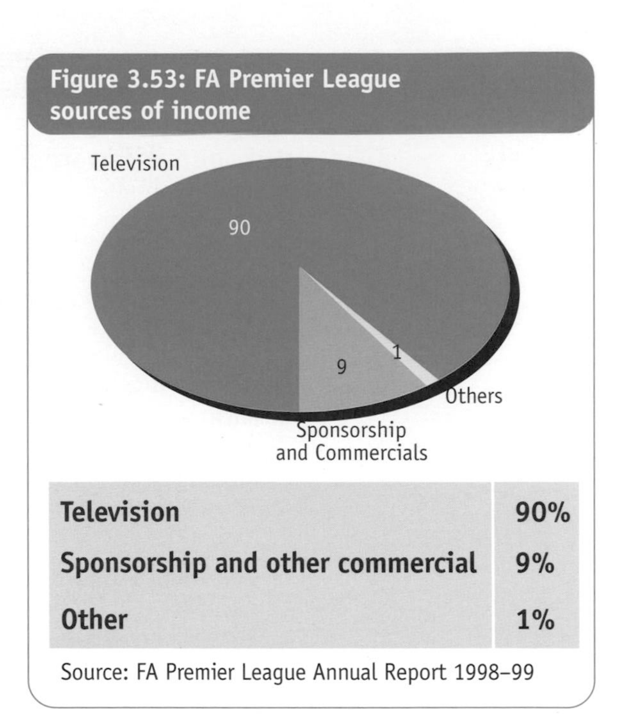

Television	**90%**
Sponsorship and other commercial	**9%**
Other	**1%**

Source: FA Premier League Annual Report 1998–99

Further evidence that the game is adapting to commercial forces can be seen in the number of clubs that have been floated on the stock market. Usually the main reason for widening share ownership in a football club is to create additional capital that can be used to fund stadia development and the purchase of players. So far 17 clubs have followed the lead of Tottenham Hotspur, the first to float in 1983. The share prices for selected clubs are given in Figure 3.54.

Figure 3.54: Share prices of selected football clubs floated on stock exchange

Club	Share price (pence) 29/03/00	52 week price (pence) High	Low
Leicester City	38 (11)	56	35
Manchester United	402 (1)	412	170
Sunderland	435 (5)	702	435
Newcastle United	63 (10)	88	56
Tottenham	66 (6)	80	60

Source: Daily Telegraph, 29 March 2000 Brackets denote league position

Figure 3.55: The distribution of television income to Premier League clubs 1998/99 seasons

Club 1998/99	TV appearances		Merit award £	Facility fee £	Equal share £	Total £
Arsenal	12	15	3,522,429.00	3,893,208.00	3,544,394.00	10,959,986.00
Aston Villa	8	11	2,780,865.00	2,622,712.00	3,544,394.00	8,947,926.00
Blackburn Rovers	6	7	370,782.00	1,932,984.00	3,544,394.00	5,848,115.00
Charlton Athletic	4	8	556,173.00	1,379,456.00	3,544,394.00	5,479,978.00
Chelsea	10	9	3,337,038.00	3,149,000.00	3,544,394.00	10,030,387.00
Coventry City	3	7	1,112,346.00	1,061,832.00	3,544,394.00	5,718,527.00
Derby County	4	3	2,410,083.00	1,243,256.00	3,544,394.00	7,197,688.00
Everton	4	5	1,297,737.00	1,297,736.00	3,544,394.00	6,139,822.00
Leeds United	5	5	3,151,647.00	2,432,032.00	3,544,394.00	9,128,028.00
Leicester City	4	3	2,039,301.00	1,243,256.00	3,544,394.00	6,826,906.00
Liverpool	8	12	2,595,474.00	2,649,952.00	3,544,394.00	8,789,775.00
Manchester United	11	16	3,707,820.00	3,630,064.00	3,544,394.00	10,882,233.00
Middlesborough	6	7	2,224,692.00	1,932,984.00	3,544,394.00	7,702,025.00
Newcastle United	6	6	1,483,128.00	1,905,744.00	3,544,394.00	6,933,221.00
Nottingham Forest	4	4	185,391.00	1,270,496.00	3,544,394.00	5,000,236.00
Sheffield Wednesday	4	4	1,668,519.00	1,270,496.00	3,544,394.00	6,483,364.00
Southampton	3	7	741,564.00	1,061,832.00	3,544,394.00	5,347,745.00
Tottenham	6	9	1,853,910.00	1,987,464.00	3,544,394.00	7,385,723.00
West Ham United	4	9	2,966,256.00	1,406,696.00	3,544,394.00	7,917,301.00
Wimbledon	5	4	926,955.00	1,560,880.00	3,544,394.00	6,032,184.00

Source: *FA, Premier League Accounts 1998/99*

ACTIVITY

Football club share prices

Figure 3.54 gives the share prices for selected football clubs as at 29 March 2000, as well as the highest and lowest value for those shares over a 52-week period. Use a newspaper to establish the current share price for each of these clubs. Find examples of any other clubs that are listed and add them to your table.

1 What factors might cause the share price of a football club to rise?

2 What factors might cause the share price of a football club to fall?

Figure 3.56: Average player wage bill for each division

Division	Average wage bill as % of income for each division
Premier League	50%
Division 1	76%
Division 2	69%
Division 3	66%

Source: Deloitte and Touche

Although the game in the Premier League is generally in good financial health, there have been concerns about the amount of money that many players are now demanding from their clubs. Players' wages increased significantly following the abolition of the 'maximum wage' in the 1960s, but are as nothing compared with developments since the late 1990s.

Top players can now earn as much as £50,000 per week as a result of changes to transfer rules (the Bosman ruling), and the influx of money into the game from sponsors and television companies. Figure 3.56 indicates why the growth in player wages is now posing a threat to the existence of some clubs, especially those clubs in lower leagues.

Grassroots football

There are over 46,000 voluntary sector football clubs in the UK, with a combined membership of 1.6 million (see Figure 3.19, page 170). Most voluntary football clubs rely heavily on income from subscriptions, small sponsorship arrangements, donations and a range of fundraising activities. In a growing number of cases, clubs have been successful in securing grant aid from sources like the Lottery, the Football Trust and Playing Fields Associations.

Football and the media

Football has always been a sport with a high media profile. We will now investigate this relationship in more detail.

Audience size and profile

The game's enduring popularity has meant that the media have not been slow to use football as a means of attracting large audiences. We have already seen how mass-circulation newspapers like the *Sun* and the *Mirror* use football to secure their market position. The same is true for television:

- 35 per cent of all adults are interested in football ('paid to watch', 'watched on television' or 'read about' in the last 12 months), making it the number one sport in the UK.
- 16.5 million adults enjoy watching football on television, again putting it at the top of the viewing list.
- The biggest television audience for football in 1998 was the England v Argentina game in World Cup France '98, watched by 26 million people.

Source: Mintel, *Spectator Sports June 1999*

Football has a broad appeal that may be spreading further due to its continuing use of better marketing. However, this does not mean that the media fail to recognise the main characteristics of their audience. Figure 3.44 on page 200 showed how Sky Sports attempts to classify its football audience into different supporter 'types'. In addition, Sky has also looked closely at the demographic profile of its viewers in a bid to develop coverage that best suits their needs.

The demographic profile of Sky Sports' football audience can be seen in Figure 3.57.

Hours devoted to football on television

As well as commanding the largest audiences, football is also the most extensively covered sport in the media. Figure 3.41 on page 199 showed that football received the most coverage on free-to-air terrestrial channels as well as Sky Sports and Eurosport. Mintel has identified that there are

Figure 3.57: Audience profile of Sky Sports football supporters

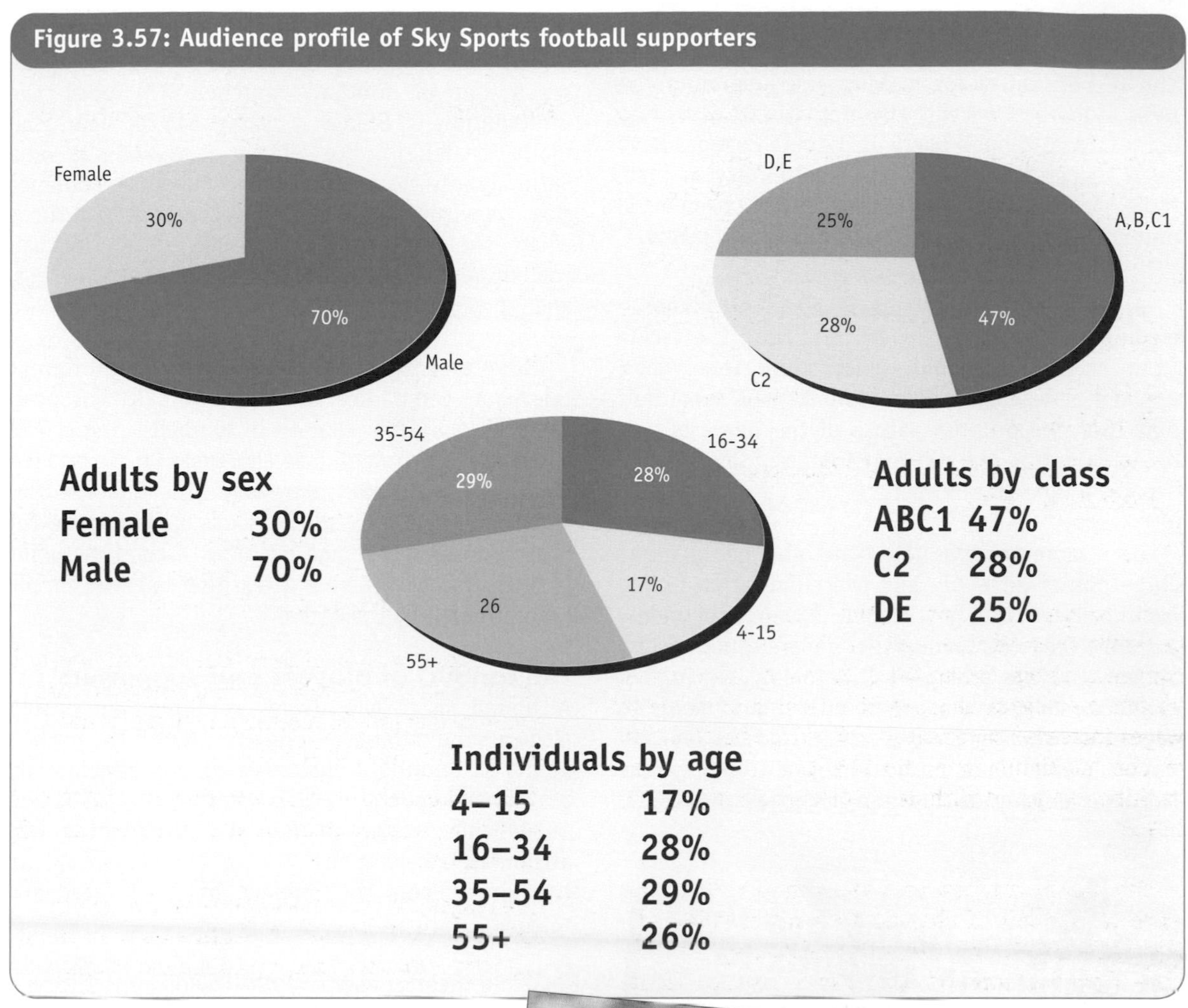

currently 2,367 opportunities to watch professional league and cup football in England each season, excluding Scottish and non-league competitions. As part of this research it was also established that football coverage is on the increase and currently accounts for 5,316 broadcasting hours a year (Mintel, *Spectator Sports*).

Effects of television on football participation

The continued growth of football as a television sport has ensured that the exploits of teams and individual players are never far from the spotlight. One of the benefits of this is the positive role that television can play in encouraging more people to become involved with the sport. Despite losing in a semi-final penalty shoot-out to Germany, England's performance in the 1990 World Cup finals and in particular Paul Gascoigne's arrival on the international stage gave many youngsters the inspiration to try to emulate their sporting heroes. The stunning arrival of Michael Owen at the 1998 World Cup finals in France had a similar effect on youngsters almost a decade later.

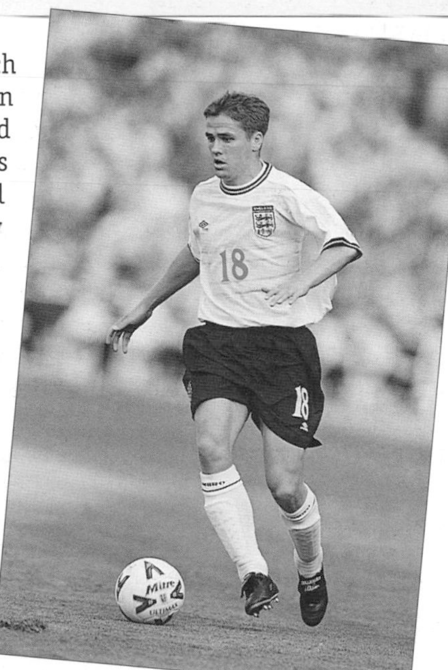

▲ Michael Owen

Rules of the game and event programming

The responsibility for making and amending the rules in football lies with its international governing body FIFA. Although many of the rule changes have been successful in improving the quality of play, some observers believe that changes have been made purely to accommodate the interests of the media.

A good example of this is FIFA's attempts to encourage attacking play by outlawing the tackle from behind. Although most supporters would applaud moves to eliminate violent play, some fans fear that the original nature of the game is now being compromised and that football may one day become a non-contact sport.

On a more positive note other changes, such as three points for a win and the elimination of the back pass to the goalkeeper, have been widely acclaimed as improving the game's quality and appeal. This has prompted FIFA to consider further changes, such as the use of goal-line cameras to adjudicate whether the ball has crossed the line and imposing time limits on goal-keepers to release the ball more quickly, as shown in the article below.

Goalkeepers to release the ball within six seconds to speed up the game

Zurich, 23 February 2000
The International Football Association Board (IFAB), the body responsible for the Laws of the Game, has approved another modification to the football rules with a view to speeding up the game and curbing time-wasting. At its 114th Annual General Meeting on 19 February 2000 in Clivedon, Taplow (England), the Board amended Law 12 – Fouls and Misconduct – by replacing the previous four-step rule with a time limit of six seconds for the goalkeeper to release the ball.

Source: www.fifa.org.

If television has brought some influence to bear on the rules it has certainly had an impact on the scheduling of football matches. Up until the intervention of BSkyB it was usual for nearly all football matches in the UK to start at 3.00 p.m. on a Saturday afternoon. In order to maximise audience size, televised games are now scheduled at times when the typical fan has no other football commitments, such as Friday and Monday evenings, and Sunday afternoons.

More recently, the deals struck by different television companies for the rights to European competitions have resulted in football being shown every day of the week (see also press article on FIFA World Cup, page 208). For some, this demonstrates television's flexibility to the needs of the viewer. For others, football coverage has now reached the point of saturation and there is a fear that fans will simply become bored by the game.

The conduct of players and supporters

Although sport has always contained an unruly element, the difference today centres on the media's ability to highlight instances of misbehaviour by players and spectators alike. During the 1970s and 1980s the decline in football attendances was attributed largely to the problem of hooliganism and has since been the subject of much academic research.

While theories about football hooliganism vary, a number of researchers have pointed to the way in which the media have used this issue either to sell more newspapers or to use certain groups, especially young working-class unemployed males, as scapegoats for wider problems in society.

Of more concern to the football authorities at the present time is the behaviour of players on the field of play. Football has always contained its fair share of disciplinary problems, but recently the debate surrounding the conduct of players on the pitch has intensified.

The views of the media on this matter are well represented in the newspaper article opposite.

Premiership marred by day of indiscipline

The Premier League's directive for referees to show more leniency and brandish fewer yellow cards was in tatters last night after a day of shame and indiscipline involving many of the game's best-known players. The highly-paid stars of Manchester United, Tottenham, Leeds, Chelsea and Wimbledon were at the centre of a number of incidents that made a mockery of any thoughts that match officials should give them their head – and hold back from reaching for their notebooks so readily.

As the champions were being soundly beaten by Bobby Robson's Newcastle, the worst side of the undoubted cohesion in their ranks was pushing to the forefront. Roy Keane was setting anything but a captain's example by being sent off for the sixth time in his United career. And the basis of his dismissal? The first yellow card came not for a hand-ball, not for a mistimed tackle, but for dissent. And where was the learning curve? Andy Cole was soon to follow into referee Steve Lodge's book for the same offence.

Source: *Sunday Telegraph*, 13 February 2000

Trends in football

There are many trends in football, including:

- changing expectations of participants and supporters, e.g. player wages; seating and ancillary facilities at football stadia
- developments in technology which have affected the design of stadia and the way games are officiated
- changing rates of participation.

In this section we will focus on one of these trends by investigating women's participation in football.

Women's participation in football

Football has traditionally been regarded as a working-class game for men, but that would now appear to be changing. In 1990 there were only 80 girls' teams, but by 1998 that figure had increased to over 1,000. The number of female players also increased from 21,500 in 1996 to 34,000 in 1998. These trends are outlined in Figure 3.58.

Figure 3.58: Female participation in football

1997/98	Number of teams	Number of players
Girls	1,000	20,000
Women	700	14,000
Total	**1,700**	**34,000**

Source: Sport and Recreation Management, February 1999

More young girls are playing football in schools and through the Professional Footballers Association (PFA) Football in the Community Scheme. In recent research MORI found that 51 per cent of all secondary-aged girls had participated in football at some time or other. Developments of this nature lay behind the FA's decision to launch its female Talent Development Plan.

The main aim of the plan is to make women's football the top female sport in the new millennium, by putting in place a system for the identification and development of talented young players from the age of 10 years through to the England senior team. This will involve the establishment of a network of Centres of Excellence for players in three age bands (U12, U14, U16).

In terms of football spectating the future appears equally bright. Although football remains the preserve of young men, the Sir Norman Chester Centre for Football Research has established that females now constitute around 12 per cent of all spectators. It also found that less than half of fans now watch the game in all-male groups.

The growing female influence in football has been reflected in some sections of the media. Results from the AXA FA Women's Premier League are widely reported throughout the press and the *Daily Express* now runs a weekly column devoted to women's football. There is also a bi-monthly women's magazine called *On the Ball* and a weekly Women's Information Bulletin going out to over 2,200 clubs in the UK.

While women's football in the UK still has to catch up on the likes of Germany and the USA, the game is currently justifying its status as one of the fastest growing sports in the UK.

▲ Female footballers in action during the Women's World Cup 1999

Useful addresses

FIFA
PO Box 85
8030
Zurich
Switzerland
www.fifa.com

UEFA
www.uefa.com

Football Association and Women's Football Association
16 Lancaster Gate
London
W2 3LW
www.the-fa.org

FA Premier League
11 Connaught Place
London
W2 2ET
www.fa-premier.com

Nationwide Football League
www.football.nationwide.co.uk

Professional Footballers Association
2 Oxford Court
Bishopsgate

ACTIVITY

Investigating football

1 Explain, using appropriate statistics, the scale and economic importance of football in terms of the numbers employed, the number of participants and financial turnover.

2 Briefly describe the organisation of football at international, national, regional and local levels. Draw diagrams to show the structure of the game in this country.

3 Explain how professional football is funded and how commercialisation has affected the game.

4 Explain how football is funded at grassroots level.

5 Describe the mass media's coverage of football and explain how the mass media benefit from this coverage.

6 Describe ways in which the mass media have influenced the development of the professional game, its players and coaches, and the spectators.

7 Compare the scale and economic importance, and the ways in which the mass media have influenced football, with one other sport of your choice. (You could use the information in the following case study about tennis to complete this question.)

8 Describe at least one major trend (other than women's participation) that has occurred in football. Support your findings with relevant information, data and examples.

Sport file: tennis

The development of tennis

Tennis is one of the UK's most popular sports, although it has had to remain sensitive to a variety of factors that affect the leisure industry as a whole. Greater personal disposable incomes have led to more people with higher expectations of service provision than ever before. In response, tennis facility providers such as the LTA, David Lloyd, local authorities and private tennis clubs have had to be ever more mindful of the service they provide. As a result, providers have become more interested in aspects such as surface technology and the range and quality of ancillary facilities on offer. Similarly, demands to make the sport a year-round activity have been influential in the recent growth of good-quality indoor facilities.

One of the main threats to tennis has been the increasing trend to participate in sport for health rather than competitive reasons. Some organisations like David Lloyd have sought to address this problem by creating additional leisure opportunities alongside their main tennis provision.

Lloyd's ace: tennis champ bounces back with new club site

New plans for a £10 million tennis and fitness centre in York were unveiled today. The College of Ripon & York St John announced it was going into partnership with Next Generation Clubs – headed by former Wimbledon star David Lloyd – to develop the centre on its playing fields just off Hull Road. Centre facilities would include eight indoor and five outdoor tennis courts, three squash courts, three badminton courts, a volleyball court, sprint track, gymnasium and fitness centre.

Source: York Evening Press, 7 March 2000

Scale and economic importance

Participation

Tennis is the most popular participant racket sport in the UK: 2 per cent of the adult population claim to play the game regularly. However, recent trends in participation point to some signs of decline. This may be due to loss of interest, time constraints, or a preference to participate in sport for health rather than competition reasons. Spectator statistics – for television viewing and at tournament events – show how tennis has maintained its position as of one of the UK's most popular sports:

- 24 per cent of all adults are interested in tennis, making it fifth sport in overall popularity in the UK.
- 1 per cent of all adults pay to watch a live tennis game; the main tennis events in the UK attracted 666,335 spectators in 1998.
- 11 million adults enjoy watching tennis on television, making it the fifth most popular televised sport.
- Wimbledon is the best-attended UK tennis tournament, drawing a crowd of 424,998 over its two weeks in June and July 1998, with a daily average of 32,692 spectators.

Source: Mintel, *Spectator Sports* 1999

Economic significance of tennis

Evidence for the economic significance of tennis is difficult to come by, although information on consumer spending and the value of volunteer labour provide useful indicators. It is thought that British consumers spend around £3.5 billion a year participating in sport, although tennis expenditure accounts for only a modest proportion of this. Total spending on goods for racket sports participation is barely £200 million, which for the average UK tennis player is roughly £30 a year. These trends are given further weight when the spending patterns of racket sports participants are compared with their team-playing counterparts, as in Figures 3.59, 3.60 and 3.61.

Figure 3.59: Spending on sports clothing during last 12 months

	Nothing (%)	£1–75 (%)	£76–200 (%)	More than £200 (%)
Racket sports	21	30	36	13
Team sports	15	26	41	18

Source: Mintel, 1998 – *The Sports Market*

Figure 3.60: Spending on sports footwear during last 12 months

	Nothing (%)	Less than £30 (%)	£31–50 (%)	£51–100 (%)	More than £100 (%)
Racket sports	18	16	16	30	18
Team sports	12	12	18	32	26

Source: Mintel, 1998 – *The Sports Market*

Figure 3.61: Spending on sports equipment during last 12 months

	Nothing (%)	£1–75 (%)	£76–100 (%)	£101–200 (%)	More than £200 (%)
Racket sports	35	28	10	10	15
Team sports	30	22	15	14	17

Source: Mintel, 1998 – *The Sports Market*

If tennis players do not contribute significant amounts of money through their purchase of tennis goods, it is interesting to see if their expenditure patterns for tennis services are any different. In this respect the evidence is more encouraging.

For example, Mintel has recently found that a family joining a private facility like a David Lloyd Leisure Club would on average be prepared to spend £1,000 on membership, activities and related purchases.

In the voluntary sector, tennis participation remains strong, which indicates that volunteer labour is still a vital element in the game's overall development. It is possible to assess the monetary value of this labour by multiplying a 'shadow wage' by the total number of volunteer hours worked. Figure 3.17 on page 169 shows that if all tennis volunteers were paid a standard wage of £8.31 per hour, their combined efforts would contribute approximately £35.5 million to the economy. Measured in this way tennis is the seventh most valuable sport in the UK.

The organisation of tennis

This section illustrates the main organisational developments in the game at international, national, regional and local levels.

International level

The three main bodies involved in international tennis are:

- International Tennis Federation (ITF)
- Association of Tennis Professional (ATP) Tour
- Women's Tennis Association (WTA) Tour

International Tennis Federation (ITF)

The ITF is the international governing body for tennis and is one of the largest sports federations, representing five regional associations and 200 national associations. It has its origins in the International Lawn Tennis Federation (ILTF) formed in 1913. Its main responsibilities include:

- administering the rules of tennis, including the technical specifications for courts and equipment;
- organising international competitions such as the Grand Slam events, the Davis Cup and the Federation Cup;
- structuring tennis by sanctioning international circuits and events like the ITF Junior World Ranking Circuit and ITF Veterans Events;
- funding a variety of tennis initiatives as part of its worldwide Development Programme.

ATP Tour and WTA Tour

The ATP Tour organises the men's professional tennis tour (excluding the four Grand Slam events). The WTA Tour is responsible for the women's professional tour which consists of nearly 60 events in 25 countries.

National level

The modern game of tennis originated in England after a Major Wingfield published the first set of rules and marketed basic equipment in 1874. Not long afterwards the Lawn Tennis Association (LTA) was set up as the sport's national governing body, a role it still plays today. In Northern Ireland, tennis is governed by a separate organisation, Tennis Ireland (Ulster Branch), whereas the associations for Wales and Scotland are affiliated to the LTA.

One of the LTA's main roles is to oversee the development of the game at all levels. It has published a four-year plan entitled 'A Strategy for the New Millennium – British Tennis and You', which contains a number of important initiatives, including:

- the provision of additional facilities through the Indoor Tennis Initiative (ITI)
- supporting the development of centres of excellence
- training coaches through the LTA Coach Licensing Scheme (see Figure 3.62).

Figure 3.62: LTA coaching awards structure

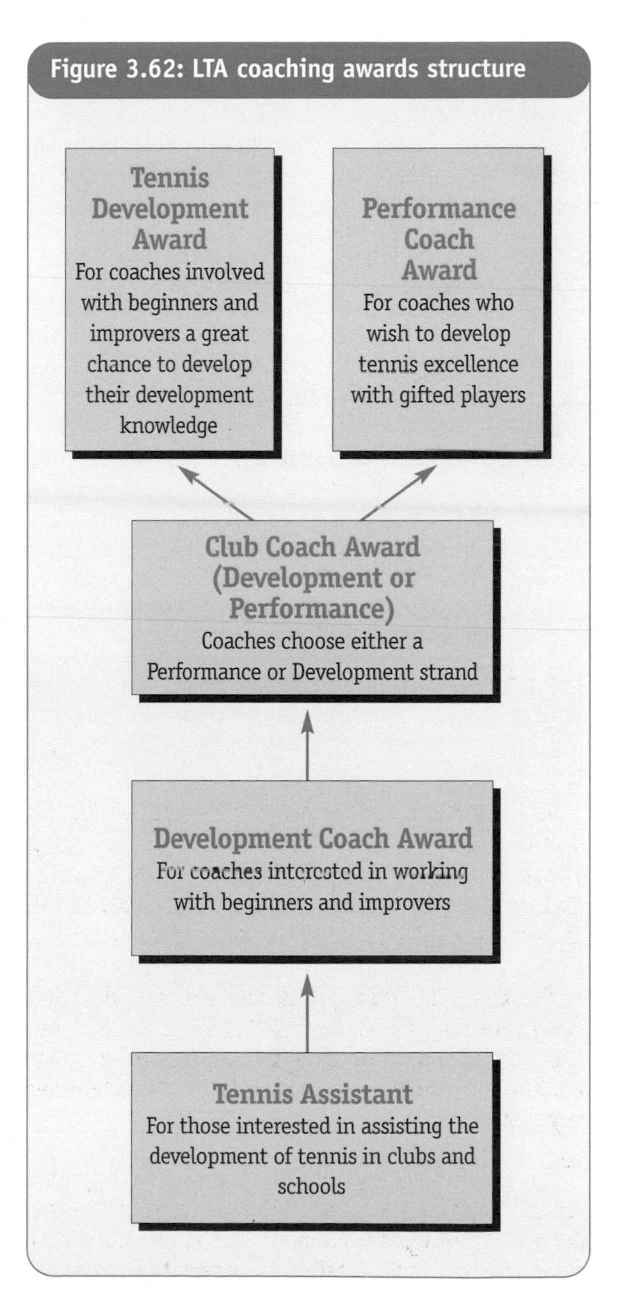
Tennis Development Award
For coaches involved with beginners and improvers a great chance to develop their development knowledge
Performance Coach Award
For coaches who wish to develop tennis excellence with gifted players
Club Coach Award (Development or Performance)
Coaches choose either a Performance or Development strand
Development Coach Award
For coaches interested in working with beginners and improvers
Tennis Assistant
For those interested in assisting the development of tennis in clubs and schools

Regional and local levels

The LTA channels much of its support for grassroots tennis through its county offices. The aim of the LTA's county administration is to provide an infrastructure which supports the development of tennis at a local level for its 2,386 affiliated clubs. The LTA is currently considering how it can assist clubs by providing resources which help them attract more members.

The funding of tennis

A more commercial approach to tennis was begun in 1968 when the tennis authorities allowed professional players into the main competitions. From this point on, the likes of Rod Laver, who had previously turned professional, returned to the tennis scene and amateurism soon disappeared from the highest levels of the game. The financial implications of the new professional era are largely dealt with by the international and national governing bodies for the sport.

As the national governing body for tennis in this country, the LTA is central to the funding of the game at all levels. A breakdown of the LTA's annual income is shown in Figure 3.48, page 205.

Tournaments and events

As the world's most famous tennis tournament, the Wimbledon Championships provide the main funding source for both the LTA and the All England Lawn Tennis Club (AELTC), whose facilities are used to stage the event (see Figure 3.63). The tournament itself generates most of its income from the sale of television rights, paying spectators and more recently corporate hospitality.

▲ The Wimbledon Championships provide the main source of income for the LTA

Some commentators have blamed the tennis authorities for placing too much emphasis on corporate guests, many of whom prefer to watch the tennis from the comfort of their hospitality tent rather than visiting the show courts themselves. As a result it has been claimed that dedicated tennis fans find it impossible to purchase tickets for important matches, even though games are often played in front of non-capacity crowds.

Criticisms have also been levelled at the LTA for failing to invest enough of its proceeds in the grassroots of the game. In response the LTA has pointed to a number of initiatives which it is now trying to implement, such as specialist indoor facilities, regional centres of excellence and Community Tennis Partnerships (CTPs).

Figure 3.63: Income from the Wimbledon Championships as a proportion of the LTA's total annual income

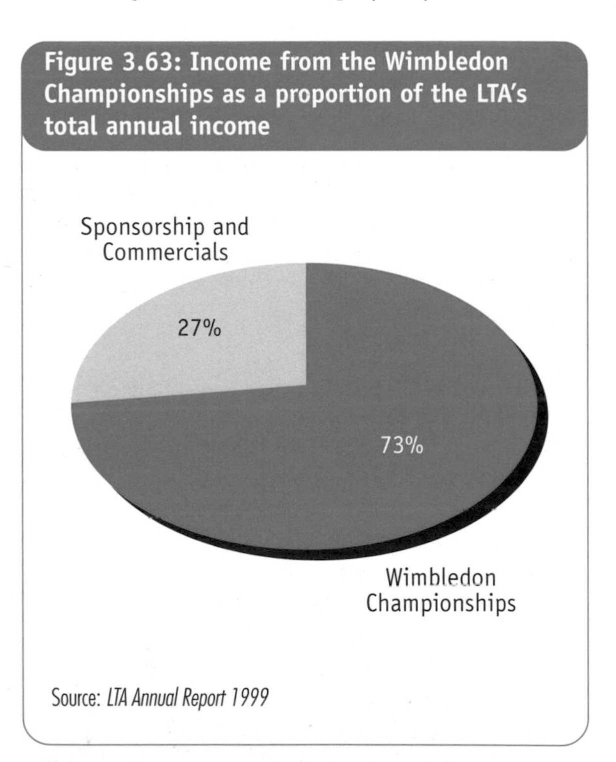

Source: *LTA Annual Report 1999*

As the LTA is a non-profit making organisation a significant amount of its income is reinvested in the game at grassroots level as part of training and coaching initiatives, and facility development.

Sponsorship

The worldwide popularity of tennis coupled with the resurgence of British talent has made the game very attractive to potential sponsors. The LTA currently receives support from 34 high-profile companies, eight of whom form part of the British Tennis Partnership (BTP). The BTP is a brand created by the LTA to promote a stronger image for the game.

Despite the influx of commercial interests in tennis over recent years, the All England Tennis Club and the LTA have steadfastly refused to embrace sponsorship of the Wimbledon Championships themselves. The authorities' determination to preserve the prestige of the world's oldest tennis tournament has pleased a number of traditional tennis fans who believe that too much commercial input might be bad for the game.

Figure 3.64: Breakdown of income from national and county associations and Registered Membership Scheme

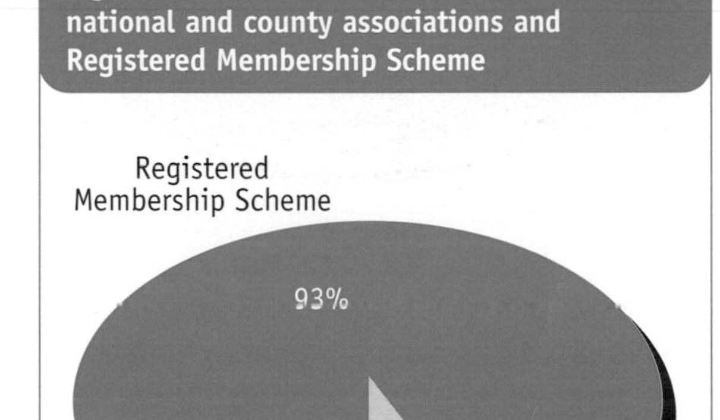

Source: *LTA Annual Report 1999*

Subscriptions

Subscription income from the national and county associations and the registered membership scheme is worth about £1 million to the LTA. A breakdown of this income is provided in Figure 3.64.

The Registered Membership Scheme is designed to provide players and supporters with a range of benefits, including the monthly Ace and British Tennis magazines. Already the scheme has attracted over 80,000 members and is growing fast.

Tennis and the media

This section investigates the media's interest in tennis and evaluates their impact on the game.

Audience size and profile of tennis fans

Although not quite as popular as football, tennis plays an important role in the media's attempts to secure large audiences. In 1998/99, 11 million adults claimed that they enjoyed watching tennis on television, making it the fifth most popular sport of those surveyed.

In this country most of the media's attention is focused on Wimbledon fortnight, when tennis dominates the back pages of newspapers and features highly in television viewing figures. The importance of the Wimbledon Championships for free-to-air terrestrial channels is shown in Figure 3.41 on page 199.

Despite some claims to the contrary, tennis spectatorship remains the preserve of the elderly middle class. This view is confirmed by research into the profile of tennis spectators, shown in Figures 3.65 and 3.66.

Figure 3.65: The profile of tennis spectators

The common characteristics of tennis spectators:

- over 55
- socioeconomic group AB

Source: Mintel, *Spectator Sports* 1999

Figure 3.66: Tennis participation rates in the four weeks prior to interview by socioeconomic group (percentage of population)

Professional	3.5
Employers and managers	2.8
Intermediate/junior non-manual	2.0
Skilled manual	1.0
Semi-skilled	1.0
Manual	1.0
Unskilled manual	0.4

Source: *General Household Survey 1996*

These findings have important implications for the media and tennis. If the media are to benefit from tennis then tennis itself needs to have a broad appeal. Similarly, tennis is equally aware that it needs the support of the media to help achieve this objective. Examples of how the media have benefited tennis can be seen in the extract from the LTA's 1999 Annual Report.

Hours devoted to tennis on television

The importance of tennis to the media is reflected in the level of coverage it receives on television. Figure 3.41 on page 199 shows that tennis coverage runs to some 1,410 hours on Sky Sports and Eurosport, plus a further 206 hours on free-to air terrestrial channels. Overall, tennis accounts for 8.1 per cent of the sports broadcasting output for free-to-air terrestrial channels and 6.4 per cent for that of Sky Sports and Eurosport.

Effects of television on tennis participation

The effects of television on rates of tennis participation would seem to be significant, although there is always a debate as to how long any such impact may last. Certainly, most tennis providers admit that their peak periods fall during or immediately after major televised tournaments like Wimbledon.

What really adds to the impact of television, however, is when home-grown players perform well in high-profile events like Wimbledon or the Davis Cup. In this respect the emergence of both Tim Henman and Greg Rusedski in the world's top ten has provided British tennis with its most successful performers for many years. What remains to be seen is whether either player has the ability to win a major tournament and the likely effect this could have on levels of tennis participation in this country.

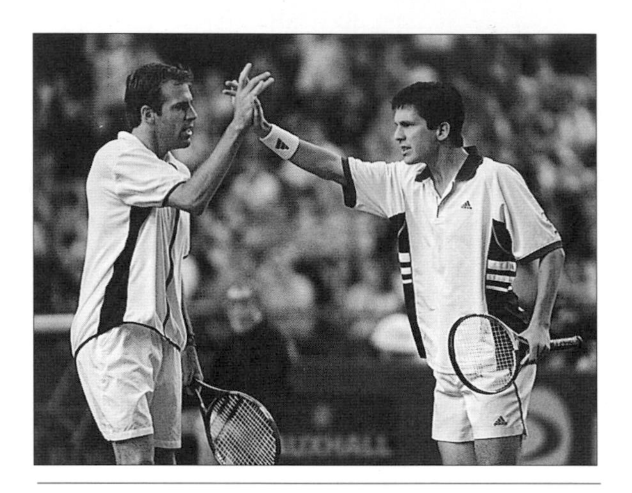

▲ Tim Henman and Greg Rusedski

In terms of both volume and content, coverage in the broadcast media improved dramatically in 1999. Tennis has been featured in a fun and dynamic light by broadcasters covering domestic events as well as in daily programming across terrestrial, cable and satellite channels. Special features, news angles, competitions and advertising campaigns have all highlighted tennis and the LTA. Thanks to this enhanced coverage, bigger audiences than ever before have been exposed to the sport.

Source: *LTA Annual Report* 1999

Rules of the game and event programming

The rules of tennis have remained largely unchanged over the years. Discussion of the future has focused on concerns that tennis has become less media friendly due to advances in racket technology and the increased physical prowess of players. Racket technology in particular has been blamed for increasing the dominance of servers, with the result that spectators and viewers have to make do with shorter rallies and a reduced variety of strokes. This has led to a consensus that tennis has become less entertaining and devoid of 'characters'.

Some of the changes which have been discussed include reducing the size of the service area in order to slow the service down, exerting pressure on the server by only allowing one serve, and making all players use the same rackets. At Wimbledon, experiments have already been conducted using lower-pressure balls, although the effects on the nature of the game proved negligible.

Tennis has not been slow to accommodate the interests of the media. At the Australian Open in 1997, for example, a number of players complained about the scheduling of matches in the heat of the mid-afternoon sun in order to accommodate the interests of television.

In another development, both the men's and the women's Wimbledon singles finals have recently been rescheduled to take place on a weekend during prime television slots. The authorities' determination to keep to the schedule, especially following interruptions for bad weather, has been questioned by a number of players who believe that they are asked to play too many games over too short a period of time.

▲ Rain stops play at Wimbledon

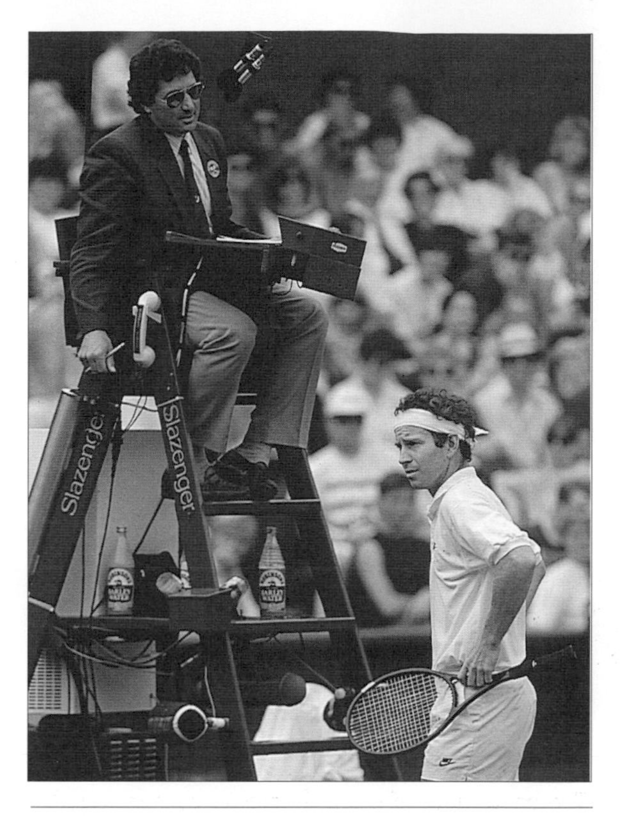

▲ John McEnroe arguing with a tennis umpire

The conduct of players and supporters

Generally speaking the conduct of tennis players and supporters does not provide the authorities with any major problems. This has not always been the case. In the 1970s and early 1980s players such as Ilie Nastasie, Jimmy Connors and perhaps most famously of all, John McEnroe, became notorious for their ill-tempered antics on court.

In response, the ITF introduced a number of disciplinary measures, whereby players are forced to forfeit points for persistent bad behaviour. These moves seem to have been successful, with fewer confrontations now taking place between players and umpires.

The notoriety of players like John McEnroe and Ilie Nastasie stemmed largely from the way they were vilified by the press. At the time the press generally took the line that players who misbehaved set a bad example to youngsters and should be punished accordingly. However, there is a sneaking suspicion that certain sections of the media were grateful for the newsworthy stories provided by such players. Evidence for this can be gained from the current popularity of veteran events, where the stars of the 1970s and early 1980s sometimes gain more media attention than their modern counterparts.

Trends in tennis

Among the many trends in tennis are the following:

- Changing expectations of participants and supporters, e.g. prize money at professional events, and seating and ancillary facilities at tennis stadia.
- Developments in technology affecting the design of rackets, playing surfaces and devices to help umpires officiate at matches.
- Rates of participation.

In this section we will evaluate the levels of participation of young people in tennis.

Participation of young people in tennis

There are currently almost 4 million tennis players in the UK, of whom more than 1 million play at least once a fortnight. Among the more frequent players there is a fairly even divide between males and females, while over half are under the age of 24.

One of the most important factors in a young person's decision to play tennis is the way in which they are exposed to the sport at school. In a recent survey conducted by MORI, it was found that the frequency of tennis participation in schools had risen from 16 per cent in 1994 to 18 per cent in 1999. Figure 3.67 shows that tennis was ranked fourth behind rounders, football and netball in schools in 1999.

Figure 3.67: Games played frequently in school lessons in the last school year

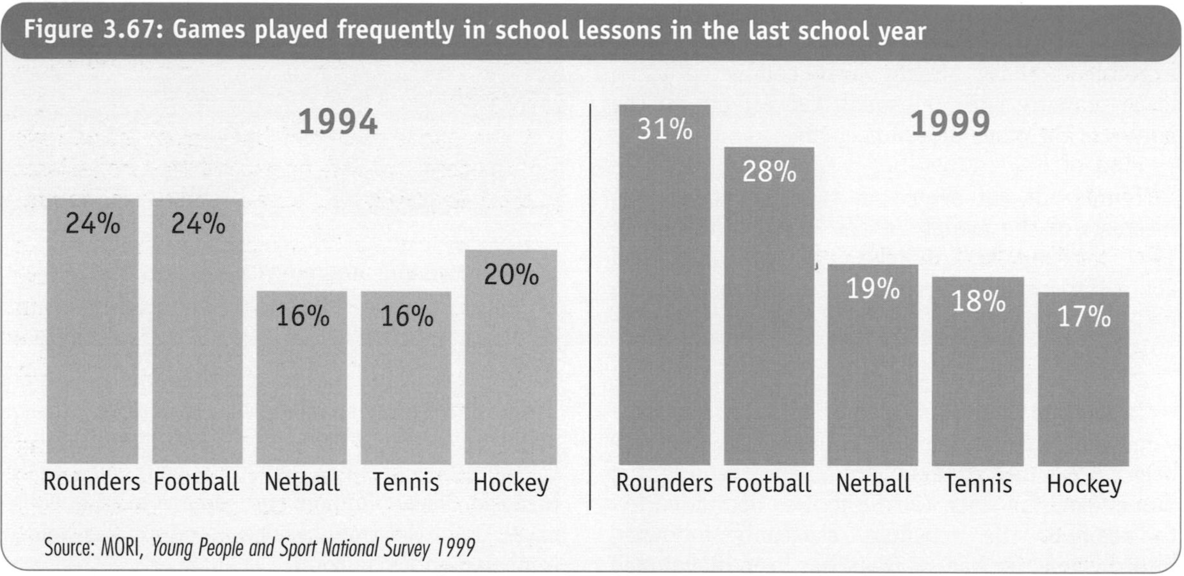

Source: MORI, *Young People and Sport National Survey 1999*

Figure 3.68: Members of sports clubs outside of school, not organised by school

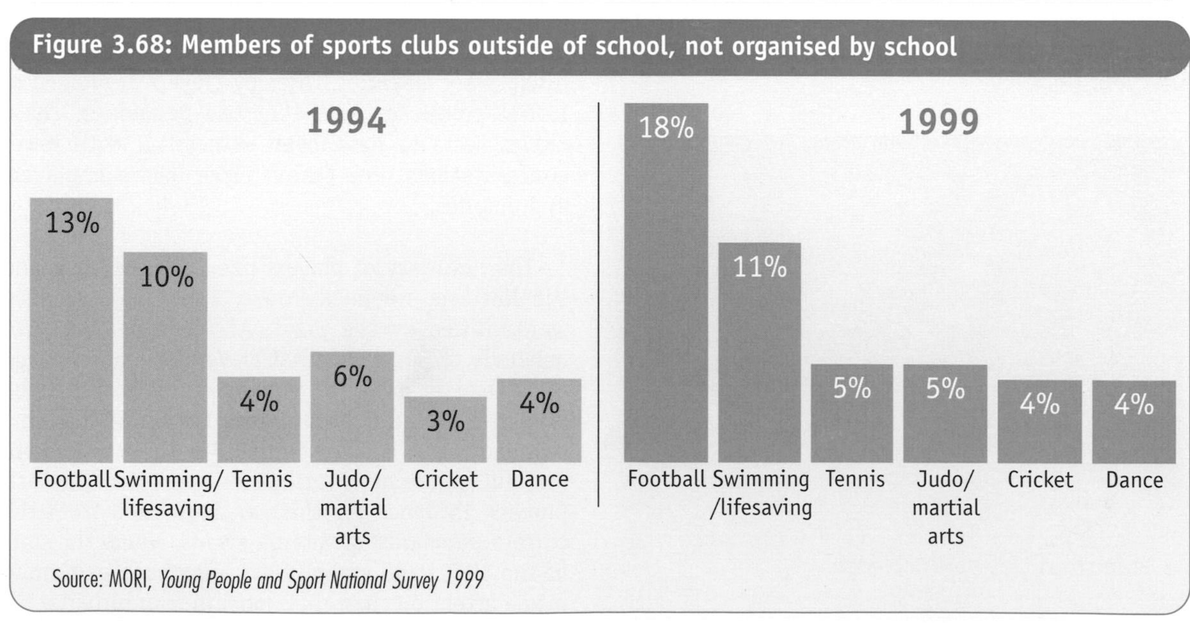

Source: MORI, *Young People and Sport National Survey 1999*

The research findings highlighted opposite demonstrate why the LTA is currently trying to initiate partnerships between schools and the wider community. At the heart of these initiatives are Community Tennis Partnerships (CTPs), which aim to create links between clubs, schools and local authorities. To date, 77 CTPs have been established, helping to make the game more accessible to young people.

Although the introduction of CTPs has generally been welcomed, some doubts remain as to whether they are being developed in the right locations. Some commentators believe that levels of tennis participation among young people will only increase significantly when facilities, equipment and coaching are provided in more deprived local areas.

Useful addresses

International Tennis Federation Ltd
Bank Lane
Roehampton
London
SW15 5XZ

ATP Tour International Headquarters
200 ATP Tour Boulevard
Ponte Vedra Beach, F1
32082
USA
www.atptour.com

Lawn Tennis Association
The Queens Club
Palliser Road
West Kensington
London
W14 9EG
www.lta.org.uk

ACTIVITY

Investigating tennis

1 Explain, using appropriate statistics, the scale and economic importance of tennis in terms of the numbers employed, the number of participants and financial turnover.

2 Briefly describe the organisation of tennis at international, national, regional and local levels. Draw diagrams to show the structure of the game in this country.

3 Explain how professional tennis is funded and how commercialisation has affected it.

4 Explain how tennis is funded at grassroots level.

5 Describe the mass media coverage of tennis and explain how the mass media benefit from this coverage.

6 Describe ways in which the mass media have influenced the development of the professional game, its players and coaches, and the spectators.

7 Compare the scale and economic importance of tennis, and the ways in which the mass media have influenced the sport, with one other sport of your choice. (You could use the information in the previous case study about football to complete this question.)

8 Describe at least one major trend (other than developing young people's participation in tennis) that has occurred in the game. Support your findings with relevant information, data and examples.

Preview

In this unit we look at the ways in which leisure and recreation providers use marketing techniques and processes to achieve their objectives. Regardless of the type of leisure and recreation organisation, or the products and services it offers, marketing has a key function in its success. You will gain an understanding and appreciation of how marketing is a continuous process that includes everything that an organisation does to attract and keep customers, identify and satisfy their needs, and continue to grow and develop successfully and effectively.

Marketing is particularly important in leisure and recreation because the industry is fiercely competitive, with providers often aiming their products and services at the same customers. Frequently, the effectiveness of an individual provider's marketing activities will determine whether or not customers choose its products and services in preference to those of a competitor.

This unit is assessed by an externally-set case study or tests.

4

Marketing in leisure and recreation

Contents

The marketing process

The Institute of Marketing describes **marketing** as:

the management process of identifying, anticipating and satisfying customer requirements profitably.

This means that those responsible for marketing within an organisation must be able to identify the needs of both existing and potential customers in order to provide products and services that satisfy those needs. The main aim is usually to maximise income and generate profits. However, it is important to note that some organisations within the leisure and recreation industry operate on a non-profit basis. For such organisations, profitability may be measured in terms of social benefit to the community, rather than in purely financial terms. For example, many council-owned parks and art galleries do not charge an admission fee and therefore do not make a financial profit.

Whatever the type of organisation and its motive for providing products and services, the principle that underpins the **marketing concept** is the same:

getting the right product to the right people in the right place at the right time, at the right price, using the right promotion.

All leisure and recreation providers need to recognise the important role that marketing plays in allowing them to reach their organisational objectives.

Getting it right is vital, because if anything is wrong customers will not be satisfied with the product or service or the way in which it is delivered to them, and it is then unlikely that an organisation will achieve its objectives. Even when an organisation gets everything right, that is not the end of the marketing process. It is necessary to monitor and evaluate progress constantly in order to ensure that products and services continue to meet customer needs.

This is particularly relevant to the leisure and recreation industry, which is characterised by strong competition and constantly changing customer expectations and needs. There is often a large number of providers for any particular leisure and recreation product and each aims to secure a large share of the market in relation to its competitors. For example, the sports footwear and clothing market is highly competitive, with providers constantly trying to develop new products that will be seen as more attractive than those offered by competitors. Another example of the competitive and dynamic nature of the industry is the continued development of new visitor attractions, such as interactive museums and exhibits based on specific themes.

▲ If organisations don't get it right, they may find it difficult to achieve their objectives

▲ The interactive Tower Bridge Experience in London

Marketing is a continuous process that starts and finishes with the customer. It embraces everything an organisation does to identify, anticipate and satisfy customer needs and expectations (see Figure 4.1).

Figure 4.1: The marketing process

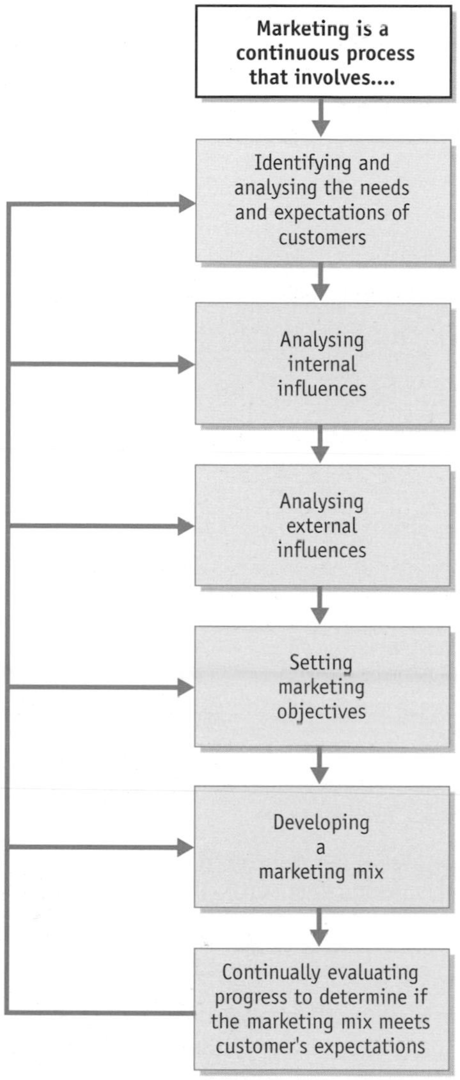

Marketing is a continuous process that involves....

Identifying and analysing the needs and expectations of customers

Analysing internal influences

Analysing external influences

Setting marketing objectives

Developing a marketing mix

Continually evaluating progress to determine if the marketing mix meets customer's expectations

We will look at this process in more detail by first identifying the specific objectives of marketing in leisure and recreation.

Marketing objectives

Before undertaking any marketing activity it is important to focus clearly on what we hope to achieve. This involves setting **marketing objectives** from the outset, then continually reviewing and monitoring them to measure progress.

Organisations may have several key marketing objectives. They may include:

- analysing market needs
- satisfying customer requirements;
- managing effects of competition
- managing effects of change
- co-ordinating a range of activities
- maximising income
- generating profit
- generating community benefit
- optimising customers' perception of the product.

Specific objectives are largely determined by the organisations's overall business objectives. Private sector operators in leisure and recreation usually gear their marketing towards achieving profit for their owners or shareholders. Consequently their marketing objectives usually include a combination of:

- achieving a target level of sales
- expanding sales revenue to a specified level
- increasing market share
- entering new markets
- achieving an overall specified level of profit.

Figure 4.2: Typical marketing objectives

The New Millennium Experience Company's objectives are:

- to deliver a once-in-a-lifetime, high-quality experience at Greenwich and a countrywide Challenge programme to time and to budget.
- to achieve at least 12 million visits to the Dome at Greenwich.
- to deliver value for money to the Millennium Commission, sponsors and paying visitors.
- to develop and implement the Experience (the Dome and the Challenge) in a way which:

  - optimises access, in the widest sense, by people of all ages, backgrounds and interests, achieving a nationally and socially inclusive event

  - involves, engages, entertains, educates and transforms the visitor and participant

  - makes best use of British and international creative talent and state of the art technology
- to create a world profile for the celebration of the millennium in the UK.
- to assist and where possible contribute to the government's policy that there will be a lasting legacy for the nation from the Experience (the Dome and the Challenge).

Public and voluntary-sector organisations that operate on a non-profit basis may also have some of the objectives listed above. However, they usually have other objectives, such as:

- generating community benefit
- targeting under-represented and disadvantaged groups in the community
- promoting a cause, such as more active, healthy lifestyles
- increasing participation.

The general purpose or direction of an organisation is usually identified in a broad **mission** or **vision statement** or **philosophy of use**. This expresses the organisation's intent and can be used as a basis for developing specific objectives. An example of a mission statement for the leisure and recreation industry is provided by the Natural History Museum:

The museum's mission is to maintain and develop its collections and use them to promote the discovery, understanding, responsible use and enjoyment of the natural world.

Setting SMART objectives

In order to achieve its overall mission, an organisation sets itself a series of short-term, medium-term and long-term marketing objectives. These are vital to the success of the operation and must be SMART:

Specific: clearly linked to a particular area of operation

Measurable: so that success and effectiveness can be gauged

Achievable: feasible and realistic, so that staff can work towards set objectives

Realistic: compatible with the organisation's mission statement

Timed: have deadlines for weekly, monthly and annual review.

Marketing objectives may cover financial, social and environmental issues. Some examples of SMART objectives are:

- increase income for the next month by 10 per cent
- reduce staffing budget by 15 per cent during January and February
- generate 50 per cent of all bookings from existing customers and repeat bookings
- achieve 10,000 paying visitors per month during the next 12-month period
- give local youth organisations and disability groups priority usage of the facility between June and September
- generate 25 per cent of all bookings from registered unemployed or those receiving income support
- give pensioners free use of the facility during off-peak periods
- reduce the number of customer complaints by 25 per cent in July and August
- increase use of park and ride scheme to 30 per cent of visitors to city centre.

ACTIVITY

Southpoint Leisure Centre

Imagine that you are one of five candidates attending an interview at Southpoint Leisure Centre for the position of marketing manager. As part of the selection process each candidate has been given the following short written test. What would be your answers?

Candidate Selection Test
Time: 30 minutes

Introduction: Southpoint Leisure Centre is a public sector leisure centre catering to the local community. The centre includes:

- a swimming pool with chutes, slides and inflatables
- an ice-skating rink
- a tenpin bowling alley
- an exercise studio
- a cafeteria serving snacks, hot meals and drinks.

The facility that generates the most revenue is the swimming pool, which is particularly busy at weekends, evenings and during school holidays. Discounts are offered at off-peak times to encourage more people to attend, but to date this has had little effect in increasing demand.

The ice-skating rink was built ten years ago and was initially very popular. However, in the last three years demand has steadily decreased with fewer young people (under 25 years) attending. A recently introduced ice-skating disco for children on a Friday night has proved popular.

The tenpin bowling alley was built at the same time as the ice-skating rink. Demand has declined over the last six months, largely due to the opening of a council-owned bowling alley nearby.

The exercise studio has only been open for three months and is already proving very successful. Customers can choose to pay per session or join as a member. The majority of exercise studio customers are aged 25-40 years and attend on their own. Average attendance is 1.2 occasions per week.

The cafeteria is used on a regular basis by many customers but largely for a snack or drink rather than a full meal. Customer feedback questionnaires have shown that 37 per cent of customers think that the food offered is not healthy enough.

Questions

1 If you were appointed as Southpoint's marketing manager what would be your first five SMART marketing objectives?
2 Write a mission statement for the company.

Analysing internal factors

One of the first activities in the marketing process that an organisation needs to perform is to analyse how effectively it is operating and what **internal factors** may influence its success. Such an analysis is commonly conducted using a SWOT approach. This stands for:

Strengths

Weaknesses

Opportunities

Threats

Strengths and weaknesses are internal factors within the control of the organisation. Opportunities and threats are outside the control of the organisation; for example, products offered by competitors, or market forces such as seasonal fluctuations in demand. A **SWOT analysis** allows an organisation to plan future activities by considering a number of questions:

- What are our strengths? How can we build on them to ensure that we offer a better product than our competitors?
- What are our weaknesses? How can we eliminate them?
- What are our opportunities? How are we going to use them to attract new customers or increase the number of products that existing customers buy?
- What are our threats? How are we going to minimise them so that they do not affect sales of our products?

Figure 4.3 on page 238 provides an example of a SWOT analysis.

Figure 4.3: SWOT analysis

Wet Wet Wet Cadbury's Concert July 1994, at Alton Towers

STRENGTHS

- Major large scale event with national coverage
- Potential increase revenue/profit
- Enhance Alton Towers' standing in event/concert management
- Unique event, demonstrating Alton Towers brand leadership
- National on pack promotion, large point of sale support
- National PR campaign covering trade, consumer and music press
- Strengthen links with on park suppliers/preferred trading partners

WEAKNESSES

- Early park close
- Alton Towers contribution to costs
- High staffing management commitment
- On pack communication of the Alton Towersbrand which associated Alton Towers with one product rather than all

OPPORTUNITIES

- High profile PR activity
- Possible third party sponsorship
- Further demonstrate Alton Towers' capacity to stage-manage successful major events
- Promotion of Alton Towers'1994 activity (eg Nemesis, Toyland Tours)
- Opportunity to create substantial database
- Possible Radio 1 coverage

THREATS

- Hostility from local residents
- Alton Towers' perception as venue only
- Antagonise theme park guests by interrupted activity
- Alienation of other trading partners within the confectionery sector
- Possible damage to Alton Towers' future developments
- 1994 Soccer World Cup Finals televised at the same time

These were the views of the Promotion Manager when asked to complete a SWOT analysis after the concert in 1994.
Source: Alton Towers Student Pack

CASE STUDY

SWOT analysis for Disneyland Paris

- Paris is the most popular city-break destination in Europe.
- The weather at Marne-le-Vallee is similar to southern England's but has quite a lot of rain throughout the year.
- There were initial problems adapting to French culture. For example, Disney had to introduce wine into their restaurants, since the French expect it as part of a meal.
- One of the big successes of Disneyland, Paris is the business travel market. Facilities are available for conferences for between 20 and 2,000 delegates. Conference delegates tend to visit at low season and are unaffected by poor weather.
- The Disney Corporation has a strong corporate image through its global operations including films, merchandising, theme parks and other activities.
- Channels of distribution include travel agents, direct selling, tour operators and ticket brokers.
- Disney can afford extensive advertising campaigns that focus on the core promise of the 'Disney Magic'. European television advertising tends to be at the end of the season to encourage visitors for the next season.

Welcome to Disneyland

Welcome to Disneyland, Paris, Europe's most spectacular theme park and resort. Into a magic melting pot, Disney has tossed make-believe and charm, entertainment and innovation, creativity and technology. Travel with us and experience the adventure and excitement of Disney, its magic and fantasy.

There is something for everyone and for all ages, be it the thrill of Space Mountain, Disney's most exhilarating ride ever, the pageantry and colour of the daily parades complete with Disney characters, or perhaps, the dazzling entertainment and nightlife.

Quality service, the highest of standards and a dedication to fun and enjoyment, complete Disney's unique recipe for an unforgettable holiday.

Source: Paris Travel Service brochure

▲ Honey, I shrunk the Audience

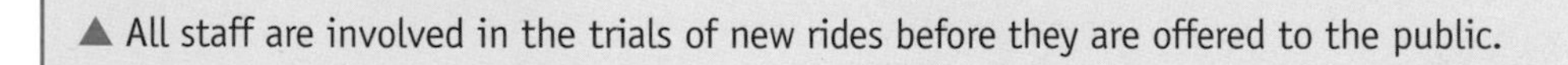

▲ All staff are involved in the trials of new rides before they are offered to the public.

- Disneyland, Paris has one of the largest gardens in Europe, staffed by 120 full-time gardeners. State of the art technology is used to regulate planting, tending and irrigating, and to predict the weather.
- Competition in Paris comes from the well-established Parc Asterix and the Futuroscope centre.
- Eighty-four per cent of visitors state that they are very or totally satisfied with their visit, while 97 per cent state that they will recommend the park to their friends. More than 30 per cent of visitors have visited the park at least once before.
- Access includes two Paris airports linked by shuttle and rail services to the park, direct motorway access and the Channel tunnel link to the UK. Disneyland, Paris has its own railway station.
- The Disney Village provides round-the-clock restaurants, bars and entertainment and is easily accessible from all the resort's hotels.

▲ The Disney Village

- Visitors to Disneyland, Paris contribute 20 per cent of all tourism revenue in the area.
- Changes in European lifestyles have meant an increase in leisure time and disposable income.
- Customer service is the main priority of the Disney Corporation and all staff are fully trained before beginning work.
- The resort hotels provide almost 6,000 rooms. A further 800 rooms have been added to other hotels in the area to cater to the Disney market.
- France currently has a low cost of living in comparison to many other European countries, including the UK, Germany and Belgium.
- Sixty per cent of visitors to Disneyland, Paris are from outside France.
- French is the first language used in the park. All cast members speak French, 70 per cent speak English and 25 per cent speak either German or Spanish.
- Shopping is a major part of the Disney experience and visitors have a vast range of themed retail outlets to choose from.
- There has been a rapid increase in the short-break and second-holiday market in Europe during the last ten years.
- Unlike Americans, the majority of Europeans only take family holidays during the school holidays - few take their children out of school during term time.
- More than 50 million people live within a four-hour drive of Disneyland, Paris. Over 300 million are within a short-haul flight designated area.
- Many of the attractions at Disneyland, Paris are covered or heated. Despite the cold weather, Christmas is one of the busiest periods for the park.

ACTIVITY

Produce a SWOT analysis

Using the descriptions, facts and figures in the case study, produce a SWOT analysis of Disneyland, Paris. You might also like to support your SWOT analysis with further research. For example, you could find information on the internet, from brochures, newspaper articles, trade press, people that you know who have visited the park, etc.

Analysing external factors

Leisure and recreation organisations do not operate in isolation. A number of **external factors** influence the products and services they offer and the extent to which customers decide to buy them. One part of the marketing process is to look at these external factors and identify the effect that they have on the organisation, its products and services, and its customers.

These factors are often referred to as market forces or market factors and can include political, economic, social, technological, cultural and legislative influences. Many organisations carry out a **PEST (or STEP) analysis**:

Political factors

Economic factors

Social factors

Technological factors

The purpose of a PEST analysis is to analyse the external environment in which the organisation operates and to identify how it should influence marketing decisions.

Political factors

The actions of governments can have major effects on business and markets, including creating or reducing demand for particular products and services. At the national level, government sets public spending levels, allocates funds for special programmes (such as the Millennium Fund), controls taxation and interest rates and is responsible for the introduction of new (or the abolition of existing) laws, regulations and licence arrangements. For example, the extension of Sunday opening hours in pubs and licensed premises in 1995 influenced the marketing decisions of many providers. In particular, day-long opening hours led to the targeting of families and the development of special children's menus and play areas.

At the local level, authorities set spending levels for the provision of leisure and recreation services in the communities they serve. In some cases this level of funding may allow for heavy subsidies for certain groups within the community, such as the elderly or the unemployed.

Economic factors

Customer demand in the leisure and recreation industry is often determined by economic factors such as the distribution of wealth and the level of national income. (See also pages 10 to 12). In other words, the amount of money that people have to spend on leisure and recreation will influence what they actually decide to buy.

Consumer spending may be controlled by a range of economic factors such as income levels, inflation, taxes, unemployment, exchange rates and mortgage rates. Figure 4.4 shows some of the economic changes that have taken place in the UK in the last couple of decades.

Figure 4.4: Economic changes in the UK, 1979-1999

	May 1979	May 1989	May 1999
Prime Minister	Thatcher	Thatcher	Blair
Inflation	13.4%	7.8%	4.6%
Interest rates	12%	13.75%	5.5%
Unemployment	4.1%	6.1%	4.6%
Women working	44%	49%	51%
Average income	£5,000	£11,700	£19,000
Average manager's income	£19,000	£25,700	£36,400
Eating out	42%	47%	69%
Holiday destination visitor numbers	Spain (1.9m)	Spain (5.7m)	Spain (7.7m)
% with videos	N/A	60%	82%
% with CDs	N/A	15%	58%

CASE STUDY

The National Centre for Popular Music

The National Centre for Popular Music

Situated in the centre of Sheffield, the National Centre for Popular Music opened in 1999. Its aim is to create a unique interactive arts and education centre that celebrates the diversity and influence of popular music.

It boasts a range of interactive exhibits specially designed to appeal to people of all ages, musical tastes and experience. 'This is not a place where you walk around looking at memorabilia', says Creative Director Tim Strickland. 'The National Centre is a place where you 'have-a-go' – play an instrument, re-mix a video or design an album cover. Our aim from the beginning was to get people involved.'

PEST analysis of the National Centre for Popular Music:

Political factors

The political framework for the development and subsequent marketing of the centre began in the early 1980s when the city council developed the Red Tape Studios, a council-run studio where the community and education groups could record music in studios for a reduced fee. There was therefore a history of linking music with education and the community in Sheffield.

In 1988, Sheffield City Council's Department of Employment and Economic Development initiated research into the concept of a popular music visitor and educational resource. At the same time some media-related businesses moved to the cultural quarter. The council policy was a help to the idea of the centre because the council's central idea was to create a media quarter in the area moving from private to some public access areas. This is a different direction to that taken by other big cities at the time. Places like Glasgow, Manchester, Birmingham and Leeds went for big cultural festivals and they are now trying to get local businesses to relocate in the areas they cleared for the big schemes. In Sheffield the council supported local, small businesses and helped them to relocate to the Cultural Industries Quarter. Now the city is developing the tourist potential.

Possible funding from local government dried up in the late 1980s when the Conservative government wanted funding for projects to be more centrally controlled. Money became available through the private sector (via trusts) and through government sources like the Urban Programme and the Yorkshire and Humberside Tourist Board. The Urban Programme gave a one-off grant of £45,000 and this was spent on consultancy fees in 1991 paid to Coopers and Lybrand. In 1993, after a positive report from the consultants, over 30 applications were made to charities and trusts for development funding.

Economic factors are often combined with political factors. For example, government changes in the amount of VAT levied on certain products can affect demand. It is important to understand that when people have less money it does not necessarily mean that all leisure and recreation products and services will suffer. Less money will usually mean that customers are more likely to buy alternative leisure products. For example, a customer with a reduced income may not go to the cinema on a regular basis but instead hire videos to watch at home with friends. Therefore, while cinema owners may suffer a decrease in demand, video hire shops will benefit.

A further issue that needs to be considered is the impact of a recession and rising unemployment on leisure activities. While people may not have as much money to spend on such activities they will usually have more time. Therefore, affordable leisure activities are likely to benefit from an economic recession.

Social factors

Social trends are important because they have a direct influence on the demand for particular types of product. For example, the UK has an ageing population because people are having fewer babies

In 1994 Sheffield's new partnership body (private and public representatives) provided a plan for the future of Sheffield. The centre was a major stimulus to regeneration in the area. In 1995 an application to the European Regional Development Fund was made and the submission to the Millennium Fund was completed. Later that year both applications were approved.

Economic factors

The overall depressed state of the economy in South Yorkshire has not been a factor in the development of the centre. The reduction in interest rates at the beginning of 1999 has been an advantage because the centre borrowed £1 million from English Partnerships which is being paid back over ten years. Repayments have dropped along with interest rates. This is the only money that has to be repaid from the initial funding. All the rest came as grants.

Social factors

Demographic patterns were taken into account in the initial research. This assessed the extent to which people found the centre interesting and the proportion who thought they were likely to visit. A second aim was to look at the attitudes of those likely visitors to the exhibition areas and proposed changes. A third aim was to establish the socio-demographic and leisure interests of likely visitors. The gender, age and socio-economic profile of the total population living within a two-hour drive was analysed.

The gender mix has almost equal numbers of males and females. The age profile of those likely to visit is markedly younger than the age profile in the catchment area, the two most important age groups being 25-34 year olds and 35-44 year olds. Retired people are a smaller proportion of likely visitors than they are in the catchment area. The two largest socio-economic groups (see page 266) among likely visitors are A/B and C2. Compared with the catchment area population, the people who think they are likely to visit the centre includes a slightly lower proportion of A/B households and a slightly higher proportion of C2 household heads. For those that said that they were likely visitors to the centre, the most common leisure interests were visits to pop and rock concerts, indoor sports events, nightclubs, jazz and outdoor sports events.

Technological factors

There is a core commitment to the use of technology in the development of the centre. This is reflected in the building design, the interactive nature of the activities and the constant commissioning of musical artists to use the technology. It is the use of technology that makes the centre unique and has been at the forefront of its marketing. The ability to update technology has been built into the design and forward planning.

Source: *NCPM Student Resource Pack*

and are living longer. By 2021 it is estimated that one in five of the population will be aged over 65, compared to only one in ten in 1951. In recent years, many leisure and recreation providers have recognized this market opportunity and developed products and services aimed specifically at older customers. A good example is the recent increase in the popularity of crown green bowling.

Changes in population also have significance for marketing. Regions where the population is increasing may offer new market opportunities for leisure and recreation providers. Conversely, a fall in population may provide a threat to organisations, as the size of their potential market diminishes. Further social changes can be seen in the increased amount of leisure time that many people now enjoy.

Technological factors

Developments in technology give rise to new products and market opportunities. The rapidly growing use of computerised reservations systems, for example, allows customers to select and purchase theatre tickets and tickets for sporting events over the telephone. Many new leisure and recreation products such as computer games, video systems and virtual reality games are only available because of technological developments.

Transport, too, has been revolutionised by advances in technology. Thirty years ago it was unthinkable to travel over 100 miles to go to a theme park for the day, but improvements in road travel have made this a realistic option for many. Further examples of the impact of technological change can be seen in the development of the internet and the effect that this has had on the way in which we are able to view and purchase leisure and recreation products.

All four of these factors - political, economic, social and technological - were used in the PEST analysis carried out by the National Centre for Popular Music in Sheffield, as the case study shows.

ACTIVITY

Virgin Active Health Clubs

Read the following information about Virgin Active health and fitness clubs.

As a group, discuss how PEST factors may influence the success of the Virgin Active clubs. For example, do you think that social changes have resulted in family groups spending more or less time participating in joint leisure activities? Try to find statistics in textbooks and newspapers to support your arguments.

Virgin

Within the last 30 years, Richard Branson's Virgin Company has expanded into an empire of more than 200 diverse companies with annual combined sales of £1.3 billion. Many of the companies cater to the needs and expectations of the leisure and recreation market.

In August 1999, Branson invested £25 million in the creation of a new brand of health club called Virgin Active. The 30 new clubs are aimed at the family market, with emphasis on family groups getting fit and healthy together. Prior to opening, more than 3,500 people had already become members of the first Virgin Active club in Preston, Lancashire.

Virgin's research showed that only 5 per cent of the UK population actually used health clubs. It also found that 90 per cent of the population did not use health clubs because:

- there were poor family facilities
- staff were uninterested
- the focus at clubs was purely on fitness activities
- clubs often charged high joining and membership fees.

Virgin Active clubs aim to dispel some of these poor opinions of health clubs. Use of the club costs less than £10 per week and there is no joining fee, deposit or annual membership fee. Facilities include:

- a gym equipped with over 200 pieces of exercise equipment
- two aerobic studios
- beauty treatments
- three swimming pools
- a library with books on leisure, lifestyle and fitness
- 'Kidsville' featuring computer games, basketball courts, videos, craft areas and play areas.

The Virgin Active concept is to offer a product that will appeal to the whole family in providing a fun day out that will have the added benefit of getting them fit.

Virgin companies by sector

SECTOR	BUSINESSES
Travel and tourism	Virgin Atlantic; Virgin Express; Virgin Clubs and Hotels
Retail and cinema	Virgin Retail; Virgin Cinemas; Virgin Brides
Media	V2 Music Group; Virgin Communications
Consumer products	Virgin Cola; Virgin Spirits; Virgin Jeans; Virgin Cosmetics
Finance	Virgin Direct
Design and modelling	Storm model agency

The way the National Centre for Popular Music used a PEST analysis to help in the planning and development of the centre can be used by any leisure and recreation provider to analyse any stage of product development. For example, a PEST analysis will provide useful insight into the reasons why organisations such as Virgin have been so successful in breaking into the fitness market.

Identifying customer needs

The next stage of the marketing process is to identify the specific **needs** and **expectations** of the organisation's customers. This can be a long, complicated process, especially when those needs are implied rather than clearly expressed.

▲ Customers at an aerobics class may have many needs and expectations

For example, a customer who joins an exercise class may do so primarily to become fit and healthy. However, there may be other, unstated factors to take into account, such as the status and recognition attached to participating in such an exercise class or the opportunity to socialise and make new acquaintances. Organisations strive to identify both expressed and implied customer needs and expectations and use this information to develop products that satisfy or exceed those needs and expectations. This is known as the **customer-oriented approach**

Identifying the needs of customers only indicates the types of product that they are likely to buy. It is also necessary to understand what makes them want one product rather than another, or why they will use one service in preference to another. In other words, organisations need to know what specific product or service features and qualities will satisfy the customer. These features are known as **unique selling points (USPs)** and help to distinguish one product from another.

Customer satisfaction means that a product or service meets or exceeds the needs and wants of the customer. This is clearly an important principle because an organisation does not usually aim to sell a product or service just once to one customer. Rather, it strives to ensure that customers will continue to use the product again and again.

Often, the leisure and recreation experience is a product that cannot be guaranteed in advance and may not be the same for two different people. Many leisure and recreation products and services rely on the reasonable behaviour of participants/customers to enable the product to be enjoyed by all. For example, when supporters go to a football match they have an expectation of the experience that will follow. If on the day there is crowd violence or the team play badly this will greatly affect the customers' assessment of the product.

Targeting and positioning

One of the main reasons for identifying customers' needs and expectations is that it allows products to be targeted at a specific market. **Targeting** is usually based on tailoring products and services to the needs of specific market segments. (Market segmentation is discussed in more detail on page 266.)

If an organisation can identify the specific needs and expectations of its customers, it can ensure that its product is tailored to meet them. For example, if a sports centre identifies that many of its regular customers use the facilities because it provides an opportunity to meet people and make friends, the centre may provide a cafeteria or bar to promote the social aspect of the product that they offer.

By targeting a particular type of customer, organisations are able to **position** themselves in a particular market. For example, McDonald's is positioned in the fast-food market, whereas Hilton International is positioned in the exclusive hotels market.

This is an important aspect of marketing. By establishing a strong market position, an organisation can ensure that its product is identified as meeting the needs of customers in that market.

BUILD YOUR LEARNING

Keywords and phrases

You should know the meaning of the words and phrases listed below. If you are unsure about any of them, go back through the last 12 pages to refresh your understanding.

- Marketing
- Marketing concept
- Marketing objectives
- Mission statement
- Philosophy of use
- Internal factors
- SWOT analysis
- External factors
- PEST or STEP analysis
- Needs and expectations
- Customer-orientated approach
- Unique selling points (USPs)
- Customer satisfaction
- Targeting
- Positioning

End of section activity

Select a leisure and recreation organisation such as a sports centre, heritage site, cinema, visitor attraction, etc. Write to them or arrange a visit in person to find out:

- the organisation's mission
- the organisation's marketing objectives
- the main strengths, weaknesses, opportunities and threats (SWOT)
- how external forces (PEST) influence their marketing activities
- which market segments they target
- the needs and expectations of their target customers
- how they evaluate their marketing activities to ensure that they meet customers' needs and expectations.

Once you have gathered sufficient information, answer the following questions.

1 Describe the strengths, weaknesses, opportunities and threats that exist for the organisation. Provide an explanation of the internal and external business environments that specifically affect the organisation and outline how the organisation makes use of such information.

2 Describe the current marketing objectives and identify and explain the political, economic, social and technological factors that influence the organisation's existing customers. How has the organisation responded to these factors?

Developing a marketing mix

The **marketing mix** refers to the factors that need to be combined for an organisation to achieve its marketing objectives. These factors are known as the four Ps:

- Product
- Place
- Price
- Promotion

The four Ps involve matching the product or service to consumer needs, determining the price, deciding where and how the product or service should be placed (distributed) in the market and promoting it through advertising, sales promotions and public relations.

Product

In marketing, **product** refers to both goods and services. Goods are physical objects, such as sports clothing, home entertainment equipment or food and drink. Services involve a combination of skills, information or entertainment, such as a football match, use of a swimming pool or a theatre production. There are three important factors to consider when developing a product:

- product characteristics
- brand image of the product
- position of the product within the product life cycle.

Product characteristics

When developing a marketing strategy for a product, it is important to identify precisely what is being purchased in terms of the **product characteristics** and how these help to satisfy a particular customer need. Product characteristics are the specific features of a product or service that the customer sees as important and which attract them to buy or use it. For example, a pop concert is a product that evokes a range of emotions, the end result being the total customer experience. The determinants of this experience might include the range and quality of performers, the special effects such as lighting and video walls, the range of souvenirs, etc.

Competition among leisure operators is becoming increasingly fierce as more and more providers enter the market. One of the inevitable results is that individual providers look for new and innovative ways of developing unique product characteristics to attract customers. Such developments include interactive exhibits, computerised attractions and promotional activities.

▲ The London Dungeon 'product' is a leisure experience

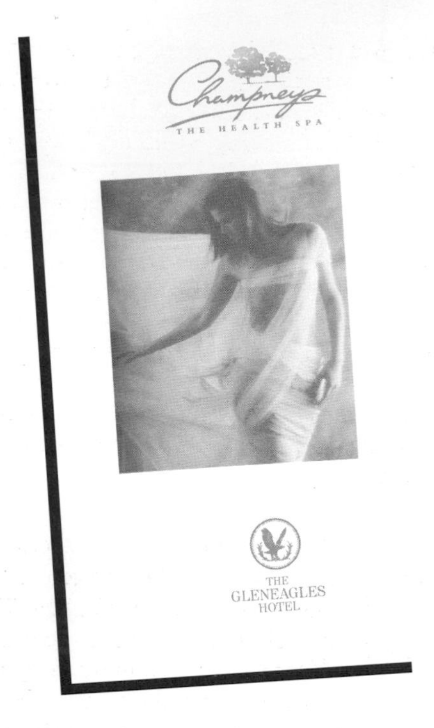

ACTIVITY

Product characteristics

In 1999 *Holiday Which* carried out research to evaluate how a range of visitor attractions compared. High scores were awarded to Castle Howard, Chatsworth House, Alton Towers, the BBC Experience, the Roman Baths and the Natural History Museum for the range of facilities offered and the overall visitor experience.

Buckingham Palace did not fare so well. Comments ranged from complaints that it is sterile, stuffy and staid to there being little that told visitors about the history of the house. A spokesperson for Buckingham Palace was understandably annoyed, claiming that as the headquarters of the British monarchy it could not be compared with a theme park.

To what extent do you think there is a conflict in trying to develop new product characteristics for a historical attraction such as Buckingham Palace to enable it to attract a wider market? For example, are the characteristics of being 'staid, sterile and stuffy' actually in keeping with the historical nature of the attraction, thus reinforcing the image of the product? If Buckingham Palace were to develop some of the more modern characteristics of other attractions, such as interactive displays, would it spoil the original appeal?

Branding

Branding is the marketing process of giving a product or service a distinctive identity with the aim of creating a unique image that will make it easily identifiable and separate from its competitors. A product's brand image can be created and reinforced by its name, logo, advertising, packaging, price, use of specific colours, etc. For example, look at the brochure cover for Champney's health spa and see how a particular leisure product has been given a brand image. What kind of image do you obtain of Champney's from looking at the brochure?

Four useful branding terms are:

- **Brand awareness** means that a customer is able to identify a particular brand and its characteristics as opposed to others.
- **Brand leader** refers to the brand with the highest share of the market in its category. For example, Manchester United is the brand leader in Premiership football clubs.
- **Brand extension** is when an existing strong brand is used to create other products that carry the same brand title and image. For example, football teams such as Manchester United, Leeds and Chelsea are diversifying into hotels, mail order clothes, financial services and travel services.
- **Brand loyalty** means that a customer is loyal to a particular brand and will buy it on a regular basis.

Following the lead set by supermarkets, many leisure and recreation providers are seeking to increase customer loyalty by introducing loyalty schemes. For instance, many theatres offer loyalty schemes whereby theatregoers pay an annual subscription in return for a number of special benefits, as the Webstract opposite shows.

WEBSTRACT

Loyalty schemes at the Stephen Joseph

Make Friends with Stephen Joseph Theatre

Sign up to become a Friend...

The Friends provide the Theatre with a committed core audience who provide audience feedback and promote the work of the Theatre by word of mouth. It is also a fund raising organisation which over the years has raised tens of thousands of pounds to provide computers, fax and copy machines, lighting and many other items which help our theatre in maintaining such high standards. Since the Stephen Joseph Theatre moved to its current location, the Friends have donated over 70,000 pounds.

Your membership will help continue this good work and will provide you with:

- Money off tickets to SJT productions
- A Gold Card entitling you to 10% off The Restaurant bills
- Membership of the Theatre Bar
- Advance programme mailing and priority booking
- Newsround, a regular Friends newsletter
- A variety of fund raising events
- An interest in the running of the Theatre through an observer on the Trust Council

ACTIVITY

Stephen Joseph Theatre

Read through the details of the Stephen Joseph Theatre loyalty scheme and discuss what benefits the scheme might have for the theatre.

Branding is a very powerful marketing tool and has a strong influence over the products and services that we buy. For example, in blind tests 51 per cent of people prefer Pepsi. However, when customers can see the brand that they are drinking, 65 per cent say that they prefer Coca-Cola. What these 65 per cent of people are in fact saying is that they prefer the brand represented by the Coca-Cola image rather than the product itself. Branding is used both to establish customer awareness and loyalty and to target specific segments of the market in order to achieve a higher market share. For example, magazine publishers such as IPC often produce a wide range of different branded magazines aimed at different markets.

Many leisure and recreation providers experience problems when the public's perceived image of the brand is not what the organisation would like. This can be for any number of reasons, such as the public clinging to an old brand image when the actual product or service has in fact changed or is being targeted at different markets. The article and Webstract overleaf show how the English Tourism Council (ETC) hopes to create a new and distinctive 'brand image' for walking activities.

▲ A selection of IPC's branded magazines

WEBSTRACT

Branding: walking in Britain

WELCOME TO WALKING BRITAIN

For anyone interested in walking or planning a walking holiday in Britain, this site will help you find out everything you need to know from where to stay, how to get there, suggested walks and itineraries and much more.

Without doubt the best way to enjoy Britain's beautiful and varied countryside is on foot. There are walks to suit everyone from a one-hour ramble to a full day's trek, so don't be put off by thinking that Britain is only suitable for experienced walkers.

There are coastal paths with breathtaking views of sea and sky, tracks following disused railway lines or canal towpaths which follow an industrial archaeology theme; lake and riverside walks, with plenty of wildlife to watch - the ideas and opportunities are limitless.

Climb steep paths around rocky coves carved out by the wind and sea in England's West Country, clamber over hills in National Park in Wales, or tackle a rugged mountain trail in the Scottish Highlands - a vast network of public footpaths, bridleways and ancient trackways run through Britain giving you, the walker, a huge choice.

Source: http://www.visitbritain.com

ACTIVITY

Brand image: walking

As a group, discuss the extent to which you think the ETC's website on walking gets away from the old brand image of walking activities as 'bobble hats, compasses and maps'. Can you identify any sections that would particularly appeal to:

- young socialisers?
- young leisure adventurers?
- family actives?

ETB makes strides to attract 'new' walkers

Marketing shifts away from bobble hat and compass image

The English Tourism Council wants to shake off the staid and serious image of walking by targeting families and young groups of friends.

It has identified several key markets for walking activities - 'young socialisers', who are informal groups of friends aged between 16-34 looking for a short activity break; 'young leisure adventurers', who are typically couples aged 18-35 seeking a weekend away to unwind; and 'family actives', who are parents with young children who want to spend a week walking in the countryside.

ETC development executive, Amanda Sillito said, 'We're not dismissing the serious walker but there is a potential to target other markets. If we can understand what these groups require, the industry can work together to develop walking activities that are appropriate and popular.

'We're looking into the branding that would attract these new groups and have found that the current images of bobble hats, compasses and maps are alienating people who are otherwise keen walkers. We're looking for the industry to present walking in a fresh way, by selling the benefits such as the different pace of life and relaxation, the sense of achievement you feel on completing a walk and the magic in nature.'

Source: Travel Weekly

Product life cycle

The concept of a **product life cycle** (PLC) is based on the idea that all products pass through four distinct stages:

- Introduction. When a product is first introduced, demand may be low initially, as customers gradually become aware of the product characteristics and its brand image.
- Growth. As more customers become aware of the product and its image and characteristics, sales start to rise rapidly. This may be due to word-of-mouth recommendations and the beginning of some customer loyalty.
- Maturity. At this stage of the PLC, sales are at their highest but tend to remain stable. Most of the demand will come from repeat customers who are loyal to the particular brand.

- Decline. At this stage demand starts to decline. This can be for a number of reasons, such as increased competition, changing customer needs or any of the factors discussed in the section on PEST analysis on page 241.

In some circumstances there may be a fifth stage of 'revamping', when the organisation tries to stimulate increased sales by changing the product's characteristics or brand image. For example, as can be seen in Figure 4.5, since the late 1980s there has been an increase in cinema attendance after a steady decline from the 1950s.

Figure 4.5: Cinema attendances 1937–97

	Millions
1937	954
1947	1,460
1957	915
1967	265
1977	105
1987	80
1997	140

Source: British Film Institute, Screen Digest, Key Note

One of the main reasons for this growth is the development of national chains of large multi-screen cinemas such as MGM, Virgin and Warner Brothers.

▲ The changing face of British cinemas

Some other examples of leisure and recreation products which have been revamped and relaunched following periods of decline include:

- holiday centres: eg. Butlins Holiday Worlds.
- indoor swimming pools with slides, chutes and wave machines.
- museums redeveloped to include interactive displays and simulators.
- football : many professional clubs now have modern purpose-built stadia and the old football league has been restructured into the 'Carling Premiership' and three divisions in the 'Nationwide League'.

The change in product image or characteristics may be accompanied by an organisation targeting a different type of customer. For example, declining demand for traditional full-season 'end-of the pier' seaside shows has resulted in many local councils offering a wider range of one-off entertainments aimed at different markets throughout the year.

ACTIVITY

Changing popularity

Select a well known sport that has been re-launched or revamped in recent years in order to increase its mass market appeal. You could chose from football, cricket, rugby league, rugby union or athletics, as all of these sports have undergone changes to increase their market appeal. Describe the things that have been done, such as changes to the way in which the sport is organised, played, televised and sponsored.

Figure 4.6 shows each of the stages of the product life cycle as being of equal length. In reality, each stage may last a different length of time. A basic product such as milk or bread has been in the maturity stage for a very long time, whereas the skateboard had initially a relatively short maturity stage and then quickly declined in popularity. Most organisations will aim to keep the introduction stage as short as possible, as it tends to be the least profitable due to the large amount of advertising needed to attract new customers. In fact, a lot of smaller leisure and recreation organisations underestimate the costs involved and may go out of business before reaching the growth stage, as they cannot afford to maintain the amount of promotion needed.

The growth and maturity stages of a product life cycle are the most desirable as they represent increasing demand, customer loyalty and profitability. Successful leisure and recreation organisations, which understand the concept of the product life cycle, will continually develop and offer a range of different products to ensure that they have products placed at each stage of the cycle.

Before looking at the other three Ps of the marketing mix, it is important to stress that the product is vital. It does not matter how well it is placed, priced or promoted if the product is not right, for it will not meet customers' needs and they will not buy or use it.

Place

Place describes the location and availability of a product or service and the method by which it is distributed to customers.

Location

When Charles Ritz, founder of the famous Ritz hotel, was asked what was important when opening a new

Figure 4.6: The product life-cycle

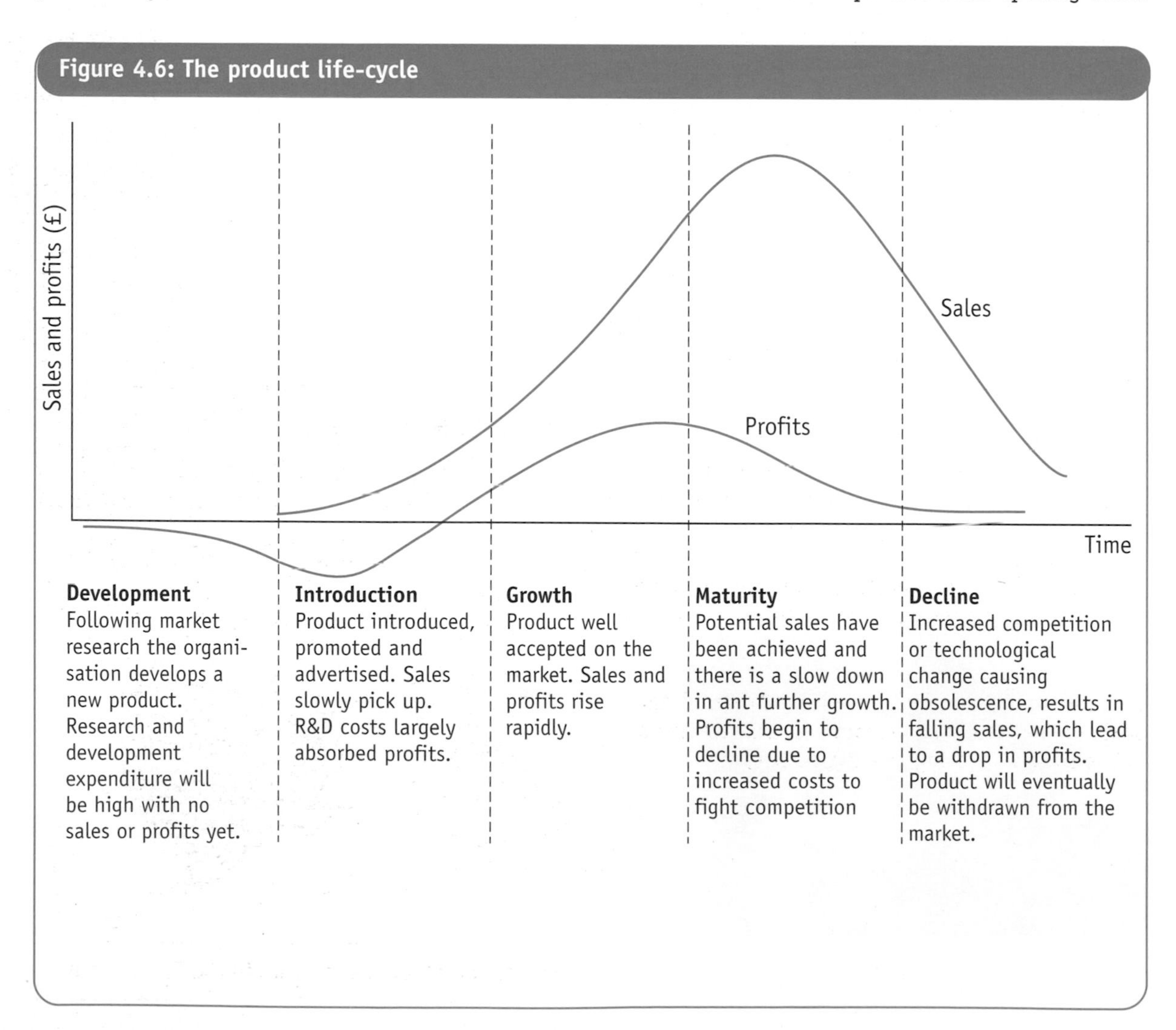

Sales and profits (£)
Sales
Profits
Time
Development
Following market research the organisation develops a new product. Research and development expenditure will be high with no sales or profits yet.
Introduction
Product introduced, promoted and advertised. Sales slowly pick up. R&D costs largely absorbed profits.
Growth
Product well accepted on the market. Sales and profits rise rapidly.
Maturity
Potential sales have been achieved and there is a slow down in ant further growth. Profits begin to decline due to increased costs to fight competition
Decline
Increased competition or technological change causing obsolescence, results in falling sales, which lead to a drop in profits. Product will eventually be withdrawn from the market.

ACTIVITY

The product life cycle

The marketing manager for Southlands leisure and amenities department has recently evaluated a number of the key sports and leisure facilities within the Southlands area. Based on her research she has decided to present the information to her colleagues in the form of a product life cycle showing where she thinks each facility fits in. Based on the information below, where in the product life cycle would you place the selection of facilities shown?

- Southlands crazy golf park, established in 1967 when crazy golf was particularly popular. Admissions peaked during the late 1980s, since when admissions have declined each year.
- Gothic Tales, a privately owned interactive attraction that opened six months ago. Themed on Southlands' association with the filming of a major horror movie, the attraction takes visitors through a series of macabre film sets with actors playing the parts of famous horror movie stars. Initial admissions were low but in the last three months they have doubled.
- Racers, an outdoor watersports centre offering jet-skiing, water-skiing and paragliding. Initial interest was high but it is too early to predict whether this will be sustained.
- Aqua-experience, a marine-life attraction that has been operating for nine years. It is part of a national chain pledged to invest large amounts of money in the next two years developing further exhibits at their centres. Admissions have remained stable for the last two years.
- Southlands all-weather tennis courts, opened two years ago and already with a long waiting list for membership.
- Southlands Art Gallery, first opened in 1966 but closed in 1998 due to declining attendance. In the last two months it has been renovated and now exhibits the work of local painters and hosts a range of art workshops for all age groups.

hotel he replied that there were only three things that needed to be remembered: 'Location, location and location'!

While it is an exaggeration to say that **location** is the only important factor, it is clearly something to which leisure and recreation providers need to give a lot of thought. If a product or service is not accessible to potential customers, then no matter how well it has been developed, or how attractively it has been priced and promoted, it will not be successful.

The case study overleaf on Alton Towers details some of the factors about location that were considered when creating the theme park.

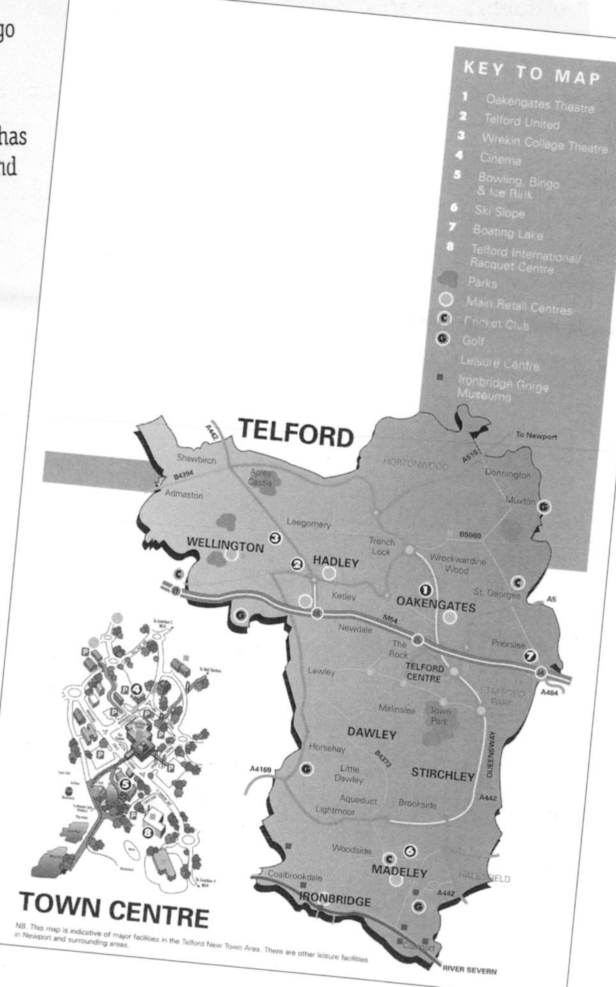

▲ The location of leisure facilities in the Telford area

CASE STUDY

Creating a theme park

Student
Information
Pack
Alton Towers
Where The Magic Never Ends!

Before undertaking a capital project such as Alton Towers, an in-depth study is essential. Certain criteria must be met before a very considerable investment is made.

The attraction must have a suitable catchment area. Alton Towers is a national brand and attracts visitors from all over the country and overseas. It is the UK's leading theme park and has a central position between the M1 and M6 motorways, making it easily accessible.

Smaller regional theme parks can operate with a more restricted catchment area. These parks have lower capital investment and overhead costs, so fewer visitors are required to meet company objectives. The average catchment area for regional parks tends to be within 90 minutes' drive.

In choosing the location of the park, its planned size and design and the mix of attractions, services and car parks need to be taken into account. Also important are access to the park - road and rail links - and the impact on the local community. It is a question of assessing whether a chosen area is sufficient or not to accommodate these components.

As a rule, major theme parks require a minimum ride and attraction area of 50 acres, but require considerably more to cater for the additional facilities, such as restaurants, snack bars, toilets and shops. For example, Disneyland in California has an attraction centre of 50 acres out of a 250-acre total area. Alton Towers is a 500-acre complex, part of which is gardens and parkland.

Source: adapted from the Alton Towers student information pack

Chain of distribution

Another important aspect of place is the **chain of distribution** an organisation uses to bring its products and services to the market. Traditionally, manufacturers have sold products to wholesalers that are then sold to retailers in smaller quantities, who then supply customers. This system can be seen in the way many films are brought to the market, as shown in Figure 4.7.

Many products are sold direct to the consumer rather than through third parties. For example, sports clothing and footwear are frequently sold through catalogues mailed to customers. Many services are generally inseparable from the 'manufacturer' and are sold direct to the consumer. For example, restaurants, hotels, cinemas and museums all provide services direct to their customers.

Figure 4.7 The chain of distribution of films

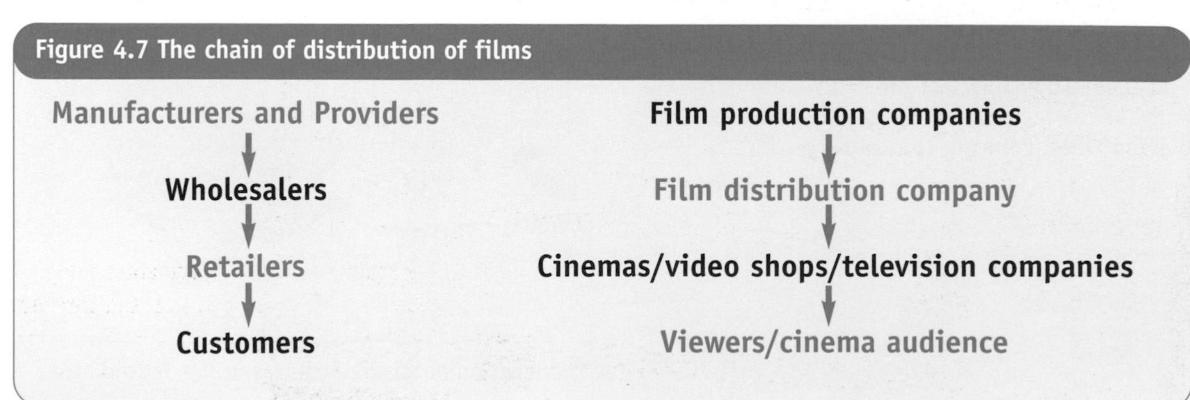

ACTIVITY

Selecting the right location

Josie Peters is planning to open a video rental shop and has narrowed down her search for suitable premises to three properties. Look at the following extracts from estate agents' descriptions of each property. Based on the information given, which of the three do you think she should choose and why?

Property 1. This highly desirable property is situated on the outskirts of the town centre near to local offices and factories. There is ample local free parking and a regular bus service passes outside. Accommodation comprises a large shop frontage with sales room, rear office space and extensive first-floor accommodation. The property enjoys the benefit of being in a quiet area at weekends and evenings due to the mainly industrial nature of the area.
Asking price: £65,000.

Property 2. Situated on the main high street, this extensive first-floor property has all of the commercial benefits that you would expect from a town centre location. Accommodation includes three separate offices and toilet facilities. Adjacent to a multi-storey car park that provides parking for the nearby covered shopping mall, it enjoys an all-year passing trade. The ground floor property is currently occupied by a card and gift shop.
Asking price: £72,000.

Property 3. Situated in the centre of the town's shopping mall on the second floor, this prime location is adjacent to many of the well-known household stores, including nine national clothing retailers, four electrical retailers, two catalogue shops and a range of financial services. The centre is open six days a week with late-night opening on a Thursday. Accommodation comprises a single sales area with small store-room facilities at the rear. The centre also has comprehensive catering and security provision as well as a 'pay and display' car park.
Asking price: £102,000.

The growing use of the internet is having a major impact on the chain of distribution of leisure and recreation products. Previously, for example, customers wishing to buy books and magazines had two options: they could either buy directly from the publisher by mail order, or they could make their purchase at a bookshop or newsagent. Now internet-based systems allow customers to search for and buy books on-line and even read parts of novels to see if they like them before making a purchase.

One of the biggest book suppliers on the internet is Amazon, which is able to offer huge discounts of up to 50 per cent on UK bestsellers. Customers can search through thousands of book categories, purchase books that they like and even have them sent directly to someone else as a present.

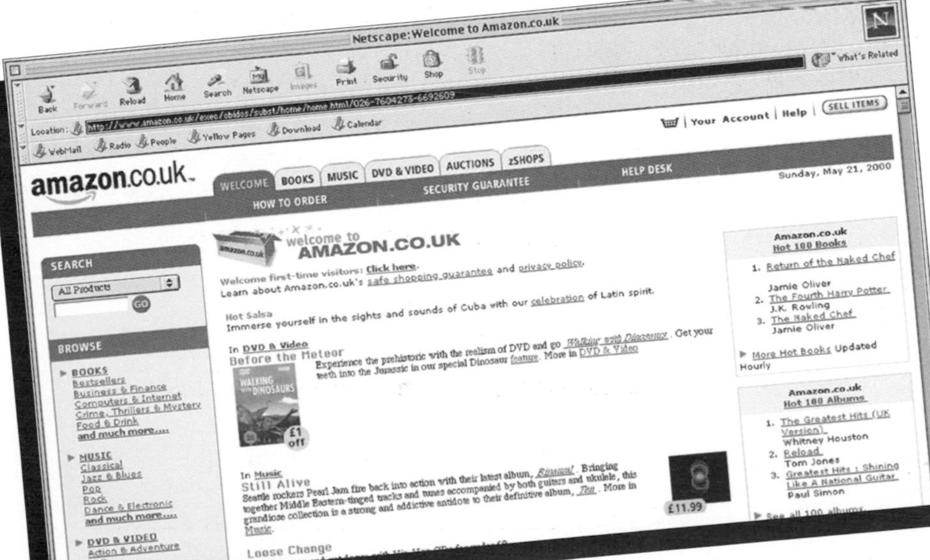

Amazon's home page on the internet

ACTIVITY

Influence of the internet

The development and use of internet services such as Amazon will clearly have profound effects on the traditional channels of distribution of books and magazines. From a marketing point of view what do you think are the benefits and/or disadvantages of these systems? You could consider this from a number of points of view, for example:

- customers
- publishers
- retail booksellers.

Price

Once an organisation has identified a product or service, it must decide on the **price** at which it is going to be offered to customers. Decisions on price need to consider two main factors:

- price determination
- pricing policies.

Price determination

Whatever the price selected, it has to appear to customers as the right price – in other words, customers should believe that the price offers value for money. Costs involved in providing the product or service usually set the minimum level of the price. This is known as the **breakeven price**. The upper level is determined by:

- what customers are prepared to pay
- the market conditions, such as supply, demand, competition and seasonality
- the brand image of the product.

However, leisure and recreation providers may consider a number of other factors when determining prices. Figure 4.8 shows the criteria that are considered important by heritage site providers when determining prices.

It is important to remember that lower prices are not always more attractive to customers. This is because the price charged will often help to reinforce a product's brand image. For example, customers may be suspicious if a price seems to be too low and assume that the product is of poor quality.

Because of the high level of competition within the leisure and recreation industry, the determination of price is often based on what competitors are charging. For providers of visitor attractions, a comparison of admissions charges is looked at in relation to how long a visitor stays at the attraction – a concept known as **dwell time**. So, for example, a theme park may charge £12.00 admission with the average length of visitor stay at 7

Figure 4.8: Admission price criteria at heritage sites

	Not important %	Quite important %	Very important %	Extremely important %
Keep our prices in line with those of our competitors	14	45	22	12
We charge as much as we feel the market will bear	17	31	33	10
We have to keep our prices as low as possible in order to maximise our volume of admissions*	53	32	6	3
We have a moral obligation to keep our prices as low as possible so that no one is excluded from visiting	33	37	15	10
We try to set our prices so as to maximise our end-of-year surplus/profits	24	28	26	6
We try to maximise our end-of-year revenues	13	30	34	10
Our prices are set in order to achieve revenue targets	18	24	33	15
We have to keep our prices high in order to keep visitor numbers down to reasonable levels	67	19	4	3

Note: percentages exclude 'Don't know' and 'No response' responses hours, whereas a museum may charge £4.50 with the average visitor stay at 1.5 hours. In terms of dwell time the theme park works out at £1.71 per hour and the museum is £3.00 per hour. Dwell time is an important issue in terms of the customer's perception of a leisure and recreation product offering value for money.

Pricing policies

Getting the **pricing policy** right determines both the financial success of a particular product and, in part, the long-term success of the organisation. The exception to this is where an organisation provides free or subsidised products and services for its customers. For example, council-owned leisure facilities often provide free or subsidized services for certain groups within the communities they serve, such as pensioners, the unemployed, students and people on low incomes.

The type of organisation and the sector in which it operates have a direct impact on the formulation of pricing policies, such as the need to make a profit, break even or operate at a loss. Several different pricing policies can be implemented by leisure and recreation organisations.

- *Market penetration pricing.* This is usually used by organisations wanting to break into a new market in order to establish a product. It might involve setting a lower price to attract new business or to undercut competitors. For example, on Sunday nights LA Bowl in Leeds offers five activities for £9.95, representing a considerable reduction in the normal prices. This policy encourages more new customers to visit and hopefully to return at other times when they will pay the normal higher rates.

ACTIVITY

Dwell time

Look at this information on the average dwell time and admission prices of six major visitor attractions in the UK. Which represents the best value for money in terms of dwell time for adults, children and families?

Rock Circus, London
Average dwell time: 4 hours
Adults: £7.95
Children: £6.00
Family: N/A
Students/senior citizens: £7.25

Royal Armouries, Leeds
Average dwell time: 4 hours
Adults: £7.95
Children: £4.95
Family: £23.95
Students/senior citizens: £3.90

NCPM, Sheffield
Average dwell time: 2.5 hours
Adults: £7.25
Children: £4.50
Family: £21.00
Students/senior citizens: £5.50

Cadbury's World, Birmingham
Average dwell time: 2.5 hours
Adults: £6.25
Children: £4.50
Family: £18.60
Students/senior citizens: £5.75

Jorvik, York
Average dwell time: 1 hour
Adults: £7.95
Children: £3.99
Family: £16.60
Students/senior citizens: £5.00

National Railway Museum, York
Average dwell time: 3 hours
Adults: £4.95
Children: £3.50
Family: £14.50
Students/senior citizens: free

- ***Cost-plus pricing.*** This involves establishing the total costs of producing a particular product, adding a standard margin or mark-up and pricing the product accordingly. A retail sports outlet, for example, will typically have margins of 60-100 per cent on most of its product lines.
- ***Competitive pricing.*** Often the competition within the market dictates the price an organisation can set. Where competitor prices are low this strategy may lead to very low profit margins and even to financial ruin. For example, the profit margins of many visitor attractions are shrinking due to the fiercely competitive nature of the business and over-capacity in many areas. Over-capacity refers to a situation where the amount of a product or service available is greater than the number of customers who want to buy it. The combined effect of these factors is a reduction in prices so as to appear to be better value for money than competitors.
- ***Discount pricing.*** This involves offering a reduced price for certain types and groups of customers. Discount pricing is widely used in the leisure and recreation industries and includes numerous sales promotions and special offers, such as two for the price of one, 10 per cent off, summer sales and so forth.

▲ Discount pricing on sports shoes

- ***Variable pricing.*** Organisations can vary price according to customer types, levels and quality of service, times and days, seasons, and so on. For example, an art gallery may set lower prices for such groups as the unemployed, students and pensioners. Similarly, prices may vary according to peak and off-peak times during the day, week or year. The example of variable pricing at the Earth Centre in Doncaster in Figure 4.9 is particularly unusual. As a result of its environmental and ecological aims, it offers discounted rates of admission to visitors who travel to the centre using environmentally-friendly transport or in shared transport such as a coach.
- ***Market skimming strategy.*** Some products are not as price-sensitive as others. In other words, customers will still buy them if the price increases. This may be because there is limited competition or customers may be prepared to pay high prices for the quality and status associated with their use. Health farms and country clubs often adopt a high price strategy to retain their exclusivity, status and high-quality image. A further example can be seen in the way that football replica kits are sold. Most top teams have three kits and they change them every season. Most fans purchase these kits because they are brand-loyal. Oasis Holiday Centres charge considerably more than some other holiday centres such as Butlins, Pontins and Haven. They strive to create a brand image of luxury which is reinforced by the prices charged and subsequently the customers who can afford the product.

Figure 4.9: Variable pricing at the Earth Centre

Cost of admission	
Adults	£8.95
Children (under 14)	£6.95
OAPs and unemployed	£4.95
Family ticket	£30.00
Adults by coach (no minimum numbers)	£5.95
Children by coach	£4.95
Visitors by rail or bike	£4.95
Schools (per pupil, one in ten free)	£3.99

▲ Oasis luxury is reinforced by its pricing strategy

ACTIVITY

Peak and off-peak pricing

Many leisure facilities and visitor attractions offer a range of admission charges. One of the reasons for this is to spread demand and encourage more people to visit at off-peak times when demand is low. Look at the following extract from Eureka's admission price list. From the information provided, can you identify its peak and off-peak periods?

Adults and children over 12	£5.75
Children aged 3 - 12	£4.75
Children aged under 3 admitted free	
Saver Ticket	£18.75

(Admits up to four visitors including a maximum of two adults/children over 12.)

Pre-booked groups
Schools during term time £3.10 (Per child)
Other groups
Weekends and holidays £3.75 (Per person, in groups with ten or more children)

Special offer
Mondays to Fridays inclusive, visitors are admitted for half-price after 3.00pm during Eureka! Term time.

Whatever pricing policy an organisation uses, it should be based on:

- the customers' perception of what constitutes value for money;
- how much they can afford to pay
- what competitors are charging.

Promotion

Promotion is a vital component of the marketing mix. It includes all those activities used to communicate with existing and potential customers. For promotion to be effective, an organisation must be talking to the right people about the right product and convincing them that the price is right. The ultimate aim of promotion is to encourage consumers to buy or use a product or service. In order to achieve this aim, promotional activities need to:

- create brand awareness of the product or service
- enable consumers to understand the characteristics of the product or service
- persuade them to buy the product or use the service
- encourage them to develop brand loyalty and therefore prefer it to alternatives provided by competitors
- encourage them to continue to buy the product and to recommend it to others.

In order to persuade consumers to go through these stages, organisations must identify who it is they are attempting to reach and target the promotion accordingly. Promotion therefore has an important role to play in positioning products in a market to specific target groups. The more precise the positioning and targeting, the greater the chance of the target audience buying the product.

Once an organisation has identified who is going to be approached, it must then decide how to approach them. This involves selecting a suitable medium to reach the target audience. For example, a local sports centre could reach its target audience by placing a leaflet in a local free newspaper delivered to every household in the area. This approach would not be suitable for a larger organisation with a national target audience, such as a major theme park and on-site hotel like Alton Towers, which would probably need to place advertisements in national newspapers or on television.

The choice of promotional activity is ultimately determined by:

- the budget (what the organisation can afford to spend)
- the type of product
- the target audience.

Most leisure and recreation organisations use a combination of promotional activities. These include:

- advertising
- direct marketing
- public relations
- sales promotions
- sponsorship.

The combination of these activities is known as the **promotions mix.** We will look at them in greater detail in the section on marketing communications on pages 288-313.

▼ Some examples of promotional activities in leisure and recreation

Evaluating the marketing mix

We have looked at the four factors within the marketing mix and their importance for ensuring the success of a leisure and recreation organisation. However, it is not enough for an organisation simply to formulate an effective marketing mix: it needs continually to evaluate its effectiveness and make changes when necessary. For example, customer needs and expectations may change so that products or services need redevelopment; competitors may change their pricing policies so that an organisation may need to revise its own prices to remain competitive; promotional techniques may decrease in effectiveness.

We will look at some of the ways in which organisations can **evaluate the effectiveness of the marketing mix** in meeting customers' needs and expectations in the section on marketing research (page 264). However, you need to understand that such an evaluation should focus on how effectively the marketing mix is able to meet the organisation's marketing objectives. For example, if one of an organisation's aims is to increase the number of new customers it attracts, an evaluation of its marketing mix might ask some of the following questions:

- Do our products and services meet the needs and expectations of the identified new market?
- Are the brand image and product characteristics appropriate for this market?
- Are the location and channels of distribution suitable for the new customers?
- Are our prices acceptable to the new customers?
- Is our promotion effective in attracting new customers?

CASE STUDY

Marketing mix at McDonald's

McDonald's is part of the British way of life, but in fact the famous red-fronted restaurants have only been with us for the last 25 years. The first restaurant opened in Woolwich in 1974. By 1977 there were 10 restaurants, rising to 200 in 1985 and 738 in 1996. The thousandth McDonald's opened its doors in the UK in 1999. Globally, McDonald's operates 23,000 outlets in 109 countries with over 38 million people in the world eating at McDonald's each day.

In its vision statement, McDonald's summarises its mission in these five global strategies:

- Develop our people at every level of the organisation, beginning in our restaurants.
- Foster innovation in our menu, facilities, marketing operations and technology.
- Expand our global mindset by sharing best practices and leveraging our best people resources around the world.
- Long term, reinvent the category in which we compete and develop other business and growth opportunities.
- Continue the successful implementation of changes underway in McDonald's USA.

McDonald's marketing mix is as follows.

Product

McDonald's product characteristics have been firmly embedded in their customers' minds through the extensive use of standardisation throughout its operations. Staff training, food and drink products, packaging and the design and decoration of restaurants are consistent in all of their outlets..

Research carried out by Interbrand found that the McDonald's brand was recognised by more people throughout the world than any other brand, including Coca-Cola's. The brand image has consistently been one of fast service, cleanliness, value for money and a fun experience for all the family.

The introduction of the McDonald's product to the UK aimed at the family market by offering catering as a leisure experience. While it still generates considerable revenue from this market, McDonald's has continuously developed new products to meet changing customer needs. Trends in healthy eating and the growing popularity of vegetarianism have led to the introduction of fish and bean burgers. More recently, ethnic influences have led to the development of Indian-style products. Targeting children, with the view that they are tomorrow's adult customers, has also been a prime objective, with the development of the hugely successful Happy Meals offering food, a soft drink and a free toy.

Place

McDonald's restaurants seem to be located on every high street throughout the UK. The company has also developed outlets at airports, on ferries, at football grounds and even in hospitals.

Price

Price determination at McDonald's has always been governed by the desire to reinforce a brand image of good value for money. Frequent special offers are made, such as the very successful 'two for the price of one Big Mac' offer in 1999; so successful, in fact, that when customer demand for Big Macs increased by 800 per cent it ran out of burgers and had to place apologies in the national press!

Promotion

A strong promotional strategy has always been one of the keys to McDonald's success. In 1974 the original advertising slogan promised 'There's a difference at McDonald's you'll enjoy' and was aimed at persuading potential customers that the company was offering a new and fun product. In 1998 the company spent £44 million on advertising campaigns compared to the £15.6 million spent by their competitor Burger King.

Much of McDonald's promotion comprises advertising on television and in national newspapers and is designed to reflect the humorous side of the British way of life, with McDonald's at its centre. McDonald's also uses promotional tie-ins extensively, particularly when targeting the children's market. In 1996 the company reached a ten-year agreement with Disney for the exclusive rights to merchandise based on new Disney films such as *A Bug's Life* and *Pocahontas*. Point-of-sale displays and posters are also used at outlets to entice hungry passers-by.

McDonald's undertakes a great deal of sponsorship, particularly sporting events such as NASCAR racing and the France '98 World Cup.

McDonald's has 75 per cent of the UK hamburger market. Its nearest competitor is Burger King with just 15 per cent of the market.

McDonald's promotional activity in conjunction with Disney

BUILD YOUR LEARNING

End of section activity

Read through the McDonald's case study.

1 Produce a SWOT and PEST analysis for McDonald's. You may find it useful to base your analysis of the business environment on a McDonald's outlet in your area.

2 Evaluate how McDonald's uses the marketing mix to satisfy its customers needs and expectations.

3 Make recommendations as to how the marketing mix for McDonald's could be improved.

4 Suggest any future trends that could affect McDonald's marketing mix, giving your reasons.

Keywords and phrases

You should know the meaning of the words and phrases listed below. If you are unsure about any of them, go back through the last 16 pages to refresh your understanding.

- Marketing mix
- Product
- Product characteristics
- Branding
- Product life cycle
- Place
- Location
- Chain of distribution
- Price
- Dwell time
- Breakeven price
- Pricing policy
- Promotion
- Promotions mix
- Evaluate the effectiveness of the marketing mix

Market research

Leisure and recreation organisations need to know who their customers are and the type of products and services that they want. Effective **market research** is crucial in achieving this - the planned process of collecting, analysing and evaluating information and data about customers and markets.

▲ Market researchers are often seen in busy high streets

Effective market research helps organisations to make decisions about the types of products their customers want, the price they are prepared to pay, where they prefer to buy the product and how it should be promoted. The market research process is therefore closely linked to the development of an effective marketing mix. By carrying out market research, organisations can identify key factors which contribute to achieving customer satisfaction, thereby increasing their competitiveness and improving performance.

Objectives

Market research can be used to obtain a wide range of information. Its objectives commonly involve identifying:

- customer needs
- markets
- trends and fashions
- changes in markets
- opportunities for market and product development
- competitors
- effectiveness of promotional activities.

Identifying customer needs

In order to be customer oriented, organisations must gather a range of information about what their customers want and how best to provide it. For example, by obtaining suitable information about the needs of the short break family market, Center Parcs has dominated the year-round holiday centre market since the 1980s. Such information led to the identification of a need for all-weather facilities, quality accommodation and facilities, and breaks based on a range of booking options such as weekend, mid-week and full week stays.

Identifying markets

Before offering a new product, most organisations carry out research to identify the market at which the product should be aimed. For example, a hotel may identify its potential market as business, conference, leisure or overseas visitors. This is clearly important information, since it allows the hotel to target its products precisely.

Alton Towers has identified its main markets as general customers (individuals and families) and trade customers (group organisers, coach operators, corporate companies, school parties and hotels).

▲ The main market at Alton Towers includes general customers and trade customers

Identifying trends

Market research can be used to identify trends and therefore predict future markets. The customer profile of Meadowhall shows that there is a continuing trend towards younger shoppers using the centre, whereas in the UK generally older shoppers comprise a higher proportion of the shopping market.

Figure 4.10: Visitors to Meadowhall

	1997	1998	1999
Age			
16–25	23	23	26
25–44	55	55	46
45+	23	23	29
Social grade			
ABC1	62	62	63
C2DE	36	36	36

One of the major trends affecting the leisure and recreation industry is the growing interest in health and fitness and the subsequent pursuit of a healthier lifestyle. This has given rise to a rapid growth in health and fitness centres, both in the public and private sectors.

Changes in markets

Trends usually result in changes in the market or in some cases the creation of entirely new markets. The leisure shopping market is a relatively new one that has been encouraged by the development of large, out-of-town shopping malls. Leisure and recreation providers have been quick to recognise this and develop their own products to fit in. For example, many shopping malls contain facilities such as multi-screen cinemas, catering outlets, tenpin bowling alleys and even small funfairs.

Opportunities for market and product development

By identifying markets and their characteristics and the influence of trends, organisations are able to identify opportunities for developing new and existing products and markets. For example, many Premiership football clubs now offer a wide range of products and services, such as financial services, travel, leisurewear, corporate hospitality and catering, in addition to the core business activity of football.

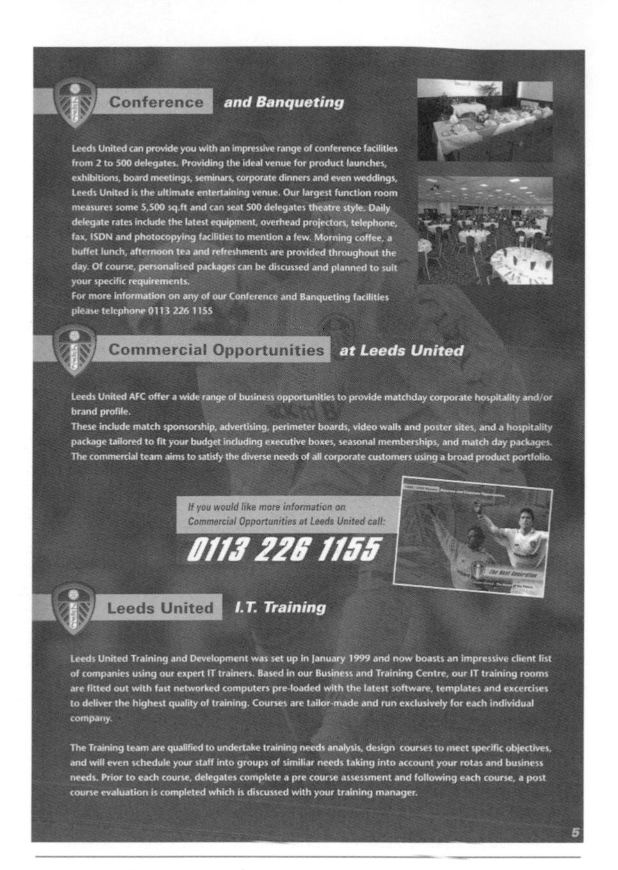

▲ Some services offered by Leeds United

Competitors

Market research can be used to identify an organisation's main competitors and the way they affect its products and markets. This information is important when identifying opportunities for developing new products and markets, as organisations must be able to gain a large enough market share to meet their financial performance targets. Research involves identifying the type of products offered by competitors, the people who buy them, their share of the market and their pricing strategy.

Effectiveness of promotional activities

Most organisations use some form of promotion to help sell their products and this can often be expensive. It is therefore important to identify how effective the promotion is in terms of meeting its objectives. For instance, did it attract new customers, and if so how many? Did it improve customers' perception of the product and organisation? Which types of promotion were the most cost-effective? For example, an organisation may ask customers how they heard about the product and services offered, in order to evaluate which of its promotional techniques were the most effective in attracting new customers.

ACTIVITY

Questionnaires

Obtain a questionnaire from a leisure or recreation organisation. They are often freely available at the reception desk for customers to complete. Alternatively, many organisations will supply copies of past questionnaires they have used.

Discuss what you think the objectives of the questionnaire might be. For example, if the questionnaire asks for details of how customers heard about the facility, product or service, one objective of the research might be to evaluate the effectiveness of promotions.

Classifying customers

Although it is vital to identify markets, it is equally important to understand the characteristics of customers within a market, so that products can be developed which meet their needs. Market research plays a key role in identifying customers and **classifying customers** into key **market segments** through a process known as **market segmentation.**

Market segmentation involves dividing the overall market into segments or groups of customers who are sufficiently alike to suggest that they will have similar needs for products or services. There are several ways markets can be segmented:

- socio-economic groupings
- age
- family circumstances
- lifestyle

Socio-economic groupings

In marketing, social class (or **socio-economic grouping**) is often used to differentiate groups according to income and occupational status. One of the most widely used classifications based on social-economic class is that developed by the Institute of Practitioners in Advertising. This divides the population into six groups.

- **Class A:** Senior managers and professionals, such as managing directors of large firms, doctors and lawyers.
- **Class B:** Intermediate or middle-level managers and professionals, such as managers of leisure centres, teachers and accountants.
- **Class C1:** Supervisory or junior management, administrative or clerical positions, including office managers, receptionists, computer operators and qualified fitness advisers.
- **Class C2:** Skilled manual workers, such as electricians and carpenters.
- **Class D:** Semi-skilled and unskilled manual workers, such as cleaners and construction workers.
- **Class E:** Others on low incomes, including casual workers and those dependent on state benefits and pensions.

In broad terms, people in these groups tend to have similar tastes, preferences and lifestyles. For example, As and Bs generally buy *The Times*, whereas C1s and C2s prefer the *Daily Mail* and the *Daily Express*, while C2s and Ds choose the *Sun* and similar tabloid papers.

Many leisure and recreation products are seen to be attractive to a particular class. Bingo is seen as a mainly working-class activity, for example, while golf is an activity of As and Bs. However, in recent years, many traditional preferences have become blurred, in part due to changing income patterns. Some manual workers have high earnings and can afford private health club membership, whereas public sector professionals including teachers and nurses may have cheaper pastimes.

Age

Many products and services are aimed at people in a particular age group. Carrying out market research into the age segments using particular products and services can help an organisation develop products and services to meet their customers' needs. Frequently this will mean adapting existing products or developing new ones to meet the needs of new and different age groups of target customers. The case study opposite shows how alcopops have become popular with a particular age group.

CASE STUDY

The rise of alcopops

The rise of alcopops

The consumption of alcohol, both as a home-based and away-from-home activity, is a key feature of many leisure activities. Prior to the early 1990s, alcoholic drinks manufacturers mainly targeted the older adult market, with few products aimed at 18-25 year olds. In 1993, when there was a glut of lemons, an Australian farmer made a fermented drink from surplus lemons which resulted in an 'alcoholic lemonade' later branded as Two Dogs. The new drink was an overnight success and led other drinks manufacturers to develop rival products. Bass developed Hooper's Hooch and immediately took a 55 per cent share of the market. In 1996 Whitbread launched Shotts and many other alcopops have followed. The drinks have three things in common:

- a taste similar to a sweet soft drink
- a high alcohol content
- an appeal to younger people.

Since their launch, alcopops have not escaped criticism. Many argue that they encourage under-age people to drink alcohol because of their sweet taste. Research indicates that drinkers under the

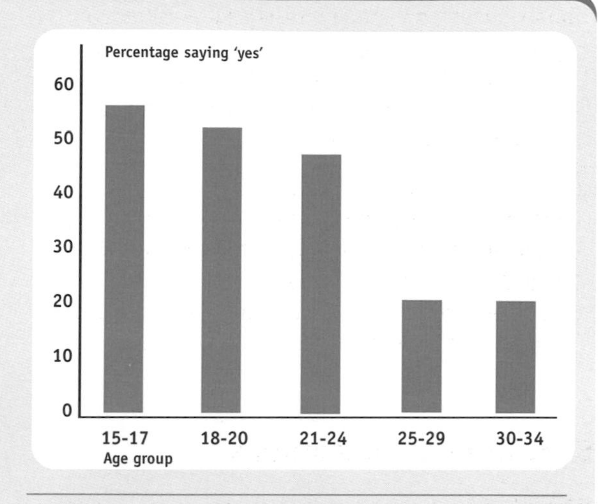

▲ Age groups who drink alcopops

age of 20 years were far more likely to drink alcopops than those over 30 years.

Added to this is concern about the alcohol content, which is considerably higher than many beers and lagers. However, no one can dispute the huge success of alcopops. Initial forecasts for sales up to the end of 1997 proved an underestimation, as shown below.

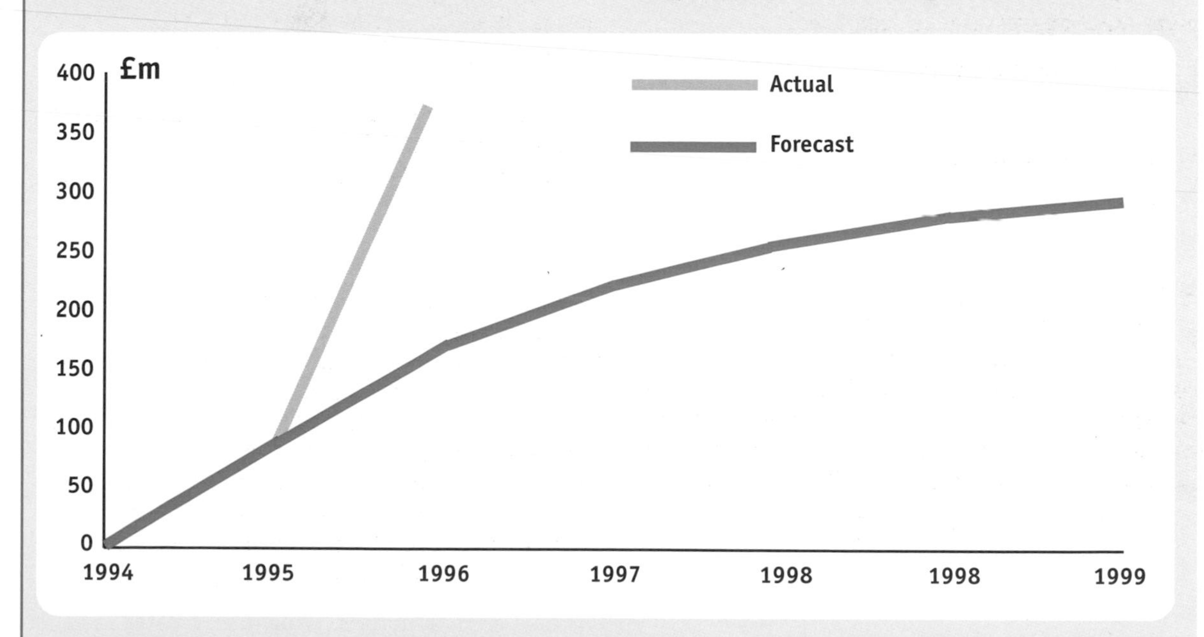

▲ Forecast v actual sales of alcopops

ACTIVITY

Market segments

Look at the list of sports below and for each identify the main market segments that you think take part in it.

football

cricket

rugby union

rugby league

crown green bowls

tennis

fishing

hockey

polo

Family circumstances

Customers frequently experience leisure and recreation products and services with friends, partners or family members rather than on their own. This means that the market segment for many leisure and recreation products is not an individual but a group of customers, each with a range of individual needs.

Family circumstances market segmentation classifies customers according to their stage in the **family life-cycle**. These stages can vary, but generally include most of the following for the majority of people at some stage in their life:

- child
- young adult
- young couple
- early nesters, i.e. young couple with baby/young children
- settled nesters, i.e. couple with growing family (aged 5-18 years)
- empty nesters, i.e. couple whose children have recently left home
- elderly couple
- single elderly person.

Leisure and recreation organisations may find through market research that their customers are from specific life cycle segments and therefore tailor their products and services to meet these segment needs. For example, over the last 10-15 years there has been a large increase in the number of young couples with babies and couples with growing families using leisure and recreation products as a family group. This has led to many tourist attractions introducing special family-priced entrance tickets and the development of specific children's areas and facilities in pubs and hotels. Similarly, there has been a growing trend for people in their 50s to take early retirement, resulting in the empty nesters having more time to pursue leisure and recreation interests.

The key market segments identified by Madame Tussauds are shown on page 281.

ACTIVITY

Family market segments

As a group, identify two leisure or recreation facilities, products or services that particularly appeal to the following groups of family circumstances:

- children
- young adults
- young couples
- early nesters
- settled nesters
- empty nesters
- elderly couple
- single elderly person.

For example, theme parks appeal particularly to young adults/couples, early nesters and settled nesters.

Lifestyle

A more complicated method of market segmentation is to identify how customers' lifestyles influence the types of products that they buy. This is particularly useful when looking at leisure and recreation products because they often form an integral part of the customer's lifestyle. For example, in recent years there has been an increasing tendency for people to spend a larger proportion of their spare time on home-based activities. This has created a huge market for home entertainment products such as videos, computers, digital television and music systems (see Figure 4.11).

Figure 4.11: Access/use of home entertainment

	Access		Use	
	% at home	% in own room	% used	Minutes spent per day
Television	100	63	99	147
Video	96	21	81	39
Computer games	67	34	64	45
Radio	95	59	86	76
Hi Fi	96	61	86	76
Personal stereo	83	68	86	76
PC (not games)	53	12	42 / 88 *(home) (school)*	31
Books	87	64	31	28

Source: *Daily Mail* March 19, 1999

The concept of **lifestyle segmentation** has led many organisations to give titles to their main segments that describe the general way in which those segments work, spend their money and use their leisure time. You have probably heard of one of the first lifestyle segments to be identified – the yuppie. The term arose in the 1980s and describes a young (25-35 years), single, successful, professional person who earns a high salary and spends their money on expensive products, including leisure activities such as skiing and watersports.

One of the more recently identified lifestyle segments in the leisure and recreation market is the juggler. Typically, a juggler is a 35-45 year-old woman with a demanding full-time career. She usually has a partner in a high-profile job and a number of school-aged children, as well as a large house to run (albeit, often with help from a cleaner, gardener, etc.). In other words, this type of lifestyle customer is continually juggling the many aspects of her busy life.

ACTIVITY

Lifestyle segmentation

As a group, discuss which particular leisure and recreation products and services the juggler will be attracted to. Bear in mind that she will often experience them with others, such as a partner and/or children.

In this activity you might also like to consider another lifestyle concept: money-rich, time-poor. This describes people who earn large salaries but have such demanding jobs and other commitments that they have very little leisure time.

Organisations may differentiate market segments on the basis of several other factors, such as:

- gender
- place of residence
- personal characteristics of their customers.

It is important to remember that identifying market segments is only an approximate way of targeting customers. However, increasingly sophisticated market research is allowing the identification to become more and more precise.

Primary market research

There are two basic types of market research, primary and secondary. **Primary market research** is also known as **field research**. It refers to any research that involves contact with past, existing or potential customers. Primary market research is what most people think of as market research and includes methods such as

- surveys
- observation
- focus groups.

Before looking at each of these in turn, it is important to understand the difference between qualitative and quantitative research. **Qualitative research** looks in depth at consumers' feelings, attitudes, desires and perceptions, whereas **quantitative research** provides more structured information that is statistically measurable.

Although qualitative research can provide more detailed in-depth information, it is often difficult to present statistically or to come to any general conclusions. For example, if you asked 200 people how the customer service provided by a sports coach could be improved, you could receive 200 different answers. Using all this information could be difficult. Quantitative research, on the other hand, can enable researchers to draw specific conclusions from the results. For example, if you asked if customers were satisfied with the customer service, it might lead you to find that, of those surveyed, 43 per cent were satisfied with the customer service and 57 per cent were dissatisfied. It does not, however, give any detailed information to explain why those 57 per cent were dissatisfied with the customer service.

Generally speaking, quantitative research results become more accurate as the sample size increases. Qualitative research, on the other hand, works better with a small sample size. Many organisations use a combination of both. Questionnaires, for example, are often used to produce quantitative information. Group discussions and in-depth interviews are usually used to produce qualitative information.

Market research questions can be phrased as open or closed questions. Closed questions require a single word or brief answer. Open questions require an explanation as an answer. In the Sea Life survey (Figure 4.12), most of the questions are closed, producing a wide range of quantitative information. Respondents are also given opportunities to make detailed comments about aspects of their visit that failed to meet their expectations.

Surveys

Surveys are usually conducted as a quantitative research method based on a questionnaire given to a large sample, such as the Sea Life example. **Questionnaires** are one of the most widely used research methods in the leisure and recreation industry because they are relatively quick and easy to administer and analyse.

The success of a survey depends to a large extent upon the quality of the questionnaire. A well-designed questionnaire, including structured questions with answers classified into predetermined categories, is quick to administer and the resulting data is easy to process. By contrast, a questionnaire made up of open-ended questions creates problems of interpretation and analysis, as well as for recording the data.

Figure 4.12: Sea Life survey

SEA LIFE

Sea Life Centres are constantly monitoring visitor response, to ensure you all receive maximum enjoyment. To assist, kindly complete this short survey. Please answer each question fully by ticking the relevant box(es). Thank you.

Visitor Survey

Date of visit

What are the main reasons for this visit? You may tick more than one box.

- To see the sharks (only centres with sharks)
- To see all the sea life / fish
- Recommended by a friend or relative
- Just passing
- To see the seals (only Centres with seal rescue facility)
- A place to go on a dull / rainy day
- Promotional Offer
- Visit a new attraction
- Family outing
- Enjoyed a previous visit and wanted to visit again
- Saw an advertisement

Other (please specify)

Publicity

How did you see or hear about Sea Life before your visit? You may tick more than one box.

- Tourist Info. centre
- Holiday Guide
- Cinema
- Road sign
- Television Commercial
- Television News
- Local Newspaper
- Sea Life Leaflet
- Posters
- Radio
- National Newspaper
- Promotional Offer

Other (please specify)

If you saw a Sea Life leaflet before your visit, where did you see it?

- Hotel
- Holiday Park / Camp
- Tourist Info Centre
- B & B / Guesthouse
- Self Catering
- Pub / Restaurant

Other (please specify)

Did you (or anyone in your party) use a promotional voucher / offer when you entered the Centre — Yes / No

If yes, where did you get the voucher? — The Daily Mirror / Iceland

Other (please specify)

About your visit

How satisfied are you with your overall visit?

- **Very satisfied**
- **Quite satisfied**
- **Neither satisfied nor dissatisfied**
- **Quite dissatisfied**
- **Very dissatisfied**

Would you recommend a visit to friends or family? — Yes / No

Did you talk to any staff as you were going round the Centre? (other than in the shop or restaurant) — Yes / No

Did you or anyone with you buy any goods from the shop? — Yes / No

Did you use the restaurant / catering facilities? — Yes / No

How well did the following live up to your expectations?

	Excellent	Good	Fair	Poor	Very poor	Did not use/ see
Displays / Creatures						
Restaurant / Catering						
Shop						
Staff efficiency / friendliness						
Talk / Presentation						
Value for money						

Compiling a questionnaire

This is a skilled process that needs careful consideration. You need to consider:

- how to frame the questions
- how long the questionnaire should be
- how the questionnaire should be laid out
- how to record the answers.

Framing questions

One of the most difficult aspects of compiling an effective questionnaire is writing questions that are easily understood and interpreted in the same way by all respondents. General rules for writing questions are:

- Keep language simple and specific.
- Avoid jargon, slang or local terms.
- Do not ask more than one thing in a single question.
- Make sure questions are unambiguous, i.e. that they cannot be interpreted in different ways by different respondents.
- Do not ask respondents to make complicated calculations or recall events that happened a long time ago.
- Only include questions that are totally relevant - it is easy to get side-tracked and forget what you are actually trying to find out.
- Do not ask respondents to speculate or imagine something that they have not experienced - their answer will only be a guess and not very helpful!
- As a general rule, avoid very personal questions - people will either refuse to answer or lie!

Length of questionnaires

When designing a questionnaire you need to consider how long it should be. There is no definitive answer to the question of length because it largely depends on the situation in which someone is replying. For example, someone stopped in the street may only be willing to spare a couple of minutes for a face-to-face interview, whereas a customer at a health farm may be more willing to spend half an hour filling in a survey.

Layout of questionnaires

The way that a questionnaire is laid out is very important. Questions need to be in a logical sequence so that one question leads directly to the next. This helps the respondent to focus their thoughts and concentrate on each section.

ACTIVITY

Framing questions

Look at this extract from a questionnaire. Its market research objectives are to identify the types of exercise taken by respondents and the reasons for their choice. All of the questions break some of the rules already discussed. Can you rewrite the questions to make them more effective?

1 How much do you earn?

2 What forms of exercise have you participated in over the last two years?

3 If you were asked to summarise the main features that you look for in exercise what would your three main priorities be?

4 How much do you spend on exercise each year?

5 Have you ever used a media direct response line to find out more about a particular type of exercise?

6 In your opinion which leisure providers offer the best service?

7 How old are you? Under 18, 18-25, 25-40, 40-55, over 55.

8 How do you decide what exercise to take and what factors do you consider?

9 If you won the lottery, in which types of exercise would you participate?

10 Do you own/drive a car?

If you really want to ensure that your questionnaire is effective, you need to carry out a pilot survey. This means testing the questionnaire on a small group of respondents to make sure that all the questions are easily understood and not misinterpreted. You will probably find that some of the questions need rewording to make them more effective.

ACTIVITY

Sequencing questions

Look at these questions taken from a questionnaire given to visitors at a visitor attraction and rearrange them so that they are in a more logical sequence.

1 How did you hear about Black Tunnel Mining Museum?

2 Will you recommend friends to visit Black Tunnel Mining Museum?

3 Have you enjoyed your visit to Black Tunnel Mining Museum?

4 Is this your first visit to Black Tunnel Mining Museum?

5 Have you seen our newspaper advertisements?

6 If you have visited before, how many times have you been in the last year?

7 Did a friend recommend Black Tunnel Mining Museum to you?

8 Have you used discount vouchers from the local newspaper for your visit?

9 Have you seen copies of our brochure at a tourist information centre?

10 Will you visit Black Tunnel Mining Museum again?

Recording answers

The method used to record answers depends on whether the research is qualitative or quantitative. In qualitative research, answers will usually comprise detailed written explanations. However, in quantitative research there are a number of options. By far the easiest is 'yes or no', but this can only be used for a limited number of questions and obviously also gives limited information. Multiple-choice is a widely used method in which respondents are given a range of answers and asked to tick the one or ones that apply. An example of this type of question is shown in Figure 4.13.

Figure 4.13: Extract from the Research Opinion Poll Survey

66 Tick all the hobbies, activities and interests that you/partner have:

01 ☐ Exercise/Active Sport
02 ☐ Fishing
03 ☐ Golf
04 ☐ Hiking/Walking
05 ☐ Antiques/Art
06 ☐ Collecting/Collections
07 ☐ Fashion/Buying Clothes
08 ☐ Reading Books
09 ☐ Music-CDs/Tapes
10 ☐ Self Improvement
11 ☐ Shares/Stock Market
12 ☐ Investments/Savings
13 ☐ Environment/Wildlife
14 ☐ Religious Activities
15 ☐ National Trust
16 ☐ Theatre/The Arts
17 ☐ Sewing/ Needlecraft
18 ☐ Eating Out
19 ☐ Cooking/Baking
20 ☐ Health Foods
21 ☐ Wines
22 ☐ DIY/Do-It-Yourself
23 ☐ Gardening
24 ☐ Grandchildren
25 ☐ Pets
26 ☐ Home Computing
27 ☐ Foreign Travel
28 ☐ Charity/Voluntary Work
29 ☐ Competitions
30 ☐ Going to Bingo
31 ☐ Doing the Pools
32 ☐ Playing the Lottery
33 ☐ Weekend Breaks
34 ☐ Stamp Collecting
35 ☐ The Internet
36 ☐ Reading Historical Works
37 ☐ Watching Videos
38 ☐ Crosswords/Puzzles
39 ☐ Home Decorating
40 ☐ New Technology

Please look at the boxes you've ticked and **write down** the numbers of the **5 favourite** activities for:

You 1 ☐☐ 2 ☐☐ 3 ☐☐ 4 ☐☐ 5 ☐☐

Partner 1 ☐☐ 2 ☐☐ 3 ☐☐ 4 ☐☐ 5 ☐☐

Figure 4.14: Family Activity Match

Would your family like to do something that's more or less active?

Some activities require a fair amount of exertion of physical activity, whereas others can be done quietly sitting in a chair. Specify the level of intensity you'd like an activity to have.

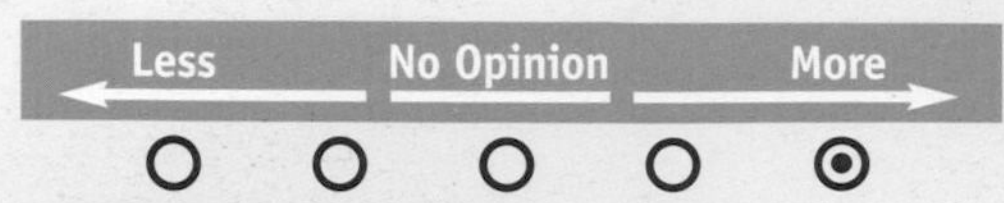

How do you feel about messy activities?

Put some paint, glue, or food in your child's hands, and you've got a potential mess waiting to happen. This may or may not be a problem depending on your patience level and how much time you'll have to clean things up. Indicate how you feel about activities that could be potentially messy.

Won't Accept — No Opinion — Like — Love

O O O O O ⊙ O

Would you prefer to be indoors or outdoors?

In the mood for some fresh air or would you rather just hang out in the family room? Indicate the degree to which you'd like to do something indoors or outdoors so only appropriate activiies will be suggested.

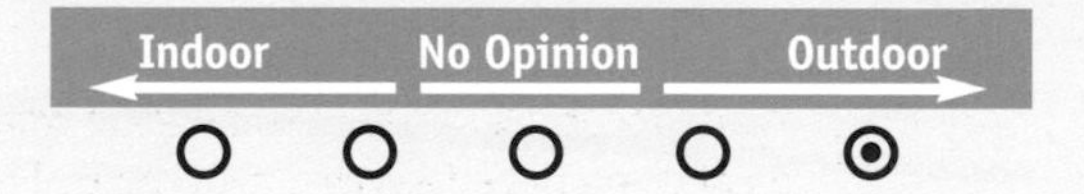

Another way of recording answers is to use a method known as 'semantic differential', in which respondents select the phrase or word that most closely describes their opinion. An example is shown in Figure 4.14, which asks respondents to rate the importance of various aspects of family leisure activities.

Sometimes this method is used with a numerical scale, so that respondents circle a number on a scale from 1 to 5. For example:

How often do you use a snack bar at a sports centre?
Please rate on the scale:
1 = never, 2 = occasionally, 3 = quite often, 4 = nearly always, 5 = always.

1 - 2 - 3 - 4 - 5.

In selecting the method of recording answers, it is important that the researcher considers the reaction of the respondent. If he or she uses a range of different methods, respondents are likely to become confused and may give inaccurate answers.

Contact methods

There are three main ways (contact methods) in which survey information can be gathered: by mail, telephone or personal contact.

ACTIVITY

Design a questionnaire

Design and implement a short survey questionnaire to identify the main market segments using a local sports facility or service. Once you have completed the survey, discuss with the rest of the group how your questionnaire could have been improved. For example, was the sample accurate, did all respondents understand the questions, were there questions that you should have added or left out, etc?

Many organisations send questionnaires through the post. The advantages of this method of research is that it is quick to administer and that a large sample can be reached relatively cheaply. The drawback is that the reply rate can be very poor - as low as 3 per cent in many cases.

Ways of encouraging people to reply include enclosing a stamped addressed envelope and offering incentives for respondents who reply, such as entry into prize draws. Even when this is done there is a problem that certain types of people are more likely to reply than others, making the sample unrepresentative.

▲ Face-to-face contact produces a higher response rate

Some organisations carry out surveys by asking respondents questions over the telephone. This is more expensive and time consuming than using the mail, but usually has a higher response rate. However, because so many organisations use the phone as a sales tool, respondents are often suspicious, thinking that the purpose is to sell them something.

Many surveys are conducted through personal contact between the researcher and the respondent. Face-to-face contact is clearly more time consuming and therefore expensive, but the response rate is usually higher than responses to mail and telephone surveys. It is extremely important for the researcher to be fully trained in research techniques and understand the ways in which his or her behaviour and attitude should be controlled. For example, if the researcher appears to agree or disagree with answers or prompts the respondent, he or she may influence the way that the respondent answers further questions.

The contact method used depends largely on the type of research being conducted and the amount of time and money available. A further consideration is the skill of the people who are going to carry out the research. Above all, the information collected needs to be objective, unbiased and truly representative if it is to be of any real value.

ACTIVITY

Observation

Observe and record how customers decide what to eat in a cafeteria or self-service restaurant. For example, do they:

- look at the menu and then decide?
- go straight to what they want?
- ask the counter staff for advice?
- look at all of the dishes on offer and then make their decision?
- choose in another way?

You will need to design a suitable form to record your observations. If your college or school has a self-service canteen you can carry out this activity there. Alternatively, you could visit a local self-service restaurant and conduct your observational research there, but remember to get the permission of the manager first!

Observation

Observation is a research method in which information is obtained by observing customers' behaviour or events taking place. For example, much research into road traffic is conducted by researchers placed at strategic road junctions counting the number of cars that pass at various times.

In leisure and recreation there are many situations in which observation methods can be used to provide valuable information. For example, observation at marine exhibits has shown that customers enjoy physical contact with the fish and other sea life rather than simply viewing them in glass tanks. This has led to some providers, such as Sealife Centres, providing touch pools where visitors can actually stroke the fish and special demonstrations that allow customers to handle live exhibits.

Focus groups

In **focus group** research, groups of people are encouraged to discuss their opinions and feelings about a particular organisation, product, service or topic that affects an organisation's marketing activities.

The great advantage is that the information collected is qualitative and therefore very detailed. However, it is extremely expensive and the information collected is based on a very small selection of respondents.

You should also appreciate that focus group research is a highly skilled technique that is often carried out by qualified psychologists. This is because the researcher must be able to encourage the respondents to talk freely about the topics that are of interest without leading them to say something that they do not really mean. In other words the researcher needs to be a part of the discussion group but ensure that their own feelings and opinions do not influence the respondents.

ACTIVITY

Focus group research

Carry out focus group research into the brand image of a selection of visitor attractions. You will need up to seven visitor attraction leaflets targeting a range of market segments, for example families, youth, older people, special interest, etc. Find at least five volunteers to make up your focus group; these should be people that you do not know very well, such as other students or tutors. Set a time limit for the group session of 20 minutes.

At the beginning of the session explain to the group members that you are interested in their ideas about the type of customers each visitor attraction is trying to attract. Give them a few minutes to look at the leaflets. Then ask them to discuss the customers targeted by each leaflet and explain what it is about the leaflet that appeals to this particular type of customer.

After the focus group session evaluate its success:

- Was the information that you collected useful?
- Were there any factors that reduced the effectiveness of the session, such as one member dominating the discussion or influencing other members?
- How difficult did you find it to resist the temptation to voice your own opinion or lead the members' answers?
- How would you conduct the session differently if you had to do it again?

CASE STUDY

National Centre for Popular Music

On page 242 we looked at the PEST analysis carried out by the National Centre for Popular Music in Sheffield. The centre also carries out extensive primary research.

The centre commissioned Sheffield Hallam University to carry out systematic quantitative research, which was conducted in six towns within a two-hour radius of Sheffield. The sample selected was based on age, gender and socio-economic groupings and involved face-to-face interviews. These were some of the findings:

- The most likely people to visit the centre were couples (25.2 per cent), groups of friends (35.8 per cent), students (11.7 per cent) and families (30.6 per cent).
- The most likely common leisure interests of those likely to visit the centre were visits to pop and rock concerts, indoor sports events, nightclubs, jazz and outdoor sports events. Sports events and music-related activities have therefore become target areas for marketing the centre.

The university also designed an exit questionnaire for visitors to complete after their visit to the centre.

More recently the centre has produced its own short feedback questionnaire, which is available at various points throughout the centre.

After the results of the quantitative research were analysed, Sheffield Hallam University conducted a number of focus groups. The quantitative research had identified adults aged 19-45, parents with children aged 5-14, and educators as three target market segments. Two focus groups were constructed for each of these three market segments (a total of six). Each focus group had 20 people who were prompted with material to encourage discussion. Much insight was gained from the focus groups on the overall product of the centre, proposals for a newer and shorter name, responses to exhibition areas, main considerations when planning visits, motivations for visiting and on benefits sought from visits. The centre also carried out observational research prior to opening by inviting 200 local school children to visit and use the exhibits. This research revealed a number of issues, including the fact that the 'unbreakable' interactive exhibits were all promptly broken by the visiting children! This was a very valuable piece of observational research, since it allowed the centre to redesign the exhibits to be truly unbreakable before it opened its doors to the general public on 1 March 1999.

THE NATIONAL CENTRE FOR POPULAR MUSIC

VISITOR SURVEY

SHEFFIELD HALLAM UNIVERSITY

WIN £50 HMV VOUCHERS AND A GUINNESS ROCKPEDIA

Dear Visitor

Welcome to The National Centre For Popular Music. We would be very grateful if you would take the time to answer some questions about your visit. The questionnaire should only take a short while to complete. Most questions only require you to mark a box like this [X] against the option which most closely represents your answer. The information will help us to improve our service.

All completed questionnaires will be entered in a **free prize draw** to win one of two prizes of a **£25 HMV music voucher and a Guinness Rockpedia book.**

▲ Extract from the NCPM's feedback questionnaire

ACTIVITY

NCPM's market research

As a group, discuss how you think the information gained from the NCPM's research might affect its marketing mix in terms of product, price, place and promotion.

Secondary research

Secondary market research is also known as **desk research** and involves obtaining information from sources that are already published or easily accessible. It is economical and comparatively quick to undertake, and can be conducted with complete confidentiality - in other words, without competitors finding out! On the other hand, because the information yielded by desk research is not generated for the particular purposes of the organisation conducting the research, it may not be sufficiently relevant: more specific (primary) research may be required.

There are two main sources of secondary research, internal and external.

Internal sources

Organisations can avoid the need for expensive market research if they use **internal sources** of information wisely. For example, by checking guest registration cards, a large hotel in North Wales identified that most of its customers came from areas of Greater Manchester. A promotional campaign was then targeted specifically at newspapers local to these areas, such as the Bolton Evening News. Let's look at some of the most commonly used sources of internal market research.

Sales records and usage figures

Sales records provide information on the quantity and frequency of products sold over a given period and can often be used to provide a comparison between current and past performance. Some organisations maintain detailed sales records showing combinations of products bought by customers.

This information is available from a number of sources, such as customer bills and cash till records. This is one of the reasons why loyalty cards are so useful, since they allow the organisation to evaluate the combination of products and services purchased by customers. The information can be useful in a number of ways, for example to identify the average spending of customers, the types of customers who spend the most, peak sales times and which products have the highest sales.

Many organisations maintain information about the number of people using a facility. For example, a library provides many of its services free of charge, so it keeps usage rather than sales figures. In complex facilities where a range of products and services is provided, usage figures are particularly useful in giving overall information about the number of customers. For example, Meadowhall has an electronic counting device on all the main entrances so that figures can be kept on how many customers visit at any time.

Many organisations compile financial information and customer databases. Financial information includes information on customers' accounts, methods of payment and credit arrangements. Much of this information may be stored on computer, making the research data much more accessible and easier to analyse. For example, organisations such as health clubs maintain records of visitors. Information may include the number of customers using the club, which facilities they used and the dates/times that they used facilities.

Much of this information is obtained when customers fill in booking forms or registration forms. For example, on page 250 we looked at the ETC's drive to improve the brand image of walking activities. Customers who visit the ETC web site and want to receive brochures have to complete a booking form. The information on the booking form can be kept to provide a database of information about the customer. Details from these forms may provide general information on the organisations that customers visit, their location, the type of people in each group and so on.

The amount of internal information that an organisation has varies according to the type of product and the ways in which a customer buys and uses it. A cinema may have limited information because customers purchase tickets over the counter, usually without giving any personal details. However, a private leisure club may have considerably more information if customers have to complete detailed membership forms.

Use of internal information

Look at these two extracts from a leisure centre's database containing information on attendance figures from 1993 to 1999. As a group, discuss what trends you can identify and how you think the leisure centre could use this information. For example, should it be targeting 26-40 year olds?

ANNUAL ATTENDANCES BY AGE GROUP (1,000S)

	0 - 16	17 - 25	26 - 40	41 - 65	65+
1993	32.7	48.3	49.8	50.1	31.9
1994	33.1	48.7	51.7	52.7	33.7
1995	37.4	49.2	53.6	54.2	35.9
1996	38.3	51.6	54.2	56.5	37.4
1997	36.5	52.9	56.3	54.8	39.8
1998	32.9	53.1	57.9	57.5	41.3
1999	30.8	54.6	59.4	58.9	44.8

FACILITY USAGE (1,000S)

	Swimming Pool	Squash	Badminton	Aerobics	Health club	Roller Disco
1993	33.8	17.6	2.9	50.1	N/a	N/a
1994	34.1	18.2	2.75	2.7	N/a	N/a
1995	32.4	19.7	3.6	54.2	25.9	N/a
1996	31.6	21.8	4.2	56.5	27.4	N/a
1997	29.3	23.5	6.3	54.8	29.8	6.2
1998	27.4	29.4	7.9	57.5	31.3	7.1
1999	25.3	32.8	9.4	58.9	34.8	9.6

External sources

There are many **external sources** of information, including:

- government publications
- newspapers, magazines and trade journals
- professional associations
- national organisations
- organisations which specialise in collecting commercial data in a particular business sector, such as Mintel and Gallup.

Government publications

Both central and local government carry out research and publishes the results. The Office for National Statistics (ONS) publish several very useful volumes of statistics, trends, demographic and census-related data. This includes the *Annual Abstract of Statistics, Family Expenditure Survey, Regional Trends* and *Social Trends,* and the annual *General Household Survey (Living in Britain)*. It also has an internet service that provides information. In all, the government publishes 400 series of statistics and many publications have specific sections on leisure and recreation. (See Resource and internet directory.)

Local government also publishes information collected through research. This may include information of direct interest to leisure and recreation providers, such as visitor numbers or usage of facilities.

Trade journals, newspapers and magazines

A trade journal is a publication produced for a particular occupation or industry. Many, such as *Caterer and Hotelkeeper, Leisure Management* and *Leisure Opportunities*, carry out research and publish the results. Mainstream newspapers and magazines also frequently contain the results of research, such as the example below dealing with the topics that interest 11-19 year olds in teenage magazines (see Figure 4.15).

▲ *Leisure Manager* is published by ILAM

Figure 4.15: Magazine topics of interest to 11-19 year olds

GIRLS	%
Clothes/fashion	72
Music	68
TV/pop stars	66
Problem/advice pages	49
Skincare/grooming	45
Relationships	30
Food/diet	27
Sex/contraception	20
Computers/Internet	13
Football	13
BOYS	**%**
Football	64
Music	54
Computers/Internet	50
TV/pop stars	42
Clothes/fashion	25
Problem/advice pages	12
Food/diet	11
Sex/contraception	9
Relationships	6
Skincare/grooming	2

Source: *Financial Mail on Sunday* September 6 1998

Professional and national associations

Professional associations are organisations that perform a co-ordinating, informing or leadership role. Within the leisure and recreation industry they include the Institute of Leisure and Amenity Management (ILAM), the Central Council of Physical Recreation (CCPR) and the Institute of Sport and Recreation Management (ISRM). Members of these associations pay a subscription in return for a range of services, which frequently includes market research information.

National organisations, often set up by government, manage various functions relating to different industries. In leisure and recreation they include Sport England (formerly the Sports Council), the Arts Council and the national park authorities. For example, many national parks carry out a number of research projects and publish the results. Figure 4.16 shows results from the research undertaken by Peak District National Park into the reasons why people visit national parks.

Commercial data

Extensive research is carried out by market research organisations such as Mintel and Gallup. For example, research undertaken about the sports industry by Mintel is shown on pages 00, 00 and 00. Leisure and recreation providers can commission research organisations to carry out specific research for them, or can buy information that has already been collected.

Figure 4.16: All Parks Visitor Survey

	All reasons %	Main reason %
Scenery/landscape	61	39
Enjoyed earlier visit	37	9
Easy to get to	33	7
Peace and quiet	28	4
Outdoor activity	18	11
Event/attraction	16	10
As it is a National Park	15	3
Come every year	9	3
Visit friends/family	5	3
Own accom. in area	4	2
Other	20	10

Source: *www.peakdistrict.org*

Analysing the findings

Analysing market research findings means extracting the relevant information and reaching some conclusions where possible. This is known as **data analysis**. One of the dangers in the analysis of market research data is that researchers are often so eager to 'prove something' that they may come to a conclusion that is not wholly supported by the findings.

Survey results

Once research data has been analysed, it needs organising into a usable form to produce **survey results**. With quantitative information, such as that gained from a questionnaire, this usually means producing statistical data. This information can then be presented in a number of ways so that it is easier to evaluate. It can be shown as a table with various columns, as a pie chart, a bar chart or a line graph.

A pie chart can be a good way of showing the distribution of response because it is easy to see the largest shares, as long as there are not too many categories.

Data analysis

Look at this research information and decide which, if any, of the statements that follow it is absolutely true.

Research information

- 75 per cent of respondents said that they went to at least one cinema film a year.
- Of the respondents who went to the cinema, 17 per cent went on their own, 34 per cent went with a friend and 59 per cent went with their family.
- 27 per cent of respondents were not satisfied with the service offered by the cinema.
- 61 per cent of respondents had been to an evening screening and 14 per cent to a matinee performance.
- 12 per cent of those who had been to the cinema had booked over the telephone, while 63 per cent bought tickets on the door.

Statements

1 27 per cent of cinema customers were not satisfied with the service provided by the cinema.

2 25 per cent of respondents did not go to the cinema.

3 63 per cent of customers who went with their family bought their tickets on the door.

4 41 per cent of people with families did not go to the cinema.

5 People who went to the cinema on their own were less likely to be dissatisfied with the service provided by the cinema.

Figure 4.17: Visitors to Madame Tussaud's

Origin	
Domestic:	30%
Overseas:	70%
Europe	60%
North America	15%
Rest of the World	25%
Age	
Under 16	20%
16–24	26%
25–34	23%
35–44	17%
45–54	7%
55+	7%
Social Class	
AB	20%
C1	44%
C2	25%
DE	11%

Bar charts are used in a similar way to pie charts and allow comparisons to be made easily. A bar chart is usually a better choice if there is a large number of categories. Figure 4.18 shows the information on age from Figure 4.17 as a bar chart.

Figure 4.18: Visitors to Madame Tussaud's

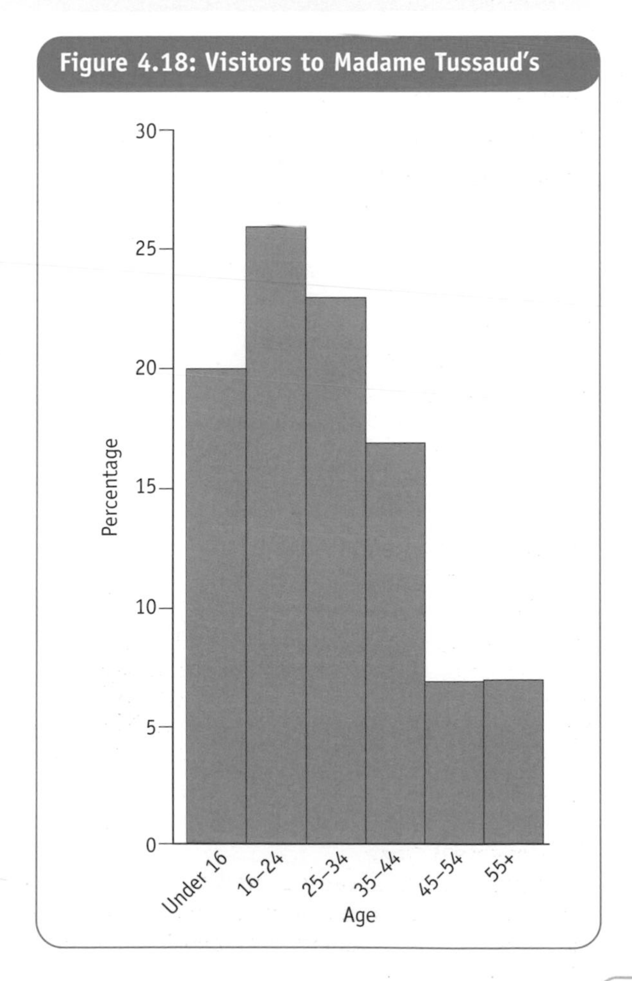

Figure 4.19: Using a line graph to show trends

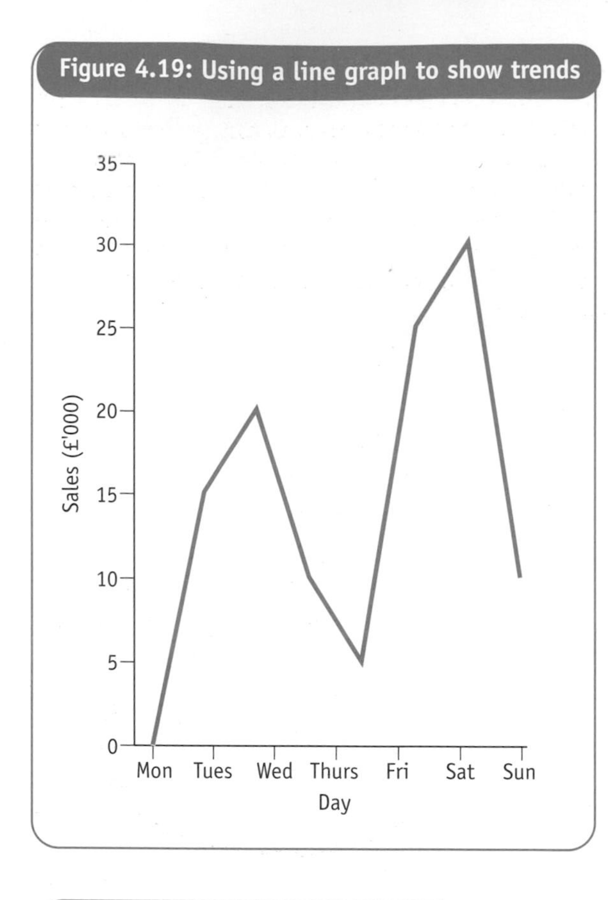

Line graphs are used to show how something fluctuates over time, for example an organisation's sales over a week.

Any information that can be shown as a line graph can also be shown as a pie chart or bar chart, but the reverse in not true. For example, it would be meaningless to show the age bar chart as a line graph, because each point on the graph is a separate piece of information unrelated to the others.

Although qualitative research can sometimes be represented in one of these graphical formats, it is unusual. Collating and presenting qualitative information normally requires a technical presentation in which the results are explained as a summary of opinions. This is because the responses are in-depth and highly personalized and therefore difficult to express graphically.

Whatever method of research is employed, in nearly all cases a written report is produced with an analysis that sums up the findings. Figure 4.20 shows the results of research into people's preferred form of leisure activity.

From these findings we could produce the following analysis. Walking is the most popular

ACTIVITY

Presenting data

Imagine you are the marketing manager at a heritage museum. Using the data below, produce:

- a pie chart showing the breakdown of admissions by type of visitor
- a line graph showing the total number of admissions during each month of the year
- a bar chart showing the total visitors in each category for the whole year
- a brief written summary of the main market segments and trends in admission levels over the year
- recommendations on how the data could be used to influence the museum's marketing mix.

Number of admissions: by month

Type of visitor	Jan	Feb	Mar	Apr	May	June	July	Aug	Sept	Oct	Nov	Dec
Adult	190	367	566	940	1,070	1,108	1,670	1,890	762	788	512	401
Child	78	290	203	1,363	992	876	1,761	2,445	535	734	269	276
OAP	38	192	314	410	435	512	420	412	396	304	188	58
Coach group booking	40	126	328	764	645	960	1,320	1,526	1,710	596	162	124
School group booking	68	160	522	496	570	610	382	145	62	242	208	95

leisure activity (with 58 per cent participating at least once a week) and accounts for 75 per cent of the total hours spent on the leisure activities listed. Swimming is the second most popular weekly activity (26 per cent) and accounts for 14 per cent of the total hours spent on leisure activities, but has the highest spending (75 per cent). Whereas the amount spent on walking is the second lowest at 6 per cent. Cycling is third in terms of the number of times per week (12 per cent) and the hours spent (8 per cent), but second in terms of overall spending (16 per cent).

What the analysis could not say is 'The reason why most people choose walking as their main activity is because it is free, as can be seen from the low amount of spending'. While this may well be true, there is no evidence in the research to support it. You would need to carry out further research to find out why people choose walking in preference to other activities before you could make any further statements.

Figure 4.20: Leisure activities

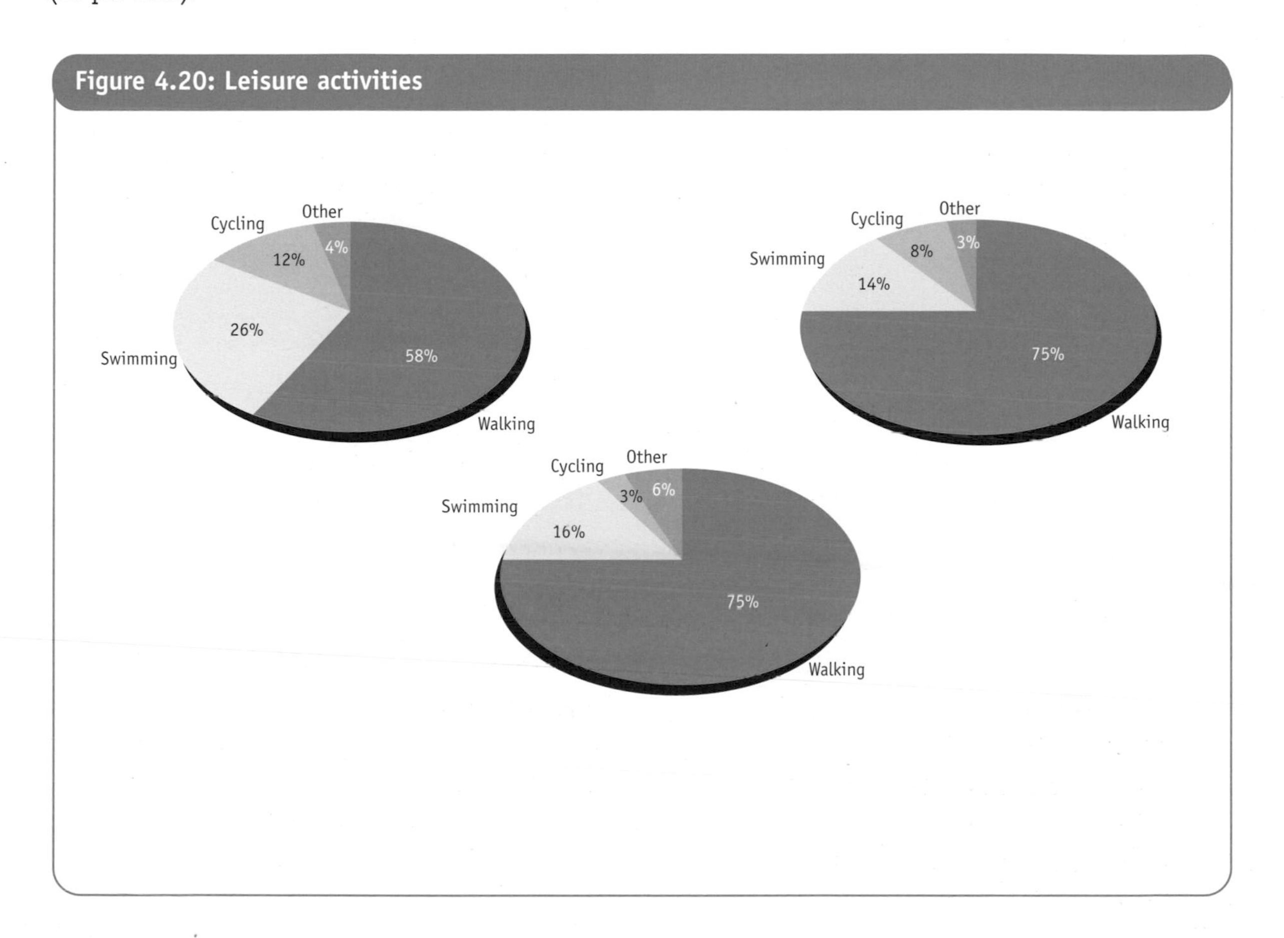

ACTIVITY

Analysing attendance data

The table compares visitor attendance figures in 1997 and 1998 at the top 20 UK visitor attractions that charge admission. Write a brief analysis (approximately 200 words) outlining the main findings from the figures. You might choose to analyse the figures generally, or to compare specific types of attractions such as theme parks or historic attractions. You may find it helpful to begin by calculating the percentage increase or decrease in attendance for each attraction, which will give you a better basis for evaluation. For example, Alton Towers = change (+80,055) divided by 1997 figures (2,701,945) multiplied by 100 = 2.96 per cent increase in attendances. Using this information, predict the rank order of the top 20 attractions for the next 12 months.

Top 20 UK visitor attractions 1997/1998

	1998	1997	Change
1 Alton Towers	2,782,000	2,701,945	+80,055
2 Madame Tussaud's	2,772,500	2,798,801	-26,301
3 Tower of London	2,551,459	2,615,170	-63,711
4 Natural History Museum	1,904,539	1,793,400	+111,139
5 Chessington World of Adventure	1,650,000	1,750,00	-100,000
6 Science Museum, London	1,599,817	1,573,151	+62,666
7 Legoland	1,510,363	1,297,818	+212,545
8 Canterbury Cathedral	1,500,000	1,613,000	-113,000
9 Windsor Castle	1,495,365	1,129,629	+365,836
10 Edinburgh Castle	1,219,055	1,238,140	-19,085
11 Victoria and Albert Museum, London	1,110,000	1,040,750	+69,250
12 Flamingo Land, N. Yorks	1,105,000	1,103,000	+2,000
13 St Paul's Cathedral	1,095,299	964,737	+130,562
14 London Zoo	1,052,000	1,097,017	-45,637
15 Drayton Manor Park	1,003,802	1,002,100	+1,702
16 Kew Gardens	1,000,000	937,017	+62,983
17 Windermere Lake Cruises	950,000	1,131,932	-181,932
18 Chester Zoo	920,000	829,800	+90,200
19 Royal Academy, London	912,714	858,854	+53,860
20 Royal Baths and Pump Room, Bath	905,426	933,489	-28,063

If you visit the StarUK website (www.staruk.org.uk) you will be able to access the latest visitor attraction data to see how accurate your forecast has been.

Choosing research techniques

Clearly, there are many techniques available to collect market research information. Leisure and recreation organisations need to identify which techniques are the most suitable for their particular research needs. A number of factors need to be considered when selecting a research method:

- cost
- time
- accessibility
- validity and reliability
- fitness for purpose.

Cost

Research methods that use a lot of personal contact, such as interviews, are generally more expensive than those that do not, such as postal questionnaires. Costs to consider include the expense of staff time, producing materials, postage and telephone charges. The larger the sample size, the higher the costs will be, both in collecting and analysing information.

Time

The amount of time spent in preparing, conducting and analysing marketing information can vary enormously according to the method used and is directly related to cost. If a leisure and recreation organisation has relatively little time to conduct research then techniques such as simple, self-completion questionnaires or telephone surveys may be most effective. Alternatively, secondary research may provide quick and relevant information.

Accessibility

The extent to which the sample is accessible also influences the choice of research methods. For example, if a members-only health club wants information about its current customers the sample could be easily accessed because the company will have contact details on its customer database. However, if the club wants information on potential customers it would need to use alternative methods, such as mailing questionnaires to a sample of the local population or conducting household interviews.

Validity and reliability

Depending on the type of information required, some research methods will have greater validity than others and therefore produce more reliable information. For example, a questionnaire is a more valid method of obtaining quantitative information than a group discussion. Generally, the reliability of information collected depends less on the method used and more on the way in which it is used. A badly worded questionnaire will not produce reliable information and it would be foolhardy to base marketing decisions on it. Similarly, if the sample used is not truly representative of the market then the information cannot be used for general marketing decisions.

Fitness for purpose

The research method selected should be fit for the purpose intended. In other words, it should achieve the objectives set by producing reliable information. It is often possible to use simple, inexpensive methods and still produce reliable information. For example, comment cards (see Figure 4.21) on tables in a restaurant are a simple way of evaluating the level of customer satisfaction.

Figure 4.21: Deep Pan Pizza's customer card

DEEP PAN
PIZZA CO.

"It is our policy to entertain our guests, to make your meal a quality experience with the best possible product, service and atmosphere."

Please take a minute to give us your comments about our restaurant and tell us how you think we measure up to the above statement.

PLEASE TICK ✓	EXCELLENT	GOOD	FAIR	POOR
WELCOME				
SERVICE				
COURTESY				
QUALITY OF FOOD:- PIZZA				
PASTA				
SALAD				
DESSERT				
VALUE FOR MONEY				

Please drop this card in the box located in the restaurant.

DAY________ DATE________ TIME OF VISIT________

Figure 4.22 overleaf lists the different types of research techniques and the main strengths and weaknesses of each. Leisure and recreation organisations will usually have a wide range of information needs and will have to use different research techniques for each.

Figure 4.22: Comparing the strengths and weaknesses of research techniques

Research technique	Cost	Time	Accessibility	Validity and reliability	Fitness for purpose
Survey	Cost depends on survey and sample size, can be very low	Can be very quick to implement	Can access a wide geographical area	Good if survey questions are well constructed	Especially good for quantitative research
Observation	Cost can be low for quantitative research but rises for qualitative	Time consuming for qualitative, fairly quick for quantitative	Usually fairly limited accessibility localised area only	Good if well-controlled	Can be used for qualitative and quantitative research
Focus group	Very high in terms of time and the need for researchers	Very time consuming	Usually fairly limited accessibility to localised area	Good if well-controlled, but requires highly skilled researchers	Usually only used for qualitative research
Internal secondary	Minimal since data is usually readily available	Can be very quick if accurate internal records are kept and are computerised	Very accessible	If records are accurate, will be highly valid and reliable	Good for quantitative, may also provide some qualitative data
External secondary	Much data is freely available but can be expensive	Can be very quick, purchasing commercial data is instant	Wide access to regional, national and international data	Dependant on source	Can provide quantitative and qualitative data

ACTIVITY

Choosing market research techniques

The Randolph Theatre is situated in the centre of a large industrialised town. For the last eight years it has successfully staged a wide range of productions, including musicals, classical drama, light entertainment and children's plays.

It plans to introduce a young persons' theatre workshop to take place on Saturdays and is carrying out market research to evaluate the market potential for this new venture. It will promote each workshop with leaflets and has set the following market research objectives:

1 To identify existing theatre customers who may be interested in participating in the workshop.

2 To identify the product characteristics of similar theatre workshops already in existence in the town.

3 To identify the specific product characteristics that attract young people to the theatre with a view to using these characteristics in future promotions.

4 To evaluate the customer's reaction to the proposed leaflet for the workshops.

5 To identify other products that could be developed if the theatre workshop is successful.

As a group, discuss which market research techniques would be suitable to achieve each objective. You should consider primary research methods (surveys, observation and focus groups) and secondary research methods (internal and external sources).

In each case justify why you think your chosen research technique is the most effective in terms of its strengths compared with the weaknesses of other techniques.

BUILD YOUR LEARNING

Keywords and phrases

You should know the meaning of the words and phrases listed below. If you are unsure about any of them, go back through the last 23 pages to refresh your understanding.

- Market research
- Classifying customers
- Market segments and market segmentation
- Socio-economic groupings
- Lifestyle segmentation
- Family life cycle
- Primary market research
- Field research
- Quantitative research
- Qualitative research
- Surveys
- Questionnaires
- Observation
- Focus groups
- Secondary market research
- Desk research
- Internal sources
- External sources
- Data analysis
- Survey results

End of section activity

Select a leisure or recreation organisation and evaluate the market research techniques that it uses.

1 Identify how it uses market research to identify market segments such as socio-economic groupings, age, family circumstances, lifestyle, etc.

2 Identify the range of primary research techniques that it uses, such as surveys, observation and focus groups. Your evaluation should explain how and why the research is carried out and be supported with examples such as questionnaires.

3 Identify the range of internal and external secondary research that the organisation uses. Find out if the organisation uses secondary research and provide examples, such as details held on customer databases.

4 Explain how the organisation analyses research findings and uses the results when formulating its marketing mix. Provide detailed examples of what action the organisation has taken as a direct result of market research, for instance its effect on:

- the development of new products or services
- pricing strategies
- decisions on location/channels of distribution
- the promotional methods used.

5 Analyse the market research techniques used by the organisation and suggest how they could be improved. For example, could questionnaires be redesigned to be more effective; would a different contact method be better, such as telephone rather than post, or could the organisation use different techniques such as observation? Justify your recommendations by explaining why they would be appropriate.

Marketing communications

Most leisure and recreation organisations use a number of **marketing communications** channels in order to make customers aware of their products, influence customers' purchasing decisions and gain beneficial publicity to enhance the organisation's image. The choice of these channels of communication (known as media) varies with the type and size of the organisation, the nature of its operations and the budget it has available. The most common marketing communications media are:

- advertising
- direct marketing
- public relations (PR)
- sales promotion
- sponsorship.

Advertising

Advertising is one of the most common marketing communication techniques used by leisure and recreation organisations and ranges from national television advertisements costing many thousands of pounds to small classified ads in local newspapers costing just a few pounds. Figure 4.23 compares the amount spent on a range of advertising between 1988 and 1997.

Figure 4.23: Advertising expenditure (£m)

Year	Press	TV	Poster	Radio	Cinema
1988	4,548	2,127	244	138	27
1989	5,131	2,288	271	159	35
1990	8,137	2,325	282	183	39
1991	4,884	2,295	287	149	42
1992	4,957	2,472	284	157	45
1993	5,085	2,805	300	194	49
1994	5,800	2,873	330	213	53
1995	5,979	3,103	378	296	69
1996	8,413	3,333	428	344	73
1997	8,987	3,851	800	383	88

Practically all leisure and recreation organisations undertake some form of advertising, so it is important to understand the basic concepts involved. Advertising is used to achieve a number of objectives, including:

- to make known a new product or service
- to create awareness of an existing product or service
- to inform customers of price changes
- to combat competitors' advertising
- to describe the services available and the benefits associated with using them
- to create favourable attitudes towards the organisation
- to correct false impressions and other obstacles to sales.

Leisure and recreation organisations must select the most effective and efficient type of advertising media to achieve their objectives. The main media used are:

- the press
- television
- radio
- magazines
- the internet
- leaflets
- point-of-sale material
- posters.

The press

The British are avid readers and buyers of newspapers. In the UK there are approximately 1,300 local and regional newspapers and 21 national dailies and Sunday newspapers. On average, over 27 million people read at least one national daily newspaper and 30 million read a national Sunday newspaper. The press therefore provides significant opportunities for leisure and recreation organisations to communicate with existing or potential customers.

There are many advantages associated with advertising in newspapers. As we have already discussed in the section on market segmentation (page 266), newspapers have specific readership profiles that can enable advertisers to target and position their promotional messages to specific groups.

National press advertisements are cheaper than other forms of mass media, such as television advertising, and large national audiences can be reached. Alternatively, press advertisers can reach audiences in individual localities or regions by using local and regional paid or free newspapers.

▲ Local press advertisement

Advertising in newspapers is very flexible. Advertisements can be placed or changed at relatively short notice, while the advertising message can be read at leisure, reread or even cut out and kept for future use. Press advertisements can be used for direct customer response and mail order sales as well as for special purchase offers using cut-out coupons. Sometimes they are accompanied by editorial coverage in supplements or special features that give added impact.

There are a few disadvantages, however. The advertisements are static and cannot show products or services working. With many leisure and recreation products this is an important consideration because they are intangible experiences. For example, advertising a product such as a theme park will have greater visual impact on colour television than in a black and white newspaper. This is why theme park providers such as Disneyland, Paris often provide free informational videos to their customers in addition to glossy colour brochures.

ACTIVITY

Press advertising

Look at the newspaper advertisement for Whitney Houston's 1999 Arena Tour. How effective do you think it is? Why do you think the tour promoters chose to advertise in Sunday newspapers rather than on television?

Television

The greatest advantage of television advertising is that it can show products working. Added to this, the use of music, dialogue, personalities, colour, special effects and animation can help to create a stunning visual impact on a mass audience. However, unlike printed advertising, the exposure is very short, usually 10-60 seconds at a time. This means that the amount of information given is limited and can be missed altogether if the advertisement fails to attract the attention of the viewer.

Research showing that the consumption of electricity increases during commercial breaks indicates that many viewers use the break in programmes to make a hot drink rather than watch the advertisements. A further problem for advertisers is the use of remote control devices that allow viewers to 'zap' between channels or turn off the sound when advertisements appear.

Cinema has many of the benefits of television advertising. Although the audience at cinemas is much smaller, it is also more passive, remaining seated throughout the commercial break.

Much of the advertising appearing on television has a tremendous influence on buyers' decision-making processes. It is well planned and targeted and can reach huge audiences of potential customers. The advertising is often backed up by teletext services that direct viewers to sources of

ACTIVITY

Television advertising

Adwatch carries out weekly research to identify which television advertisements viewers remember seeing from the previous week. The table shows the results of one such survey.

Over a week, list ten advertisements that appear on television frequently. Carry out a survey of at least thirty people to see which of the advertisements that you have listed are remembered. Try to get a cross-section of people of different ages, genders, occupations, etc. When you have completed the survey, rank the advertisements in descending order according to how many people remembered them.

	Last week	Account	Agent/TV buyer	%
1	(1)	Asda	Publicis/Carat	70
2=	(2=)	BT	Abbott Mead Vickers BBDO/The Allmond Partnership	69
2=	(2=)	Andrex	Banks Hoggins O'Shea FCB/MindShare	69
4	(-)	B&Q	Bates Dorland/Zenith Media	68
5	(-)	SkyDigital	In-House/Universal McCann	67
6	(-)	McDonald's	Leo Burnett	64
7	(-)	Somerfield	RPM3/Universal McCann	56
8	(-)	Kellogg's Rice Krispies	J Walter Thompson/MindShare	55
9	(-)	Nescafe	McCann-Erikson/Universal McCann	53
10=	(-)	Surf Tablets	Ammirati Puris Lintas/Initiative Media	52
10=	(-)	Nissan Primera	TBEA GGT Simons Palmer/Carat	52
10=	(-)	Pepsi	Abbot Mead Vickers BBDO/BMP OMD	52
13	(4)	Persil Colour Tablets	J Walter Thompson/Initiative Media	51
14	(-)	Weetabix	Lowe Howard-Spink/Western International Media	49
15	(-)	Boots	J Walter Thompson/BMP OMD	47
16=	(-)	Burger King	Ammirati Puris Lintas/Carat	44
16=	(-)	National Savings	BMP DDB/BMP OMD	44
18=	(-)	Wella Shockwaves	Abbot Mead Vickers BBDO/New PHD	43
18=	(-)	Maybelline – Wonder Curl Mascara	McCann-Erikson/Universal McCann	43

further information. For many leisure and recreation providers, the single greatest disadvantage of television advertising is the expense. A 30-second advertisement at peak time on one of the larger ITV stations such as Carlton currently costs around £50,000. Many smaller providers, such as local independent travel agents and council-owned leisure facilities, cannot afford to consider any form of television advertising.

Radio

Many leisure and recreation providers use local commercial radio stations to promote products to the local population. It is a lot cheaper than television and has the advantage that music, dialogue and sound effects can be used. However, since radio is not a visual or printed medium, the messages rely totally on the effectiveness of oral communication. This is often a drawback for advertisers for many people the radio is something that is on in the background and ignored unless it is particularly interesting. On the other hand, radio advertising is often an effective means of promoting specific products and local events, particularly when it can be linked to public relations activities such as live radio coverage of an event.

Magazines

Advertisements in magazines have similar advantages and disadvantages to newspapers since they are also a printed medium. Print quality varies but in nearly all cases it is vastly superior to newspapers, with the use of full colour commonplace. As many magazines are published weekly, monthly or quarterly, magazine advertisements tend to have a longer lifespan than those placed in newspapers.

▲ Magazine advertising

A vast selection of special-interest magazines is available aimed at particular hobbies, interests or leisure and recreation activities. Examples include *Homes and Gardens, Empire, Movie Magazine, Shoot, English Heritage, New Musical Express* and *Theatre Print*. Perhaps the most useful aspect of advertising in special interest magazines is that leisure and recreation organisations can target the specific audiences most likely to buy or use their products.

Trade news-sheets, journals and magazines also provide opportunities for leisure and recreation organisations to communicate with the trade and inform them of new product and service developments. Some of the better-known trade journals include:

- *Leisure Manager*
- *Leisure Management*
- *Health Club Manager*
- *Leisure Week*
- *Sports Management*

The internet

The rapid increase in use of the **internet** has meant that many leisure and recreation organisations have realised the benefits of using it as an advertising channel. It combines many of the advantages of both printed and visual advertising media. Customers have the opportunity to browse through a large amount of information at their own speed and print specific pieces of information that interest them. In addition, many leisure and recreation web sites incorporate video footage and sound to enhance the products that they are promoting. A further advantage is that customers are frequently offered the opportunity to buy products on-line.

Of course, the internet is not without its disadvantages as an advertising medium. Many people do not have access to it or are reluctant to give the personal details required to make an on-line purchase or reservation. A further disadvantage is that there is such a large amount of information on the internet it can sometimes be difficult for a customer to locate what they are looking for.

ACTIVITY

Advertising on the internet

Obtain a copy of a leisure or recreation provider's brochure containing their website address (for example, Granada Studios, Blackpool Pleasure Beach, Alton Towers). Visit their website and compare its relative strengths and weaknesses with the information provided in the brochure. For example:

- Was it quicker to find information in the brochure or on the internet?
- What could the internet offer that the brochure could not?

Some useful website addresses are provided in the Resource and internet directory.

Leaflets

Leaflets are probably one of the most important promotional channels for leisure and recreation organisations. They are used extensively to promote many sporting facilities and venues, visitor attractions, entertainment venues and special events.

Leaflets have the same advantages as other printed media, but are often slightly better because they are more accurately targeted to specific markets and are (usually) more colourful than newspaper advertisements. The increasing use of computers has also meant that many leisure and recreation organisations are now able to produce their own leaflets using simple desktop publishing software. This has meant that leaflets can be produced relatively cheaply for specific market segments and products.

▲ Leaflets are used to promote many visitor attractions

ACTIVITY

Use of leaflets

Visit a tourist information centre or local visitor attraction/hotel that has a leaflet rack. Collect examples of leaflets of leisure and recreation facilities in the area and compare the relative features that make leaflets effective. You might like to make your comparisons using the following criteria:

- overall design
- use of colour
- pictures, diagrams and photographs
- text and use of font
- layout
- type of paper and the way in which the leaflet is folded.

Point-of-sale material

The term **point of sale** refers to the place that the customer actually buys a product, such as a ticket or reservation desk, a shop counter or the reception area in a leisure centre.

It has the advantage that it is targeted at customers who are clearly interested in the product. Its main disadvantage is that it rarely reaches new markets. It is often used when the marketing objective is to develop existing markets or products. For example, a point-of-sale promotion at a cinema might promote a newly released film. The materials used can include displays of products, posters, leaflets and brochures. In many situations sales staff are present to answer customers' questions and enquiries.

Posters

Posters are the oldest form of advertising and they are still used extensively by leisure and recreation organisations. They are often used in combination with other advertising media to reinforce a particular message. This is because the amount of information that they contain is limited by the fact that people often only glance at them in passing.

One of the main considerations with poster advertising is that its effectiveness depends largely on where it is located. Posters can be displayed on billboards, bus shelters, on transport such as underground trains, at sports stadia or simply on the wall of the provider's own facility. The choice of location should be based on three factors:

- how many people will see it
- who will see it
- how long they will see it.

For example, a poster advertisement on the London Underground will be seen by a lot of people and they will probably have time to read it properly during their journey. However, it will be a very broad market. A poster outside a tourist attraction such as a museum will have a limited audience but the targeted market may stop to read it fully.

▲ Advertising on London buses

WEBSTRACT

Victoria and Albert Museum

The Victoria and Albert Museum aims to attract people from all walks of life. As part of this mission the V&A seeks to inform people that it caters for everyone - not just art specialists - and that its exhibits are as much about the future as they are about the past, as can be seen in the following press release.

In 1999 the V&A launched a new advertising campaign on London tube trains, supported by advertising in popular tourist guides. The main objectives of the campaign were to:

- increase visitor numbers during the summer months
- establish the V&A as a vibrant and relevant place to visit
- create a fun, positive image about visiting the museum.

The campaign was aimed at tourists in London as well as Londoners, particularly:

- 25-54 year olds
- ABC1s
- those with broad cultural interests
- those who may have visited in the past.

The campaign slogan 'Find Yourself at the V&A' was intended to create a sense of urgency in visiting and to encourage visitors to start looking for the beautiful things in life among the exhibits at the V&A. The following six advertisements were designed for the campaign:

- A genteel lady exclaiming next to a rather racy Yves St-Laurent Mondrian-inspired cocktail dress.
- A large man, hands on hips, grinning next to the awesome plaster reproduction of Michelangelo's David.
- A cheeky child wearing a pair of 3-D spectacles next to a stunning stained-glass window of Joanna of Aragon.
- An older woman hugging her much loved cat next to one of the more voracious members of the feline family, the tiger - more importantly the famous 'Tippo's Tiger', which shows the tiger devouring an English soldier.
- A happy builder with a mug of tea next to one of the most fancy silver teapots of the 1700s.
- A man dressed in a pinstripe suit having a hair-raising encounter with the classic smooth curves of a 1920s MT8 table lamp.

Source: ww.vam.ac.uk

Swell - the designs of Inflate October 1998

The V&A is mounting a display of exciting an innovative designs by Inflate, one of Britain's leadin contemporary design companies from 16 October 199 to April 1999 in the Twentieth-Century Gallery.

Since their launch in 1995, the young design team ha achieved considerable commercial and critical success with a range of fun, functional and affordable PVC-moulded designs in shades of lime, orange, lemon, fuschia pink and indigo. Ranging from inflatable egg-cups and fruit-bowls to digital grass toasters, luna ashtrays and Mr & Mrs Prickly salt and pepper dispensers, their colourful designs have become iconic objects of the mid-1990s.

The display will showcase some twenty Inflate products from the last three years, including prototypes and production models. The design process from conception to realization will also be included.

Capturing the spirit of fun and experimentation central to the 'swinging sixties', Inflate are central to a new Pop sensibility in contemporary British design. 1960s inflatable architecture and furniture defined the look of Pop products as disposable, iconoclastic and youthful. With the advance in chemical technology and the 1970s oil crisis, plastic has been revived as an acceptable product material in the 1990s.

The installation designed by Inflate and curated by Gareth Williams of the Furniture and Woodwork Department of the V&A, will combine one-off and specially produced objects to create an exciting and unified space.

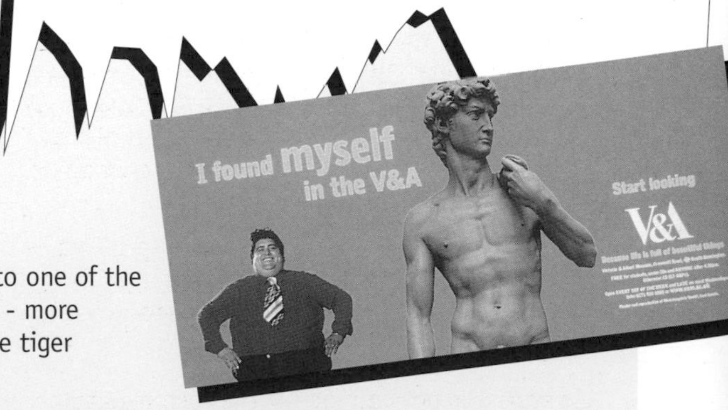

ACTIVITY

V & A poster campaign

As a group, try to think of a seventh poster advertisement that would fit the general objectives and image of the V&A's promotional poster campaign given in the case study opposite.

Direct marketing

Direct marketing is so called because it operates through personal channels of communication where the target market is, in effect, a single customer. It is one of the fastest growing methods of marketing communication and can be used either as the sole method of promotion or in combination with other methods. One of its main benefits is that it enables organisations to target products at specific markets, as when a theatre sends a list of its forthcoming productions to past customers, for example. There are a number of ways in which direct marketing can be carried out, such as:

- direct mail
- telemarketing
- door-to-door distribution
- media direct response.

Direct mail

The process of sending promotional material to a potential or existing customer is known as **direct mail** or a mailshot. The number of direct mail letters from 1987 to 1997 rose by 126 per cent and now represents 11.8 per cent of all advertising. Figure 4.24 compares the number of people who made a purchase following different types of advertising. As we can see, direct mail is the second most effective medium after press advertising and a long way ahead of leaflets, radio and the internet.

One of the misconceptions about direct mail is that everyone throws it away without reading it. In fact research shows that this is not the case, as Figure 4.25 shows.

However, it is not enough for the customer simply to open a direct mail letter and read it. The promoter also wants the customer to buy the product as a result of reading the mailshot. The Consumer Direct Mail Trends Survey (1997) found that the average response rate to direct mail letters was 5.2 per cent, which works out at an advertising cost of £8.72 for each customer who makes a purchase.

Figure 4.24: Purchasing from all media

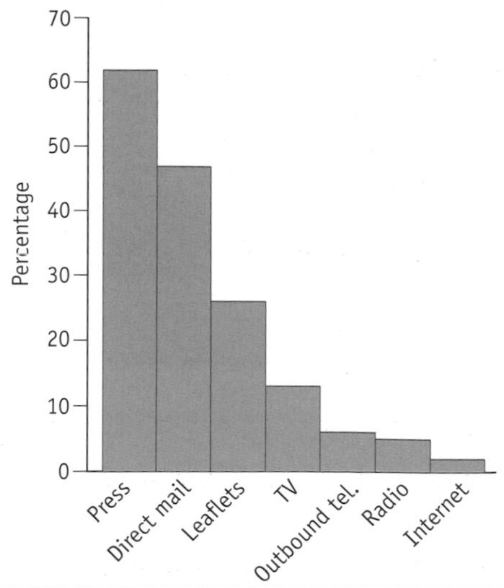

One drawback with direct mail is that people receive so many mailshots that they sometimes throw them away without reading them. Therefore direct mail needs to be carefully designed to encourage customers to read the literature. It is common practice to include a letter in the mailshot explaining the contents of sales literature. The letter may include some form of sales promotion, perhaps offering a discount or prize if an order is placed within a certain period. Research has shown that including what are known as power words increases the likelihood of a mailshot's success. Power words are terms like 'new', 'free', 'announcing', 'special' 'successful', 'exclusive', 'limited number', 'selected' and 'important'.

Figure 4.25: 'Who opens or reads direct mail'

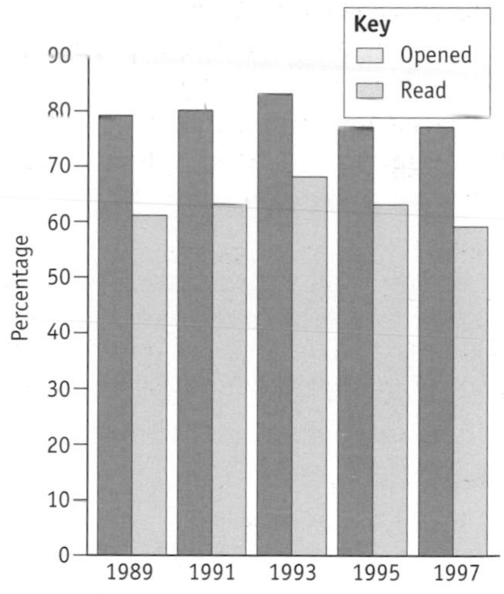

Source: Royal Mail website

ACTIVITY

Direct marketing

Yale University in the USA conducted research into the power of words. It concluded that the following twelve words are the most powerful in the English language:

- **you**
- **money**
- **health**
- **proven**
- **results**
- **guarantee**
- **safety**
- **love**
- **easy**
- **save**
- **free**
- **new**

Use of these words can have a positive and persuasive effect on the reader. Look at the mailshot on the right and rewrite it using as many of the power words as are appropriate.

Dear Valued Customer

This year we have opened an additional beauty therapy centre at Cramford Grange Health Farm offering a wide range of treatments. We are sure that customers will feel the benefits of the services offered - research shows that many of the treatments help people to relax and feel better as well as looking good!

In addition, we are continuing to offer our high standard of accommodation and catering, as well as an extensive range of activities and exercise classes.

Early booking (by the end of April) entitles existing customers to a 20 per cent discount on all treatments at the beauty therapy centre as well as a complimentary Indian Head Massage.

Yours sincerely
K. R. Holdsworth
Manager

Mailshots are also more effective if they appear to have been written to an individual rather than to dozens of customers. Using the word 'you' is effective in this respect, as is addressing the recipient by name rather than as Sir or Madam. Finally, it is important to remember the phrase 'The more you tell, the more you sell!' Mailshots need to include all of the relevant details about the product, but describe it in such a way that customers perceive it as meeting their needs and expectations.

Mailshots are often very successful because they are sent to past customers who are known to have bought products before and may therefore be interested in similar ones in the future. But how does an organisation know to whom to send mailshots?

Mailing lists are compiled by using information already held on people who have either bought or enquired about a product, or by targeting specific groups of people, for example by using the post code system. A computer-based system known as ACORN (a classification of residential neighbourhoods) uses post codes to provide a profile of the types of people likely to be living within any specific postal code area. So, for example, using the ACORN system an organisation could create a mailing list and target specific geographical areas where the population has the particular characteristics that make them likely customers.

Telemarketing

Like direct mail, **telemarketing** is an increasingly common marketing and has the same kind of drawbacks: many potential customers are suspicious of unsolicited sales calls and are therefore unwilling to engage in a conversation. However telemarketing, in which customers are contacted by telephone with the aim of promoting a particular product, can be successful if properly conducted and targeted. This means selecting customers who are likely to be genuinely interested and explaining the reason for the call in such a way that they will want to listen to what you have to say.

The beginning of the call is most important, since many customers will realise that it is a sales call and may say that they are too busy to talk. The trick is to get the customer to talk to you by asking them questions, so that they are more likely to listen to you. For example: 'Good morning, Mrs James, this is Paula from Westly Manor Health Farm. I am just calling to see if you enjoyed your stay with us.' This opening is likely to encourage an answer from Mrs James so that Paula can go on to talk about further visits to Westly Manor.

In the leisure and recreation industry telemarketing is used more for trade promotions than as a means of reaching individual consumers.

Door-to-door distribution

Many organisations deliver direct marketing materials to customers' homes in person. Such **door-to-door distribution** can work out a lot cheaper than mail or telephone. It also provides the opportunity for personal face-to-face contact with potential customers, which can encourage customers to try a product or service. For example, a restaurant may send staff out to local houses with discount vouchers, to make contact with residents and ask them if they would be interested in using the restaurant.

One of the disadvantages of this method is that it can be impersonal, resulting in potential customers taking little notice of the materials. For example, with a large-scale leaflet drop, when standard material is posted through a lot of letterboxes, many people may simple throw the materials away. As a general rule people are far more likely to look at direct mail materials if they are addressed to them personally.

Media direct response

Media direct response allows customers to place a direct order for a product without having to go to an intermediate supplier such as a shop. It can be used in any medium such as television, radio, newspapers and magazines. Customers can call a fax or telephone number, write to an address or even contact the organisation over the internet to place their orders. Apart from persuading a customer to buy a product immediately, direct response also allows an organisation to evaluate how effective each advertisement is by logging the number of responses it receives. The advertisement for Gelert gives potential customers four options to respond directly: a telephone number, a fax number, an e-mail address and a web site address.

▲ Gelert direct-response advertising

The increasing use of credit and charge cards has resulted in more direct response promotions with customers able to make instant purchases of many leisure and recreation products, such as sports clothing, theatre tickets and home entertainment.

ACTIVITY

Activate Leisure Centre

Read the conversation between Carla Andrews, manager of Activate Leisure Centre and Jason Barnes, her newly appointed marketing manager.

Carla: *Well, Jason, you've had a few weeks to find your feet at Activate. I'd like to start thinking about promotional ideas for some of our new products and services.*

Jason: *I'd welcome that opportunity Carla. I've had plenty of time to get to know the company and its products. Where do you think we should begin?*

Carla: *I'm particularly keen to promote corporate membership of our fitness studio. By that I mean offering special discounted rates to employees of local companies in return for the companies encouraging their employees to join.*

Jason: *I agree. I think that there is huge potential in this market. I think that if people could get a reduced membership by joining as an employee and perhaps attending sessions with their colleagues they would be encouraged to come along. And then, of course, there is the added benefit that they will probably persuade their friends and family to join us well. How about using newspaper advertisements?*

Carla: *That might work, but I'm not sure that it is necessarily the most effective means of advertising. I was thinking more of using direct marketing such as mailshots, door-to-door delivery to organisations and perhaps telemarketing. We already have a customer database which gives details of current members and which local organisations they work for. Plus we have a lot of local council information on the location and size of companies in the area. Get back to me with a some ideas in a few days on how we could approach this.*

Imagine that you are Jason. What suggestions would you make? You should specify whom you intend to contact and the contact method.

Draft a mailshot and specify what additional information you would include. If you decide to use telemarketing as one of your methods, outline what sales staff should say as an opening statement.

You can assume that Activate has a fax, e-mail and website.

Public relations

The Institute of Public Relations (IPR) defines **public relations** as

the planned and sustained effort to establish and maintain goodwill and mutual understanding between an organisation and its public.

In this definition 'public' means the whole range of people who come into contact with the organisation, not just its customers and employees. These may include trade unions, suppliers, press, shareholders or councillors, for example. In 1999 the IPR extended its original definition:

PR is about reputation, which is the result of all you say, all you do and what others say about you.

In other words an organisation continually communicates messages to the public, whether it wants to or not. Let's look at some of the ways in which this is done.

In many cases public relations (PR) involves the positioning of information about an organisation in a suitable publication which may be read by its existing or potential customers, or obtaining free favourable presentation of its activities on radio, television or elsewhere. PR can include:

- media inclusion
- press releases
- community relations
- lobbying
- corporate communications.

ACTIVITY

Impact of negative PR

Read the extract on the right from a report on a Watchdog item about customers' dissatisfaction with the service they received from the Boyzone Fan Club.

How many providers do you think will have suffered from negative PR as a result of people seeing this programme? What do you think each of them could do to turn it into a positive PR opportunity?

BOYZONE

Boyzone has an estimated two and a half million fans in Britain. Their biggest following is amongst teenage girls. When the band announced their three week, 18 concert tour, the fans were eager to find out how to obtain tickets.

About 20,000 of Boyzone's fans are members of the official Boyzone fan club. It costs £11 a year for which you receive a membership card, a pen, a badge, photos of the fab five and a quarterly magazine.

Last April fan club members received a flyer through the post saying 'The fan club has arranged a priority booking facility which will enable you to purchase your tickets before they go on general sale.' 'You can get the best seats at all shows on Boyzone's tour.'

Kajal Ruia, who has belonged to the fan club for two years, phoned the members' priority booking line. She spent £37 on two tickets for the concert at The Manchester Evening News Arena. She was sold tickets in row Q, 17 rows back from the front. Kajal's sister waited until the tickets went on sale to the general public and got tickets only 6 rows from the front, at the side. Kajal wasn't very pleased that her 'priority booking' hadn't given her better seats than her sister's.

The same thing happened to another fan club member, Jodie Culpin, when she got a 'priority booking' to see Boyzone at Wembley Arena. Her friends got better seats by buying direct from the box office.

When the fan club started receiving complaints from their members they passed them on to Triple A Entertainment, the concert promoters who are in charge of allocating the tickets. Triple A have sent out a letter saying that they did offer the fan club members a chance to get the best seats but 'did not offer best seats exclusively'.

According to the Concise Oxford English Dictionary the word 'priority' does mean 'first' but not necessarily best.

Media inclusion

Media inclusion refers to the inclusion of a leisure and recreation product in a screened or broadcast film or programme. An obvious example is the featuring of a particular visitor attraction or leisure and recreation facility or event in a televised documentary about a particular area. Of course, sometimes this can have a negative PR result, such as many of the leisure and recreation items featured in consumer programmes like the BBC's Watchdog.

Media inclusion is mostly welcomed by leisure and recreation providers and used as part of their marketing communications. For example, the leisure market in Torbay is partly promoted through the PR benefits of the area being used as a film and television programme location.

Productions made in Devon

The beautiful scenery of the English Riviera has long attracted film and television companies to use the area as a backdrop. In recent years, Torbay has been the setting for several major television programmes including Brookside, GMTV, Songs of Praise, Noel's House Party and Working Lunch. In addition, the English Riviera is frequently featured on travel-related programmes such as Travel Show, Wish You Were Here and Holiday. Other television productions include:

Edward the Seventh

Location: Oldway Mansions, Paignton

Starring Anette Crosbie as Queen Victoria, Robert Hardy as Prince Albert, John Gielgud as Disraeli and Timothy West in the title role.

Monty Python's Flying Circus

Locations include Paignton Beach and Broadsands Beach, as well as an open-top bus ride to Babbacombe by John Cleese.

Fawlty Towers

It was while John Cleese was filming with the Monty Python team at the Gleneagles Hotel, Torquay that he was inspired to write Fawlty Towers.

Source:www.swtourism.co.uk

This is a growing trend as local authorities realise the great PR benefits of film crews using their towns, cities or areas as the backdrop for productions. *The Full Monty* encouraged a large increase in visitors to Sheffield and *Little Voice* had a similar effect in Scarborough. Similarly, individual organisations have benefited from being the subject of 'fly-on-the-wall' documentaries, such as the Adelphi Hotel in Liverpool, Blackpool Pleasure Beach, Butlins and London Zoo. In fact some leisure and recreation organisations maximise the effectiveness of this media inclusion by prompting potential customers to watch programmes in which they feature, as can be seen in the press advertisement for Butlins.

▲ Butlins has benefited from media inclusion

For organisations with a limited promotional budget, PR activities often form an extremely important part of their promotions mix. For example, a leisure centre unable to afford expensive advertising may find that the public relations exposure of, say, sponsoring a local football team is an effective way of promoting the organisation. One of the ways in which organisations ensure that the public are aware of their public relations activities is by issuing press releases.

Press releases

A **press release** is a statement written by an organisation describing a particular event, occasion or piece of interesting news which is sent to the media in the hope that editors will consider it of interest. In many newspapers, particularly local ones, a large proportion of the editorial (articles) is in fact made up of stories based on press releases rather than articles written by reporters. The decision as to whether or not to use a press release depends not only on its content but also on the relationship that the organisation has with the paper. Therefore, part of PR requires maintaining a good relationship with media staff to ensure that they look favourably on news items submitted. Apart from the fact that it is free, the main advantage of getting editorial coverage based on a press release rather than, say, advertising, is that people are likely to read it properly without thinking that it is trying to sell them something.

When writing a press release there are a few simple guidelines to follow.

- Provide a contact name and number for further information if required.
- Include all of the necessary details, such as times, prices and special features.
- Make the title and first line interesting and eye-catching to draw the reader's attention.
- Write an introduction, middle and conclusion like a proper news story. Make sure you supply the main news point in the first paragraph.
- Keep it short, to the point and interesting.
- Always try to include at least one quotation, as it makes the story more realistic and enables you to say a lot in a few words. It also lets you sound really enthusiastic and excited about the subject. For example: 'Joe Shepherd, waiter said, "We are all really excited about the new restaurant and menu. It has been a challenge getting everything ready for the opening, but we are sure that customers will love it."'
- Date the release and indicate whether there is a date before which it cannot be used.

Community relations

Maintaining a good relationship with the local community (**community relations**) is an important part of PR. This is often achieved by providing support to various groups or participating in events. For example, a hotel may allow its premises to be used free of charge by a group of retired people for their Christmas party, give guided tours of the premises to schools and colleges, or participate in local events, such as entering a float in a street carnival parade.

ACTIVITY

Attracting customers

Look at these two press cuttings. One is a press release and one an advertisement for the same product. Discuss which you think might be the most effective in attracting customers. Explain your reasons.

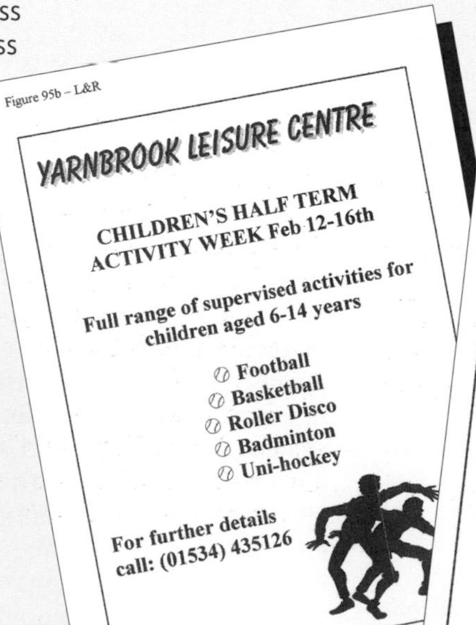

Figure 95b – L&R
YARNBROOK LEISURE CENTRE
CHILDREN'S HALF TERM ACTIVITY WEEK Feb 12-16th
Full range of supervised activities for children aged 6-14 years
Football
Basketball
Roller Disco
Badminton
Uni-hockey
For further details call: (01534) 435126

NO BORED KIDS AT HALF TERM!

Parents worried about how to keep their children occupied during the February half term break need look no further than their local leisure centre. Staff at Yarnbrook Leisure Centre have organised a fun-packed week of activities designed to suit children of all ages from 6-14 years. Centre manager, Leslie Bartok says, "This is the third year that we have offered an activity week for local children and demand keeps on growing. I think that parents often run out of ideas about how to keep their children occupied when the weather is poor and welcome the chance for them to make new friends and burn off a bit of energy at our centre. All of the activities are supervised by our qualified staff and the children all seem to have a great time".

This year's activities include football, basketball, roller disco, badminton and uni-hockey, with all equipment supplied by the centre.

Details of the week's programme and how to reserve places can be received by ringing: (01534) 435126

ACTIVITY

West Midlands Safari Park

The press release on the right from West Midlands Safari Park gives details of the first exhibit in the UK of Bengal White Tigers. It does not contain any quotes from zoo staff that enhance the 'excitement and enthusiasm' aspect. Can you add some quotes to make the press release even more effective? Compare your quotes with those written by other members of the group and identify any key words and phrases that are effective in conveying excitement and enthusiasm.

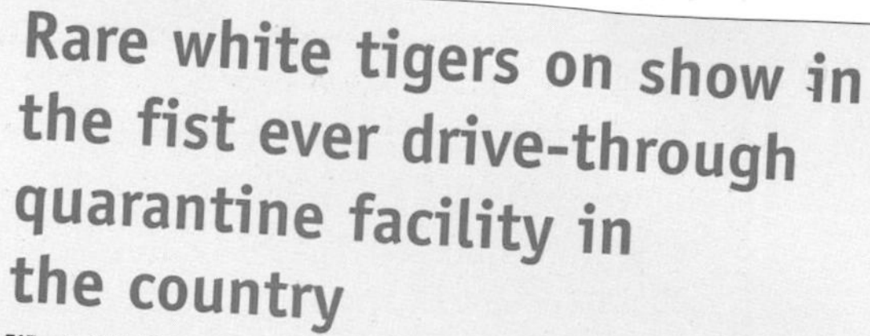
Rare white tigers on show in the fist ever drive-through quarantine facility in the country

West Midland Safari & Leisure Park have two rare white Bengal Tigers on show to visitors for the first time. The pair, which are just 18 months old, were imported from Junsele Zoo in N.E. Sweden in December and were transferred to purpose-built rabies quarantine quarters in Bewdley. Following a ,landmark decision by M.A.F.F., the Park now have the first ever drive-through quarantine facility in the country, costing in excess of £1/4m. The area has been totally landscaped and allows visitors to drive through the entire area.

The White Tigers, called Tahas and Tikua, have been integrated into a small group of young Bengal Tigers which have been born at West Midland Safari Park and it is anticipated that a further four will join them at a later date. White Tigers are neither albinos, nor a separate species. They are rare white Bengal Tigers of which barely 150 exist in the world, with no more than 12 being found in this country. Most of them have black stripes of varying distinction and blue eyes. These rare and extremely beautiful Tigers will be on show throughout the Whitsun Bank Holiday

West Midland Safari & Leisure Park is open 7 days each week, from 10.00am, until 31st October 1999. Further information from: The Press Office (01299) 402114

Release date: 24th May 1999

Lobbying

When a group of people with a common interest join together in an attempt to influence or change opinions or policies this is known as **lobbying**. For example, in the last few years reports of polluted British coastal areas have resulted in many seaside leisure and recreation providers joining forces and lobbying for action to clean beaches. Some large organisations lobby independently on specific issues, like the Ramblers Association's campaign on access to the countryside for recreational use. From a PR perspective, the benefit of lobbying is that the organisation can be seen by the public as caring about wider issues than simply making a profit.

Corporate communications

Many organisations partly establish their corporate image through their communications. **Corporate communications** use consistent and recognisable formats and images such as logos, colours and typefaces on their leaflets, bills, faxes and advertising. The logos on this page are all well known to consumers because each of these organisations has invested huge sums of money in order to establish a high-profile corporate identity, despite the fact that they target similar market segments.

Establishing effective corporate communications is important for most organisations, not just major companies. Although some methods of PR, such as providing extensive free use of facilities, may be too expensive for smaller businesses, most can afford some form of PR activity to ensure that they maintain a positive corporate image and good relationship with the public.

It should be mentioned at this point that sponsorship is frequently seen as a key part of an organisation's public relations activities. We look at **sponsorship** in detail on page 306.

ACTIVITY

Hanworth Grange

Hanworth Grange is a privately owned stately home in Norfolk. It attracts visitors from a wide geographical area and targets resident markets and visiting tourists. Research has shown that its main market segments are:

- families (35 per cent)
- couples (21 per cent)
- school groups (17 per cent)
- special interest groups (15 per cent)
- other (12 per cent).

Based on the fact that at least 52 per cent of its market includes groups with children (families and school groups) it has recently invested £12,000 in the development of a children's outdoor play area in the grounds. With a very limited advertising budget and the opening of the play area set for the beginning of June, the owners are keen to maximize the PR opportunities available. It has been decided that the opening should be marked by a special event to be covered by the local newspaper. Staff were asked to provide suggestions and the following were received:

- A famous actor lives in a nearby village and would agree to open the play area for a fee.
- Invite a selection of past customers for a free barbeque and firework display to view the new play area.
- Hold a competition in the local newspaper to invite selected guests to the opening. The newspaper has agreed to print the competition entry forms free of charge.
- Invite all local primary school children from a nearby village to attend the opening and use the facilities free of charge.
- Stage a sponsored 'play' for the longest time spent on a swing to raise funds for the local hospice. Local students have said that they would be willing to organise the event.

As a group, discuss and decide which of the options offers the best PR opportunities. Based on the option you select, try to think of any other ways in which the event could be improved at minimal cost to the owners. Then write a press release for the local paper outlining the opening event.

Sales promotions

A **sales promotion** is a short-term activity aimed at generating sales or improving public perceptions of a product or service. It can be aimed either at consumers or trade clients. Sales promotions are often undertaken in response to the activities of competitors so that an organisation can keep its market share. It has become common practice for a range of sales promotions to accompany the release of major Hollywood 'blockbuster' films. This not only allows the studio to promote its film, but also generates extra revenue from the sale of merchandising rights to other companies. For example, the 1999 release of *Star Wars, the Phantom Menace* created a massive opportunity in special merchandising through sales promotions. These sales promotions were implemented by a number of other companies such as Heinz, Cadbury's, Pizza Hut and the *Daily Mirror*.

Star Wars sales promotion ▲

Sales promotions targeted at consumers

Sales promotions usually form part of a promotional campaign and are supported by advertising, personal selling, direct mail and public relations activities. In the leisure and recreation industry a wide variety of sales promotions is commonly used.

- **Price reductions (discounting).** Discounts are offered to increase sales or usage, often at periods of low demand. For example, a leisure centre may offer limited discounts in January to encourage new customers who have made a New Year resolution to get fit and healthy.

▲ An organisation may offer price reductions at certain times to boost demand.

- **Free gifts and incentives.** These are used to encourage consumers to purchase products or services. Increasingly, leisure and recreation organisations are realising the effectiveness of offering a free gift to customers to provide an incentive.

▼ Many sports clothing providers offer a free gift with a customer's first order.

- **Special offers.** This is another form of discounting. Special offers are often made in conjunction with some form of advertising campaign in which consumers have to produce the advertisement (or coupons) to qualify for the offer. For example, many leisure and recreation organisations provide money-off vouchers in both local and national press. Customers often have to collect a token or coupon in the newspapers to qualify for the special offer.

▼ Special offer coupons

STAINTONDALE
SHIRE HORSE FARM
HORSE AND PONY SHOW
Well signposted from A171 Scarborough to Whitby road
ADMIT ONE CHILD
WITH TWO PAYING ADULTS
PICK UP A FULL COLOUR BROCHURE FROM
SCARBOROUGH TOURIST INFORMATION CENTRE,
OR TEL/FAX (01723) 870458
Valid until 19th September 1999

ROX™ FREE ROX RECORD BAG!
(WORTH £23.99) WITH EVERY ORDER OVER £60*

7. ROX LOGO 99
PICS: Charcoal & Stone Long Sleeve T-shirts £24.99
Woof! Stone Baseball Cap £14.99

2. AIR-Just get High
PICS: Stone & Charcoal Long Sleeve T-shirts £24.99
Woof! Dusky Green Baseball Cap £14.99

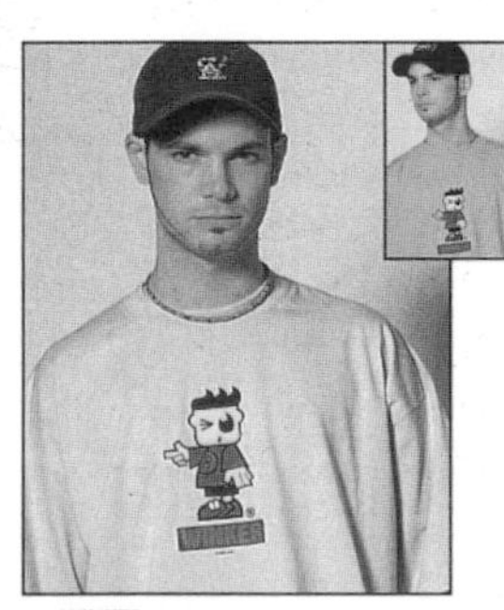

10. WINKER
PIC: Sand & Mushy Pea Short Sleeve T-shirt £19.99
Woof! Olive Baseball Cap £14.99

5. CLUBBER
PICS: Denim Short Sleeve T-shirt £19.99
Mocha Long Sleeve T-shirt £24.99

- **Competitions.** Many leisure and recreation organisations run free competitions to encourage consumers to buy their products and services. Prizes include a wide range of products, services, memberships, activities and holidays. One approach to competitions that has become particularly popular is the use of scratchcards, which can easily be inserted into newspapers and magazines.

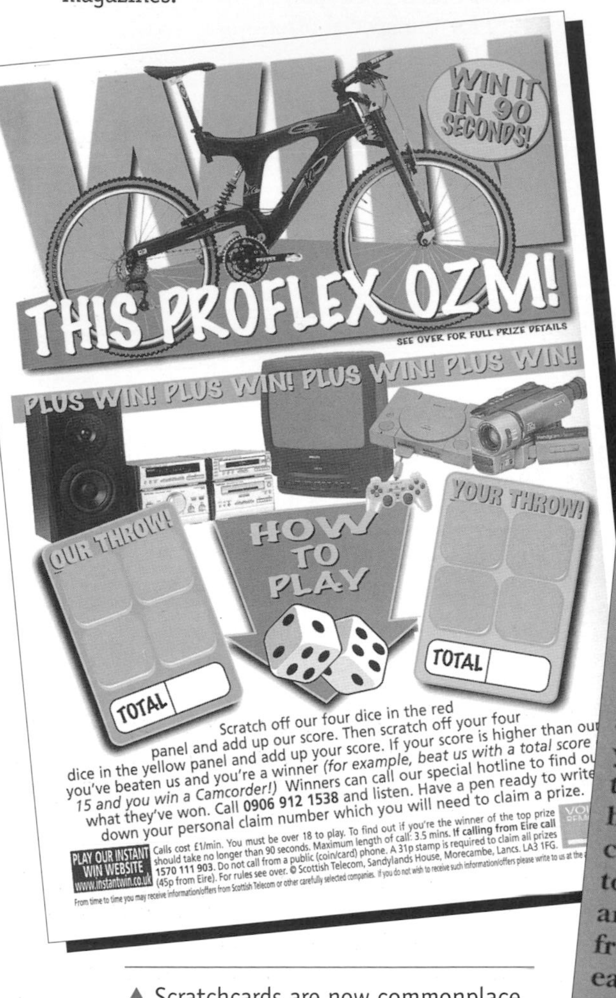

▲ Scratchcards are now commonplace

▲ VIP passes are an example of a loyalty incentive

- **Loyalty incentives.** Many organisations use a range of loyalty incentives to retain their customers. For example, Drayton Manor Theme Park offers regular customers the chance to buy a year-round VIP pass that includes a number of price concessions as well as reduced entrance charges.

▲ Escape, the travel book club, offers extra products as a sales promotion

Figure 4.26: Selected trade and public exhibitions

Exhibition and venue	Type of show	Duration	Number of exhibitions	Visitor attendance figures
BBC Holiday Line Olympia	P	6 days	230	13,000
Holiday World. The Kings Hall	TP	5 days	119	31,400
International Holiday Travel Show Bournemouth International Centre	P	2 days	78	41,500
Northern International Holiday and Travel Show, Manchester	TP	4 days	287	41,000
World Travel Market, Earls Court	T	4 days	3,254	11,069
International Food and Drink Exhibition, Earls Court	T	4 days	550	3,897
International Boat Show	TP	12 days	546	172,813
British Craft Trade Fair, Harrogate Exhibition Centre	T	3 days	667	n/a
Boat Caravan and Leisure Exhibition, National Exhibition Centre, Birmingham	P	9 days	386	112,455
Daily Mail International Ski Show, Olympia	P	9 days	175	96,700
Leisure Industry Week	T	4 days	538	16,279

Source: The UK Exhibition Industry Federation, 1994
Note: T = trade only, P = public show, TP = trade and public

- **Extra products.** This is another form of special offer. Customers are provided with extra products or services at no extra charge. A free bottle of wine with your meal, or three weeks' holiday for the price of two are just two examples of extra products being used as incentives to persuade consumers to purchase products.

Sales promotions targeted at the trade

Trade clients are those who work in the leisure and recreation industry and who are in a position to recommend or sometimes sell an organisation's product to customers. For example, someone working in a tourist information centre recommends local accommodation, catering and attractions.

Organisations often use sales promotions to encourage the trade to recommend their products to customers by offering discounts, allowances and free products and gifts. For example, sports clothing suppliers may provide free samples of their goods to shop staff so that they can provide customers with detailed product information.

Theatres use similar sales promotions by giving free press passes on opening nights together with complimentary refreshments, hoping that critics will recommend the performance in their newspaper.

Trade exhibitions are another way in which organisations promote their products to other staff within the trade. The exhibition industry is a rapidly growing area of leisure and recreation and now encompasses a very wide range of specialist exhibitions. Figure 4.26 gives some examples of major trade and public exhibitions in the leisure and recreation industry.

By now you should understand that there are many examples of sales promotions in use in the highly competitive leisure and recreation industry. As with all other forms of marketing activity, it is vital that organisations are able to measure accurately the effectiveness of a sales promotion. This involves measuring results against predetermined objectives, such as increasing sales by 10 per cent or increasing market share over a specific period.

ACTIVITY

Promoting Pizza Park

1. The extract opposite from the Granchester Evening News is about a new local restaurant, 'Pizza Park'. The editorial text was supplied by the owners of Pizza Park as a press release and has been printed alongside their advertisement. How many examples of sales promotion can you identify in the extract?

2. Three months later, in early November, the Pizza Park is already a success but is aware that there is strong local competition for the Christmas market of office parties. The owners have decided to run a similar series of sales promotions to those carried out for the opening. Can you suggest suitable sales promotions and redesign the newspaper spread based on your suggestions? You will need to write a new press release bearing in mind that the restaurant is now well established with a number of loyal customers.

Pizza Park set to open

Grantchester's newest restaurant is all set to open on 1 August 2000. Housed in the former library building on the High Street, Pizza Park's owners have completely redesigned the interior to bring a touch of Italy to the East of England. The exciting new menu features a range of pizza, pasta and seafood dishes as well as a mouth-watering choice of desserts. Reasonably priced Italian wines and soft drinks are also offered to complement the meal. In addition, throughout August they are offering a free children's meal for every child accompanied by two adult diners.

Pizza Park is able to offer Evening News readers a tremendous offer available for the entire month of August. Simply cut out and collect 10 vouchers from the Evening News and you can have two main courses for the price of one. The first two vouchers are printed above and further vouchers will appear during the next two weeks.

Grantchester Evening News
17 July 2000

▲ Foster's Lager sponsorship and sales promotion

Sponsorship

Sponsorship is the provision of financial support by one organisation to another organisation, individual or event in order to gain prestige and status from their association with them. It is often included in an organisation's public relations activities, since it indirectly enhances the customer's perception of the organisation or its products and services.

There are many examples of sponsorship in the leisure and recreation industry. Often one organisation will sponsor another because they target similar customers. The aim is to reinforce the overall brand image of both organisations with the customer. For example, Foster's Lager sponsors Grand Prix and links its sponsorship to its sales promotions with competitions offering Grand Prix holidays as prizes.

On a smaller scale, a small business may gain PR benefits by sponsoring local or regional organisations, events, facilities or services. For example, many local businesses sponsor local charitable causes that can lead to enhanced community relations for the sponsor.

The main concern with sponsorship is that an organisation needs to have a clear idea of what it wants to achieve and how it is going to achieve it. So, for example, it might ask:

- How much can we afford to pay out in sponsorship?
- Which sponsorship causes do we want our name associated with?
- Will these causes create a positive image for existing and potential customers?
- How are we going to ensure that existing and potential customers know about our sponsorship activities?

Many leisure and recreation organisations receive a large number of requests for sponsorship. The amount of money requested may vary from thousands of pounds to just a few pounds. Organisations need to decide how best to spend their sponsorship funds.

All of the marketing communications that we have looked at in this section help an organisation achieve its marketing objectives. In particular, effective marketing communications can:

- be an effective tool to increase consumer awareness
- prompt sales and take-up - in other words encourage consumers to actually buy the product or service.

While each type of marketing communication has its individual benefits and uses, most organisations use a range of communications to achieve their marketing objectives. This is because different types of communication will influence different customer segments. Similarly, different products and services will benefit from different types of marketing communications. For example, a theme park may use the following:

- leaflets to target customers who go to a tourist information centre or write and ask for details.
- press advertisements to attract new customers.
- television advertisements to raise general consumer awareness of the products that are offered.
- point-of-sale posters for sales promotions.
- direct marketing to past customers, etc.

The use of a range of marketing communications is known as the **promotions mix**. The following case study shows how Cadbury World uses marketing communications.

CASE STUDY

Cadbury World

Cadbury WORLD

Cadbury World in Birmingham was one of the first organisations to realise the potential of turning a consumer product into a tourist attraction. Apart from generating a great deal of revenue from the attraction itself, the creation of Cadbury World also helps to promote the company's core product of chocolate.

Cadbury World does not have a large advertising budget and thinks that it cannot justify national advertising. Therefore marketing communications are focused on the Midlands area. When identifying the promotions mix, Cadbury World aimed to achieve four marketing objectives:

- to communicate what Cadbury World is
- to communicate what Cadbury World is not
- to highlight new developments at Cadbury World
- to encourage return visits based on the new developments.

The promotions mix encompassed six main forms of marketing communications.

1 Brochures and leaflets designed for consumers have grown from 600,000 in the early days to a current 1.25 million. While still providing basic product information and details on how to organise a visit, each new print-run of leaflets has included details of new developments.

2 Regional press advertising. Cadbury World uses regional newspapers to advertise its facilities, products and services. Through experience, it has decided that discount vouchers in the press are largely ineffective, as they take up a large amount of advertising space but do not guarantee that readers will necessarily decide to visit.

3 Radio. Initially the effectiveness of radio advertising was marginal. However, more recently, Cadbury World has found this to be a highly effective advertising medium, to the extent that some radio advertisements have resulted in such a huge increase in visitors that the extra volume has been difficult to deal with. A further advantage has been improved evaluation of its effectiveness in different areas: visitors are asked to provide their phone numbers, which are then used to identify which radio areas are attracting the most visitors.

4 Poster advertising. Cadbury World uses both four- and six-sheet posters as well as posters on the sides of local buses. The effectiveness of posters as an advertising medium has been supported by word-of-mouth and observation, although it is difficult to evaluate just how effective this form of advertising is.

5 Public relations was used extensively in the pre-launch of Cadbury World and a great deal of television coverage was gained outlining the new tourist attraction and the products and services offered. This was particularly useful in launching Cadbury World into the introduction and growth stage of its product life-cycle.

6 Sales promotions. Half of the Cadbury World advertising budget has been spent on sales promotions with offers linked to discounted admission charges. Sales promotions are primarily used to increase customer awareness and support the other marketing communications used. Sales promotions were also used on Cadbury's chocolate product wrappers.

Source: *Cadbury World Student Pack*

The most appropriate type of marketing communication will depend on the products and services offered and the target markets, as well as the amount of money that an organisation can afford. However, there are three further, very important considerations when planning marketing communications:

- AIDA
- timing
- legal requirements.

AIDA

Identifying suitable communication channels is only the first step in successful marketing communications. The next stage is the actual design of marketing communications materials. For example, local press advertisements may be identified as the best way of communicating with certain local market segments. Unless the actual advertisement is well written and eye-catching, it is unlikely to be successful. Most advertisers use a model known as **AIDA**, which stands for:

Attention

Interest

Desire

Action

ACTIVITY

Cadbury World

As a group, discuss any further marketing communications that you think would be effective for Cadbury World. For example, could it use direct marketing or sponsorship?

The AIDA approach to advertising is designed to draw attention and create interest in order to produce a desire and demand for the product or service in the target audience. This desire should then be translated into action by customers purchasing the product or service.

Advertisers applying AIDA to the design of advertising material frequently attract *attention* through the use of slogans, bold headlines, well-known personalities or celebrities, vivid use of colour and eye-catching graphics. The message is kept clear, concise and understandable to maintain *interest*. Highlighting the benefits and incentives of purchase creates *desire* for the product. Prompt *action* is encouraged by providing instructions on how to purchase or use the product, providing booking information or directions and opening times.

ACTIVITY

AIDA

Look at the leaflet and identify how it achieves AIDA.

Get your hands on a
DINOSAUR
in Dorchester
at Britain's
one and only
Dinosaur
Museum
AWARD WINNING MUSEUM
Dorset's Best Family Attraction 1997
Open Every Day
7 days a week 9-30 - 5.30
THE
DINOSAUR
MUSEUM
en Way, Dorchester, Dorset. Tel:01305 269880
ASK FOR OUR
SPECIAL FAMILY SAVER TICKET

Timing of marketing communications

One problem that many leisure and recreation providers face is that demand for their products varies throughout the year and is therefore subject to seasonality. For example, cinemas and theatres have peak demand at weekends. The demand for UK-based watersports peaks in July and August, whereas the demand for skiing in Scotland peaks between January and March. Leisure and recreation organisations need to time their market communications to fit into the particular seasonality of their products and services.

The important issue that we need to bear in mind is that the chosen marketing communication method needs to be timed for when the consumer decides to buy the product, not necessarily when they actually experience it. So, for example, many potential leisure centre customers decide to take exercise in January based on New Year resolutions to get fit! Therefore promotions may intensify at this time. A further advertising drive may be set in May as the weather becomes better and people become more willing to venture out in the lighter evenings.

Any number of external factors may alter the timing of a consumer's decision to buy a product and therefore affect the timing of promotions. For example, the hype surrounding the new millennium resulted in many hotels and restaurants advertising New Year celebrations as much as three years in advance.

With other leisure and recreation products, the decision to buy may be much nearer the time of actually experiencing the product or service and the timing of promotions needs to reflect this. For example, the decision to go to a particular film may be made during the week before the visit by reading a local paper and seeing what films are being shown. Alternatively, the decision to visit an indoor swimming pool may be made on a rainy day by a tourist in a local tourist information centre looking for something to do. Leisure and recreation organisations need to have a clear idea of when consumers decide to purchase their products so that their promotional material is available at the appropriate time to influence the buying decision.

ACTIVITY

Timing

As a group, suggest the most effective time of the year to promote the following. For each item you need to consider when the target market segment is likely to buy the product or service. For example, at what time of the year are people most likely to think that joining a health and fitness club is a good idea?

- Campaign to increase membership at a health and fitness club
- Season ticket sales launch for a football club
- Season ticket sales launch for a county cricket club
- Campaign to increase membership of a golf club
- Promote a local summer sports coaching scheme for children

Legal requirements

When designing marketing communications materials it is important to remember that there are certain restrictions on what can and cannot be included. A number of laws restrict what advertisers can include in promotional materials:

- Trade Descriptions Act 1968
- Consumer Protection Act 1987
- Data Protection Act 1984

Some of these Acts affect activities other than just marketing, but let's look at their impact on the marketing communications of leisure and recreation organisations.

Trade Descriptions Act 1968

This Act states that any description of a product or service must be truthful at the time that it was written and that if circumstances change the organisation must inform customers of the changes. Therefore, it would be a contravention of the Act if a brochure described a hotel as 'quiet and peaceful' if the hotel was adjacent to the main airport and frequently subject to aircraft noise. Similarly, a theme park could not claim to have a new ride opening at a certain date if there were merely plans to open the ride. This would need to be made clear in its communications.

Consumer Protection Act 1987

This Act requires organisations to display accurate prices for products and services and describe their products and services honestly and realistically. Sales promotions which offered a discount on sports centre membership which in fact was more expensive than advertised would therefore contravene this Act.

Data Protection Act 1984

The Data Protection Act has particular implications for direct marketing, as it affects all organisations that hold personal details on customers. There are eight general principles to the Act. In particular, an organisation is only allowed to keep relevant information on customers for the purpose for which it was collected and no longer than is necessary. So, for example, a theatre which collects names and addresses of customers when they enter a competition cannot keep the data and use it for other promotional activities unless the customer has given permission. Neither could the theatre sell the data to another organisation.

Regulatory bodies

When designing and implementing marketing communications, organisations need to conform to regulations set down by advertising bodies such as the Independent Television Corporation (ITC) and the Advertising Standards Authority (ASA).

Independent Television Corporation

The ITC regulates all advertising on commercial television and sets over forty different standards with which advertisers must comply. (If you are interested in looking at some of these standards you can find a detailed description of them on the ITC web site: www.itc.org.uk.) Some examples of standards that could affect leisure and recreation providers include:

- Advertising must comply with the Race Relations Act and Sex Discrimination Act.
- Advertisements for alcohol, the Lottery, Pools or bingo cannot be directed at people under the age of 16 years (18 for bingo and alcohol) or use treatments likely to appeal to them.
- Advertisements cannot unfairly attack or discredit other products or services.
- A product cannot be described as 'free' unless there is no cost other than postage and packing.
- No advertisement may suggest that drinking alcohol is an essential attribute of masculinity.
- No advertisement may lead children to believe that if they do not have a product or service they will be inferior to other children.

Advertising Standards Authority

The ASA is responsible for ensuring that all advertising conforms to the British Code of Advertising Conduct. If an advertisement is found to contravene the code it has to be withdrawn. The webstract opposite shows key ASA definitions.

ACTIVITY

GOALS Football Academy

Jimmy Tomlinson is a keen footballer and has played for the Stanley junior team prior to retiring from the game because of a knee injury. He has continued to maintain his interest by coaching a local amateur team. Jimmy has decided to go into business on his own running football coaching weeks during the school holidays for local school children: it will be called GOALS Football Academy. He is currently in negotiation with two local organisations for the use of their pitch facilities. The local leisure centre has a new all-weather pitch with excellent changing rooms and is willing to rent the pitch to Jimmy for the week he requires. However, he cannot afford the amount they are asking for rental, but is hopeful that they may reduce the price.

The alternative is to use the playing fields at the local secondary school. This is considerably cheaper but the facilities are far inferior. At the time of writing his promotional materials, Jimmy was still not sure which of the pitches he would be using.

Jimmy hopes to attract more than 60 school children to the coaching week. He intends to coach the eldest group of children himself, while the remaining children receive coaching from three leisure and recreation students that he will employ for the week. He was keen to offer prizes to all participants and was therefore delighted to find that a local toy manufacturer made plastic footballs printed with the signatures of the Manchester United team. After some discussion he was able to buy 70 footballs at the discounted price of £3.00 each.

To ensure high numbers, Jimmy decided to offer a special deal to families with more than one child enrolled on the coaching week. Therefore he decided to offer two places for the price of one, with the second child only having to pay £5 per day for insurance, lunch and snacks - a saving of £40.

Look at Jimmy's local newspaper advertisement and discuss how he might be contravening any laws. Is there anything that he should make clear to enquirers who contact him for more details?

WEBSTRACT

The Advertising Standards Authority

The ASA requires all advertising materials to be legal, decent, honest and truthful. Below is the ASA definition of these four words.

Legal
Advertisers have primary responsibility for ensuring that their advertisements are legal. Advertisements should contain nothing that breaks the law or incites anyone to break it, and should omit nothing that the law requires.

Decent
Advertisements should contain nothing that is likely to cause serious or widespread offence. Particular care should be taken to avoid causing offence on the grounds of race, religion, sex, sexual orientation or disability. Compliance with the Codes will be judged on the context, medium, audience, product and prevailing standards of decency.

Advertisements may be distasteful without necessarily conflicting with the clause above. Advertisers are urged to consider public sensitivities before using potentially offensive material. The fact that a particular product is offensive to some people is not sufficient grounds for objecting to an advertisement for it.

Honest
Advertisers should not exploit the credulity, lack of knowledge or inexperience of consumers.

Truthful
No advertisement should mislead by inaccuracy, ambiguity, exaggeration, omission or otherwise.

Source: www.asa.org.uk

Advertising Standards complaints

Examine the following four cases referred to the ASA. Decide in each case whether or not the leisure and recreation organisations have contravened ASA rules. You can find the correct answers on page 461.

Is it legal?

Organisation: Satellite Technology
Media: Regional press
Complaint: Objection to a regional press advertisement that was headlined 'FREE SATELLITE VIEWING' and continued 'Novelty satellite cards. New and exclusive. Call Satellite Technology. Warning: the use of this product to receive satellite pictures is illegal in the UK.' The complainant also objected to follow-up literature that claimed 'FREE Movies, Sports, Soaps, etc. FREE SATELLITE VIEWING GUARANTEED. Warning: It is an Offence to obtain free viewing on Sky in the UK and we will not be held responsible for any misuse with our satellite cards we dispatch to the public. All cards sold are for novelty purposes only and provide alternative viewing outside the United Kingdom.'

- The complainant, who bought a card and found that it did not work, challenged the impression that customers could have free satellite viewing.
- The ASA challenged whether the advertisement and follow-up literature encouraged people to break the law.

Is it decent?

Organisation: Capital Shopping Centres plc, trading as Lakeside Shopping Centre
Media: National press
Complaint: Objections to an advertisement for a large shopping centre in the *Daily Express, The Times, Evening Standard, Cambridge Weekly News* and *Southend Yellow Advertiser*. It featured the Three Wise Men looking into the distance at a building with a bright star shining over it. The advertisement stated: 'From November 11th, wise men and women will visit Lakeside on weekdays between 10 a.m. and 10 p.m. when they can avoid the crowds.' The complainants objected that the advertisement was offensive because it trivialised the Christmas message.

Is it honest?

Organisation: High Legh Park Golf Club
Media: Leaflet
Complaint: Objection to a leaflet that promoted a limited number of memberships of a new golf club. The leaflet claimed, '50 REMAIN Membership Closes Sunday 21st June 1998 at 8 p.m.' The complainants objected that the leaflet was misleading because, having joined the club before the stated deadline believing that only twelve spaces remained, they discovered that the advertisers had continued to invite new members.

Is it truthful?

Organisation: British Field Sports Society
Media: Magazine
Complaint: The League Against Cruel Sports objected to an advertisement in a special interest magazine that claimed: 'If you're not helping to fight the growing threats against angling, you're effectively helping to kill your sport.' The advertisement continued: 'As the League Against Cruel Sports' Chief Spokesman has said, "The League accepts that fish are capable of suffering and therefore opposes angling for sport."' The complainants objected that the person responsible for making the statement had done so in 1982 when he was not employed by the League Against Cruel Sports. They asserted the advertisers were aware that the quote had since been corrected and did not represent the League's neutral stance on fishing. They believed the advertisement was misleading.

BUILD YOUR LEARNING

End of section activity

Each member of the group should select a different leisure or recreation organisation. Investigate how your organisation uses marketing communications, including:

- advertising (press, television, radio, magazines, internet, leaflets, posters, point of sale)
- brochures
- direct marketing (direct mail, telemarketing, door-to-door distribution, direct response advertising)
- public relations
- sales promotions
- sponsorship.

Collect as many examples as you can of the organisation's marketing communications materials. As a group, make up a display board of your marketing communications materials. Use the six categories specified above as headings.

Evaluate how effective you think the various materials are and make recommendations as to how they could be improved.

Keywords and phrases

You should know the meaning of the words and phrases listed below. If you are unsure about any of them, go back through the last 25 pages to refresh your understanding.

- Marketing communications
- Advertising
- Internet
- Leaflets
- Point of sale
- Direct marketing
- Direct mail/mailshot
- Telemarketing
- Door-to-door distribution
- Media direct response
- Public relations
- Media inclusion
- Press releases
- Community relations
- Lobbying
- Corporate communications
- Sales promotion
- Sponsorship
- Promotions mix
- AIDA

Preview

The main focus of all leisure and recreation organisations, whether they operate to make a profit or are non-profit making, is on ensuring that customers want, and therefore buy, its products and services. One of the main ways of ensuring this is to provide excellent customer service, which leads to high levels of customer satisfaction, encourages customers to return and predisposes them to recommend the organisation to others.

In this unit we explore the various ways in which leisure and recreation organisations and you, as a member of staff, can provide excellent customer service.

The assessment requirement for this unit is shown on page 457.

5

Customer service in leisure and recreation

Contents

The importance of excellent customer service

Customer service is broadly concerned with looking after customers. However, this is a very general definition; we need to be more exact about what we mean. Customer service includes all of the components shown in Figure 5.1.

Customer service is very much a team effort and it is vital that all team members recognise the important contribution that they are expected to make. This is why many leisure and recreation organisations provide staff with training in customer service skills. Providing excellent customer service is an important part of everybody's job, but it is particularly important in the leisure and recreation industry, as there are many organisations that provide similar products or services; often, it is the quality of customer service which distinguishes one from another.

Good customer service leads to customer loyalty, which in turn increases repeat business. For example, an exercise studio may offer various incentives for regular customers. These might include priority booking, discounts on selected facilities and other perks to encourage customer loyalty.

Many leisure and recreation organisations outline their customer service strategy in what is known as a customer promise or charter, such as the one shown in Figure 5.2.

The term **customer service** refers to all elements of the customer interface and includes all direct and indirect contact with the customer, as well as the products, services, systems and strategies that support the customer service process.

Figure 5.1: Components of customer service

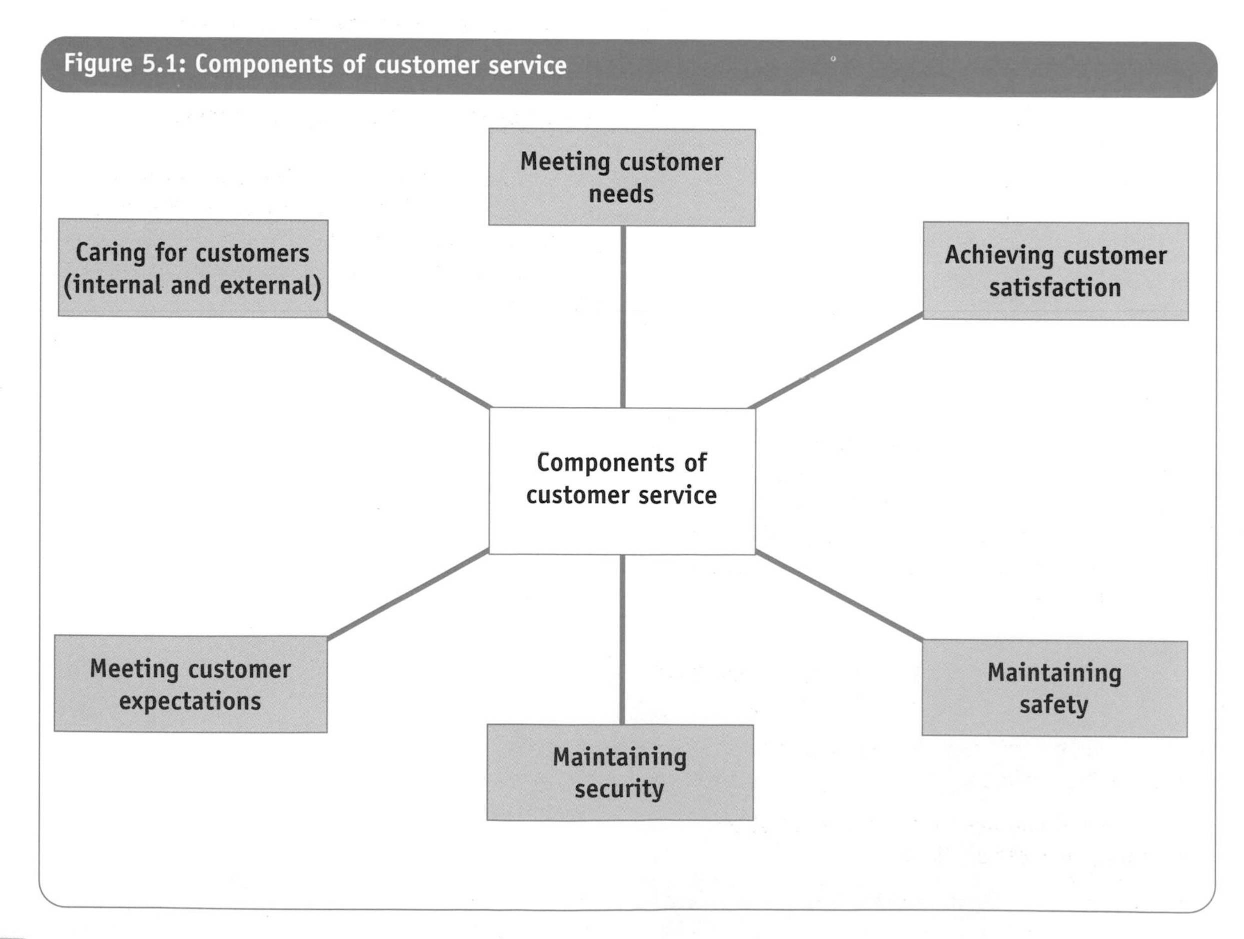

Figure 5.2: Sport England's Customer Promise

Our aspirations

We will seek the views of our key partners in the sport development business and take account of them in our work.

In particular we aim to:

- listen carefully to what is being said
- value, and consider carefully all views expressed
- treat you with respect and credibility
- communicate the outcome of our deliberations and explain the reason for our decisions.

We will be personally responsible for our actions and appearance.

In particular, each of us aims to:

- provide a quick and satisfactory service, whenever possible
- treat people fairly and equally
- be courteous and polite
- be helpful in our attitude
- meet agreed timescales
- arrive on time for appointments
- be neat and tidy in our appearance
- be efficient in our duties
- be informative in our responses

The attitude and behaviour of staff is the foundation of all excellent customer service. It means that staff really have to care about their customers and try to anticipate and satisfy their needs. To achieve this, staff have to be able to put themselves in the position of their customers and see the service from a customer's point of view. For example:

- How would you feel if you were kept queuing for half an hour to get into a football match?
- What would your attitude be if your squash court was double booked?
- How would you react if an attendant at a bowling alley was off-hand?

What would you expect staff to do and say in any of these service situations? If you can put yourself in the customer's position, most aspects of excellent customer service will come easily to you.

You probably already have some ideas about what customer service is, based on your own experience as a customer. You may have experienced excellent service that is worth copying. Alternatively, you may have received bad service on occasions and therefore recognise what you should not do.

Customer service is the most important part of a leisure and recreation organisation's business because, quite simply, without customers there would be no business! But what are the specific benefits to an organisation of training its staff in good customer service skills? There are many, but seven key and interlinked benefits can be highlighted:

- increased sales
- more customers
- better public image
- an edge over the competition
- happier and more efficient workforce
- satisfied customers
- customer loyalty and repeat business.

Before we look at each of these in detail, read the case study on the English Tourist Board's Welcome Host programme, which will give you a general overview of the benefits of providing excellent customer service to customers.

CASE STUDY

ETB Welcome Host programme

The Welcome Host programme was developed by the English Tourist Board (now known as the English Tourism Council) in association with the regional tourist boards to improve the level of customer service in the leisure and recreation industry. Its aim is to improve levels of customer service throughout the industry by encouraging staff to take professional pride in their work.

The one-day course covers a range of topics including communication skills, complaint handling, making a positive first impression and providing information and guidance to customers. In 1998, almost 28,000 people successfully completed Welcome Host.

Successful course attendees receive a Welcome Host certificate and badge on completion of the course. If you visit a tourist information centre you will probably see most of the staff wearing their Welcome Host badges.

In 1999 the English Tourist Board commissioned independent research to look at the benefits to organisations of offering the Welcome Host programme to their employees. The results were overwhelming, both in terms of enthusiasm for the programme and in listing a number of very important benefits.

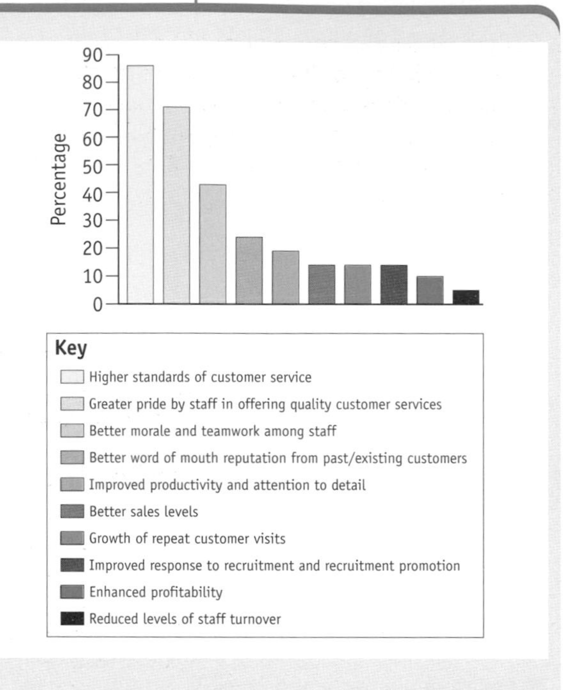

The English Tourist Board offers a number of other Welcome programmes including:

- Welcome Line, which focuses on telephone skills.
- Welcome All, which deals with customers with specific needs or disabilities.
- Welcome Management, aimed at managerial and supervisory staff with responsibility for customer service.
- Welcome International, focusing on the needs of foreign visitors.

The Welcome Host programme is available to any leisure and recreation organisations, with specially adapted programmes tailored to the needs of individual providers, as the following article shows.

ACTIVITY

Customer service training

If your local taxi drivers were about to be given training similar to that provided in Bristol, what specific leisure and recreation facilities and services do you think they should be aware of? Bear in mind that they cannot be expected to know about everything, so you need to be selective.

Training shows taxis the route to more profit

'Are you good enough to become an ambassador for Bristol?' This is the question being asked of 420 registered taxi drivers in the famous West of England city, in an initiative which has captured the attention and support of local people. Based upon Welcome Host, the programme has been drawn together by Bristol Tourism in an initiative which will shortly spread to Bath through the tourism department.

The cab drivers are being encouraged to complete two days of learning, the first hinging on the Welcome Host for transport variation of Britain's most popular customer service award, whilst the second is devoted to Bristol Awareness, with presentations from some of the city's top attractions and leisure and recreation providers.

The initiative began in January, led by Carol Wager of Bristol Tourism, with the enthusiastic support of local taxi-driver leaders. Approximately ten drivers are recruited on each programme, which is free thanks to European funding.

'At the beginning everyone was pretty sceptical,' said Carol. 'But those opinion-formers on the original programme worked hard in spreading the message that the training is worthwhile and the feedback indicated that they had learned a lot.'

Source: *Trailblazer* magazine

Increased sales

Increased sales is one of the key measurements of success. Excellent customer service means that customers will buy more and recommend products and services to others, which will increase sales still further. Selling skills therefore form an essential element of effective customer service delivery. We look at selling skills in detail on pages 346-351.

More customers

While sales are clearly very important to leisure and recreation organisations, many of them also measure their success in terms of **customer numbers**. This is particularly true of non-profit making or subsidised organisations. For example, a public swimming pool may not aim to make a profit and may instead measure its success in terms of community benefit and therefore the number of local people who actually use the pool. This might include encouraging minority or other groups to use it, such as the elderly or unemployed.

ACTIVITY

Increasing sales

The quiz on the right is given to staff in a tourist attraction to show them how important customer service is in ensuring sales. Try the quiz yourself and find out how much a single member of staff might contribute to sales by providing excellent customer service.

- C = £
- D = £
- E = £
- F = £
- Final total = £

What do you think......

...your customers are worth?

And how much are you worth to the company?

Try this exercise

(A) Your average customer spends: £10.75

(B) You handle approximately 30 customers a day

(C) Therefore each day you earn the company: £ ....? (A and B)

(D) You work 5 days a week, so multiply C by 5: £.........

(E) On average you work 46 weeks a year so multiply D by 46: £.......

(F) If you give good service they remain loyal for 5 years, so multiply E by 5: £.........

If they really like the service that you give they will tell up to five friends who will also become loyal customers, so multiply F by 5: £....

THAT IS WHAT YOU ARE WORTH TO THE COMPANY WHEN YOU PROVIDE EXCELLENT CUSTOMER SERVICE

PRETTY GOOD, ISN'T IT?

What are you left with?

Lots of very happy smiling faces, both with your customers and especially Head Office!

Customer service plays a part in attracting customers in two ways. First (and probably most important), there is the powerful influence of word of mouth. Existing customers who are impressed by the customer service they receive will tell others about it. This means that an organisation keeps its existing customers and also attracts new customers.

Research shows that the greatest influence on customers' decisions to buy or use one leisure and recreation product as opposed to another is the recommendation of people they know. This influence is far greater, in fact, than the influence of any amount of expensive advertising.

Second, customer service helps to attract customers by emphasising customer service policies and making them a major part of any promotional material and information. Promotional material is often used to formulate the customer's expectations while explaining how their needs will be met. Center Parcs, for example, uses the coveted Hospitality Assured marque on all of its promotional materials to reassure customers that they can expect the highest standards of customer service.

Center Parcs wins major customer service accolade

Center Parcs is the first company in the short-break sector to receive Hospitality Assured accreditation, in recognition of its high standards of guest service and management. Hospitality Assured is the quality marque developed by the Hotel and Catering International Management Association (HCIMA) to recognise and reward commitment to and achievement of service excellence. It is a new industry standard and is awarded only to organisations in the leisure and hospitality sector – hotels, restaurants and other catering establishments – which demonstrate delivery of the highest standards of service across all areas of their business.

'Without doubt, it is the professionalism, commitment and enthusiasm of each member of staff that has won this recognition for Center Parcs. We genuinely strive for excellence in every facet of our experience, and I am delighted that our teams have now been recognized as leaders in their fields through gaining this Hospitality Assured accreditation,' comments Peter Moore, Managing Director of Center Parcs.

To gain accreditation, a score of more than 50 per cent in each category is required and Center Parcs scored an average of 81 per cent throughout. During the external audit, individual on-site interviews were held with staff and the process was communicated to its 3,000 company-wide staff.

David Wood, Chief Executive of HCIMA, adds: 'We are delighted that the brand leader in the short-break market is now part of the Hospitality Assured stable.'

Source: Extract from HCIMA press release

Improved public image

The overall effect of an effective customer service policy is that customers will view the organisation and its products or services in a positive light. Thus, the image of the organisation will be enhanced by the standard of customer service. This is very important for:

- attracting new customers
- retaining existing customers
- reinforcing customer satisfaction
- securing repeat business
- gaining an edge over the competition.

But what is meant by an organisation's **public image**? It is the mental picture that we have of an organisation. It can be based on our own experience of the organisation, or on what others have told us about it, or on what the organisation itself has told us via its marketing activities such as advertising and public relations.

Increasingly, television consumer programmes such as the BBC's Watchdog also help form the image of organisations, especially when such programmes report viewers' complaints. The extract below from Watchdog's website is based on a report on Holmes Place Health Clubs. What effect do you think the report will have on the image of the clubs?

ACTIVITY

Public image

In small groups, discuss the image you have of each of the following organisations and the factors that have influenced that image.

- Alton Towers
- Center Parcs
- Manchester United Football Club
- Disneyland, Paris
- McDonald's
- Madame Tussaud's
- Millennium Dome
- London Zoo
- Legoland, Windsor
- Ramblers Association
- Rugby Football Union
- Lawn Tennis Association
- International Olympic Committee
- FIFA

WEBSTRACT

Holmes Place Health Clubs

If you're a man and you like to wear sports vests when you're working out, then you may not be welcome at the Holmes Place chain of health clubs, which has 18 gyms around London and the South East.

Accountant Bill Fell and heart surgeon Mo Adiseshiah regularly wore their vests at the Broadgate Club West. But last month when Holmes Place bought their gym, they received a letter saying that men will no longer be able to wear vests as the company deem them to be threatening and unhygienic. Vests are OK for women, but for men its strictly T shirts only in the gym. When Mo Adiseshiah turned up with his vest on, he was called in by the management and told he'd be thrown out if it happened again. Alan Fisher, Managing Director at Holmes Place, says that the company has a dress code policy appropriate to the style of its business.

Source: *www.holmesplace.co.uk*

Good customer service can also enhance the image of an organisation's individual products or services. For example, customers may have a positive image of a sports centre, but also have a positive image of individual products and services such as the reservations system and changing facilities.

Competitive advantage

Good customer service is vitally important in giving an organisation a **competitive advantage**. This means that you offer something that your competitors don't. If you have a similar product to your competitors, you can gain an advantage by offering a better quality of service or advertising your product at a lower price. You will then have a greater chance of attracting customers from your competitors.

Physical resources play a large part in gaining competitive advantage. For example, a small local swimming pool may have little chance of competing with a large leisure pool with water flumes, slides and wave machines. However, where the facility is similar to that of its competitors, good customer service becomes crucial. In some circumstances, as the case study of Activate shows, good customer service has led to a competitive advantage even where the physical resources of the company are inferior to those of competitors.

ACTIVITY

Competitive advantage

Compare two facilities known to you, such as two nightclubs, two fitness centres or two visitor attractions. Identify which, in your opinion, has achieved a competitive advantage, and give reasons for your choice.

CASE STUDY

Customer service and competitive advantage

Activate is a single-operation, privately owned indoor activity centre aimed at children aged from 5–14 years. The centre is situated on the main street of a northern town. One of Activate's most popular products are children's birthday parties, which include full use of the facilities and a party tea. In the same town there are three other larger sports facilities offering similar children's birthday parties. The larger companies have more extensive premises, a wider range of activities and advertise frequently in the local and regional press. Activate has a much smaller facility and cannot afford to place large advertisements in the press.

The owner of Activate was convinced that, despite the apparent competitive advantage of the larger facilities, he could gain an advantage over them if he could offer a better level of customer service. He visited all of the competitors in the guise of a potential customer to discover if Activate's service could be improved. He soon realised that customers expected to remain with their children during the party to check that all went well. At many parties (especially those for smaller children) the parents of party guests would also stay. He noted that while the children were well supervised by the centre's staff and were kept occupied, the parents tended to stand around the edge of the room and grow increasingly bored.

The owner of Activate immediately saw an opportunity to secure a competitive advantage. He reorganised the way his centre was laid out. Although there was relatively little space available, there was enough room to create a small seating area where he put some comfortable chairs and a coffee table. He bought a coffee machine and asked a member of staff to ensure that coffee, milk, sugar, biscuits and clean cups were always available. Next, he bought a range of current magazines and newspapers, which he placed on the coffee table.

He then redesigned his birthday party leaflet to include the following section: 'If you would like to stay with your child during a birthday party please make yourself comfortable in our lounge area. Relax with free coffee, biscuits and magazines while you are waiting.'

Three months later, Activate's owner was able to congratulate his staff on record sales. The manager of one of the larger facilities remarked to her staff, 'Activate seems to be stealing our customers. Let's see what new equipment we could install to gain a competitive edge!'

A happier workforce

A further benefit of excellent customer service is that it creates a much more pleasant working environment. If customers receive excellent service they will generally respond by being friendly and appreciative. If you have worked in a customer service role you will know how much more enjoyable the work is when customers thank you for the service you have given them. Similarly, if you treat your colleagues well, they will treat you well in return.

Figure 5.3: Customer and staff satisfaction

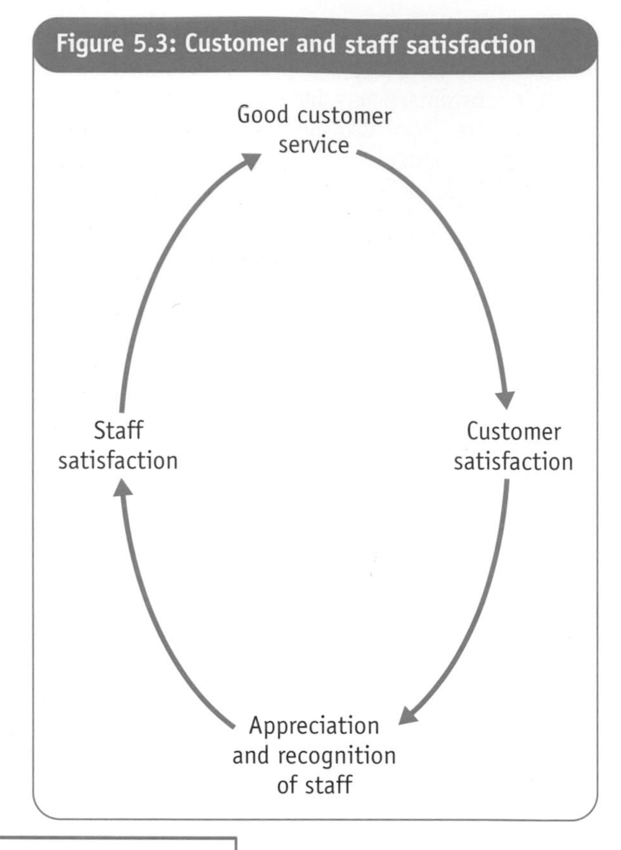

CASE STUDY

Woburn Safari Park

Preparations for the 1999 season at Woburn Safari Park are accelerating in a visitor attraction with a remarkable record of growth and awards recognition. For the second consecutive time in 1998, the park was named as the East of England Tourist Board Visitor Attraction of the Year. The seeds of achievement are people performance and the responsiveness of staff in putting customers first without sacrificing any of the vital responsibilities in the care and well-being of a variety of animals.

Six years ago there was a culture of resistance to training among employees and Chris Webster found himself having to impose a three-line whip to get the participation of all in identifying needs and prioritizing. 'It was clear that both communication and customer services were areas where improvement was necessary to help lift the business, improve the customer experience and provide better value for money,' said Mr Webster.

Today, at least two thirds of the growing staff of 51 full-time and 120 part-time claim to enjoy the training and over the last three winters a total of at least 18 days have been devoted to the running of courses. The process has been assisted by job swaps introduced in 1996, giving more people greater levels of skill in the different specialisms of work and understanding the business as a whole.

In 1997 the first comprehensive market research into customer attitudes to their visits to Woburn was complete and results were widely shared internally. This form of benchmarking, repeated up to four times a year, is now linked to the park's quality measurement scales with a linkage to both appraisals and individual job performance measurement. This includes input into a bonus scheme for seasonal staff, who can earn bonus payments of up to £70 every six months if they are clearly shown to be contributing to the success of the totality of Woburn Safari Park through their customer service skills.

Source: *Trailblazer* magazine

ACTIVITY

Woburn Safari Park

As a group, identify the ways in which the customer service initiatives at Woburn Safari Park could help to create a happier, more efficient workforce.

Satisfied customers

The main aim of providing excellent customer service is to make sure that customers are totally satisfied with the service they receive. This is known as **customer satisfaction**

This means that the service provided must meet **customers' needs** and **expectations.** The terms needs and expectations are often used interchangeably, as if their meaning were the same. In fact, there is a subtle difference. A need is the reason why a customer is buying a product or service. An expectation is what he or she expects that product or service to be like. For example, a customer's need might be for a ticket to a pop concert. The customer's expectation of the concert will be influenced by a number of factors, such as past experience, advertising or what friends have said. Clearly, it is just as important to meet customers' expectations as it is to meet their needs.

Which? magazine evaluates all the letters it receives and identifies the top ten tips for providing excellent customer service. This provides a good insight into the general needs and expectations of customers and the factors that contribute to customer satisfaction. The results can be seen in the webstract.

WEBSTRACT

Keeping customers happy

Here are ten tips, based on letters from Which? members, on how organisations can keep their customers happy.

1 Ensure that staff are well-informed, polite, and attentive.

2 Introduce customer-friendly after-sales service systems.

3 Provide easy and quick access to tills and customer service points.

4 Provide reliable guarantee and warranty clauses, without any exclusions hidden in the small print.

5 Make sure that phone lines are easy to get through to.

6 Phone queuing systems should let callers know how many people are being kept waiting.

7 Label goods clearly.

8 Ensure that promised levels of service are honest and clear. Charters and pledges are good, but they should come without disclaimers and small print.

9 Keep people informed about how their complaint is progressing, and ensure that phone calls are returned and letters answered.

10 Avoid piped music.

Source: www.which@which.net

ACTIVITY

Customer needs

Decide what the needs of customers might be when they buy the following services or products. Remember, most customers have more than one need when buying a service or product.

Product or service	Needs
Attending a football match	e.g. Quick and efficient entry to the stadium
A meal in a fast-food restaurant	
An aerobics session	
A day at a theme park	
A swim in a local pool	

ACTIVITY

Keeping customers happy

Look the 10 points in the webstract on page 325 and think of two examples in leisure and recreation where each particularly applies. Some, such as the first, would apply to any leisure and recreation provision. However, others are more specific to certain organisations. For example, which leisure and recreation organisations use piped music and does it improve or worsen the customer's experience?

Discuss why you think these ten points are particularly important in ensuring customer satisfaction.

Customer loyalty

Excellent customer service can help reinforce customers' loyalty to an organisation with each visit they make. Past customers remain loyal and become future customers. This is known as **customer retention** or **loyalty.**

WEBSTRACT

The Royal Mail and customer loyalty

It used to be thought that a good product backed with good service would automatically lead to repeat sales. Nowadays, research tells us that those customers who pronounce themselves as satisfied are often the most fickle when it comes to brand loyalty. That's why it pays to communicate with your customers – to build relationships with them. Just because a customer has bought something form you once doesn't mean that they'll buy from you again. There are dozens of reasons why customers might not buy from you again, and only really two why they would.

The first is a negative reason. He or she can't be bothered to look elsewhere (but they might well in the future). The second reason for staying with you is positive. You give the customer a reason to stay loyal. Not just by selling a good product or service, but by initiating a relationship, by taking the trouble to communicate, and by finding out what he or she wants and then offering it.

Source: http://www.royalmail.co.uk

It is estimated that it costs five times as much to attract a new customer as it does to retain an existing customer, so it makes sound business sense to adopt a customer service approach that aims to keep existing customers by encouraging their loyalty. Such loyalty is based on the knowledge that:

- the organisation can satisfy their needs
- they will not be pressurised to buy something that they do not want
- they are made to feel important and valued customers whenever they visit
- the advice and information they get is accurate and tailored to their requirements
- they can trust staff to meet their expectations of the organisation on each and every occasion.

Even if a customer has been dissatisfied with some aspect of the service provided, it need not mean that the organisation will lose their custom. Survey evidence suggests that 82 per cent of customers are likely to return if their complaints are answered successfully. However, failure to deal with complaints can have severe consequences. Research indicates that on average a satisfied customer tells three people of their experience, whereas dissatisfied customers share their experience with an average of 15 others.

If customers are loyal they are likely to return. A **repeat customer** is someone that you know. You know their needs and expectations and are therefore able to satisfy them better. At best, you will have created loyal customers who would not consider going anywhere else because they know that their needs and expectations can be met fully by the service you provide. Think of a popular restaurant in your locality. It is probably popular because it has achieved customer satisfaction and has built up a large number of regular customers. Figure 5.4 shows the reasons why customers chose a particular hotel. As you can see, more than a third are either repeat customers or have received recommendations about the hotel from loyal customers.

Figure 5.4: How accommodation is chosen

Word of mouth	19%
Stayed before	19%
Travel agent	10%
Guidebook	9%
Arranged by holiday company	8%
Tourist board/TIC	7%
Saw a sign	6%
Newspaper/magazine	3%

Source: ETB *Insights* magazine, March 1999

We have looked at why excellent customer service is important to an organisation and focused on its benefits. However, it is important not to view these benefits as separate, for they are all closely related. For example, customer satisfaction results in repeat business, increased sales and more customers. This in turn leads to an enhanced image and competitive advantage. All of these benefits are likely to create a happier and more efficient workforce.

Effects of poor service

We have looked at the main benefits of excellent customer service. What about the effects on an organisation whose customer service is poor? As well as losing the benefits, it will probably suffer from:

- decreased sales
- fewer customers
- a poor public image
- an absence of competitive edge
- an unhappy and less efficient workforce
- dissatisfied customers
- lack of customer loyalty and repeat business.

ACTIVITY

Effects of Poor Service

The article opposite raises a number of interesting issues about the effects of poor customer service; for example, the fact that customers aged 15–34 are the most dissatisfied.

As a group, discuss why you think these customers might have particular grounds for complaint. What could be the long-term effect on the organisation of alienating this group of customers? Consider the volume of sales and customers, as well as public image, competitive edge, customer satisfaction and loyalty, and repeat customers.

The development of out-of town shopping malls and retail outlets, and the regeneration of inner cities, has meant that shopping is one of the fastest growing areas of leisure spending. Added to this is the huge number of souvenir shops and outlets at visitor attractions, sports centres and hotels and restaurants such as Planet Hollywood and Hard Rock. The following newspaper article shows how the quality of customer service in shops is a crucial determinant of whether customers will be satisfied and consequently come back.

It is the question posed by shop staff millions of times every week: 'How can I help you?' The answer, according to many customers, is this: 'Buck up your ideas.'

A survey published today reveals that one in six shoppers have been put off making a purchase because of the way they were treated by staff. The poll found that poor staff attitudes damage consumer relations and that businesses need to improve service standards.

Mori questioned over 1,000 consumers over the past three months. Younger and more affluent consumers appeared the most dissatisfied. Nearly a quarter of those aged 15–34 and a similar number with an annual household income of more than £30,000 said that they had left a shop empty-handed after being badly treated by staff. In describing their dealings with shop staff, only 20 per cent of consumers said that employees showed appreciation that they were buying something from their shop and just 12 per cent said staff were enthusiastic about their products or services. Consumers who feel that staff are interested in helping them are more than twice as likely to make a repeat purchase and more than three times as likely to recommend the company to others.

The survey also tried to determine what were the main factors influencing repeat purchases. Whilst quality and price came out top, the third most important factor was how they were treated by staff. This came out well ahead of advertising and brand reputation. The report also found that only one in 26 customers complained before shopping elsewhere – because customers only complain when they want to have a continuing relationship with the company.

Source: *Daily Mail*, 28 May 1999

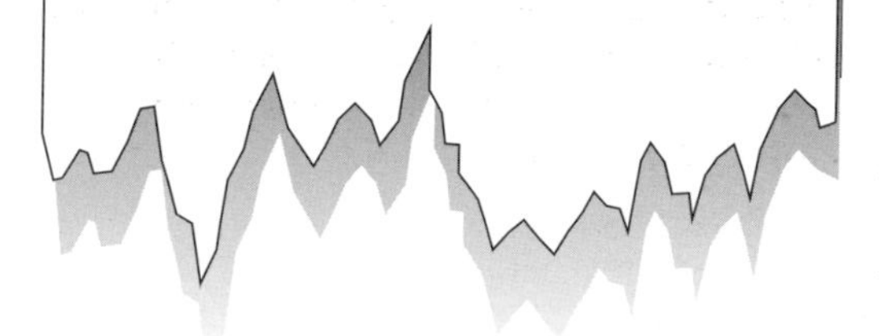

Figure 5.5: Importance of customer service

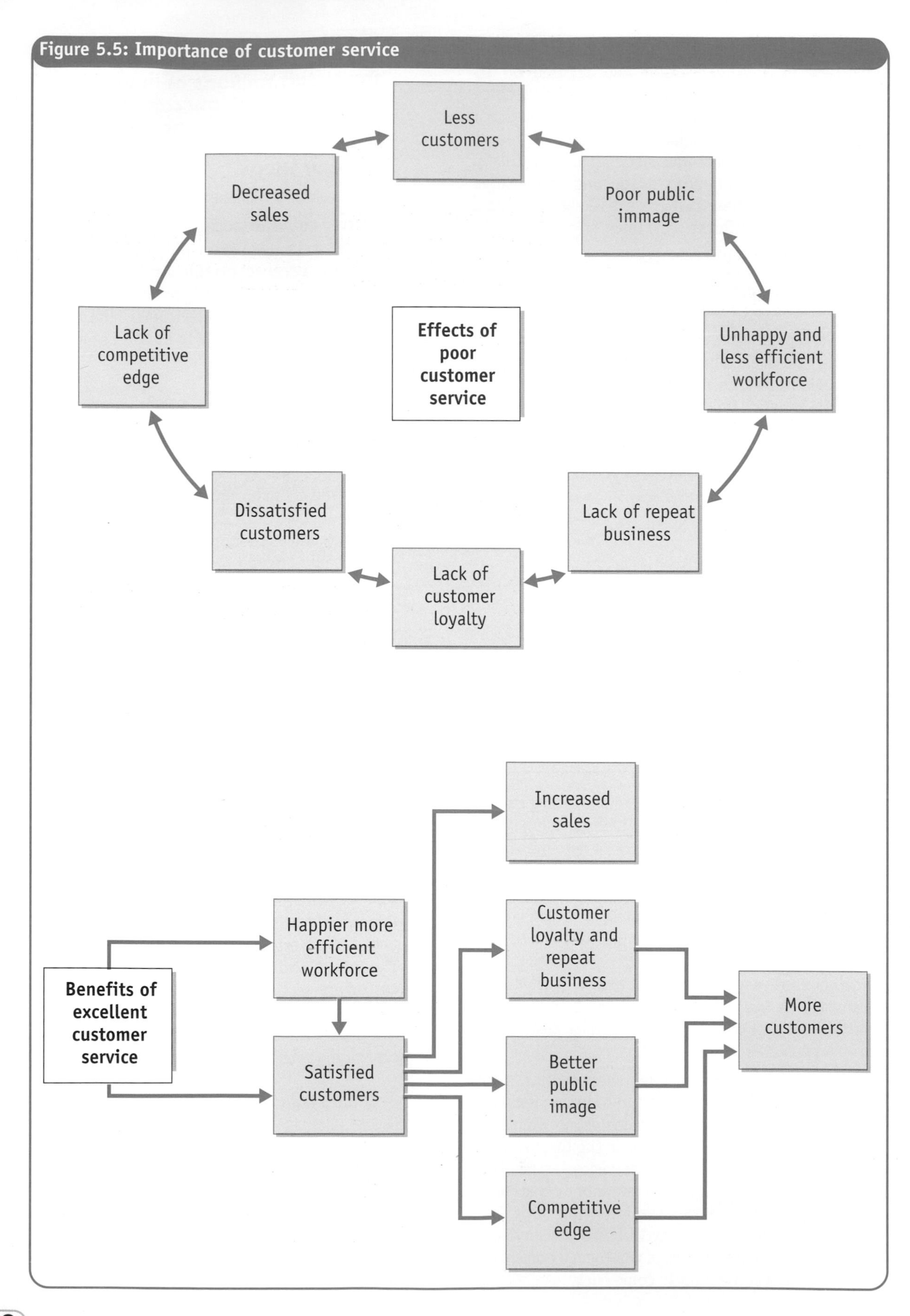

BUILD YOUR LEARNING

End of section activity

Select two leisure and recreation organisations and identify why customer service is important for each of them. Provide specific examples of how the following benefits are achieved through the effective use of excellent customer service:

- increased sales
- more customers
- a better public image
- an edge over the competition
- a happier, more efficient workforce
- satisfied customers
- customer loyalty and repeat business.

If you think that the organisations could increase such benefits by offering even better customer service, give examples of how this could be achieved.

Keywords and phrases

You should know the meaning of the words and phrases listed below. If you are unsure about any of them, go back through the last 13 pages to refresh your understanding.

- Customer service
- Increased sales
- Customer numbers
- Public image
- Competitive advantage
- Customer needs and expectations
- Customer satisfaction
- Customer loyalty or retention
- Repeat customers

Personal presentation

When working in the leisure and recreation industry you will be at the heart of customer service delivery. The way you present yourself – your **personal presentation** – will directly influence customers' satisfaction and the image they have of the organisation for which you work.

You never get a second chance to make a first impression. The **first impression** that you give to customers communicates a great deal about yourself, what you think of them and how you view your job and your employer. It sets the tone of customers' dealings with the organisation and its staff and their enjoyment of the experience. A customer's impression of you and the organisation you represent will usually be formed within the first 30 seconds of contact.

ACTIVITY

First impressions

Think about an organisation that you encountered for the first time recently. This could be a shop, a sports centre or visitor attraction. What was your first impression when you met a member of staff? What influenced that impression? If you cannot remember your first impression, this in itself is important. Why do you think the member of staff failed to make any impression?

Discuss your ideas and experiences with the rest of the group.

▲ Staff working in leisure and recreation are often required to wear a uniform

Personal presentation includes four key areas:

- appearance
- personal hygiene
- personality
- attitude

Appearance

Appearance covers everything from clothes and footwear to hairstyle, make-up and jewellery. Why do you think so many leisure and recreation organisations provide their staff with uniforms? From a customer service point of view there are many advantages.

- It helps create a positive first impression.
- Staff are recognised instantly as working for a specific organisation.
- It is easy to identify a member of staff when a customer needs advice or assistance.
- It can indicate the department in which a member of staff works.
- It helps to create a professional corporate image.

It is becoming more common for organisations to provide some sort of **uniform**. Organisations also rely on the good judgement of their staff in deciding what is and is not acceptable in terms of appearance. Some organisations set ground rules and to a large extent these will reflect the nature of the organisation and the type of customers it serves.

For example, a five-star hotel will have strict rules about the appearance of all front-of-house staff, which will usually include the requirement to wear a uniform, and may include rules on appropriate footwear, hairstyling and make-up. Other leisure and recreation organisations may have less stringent requirements, such as those shown in Figure 5.6.

Figure 5.6: Staff appearance

Neptune Water and Adventure Park

Staff Appearance

Whilst on duty all staff are expected to conform to the following rules on appearance:

- Neptune T-shirt (supplied)
- Neptune Sweatshirt (supplied)
- Black shorts or tracksuit trousers
- Trainers (white soles)
- Hair tied back if shoulder length or longer
- No jewellery except stud earrings and wedding ring

Staff are responsible for ensuring that their clothes are laundered and kept in good condition.

The most important point is that dress and general appearance should suit the job, the organisation and the customer's expectations. Similarly, an organisation should ensure that uniforms are comfortable, easy to maintain and look appropriate for staff of all builds.

ACTIVITY

Staff Uniforms

Yannis Demetriopolus is about to open his own fitness studio and wants to provide all staff with a uniform. He has decided to spend a maximum of £175 per uniform. The colour scheme of the studio and fittings is red and dark blue. He has employed five fitness instructors: three women and two men.

Look at some mail-order clothing catalogues and suggest a suitable uniform that does not exceed his budget and suits the general image of his company. Bear in mind that staff will need at least two of each item of clothing to allow for washing. You are not expected to buy shoes, etc. Present your ideas in a file, together with a checklist of general requirements for staff appearance. You should also include a breakdown of the total cost.

Personal hygiene

Anyone serving customers should have excellent standards of **personal hygiene**. No customer will be impressed by a lifeguard who smells of garlic or a waiter with dirty finger nails! Equally, dousing yourself with perfume or aftershave when you have not had time for a shower, or chewing gum after a curry, is just as off-putting for customers.

Some jobs in leisure and recreation will have stricter requirements for personal hygiene than others due to the nature of the work. For example, someone employed in food preparation will be expected to wash their hands dozens of times a day between separate food preparation activities in order to avoid cross-contamination.

ACTIVITY

Personal hygiene

Look at the drawing on the right and identify the key personal hygiene concerns.

Personality

The first impression you give to customers also depends on your **personality** and how you project it. Your personality will influence the image that the customer forms of the whole organisation. The difference is that only you can actually influence your personality and determine whether the customer is going to see it positively. The importance of projecting a good personality is summed up in the following extract from a training session given by a personnel and training manager for Forte Hotels.

Most of us spend our social lives trying to be attractive, friendly and likeable people – we want others to like us and to see our best side. So why should we behave any differently at work? Treat every customer as the person you most want to impress – and impress them totally! Make sure that they walk out of the door wanting to come back – because they liked you!

Of course, different jobs in leisure and recreation require different types of personality. The sort of personality required to work as a children's sports coach will be different to that required of a personal fitness instructor at an exclusive health spa.

ACTIVITY

Personality types

Look at the following leisure and recreation jobs and discuss the specific types of personality that you think each would require.

- A professional sportsperson
- A lifeguard at a swimming pool
- A guide at a heritage site
- A sales assistant in a sports clothing shop
- A bingo caller

Attitude

Your **attitude** towards the customer is crucial to your ability to deliver excellent customer service. All customers are sensitive to the way you feel about them. For example, imagine that you go into a sports centre to ask for advice about the facilities available and the receptionist informs you that they are just going off-duty. As you require a lot of information, they will hand you over to the assistant on the next shift who starts in five minutes. In this situation you might feel that:

- you are asking for too much
- the receptionist can't be bothered to handle the enquiry
- the receptionist does not really care about the job or the customers because they want to go home.

In short, the receptionist's attitude gives the impression that they are not interested in you, the customer.

ACTIVITY

The 'attitude scale'

Your attitude towards and understanding of particular customer service situations say a lot about your attitude generally. Here is a quick quiz to see how you score on the attitude scale.

Consider the following statements and decide whether they apply **always, never** or **sometimes.** If you decide the answer to a question is 'sometimes', explain the situations in which this would apply.

1. It is all right to call a customer by their first name.
2. A member of staff should always stand up when dealing with a customer.
3. It is acceptable to chew gum when talking to a customer.
4. You should always wait for a customer to start a conversation.
5. You should maintain eye contact when dealing with a customer in person.
6. It is old-fashioned to address a customer as sir or madam.
7. It is acceptable to get angry with a very difficult customer.
8. It is wrong to complain about one customer to another customer.
9. Customers will understand if you are tired or unwell and make allowances.
10. All customers are equally important.
11. Your attitude and behaviour towards the customer will affect the extent to which he or she is satisfied.
12. The customer is always right.

Score rating

8–12 correct answers: an excellent attitude;

4–7 correct answers: not bad, but you probably need a bit more practice

0–3 correct answers: oh dear, perhaps you should read this chapter again – slowly! Answers are given on page 462.

ACTIVITY

Do you have the right attitude?

Look at this advertisement for a recreation assistant.

Fareham Borough Council
Fareham Leisure Centre

Recreation Assistant

Salary £8,412 to £12,663

Fareham Leisure Centre is one of the busiest centres in the southern region. It offers a comprehensive range of facilities including two swimming pools, sports halls, health and fitness suite, squash courts, sauna, solarium, creche, café and bar areas.

This is an exciting opportunity to be involved in all aspects of the Leisure Centre's operations, and play a key role in quality and service provision.

Experience of working within the leisure industry is essential, as is the possession of sound knowledge and good working practices. You should have excellent interpersonal skills and the desire to work as a team member showing flexibility and commitment. Ability to teach and supervise an extensive range of activities to various age groups, and the willingness to develop your sports coaching skills will be advantageous.

A relevant leisure qualification and various coaching/teaching awards are desirable. Possession of the R.L.S.S. Pool Lifeguard award, and a first aid certificate are essential.

You must, as part of a shift system, be prepared to work flexible and variable hours to cover the operational requirements of the centre. The salary has been set at a level sufficient to incorporate all necessary remuneration for evening and weekend work.

Identify the specific type of attitude looked for in the successful applicant.

Imagine that you are at an interview for the position of recreation assistant. What questions do you think you may be asked in order to evaluate whether or not you have the right attitude for the job? Think of some examples you could give in your answers to these questions. For example, could you give examples of your ability to work as a team member?

Your attitude towards customers may vary according to the situation. For example, it may be acceptable to be less formal with a child than you might be with an adult; you might address children by their first name but call adults 'sir' or 'madam'. However, there are some general rules about attitude that should apply to all customers, whatever their age or circumstances. These include being:

A ttentive
T houghtful
T olerant
I ndividual
T horough
U nflappable
D ependable
E nthusiastic

Personal presentation is important in any situation involving contact with a customer, whether it is face-to-face, in writing or over the telephone. On pages 352-367 we look at the specific features of these three methods of communication in detail.

ACTIVITY

Personal presentation role play

Think of a situation involving a member of staff and a customer in a visitor attraction. Be as inventive as you can. For example, the customer might be complaining, unable to speak English, have special needs or an unusual request.

Take turns to role-play the customer and the member of staff. Do not tell the staff member beforehand what your request will be, as it is important for it to be a surprise! You might like to plan this role play in advance and also dress appropriately for someone working in a visitor attraction. You may also be able to use this exercise for your unit assessment.

It would be useful if you could video each role play in this activity. You could then show the video to give group members an opportunity to evaluate the way in which their personal presentation affected the service they gave.

BUILD YOUR LEARNING

end of section activity

1 Select two different sorts of leisure and recreation organisation, i.e. ensure that they are not both sports centres, for example. Visit them as a customer and evaluate the staff's personal presentation based on the following criteria:

- first impressions
- appearance
- personal hygiene
- personality
- attitude

2 As a group, write a letter to each organisation and telephone them to ask for details about their products and services. The reason for your visit, letter and telephone call could be to ask about opening hours or discounts for groups, for example.

Identify the areas of good practice in staff presentation skills and make recommendations as to how they could be improved.

Keywords and phrases

You should know the meaning of the words and phrases listed below. If you are unsure about any of them, go back through the last four pages to refresh your understanding.

- Personal presentation
- First impressions
- Appearance
- Uniform
- Personal hygiene
- Personality
- Attitude

Types of customer

We have already seen how it is important to meet the needs of customers and achieve customer satisfaction.

Customers have different needs depending on who they are and the circumstances. For example, the needs of a customer on a conference in Disneyland, Paris will be different to those when they visit with their family for recreation.

It is important to be able to identify the different **types of customer** using a service, product or facility and understand how their needs may vary. First, let's begin by making a distinction between internal and external customers. **Internal customers** are members of staff or outside suppliers who contribute towards the service provided to external customers. They include:

- Colleagues. These are the people you work with directly and who have a similar status to you.
- Management and supervisors. Most employees have a direct line manager in the organisation – either a supervisor, head of department or manager.
- Staff teams. These are groups of staff who form a team to undertake specific functions or jobs. For example, a leisure centre may have a health and safety team comprising staff from different departments. Many hotels have a fire evacuation team that works to evacuate the building if the fire alarm sounds.
- Employees. If you are self-employed or own a company you may employ people to work for you.
- Staff in other functional departments or organisations who do not work directly with you but contribute to the job you do. For example, the personnel, finance, administration and maintenance departments in a local authority provide services to employees in the authority's recreational and sports facilities.

Organisations must provide effective customer service to internal customers in order to establish good working relationships between colleagues, managers and staff teams.

External customers are the people who actually buy or use an organisation's products and services. There are many ways of categorising external customers, depending to a large extent on the type of organisation and the nature of its business. Common ways of categorising types or groups of customers include by:

- individual
- group
- age
- culture
- language spoken
- specific needs, such as wheelchair access, sensory disabilities and people with young children.

Individuals and groups

It is important to realise that although customers may use a product or service on an **individual** basis, they may also do so as part of a **group**. For example, customers taking exercise classes may do so in the hope of meeting and socialising with others. Other customers may appreciate the fact that they are on their own and prefer to be treated individually rather than grouped together with others. Guests at a private health club such as Champneys in London, for example, pay for the privilege of individual and personal service.

Many organisations identify specific types of individual and groups that use their products and services in order to provide the level of service that meets their needs and expectations. For example, Crest Hotels saw that there were more and more businesswomen who needed to travel and stay in hotels on their own. The chain introduced Lady Crest rooms, furnished and decorated with fabrics, ornaments and pictures it believed would appeal to such women. Crest provided a range of toiletries, magazines and provisions to appeal to female guests in addition to those facilities that businessmen received such as a desk, stationery and mini-bar. The scheme was a success because the level of service exceeded customer expectations and therefore gave Crest Hotels a competitive advantage over its rivals.

ACTIVITY

Jane's internal customers

Jane is the front-of-house manager in an hotel that is part of a national chain. She supervises three receptionists, a telephonist, a cashier and two hall porters. The hotel has a general manager and a deputy manager to whom Jane reports. She liaises on a day-to-day basis with other heads of department. She is part of the hotel's quality review group and also the front-of-house representative for the hotel's staff consultative committee which meets once a month to discuss general issues. Many reservations come from the company's central reservations department at head office or through recommendations from the local tourist information centre.

Jane works closely with the hotel's marketing manager on promoting the hotel's facilities, but receives most of the promotional leaflets and brochures from the head office marketing department. She has recently set up a customer service advisory group in the hotel, meeting with a member of staff from each department to discuss how customer service could be improved. Jane carries out most staff training within her department herself but sends key members of staff to residential training courses run by the company's training office.

Fill in the following boxes to show all of Jane's internal customers. Be specific, for example, under 'colleagues', specify the departments concerned.

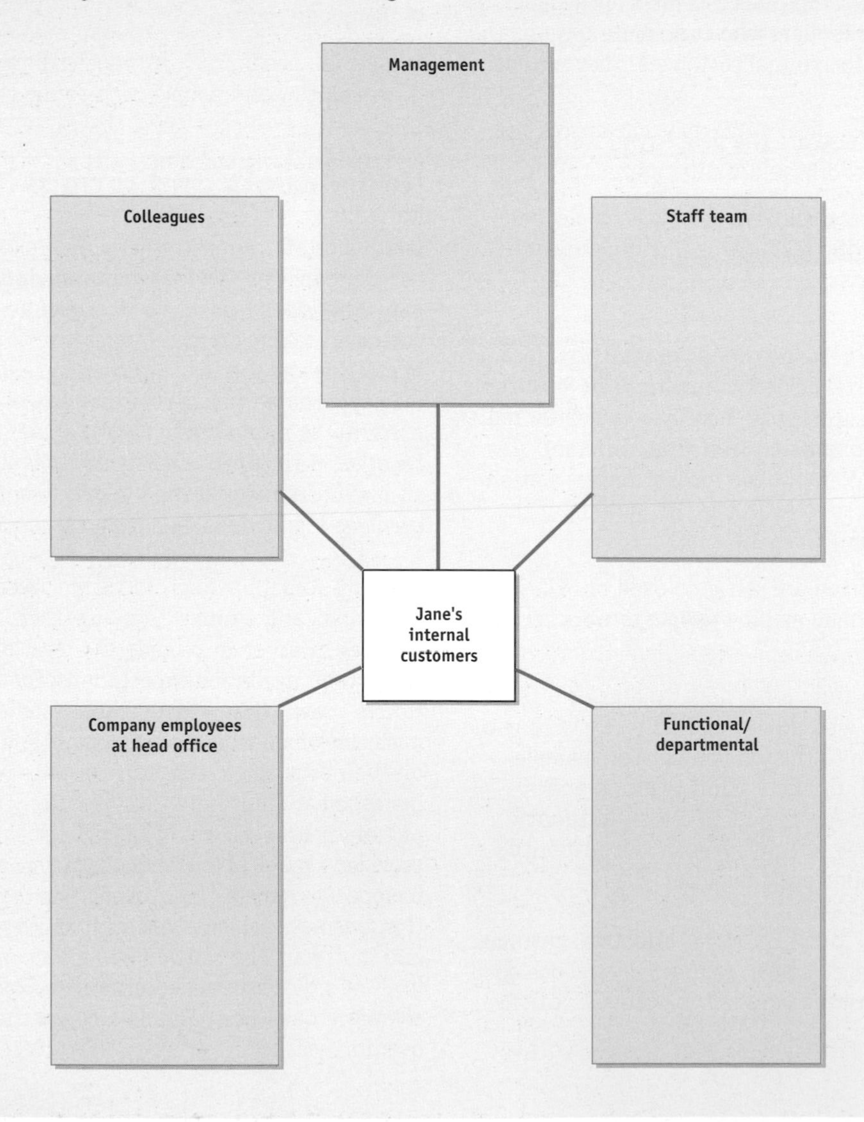

Many leisure and recreation providers serve groups and the individuals who comprise them in ways that enhance and promote customer service. For example, the exclusivity of the service offered to members of Wentworth Golf Club is a key part of its attraction, as the case study below shows.

CASE STUDY

Wentworth Golf Club

Mention the name 'Wentworth' and a whole host of associations springs to mind. It's not just the golf; Wentworth feels like something bigger – tradition, Englishness, exclusiveness and status. 'This is not just a golf, tennis and health club,' says Julian Small, managing director of Wentworth. 'This is the Wentworth Club. We are a twenty-first century facility and have taken ideas from many of the leading health clubs to create a club for the whole family and the individual.'

The club retains its exclusivity while being relaxed, friendly and non-intimidating. The membership selection procedure is an interesting Wentworth idiosyncrasy in itself. There are three stages to the process: a prospective Wentworth Tennis and Health Club member must be proposed by an existing member. The applicant then has to go through an informal interview with Julian Small and a member of the Tennis and Health Club Committee – the club's advisory body. After this formality, the name of the prospective member goes up on the club noticeboard for seven days, during which time any member has an opportunity to raise an objection. No objection, and Wentworth welcomes its new member.

Says Small, 'Members of Wentworth are successful people in their own right and come here to enjoy their leisure time. They are not honed athletes and don't join with a singular agenda of losing weight, for example; they are buying into a lifestyle. You'll find there is more Pimms served on the tennis courts than aces!

'We want to achieve a clubby feel,' says Small. 'It is important that it doesn't come across as stark. We are hoping to put up some pictures of people enjoying the club; famous people who play here. That will bring a sense of place and community.'

Fully qualified fitness consultants (not instructors) are available if members require one-to-one tuition and the fitness adviser is Josh Salzmann, who is the personal trainer to the stars, and invites clients like Kenneth Branagh and the Duchess of York to train at Wentworth.

'Treating people as individuals is exceptionally important. All members fill in a health questionnaire on joining, and we invite them to have a fitness consultation, where they fill in a programme questionnaire – this consultation lasts just 15 minutes. We use the word "consultation" rather than "assessment", because that is more like an interviewer and interviewee situation. We want to listen to what they say.' Small develops this further, using the analogy of the member driving the car, while the fitness consultant holds the map. 'On the programme questionnaire we don't suggest a fitness test; we ask open questions. The aim is to help the individual set achievable objectives.'

Further facilities are provided for the enjoyment of family groups and juniors – the junior lounge and crèche. The junior lounge is a social space for children on the lower-ground floor with a television, video game and table football. There is plenty of comfortable seating, and Simpsons posters on the walls. Demand from families is great, as people are drawn to this area of Surrey by the good schooling, says Small. However, the sale of junior memberships needs to be handled sensitively, as many more could create potential problems for adult members.

The fully staffed crèche is provided as a service to Tennis and Health Club members only, who must be on site while their child is in the crèche. It can take up to 16 children in a planned programme of activities. There's also a private secure garden. 'We have made living at Wentworth like living on a resort,' says Small. 'It's paradise!'

Source: *Leisure Opportunities*

ACTIVITY

Wentworth Golf Club

Read the case study on Wentworth and discuss the different ways in which the club meets the needs of both individuals and groups.

People of different ages

Customer age groups can be classified as:

- children: babies, toddlers, older children, teenagers
- adults: young adults, middle-aged adults, senior citizens.

However, customers will often be in the company of friends or relatives, so that a group may comprise a combination of ages. Some common combinations are:

- parents with young children and/or babies
- parents with teenage children
- adults with grandchildren
- adults with senior citizen parents.

Although the age of customers is important, it is equally important not to make assumptions about customers' needs based solely on their age.

▲ A group of customers may comprise a range of ages

Many leisure and recreation organisations promote specific facilities and services for people of **different ages**, particularly young children and babies. This can be effective in encouraging customers to visit, as they are reassured that their needs will be met. The extract below shows the special services offered to parents with babies and toddlers who visit Alton Towers.

Babies and toddlers

Baby changing facilities are available across the park – see the map for details. A free milk warming service is available in the Medical Centre and nappies are sold in Towers Street and Festival Park - see the map for locations.

Why not hire a pushchair from the Guest Facilities Office at the top of Towers Street? There's a lot of walking to do. As proud winners of the Tommy's Campaign 'Parent friendly' award for 1995, Alton Towers tries to make sure that the needs of guests with babies and toddlers are well catered for.

Source: Alton Towers leaflet

ACTIVITY

Customer age groups

Look at this list of customers and discuss what you think their specific customer service needs might be.

- Young, single adults going to a three-day music festival.
- Two elderly grandparents taking their three young grandchildren to a theme park.
- Two 50-year-olds taking a beginners' swimming class.
- A couple with a six-month-old baby at a National Park.
- A 70-year-old woman at a theatre.

Different cultures

It is often important to categorise customers by their cultural background in order to provide them with effective customer service. **Cultural background** influences people's traditions, tastes, preferences and opinions and it will therefore affect the type and level of service they need and expect. For example, some cinemas show films in different languages to cater for large ethnic populations in their areas.

As with different age groups, the cultural background of customers is useful in identifying their needs, but it is equally important not to make assumptions based on culture. At best, this may result in customer dissatisfaction; at worst, it may offend and upset the customer. It is very useful, however, to understand some of the more common cultural differences, such as the way in which different cultures use gestures (see Figure 5.7).

Language

Foreign visitors are an increasingly important part of the UK tourism market. Many such visitors may speak little or no English, but will expect staff to be able to deal with their needs despite the language barrier. Large organisations often employ multi-lingual staff to communicate with **non-English speaking** visitors. However, even if you are not proficient in other languages there is still a great deal that you can do to help the communication process, such as:

- using gestures when pointing out directions
- using diagrams and pictures
- keeping copies of dictionaries so that you can translate key words
- making the effort to learn a few simple phrases in some common languages. An ability to say hello, goodbye, please and thank you in two or three foreign languages will please your foreign guests and show that you care enough to make the effort.

You should not forget that even foreign visitors whose native language is English may still have difficulty in understanding some words. For example, American English differs from British English in important ways, including different names for everyday items, which can lead to confusion.

Figure 5.7: Watch your hands

In Greece, Spain and Turkey the fig gesture (fist with thumb protruding between index and middle fingers) is considered very rude

In Egypt the right hand over the heart means 'no thank you'

In Greece an open palm and extended fingers (like a 'five' sign) can be insulting

In Japan, Korea and Mexico making a circle or semi-circle with forefinger and thumb is a symbol for money; in France the same gesture means something worthless; in Brazil it is very rude; in the US it means OK

In Morocco and parts of the Middle East the thumbs-up sign is an obscenity

ACTIVITY

American English

The British Tourist Authority provides a guide to the English language for visiting American tourists called *Talk Like A Brit!* Look at the 14 American words listed below. If an American asked you for these would you know what they meant? (Answers on page 462.)

- traffic circle
- divided highway
- freeway
- sidewalk
- second floor
- faucet
- jelly
- check
- liquor store
- chips
- restroom
- ATM
- pocket book
- bandaid

Specific needs

Some customers have **specific needs** that may require special customer service in addition to that provided to meet the general needs of everyone. These include:

- sensory disabilities such as visual impairment, hearing impairment or speech impairment.
- mobility problems such as the need for a wheelchair, zimmer frame or walking stick.
- literacy and/or numeracy difficulties.
- dietary requirements such as vegetarianism, nut allergies or religious restrictions.
- people with young children.

There is often a lot of misunderstanding about people with specific needs. This may lead to inappropriate service delivery. Many people are even unsure as to how to refer to a customer's special needs and may use 'labels' that are offensive. Figure 5.8 lists some key do's and don'ts.

Figure 5.8: Avoiding offensive language

Don't say	Say instead
A cripple	Disabled person
Invalid	Disabled person
Handicapped	Disabled
Mentally retarded/handicapped	Person with learning disabilities/difficulties
Deaf aid	Hearing aid
The disabled	People with impaired mobility/a disability
Spastic	Person with cerebral palsy
Suffering from/afflicted by/a victim of Confined to a wheelchair/wheelchair bound	Wheelchair user
Deaf and dumb	Profoundly deaf
Disabled toilet	Accessible toilet

People with specific needs require special service, but they do not want to be made to feel different, stupid or a nuisance. They want the same level of service that every customer receives, plus a little extra care and consideration for their particular needs. Remember that people are often disabled, not by their impairment, but by the environment and the attitudes of the people they encounter.

There are also legal requirements and guidelines for people with disabilities or specific needs. For example, the government's National Tourism Strategy emphasises the need for England and Wales to improve the way in which experiences and attractions are provided to **people with disabilities** and specific needs. One of the main reasons for this is to attract more foreign visitors and to improve the quality of tourism for an ageing population.

In addition, the **Disability Discrimination Act 1995** was introduced to end discrimination against people with disabilities. Of particular relevance to the leisure and recreation industry is the section of the Act that deals with access to goods, facilities and services.

Some of its main requirements are as follows:

- Service providers cannot refuse a service or offer a lower standard or terms of service to a person with a disability for a reason relating to that disability.
- Providers must consider making changes to the products or services that they offer so that customers with disabilities are not excluded.
- From 2004, providers must take reasonable steps to remove any physical barriers that make it unreasonably difficult for customers with disabilities to gain access to goods and services.

It is important to realise that, while removing physical barriers is a positive move, the attitudes of staff are much more significant. An excellent example of the way specific needs can be met through caring customer service is provided by York's Theatre Royal, which provides a special leaflet outlining the wide range of facilities and services that it offers to customers with specific needs (Figure 5.9).

Figure 5.9: York Theatre Royal's guide at a glance

A guide at a glance

- There is level access from St Leonard's Place into the Box Office, Foyer and Stalls and a wheelchair lift to the Café Bar and payphone.
- Car parking spaces are available nearby in Bootham Row, Union Terrace and Marygate car parks.
- Spaces for up to 10 wheelchair users are available in the Stalls.
- There is a toilet suitable for wheelchair users.
- There is a Sennheiser infrared system for deaf people and those who are hard of hearing.
- There are sign language interpreted and audio described performances for each of the Theatre Royal's own productions and for many visiting companies.
- Taped and large print copies of the theatre's season brochure are available.
- Guide and hearing dogs are welcome at the theatre.
- If you would like to be kept up to date on the Theatre Royal's facilities and services for disabled people, please let us know and we will place you on our free mailing list.
- Disabled people can claim the concessionary ticket price for themselves and one other person.

ACTIVITY

Special facilities and services

Visit a leisure and recreation facility such as a leisure centre or visitor attraction. Make a list of any special facilities or services for people who have visual impairments, mobility problems and hearing impairments, and for non-English speakers.

Do you think the facilities and services provided meet the specific needs of these customers?

People with specific needs also include customers with young children. In recent years leisure and recreation organisations have been quick to respond to the growing pressure to provide better facilities and services for this type of customer. Well-equipped changing and feeding rooms, baby-food and bottle-warming services, and free pushchair loans are commonly offered by many organisations.

Depending on the nature of the leisure and recreation product or service on offer, any group or individual customer can have specific needs that need to be identified and satisfied. The case study below highlights some of the specific needs that women may have when participating in sporting activities.

CASE STUDY

Women and sport

In 1999 Sport England established a steering group to look at women's participation in sport. One of the main aims was to explore the perceived 'gender gap' in sports participation that results in only two women for every three men actually participating in sport. Research, conducted by Kit Campbell Associates, led to the development of guidance notes for recreation managers and local authorities. The main recommendations from the research highlighted four key barriers to women's participation:

1 **Confidence.** Many women think that sporting activities are male-dominated and they lack the necessary confidence to start. They are also reluctant to be seen in sports clothes and believe that they will be regarded as unfit.

2 **Comfort.** Many women had real concerns about personal safety when travelling to and taking part in sports activities. This was particularly true when they were on their own or using public transport.

3 **Choice.** Some women believed that there was little real choice for women when it came to sports activities. This problem was made worse by concerns about childcare at times when activities were available.

4 **Convenience.** Because women's leisure time tends to be more fragmented due to work, child and domestic commitments, many felt unable to commit themselves to a regular sporting activity that took place at a set time each week.

Source: adapted from *Leisure Opportunities*

ACTIVITY

Women and sport

As a group, discuss what sports providers could do in terms of customer service to meet the specific needs of women and overcome some of the barriers listed above. For example, providing 'mother and child only' parking spaces adjacent to the main entrance could help overcome some concerns about personal safety.

When dealing with customers with specific needs, it is not only the provision of extra facilities that is important. Staff need to be trained in appropriate skills so that they can advise and help customers to use facilities. For example, the Scottish Tourist Board produce an excellent book entitled *Tourism for All* that gives clear advice on meeting the needs of customers with specific needs. An extract is shown on the next page, giving guidance to staff in leisure, health and sports facilities.

We have looked at the range of different types of customer and how their specific needs and expectations can be met. Of course, it is often very different when you are faced with real-life situations, particularly at the beginning of your career, so you may feel apprehensive.

Practice and experience will help you deal effectively with all customer service requirements and in time you will discover that your confidence and expertise have grown. The activity on page 344 gives you the opportunity to start gaining some experience by carrying out some realistic role plays and evaluating how well you perform.

Providing Services for All - Section 2 - YOUR ROLE WITHIN THE ORGANISATION

10 YOUR ROLE WITHIN THE ORGANISATION

1 Guidelines for all staff

These guidelines will help everyone working in the tourism industry to respond to the needs of disabled customers. The suggestions below are based on the principle that all of your customers are special and have varying needs – whether they require a vegetarian meal, a fax point in an accessible position, a nappy changing facility, a wheelchair accessible bathroom or shower, a no-smoking bedroom, a vibrating alarm pillow pad, a buffet selection within easy reach, an induction loop, a telephone with an inductive coupler or a meal for their guide-dog or service animal.

As a starting point, people working in tourism should also know whether their establishment has been inspected under the Tourism for All National Accessible Scheme and should be familiar with the relevant Standard, as set out on pages 41-48.

ALWAYS ASK GUESTS, *'MAY I HELP YOU'.*

- Listen carefully to what guests say about their requirements.
- Have a pad and pen handy to write down information when verbal communication is difficult.
- Be ready to give clear directions to accessible toilets, lifts, emergency exits and public areas.
- Face disabled people, speak to them at a normal volume and speed.
- Be aware that most blind people have some sight.
- When communicating with someone who lip-reads, you will need to face the light and avoid speaking with exaggerated lip movements.
- Be clear when giving directions and remember blind and visually impaired guests will be unable to see gestures, but deaf people will find them helpful.
- Make no assumptions about guests who have limited mobility, a sensory disability or speech and language dificulties.
- Do whatever is required without drawing attention to the guest
- Always ask guests.'May I help you?'

Source: Tourism for All, *Providing service for all*, Scottish Tourist Board

ACTIVITY

Customer service role plays

These role plays involve all the different types of customers that we have discussed. Each member of the group should select and perform a range of role plays in order to practise dealing with different types of customers. You can use this activity for your assessment evidence. You can record your performance on a proforma like the one shown on page 460.

1 Mr Jones is an elderly gentleman on a coach trip to an industrial museum. He likes to sit in a front seat because there is more room. When he boards the coach, the front seats are already occupied: two by other passengers and two by couriers who have to be next to the microphone situated at the front of the coach.

Roles: Mr Jones, two passengers, two couriers.

2 Lizzie is three years old and very excited about her first visit to a water park with her parents. She is running around the edge of the pool and collides with a lifeguard, falling over and cutting her knee. There are clear signs asking customers to refrain from running.

Roles: Lizzie, Lizzie's mother and father, the lifeguard.

3 Wayne is attending a karaoke night at the local rugby club. He has had too much beer and is trying to start a fight with another man who Wayne claims has taken his girlfriend. The worried girlfriend asks the bar staff to help.

Roles: Wayne, other man, two bar staff.

4 Maureen is a guide at a stately home. She is showing a group of visitors around when one of the guests faints. A cleaner is working nearby.

Roles: Maureen, fainting visitor, cleaner, rest of tour group.

5 An American couple makes the restroom their first visit at a theme park but are disgusted to find it dirty, with no soap or

towels. They complain to a member of staff who tells them to go to the customer service desk.

Roles: American couple, customer service assistant.

6 A party of visitors arrives at a football match with a member who is in a wheelchair. They have written in advance asking for assistance in gaining access. When the party arrives, the main car park is full and the only available parking spaces are on a lower level reached by 30 steps.

Roles: visitor in wheelchair, car park attendant.

7 A hotel fire alarm has sounded at 10.30 p.m. All the guests have evacuated the building, apart from Mrs Simcox, an elderly lady who is standing at reception in her dressing gown and slippers refusing to go outside because it is snowing.

Roles: Mrs Simcox, receptionist.

8 Mr and Mrs Rodriguez are from Spain and speak very little English. They have entered a fast-food restaurant to ask for directions to the main shopping area.

Roles: Mr and Mrs Rodriguez, counter assistant.

9 Mr and Mrs Cohen are interested in booking a wedding reception for their daughter at a hotel. As devout Jews they abide by strict dietary laws. They would like the hotel to permit an outside chef to oversee food preparation to ensure that it is kosher. The hotel's chef is not very keen on the idea of an outsider running his kitchen, even if it is only for one day.

Roles: Mr and Mrs Cohen, hotel manager, hotel chef.

10 Miss Carmichael has gone to a sports centre to find out about hiring a badminton court. She has a profound hearing impairment but can lip-read.

Roles: Miss Carmichael, sports centre receptionist.

BUILD YOUR LEARNING

End of section activity

Select two leisure or recreation organisations. Identify the different types of customers that they serve and evaluate how each organisation meets the particular needs of different customers, including:

- individuals
- groups
- people of different ages
- people from different cultures
- non-English speakers
- people with specific needs, e.g. wheelchair access, sensory disabilities and people with young children.

You will need to decide the criteria you are going to use for your evaluation. For example, you might decide that some of the specific needs of people with young children are pushchair access, changing and bottle-warming facilities, children's menus, etc.

Make recommendations as to how each organisation could improve the service it offers to these types of customers. Compare the effectiveness of the two organisations in meeting specific customer needs.

Keywords and phrases

You should know the meaning of the words and phrases listed below. If you are unsure about any of them, go back through the last 10 pages to refresh your understanding.

- Types of customers
- Internal customers
- External customers
- Individuals
- Groups
- Different ages
- Cultural background
- Non-English speaking
- Specific needs
- People with disabilities
- Disability Discrimination Act 1995

Selling skills

Selling skills are an important part of customer service. Providing good customer service should always be more important than simply selling a product or service to the customer. As a member of staff, your main **sales objective** should be to satisfy customers by meeting their needs and expectations. In doing this you will almost inevitably sell the customer a product or service. But the selling aspect of your relationship with the customer should only be the end result, when appropriate, of good customer service.

Staff must be able to conduct sales transactions in a variety of situations. **High-quality sales service** means ensuring that the advice, information and recommendations you give to a customer suggest that you fully understand a product or service and are confident it will meet or exceed his or her needs and expectations. Selling is not just the responsibility of designated sales staff: all staff need to understand the importance of effective selling skills and put them into practice.

Every time a customer asks you for advice or information you are probably in a selling situation. The advice or information you supply is part of selling and customer service.

In many circumstances you may not realise that you will be selling something until the customer approaches you. For example, a person may approach a lifeguard at a swimming pool and ask about lessons for children. In other situations, for example when a person makes an appointment to discuss a possible wedding reception at a restaurant, you will have advance notice.

Clearly, your task is easier if you know about the situation beforehand, because you can then make sure you have all the necessary information. However, in any selling situation there are certain steps you can take to ensure that you meet the customer's needs and expectations.

Generally, you should have excellent product knowledge. This means being completely familiar with the products or services that your organisation offers. In addition, in order to carry out their duties and responsibilities, staff also need certain personal qualities. Figure 5.10 shows some of the personal qualities required.

Figure 5.10 Personal qualities of sales staff

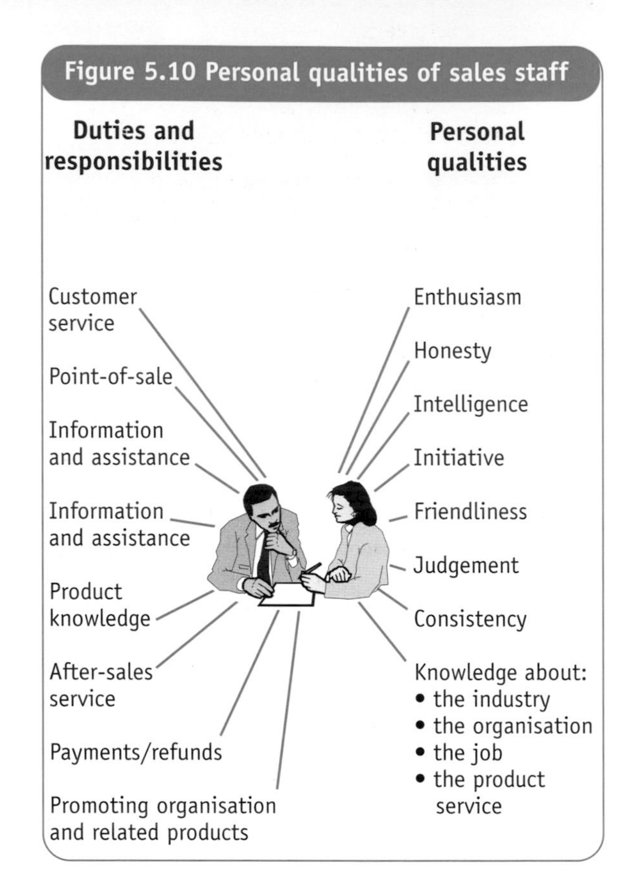

Let's look at some of these qualities in more detail.

- **Enthusiasm**: showing that you are enthusiastic about your job, the organisation, its products and the customers.
- **Honesty**: giving truthful advice and information to customers to ensure that the product they buy will meet their needs and expectations.
- **Intelligence**: showing that you have really thought about the customers and understand how to meet their needs.
- **Initiative**: able to react quickly and efficiently on an individual basis.
- **Friendliness**: showing that customers are welcome, not a nuisance or an interruption.
- **Judgement**: able to assess a situation and the needs of the customer so that the service is appropriate.
- **Consistency**: ensuring that you always give the same high level of customer service regardless of the situation or needs of the customer.
- **Knowledge**: knowing enough about the leisure and recreation industry, your organisation, your job and the products and services that you offer, to provide any advice, information or assistance that the customer requires.

There are a number of selling skills used by the leisure and recreation industry:

- raising customer awareness
- establishing rapport with the customer
- investigating customer needs
- presenting the product or service
- closing the sale
- delivering after-sales service.

Raising customer awareness

Frequently, customers do not buy particular products and services from an organisation simply because they are not aware that they exist. Therefore, one of the key selling skills that you need to acquire is the ability to raise customers' awareness by highlighting products and services that you think might satisfy their needs and expectations. For example, staff in a sports clothing shop may suggest that a customer buying a pair of trainers might be interested in a specific cleaning product. Bar staff in a theatre bar might suggest to theatregoers that they pre-order their interval drinks.

However, you need to make sure that you only highlight suitable products or you risk giving the impression that you do not understand the customer's needs and are merely trying to increase sales. Disneyland, Paris produces a sales manual for staff to enable them to sell the park to customers. The extract below is from the section about answering customers' questions and therefore raising awareness of what is offered. See how much you learn from reading it and note the extent to which it raises your awareness of what Disneyland has to offer.

CASE STUDY

Disneyland Paris sales manual

What is Euro Disneyland, Paris?

Euro Disneyland Paris is more than just a theme park, it's a complete destination. The exciting and unique theme park is complemented by top quality entertainment and dining, excellent sport and leisure facilities, 27 holes of golf, a state of the art convention centre, and six beautifully themed hotels.

Isn't Euro Disneyland, Paris just for kids?

No, Euro Disneyland Paris is not just for children. It's a fun destination for all age groups. It is designed to have something for everyone, sparkling shows, themed architecture, fascinating technology and, of course, thrilling rides. With hotels ranging from economy to luxury, and self-catering, there is something to fit every taste and budget.

Why go to Euro Disneyland, Paris?

People go to Euro Disneyland Paris to have fun and nobody has more experience in providing fun than Disney. Euro Disneyland Paris is perfect for a short-break and it's a great place to celebrate a birthday, anniversary or some other special event. It is also an ideal add-on to a longer trip to France or Europe.

When should we go to Euro Disneyland, Paris?

Euro Disneyland Paris is open 365 days a year, so it can fit into everybody's schedule. The entertainment changes seasonally so there's always something new to see. Some 80 per cent of the attractions are covered and almost all facilities are well adapted to cooler seasons, plus seasonal pricing means even better value for money for your clients.

Establishing rapport

Establishing rapport with the customer means encouraging a conversation in which you are both communicating on the same level and establishing your sympathetic attention to the customer's needs. This requires good judgement, for while no customer likes to be ignored, neither do they like to feel pressured or rushed by over-enthusiastic sales staff. It is usually possible to tell from a customer's body language and behaviour whether they feel comfortable talking to you and want to pursue the conversation. However, in any situation it is important to greet each customer and ask if you can be of help.

Identifying customer needs

To begin with, the easiest way of **identifying customer needs** is to ask: 'Can I help you?' The reply will indicate what further questions you need to ask to identify the customer's specific needs. For example, if a customer expresses an interest in booking hotel accommodation you might ask about preferences for type of room, facilities required, any special requests, etc.

ACTIVITY

Selling the 'product'

Imagine that you work at the Dorchester Leisure Centre, which offers the exercise classes listed opposite. With a colleague, role-play the parts of a potential new customer and the centre's receptionist. The customer should decide in advance the type and level of exercise class that interests them. As the receptionist, identify the customer's needs and suggest suitable classes. Talk through the proposal with your customer. Can you sell them the product?

DORCHESTER LEISURE CENTRE

Programme of classes

Fitness levels 1 (lowest) – 5 (highest)

Beginners Aerobics – Tuesday/Thursday 7-8pm

Fitness level: 1

Intermediate Aerobics – Monday/Wednesday/Friday 5.30-6.30pm

Fitness level: 2-3

Advanced Aerobics – Monday/Thursday 6-7pm

Fitness level: 4-5

STEP Aerobics – Monday/Saturday 10-11am

Fitness level: 3

Spinning (using exercise bikes to music) – Thursday/Friday 8-9pm

Fitness level: 4-5

Pilates (low impact) – Wednesday 9-10am/Thursday 5-6pm/Saturday 3-4pm

Fitness level: 1-3

Yoga – Monday 6-7pm/Thursday 11-12 noon/Saturday 2-3pm

Fitness level: 1

Presenting the product or service

Staff need to be able to **present the product or service** to the customer in a way that satisfies the customer's needs. This process usually involves considering the available options and possibly suggesting compromises. For example, a customer may wish to book a week in a luxury lakeside lodge in a holiday centre such as Center Parcs or Oasis, but be unable to afford it. The reservations clerk may be able to suggest less expensive accommodation, staying at a cheaper time of year, or a short-break stay rather than a whole week's holiday.

ACTIVITY

Presenting the product

Obtain some leaflets from visitor attractions and heritage sites. Take it in turns to role play the presentation of suitable products to the following customers:

- an elderly couple
- two young adults
- a family with a baby and young child
- a couple in their mid 30s
- a middle-aged couple from America

Make sure that you choose to present the attractions you think would suit each particular customer and describe them in a way that reflects customer needs. After each role play discuss the extent to which you gave an honest and realistic presentation of the products.

Closing the sale

Closing the sale means actually getting the customer to buy the selected product. Not all sales can be closed straight away. Often the customer may wish to go away and think about it or discuss it with someone else. In these circumstances, it is frequently acceptable to suggest that you reserve the product or service for the customer until he or she decides whether or not to buy it. You might also suggest that you contact the customer in a few days for a decision.

A further aspect of closing the sale is taking a customer's payment. It is a duty of staff to ensure that customers pay the correct amount for products and, from a service point of view, it is important to consider the way payment is asked for and handled. One well-known credit card company used the advertising slogan: 'That will do nicely'. This phrase sums up the sort of attitude that is desirable when accepting customers' payments: cheerful, friendly, polite and grateful.

There are four basic steps to accepting payment from customers:

- **C**alculate accurately. Make sure that the bill is added up correctly and laid out clearly so that the customer understands it.
- **A**sk politely. Saying '£4.50' is not polite. A far better request might be: 'That will be £4.50 please, madam.'
- **S**ay thank you when the customer hands you their payment.
- **H**and over the change and a receipt.

The first letters of these four points spell out the word cash. However, there are many other ways that a customer can pay, such as by cheque, traveller's cheque, credit card, debit card or company account. You need to know how to deal with all these forms of payment, since a mistake can prove very costly for your organisation and result in dissatisfied customers.

After-sales service

Good customer service does not end when customers hand over their money. The service should continue after the sale has been made to show that you care about the customer. Sometimes the **after-sales service** will be immediate, such as asking customers if they have enjoyed their visit to a museum and listening to the comments that they make.

In other situations, there may be a need for service a long time after the sale has been made. For example, a customer subscribing to satellite television may require after-sales support and help in using the system. Figure 5.11 shows the after-sales help provided by Sky customer services.

Figure 5.11: Sky after-sales services

How to get further help
If you have problems and the above steps don't work, call Customer Services:

- Write down your receiver make and model number. Then call Customer Services on 0990 10 20 30 and select option three from the menu. A member of staff will try to help you solve the problem over the phone.
- If your equipment needs repair and is still under warranty, we'll help you get in touch with your warranty service company.
- If your equipment needs repair and the warranty has run out, we can arrange for a Sky In-Service engineer to visit your home for a reasonable cost. And while we are repairing your equipment, we will loan you a replacement at no extra charge.
- If your equipment can't be repaired, we will help you choose a replacement from a range of reasonably priced options.

It is important to remember this maxim: 'Once a customer, always a customer'. In other words, once you have established a relationship with a customer, he or she is entitled to receive good service from you in the future, even if you are not in a position to sell them something.

AIDA

In marketing, a technique known as AIDA is used in the design of advertising and promotional materials (see Unit 4, page 308). This technique is of equal value when considering effective selling techniques. **AIDA** is a mnemonic that stands for

Attention
Interest
Desire
Action

AIDA is useful because it expresses the process of selling in simple terms. The first stage of selling is to ensure that you have the full attention of the customer. Having achieved this, you need to create interest by describing the product in a way that sounds attractive. This will result in the customer desiring the product and therefore taking action by buying it.

ACTIVITY

Selling skills role play

Obtain a *What's On* guide for your area or a local newspaper that lists leisure and recreation facilities and events (the weekend editions are usually best). Imagine you are on work placement at a local hotel and the following guests have asked you for recommendations as to what they could do for the day.

- Mr and Mrs Jacob, senior citizens. Have never visited the area before. They particularly like anything historical. Mr Jacob is in a wheelchair.
- Miss Shogbesan and Miss Adanouga, both 18 years old. Have limited spending money, but both enjoy sports and outdoor activities.
- Mr and Mrs Wallis and their 5-year-old twins. They are particularly concerned about how to occupy the children during the poor weather.
- Miss Carruthers, 55 years old. Would like something active but is worried about visiting a facility on her own.
- Mrs Walton and her daughter, Louise (19 years old). Louise likes watersports but her mother does not.
- Mr and Mrs Fortune, both 30 years old. Are seeing friends all day but would like something to go to the cinema in the evening.
- Mr Nolan, 25 and Mr Wong, 26 . Would like to go ten pin bowling.
- Mr and Mrs Cook and their two children, Ben (12) and Samantha (15). Samantha did not want to come to the hotel with her parents as she thinks that they will spend all day looking at museums and art galleries.

Take turns at role playing the customers and the hotel receptionist, advising each customer on suitable leisure and recreation activities. You should try to

- establish a rapport with each customer
- raise customer awareness about the different excursions that might meet their needs
- investigate each customer's specific needs
- present the possible activities
- close the sale.

Selling is an important part of excellent customer service because it helps to ensure that customer needs and expectations are met. However, it is equally important to understand that making a sale is never the only objective in a selling situation. Pressurising a customer to buy a product or service that they do not really want may result in a short-term gain, but the end result is almost certainly a dissatisfied customer who will probably not return.

BUILD YOUR LEARNING

Keywords and phrases

You should know the meaning of the words and phrases listed below. If you are unsure about any of them, go back through the last five pages to refresh your understanding.

- Selling skills
- High-quality sales service
- Sales objective
- Raising customer awareness
- Establishing rapport
- Identifying customer needs
- Presenting the product or service
- Closing the sale
- After-sales service
- AIDA

End of section activity

1 Select two leisure or recreation organisations and evaluate the selling skills of their staff by visiting each as a customer. For example, you could visit:

- a local museum or art gallery and ask about special events or exhibitions
- a leisure centre and ask about exercise classes
- a cinema and ask about future screenings that are suitable for under-18 year olds
- telephone a visitor attraction and ask about discounted rates for student groups.

2 For each organisation, identify and evaluate how the staff used the following sales skills:

- raising customer awareness
- establishing rapport with customers
- investigating customer needs
- presenting the products or services
- closing the sale.

3 Use AIDA to identify the effectiveness of the selling skills of staff in each organisation. Give examples of how the staff could deliver after-sales service.

4 Following your investigation, suggest ways in which the staff could improve their selling skills.

Dealing with customers

Nearly everyone who works in the leisure and recreation industry is required to deal with customers on a regular basis. The contact might be face-to-face, on the telephone or in writing.

Face-to-face communication

Face-to-face communication has many advantages but only if you understand how to use it well. For example, your appearance can help create a positive impression.

You can also use facial expressions and gestures to help you communicate more effectively. Different communication skills will be required for situations involving groups and individuals. For example, when communicating with a group you will need to ensure that all group members understand you. This can often be difficult with mixed groups, such as a tour group with adults and small children: the adults may want detailed information, whereas the children will quickly become bored if the tour is too formal and factual.

ACTIVITY

Appealing to children

Look at the text below from the leaflet for the Mysteries of Egypt exhibition at Goodwood House.

Most young children are fascinated by ancient Egypt and study it in depth at primary school. However, this leaflet is clearly written for adults. Imagine that you are a tour guide for the exhibition and have a school party of 15 nine-year-olds to show around. Can you rewrite the leaflet so that it would appeal to this group? You can make up some stories and details if you like, but try to keep them realistic! Try role playing the tour, using your new text with the rest of the group.

Mysteries of Egypt at Goodwood House

The Regency splendour of Goodwood's Egyptian State Dining Room is guaranteed to make visitors catch their breath.

Soon after Napoleon's campaign on the Nile, the third Duke of Richmond decorated his dining room with this striking scheme.

Now, 200 years later, it can be seen again. Thanks to the Earl of March, who now lives in Goodwood House, we can marvel at this dramatic recreation of the Egyptian scheme after two years of intensive restoration.

The stunning scagliola marbled walls reflect the light both by day and by night, making this a room full of beautiful, exotic mystery exactly as the 3rd Duke had planned. Majestic purple drapes highlighted by flashes of Egyptian turquoise frame the windows beneath their gilded temple pelmets while golden scarabs, cobras, vultures and crocodiles add exotic interest to the stunning cornice.

Goodwood House has taken on new life. The grand Yellow Drawing Room forms a glowing heart to the house with its ottomans, sofas and French chairs beautifully covered in newly-woven yellow silk. Every painting from the vast collection has been rehung. The Ballroom arrangement faithfully follows a sketch laid down – but never realised – by the Duke before his death in 1806. The English paintings, including works by Van Dyck, Stubbs, Canaletto and Reynolds are unrivalled as a group and the Sèvres porcelain dinner service has been superbly redisplayed.

The family's French descent is reflected in the 18th century furniture and tapestries while the Scottish history can be seen in portraits and landscapes. New gilding provides the perfect setting for these old favourites.

Today, whilst still being used by Lord and Lady March for private entertainments, especially during the world-renowned Festival of Speed in June and for Raceweek in July, the State Apartments are available throughout the year for private parties, weddings or corporate functions.

Once experienced, visitors will never forget the unmistakable atmosphere – both friendly and grand – which permeates the Goodwood Estate.

Telephone communication

Most organisations use **telephone communication** in providing part of their customer service. Indeed, some organisations such as hotel central reservations offices use the telephone as the main method of communication when dealing with customer enquiries.

ACTIVITY
Telephone communication

1 Using your own experience of telephoning an organisation, make a list of the things that annoy or frustrate you. You should consider such things as the way in which the call is answered, the telephone manner of the person answering, the process of being connected to someone else within the organisation, how delays are dealt with, the way in which the call is terminated and the effectiveness of message-taking.

2 Look through the items you have listed to see how many are technical matters (e.g. a bad line or wrong number) and how many are due to poor customer service. You will probably find that most of the things that annoy you could be avoided with better staff communication skills and customer service.

With good telephone skills we can usually meet or exceed the standard of service that customers expect. Many of the skills needed are the same that you would use in any customer service situation. For example, you need to be polite, friendly, attentive and efficient. However, additional skills are needed when using a telephone because the customer cannot see you and you cannot see the customer. You cannot use facial expressions or bodily gestures to help the communication process, but must rely totally on your voice and your ability to listen carefully. Here are some basic rules for using the telephone effectively.

- **Speak clearly.** Do not eat, drink, chew gum or smoke while on the telephone, as this will distort or muffle the sound of your voice.
- **Take notes.** Always write down full details of what the customer wants, particularly if the message is for someone else.
- **Identify the caller's needs.** Remember that the caller is paying for the call and wants to be dealt with quickly and efficiently.
- **Listen carefully.** Do not interrupt when the caller is talking.
- **Explain what is happening.** If you transfer the caller to someone else, state what you are doing.

ACTIVITY
Telephone communication role play

In pairs, role play a caller and telephonist. Decide who is going to be the caller and the telephonist. With your backs to one another, role play the following telephone calls to a large leisure centre.

- A customer wanting to know what activities are suitable for elderly customers.
- A customer who has not received confirmation of his son's birthday party at the centre next week.
- The mother of a member of staff wanting to talk to her daughter who is on her lunch break.
- A student wanting some general information about the company.
- Someone calling about a recent job advertisement for a receptionist.
- A vending machine salesperson wanting to speak to the catering manager, who has the day off.

For each role play, the telephonist should record all necessary details and state what action he or she will take after the call.

Identify the extent to which the information recorded was sufficient. For example, did the telephonist record the full name, telephone number and extension number (if appropriate) of the caller, the time of the call and establish whether it was a matter of urgency?

Written communication

For some organisations, **written communication** is the main way of keeping in contact with customers. For example, many customers may rarely visit a branch of their bank to talk to staff; instead, they will obtain money from a cash dispenser and receive details of their accounts by mail. Much of the image that they have of the service offered by the bank will depend on its written communications.

Examples of written communications used by leisure and recreation organisations include:

- menus
- tariffs or price lists
- letters

- bills
- brochures and leaflets
- advertisements
- signs
- notice boards
- programmes
- tickets
- faxes
- e-mails
- the internet
- timetables.

The same standard of care needs to be given to written forms of communication as to any other aspect of customer service. The quality of written communication will affect the customer's image both of you and the organisation. For example, a customer in a sports centre may be very impressed by the friendly, enthusiastic attitude of the receptionist, but that impression may change if he or she is handed a crumpled and badly photocopied programme. However, if the programme looks professional and attractive then the previous positive impression will be confirmed.

ACTIVITY

Written communication

Imagine you are the manager of a sports centre.

1 Write a letter welcoming new members to the centre.
2 What other information could you provide for new club members? You may find it useful to visit a sports centre to obtain examples of information provided.

Most leisure and recreation organisations use a combination of communication methods, so it is important that all staff are trained appropriately. Even if it is not a normal part of someone's job, they may still need such skills on odd occasions, as the following telephone call to a children's residential activity centre demonstrates.

Not a good impression for the customer, but no doubt one that will be remembered! Many leisure and recreation providers have written standards for communicating with their customers, such as those outlined below.

Our aspirations

We will answer telephone calls promptly and efficiently. In particular, we aim to:

- answer phone calls within five rings, but if not possible ensure that the answering service is activated after five rings.
- answer politely, giving our name and unit.
- take personal responsibility for responding to requests for information and assistance.
- ensure that when we cannot resolve the matter ourselves a response will be provided within 24 hours, or as promised.

We will deal with all correspondence promptly. Written responses will be clear and concise and contain accurate information. In particular, we aim to:

- respond within the writer's specified deadline or within ten working days, giving details of why there is a delay and when a full response can be expected.
- acknowledge, by phone or writing, within three days of receipt, if a reply is unlikely within ten days, giving details of why there is a delay and when a full response can be expected.

We will process grant applications effectively. We will produce communications which are concise, easy to understand and avoid the use of jargon. In particular, we aim to:

- ensure that all communications are of a high and consistent quality in terms of presentation and clarity of purpose.
- avoid the use of acronyms.
- ensure that all communications produced by Sport England and its units are consistent in presentation and purpose, and appropriate for the key audience at which each is aimed.
- apply the corporate identity to all communications.

We will communicate changes in our policies and operation at the earliest opportunity. In particular, we aim to:

- inform pertinent individuals and organisations of imminent staff changes and responsibilities, together with transitional contact arrangements as soon as they are known.
- promote widely our policies, and, as soon as they are agreed, any changes or additions to them.

Source: *Sport England*

ACTIVITY

Communications

Select a leisure and recreation information desk at a cinema, leisure centre, hotel, etc. Evaluate the staff's dealings with customers face-to-face, in writing and over the telephone. You will need to think of a reason for an inquiry. For example, you might try to find out what facilities are available for children.

Communication skills are not just spoken or written. They can be **verbal** and **non-verbal.**

Verbal communication

Verbal communication is central to many of the communication methods we have considered. It is part of face-to-face, group and telephone communication and it influences your personal presentation and the first impression that you give to customers.

The ability to speak well does not mean using a posh accent. Of far greater importance is the ability to speak in a way that is comprehensible and acceptable to your customers. 'Comprehensible' means speaking in a way that is understandable and easily followed by the customer. 'Acceptable' means that the way you express yourself should fit the personal image that you are trying to convey. As a quick guide, the following points are worth considering.

- Express your thoughts clearly. Do not mumble or ramble.
- Avoid slang and jargon. In other words, use language that is likely to be familiar to the customer.
- Vary your tone of voice. It makes it more interesting and shows that you are interested.
- Listen to the customer. Good communication skills also involve the ability to listen carefully to customer requests and respond to their needs.
- React with interest by using suitable facial expressions as well as your voice.

Effective verbal skills are often a matter of experience and practice. One situation that frequently makes staff nervous is making a speech or presentation. You may have experienced this already if you have been required to give a presentation to other students. You will know that it can be a nerve-racking experience, but will have learned that good planning and preparation gives confidence and helps you to communicate effectively.

The same advice can be applied to any situation where you have to speak to a number of customers at the same time. For example, many hotels and cinemas use public address systems. The steps set out in Figure 5.12 will help you to create a professional and calm impression.

Figure 5.12: Using public address systems

1 Plan what you want to say.
2 Gain attention.
3 Relay the message.
4 Repeat key points.
5 Say thank you.

ACTIVITY

Verbal communication skills

Practise your verbal skills by role playing the following public address messages. It will help if the rest of the group have their backs to the announcer.

1 A swimming pool is due to close in 30 minutes. Make the announcement to customers.

2 The cafeteria at a heritage centre will be open at 10 a.m., serving drinks, snacks and hot and cold meals. Make the announcement to visitors at the heritage centre.

3 Staff have found a small boy called Tom in a visitor attraction. He is waiting for his parents at the customer service desk. Make the announcement to all visitors at the visitor attraction.

4 Give a standard security warning in a large sports stadium telling spectators to evacuate due to a bomb alert.

5 The start of a football match has been delayed by 15 minutes due to a pitch inspection. Make the announcement to the crowd waiting for the start of the game.

6 The owner of a Blue Renault Espace, licence number L177 HRO has parked their car in the emergency vehicles bay at an art gallery. Make the announcement to visitors and staff.

Non-verbal communication

Non-verbal communication comprises all forms of communication that are not spoken or written down. We all tend to focus on what we say or write and overlook the importance of what we communicate non-verbally. Research indicates that as much as 80 per cent of communication is non-verbal, so it is clearly an important part of customer service.

Body language is one kind of non-verbal communication and refers to the way we use our body to send messages to someone else. Body language includes posture, mannerisms, gestures and facial expressions, all of which communicate messages about what we really think and feel. The subject of body language is too complex to discuss in detail here. However, as far as customer service is concerned, it is useful to be aware of what is known as open and closed body language. Open body language suggests to a customer that you are interested in them, that you are not hostile or aggressive and that you want to listen to them and please them. Closed body language suggests the opposite: that you are uninterested, may be hostile or aggressive and are unwilling to listen to them or satisfy their needs. Figure 5.13 gives examples of open and closed body language.

Figure 5.13: Open and closed body language

Open	Closed
Smiling	Frowning
Standing up straight	Slouching
Arms loosely at your side or behind your back	Arms crossed in front of you, or hands on your hips or in your pockets
Head held with chin level to floor	Chin up or down
Eye contact with customer	Avoiding eye contact with customer
Remaining in a comfortable position	Fidgeting, moving from foot to foot, crossing and uncrossing legs
No obvious mannerism	Fiddling with your hair, hands, clothes
Using gestures that help you to explain what you are saying	Using gestures excessively or for no apparent reason
Showing interest	Showing no feeling at all
Showing concern	Showing lack of concern

Smiling is the single most important aspect of non-verbal communication. It says that you like and take pride in your job and that you like the customer and want to meet their needs.

Good communication skills, both verbal and non-verbal, are important in all situations involving customers, for example when:

- providing information
- giving advice
- taking and relaying messages
- keeping records
- providing assistance
- dealing with problems
- handling complaints.

Providing information

Providing information is important in ensuring that the customer can select the product or service that meets his or her needs. The type of information provided will largely depend on what the customer asks. They may want to know about products, services or facilities. Alternatively, they may require information on prices or directions on how to get to somewhere. Many organisations include detailed directions in their promotional materials, as the very thorough example from London Zoo shows.

Getting There

London Zoo is open every day – except Christmas Day – from 10 a.m. To get to the Web of Life use the map and instructions below.

Using London Transport

By Underground – The nearest station is Camden Town (Northern Line). Follow the signs up 'Parkway' to the Zoo (12 minute walk).

By British Rail – the nearest station is Euston. Take the Underground (Northern Line) from Euston to Camden Town.

By Bus – Services run from Oxford Circus and Baker Street (no. 274), to Ormonde Terrace. Pick up the C2 from Oxford Circus or Great Portland Street, to Gloucester Gate.

By Waterbus – The London Waterbus Company runs a scheduled service along the Regent's Canal between Camden Lock or Little Venice and London Zoo. For full details call the London Waterbus Company: 020 7482 2550.

By London Pride Sightseeing Bus – Hop on a 'No. 1 for Attractions' London Pride Sightseeing Bus oin the centre of London, at any London Pride bus stop. All-inclusive price. Arrives at the Zoo every 15 minutes. For full details call London Pride: 01708 631122.

By Car – The Zoo's Main Gate is situated on the Outer Circle of Regent's Park, NW1. Parking is available in the Zoo's Gloucester Slips car park at £5 per car, per day. £12 is payable at the car park, with £7 when paying to get into the Zoo.

Just as the leisure and recreation industry is very diverse, so too are customers' information requirements.

ACTIVITY

Providing information

Here are some FAQs (frequently asked questions) by American visitors to the UK. See how many of them you can answer. You might need to use reference books, manuals, guides or the internet.

1 How do I get from London's Heathrow Airport to Gatwick Airport?

2 What's the most convenient airport if I want to visit Shakespeare country and the Cotswolds?

3 I'd like to stay in a Bed and Breakfast, how can I arrange this?

4 How can I book theatre tickets in the USA for London shows?

5 I am arriving at Southampton on the QE2. How can I get to London?

6 When does the Ceremony of the Keys take place and how can I get tickets?

7 How can I claim back the VAT tax on my purchases?

8 When does the circus start in Piccadilly?

9 What's the weather going to be like in York during July?

10 We would love to see those shaggy brown cows while in Scotland. Where can we find them?

Answers can be found on the British Tourist Authority's web site at www.Usagateway.visitbritain.com

Of course, no one can be expected to know the answers to all questions. However, what is expected is that you know where and how to find out information so that you can answer customers' questions. A wide range of sources is available, including:

- manuals
- brochures and leaflets
- reference books
- guide books
- computerised information systems
- timetables
- recorded telephone information lines
- tourist information centres
- Yellow pages
- telephone directories
- the internet.

Knowing where to find information quickly is an essential part of excellent customer service.

ACTIVITY

Using references

The left-hand column below lists some sources of information. The right-hand column lists some examples of typical requests for information. Can you match the information request with a suitable source of reference? There may be more than one source of reference for some of the requests.

Source of reference	Request for information
Yellow Pages	Telephone numbers of local tennis clubs
Visitor map of area	Five-star hotels in London
Directory enquiries	Film showing at local cinema
Railway timetable	Name of a plumber
Local newspaper	Stately homes in the area
RAC hotel guide	Nearest public swimming pool
Telephone directory	Times of trains to Granada Studios, Manchester
National Trust book	Location of local nightclubs
What's On magazine	Late opening for the area chemists

In any customer service situation **product information** should be impersonal, accurate and objective.

- **Impersonal** means your own tastes and preferences should not limit or restrict the sort of information you give. For example, a customer visiting a sports centre expects product information about sporting activities suitable for his or her needs, not about activities that the assistant would like to do.
- **Accurate** means making sure that everything you say is true. If you are not sure about something, say that you will check the information and then let the customer know. For example, saying that a cinema film is suitable for young children when you are not really sure could result in some very dissatisfied customers.
- **Objective** means including all the information that customers need to know, even if you think that it might put them off buying the product. Sometimes this may mean referring potential customers to a competitor, but the reputation that you gain for good customer service will mean that customers will come back another time.

Impersonal, accurate and objective information is important in all situations if you are to satisfy customers' needs and ensure that they return. Sometimes giving the wrong information can result in customers not being able to buy a product or service at all. For example, providing inaccurate information on opening times might result in a customer arriving too early or too late.

Many leisure and recreation providers outline the ways in which they offer information as part of their promotional materials, such as the example (opposite) of the National Railway Museum.

Giving advice

Giving advice is really an extension of giving them information. However, while information may be purely factual, advice requires you to make appropriate recommendations and suggestions. For example, a reservations clerk at a holiday centre may provide a customer with information on accommodation and facilities by giving them appropriate brochures and possibly a video. The customer may then ask for additional advice on what would best suit their particular needs. For example: 'Which of the centres would you recommend for young children who enjoy lots of sporting activities?' or 'Do you think I should book full or half-board?' Advice should always be impersonal, accurate and objective.

WE PROMISE

Up-to-date information about the Museum.
Staff at the Ticket Points and Information Desks are there to help you. We produce a 'What's on' Leaflet twice a year. Copies are available from the Information Desks. If you would like us to send you 'What's on' Leaflets, please ask at our Information Desks. Summarised guide books are available in five languages. Please listen for announcements about today's programmes on the public address system, and read about them at both entrances.

A prompt and helpful response to enquiries.
We aim to respond promptly to all enquiries. Our switchboard (01904 621261) is open between 08.30 and 17.30 Monday to Thursday and 08.30 and 16.30 on Fridays. At all other times calls are directed to our control room. Our address, telephone and fax numbers are given at the end of this leaflet. Whether you write or telephone, all staff will give their name and either help you immediately or agree a response time with you.

▲ The National Railway Museum promises information to customers

Many leisure and recreation products and services are complex, with lots of different aspects. The first-time customer can often find this quite confusing and it may spoil their enjoyment of the product if they have difficulty understanding how it is delivered. Consequently, many organisations have to provide their customers with sufficient advice on how services are delivered and used. For example, package holiday customers will be sent pre-holiday advice about when and where they check-in for their flight. Once customers arrive they will usually be given advice on health and safety issues such as the use of lifts, swimming pools, hotel balconies, etc.

One excellent example of an organisation providing clear and effective advice to their customers is the system used by the Brewers Fayre public houses for customers wishing to eat (see case study on page 360).

CASE STUDY

Customer information at Brewers Fayre

Brewers Fayre offers an extensive menu aimed primarily at the family market. Meals are selected from a menu, ordered and paid for at the bar and served at the customer's table by waiting staff. One problem that could have arisen at busy times is customers ordering a meal but then be unable to find a table. Brewers Fayre uses a simply but very effective system to ensure that this does not happen and provides customers with clear advice on how the system operates.

All tables have menus and a tent card giving advice on how to order food.

HOW TO ORDER YOUR MEAL

- Find a vacant table and note the table number
- Place your order at the food counter, quoting your table number
- Please pay for your food when you order
- Our staff will serve your order to the table
- Please purchase drinks at the bar

TO SHOW THAT YOUR TABLE IS OCCUPIED SIMPLY REVERSE THIS CARD.

NOWHERE'S FAIRER THAN A BREWERS FAYRE.

Customers then fill in their order and table number on the order form.

TABLE NUMBER

STARTERS

SIDE ORDERS	DRINKS

MAIN MEALS	CHOICE OF CHIPS/POTATOES OF THE DAY

WINE

There are even reminders about drinks, wine, side orders and whether the customer wants chips or the potatoes of the day. While the customer goes to the bar to order food, another tent card is placed on the table to show that it is already taken.

SORRY BUT THIS TABLE IS OCCUPIED

– we have gone to order our meal

NOWHERE'S FAIRER THAN A BREWERS FAYRE.

The case study on Brewers Fayre shows one way in which a leisure and recreation provider gives advice so that customers can fully enjoy a product or service.

ACTIVITY

Customer advice

Customer feedback at theme parks indicates that one of the biggest complaints is the length of queues for the big rides. As a result, some parks are introducing 'virtual queuing', where customers obtain a ticket with a time at which they will be guaranteed a place on the ride. In the meantime they are free to wander off and see other attractions, rather than waste time standing in a queue.

Design a form that tells customers how this system works. It should include blank spaces to allow customers to fill in the times at which they are booked on a number of different rides at the park.

Taking messages

Taking and relaying messages is an important part of customer service for both internal and external customers. There are many times when it may be necessary to take messages:

- A customer telephones a conference centre wanting to speak to one of the delegates.
- A customer in a leisure centre complains about the service and wants the manager to contact him about it when she returns.
- Someone leaves a package for a customer at the reception desk of a sports centre to be given to the customer on arrival.
- A member of staff phones to say that he is unwell and will not be in for work.

Failing to take accurate messages and ensuring that they are passed on to the right person promptly can have disastrous effects on the customer's perception of the overall level of service. For example, a hotel guest may be very impressed by the friendly, enthusiastic attitude of the receptionist, but that impression may change if he or she is handed an illegible handwritten message on a scrappy piece of paper. If, however, the message is presented in a professional manner, then the previous positive impression will be confirmed.

Figure 5.14: Good and bad message taking

TELEPHONE MESSAGE

Message for: Mr Sinclair   Date: 26/9/96
Message from: Miss J Collins   Time: 3.40 p.m.

Message:
Please call me at the office before 6:00pm tonight.

Telephone number: 01723 562189 Ext.126

Message taken by: S Rawlins

Mr Sinclair
Please call Miss Collins
at the office this afternoon
Tel no. 01723 592189
x 129

ACTIVITY

Taking and relaying messages

Megathrills Theme Park often receives phone calls at its customer service desk from people who are due to meet friends for the day but have been delayed. The park covers several acres of land and can become very crowded. There is no public address system, which has meant that relaying such messages has proved very difficult. The manager has decided to introduce a 'meeting point' notice board at the customer services desk. After each telephone message, customer service staff will complete a pre-printed card and display it on the board.

1 Design the layout of the card with spaces left for customer service staff to fill in the relevant details. Try to think of all the information that you would want if it was your friends who were delayed.
2 Design a checklist for staff, showing how they should fill in the card and what information is appropriate for public display. You will need to consider confidentiality and tact. For example, it would not be appropriate to have a card that read: 'Reason for delay: Your mother has had a heart attack' or 'John has been stopped for drinking and driving'!

Keeping records

As we have already seen, excellent customer service involves giving information to customers. Another key part of the process involves **keeping records** of information needed by other staff to help them provide good service to customers. For example, a hotel receptionist may record a guest's reservation, including the following information that would be passed on to relevant staff:

- double room with cot in bedroom – head housekeeper
- table for two for dinner at 8 p.m. – head waiter
- one guest cannot eat any dairy products – head waiter and head chef
- early morning alarm call at 7 p.m. – early shift receptionist
- mini-bus transfer to the airport – hall porter.

All leisure and recreation organisations keep records on their customers. Understanding how to maintain and use these records is an essential part of excellent customer service. Customer records can be kept for a wide range of functions, such as:

- details of financial transactions
- details of complaints and compliment letters
- accidents and emergencies.

Most leisure and recreation organisations have standard procedures for keeping records, which may be paper-based or stored on a computer. For example, a private sports centre may have paper-based customer files which contain copies of completed membership forms, health questionnaires, written correspondence and payment details. It will probably also store specific details on a computerised database.

Many leisure and recreation providers have to keep specific records by law or because of professional codes of conduct. For example, members of STAR (Society of Ticket Agents and Retailers) are required to keep detailed records of all bookings and reservations made by customers. This can have considerable benefits for customers who have lost tickets, since they are able to obtain replacement tickets once the provider has checked the records and verified that the tickets have been purchased.

Customer records are vital to ensure that you know who your customers are, what their needs are and how you have satisfied them in the past. They are also a very necessary part of the process of being able to answer a customer's inquiry quickly and efficiently.

ACTIVITY

Customer records

Castleford Health Spa is a privately owned, exclusive residential health club. Most guests are regular visitors who appreciate the extensive facilities offered. Sporting facilities and events include the following:

- An indoor and outdoor swimming pool. The indoor pool offers gentle exercise sessions in the form of aqua-aerobics and more strenuous lane-swims.
- An exercise studio with a wide range of high-tech equipment.
- Outdoor crown green bowls.
- Two squash courts with league games for guests.
- Accompanied daily jogging and mini-marathon sessions over 5–12 miles.
- Cycle rides for beginners and experienced cyclists.
- Aerobics, yoga and meditation sessions.

All new guests are sent a detailed health and fitness questionnaire to help staff provide advice on suitable exercise. The questionnaires are entered into the company's database records and updated after each guest stay. Look opposite at the recently returned questionnaire of Mr Butler, who has not been to Castleford before. What activities do you suggest would be particularly suitable for him, based on the information in the completed questionnaire?

CASTLEFORD HEALTH SPA

Please complete and return this questionnaire prior to your first visit

Name: Michael James Butler

Address: The Oaks
Meadow Lane
Chichester

Date of Birth: 8.12.47 Height: 5ft 10 Weight: 17st 10oz

Do you suffer from any of the following:

Heart Condition no

Epilepsy/blackouts no

High blood pressure no

Back Problems no

Respiratory condition Yes

Arthritis/rheumatism no

If 'yes' to any of the above, please give details:

I suffer from asthma

Have you had an operation or received hospital treatment within the last five years, if 'yes', please give details.

I spent three days in hospital last year following a car accident which resulted in a broken leg and concussion.

Are you pregnant or have given birth within the last twelve months?

I hope not - that would be one for the Guinness Book of Records!

Please outline how much exercise you take on average per week and what it consists of:

A short walk on the beach with the dog each morning and a bit of light gardening when I have time!

Providing assistance

We have already looked at how some customers may have specific needs and the ways in which excellent customer service can meet those needs. Any customer may have a specific need for extra assistance at any time; for example, the football spectator who cannot find his seat; the conference organiser who wants assistance in working the overhead projector; the mother with young children who needs help in getting a pushchair up a flight of stairs to the swimming pool changing rooms.

In situations such as these, it is your responsibility to anticipate when customers might need assistance and provide it. For example, if you see a mother struggling with a pushchair you should not wait for her to ask for help: offer assistance quickly to show that you really care and have anticipated her needs.

ACTIVITY

Providing assistance

Sam is having a very stressful day as a customer services assistant at the Grangemouth Recreation and Leisure Park. Throughout the day she has been called on by a number of customers to provide assistance in the following situations:

1 A customer's young child has become badly sunburned while playing in the children's adventure area.

2 A customer's wife has not turned up at the agreed meeting place and her husband is anxious to find her.

3 An American customer has left her handbag in the park's restaurant. It contained her passport, money, car keys, driving licence and credit cards. A call to the restaurant has failed to find the missing bag.

4 A vegetarian complains that, apart from salad and chips, the restaurant offers nothing he can eat.

5 A customer walking beside the stream has fallen in. He does not have any other clothes for the two-hour journey home.

What assistance do you think Sam should provide in each case? If you do not know, now is the time to find out! For example, what is the best help for a young child with sunburn? What is the first thing that someone should do if they lose their credit cards and passport?

Dealing with problems

Dealing with customers' problems overlaps with giving them assistance. However, problems are frequently outside the control of the customer – sudden illness, for example, or stolen belongings.

These problems are very stressful for the customer. They require tact and careful handling. Often the customer will be anxious, upset or even angry. It is your responsibility to reassure them and show that you are confident and in control of the situation.

ACTIVITY

Dealing with problems

Two very common customer problems are for a member of a group to go missing (especially small children) and personal belongings to be lost or stolen.

Discuss how you would resolve the problems listed below and the specific factors you would need to consider in each situation.

1 A young child is missing in a large shopping complex. There are six different entrances. The child was last seen outside McDonald's.

2 A teenage son has not met up with his parents, as arranged, at the car park of a theme park.

3 A 10-year-old girl is missing at a swimming pool. The pool is very busy and the girl was last seen in the children's area.

4 A customer at a leisure centre has returned to his locker to find that his belongings have been stolen.

5 A businesswoman has left her coat in the unstaffed cloakroom at a conference centre and the staff cannot find it.

Depending on the complexity of the problem, a staff member may need to check repeatedly that it has been resolved and that there is nothing more that they can do. For example, if a customer at a theme park has an accident and ends up in hospital, the park's staff will have a number of different problems to resolve:

- providing first aid
- ensuring that the customer gets to hospital
- possibly visiting the customer in hospital to see how they are and whether they need anything
- notifying next of kin if the accident is serious
- ensuring that others accompanying the injured guest are all right and can get to the hospital.

In any situation involving customers it is vital to remain calm and listen carefully, so that you can accurately identify their needs and provide the best possible customer service.

ACTIVITY

Leisure or sports centre problems

One of the key responsibilities of staff in a leisure or sports centre is to deal with customers' problems. As a group, brainstorm a list of problems that you think staff will frequently be asked to deal with and suggest ways in which they could be handled.

You might like to draw on your own experiences of using a leisure/sports centre and any problems that you have had. Alternatively, you could speak or write to the manager of a leisure/sports centre and ask them to outline common customer problems.

You could use the table below to list the problems you think of and how you think they should be dealt with.

Description of problem	Customer's needs/expectations	How problem could be handled effectively

ACTIVITY

Customer role play situations

1 Swimming pool lifeguard
A group of young adult men have been causing disruption by running along the side of the pool, pushing each other in and generally upsetting other swimmers with their rowdy behaviour. You suspect that they might have been drinking before they came to the pool.

2 Concert booking agency clerk
An Italian visitor wants to reserve seats for an open-air pop concert in Hyde Park, London. In fact the concert is free and there are no seats. He does not speak much English.

3 Sports centre receptionist
A customer would like to start taking some form of exercise class or sporting activity. Their preference is for an activity where they will meet other people while getting fit. Their hearing is impaired, so they need advice on suitable activities.

4 Leisure centre receptionist
A customer has just returned to his locker and found that his wallet has disappeared. He claims that he is sure that he locked the door. The only other person with a key to the locker is the duty manager.

5 Ride operator
A customer and her two children have been queuing for the Log Flume for 45 minutes. Just as she gets near the front of the queue the maintenance engineer decides that the ride has to be closed temporarily due to a suspected fault.

6 Assistant in a children's soft play area.
A customer is concerned that she is not allowed to accompany her young children into the ball pool and soft play area. Her concern is increased by the fact that the area is quite large and therefore it is not possible for parents to actually see their children at all times. She is worried about the safety of such an arrangement, particularly since the area is very busy and she is not convinced that the assistants will be able to keep an eye on her children.

7 Conference centre receptionist
A new customer telephones to speak to a delegate attending a conference at the centre. First make a public address announcement. The delegate does not respond to this, so you will need to take a message to pass on to them. (You need a pen and paper for this one!)

8 Cinema attendant
An elderly customer at the cinema would like to sit at the rear of the auditorium near to the toilets, as she has difficulty moving around. The cinema is already very busy and there are no vacant seats in the area that she would like. She did not know that she could have reserved a specific seat in advance.

9 Stately home souvenir shop sales assistant
A customer has returned with a recently bought video of the stately home. There is nothing wrong with it but the customer is disappointed that the video only features the interior of the house and not the grounds. He says this should have been made clear in the description.

10 Fast food assistant
Lucy is having her sixth birthday party at your fast-food restaurant. She and her ten friends have finished their meal and become bored. They have started running around the restaurant and disturbing other customers. With another half an hour to go, the manager has asked you to think of an activity that will keep them occupied (and relatively quiet).

11 Shop assistant in a heritage museum
A Swedish visitor would like to buy some souvenirs but is unfamiliar with English currency. The total cost of his purchases is £46.23, but he has given you three £50 notes. The customer would also like a receipt.

12 Hotel night porter
A guest rings down in the middle of the night and asks for some indigestion tablets. He claims that the fish he had in the restaurant was not cooked properly and has made him ill. It is against company policy to give guests any form of medication. There are no all-night chemists in the area.

13 Jet-ski centre manager
A customer has booked herself and her sister on a day's jet-ski course. On the day of the course the sister is unwell and both customers want a full refund. The booking form states clearly that no refunds will be given if cancellations occur less than 24 hours prior to the course.

14 Video shop sales assistant
A customer would like to become a member of your video rental shop. You need the following information: name, address, telephone number, age (to ensure that they are over 18) and proof of identity. They also need to be told about the conditions of renting a video (e.g. the extra cost if videos are returned late, charges made if they damage a video, etc.).

15 Private sports club attendant
A new member has arrived to play a pre-booked game of badminton. Unfortunately, they did not realise that the club has strict rules on appropriate footwear to avoid damaging the court and have not brought trainers that are acceptable.

BUILD YOUR LEARNING

End of section activity

Select at least four of the situations outlined on page 365 and role play them in front of the rest of the group. Evaluate your performance with the help of the group and make recommendations as to how you could improve your customer service skills. Copy and complete the form on page 365 as evidence of your customer service skills and evaluation for each of your role play situations.

Keywords and phrases

You should know the meaning of the words and phrases listed below. If you are unsure about any of them, go back through the last 15 pages to refresh your understanding.

- Face-to-face communication
- Telephone communication
- Written communication
- Verbal and non-verbal communication
- Body language
- Providing information
- Giving advice
- Taking and relaying messages
- Keeping records
- Customer records
- Dealing with problems

Handling complaints

Strange as it may seem, **dealing with customers' complaints** also forms part of excellent customer service. This is because if a complaint is handled well a good relationship will be established and the customer may well return in future.

Why it is important

Research into customer complaints reveals some interesting facts:

- A happy customer will tell four other people about the good service they receive.
- A dissatisfied customer will tell at least 15 people about the bad service they receive.
- 94 per cent of customers do not complain, but simply walk away and don't come back.
- Most organisations lose between 45–50 per cent of their customers every five years through complaints.
- Replacing lost customers costs a company five times more than it does to keep them.

If you still need convincing about the huge benefits of effective complaint handling, read this extract from the Strategic Planning Institute:

> Those companies who actively encourage customers to complain can increase customer retention by 10 per cent. Actually responding to that complaint can boost retention by up to 75 per cent. And if the customer is very satisfied, retention increases to 95 per cent.

Most organisations have a **complaints procedure** which staff must follow when dealing with customer complaints. This procedure is usually described in an organisation's customer charter. The extract from the customer charter issued by the Newcastle City Council (Figure 5.15) outlines what action the council will take when dealing with complaints.

Figure 5.15: Newcastle's complaints policy

We will:

- always treat you fairly and with respect
- always offer a friendly and polite service
- see you promptly when you visit our offices
- answer your letters and phone calls promptly
- listen to you and be sensitive to your needs
- do our best to help you and let you know how quickly we can act
- provide easy-to-understand, useful, information
- keep you informed about services we provide
- deal with your comments and complaints positively and quickly
- respect your confidentiality
- make sure our staff have the skills they need to do their jobs properly and considerately
- listen to and consult you as our customers, and be prepared to change our policies and practices whenever possible

Complaints

We recognise that things can go wrong and that

- we can only put them right if customers complain – so we treat every complaint as an opportunity to improve our service
- we will try to deal with any complaints about our service informally, quickly and through the most suitable person
- you have the right to complain formally if you are not satisfied with the service you have received
- we will investigate your complaint fully, and you will receive a full reply or a progress update in writing within 15 working days of us receiving your complaint
- you can get copies of our complaints procedure from all our offices and receptions

Effective complaint handling

No one likes dealing with customer complaints because it can suggest that you or a colleague have not done your jobs properly. Research carried out by the English Tourism Council shows that the four most common reasons for complaints in the leisure and recreation industry are poor service, delays, incorrect information and standards not meeting customers' expectations.

Even when a complaint is about something totally beyond your control, you may still be concerned that the customer is disappointed. Sometimes a customer may be angry or they may criticise you directly. They may even shout at you. The ability to deal with such situations is all part of good customer service, although on the first few occasions you may find them difficult to handle. Here are some useful tips:

- **Listen** carefully to the customer.
- **Apologise** in general terms for any inconvenience caused.
- Let the customer know that the matter will be fully **investigated** and put right.
- Try to see the problem from the **customer's point of view.**
- **Keep calm** and don't argue with the customer.
- **Find a solution** to the problem or refer the issue to a supervisor/manager.
- **Agree the solution** with the customer.
- **Take action** and make sure that what you promised to do gets done.
- Make sure that you **record details** of the complaint and actions taken.

Many leisure and recreation organisations outline the way in which they handle customer complaints. For example, Sport England includes the following procedure in its Commitment to Service:

> We will welcome comments on our performance and investigate complaints thoroughly. In particular, we aim to:
>
> - treat your complaint courteously and in confidence;
> - acknowledge and investigate your complaint quickly;
> - give the name of the person dealing with the matter;
> - apologise if we have made an error and make every effort to put things right.

In addition, Sport England explains the procedure for customers to make a complaint.

How you can make a complaint

Step 1 Initial complaint
If you are dissatisfied with any aspect of the service received, you should initially speak with the member of staff concerned. We hope that most complaints can be settled quickly and as close to the source of the problem as possible.

Step 2 If you are not satisfied
If you are dissatisfied with the initial response, you should either write to or telephone the Head of Unit in which your complaint originated. You will receive an acknowledgement within three working days and a full response within ten working days. Your complaint will be investigated personally.

Step 3 Formal complaint
If you believe your complaint requires further attention, you should write to the Chief Executive (Derek Casey) at Sport England, 16 Upper Woburn Place, London, WC1H 0QP. You will receive an acknowledgment within three working days and a full response within ten working days. Your complaint will be investigated personally.

Step 4 If you are still not satisfied
If still not satisfied with our response, you can write to your MP with a request that the matter be referred to the Government Ombudsman.

Similarly, we would like to hear from you if you have any suggestions as to how we can improve our service or are pleased with the service provided.

Types of complainers

The English Tourism council's Welcome Host programme identifies four different types of complainant, each of which need handling in a slightly different way.

The aggressive complainer

This customer is likely to be angry, raise their voice and possibly shout at you. Often there will be a very good reason for their anger. The worst approach to the aggressive complainer is to shout back or interrupt, as this will simply make them angrier. Allowing them to let off steam is the best solution, as they will soon calm down if you remain calm and in control. It also helps to suggest that you discuss the complaint in a private area. Apart from preventing other customers from hearing all of the details, you will also find that an aggressive complainer often calms down more quickly if there is no audience.

Once the customer has calmed down you are then in a position to identify exactly what they are dissatisfied with and find a solution. Needless to say, if this type of customer is physically aggressive or abusive you would not be expected to deal with the situation on your own and should call for assistance from a supervisor at once.

The passive complainer

This type of complainer is by far the most common. They will often not tell a member of staff about their complaint but simply leave dissatisfied. A typical passive complainer's conversation might go something like this:

'Is your meal all right, mother?'

'Not really. I asked for the steak well done and it's still raw in the middle.'

'Why don't you tell that nice waitress? I'm sure that she would get it changed for you.'

'No, I don't want to cause a fuss and anyway she is so busy.'

The obvious way that this complaint could have been identified and solved would have been for the waitress to check that the customers were enjoying their meal. All customers need observing to see whether they appear satisfied with the product or service that they are using. You can usually tell by a customer's body language when they are not happy. The passive complainer may often need coaxing to actually voice their complaint and should be made to feel comfortable about the situation rather than a nuisance.

The constructive complainer

This type of complainer often raises general issues that will be of concern to other customers. Their main reason for complaining will be because they want some action taken and may often offer constructive advice on what they think you should do. A typical complaint from a constructive complainer might be:

'Excuse me, I've just used your women's toilet and it's in a terrible state. Someone's left the taps running and thrown toilet paper all over the floor. You might like to get someone to clear it up before you get any complaints.'

The professional complainer

Unfortunately, not all complaints are genuine and there exists a small group of people who complain because they hope to get something free in return. This situation has arisen largely because organisations are becoming very good at dealing with complaints and are keen to ensure that the customer leaves totally satisfied. The customer who has not been charged for his visit to a visitor attraction on one occasion after complaining, might be tempted to see if he can do it again in another similar attraction! However, you should always assume that a complaint is genuine and listen carefully to the details before jumping to conclusions.

Dealing with complaints

We have looked at general guidelines for dealing with complaints in a face-to-face situation and some of the specific types of complainers that you may encounter. Two further methods of dealing with a complaint are over the telephone and in writing. Both or either of these methods may be necessary when:

- following up a **face-to-face complaint** that could not be resolved at the time
- responding to a **telephone complaint**
- responding to a **letter of complaint.**

Deciding which method is preferable will depend on the situation. The Strategic Planning Institute found that:

95 per cent of customers prefer a letter to a phone call when you are dealing with their complaints. This is because a letter is more personal, it demonstrates a greater commitment on behalf of the company and its tangibility suggests that the complaint has been taken seriously and is concrete evidence that something will be done.

However, there will be some situations when a phone call is the most appropriate first method of contact. The great advantage of telephoning a complainer is that it is immediate and ensures that the customer knows that you are taking the complaint seriously.

The policy of many leisure and recreation organisations is to phone the customer immediately they receive a letter of complaint in order to confirm that something is being done about it. They then write a letter to describe the action that has been taken.

The advantage of a written response to a complaint is that considerable thought can be given to the planning and content of the letter to make sure that it is absolutely right. However, even then some organisations do not get it quite right, as the activity below demonstrates.

ACTIVITY

Handling Complaints

The letter below is the genuine response of a theme park manager to a leisure and tourism tutor who wrote to complain about the poor customer service that she and her group of students had experienced while on a visit.

Read the letter carefully and discuss the following points.

1 Do you think that it is adequate to 'duly note' the complainant's comments?

2 Is it justifiable to argue that it is easier to provide good customer service at a smaller tourist attraction because staff morale is higher and staff turnover lower?

3 To what extent is it helpful to suggest that a complainant is being hypercritical because they were part of a leisure and recreation group?

4 Is it acceptable to suggest that because the complainant received a group discount on the admission price they should be 'grateful' for the good value for money – the implication being that they should therefore not complain about poor customer service?

5 To what extent do you think the complainant will share the theme park manager's confidence that a return visit 'will more than match your expectations'?

Based on your discussion of the five points above, rewrite the letter to make it more effective.

Dear …

I am in receipt of your letter regarding your group's visit to our theme park. Your comments concerning employee apathy and sullenness have been duly noted.

I concede that it is sometimes difficult to keep young, part-time staff motivated. However, we have had much success with improved induction courses and staff training. On the whole, feedback concerning staff has been generally good this season.

The comparison which you have used between our operation and other operations in the region has also been noted. I have to say that I find this comparison unrealistic. There is no other leisure facility in the region which is remotely close to the magnitude of our theme park. Running a small concern and keeping staff morale high and staff turnover low is relatively non-complex. The situation becomes more obtuse when an operation grows to become the fourth most visited theme park in the country and attracts in excess of one million visitors per annum. Perhaps being part of a leisure and recreation trip has made you hypercritical. If you were part of a prepaid group you would have enjoyed all of our facilities for £6.50 each. Perhaps the many positives such as the aforementioned value for money should be remembered as well as the negatives.

Please be assured that much effort and resources have been allocated towards improving staff training and in particular customer service. The impression of our staff which you have been left with is by no means normal operating standards. I am confident that if you make a return trip to Flamingo Land our operation will more than match your expectations.

Regards

General Manager

Deciding on action

One difficulty that many staff have when dealing with complaints is deciding what action is most appropriate and whether or not they have the authority to take that action themselves. For example, the new receptionist at a sports centre may be unsure whether or not she is allowed to make a deduction from a customer's bill if they are dissatisfied with the facilities. If you are ever unsure about the appropriate action to take, always ask a supervisor for help.

The best course of action will depend on the type of customer, the nature of their complaint and its seriousness. It is very important to identify correctly what the customer would find acceptable, or you may risk making them even more dissatisfied or even insulting them. For example, the constructive complainer will usually be satisfied if he knows that his complaint has been taken seriously and something will be done about it. Offering him his money back may be totally inappropriate and give the impression that you are trying to get rid of him with a bribe.

Many complaint situations will result in the customer being given some form of compensation, such as a refund or complimentary product. The scale of the compensation should reflect the severity of the complaint. For example, customers at a holiday camp who had to wait for an hour to check in because of a reservation mistake may be given a complimentary drink, but they would not expect to have the cost of their stay refunded in full. On the other hand, customers who are unable to play a pre-booked game of squash at a sports centre because of a double booking may be offered a free game on another occasion. There are great advantages in providing compensation in the form of a free return visit, since it ensures that the customer will come back and gives the organisation the opportunity to show that they can get it right.

ACTIVITY

Putting things right

Imagine that you are the duty manager at a theatre and have come on duty to find the following information in the management handover book.

Friday 15 September

A Mr and Mrs Jarvis will be attending tonight's performance with complimentary tickets. The tickets were given to them after they complained about their last visit to us. The basis of their complaint was that they had given us advance notice that Mrs Jarvis would need help getting to her seat and further assistance at the interval, as she is in a wheelchair. Unfortunately, due to a breakdown in communication, no help was offered and Mrs Jarvis missed the beginning of the performance and was unable to get to the first-floor theatre bar for an interval drink, as she was unaware that we now have a lift. They will collect their tickets from the box office on arrival and are seated in the stalls in D32 and D33. Please make sure that you greet them on arrival and give them every possible assistance during the evening. They are regular customers and we need to prove that their bad experience will not happen again!

What steps would you take to ensure that Mr and Mrs Jarvis enjoyed their evening and were keen to return? Which other members of staff would need to know about their visit and what would you expect them to do?

BUILD YOUR LEARNING

Keywords and phrases

You should know the meaning of the words and phrases listed below. If you are unsure about any of them, go back through the last six pages to refresh your understanding.

- Dealing with customers' complaints
- Complaints procedure
- Written complaints
- Face-to-face complaints
- Telephone complaints
- Letters of complaint

End of section activity

1 Think of a complaint for a customer at a local authority swimming pool. For example, the pool could be unclean or overcrowded, or it could have poor changing facilities and showers, etc. Try to select several grounds for complaint rather than just one. Write a letter to the local authority outlining your main areas of complaint.

2 Working with other members of the group, role play the following situations with everyone taking a turn as both the complainant and member of staff.

- The customer outlines their complaint to the receptionist at the swimming pool. The receptionist should take steps to solve the problems.
- A telephone call between the customer and the manager of the pool the following day. The customer should outline their complaint and allow the manager to deal with the complaint.
- Give your letter to someone else in the group, who should then write a response on behalf of the local authority.

After all three role plays, decide how effective the member of staff was in handling the complaint and suggest ways in which they could have improved their complaint handling skills.

Assessing the quality of customer service

For most leisure and recreation organisations, training their staff to enable them to provide excellent customer service is not the end of the process. An organisation will also continuously monitor, **assess** and **evaluate** its levels of customer service to ensure that it is meeting and, it is hoped, exceeding its customers' needs and expectations.

If the evaluation identifies areas where service is not meeting customers' expectations it gives the organisation the opportunity to make any necessary changes.

Benchmarking

Many leisure and recreation organisations use a system of monitoring and evaluation known as **benchmarking.** This involves establishing **quality criteria** or **standards** and then measuring the organisation's performance against those standards. Sometimes the benchmarks will be set according to standards offered by competitors. Rank Xerox defines benchmarking as

the continual measuring of products, services and practices against the toughest competition of those recognised as leaders.

CASE STUDY

Quest benchmarking

Quest was a quality initiative introduced in the 1990s by the British Quality Association Leisure Services Sub-Committee. Its aim is to help managers continually monitor and improve the level of customer service that they offer based on Quest's defined industry standards and examples of good practicc. Organisations participating in the Quest initiative are provided with a Manager's Guidance Pack which allows them to evaluate their facility's customer service against industry benchmarks. These benchmarks are continually updated to ensure that they truly reflect industry practice.
There are four key areas of evaluation:

- facilities operation
- customer relations
- staffing
- service development and review

These areas are evaluated using a ten-step process.
Step 1 The organisation receives the explanatory booklet and makes an internal commitment to quality.
Step 2 The organisation buys the Manager's Guidance Pack together with a self-assessment quality questionnaire (SAQQ). The SAQQ is used by the organisation's management to evaluate the quality of their operation and identify any areas of weakness.
Step 3 The organisation submits the SAQQ and receives a Commitment to Quality certificate which can be displayed for one year.
Step 4 If the SAQQ meets the minimum quality standards of Quest the organisation moves on to the next step.
Step 5 The organisation is sent a detailed checklist of the information that an external assessor from Quest will need when he or she visits to assess the organisation's quality.
Step 6 An assessor and mystery visitor are appointed and an assessment date agreed.
Step 7 The mystery customer visits the organisation and assesses aspects by taking part in activities and making bookings and enquiries.
Step 8 An on-site assessment is made by an external assessor who evaluates whether the organisation meets the benchmarked standards set out in the Manager's Guidance Pack.
Step 9 Organisations that meet the minimum standards then receive a Quest plaque which they can display. They also receive a written report based on the mystery customer's and external assessor's findings that can be used to further improve the quality of service provided.
Step 10 During the next two years the organisation will receive a further mystery visit and external assessor visit to ensure that standards are being maintained. At the end of the two years the organisation is required to go through the ten stages again.

Many larger organisations have their own internal benchmarking systems which allow them to compare separate facilities and to spread good practice.

ACTIVITY

Benchmarking

Corinthian Leisure owns 25 private health and fitness clubs throughout England and Wales. In 1999 it introduced a benchmarking system to enable each club to measure its performance against other clubs in the company and identify where improvements need to be made. The system involves sending postal questionnaires to a sample of members of each club, asking them to rate a range of factors on a scale of 0 (poor) to 10 (excellent). The results from six of the clubs, plus the average rating for all 25 clubs, are shown below.

Imagine that you work in the company's customer service department at head office. Your manager has asked you to write a brief report describing the clubs and any specific areas that need immediate attention. For example, the club in Leeds appears to have a serious problem with its staff attitude that needs addressing. Your report could include the following headings:

- Introduction: explaining what is included in the report and its purpose.
- Main areas of concern: listing the clubs involved and the specific issues for each.
- Examples of good practice: listing the clubs that scored well in specific areas.
- Conclusion: summarising the main issues that generally scored badly or scored well throughout the company.

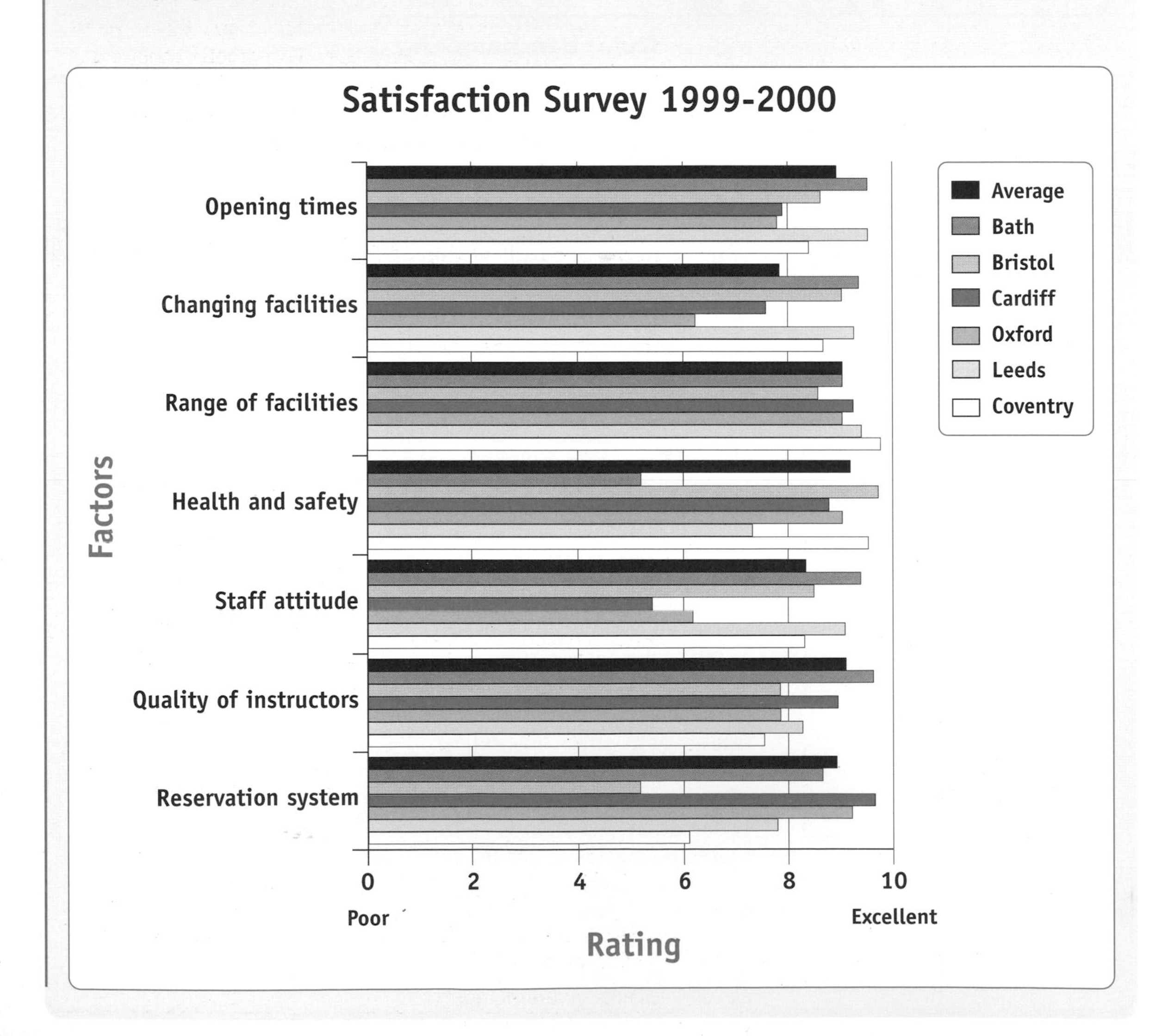

Different leisure and recreation organisations will identify different quality criteria that are important for their particular products and services. For example, providing personal attention to individual needs would be one of the main criteria for a private health spa, whereas providing value for money to groups may be one of the main criteria for a theme park.

When evaluating and monitoring the quality of their customer service, many leisure and recreation organisations rely to some extent on quality criteria identified by independent organisations. In the last activity we looked at how Corinthian Leisure used its own internal benchmarking system to evaluate customer satisfaction. However, smaller companies will not have the resources to carry out this type of large-scale evaluation and may rely on organisations such as the AA, RAC, English Tourism Council, Egon Ronay, Relais Routiers, etc. to help them evaluate the service they offer.

The AA introduced the first hotel-rating scheme, based on numbers of stars, in 1906. This was followed much later by the English Tourism Board's Roses scheme in 1974 and Crown scheme in 1987. In 1998 the ETB (now ETC) joined forces with the AA and RAC to develop a single rating system based on Diamond and Star signs which was introduced nationally in England in August 1999. The new scheme rates hotels on a 1–5 star rating (diamonds are used for 'guest accommodation' such as Bed and Breakfast houses), based on 71 individual quality criteria which cover all aspects of the guest's experience.

Before deciding on suitable criteria for the scheme, extensive research was carried out by a number of independent research organisations, including MVA. MVA's research in 1995 indicated that hotel guests had clear ideas of what was important to them when staying in a hotel. The top criteria are shown in Figure 5.16.

ACTIVITY

Rating scheme for accommodation

Identify which of the criteria in Figure 5.16 are directly related to customer service. Then give five examples for each as to how a hotel could ensure that they achieved a high rating. For example, 'Staff attentive and efficient' could be: greet all guests warmly as they enter the hotel.

Figure 5.16: Essential features in hotel accommodation

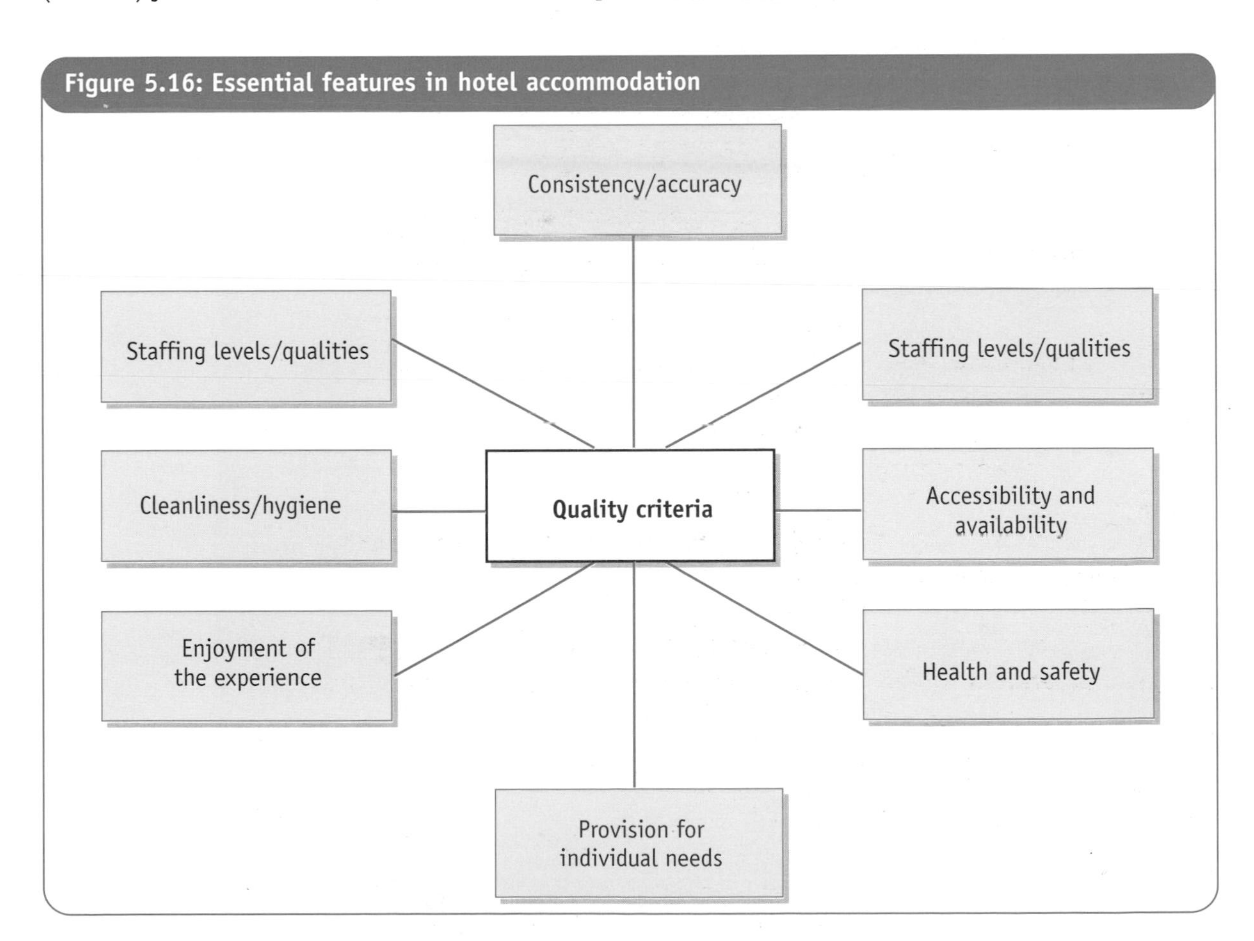

When using a benchmarking system the first stage is to identify the most important aspects of service delivery. These will vary depending on the type of organisation and the nature of the product and service being offered. Figure 5.17 shows the nine general quality criteria that are applied to most leisure and recreation products and services:

Figure 5.17: Quality criteria

- Price/value for money
- Consistency/accuracy
- Reliability
- Staffing levels/qualities
- Enjoyment of the experience
- Health and safety
- Cleanliness/hygiene
- Accessibility and availability
- Provision for individual needs

Price/value for money

Most customers have clear expectations of what they will have to pay for a particular service and will be dissatisfied if the **price** charged does not meet their expectations. This means that an organisation needs to be fully aware of the customer's expectations of price and set standards that meet those expectations by providing **value for money**. For example, if a theme park increased its entrance price from £12.50 to £25.00, it is likely that repeat customers would feel cheated by the unexplained rise.

The concept of value for money is closely related to price, but also involves other quality criteria. Value for money does not mean cheap but rather that the customer is satisfied that the service provided is worth the money paid. Many people are willing to pay considerably more for membership of a private leisure centre because of the increased levels of service offered; these customers feel that they are getting good value for money.

In understanding value for money, it is important to understand why the customer feels that the product or service is good value. A member of an exclusive health and fitness club may pay several hundred pounds in membership fees but feel that it is value for money because of the high quality service. Those setting standards in such a situation need to identify exactly which aspects of the service contributed towards the customer's impression that he or she is getting value for money.

▼ Value for money does not necessarily mean cheap

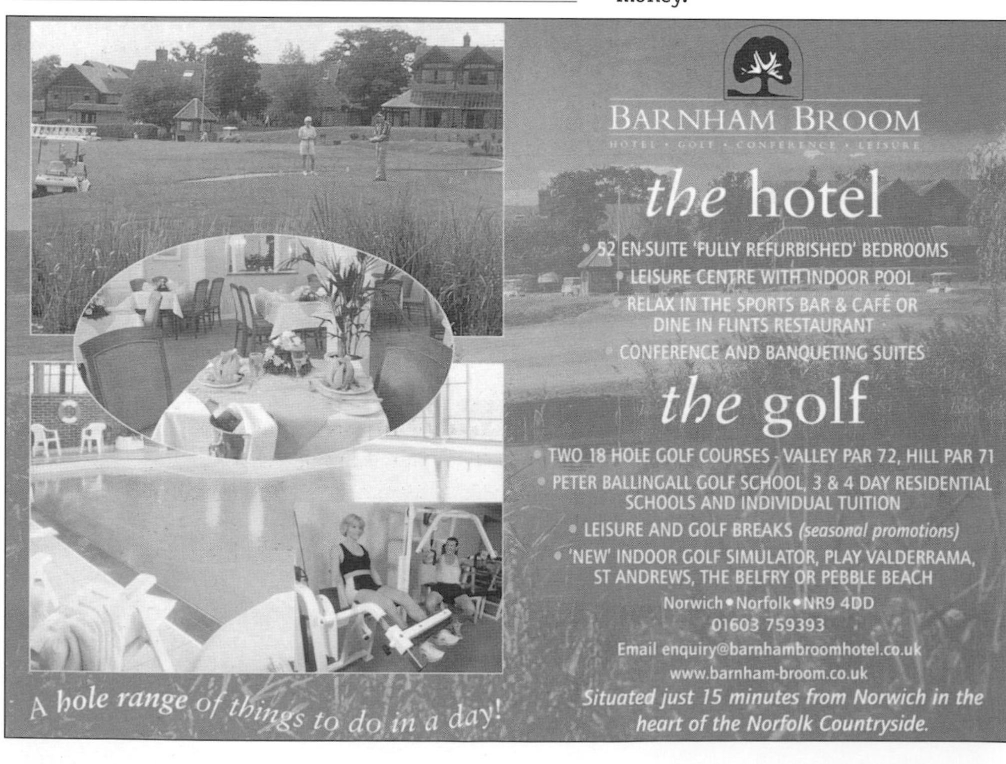

BARNHAM BROOM
HOTEL • GOLF • CONFERENCE • LEISURE
the hotel
• 52 EN-SUITE 'FULLY REFURBISHED' BEDROOMS
• LEISURE CENTRE WITH INDOOR POOL
• RELAX IN THE SPORTS BAR & CAFÉ OR DINE IN FLINTS RESTAURANT
• CONFERENCE AND BANQUETING SUITES
the golf
• TWO 18 HOLE GOLF COURSES - VALLEY PAR 72, HILL PAR 71
• PETER BALLINGALL GOLF SCHOOL, 3 & 4 DAY RESIDENTIAL SCHOOLS AND INDIVIDUAL TUITION
• LEISURE AND GOLF BREAKS (seasonal promotions)
• 'NEW' INDOOR GOLF SIMULATOR, PLAY VALDERRAMA, ST ANDREWS, THE BELFRY OR PEBBLE BEACH
Norwich • Norfolk • NR9 4DD
01603 759393
Email enquiry@barnhambroomhotel.co.uk
www.barnham-broom.co.uk
Situated just 15 minutes from Norwich in the heart of the Norfolk Countryside.
A hole range of things to do in a day!

ACTIVITY

Oasis holiday centre: Value for money

Many leisure and recreation providers offer a different range of prices for their products and services. For example, the hospitality and catering sector of the industry often provides different services charged at different rates. It is important that customers appreciate exactly what is included, so that they understand how the prices charged represent value for money and can make an informed choice as to which level of service they want. Look at these three types of lodges offered by Oasis Holidays and identify the main differences between each.

If you can obtain a brochure for Oasis and, compare the prices of each type of lodge for a given period. Which one do you think offers the best value for money?

2, 3, 4 Bedroom Forest Lodge, 2, 3, 4 Bedroom Woodland Lodge and Lakeside Apartment include:

Fully fitted and equipped kitchen including microwave and fridge/freezer (fridge with freezer in two bedroom lodges) and ironing facilities; telephone, TV with pay film channel and radio. Bathroom with bath, shower and toilet. Separate toilet and hand-basin. Towels are available for hire, please ask for details at time of booking. Private patio (or balcony for apartments and penthouses) with outdoor furniture. Brick barbecues are also provided for lodges. Bed linen is provided. Centrally heated with open fire place in lodge lounge area. High chair and folding cot provided (except in apartments and penthouses please reserve your cot at the time of booking). Three and four bedroom lodges have either a second bathroom or shower room (in two storey, three bedroom Forest Lodges this is en-suite to the master bedroom). Some of the accommodation options are also suitable for customers with special needs, please ring for details.

Cumbrian Lodge, Lakeside Lodge and Lakeside Penthouse Apartment include:

In addition to the above: Housekeeping service daily (except Sunday and Wednesday), double whirlpool bath in bathroom (single in Penthouse), bathroom towels, dishwasher and washer-dryer in kitchen. Hairdryer in the main bedroom. Higher quality of furnishings, a CD player and luxury throughout. Three bedroom lodges have a master bedroom with en-suite bathroom. A sofa-bed option is available in the Penthouse apartment, making it suitable for a family of four at no extra charge.

NEW VIP Cumbrian Lodge

Situated in prime locations central to all the facilities, VIP Cumbrian Lodges offer, in addition to the facilities shown above: An even more luxurious standard of décor, complimentary move channels, fresh fruit & flowers on arrival. Housekeeping service, daily except Sunday and Wednesday, priority VIP hotline allowing you to pre-book all bookable facilities and activities prior to arrival.

Consistency and accuracy

Consistency is concerned with ensuring that the customer always receives the same level of service, so that they are never disappointed that it does not meet their expectations. **Accuracy** means that the customer is given correct information about the products and services offered. So, for example, customers want accurate information about the opening times of a sports centre, with activities taking place at the published times. They also expect the service to be consistent, with clean and comfortable changing rooms, friendly and knowledgeable staff and efficient service.

ACTIVITY

Reliability

As a group, discuss some of the leisure and recreation facilities that you use on a regular basis; for example, a sports centre, swimming pool or cinema. Which aspects of the service do you rely on being the same on each occasion that you visit? Can you think of examples when the service did not meet your expectations and the effect this had on your visit?

Reliability

Reliability is perhaps one of the most important quality criteria because it influences all of the others. It means that customers can rely on the service being the same every time they use it. Therefore, they can be confident that it will provide value for money, be enjoyable and ensure excellent staffing levels, health and safety, etc. For example, customers who use a sports centre on a regular basis will probably do so because they know that they can rely on the organisation to maintain past standards of service. This might include:

- accuracy of programmes and descriptions of activities
- friendliness and efficiency of staff
- value for money
- high level of attention to health and safety issues
- quality of facilities.

Many leisure and recreation organisations ensure the reliability of their service by providing customers with a guarantee about the minimum level of service that they can expect, as shown in the case study below.

CASE STUDY

Customer guarantees at Meadowhall

The Meadowhall shopping and leisure centre in Sheffield has a range of leaflets outlining its guarantees to customers, motorists, people with disabilities and families.

What Meadowhall Guarantees for the Family.

MEADOWHALL GUARANTEES TO PROVIDE:

- Free parent and baby parking spaces
- A free nappy when necessary from the upper Customer Services Desk
- Baby changing facilities for both parents
- Baby bottle and food warming service in the Coca-Cola Oasis
- A daily schedule of on-mall children's entertainment
- Creche facilities for children aged between 2 and 7 years old
- Creche staff trained to NNEB/BTEC standards
- Buggy storage space for Creche customers
- A choice of free drinks for creche customers
- A change of clothes or nappies in case of an 'accident' for creche customers
- A Creche customer refund if your child is not settled in 15 minutes
- Children's play areas on mall and outdoors
- Free high chairs in the Coca-Cola Oasis subject to availability
- Free pushchair for use in the centre subject to availability
- Creche facilities for children with special needs by prior arrangement
- A 'Happy Birthday' greeting for any child by prior arrangement
- The most 'Parent Friendly' shopping centre in the UK
- Compensation to any customer suffering a breach of any Customer Service Guarantee

Staffing

In any service industry, wages are one of the most expensive overheads because a high level of staffing is required to deliver the service. Because staffing is so costly, organisations tread a fine line between providing the right **staffing levels** to deliver the service and overstaffing a facility and therefore reducing profits.

This is often made more difficult to achieve because it may be impossible to predict the number of customers on some occasions. For example, a football supporters' coach party arriving unannounced at a motorway service station at 2 a.m. will probably find that there are insufficient staff to serve them quickly.

In setting standards for staffing levels, an organisation must identify as best it can the number and type of staff required to deliver the service. It will adopt different staffing levels for different times of the day, week or year, where it can predict variation in the level of demand.

Staffing levels are often linked to health and safety standards. For example, a swimming pool must have a minimum ratio of lifeguards to swimmers to ensure safety at all times.

Setting staffing levels is not just a matter of determining the number of staff needed to provide the speed of service required. It also involves the types of service that are offered. The type of service required depends on the nature of the facility and the needs of the customer. An organisation may find that its service levels vary greatly from one facility to another, and in many cases from one product to another. In general terms (there are exceptions), the more that a customer pays for a particular product or service the 'higher' the service level is likely to be. In other words, the service is more personalised with a higher staff–customer ratio.

The actual **qualities** that staff possess is also an important quality criterion. It is important to identify the specific aspects of appearance, personal hygiene, personality and attitude as well as skills needed by staff in a particular job. Of course, this will vary enormously according to the type of organisation and the actual job. Staff must be accessible to customers so that they can provide information, help and assistance, and all these staff qualities must be seen in the context of consistency and reliability.

Any quality standards will only be as good as the minimum that is offered. If a member of staff is usually friendly and welcoming but on a bad day is offhand and uninterested, then the bad day sets the standard. This is because the member of staff cannot guarantee to be friendly and welcoming on each and every occasion. When setting quality criteria for staff, it is vital that they will always be able to live up to the standard.

ACTIVITY

Staffing levels and qualities

The owner of a museum based on a nature theme aimed primarily at children has received the following letter of complaint.

1 Identify the different ways that the staffing levels and staff qualities were inadequate.

2 Suggest what the manager should do to ensure a similar situation does not occur again.

Dear Sir/Madam

Last Saturday I brought a group of 25 scouts to your museum for the day and think that you should be made aware of some of the problems that we experienced.

I had telephoned the previous month to establish whether the museum was suitable for boys aged 9 to 15. I was told that it was suitable. However, I have to say that the exhibits and activities were largely geared towards younger children and the older boys quickly became bored.

When we arrived there was already a long queue at the ticket office because there was only one member of staff on duty. After waiting for 30 minutes, I was told by the member of staff that I should have gone to an alternative entrance for group arrivals. Her manner was offhand and discourteous; however, she agreed that the queuing system was poor and said that she had been complaining about it to the management for the last three months.

When we finally got into the museum, I asked about disabled toilet facilities as one of the boys uses a wheelchair. The member of staff was very polite but said that the disabled toilet was locked and had to be opened by the duty manager. He promised to find the key but did not return until 25 minutes later. Apparently the duty manager was now busy helping in the ticket office! When we actually got into the toilet, it was filthy and had clearly not been cleaned for some time. The duty manager apologized for the state of the toilet but explained that the cleaner had not turned up for work that morning.

At lunchtime we visited the café and had an enjoyable lunch, although one of the boys was given change for a £5 note rather than the £10 that he had paid. When I pointed this out the money was refunded, but the cashier insinuated that it was the boy's fault for not checking his change at the time.

Finally, on leaving, I asked a member of staff for directions to the town centre. The member of staff was new to the area and suggested that I ask at the police station.

I am sorry to have to write this letter, as I think that the facilities in the museum are first class and offer excellent value for money. However, I believe that you should be made aware that your staff are frequently unable to provide a level of service that matches the standards of your facilities.

Yours faithfully
R. N. Scales

Enjoyment

The reasons why customers enjoy a particular leisure and recreation experience are difficult to quantify. For example, some visitors to the Lake District may only enjoy their visit if the weather is good; others' **enjoyment** may be unaffected by the weather.

Poor weather can have such a negative effect on many people's enjoyment of a leisure or recreation activity that some providers such as theme parks partly analyse customer feedback in relation to the weather on the day of the customer's visit. This is because bad weather will often affect the customer's perceptions of all aspects of their experience and make them more critical than they would have been if the weather were good. Obviously, the weather is outside the control of leisure and recreation providers, but there are other factors that affect enjoyment which can be controlled, and can therefore be assessed in terms of quality.

The MGM multi-screen cinema complex in York lists many factors that affect its customers' enjoyment. One factor is that customers like to sit with others in their group rather than be split up. Therefore, one quality standard is that the maximum number of seats sold for any one performance at each of its screens is 40 less than the actual number of seats available. This gives it the flexibility to move customers so that they can watch the film in the company of their group.

Sometimes a person's enjoyment is not solely personal but because of the people that they are with. For example, parents may take their children to the pantomime not so much because they enjoy it, but because of the enjoyment they get from seeing their children's pleasure. The parents' enjoyment will be increased by any aspect of the service that increases their children's enjoyment, such as imaginative merchandising, or theatre staff who take the trouble to talk directly to the children.

ACTIVITY

Quality criteria

Consider the following types of customers visiting an art gallery:

- An elderly retired couple on their first visit.
- A group of teenagers and teachers on a school trip.
- A couple with two young children.
- Two 20-year-old male art students.
- A customer in a wheelchair.

For each type of customer, discuss the specific quality criteria that would affect their enjoyment of the experience. For example, the school party would require different information to that required by the art students.

Health and safety

Health and safety issues are a key concern for all leisure and recreation organisations. Failure to comply with health and safety requirements can result in an organisation not being allowed to operate. Most health and safety standards are legal requirements. Health and safety regulations have a varying impact on leisure and recreation organisations, depending on the type of service and facility provided. For example, COSHH (Control of Substances Hazardous to Health) regulations have a greater significance for swimming pools than for museums. However, all organisations must comply with the Health and Safety at Work Act 1974, which covers four main areas:

- health, safety and welfare of people at work
- protection of outsiders from risks to health and safety
- controlled storage and use of dangerous substances
- controlled emission of noxious or offensive substances.

Apart from complying with legal requirements, many leisure and recreation organisations also make it part of their customer service standards to provide customers with general health and safety advice.

NOVOTEL
NEWCASTLE
Health and safety regulations

Children under 16 years are only permitted in the Pool area when accompanied by a parent or guardian.

Food and drinks are not allowed in the Pool area.

This is a 'No Smoking' area

Ball games, jumping and diving are not permitted.

There is a life ring and emergency push button at the Pool side.

Pool depth 1.3 metres.

The maximum numbers of people allowed in the Pool at any one time is 16.

The fitness equipment area is a dry area and should not be entered when wet and without training shoes.

▲ The Novotel Hotel in Newcastle provides a leaflet for guests using the hotel swimming pool.

CASE STUDY

Health and safety guidelines

This extract is taken from a guide providing health and safety advice on swimming pools abroad.

As only the largest hotels/apartments employ lifeguards, please find out the times (if any) that your pool is supervised, and follow all pool rules and instructions. Please do not use the pool after dark or after consuming alcohol. Never dive from the pool side into water less than 1.5m deep, or where you see a No Diving sign. Do not dive or jump from any raised features around the pool, i.e. decorative rocks, bridges, islands, etc. Remember, the pool at your accommodation may have a strange design, so familiarise yourself with its layout, including depths, slopes and children's areas before you or your children swim. As in the UK, children must never use the pool unless supervised by an adult, even if there is a lifeguard. Please do not run around the pool area as floors can be slippery and accidents could occur. Swim before drinking and eating, not after!

Source: Air 2000 website

ACTIVITY

Health and safety

Another section of the Air 2000 website gives advice on health and safety on the beach and when swimming in the sea. Can you suggest the key tips that should be included?

Hygiene

Cleanliness and hygiene are often linked to health and safety criteria. For example, a chef is expected to be clean and work hygienically, but it is also a legal requirement under health and safety legislation.

As we discussed when looking at personal presentation (page 330), personal hygiene is a key factor in providing excellent customer service because it shows that you take pride in yourself and your job and care about your customers. Leisure and recreation organisations will also have quality criteria for the cleanliness and hygiene of the products that they offer and the environment in which they are delivered. For example, it is almost impossible to find a piece of litter at Disneyland because the highly efficient staff remove all litter the minute it touches the ground!

Cleanliness and hygiene also extend to the general tidiness of the working environment, such as ensuring that reception desks are uncluttered. Many organisations do not allow staff to have drinks or food in areas where they are dealing with customers because it can give an impression of lack of cleanliness. One area where cleanliness is a key quality criterion is in coastal resorts where the cleanliness of the beaches and bathing water is regularly monitored and assessed.

WEBSTRACT

Britain's beaches

The Environment Agency monitors the quality of bathing water in England and Wales between May and September. Twenty samples are taken at regular intervals throughout the season at each site, and the results are updated fortnightly on its web site at www.environment-agency.gov.uk. Agency spokes-person Rob Thomas, said, 'There have been major improvements at many beaches in recent years and in the last year alone effective sewage treatment has been provided for the first time at such popular coastal resorts as Benllech, Colwyn Bay and Llandudno. However, we will be keeping a close eye on the results and investigating the reasons if any samples fail to meet the EC standards. A number of other remedial schemes are now approaching in such areas as Harlech and neighbouring Llandanwg and we are hoping to see improvements in water quality at all local beaches.'

Beaches that pass a range of tests can gain specific awards, such as:

- Blue Flag Awards. These annual pan-European awards are given to beaches that meet the strictest guideline standard as well as various standards for beach management.
- Seaside Awards. Award-winning beaches display yellow-and-blue flags. Beaches are classified as resort or rural beaches and have to meet the mandatory (minimum) water-quality standard as well as providing good safety measures and supervision. They must also practise good beach management, such as dog controls, and offer facilities for disabled visitors at resort beaches.

Source: www.which@which.net

ACTIVITY

Blue Flag beaches

Select a coastal area in the UK. Investigate how many of the beaches in the area have been awarded a Blue Flag or Seaside Award. Why have the beaches gained the award?

Accessibility and availability

Making it easy and straightforward for a customer to buy a product or service is also an important quality criterion. A leisure centre or heritage museum will quickly lose customers if it is not open (**available**) at the times specified. It will be inaccessible to some customers if people in wheelchairs are unable to get through the turnstile, for example. Similarly, **accessibility** can be affected by the provision of car parking or public transport, as shown in the newspaper report below.

A Space Oddity

Wembley invited uproar last night when it emerged that the new £475 million National Stadium will be virtually for Londoners only. Cars are, in effect, banned at the futuristic ground, with parking slashed to only 1,500 spaces and no park-and-pay on match days. Even though Wembley's capacity will be increased to 90,000 there will be just 3,500 parking spaces, half the current provision, with 2,000 given to coaches. It is a recipe for chaos, making it more difficult for fans from all over the country to get to big games and fuelling claims that Wembley is being rebuilt solely for London's convenience.

When it was put to Chelsea supremo Ken Bates, also chairman of the company rebuilding Wembley, that the decision will make access difficult for anyone north of Watford, he said, 'The short answer is that we can't design Wembley for a few individuals'.

Fans, despite contributing £120 million in Lottery money to the project, will be forced to take coaches or trains to new Wembley in May 2003, using currently inadequate British Rail and tube connections to the stadium. It puts massive pressure on the government and Brent Council to improve services and stations in less than four years.

Privately, Wembley officials are fuming nothing has been done to help solve the transport problem. They fear time will run out, leaving them to cope with the chaos when the stadium finally opens for business. There are no plans to build new tube or railway stations near the ground and little has been done about up-grading.

Source: *Daily Express*, 30 July 1999

The timing of a service relates, in part, to availability. It focuses on offering the service at a time that the customer wants to buy it. The success of Sunday trading, allowing shops to open on a Sunday, is an example of how a service has been made available to meet customer needs. Some leisure and recreation organisations offer different prices to increase availability. For example, a visitor attraction such as a theme park that offers an experience that usually lasts several hours may have a reduced admission charge in the late afternoon to encourage customers to experience part of the product or service.

One of the factors that will greatly affect the availability of a leisure and recreation product or service is the process that the customer needs to go through to gain further information and actually buy it. The extract opposite from a leaflet by the National Centre for Popular Music is an excellent example of how a leisure and recreation organisation increases availability by providing a number of booking options. It also highlights accessibility by explaining how customers can get to the centre and also how the specific needs of visitors can be met.

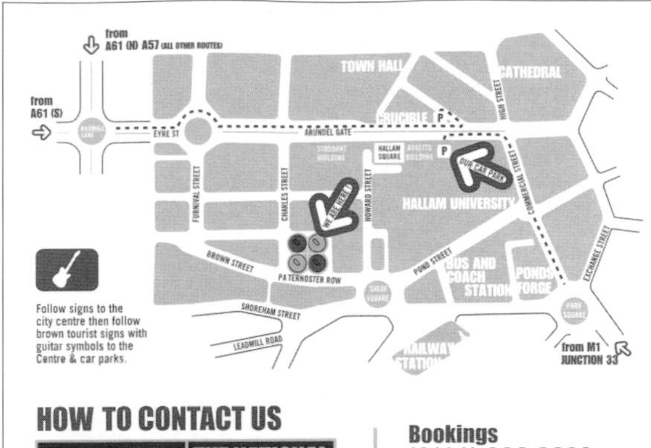

HOW TO CONTACT US

Paternoster Row Sheffield S1 2QQ

Bookings (0114) 296 2626

24hr Information Line (0114) 296 6060

Fax: (0114) 249 8886

Email: info@ncpm.co.uk

Web: www.ncpm.co.uk

ACTIVITY

Accessibility

Collect some examples of leaflets from leisure and recreation organisations and discuss how they provide accessibility.

Individual needs

One of the criticisms often directed at organisations that have well-defined quality standards is that it makes the service too inflexible and unable to meet the **individual needs** of customers. One example is the customer who asks for a hamburger without a gherkin or mayonnaise, who is told that it is not possible because all hamburgers have to be served with the standard garnishes. Fortunately, situations like this are becoming less frequent as organisations realise that quality standards are only effective if they truly satisfy the needs of all customers.

In assessing the quality of customer service, therefore, the needs of individual customers must be considered. This may be a matter of identifying the general needs of customers and then asking the question: 'But what if one customer wants something different?' For example, a sports centre may identify the general needs of customers as friendly service, detailed and expert advice and information, clean and safe facilities and value for money.

But individual needs should also be identified, by asking such questions as: 'But what if the customer

- can't speak English?
- is elderly?
- is visually impaired?
- is a child?
- wants extra information?

ACTIVITY

Quality criteria

Select a service provided by a leisure and recreation organisation. It may be one you have used yourself. In small groups, brainstorm to identify quality criteria that customers might expect when using the service.

Feedback techniques

Once an organisation has identified the quality criteria by means of which it will monitor and evaluate its customer service, it needs to decide how to go about it. There are a number of **feedback techniques** that organisations use to evaluate whether their customers are happy with the level of customer service. These are set out in Figure 5.18.

Figure 5.18: Feedback techniques

- informal feedback
- surveys
- suggestion boxes
- focus groups
- mystery shoppers
- observation

Informal feedback

All staff in leisure and recreation organisations will receive **informal feedback** on a daily basis. They may overhear customers talking or customers may voice their opinions directly to staff. Alternatively, feedback may be from other staff, management or even people who are not customers but voice an opinion about the products and services offered. For example, someone passing by a visitor attraction may comment on how untidy the outside is looking and how the plants need watering.

This type of informal feedback is very important to organisations in helping them to monitor and evaluate the service that they offer. Many customers feel more comfortable making informal comments and may not have the time or inclination to complete formal questionnaires. Remember the passive complainer described on page 370: he or she is much more likely to make an informal comment than put their complaints in writing.

Of course, informal feedback can also be positive and it is just as important to listen to this. Positive feedback tells an organisation what it is doing right and allows it to develop these areas so as to continue to satisfy customers' needs and expectations.

All staff who work in leisure and recreation organisations need to be receptive to informal feedback and ensure that it is relayed to the appropriate people so that action can be taken. Many organisations have a mechanism to ensure this, such as regular staff meetings in which staff can report on feedback received.

ACTIVITY

Informal feedback

Jo is an area manager for a chain of sports clothing and footwear shops. One of her responsibilities is to ensure high sales and her annual appraisal takes this into account. This season, sales have decreased and she is keen to identify the reasons and see if anything can be done. Therefore, she has decided to call a meeting of all her shop managers to discuss any ideas that they might have for the decline in sales. She has particularly asked them to report on any informal feedback that they have received. The following managers attend the meeting.

Antonio. His sales are the only ones to have increased this season. His customers have said that although the products may be more expensive than others, you get what you pay for. They are particularly complimentary about the advice and help provided by the sales assistants in the shop.

Julie. She is the manager of the company's largest branch situated in a busy city-centre shopping mall. One of the main complaints that she gets from her customers is that the mall gets very busy at peak times, which means that getting to the shop can take some time. She has also had complaints about the fact that customers can sometimes queue for over 20 minutes at the cash desk when the shop is busy.

Robin. He runs a high street shop near three similar shops operated by competitors. He was speaking to some customers who had bought products from one of the competitors but were dissatisfied with the quality of the merchandise. Their main complaint was that the products did not last long and that the shop assistants were unsympathetic when the goods were returned.

Dana. Her sales have shown the biggest decline of all the shops. She claims that the manager of the local sports and leisure centre is recommending competitor shops to his customers because they provide better value for money. Dana argues that they may be cheaper, but her company's products are of a better quality and the level of service is higher.

Sandra. Sales used to be high at Sandra's shop but have declined steadily over the last year. She has overheard some customers complaining about the hard sell techniques of the sales staff, such as suggesting that the customer might like to buy expensive cleaners for trainers. It is company policy to train staff to offer such additional products to customers. Recently, she has been told by her assistant manager that some of the casual staff sometimes lack the product knowledge required to give customers relevant and accurate advice. The shop finds it difficult to attract and keep staff, so relies heavily on part-timers who tend to be local students. Because these staff work few shifts it is often difficult to provide them with adequate training.

As a group, role play the staff meeting and discuss all of the feedback that you have received and what you are going to do about it. You can repeat the role play if there are more people in your group than there are roles.

Surveys

Many leisure and recreation organisations use **formal feedback** methods such as **surveys** and customer comment cards. If you have already studied Unit 4 you will have a good understanding of how questionnaires are designed and used (see page 272). Some organisations use open questions that allow customers to write their own opinions, such as the one in Figure 5.19 for Oasis.

Figure 5.19: Oasis customer care questionnaire

Oasis

"A penny for your thoughts"

Guest Questionnaire

Please help us to provide the best possible holidays for you and your family by giving us your views on this questionnaire. Your replies will be treated in the strictest confidence and will help us to improve our service. In addition, all completed questionnaires will be entered into our monthly **free** holiday prize draw.

Holiday Start Date ....

Holiday Finish Date ....

Lodge Name ....

Lodge Number ....

How did you rate your holiday at Oasis?

BETTER THAN EXPECTED ☐

AS GOOD AS EXPECTED ☐

WORSE THAN EXPECTED ☐

	VERY GOOD	GOOD	FAIR	POOR	COMMENTS PLEASE
CUSTOMER SERVICES					
How was your booking handled					
Drive Thru/Check in					
Customer Services Desk					
ACCOMMODATION					
Cleanliness on arrival					
Decor/Comfort					
Equipment/Utensils					
Maintenance Service (if used)					
Cleaning Service (if used)					
RESTAURANTS/CAFES/BARS					
The Food Court					
Cafe Vert					
Le Champenois					
Rajinda Pradesh					
Yangs					
Great American Disaster					
Pizza Piza					
Bistro Bar (Country Club)					
Burger Republic					
Tom Cobleigh Pub					
The Green Room Bar					
The Garden Bar					
The Den Bar					
ENTERTAINMENT					
Cabarets/Shows					
Woodmites/Forest Friends					
Kindergarten					
Oasis Cinema					
LEISURE ACTIVITIES					
Booking Service for Sports					
Cycle Hire					
World of Water					
Indoor Sports facilities					
Outdoor Sports facilities					
Lake Watersports					
Off - site activities					
The Sanctuary Spa					

Some organisations, like the National Railway Museum, are able to use simpler comment sheets yet still obtain useful information. Figure 5.20 shows the customer comment card used by the National Railway Museum. The completion of this sheet could hardly be made any easier for customers: they simply tick the appropriate yes/no box for each quality criterion listed. There is also a space on the back page for the customer to make specific recommendations on how customer service could be improved.

ACTIVITY

Customer comment cards

Go back to the last activity involving Jo and her shop managers. Can you design a customer comment card to find out customers' opinions of the service in the company's shops? You should bear in mind the results of your role play discussion.

Figure 5.20: National Railway Museum customer comment card

DID WE KEEP OUR PROMISE?

We aim to maintain high standards in all that we do. You can help by completing this questionnaire, which we will use to monitor our performance.

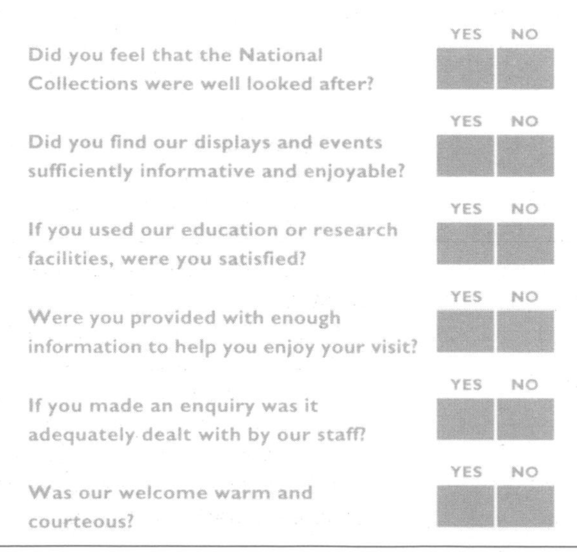

	YES	NO
Did you feel that the National Collections were well looked after?		
Did you find our displays and events sufficiently informative and enjoyable?		
If you used our education or research facilities, were you satisfied?		
Were you provided with enough information to help you enjoy your visit?		
If you made an enquiry was it adequately dealt with by our staff?		
Was our welcome warm and courteous?		

Suggestion boxes

Some leisure and recreation organisations provide suggestion boxes for their customers. As with informal feedback, this has the advantage that many customers may not want to spend time filling in a lengthy questionnaire, but would like to make a brief comment on the service they have received. A variation on the suggestion box concept is to have a visitors' book where customers can write comments. Visitors' books are particularly popular at visitor attractions, so that for many visitors the books themselves have become an enjoyable part of the experience. For example, in the Anne Frank museum in Amsterdam, visitors queue, not only to write their own comments, but also to read the moving messages from visitors from around the world.

ACTIVITY

Customer comments in visitors' books

Blackwall Heritage Centre and Country Park partly monitors and evaluates levels of satisfaction by analysing the comments that customers make in the visitors' book. Comments are generally very positive, but the manager is disappointed to find that entries for last week are not as favourable as usual. Only 7 of the 350 visitors to the park and heritage centre that week actually made a comment in the visitors' book. Here are their comments:

'Excellent outdoor facilities and parkland, but the heritage centre was crowded making it difficult to view exhibits.'

'Catering and souvenir shops a disgrace – long queues and staff who couldn't be bothered to even smile.'

'A great day even though the weather was the worst week of the summer.'

'Good value for money with an excellent range of facilities for children, but very expensive given that we saw everything in two hours.'

'Why can't you do something about the queues to buy admission tickets? We waited for half an hour in the rain because most of the customers ahead of us were paying by credit card.'

'Our day was spoilt by the large number of ill-disciplined school groups at the centre. It made it difficult to see the exhibits and the noise and disruption that they caused was unacceptable – especially since they pay so much less to get in than normal customers.'

'We had to wait 45 minutes for a guided tour of the heritage centre and then our guide did not seem to know what she was talking about. When asked any question, she apologised for not knowing the answer and said that she was new – surely the least we can expect is a knowledgeable guide!'

If you were the manager of Blackwall what key customer service issues would you think need addressing to prevent similar dissatisfied comments in the future? Can you identify any other factors beyond the control of staff that may have influenced the negative comments?

Focus groups

A **focus group** is a group of people who are encouraged to discuss their opinions and feelings about a particular organisation, product, service or topic. It has the great advantage that the information collected is very detailed, because customers can explain their feelings and opinions in depth. For example, a leisure centre may hold a focus-group discussion to identify how customers view its customer service.

Mystery shoppers

An increasingly common method of evaluating customer service is to employ a **mystery customer**. This is someone employed by the organisation, but not known by the staff, who visits the facility as a customer and analyses the extent to which service levels meet quality criteria. The mystery customer will usually have a checklist covering what needs to be looked at.

CASE STUDY

Fedback techniques at Cadbury World

Cadbury World in Birmingham uses a range of feedback techniques to evaluate the level and quality of its customer service. In 1993 it introduced a mystery visitor survey which is now run annually and involves up to 75 separate visits. Each mystery visitor is provided with a checklist of points to assess, which include eye contact, smile and wearing of name badges.

This last point is particularly important because it allows the organisation to identify which staff need further training in customer service skills. The mystery visitor scheme is linked to the staff bonus scheme and has resulted in a dramatic improvement in standards. Each department is rated separately, using a points system, and there is healthy competition between departments to achieve the highest score. The mystery visitors usually call during peak times. Interestingly, though, scores tend to be higher at these times than when the attraction is quieter and staff are tempted to stand around and chat.

Source: ETC *Insights* magazine

ACTIVITY

Cadbury World

Imagine that you have been employed as a mystery visitor to evaluate customer service in shops offering leisure and recreation products such as videos, computer games, home entertainment, music, sports equipment/clothing, etc. Design a checklist with a rating score and visit at least three shops and assess their customer service. For example:

Greeting: 1 (very poor) 2 (poor) 3 (adequate) 4 (good) 5 (excellent)

You could use a table such as this one to record your findings. Compare your results with the rest of the group.

	Name of Organisation		
Criteria	**1**	**2**	**3**
1. Greeting	Rating 1 - 2 - 3 - 4 - 5	Rating 1 - 2 - 3 - 4 - 5	Rating 1 - 2 - 3 - 4 - 5
2.	Rating 1 - 2 - 3 - 4 - 5	Rating 1 - 2 - 3 - 4 - 5	Rating 1 - 2 - 3 - 4 - 5
3.	Rating 1 - 2 - 3 - 4 - 5	Rating 1 - 2 - 3 - 4 - 5	Rating 1 - 2 - 3 - 4 - 5
4.	Rating 1 - 2 - 3 - 4 - 5	Rating 1 - 2 - 3 - 4 - 5	Rating 1 - 2 - 3 - 4 - 5
5.	Rating 1 - 2 - 3 - 4 - 5	Rating 1 - 2 - 3 - 4 - 5	Rating 1 - 2 - 3 - 4 - 5
6.	Rating 1 - 2 - 3 - 4 - 5	Rating 1 - 2 - 3 - 4 - 5	Rating 1 - 2 - 3 - 4 - 5
7.	Rating 1 - 2 - 3 - 4 - 5	Rating 1 - 2 - 3 - 4 - 5	Rating 1 - 2 - 3 - 4 - 5
General comments			

Observation

Observation is a research method in which information is obtained by observing customers' behaviour or events taking place. In leisure and recreation there are many situations in which observation methods can be used to provide valuable information about customers' reactions to customer service. For example, observing the way that customers react in an interactive museum will often indicate the extent to which they find it enjoyable and interesting. Similarly, a new waiter or waitress will be closely observed by the restaurant manager during training to check that they are delivering an appropriate level of service.

ACTIVITY

Observation

Working in groups of three, take turns to play the role of a telephone enquirer, a leisure centre manager and a trainee receptionist at the leisure centre. The trainee has been given the following quality criteria for taking telephone messages:

- Answer phone within five rings.
- Say: 'Good morning/afternoon, Anytown Leisure Centre. How may I help you?'
- Identify who the message is for. If the recipient is not available, make a record of the following details:
  - Name of caller
  - Telephone number of caller
  - Name of person to receive message
  - Message
  - Time and date of message
- Thank the caller for the message and assure them that it will be forwarded.
- Remain polite, friendly, confident and professional throughout the call.

The leisure centre manager observes the trainee take a telephone message and should give them feedback on the extent to which they met their quality criteria.

The enquirer should make up the details of the message. Each of you should have a turn at playing all three roles.

Evaluating quality criteria

Quality criteria provide a clear idea of what we need to be looking at when assessing customer service requirements. However, it is important to understand how to evaluate the criteria and the quality of customer service provided. In this context, 'to evaluate' means to identify the value or worth of each criterion in terms of customer needs and expectations. It is vital to understand:

- the perceived importance of each quality criterion to the customer
- how customers would rank each criterion in order of importance.

A customer taking flying lessons might rank health and safety as the most important quality criterion. Someone visiting a heritage centre might think that the provision of specialist guides is most important. Of course, both customers will have many other quality criteria that they rank in order of importance. Most organisations evaluate and continually monitor the customer service that they provide. They do this to ensure that their service is meeting the needs of customers, and if it isn't, that the necessary changes can be made. An evaluation of customer service focuses on the extent to which quality criteria:

- meet customers' expectations
- are met by the actual level of service provided.

In setting quality criteria, it is clearly the intention to satisfy customers' needs, but continuous evaluation is needed to ensure that those needs are met on each and every occasion. Similarly, in setting standards an organisation expects them to be met, but in reality this may not always happen. For example, one quality criterion might be that telephones should be answered within three rings. This may be impossible if staff are overstretched and trying to meet a number of other criteria at the same time, such as dealing promptly with customers waiting at the reception desk.

In essence, then, an evaluation of customer service seeks to ensure that the level of customer service is fulfilling the quality criteria, and that these quality criteria are, in turn, satisfying customer expectations.

Service delivered by competitors

Evaluation of the quality of customer service should include an assessment of the level of service offered by organisations in related markets. On page 323 we looked at the benefits of securing a competitive advantage in the provision of products and services. By analysing the level of customer service in related markets against key quality criteria, it is possible to evaluate the quality of service provided within your organisation. This is another way of benchmarking standards.

Related markets consist of organisations which offer services that may influence the customer expectations of your service provision. Organisations in related markets include the following.

- **Direct competitors**: those who offer the same things as you; for example, competing sports centres, visitor attractions, health clubs, etc. If a competitor offers customers better customer service, it is likely that it will achieve a competitive advantage which may threaten the profitability of your organisation.

- **Other organisations in the same business.** For example, an art gallery is in the same business as a museum, because they provide a service in a similar way.
- **Related service organisations.** A visitor attraction could be related to other, different leisure and recreation organisations; for example, procedures for dealing with credit card payments at a theme park could be used at a visitor attraction.

Facilities outside the leisure and recreation industry in unrelated service organisations also influence customers' expectations. For example, the use of cash machines by banks reduces queueing times. This may affect customers' expectations of how long they are willing to wait for a leisure and recreation service. Many visitor attractions now have a similar facility to that offered by banks, where customers can use a visual display unit to access information without queueing.

ACTIVITY

Benchmarking against competitors

1 Using the information provided in the table below, identify:

- customer service areas for which the attraction received low scores from customers;
- service areas where staff think they are performing better than actual customer perceptions;
- service areas where the attraction has and has not gained a competitive advantage over the competitor attraction.

2 On the basis of these findings write a brief summary of the level of customer service and make recommendations for possible improvements in service delivery that will meet customers' expectations and gain a competitive advantage in all areas.

Customer service area	Rank order	Average customer score	Average employee score	Average customer score for competitor attraction
Wide range ofexciting activities	1	8	9	9
Value for money	2	5	6	10
Attraction appropriate for all age ranges	3	5	7	8
Attraction suitable in all weathers	4	5	6	7
Good staff supervision	5	8	8	5
Friendly and helpful staff	6	9	10	6
Attraction well located and easy to find	7	10	10	7
Clean environment	8	10	10	8
Good catering service	9	9	8	7
Sufficient car parking	10	8	8	10

Making recommendations for improvements to customer service delivery

The final stage of evaluating customer service quality is to summarise any findings and make recommendations for improvements to service delivery:

Stage 1: Decide how the quality of customer service can be evaluated.
Stage 2: Evaluate quality criteria in terms of their importance and ranking based on customer expectations.
Stage 3: Evaluate (benchmark) customer service delivery against quality criteria identified by customers' expectations and actual level of service.
Stage 4: Evaluate (benchmark) the quality of customer service in related markets against key quality criteria.
Stage 5: Compare and summarise the findings of stages 3 and 4.
Stage 6: Suggest recommendations for improvements based on stages 3, 4 and 5.

Remember that the evaluation of customer service quality is based on the measurement of key customer service criteria against actual service delivery, together with a comparison of service delivery with organisations in related markets. In particular, this evaluation of organisations in related markets will focus on the level of service provided by direct competitors.

BUILD YOUR LEARNING

End of section activity

1 Identify the key service quality criteria in two leisure and recreation organisations of your choice, giving examples of the procedures and practices used by managers and staff to achieve them.

2 Using appropriate methods for measuring and monitoring, evaluate the effectiveness of the customer service delivery in each organisation.

3 Compare the effectiveness of customer service delivery in each organisation.

4 Suggest appropriate actions to improve customer service delivery in each organisation.

You may be able to use the same organisations that you choose for earlier end of section activities on pages 344 and 367.

Keywords and phrases

You should know the meaning of the words and phrases listed below. If you are unsure about any of them, go back through the last 21 pages to refresh your understanding.

- Assessing
- Evaluating
- Benchmarking
- Quality criteria/standards
- Price/value for money
- Consistency
- Accuracy
- Reliability
- Staffing levels/qualities
- Enjoyment
- Health and safety
- Cleanliness and hygiene
- Accessibility
- Availability
- Individual needs
- Feedback techniques
- Informal feedback
- Formal feedback
- Surveys
- Suggestion boxes
- Focus groups
- Mystery shoppers/customers
- Observation

Preview

Organisations in the leisure and recreation industry are continually undertaking research, and developing and testing new products and services. For example, a sports goods manufacturer may design and launch a new piece of equipment, or a leisure centre may stage a 'taster day' to try to attract new customers. Such projects are a response to the changing desires and expectations of the consumer and often produce unique and innovative results.

This unit provides the opportunity for you to work as part of a team; to plan, carry out and evaluate a real project that is of interest to you. Working as part of a group, you will agree on an event or business project related to leisure and recreation, and then assess whether it is feasible. Once the feasibility of the project has been established, you will put together a business plan and then actually carry out your planned project, rounding it all off with an evaluation of your performance. As well as producing a written business plan for your chosen project before it takes place, you will also keep a log of your involvement in the project.

Whatever you choose for this unit – short-term project or one-off event – you will need to draw on things you have learned from other units in your course, such as marketing and customer service. The title of this unit effectively sums up what you need to do to complete your assessment: put leisure and recreation into action.

The assessment requirement for this unit is shown on page 458.

6

Leisure and recreation in action

Contents

Choosing a leisure and recreation project

Project development and the staging of events in the leisure and recreation industry are widespread, as organisations strive to meet increasing consumer demand for leisure and recreation activities. A **project** or **event** refers to activities with significant requirements for planning, resources and evaluation specific to the undertaking. This can include the provision of a product or service. In the context of this unit, a project or event means a planned undertaking that is leisure and recreation related, and which will run for a designated period of time. The project or event may be short term (a week), medium term (a month) or long term (several months). The basic planning aspects of projects and events are the same, so throughout this unit we will use the term project to cover the wide range of events and projects that take place in the leisure and recreation industry.

There is an enormous range of industry projects: everything from small-scale projects such as a children's summer activity programme in a leisure centre, to large-scale projects such as the building of a giant IMAX screen, or renovating a derelict dockside area. The latter examples involve huge investment, extensive planning and many thousands of people in their creation. Examples of projects occur in all three sectors of the industry:

- voluntary sector projects, such as the building of a new pavilion or changing rooms.
- public sector projects, such as sports development programmes or the creation of a countryside trail.
- private sector projects, such as a new ride at a theme park.
- partnership schemes involving organisations from all three sectors, such as a stream clean-up campaign sponsored by the private sector, carried out by volunteers, with vehicles and resources provided by a local authority.

On a much larger scale, there are numerous examples of spectacular projects to mark the new millennium, such as the Millennium Dome and London Eye beside the Thames in London.

▲ The Millennium Dome

International sporting projects include the

- Sydney Olympic Games
- European Indoor Athletics Championships in Ghent, Belgium
- European Football Championship in Belgium and Holland
- Six Nations Rugby Championship.

ACTIVITY

Leisure and recreation projects

Make a list of leisure and recreation projects that are of:

- international significance
- national significance in the UK
- regional significance
- local importance.

When you have completed your list, discuss in small groups what it is that such projects share in common in terms of their planning and operation.

The assessment for this unit involves planning, carrying out and evaluating your own leisure and recreation project. Figure 6.1 shows the main stages you will need to complete in order to undertake this task.

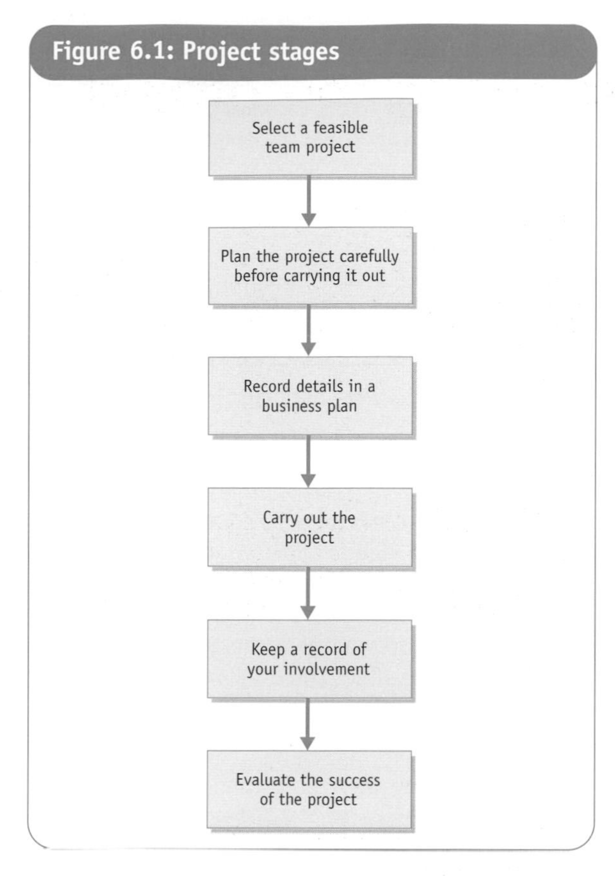

Figure 6.1: Project stages

Project organisers and co-ordinators use the same basic planning techniques and teamwork that you will need for your own project. Figure 6.2 uses a simple format to show the main stages of a project, from idea to implementation.

You should begin by selecting a few ideas that you think might be appropriate for your project. Take time to assess each idea in more detail, to see which one is the most **feasible** (possible). You will then plan the project and put together a **business plan**. A business plan should normally represent a summary of:

- what the organisation aims to achieve: its objectives
- the methods by which it intends to achieve those aims, such as marketing
- the tools or resources it requires, such as people and equipment
- the financial implications: budgets
- how success will be measured.

Recording your involvement

Although you will run the project as part of a team, you will also need to produce a **personal log** or **diary** that records your particular contribution to the team project, right from your first team meeting, through the running of the project, down to the last team meeting.

Figure 6.3 on page 400 shows a grid of the skills and attitudes you need in order to complete the project successfully. It is useful to keep this in mind throughout.

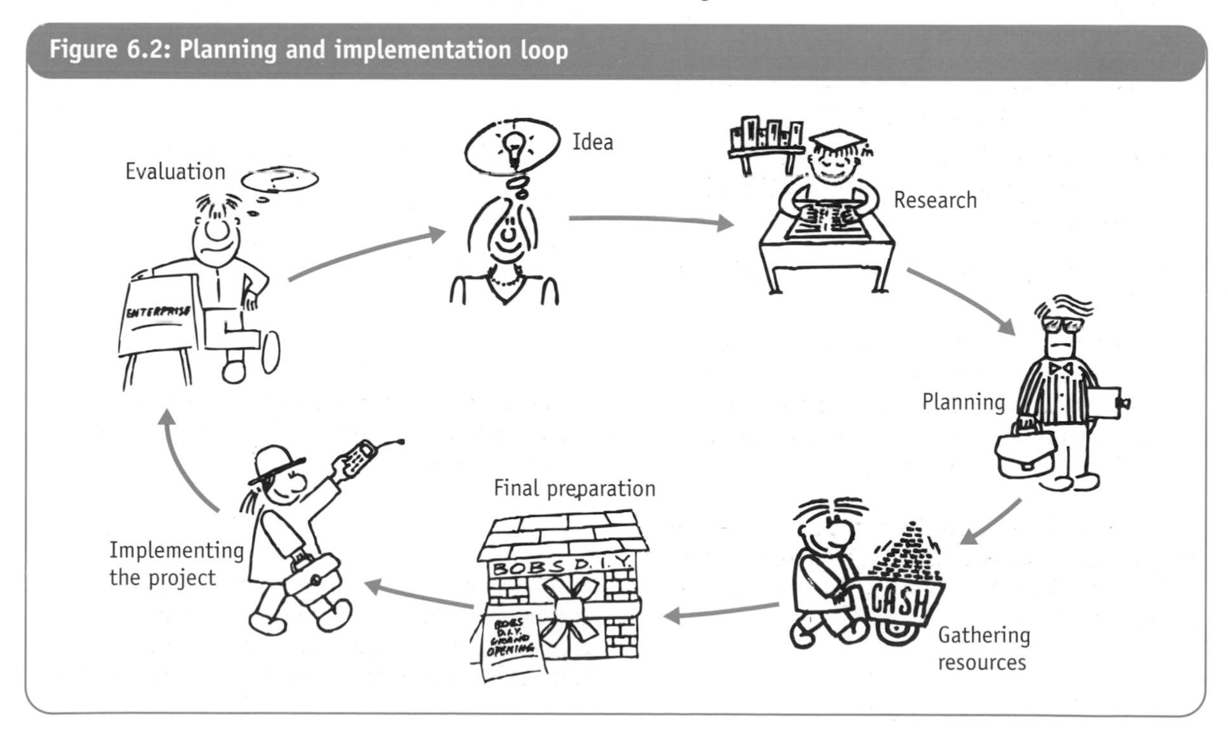

Figure 6.2: Planning and implementation loop

Your record of your own contribution and that of the team is an active process: it must be maintained throughout the whole project. It will be a vital source of evaluation and review material. You need to decide how you will record this information right at the start of the project. You could use a variety of formats and should prepare these during the planning stage, so that you become familiar with them and can fill them in efficiently during the busy project stage. Formats might include:

- ring binder divided into sections
- diary with ample pages for notes
- computer disk
- wall planner or flow chart
- video recording
- photographs or tapes
- observer comments
- participant statements
- tutor observations.

Whichever format you select, it has to cover two main areas: process and content. **Process** means all the actions or procedures gone through by the team, such as planning, tasks allocated, customer care, deadlines and any revisions made, along with notes on advice sought. **Content** means the topics covered. This must include records of:

- personal and team contributions
- how roles (briefings) were maintained
- how disruptions were handled
- how health, safety and security aspects were maintained
- how well the team co-operated and whether it adhered to the plan.

The format of the log should be discussed with your teacher to establish what is acceptable. For example, individual page headings could follow the suggestions shown in Figure 6.4.

Figure 6.3: Personal skills grid for carrying out a project

- learn by your mistakes
- communicate
- be adaptable
- keep up group spirit

- be proactive
- begin with the end in mind
- prioritise
- synergise

- manage your tasks well
- be a positive influence
- think before you speak
- use logic, not emotion, to decide issues

- respond rapidly
- don't get stressed
- do an equal share
- be part of the team

Figure 6.4: Log book headings

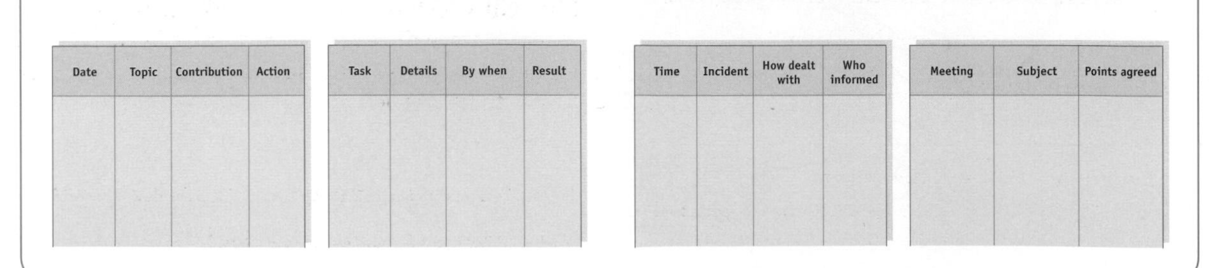

Date	Topic	Contribution	Action

Task	Details	By when	Result

Time	Incident	How dealt with	Who informed

Meeting	Subject	Points agreed

Your log should also contain copies of all relevant materials, such as:

- minutes from team meetings
- schedules of tasks
- checklists and briefings
- diary of activities
- reports on research
- costs of resources
- contacts for providers
- contingency plans
- emergency procedures.

ACTIVITY

Creating a personal log book

Create a log book suitable for recording your own contribution to the running of a project and those of your fellow team members. The log book should have enough space and section divisions to cover all the following process and content factors.

Process:

- schedule for the project
- reports on progress
- revisions or alterations made
- summary of the business plan

Content:

- own contribution
- team's contribution
- adherence to role and briefing
- maintenance of health, safety and security
- co-operation with others
- report on how closely the plan was followed
- reports on dealing with disruptions
- advice and guidance from others

You can use this log book for the activity on page 453 and on the Portfolio assessment on page 458.

All of these go to make up the complex picture of your contribution and that of your colleagues to running the project, for assessment purposes. If you are unsure if you should include certain materials, you can always present them as an appendix. This helps others to cross-check and verify your evidence, as well as showing depth. It is absolutely essential to fill in your log frequently, while your memory is fresh. There is nothing worse than trying to recall and record information long after the project is over: that is not good organisation.

Ideas and options

The starting point for your project is the ideas stage. Without initial **ideas or options** for a project, you will have nothing to plan and develop. If you look at the list opposite compiled by Project Sport Event Management (Figure 6.5), you can see how diverse its ideas and options are.

One of the best ways of identifying ideas and options for your project is to run a **brainstorming** session with everyone in your team. Everyone should put forward ideas, no matter how bizarre those ideas seem. From this long list, the best three ideas can be selected and investigated further. Here is a list of brainstormed options for projects which a local council running a leisure centre might come up with, in order to increase participation in recreational activities offered in its facilities.

- Various taster days for specific sports.
- Various taster days for specific target groups.
- Hosting a regional tournament.
- Staging a recruitment drive/display in schools and colleges.
- Staging some exhibition matches.
- Making a promotional video for circulation throughout the district.

Looking at examples of previous successful projects can also be an effective way of identifying options. It is a safer route which may not be as creative as an original idea, but which nevertheless offers opportunities for teams to stage their own version of a tried and tested formula. Projects that student groups have run successfully include:

- special events, such as children's beach games
- excursions to visitor attractions

Figure 6.5: Examples of events

- Air/Land/Sea Treasure Hunt
- Country Sports Day
- Executive Challenge
- Flying & Off-Road Experience
- Company Golf Day
- Scottish Golf Experience
- High Flyers Day
- Indoor Amusements
- Ocean Yacht Challenge
- Off-Road Driving
- Shooting through the Ages
- Sunseeker Powerboat Experience
- Riverboat Challenge
- Winter Off-Road Challenge
- Circuit day
- Rallying Experience
- White Water Rafting
- It's a Knockout
- Inflatable fun

- Bedrock Challenge
- Eggs can fly
- Executive Kidnap

- Thames Cruise
- Classical concerts
- Low Flying in Scotland
- Theatre Evenings
- Ballet/opera
- Last Night At The Proms
- Europe by Eurostar
- Pop Concerts
- Champagne Tours
- Booze Cruise
- Casino Evenings
- Christmas parties
- Evening Entertainment
- Indoor Amusement Arcade
- Mafia Murder Eveing
- Monoply Challenge
- Race Evening
- Summer Sizzler
- Family Fun Day
- Firework Event

- British Grand Prix
- Cheltenham Gold Cup
- The Grand National
- Touring Cars
- Polo
- Formula 1
- The Derby
- International Cricket
- Domestic Cricket
- Rugby League
- Tennisl
- Henly Royal Regatta
- Prix De L'arc De Triomphe
- Royal Ascot
- International Soccer
- Cowes Week
- Glorious Goodwood
- Premiership Football

Source: Extract from *Projectsport Event Management* brochure

- fundraising ventures for a charity
- an open day for prospective leisure and recreation students
- exhibitions and conferences using a leisure and recreation theme.

Whatever you finally decide to do, it's a good idea to have an alternative project just in case your first choice turns out not to be feasible.

ACTIVITY

Brainstorming

Hold a group brainstorming session with your project team to identify ideas for possible projects. Then decide on the best three ideas to create your shortlist. From this shortlist, select the best option for your project.

You will need to consider a wide range of factors in making your decision, such as time-scale, skills of the team, resources available and potential demand from customers.

Feasibility

Assessing the feasibility of a project involves asking this question: 'Can it be done within the time-scale and resources available?' The main factors that will determine the feasibility and success of a project are:

- the market (customers)
- the location(s) to be used
- scale (size of the project)
- cost
- funding sources
- method of production
- plan of operations

There is a wide range of possibilities to choose from within a leisure and recreation context. The choice is yours, as long as the project is sufficient to meet all the unit assessment requirements (see page 458-460).

There are two main benefits in ascertaining the feasibility of a project. First, it helps people to think through the project in a logical sequence. Second, a thorough plan ensures that human, physical and financial resources are not wasted on a project that cannot be implemented.

The case study highlights some of the key feasibility points that Barclays Bank advises for customers intending to start a business. The questions the bank asks are also relevant to your leisure and recreation project.

CASE STUDY

Will your idea work?

Will your idea work?

You may have the best idea in the world for a project – you may even have a product or service that nobody has thought of before – but a good idea alone will not guarantee you success. Before you begin to develop your project idea, there are some key questions you should ask yourselves.

- Are there people who will want what you propose to offer?
- Who are they and how will you market your idea to them?
- What will you charge them?
- Will it meet the targets you set?

Personal qualities

- Self-sufficiency: will your team be able to cope with pressure from others, make decisions quickly, carry responsibilities?
- Initiative: can your team spot opportunities and act on them?
- Determination: can you overcome difficulties and sustain effort?
- Resilience: can your team learn from its mistakes and keep believing the project will succeed?
- Responsibility: will you tend to blame everyone else when things go wrong?
- Imagination: can your team keep the smaller ideas flowing to meet client needs?

Skills

- Management: can your team control the project, prioritise tasks and meet deadlines?
- Finances: will your team meet its targets and keep accurate records?
- Marketing: can you meet your customer needs and cover costs or make a profit for your project?
- Production: even if you don't actually make a product, but deliver a service instead, can you deliver on time, to the right level and in style?
- Technical expertise: does your team possess or have access to any specialist knowledge it requires?

Source: Barclays Bank *Starting Your Own Business*

ACTIVITY

Will your ideas work?

Read the case study above and summarise the guidance it provides by producing six key points your team needs to consider when deciding the feasibility of your project. Once these are agreed, discuss and evaluate each of the three shortlisted ideas that you selected in the last activity and select the best option.

Developing a business plan

The most effective way of progressing your idea from the feasibility stage is to put together a **business plan**. This is covered in detail in the next section on page 407. Planning for all projects is essential. Anyone involved in carrying out a project should bear in mind two pieces of sound advice:

If you fail to plan, then prepare to fail!

Proper planning prevents poor performance.

In the following summary of a Sport England publication, you can see how comprehensive are the planning guidelines for those people who wish to plan a building project for sports activities.

Building a sports club: laying the foundations

The first step is to decide what you really want to achieve – for example, new changing rooms, courts, pitches, equipment, more teams, more members, more facilities, etc. First of all, form a small working group with a designated leader to gather everyone's views. Once this has been done, the second step for the working group is to develop an overall vision for the project – 'think long term and think quality' is the advice given.

Step three involves moving from 'vision to blueprint' by reviewing aims and priorities, problems and resources. The next stage is to 'assess local needs', meaning the views of likely partners and customers: if they fit with your vision then it is likely that your project will have a future. The guidance goes on to describe what should be included in the business plan, including funding as a key area.

In this case (the proposed building of a new sports club), permission will have to be sought from the local council. If this is obtained, building work can commence, usually by appointed architects and building contractors. Finally, consideration should be given to how the facility will be run after it is completed so that sufficient revenue can be generated to maintain operations. As work progresses, plan your grand opening and usage programmes.

In the leisure and recreation industry, a business plan forms the basis for discussions and negotiations with bankers, planners, sponsors and many others when seeking funding, support or permission to proceed with a project. Your formal business plan will show if your team has:

- considered every aspect of your project
- budgeted sensibly and realistically
- allocated sufficient resources.

Figure 6.6 shows how all the different elements fit into the **project planning and delivery sequence**, and what needs to go into the business plan.

Figure 6.6: Planning and delivery flow chart

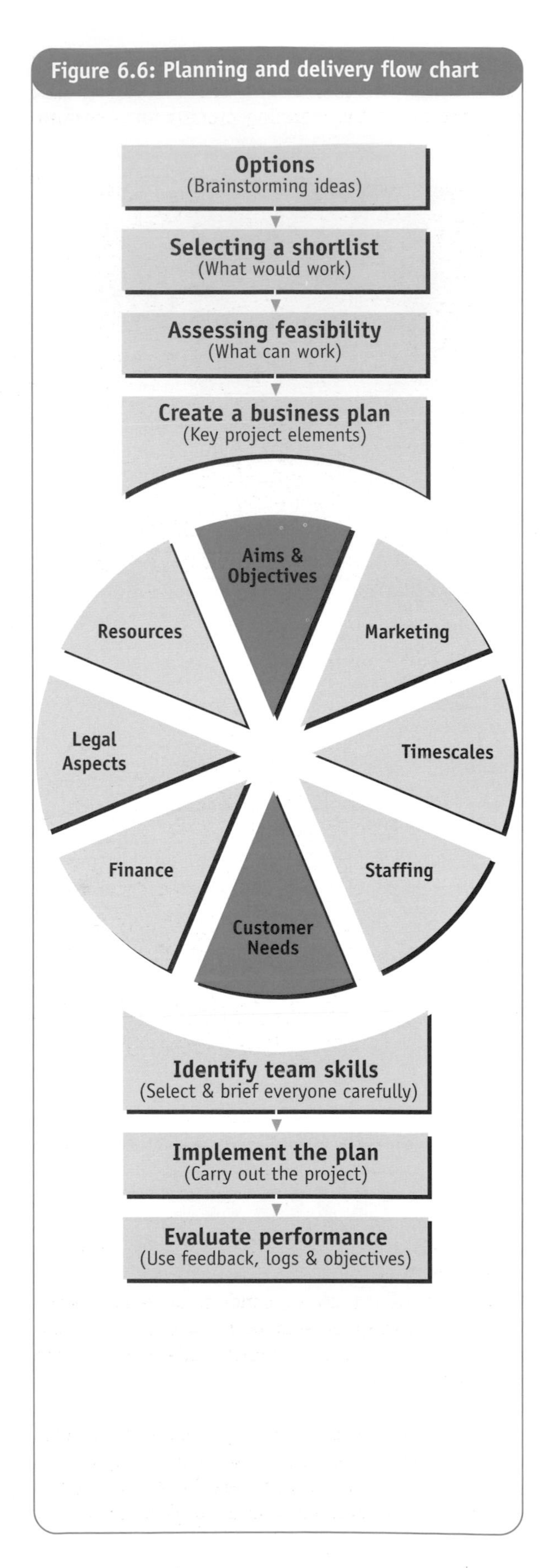

Organisations such as the English Sports Council (now Sport England) and banks all provide free guidance about the planning process for a business project.

In order to plan, co-ordinate and control the complex and diverse activities of modern leisure and recreation projects, a process called **project management** is used. Project management is used in large schemes such as the conversion of Bankside Power Station into the new Tate Gallery for Modern Art, the building of the Millennium Dome, and the rebuilding of Wembley Stadium, all in London. Such large-scale projects involve massive amounts of technology and investment and thus require extensive project management techniques.

Project management also helps teams to take into account the economic pressures to keep to budget, work safely and within the law, provide value for money, and respect the environment. Your project team will probably face similar pressures, albeit on a much smaller scale!

All projects have one common characteristic: transforming a feasible idea or activity into reality. In any project there will always be an element of risk and uncertainty. This means that the steps to completion can never be described with absolute certainty beforehand. Every effort must be made to get the details as accurate as possible – in other words, to foresee or predict all of the elements of the project, using the best information available, with back-ups included should anything unforeseen occur. This brings us to the central concept of business planning, whereby each element is calculated meticulously to help reduce uncertainty and enable the project to run smoothly.

BUILD YOUR LEARNING

Keywords and phrases

You should know the meaning of the words and phrases listed below. If you are unsure about any of them, go back through the last eight0 pages to refresh your understanding.

- Project
- Event
- Feasible
- Business plan
- Personal log/diary
- Process and content
- Ideas and options
- Brainstorming
- Planning and delivery
- Project management

End of section activity

In order to assess the feasibility of your chosen project, your team should hold a meeting to brainstorm ideas for your project or event. This meeting and its agreed outcomes should be recorded and included in your personal log or diary. The following criteria can be used to determine the feasibility of the events/projects that are suggested:

- Location and availability of facilities.
- Accessibility and suitability.
- Likely customer demand.
- Cost implications and finance available.
- Human resources available – skills/abilities/numbers.
- Time-scale.
- Scale or scope of the project: will it meet all necessary assessment criteria?
- Tutor/school or college/outside organisation approval.
- Health and safety issues.
- Achievable by the team within the time and budget.

The business plan

This section looks at each element of the business plan for your chosen project (see Figure 6.7).

Aims and objectives

An **aim** describes what an organisation intends to do. It usually states its overall purpose or direction. Devising your group's aim(s) can be undertaken through discussion. It is best to keep your aims short and memorable. A project team's overall aim could be, for example, to:

- complete the project on time and on budget
- provide a first-class service to customers
- ensure participants have a safe and happy time
- use all resources effectively for the benefit of the target group.

ACTIVITY

Statement of aims

Each member of your project team should devise a statement to convey your project's overall aims. Then, as a group, analyse each statement to find the most suitable version. Complete the task by agreeing your aims and writing them down.

Setting objectives

In order to achieve your aim(s) they require measurable dimensions. The project team needs to set specific **objectives**. These are used as the starting point for the whole business planning process and as the chief means of measuring performance at the end of the project. As a consequence, objectives must themselves be quantifiable so that they can be measured. One of the best-known ways to remember how to set appropriate objectives is to use the **SMART** approach (see also page 236).

Figure 6.7: Elements of the project business plan

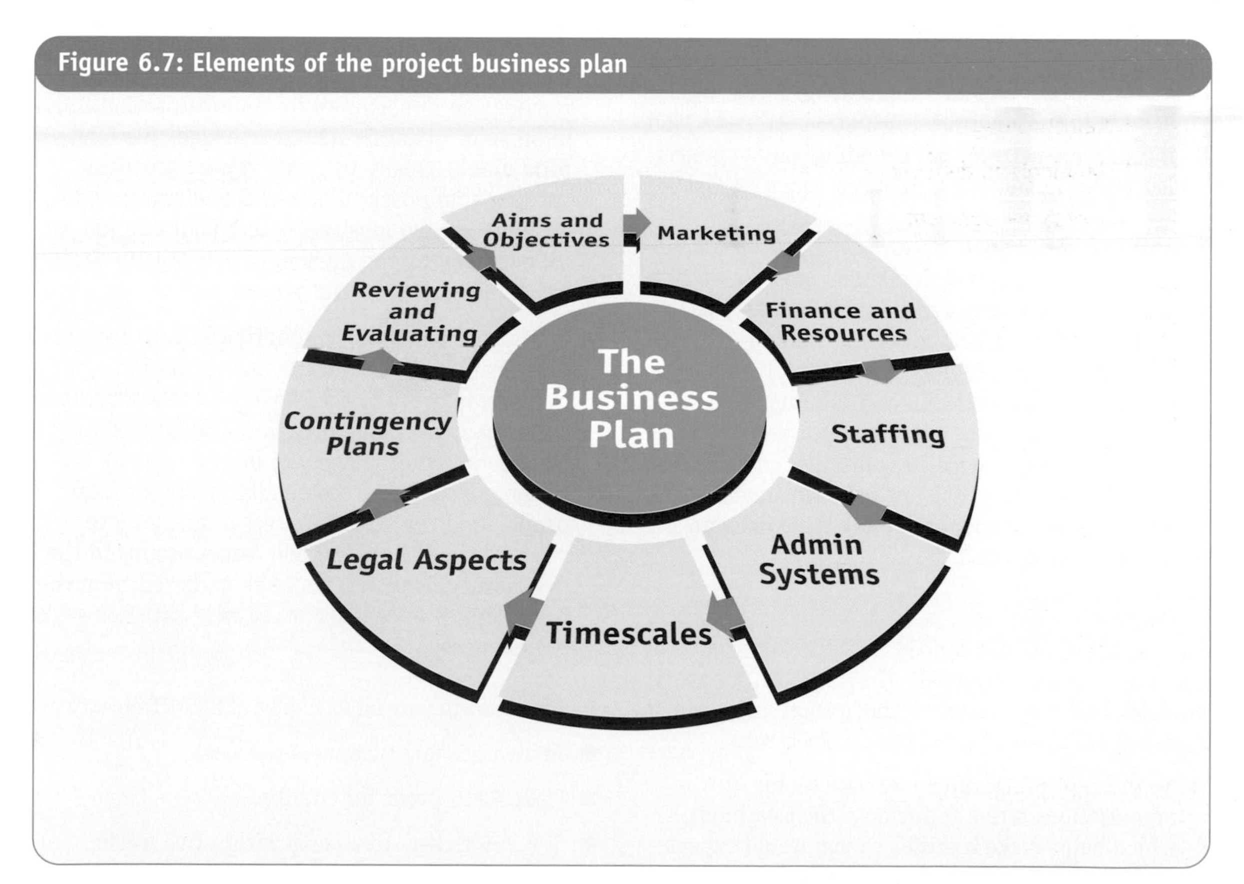

Objectives should be:

S pecific
M easurable
A greed
R ealistic
T imed

Objectives usually cover three key areas of project operation:

- performance and quality
- budget
- time to completion.

Performance and quality

The outcome of the project must be fit for the purpose for which it was intended and the specifications given must be satisfied. For example, a new ride at a theme park must function reliably, efficiently and safely, and not be an eyesore; a new line of sports products must satisfy such market requirements as durability.

Budget

The project must be completed without exceeding the agreed budget. For most commercial projects, failure to achieve this objective will lead to reduced profits and lower returns on capital invested, or actual losses. Proper attention to and calculation of costs and financial management of spending on a project, however large or small, are essential.

Time to completion

Actual progress must match planned progress, so that all the significant stages of the project take place no later than their specified date, leading to final completion on or before the planned date. For example, although the Greenwich Millennium Dome has been criticised for various reasons, its project team successfully met its budgetary objectives on time. The London Eye, however, did not open on time when it failed vital safety checks; as a result, it did not earn any income in January 2000.

Projects in the leisure and recreation industry incorporate objectives derived from the overall aims of the organisation involved, the type of service it provides and the sector of the market in which it operates. Let's look at some typical objectives.

- To increase **profitability**. Private sector organisations strive to increase their earnings, which helps make a profit, so you would expect this to be a prime objective for them. For example, a project team might set a profit objective of 25 per cent from ticket or admission charges.
- To increase **take-up** (numbers of customers). This could be an objective for providers in any sector of the leisure and recreation industry. For example, an entertainment arena might set a target of increasing visitors for concerts by 1,500 after running a series of promotions. If it is achieved it usually brings a host of benefits, such as increased income, more seats booked and more spectators. Sports development schemes often set this type of objective when targeting groups which have low levels of participation (take-up), such as ethnic minorities or people with disabilities.
- To increase **consumer interest** in products or services. A number of short-term projects can raise awareness of products and services. Local, regional and national projects therefore often attract sponsors, who see them as excellent vehicles for promoting their products and services. In this case, a percentage increase in sales, such as a target of 5 per cent, could be used to judge whether the objective had been achieved.
- To create a favourable **image**. The completion of a project in partnership with a charity group provides an opportunity for an organisation to improve or maintain its public image. The long-term aim is usually to create **repeat business** (people going back to buy or spend more) and customer/brand loyalty. Success might be judged, for example, by the number of new loyalty cards issued after a successful project.
- To provide **community benefits**. Private sector organisations in the leisure and recreation industry may try to achieve a good relationship with the local community through sponsorship; the public sector may try to do the same by working to improve the quality of life for local people, and the voluntary sector by trying to improve conditions for their target groups in the community. Feedback could be gathered from the target group to see how many were satisfied with the changes.

The following are all examples of SMART objectives:

- Attract 35 new customers per week.
- Make £110 profit for charity.
- Sell 225 tickets to a party within five weeks.

When you have agreed the objectives for your project, you should include them in your business plan, so that the outcomes can be measured. This may involve focusing each objective on a specific aspect, e.g. setting a target of 100 ticket sales, or of a 10 per cent profit, or of less than five complaints overall. You should make sure all your team members are aware of and agree with the objectives set.

It is important to decide how your team will collate the evidence and compare objectives to outcomes before you carry out the project. Figure 6.8 illustrates this process.

Figure 6.8: Monitoring objectives throughout the project

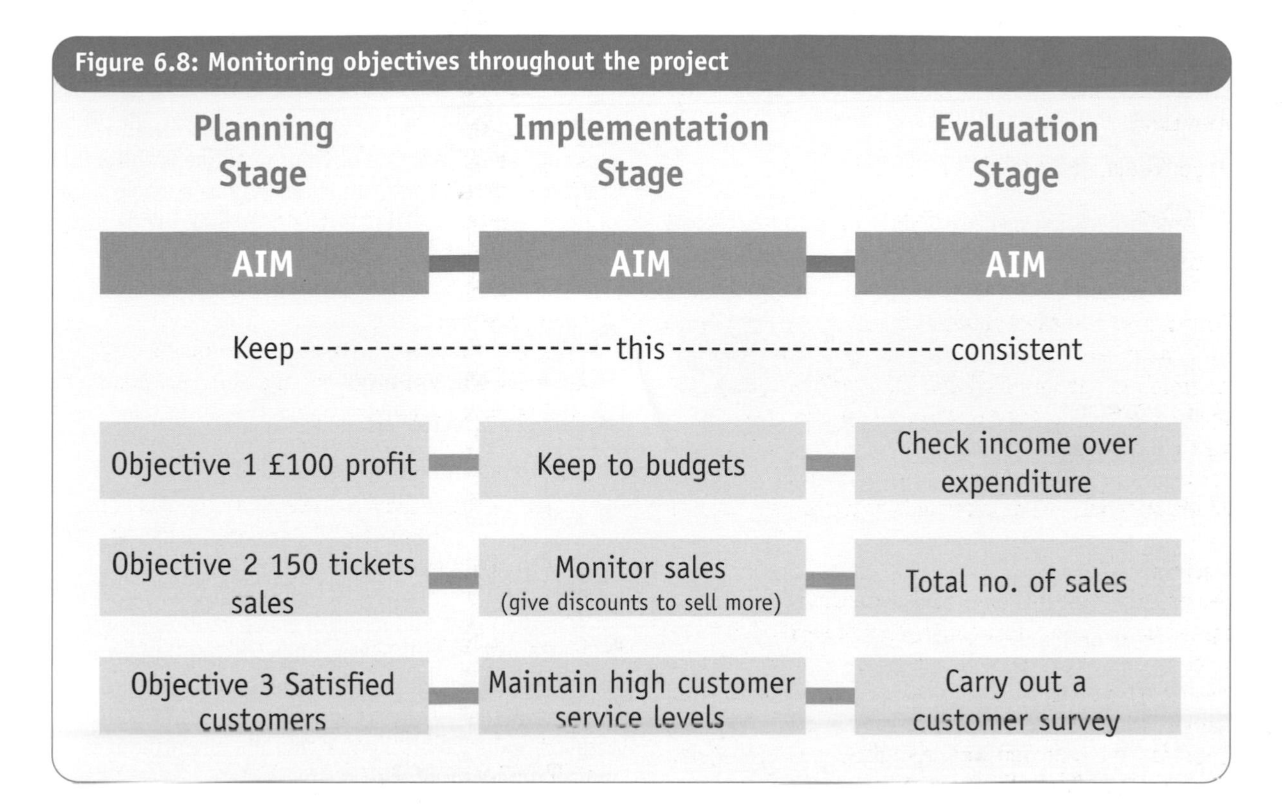

ACTIVITY

Setting objectives

1 With your project team, look at the examples of projects shown in the list below and devise suitable objectives for them, bearing in mind the SMART approach. For each objective you devise, list how you might gather information on how your team performed, or the success of the project, with reference to the objective. Some possible sources to get you started include tickets sales, questionnaires and evaluation sheets.

- A day trip to a theme park for a group from your school/college.
- A countryside outing for a group of students with physical disabilities.
- An exhibition of football memorabilia and displays.
- A sports quiz held for a charity.
- Coaching a group of young girls how to play netball.
- Arranging a hockey taster day at a local hockey club.

2 Using your own team project, devise a range of objectives that follow the SMART approach. When your team has agreed these objectives, include them in your business plan. Remember to consider how you will evaluate the project outcomes to determine if you have achieved each objective.

Project time-scales

The importance of **timing** cannot be emphasised enough. Any delays will have consequences not just for the project and the organisation, but will also affect other resources, budget estimates and business relationships. The most common delays are caused by:

- lack of information
- lack of immediate funds
- delays in other resources
- waits for approval/permissions.

Any project, irrespective of its scale or context, costs money throughout every day of its existence, for a variety of reasons:

- materials
- design time
- construction time
- inflation
- price rises
- wages
- interest on loans
- administration
- accommodation
- buying other services
- use of facilities.

When you tackle your project, remember this simple phrase: Time is money!

Deadlines

The success of your project could depend on people working to a **time-scale** (prearranged schedule) as an essential feature:

- A specific and spectacular/memorable start and finish point.
- A series of fixed or target deadlines, before, during and after the project.
- Actions needed to meet the priorities and deadlines.
- Split-second timing by the team running the project.
- Effective resource allocation to the right people at the right time.

Projects need distinctive **starting and finishing characteristics**. Most large events these days have opening and closing ceremonies, with themed displays and parades and increasingly elaborate special effects, such as fireworks or laser shows. The Olympic Games, for example, can have truly spectacular opening ceremonies. It may be possible for your project to use a starting and/or closing ceremony.

Projects always have important **deadlines** which must not be missed. The obvious deadline is the actual starting date and time, but there may be a whole series of deadlines before the start concerning a wide range of aspects of the project, including:

- publicity
- finances and resources
- delivery of materials
- confirmation of arrangements
- staff training
- health, safety and security checks.

In order to set and monitor these various deadlines, it is often necessary to establish an **implementation schedule**, which lists actions, responsibilities, dates, times and the resources required to run everything. Establishing such a schedule and documenting it is an important aspect of your business plan.

On a much larger scale, the preparations for the Sydney Olympics took over eight years and a business plan was submitted to the International Olympic Committee at the bidding stage in 1992. The webstract opposite shows that preparations for the games followed a 'Masterplan' covering four main projects, embracing not only the sports events themselves, but also other leisure and recreation requirements.

WEBSTRACT

Sydney and the Great Games in 2000: what it's all about

The development of the Olympic Games site is actually a redevelopment of an area called Homebush Bay, and the biggest programme that the State Government of New South Wales has undertaken. A masterplan sets out the mixed uses of the massive site, which is strategically located near the heart of Sydney – its long-term uses are for tourism, recreation, exhibitions and entertainment, residential and commercial uses. The masterplan divides sites into four main project areas:

- Urban core containing sporting and entertainment facilities, the show ground and exhibition precinct and commercial sites.
- Urban district which will be the Olympic village.
- A major metropolitan park.
- A waterfront development providing public access to the shoreline.

The masterplan has been revised to include changes prompted by the bad experiences of the Atlanta Olympic Games. A huge plaza with room for 300,000 people to circulate has been planned and the natural landscape has been harnessed and improved to include water features.

The Sydney games will increase tourist income for the city, not just during the games, but long afterwards as well, for the site adds another attraction to the many which Sydney already has to offer. Spectators at the games will benefit, but in the longer term the residents will gain a valuable and attractive range of leisure and recreation locations.

Source: http://webdog.com

Recording time-scales and deadlines

Timetables are the simplest form of project plans. They are useful at the feasibility stage, in order to assess roughly whether the proposal will fit into the available time-scale. However, they are not sophisticated enough for daily monitoring and control of progress, because they do not contain enough detail for a large project. You can see from Figure 6.9 overleaf how difficult it is to squeeze information onto a calendar-style timetable.

A bar chart is a better option. It displays the programme more effectively, with the time-scale along the top and each horizontal bar representing a project task. The name or description of each job is written on the same row at the left-hand edge of the chart, as you can see from the example shown in Figure 6.10 overleaf.

Bar charts are easy to construct and interpret, and are also readily adaptable to a great variety of planning requirements, especially if you can find an IT software programme that you can use. You may well see bar charts used for staff rotas or room scheduling in your school or college.

A more complex chart might be colour coded to show exactly who is to complete a task. A simple form of such an approach is a flow chart which indicates the key stages of the project in chronological or prioritised sequence, as in the Alton Towers event planner shown in Figure 6.11 on page 414.

Critical path analysis (CPA) is a planning technique that sets out the master route or sequence of key tasks (rather like the masterplan for the Olympics in Sydney). Figure 6.12 on page 413 shows how a group's network of tasks might look when applied to some project-planning sequences.

This technique can also be helpful at more complex stages, too, when several tasks are continuing at the same time, or some tasks are dependent on a key task's completion (e.g. a mailshot as task 5 depends on the prior printing of materials as task 4).

Figure 6.9: Calendar style timetable

WEEK	MON	TUES	WEDS	THURS	FRID	SAT	SUN
1	First team meeting		Aims & objs decided		Bus. plan		
2		Marketing commences		Second team meeting	Fund raising days		
3	Third team meeting		Roles decided		Bookings confirmed		
4		Publicity stunt					
5	Fourth team meeting		Final checks				
6	Project starts					Project finishes	
7	Evaluation						
8	Reports		Logs				

Figure 6.10: Bar chart for a leisure and recreation careers event

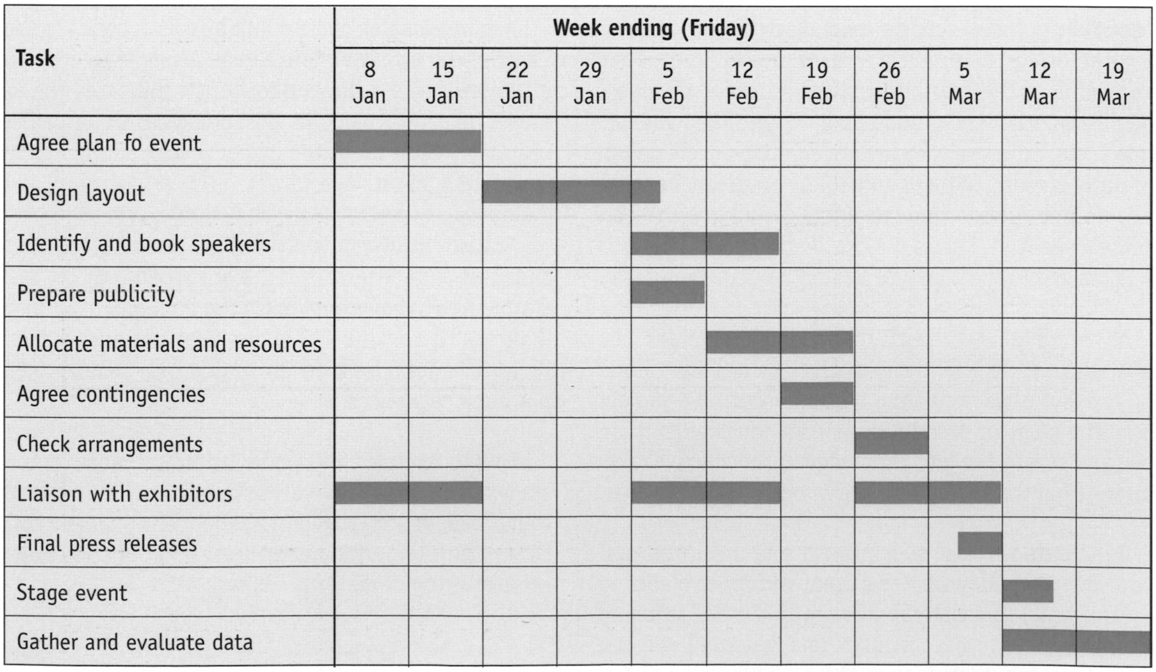

Task	Week ending (Friday)										
	8 Jan	15 Jan	22 Jan	29 Jan	5 Feb	12 Feb	19 Feb	26 Feb	5 Mar	12 Mar	19 Mar
Agree plan fo event											
Design layout											
Identify and book speakers											
Prepare publicity											
Allocate materials and resources											
Agree contingencies											
Check arrangements											
Liaison with exhibitors											
Final press releases											
Stage event											
Gather and evaluate data											

Figure 6.12: Critical path analysis

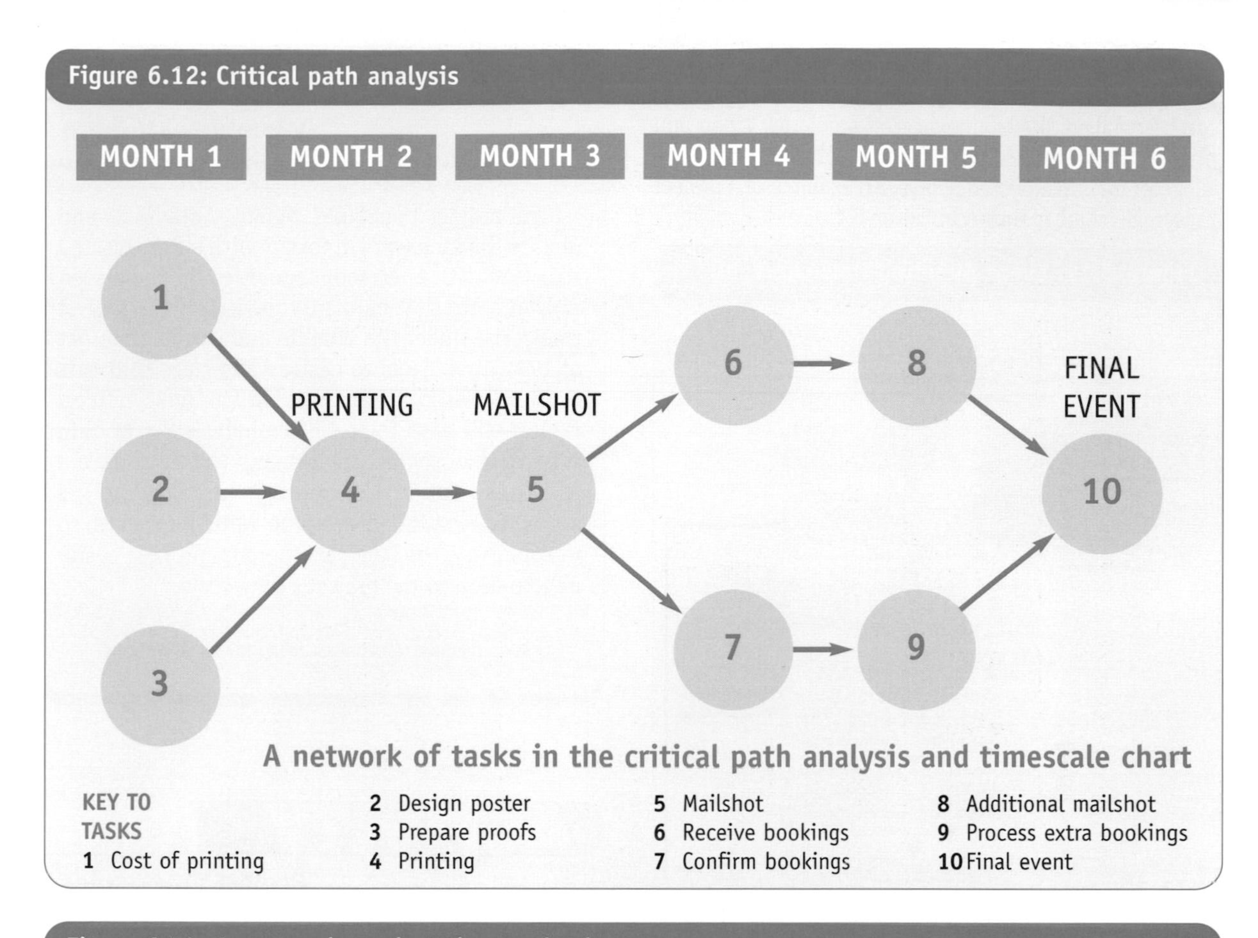

Figure 6.13: An example project time-scale chart

Tasks	January 1 → 31	February 1 → 28	March 1 → 31
1			
2			
3			
4			
5			
6			
7			
8			

The case study on the rebuilding of Wembley stadium shows how even the largest leisure and recreation projects can be delayed due to unexpected problems. When you plan your own project it is wise to build in extra time to allow for any unexpected delays. An example of a project time-scale chart is shown in Figure 6.13.

Figure 6.11: Event planning flow chart

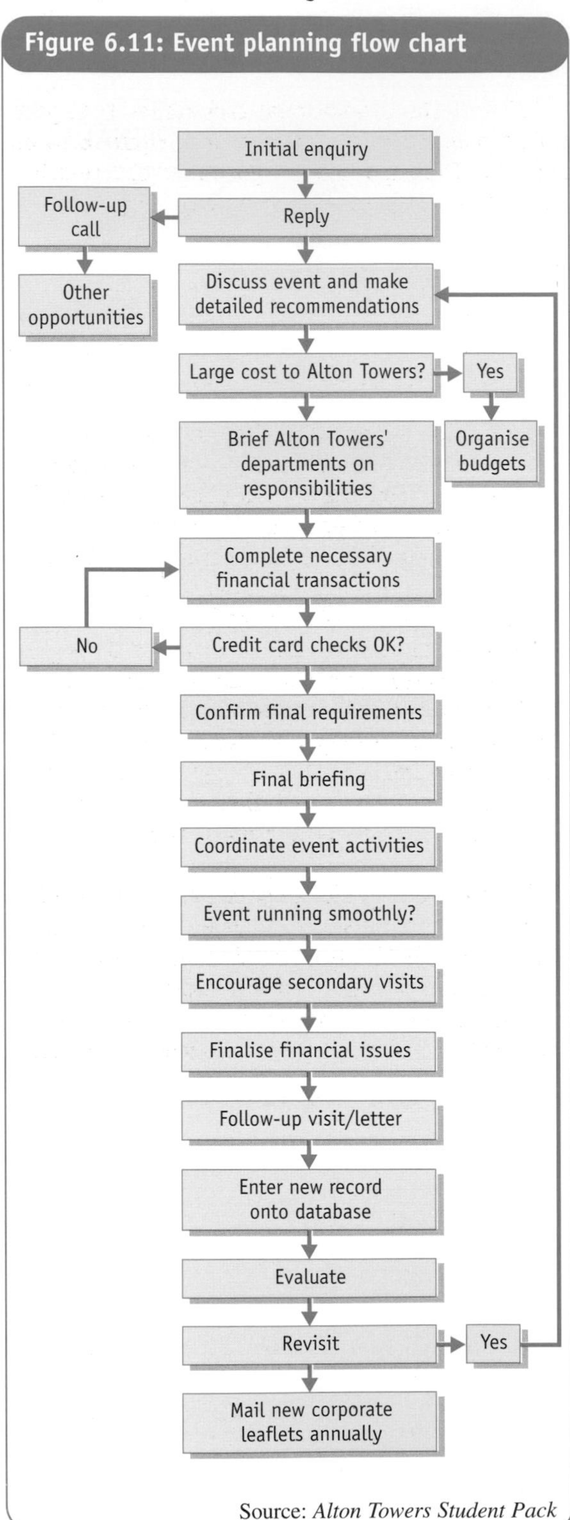

Source: *Alton Towers Student Pack*

CASE STUDY

Wembley stadium

The project to rebuild Wembley stadium, and replace the famous twin towers with a four-masted structure with a retractable roof, could be delayed after reports that bats are roosting in the roof of the arena. Under the Wildlife and Countryside Act of 1981, it is illegal to destroy any place that bats use for shelter. So progress on the £475 million project will have to come to a halt, while wildlife experts investigate. The scheme will only have a five-year building schedule if England is successfully awarded the 2006 World Cup finals, so re-colonising the bats elsewhere might be a costly interruption to the project's time-scale.

Source: adapted from an article in the *Daily Telegraph*

ACTIVITY

Project time-scales

1 To test your powers of scheduling, try this exercise. Your whole project team should attempt it first in pairs.

Using the information below about the opening of a small private gym, you and a partner should study the tasks specified for the opening, just as the manager would do. The tasks are not in the best order, nor are there any timings allocated. Reorder the tasks into a more logical sequence and allocate appropriate amounts of time on the chart, using short straight lines. Afterwards, compare your ideas with those of the rest of your team.

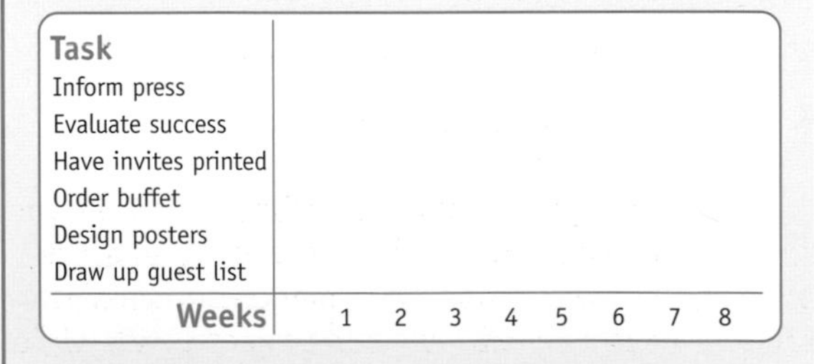

Task
Inform press
Evaluate success
Have invites printed
Order buffet
Design posters
Draw up guest list
Weeks
1 2 3 4 5 6 7 8

2 As a team, devise a detailed time-scale plan. You will need to present it as a chart that all team members can follow. It will also be a valuable evaluation tool after the project is over. An example is shown in Figure 6.13 for a project due to run over three months. You could use this example as the basis for your chart, or devise your own.

Description of the project

Your business plan should include a brief description of the project with the following details:

- Scale and content of the project, e.g. product or service, team profile, time-scale, reasons why you think you will succeed.
- Location/venue: give brief details of the site and its suitability, any constraints or difficulties envisaged.

Limiting the description to a maximum of one page makes it a more effective document. It is often known as an executive summary or project overview.

Target customers

Whatever objectives your team settles on, they need to be related specifically to the customer group(s) who have been identified through your **market research** (see Unit 4, page 264-287).

Customers are crucial to any leisure and recreation project. Consequently an early part of your business planning will involve your team identifying who the customers will be (along with their needs and expectations) and then planning how the project will actually meet those needs and expectations. You will be able to make good use of the knowledge you gained in Units 4 and 5.

You need to identify **target groups** of customers who you think would be interested in your project. You can use the following categories to help you identify your target market:

- Age: children, teenagers, adults or over 50s?
- Lifestyle: families, couples or singles?
- Location: people from a particular area?

The advantage of using this technique is that you can be more exact about who you will try to attract. In turn, this will guide your marketing activities. You will need to position your project in the right market, to maximise impact and achieve a successful outcome. Your project will need to attract the customers you have targeted and satisfy their needs and expectations. You will only have one chance to get it right!

The marketing of leisure and recreation products and services is a very competitive and creative part of the industry. Many operators seek to create unique aspects for their business in order to attract customers. You will have to do the same for your project. The case study below may help give you some ideas of how best to attract your likely customers.

Some of the promotional techniques that your project team could use are shown in Figure 6.14 on page 417. The importance of good market research is highlighted in the case study on page 416.

CASE STUDY

The art of stimulation

Steve Hill, head of marketing at Academy Expo, says, 'Technology is enabling us to use pictorial imagery a lot more convincingly, imaginatively and stylishly than was possible five years ago. Large images are relatively easy and cheap to print now. It creates a captivating, attention-seeking point of focus for people; they'll stop and look at an image which has an impact, for this gets the message across far better than words can often do. Images of lifestyle are particularly popular at the moment because people readily associate the product with a certain desirable lifestyle. Using pictures is more effective in areas where there is no tangible product, such as fun events or activities.

Tim Wheeler, professor of communication and psychology at University College, Chester, says, 'The images that have universal appeal are the ones that tend to be concerned with basic needs, such as food or comforts. 98 per cent of our senses are geared to visual imagery – it's the most important sense we have.'

CASE STUDY

Planning a new business project

As many as 40 per cent of new business projects are unsuccessful. Studies reveal that a substantial proportion of these failed to undertake adequate market research, both before they set themselves up and after they started their project. Many became complacent about their customers and rival projects, relying instead on what they thought their customers wanted rather than finding out what they actually wanted.

This kind of knowledge helps to focus efforts in the most effective and profitable ways. Knowing why your customers are interested in your project and checking with them (gathering feedback) on the details of their interest is important too, for it may enable you to:

- offer them a better service
- create additional products
- identify new customers.

A simple example of this involved a young woman who ran a hairdressing salon which also offered beauty treatments as a franchise in a large hotel's leisure complex. Two months after she started, she decided to analyse her list of customers and how much they had spent since the salon had opened. She learned that 80 per cent of her sales came from just 20 per cent of her customers. Further analysis revealed that much of her profit came from the beauty treatments and that these were enjoyed mainly by her more regular customers.

As part of this investigation, she asked her customers to answer a questionnaire on the kinds of services they would like. A significant number said they would be interested in aromatherapy treatments. Since she was getting to know her customers better, she was able to revise her business plan, focusing her attention on the customers who visited the salon most frequently, and increasing the space and staff she devoted to beauty and aromatherapy treatments. She was very successful, much to the delight of the hotel, for she had added value to its product as well.

ACTIVITY

Target groups and marketing

Using the suggestions in this section and in Unit 4 (pages 264-287), carry out the following tasks as a project team.

1 Identify the types of customer that might be interested in your project.

2 Discuss what research techniques you could use to assess customer needs.

3 If applicable to your project, determine the price that you intend to charge customers for your products or services. (Remember to ensure that your pricing strategy is in line with any financial objectives that your team has set, such as covering costs - breaking even - or making a small profit.)

4 If applicable, list the main ways in which you will promote your project to your target customers (Figure 6.14 gives you some suitable examples).

5 Create a chart similar to the one shown in Figure 6.14, but add a costs column.

6 Complete each of the three columns in the chart with:

- techniques
- how you will apply them
- accurate costs.

Resources

Identifying the range of **resources** for a project is an important task, one that forms an essential part of your business plan. For the purposes of your business plan you will probably need to consider many aspects under the following headings:

- Physical resources
- Financial resources
- Human resources.

Physical resources

Physical resources include materials, equipment, venues, premises and facilities. The materials and equipment required for projects are as diverse as the projects themselves. They can range from the simplest of things, such as paper and pens for a children's party, to high-tech lasers, simulations and computer packages for large exhibitions or shows, such as in the Millennium Dome. There are a number of ways of identifying all the resources that will be needed. You could:

- visualise each separate section and phase of the project and jot down the materials and equipment needed to resource it
- list all the requirements through discussion and consultation
- put yourself in the customer's place for every stage of the experience
- individually take an area of responsibility for the project and research what materials and equipment will be required.

ACTIVITY

Physical resources

Imagine your group has decided to run a small project in your school or college sports hall on a Saturday morning. The objective is to raise funds (£150) towards hiring a coach to take a local children's playgroup to a theme park. You have invited five teams, each with five players, to compete in a sponsored obstacle race. Your group will provide some light refreshments afterwards. Each team has worked hard to find sponsors, which will be your main source of income, and they will earn money every time a team member completes a circuit of the obstacle course. There is also a prize, donated by your tutors, for the team who gets the most people round the course in the time set.

Make a list of all the materials and equipment that you would require.

Figure 6.14: Promotional techniques

Promotional Technique	Use for a project
ADVERTISING	All appropriate and affordable means should be used: radio; TV (news reports); displays
PUBLICITY MATERIALS	Creation of a specific brochure, based on the business plan, adds credibility
PUBLIC RELATIONS	Free publicity via newspaper stories. Promotional events to publicise the project
DIRECT MAIL	A mailshot or leaflet drop directly to target customers
POSTERS	Flyers or large posters positioned at strategic points to catch the eye of likely customers
SPONSORSHIP	Use of the sponsor's name and logo on all publicity material or letters can greatly boost the project's image and attractiveness
PERSONAL SELLING	Telephone calls; presentations; one to one contact with key people

Premises, facilities and venues

Premises or facilities are usually required when undertaking a project, whether it be a pitch for a match or a venue for a comedy night or fireworks display. The premises or venue selected must be appropriate for the event, with as little improvisation or temporary facilities as possible. The factors which influence the suitability of location should be identified at the planning stage and evaluated for inclusion in the business plan. These could include:

- numbers of participants or spectators who will attend
- parking requirements for staff, spectators and participants
- specialist needs; for example, a high roof, lighting or a stage
- access for people with disabilities
- communications systems for organisers, press and customers
- permanent catering facilities
- technological support levels
- ease of adaptation or alteration
- health, safety and security considerations
- opening and closing times
- accommodation
- hire costs or facility charges.

Most project teams will create a checklist to gather all this information, then allocate individuals to assess costs, supply, availability and other factors which are specific to the resources identified. You can see an example of this in the extract taken from the Alton Towers event planning chart shown in Figure 6.15.

Figure 6.15: Operational activities, Alton Towers

Activity	
Security/medical/traffic control/stewards	✔
Medical tents/control room	✔
Stage/video screen	✔
Central control portacabin	✔
Security passes - arena/all areas/VIP	✔
Crowd management teams	✔
Power/water supply	✔
Additional radios	✔
Corporate hospitality	✔
Disabled platform access	✔
Additional catering services	✔
Fencing	✔
Additional lighting	✔
Temporary roadway	✔
Police/council buildings	✔
Information flyer to notify local residents	✔
Additional signage/information boards	✔
Temporary toilets	✔
Additional telephones	✔
Crew catering	✔
Official band merchandising	✔

ACTIVITY

Operational checklist

As a group, using a blank version of Figure 6.15 as guidance, carry out a check of the premises, facility or venue which you intend to use for your project. During this check identify resources which might be needed. Create your own list of these and opposite each one put a brief description of what action is needed to ensure it is ready for the project.

Financial resources

The financial resources of a project are all the amounts of money involved and the ways in which they are earned or spent. The control of financial resources involves:

- preparing an analysis of expected **income** and **expenditure** (forecasts of the money you hope to bring in and the money you will need to spend to generate the income)
- preparing a **budget** (the amount of money which can be spent)
- **financial monitoring** (checking and controlling) to ensure that financial objectives are achieved.

A small project may have very straightforward financial considerations. For example, taking a group on a trip to a football match or concert might only require a small amount of budgeting. Since most of the people organising this type of activity usually give their time for free, there are no staffing costs and a reasonable profit might be expected, which might be donated to a good cause.

A larger-scale project such as a pageant or parade would have considerably more budgeting implications. For very large events such as international festivals, exhibitions and other major leisure or recreation developments, budgeting may involve large sums of money and extensive accounting and financial management, as is the case for the huge development proposed at Milton Keynes for the UK's second indoor ski slope, costed at £60 million. The case study on this development provides some idea of the complexity and resource details needed for such large projects.

Keeping financial records

For any project involving finance it's important to keep accurate financial records (accounts), so that the budget (funds allocated for spending) is not exceeded. Projects which go over budget are unlikely to be repeated or supported in the future, or may be terminated prior to completion.

You will need a realistic understanding of the costs involved in implementing a project and adopt good accounting practices, especially where cash is involved. The following information on record keeping gives some guidance and examples that you may wish to use as a basis for your team's financial controls. There are three basic rules to keep in mind:

Record everything.
Keep the system simple.
Summarise your position each month.

Some general guidance follows to help you decide what is appropriate for your project.

Appoint one or two people as your treasurer or financial management team as soon as possible. As a starting point you should calculate your **break-even position**, that is, the amount of money needed to cover your expenditure compared to the income you expect to achieve. If one of your objectives is to make a profit, you can then calculate what you need to charge to meet that profit objective by adding that percentage or amount to your calculations. For example, if you need to make £100 to break even, have a profit target of £50 and expect 50 participants, you will have to charge £3 per person to achieve your objective.

You will need to hold a team meeting to agree on budgets for each area of expenditure according to what you can afford. The financial calculations and allocation of money need to be based on accurate research into the costs of every item; for example, the hire of a hall, printing of tickets or production of publicity posters. Your team will then have to decide how much of the budget can be allocated to each item or activity by establishing what is essential and what could be gathered through donations, supported by sponsorship, or obtained free of charge from your school or college.

Budget estimates made at the planning stage and agreed by the team provide guidance and control throughout the project's organisation and set the limits on spending. Once these are created they should go into your business plan. It is always wise to keep a small amount in reserve for unexpected costs. This is called a **contingency fund**.

An expenditure budget sheet for the planning and running of a student project could look like the one shown in Figure 6.16.

CASE STUDY

Milton Keynes Ski Slope

Milton Keynes will be home to the largest indoor real-snow ski slope in Europe, with the launch of Xscape, a joint venture between Capital and Regional Properties and two funds managed by PRICOA Property Investment Management. The 170-metre ski slope will be 20 metres longer than the UK's only existing slope at Tamworth.

Besides the ski slope there will also be a 16-screen multiplex, run by Cine UK, a 60,000 sq ft City Limits entertainment centre, a health and fitness club, cafés, bars, restaurants and lifestyle shops, including Diesel. Heathlands, a subsidiary of LeisureNet, will run the ski centre and health and fitness club. The £60 million complex will be the first of a number of outlets throughout Europe, with the next likely to be in Germany. The European outlets will follow the same format as Milton Keynes.

Capital and Regional's executive director thinks the idea will be a hit: 'Xscape is our direct response to growing customer demand for greater leisure and entertainment choice, at one location, as well as increased value for both money and time.'

Source: *Leisure Opportunities*

Figure 6.16: An example expenditure budget sheet for a student project

Expenditure Budget (£)

Category	Week 1	Week 2	Week 3	Week 4	Week 5
Marketing	45	40	35	30	15
Printing costs	15	12	11	10	-
Admin resources	25	18	12	9	-
Equipment	12	-	9	-	3
Hire of premises	-	-	-	28	28
Catering	5	5	5	5	25
Travel	12	12	9	6	7
Fees	15	-	-	-	25

ACTIVITY

Budget control

Study the following scenarios of project teams attempting to control their budgets and discuss what they could have done better.

One member of the team in charge of marketing has overspent on the printing of advertising materials by £40, but has no records of what exactly he spent the money on.

A group of leisure and recreation students has organised a very successful project, gaining a lot of publicity and letters of thanks, but made a loss of £133, despite intending to break even.

With only three weeks to go to the start of its project, the team learns that the hire charges for a local hall have increased after an annual review, which takes it over budget by £150.

A group of leisure and recreation students undertake a sponsored walk to raise money for a trip abroad. Unfortunately, many of the participants don't collect all of their sponsor money, so the team falls short of its target.

At the end of the project, your team may need to produce a **balance sheet** and use it as part of the evaluation process. In accounting jargon, the balance sheet should show the 'state of affairs' or 'financial position' of the project, not the value of it all. The possible contents of a balance sheet for the end of a project are shown in Figure 6.17. Software packages can help create spreadsheet projections and up-to-date records which can be easily adjusted and printed.

Sponsorship

Many organisations in the leisure and recreation industry strive to attract **sponsorship** to support their efforts. Financially sponsored events and projects often have a greater chance of success, as the sponsor can pay for additional resources or promotional activities. The sponsor will of course want to be associated with success and good organisation, which enhances their image and the products or services that they provide. The examples included in the following article (Medisport sponsor 'Fit for TOPS') illustrate how many sponsors are involved in leisure and recreation sports projects.

Project teams working with a sponsor need to ensure they account for all monies spent, as the sponsor will not only want value for money, but will also want to know on what the money has been spent!

Figure 6.17: Sample of an end-of-project balance sheet

Balance Sheet

	Debit £	Credit £
"Saturn Event" End of project, June 2001 net closing balances		527.74
Bank balance	107.72	
Petty cash	36.43	
Sales account	380.37	
Purchase account		390.34
Sales		311.84
Other income		177.26
Fees	206.67	
Light and heat	76.90	
Travel expenditure	52.90	
Materials	375.68	
Sundaries	16.22	
Office	42.50	
Printing and stationary	111.79	
	1407.18	1407.18

Medisport sponsor 'Fit for TOPS'

Medisport, one of the country's leading suppliers of sports care products to the sports medicine market, have become sponsors of the Youth Sport Trust 'Fit for TOPs' programme. Fit for TOPs, developed in conjunction with the YMCA and Sport England, is designed to complement BTTOP sport for 7-11 year olds by encouraging young people to adopt an active lifestyle in parallel with the development of their sporting skills. Medisport's sponsorship of Fit for TOPs comes at a time when the Trust is receiving increasing demand from schools for the Fit for TOPs training resources. Medisport's support has been recognized by an award of £50,000 under Sportsmatch, the business sponsorship incentive scheme that is administered by the Institute of Sports Sponsorship on behalf of the Department of Culture, Media and Sport.

John Malins, brand manager for Medisport, is enthusiastic about the association: 'The Medisport Fit for TOPs programme is an excellent opportunity; unique in its approach and managed by people who care about children, are passionate about sport, and committed to making it work.'

Source: *TOPs newspaper*

ACTIVITY

Financial targets

As a group, set appropriate financial target(s) for your project, then devise and draw up a cash-flow forecast sheet, detailing every category of income and expenditure that you envisage will occur during the lifetime of the project, which will allow you to meet your target(s). You may be able to use a software package to assist you. Also prepare other record sheets or books that you think your group will need.

Human resources

The success of virtually every leisure and recreation project relies heavily on the people who run it. These are known as human resources. It is essential to get the right people in the jobs for which they are best suited and to allocate their tasks effectively. The process of matching skills to jobs may even mean that adjustments to the tasks or the actual format of the proposals must be made in order to get the best out of everyone. You can see how one leisure and recreation activity training organisation regards staffing from the way it is highlighted in its brochure:

Sir Chris Bonington, CBE, Outward Bound Trustee and chairman of the Risk Management Committee:

> *'Outdoor Adventure provides a vivid learning experience for all ages because they combine the opportunity for personal growth and greater co-operation between individuals.*
>
> *'To ensure that all course members gain the maximum benefit, Outward Bound invests a great deal of time and effort in providing the highest standard of safety and care.*
>
> *'We take the greatest care in selecting, training and monitoring our staff because they are the key link in the chain of delivery that runs through all activities. Staff at our centres have built up an impressive depth of knowledge about the environment in which they work.'*
>
> *Source: Outward Bound brochure*

Success very often comes down to individual skills and the time, effort and teamwork put into the tasks which make up the project. The following principle can be applied to any project management team:

Time and effort + skills and motivation = success

At the initial planning stage, team members have responsibilities for researching options and considering the feasibility of those options. During the project itself all staff members must play their parts by undertaking specific **tasks**. In the evaluation phase following the project, it is vital to assess how effective individuals and the team have been in completing these tasks.

Once all the tasks required to meet the objectives of the project have been identified, then the allocation of roles and responsibilities can begin. People may have preferences, or certain constraints, which will help to determine who takes on which tasks. Where skills required for key tasks do not exist within a team, then other people may have to be sought to carry these out. Identifying tasks helps to create your team's operational structure (described on pages 436-437), for you can group similar tasks under one heading, such as finance, marketing, security, administration and so on.

ACTIVITY

Allocating tasks

You can begin to identify the range of tasks involved in your project by imagining you are in charge of one of the following aspects of the project:

- Finance
- Marketing
- Security
- Physical resources
- Human resources
- Administration

Brainstorm every single task - large or small - which you think might need doing. Put these down in a checklist, then pass the list to a colleague for comment. If everyone in your team participates you will be able to cover many of the tasks in your project. Analyse the final checklists and place the tasks under the headings provided. This exercise can be repeated every time a new planning aspect occurs.

Roles for the project

A role is the part or function a team member has in the project and is especially significant in any group. The following guidelines and those on page 438, provide you with some help in effectively allocating roles for your team members.

- Definition of roles must be clear, so that a team member knows what is expected of them (a copy may be put into your personal log for reference).
- People need clear guidelines on leadership/co-ordination within the team.

When allocating tasks to team members, it is important to ensure that they fully understand what is involved and have a chance to ask questions about their tasks. Once everyone is clear about responsibilities, these should be entered into the business plan, along with your team structure, functions and roles, so that they are recorded to guide each person. See page 435 for an example of a project team structure.

Allocating resources

One of the most difficult tasks for any project management team is to allocate its resources as efficiently as possible. Deciding on the factors which will determine how resources are allocated may involve lengthy discussion at team meetings and consideration of such questions as:

- What resources do we have available?
- What additional resources are needed?
- What skills or abilities are needed to use the resources?
- For how long are the resources available?
- How much finance will the resources require?

Most projects are unique, so there is no single formula for calculating and allocating resources. However, you can use the following guidelines to help your team make decisions.

Physical resources may well be in short supply and represent a considerable cost, so your team will have to identify exactly what is needed and match that to a definite source so that its availability and cost can be assessed. Your school or college may make a lot of resources available to you at no cost, such as venue, photocopying, staff and so on. In such cases it is important that your team still appreciate what the costs would have been had such things not been provided free of charge. Where the cost involved is prohibitive, you may have to negotiate discounts, arrange for free use or sponsorship, or perhaps change your plans altogether. Finally, care needs to be taken not to waste or duplicate resources due to lack of communication. The business plan should itemize the agreed allocations clearly for everyone to see and follow. This record will also provide a source of evaluation after the event, so that the efficiency of the use of resources can be judged.

ACTIVITY

Identifying resources

Imagine that your team is running a day visit programme to your locality for a group of visiting foreign students. Devise a one-day programme that includes a fun activity for everyone based in your school or college, plus a visit to a leisure location in your area. Once you have done this, identify all the physical resources needed, how you will staff the programme and any costs involved.

Administration

All organisations need clearly established systems (procedures to follow) to support their functions (ways of working) and to allow them to operate smoothly. For the purposes of running your project, the two most important systems to consider at length are administration systems (described below) and communications systems (incorporated into the teamwork section on pages 435-446).

Administration systems

A good administration system identifies exactly what information it is necessary to record and the most effective method of recording it. Usually, it is the simple systems, which are thoroughly understood by those who operate them, that are most effective. The overall objective of a project administration system should be to save time and money by helping the people involved to work well together. The procedure for collecting and recording information should be simple and easily applied.

From examples of administration systems within the leisure and recreation industry we can adapt or adopt those most suited for use with a project. They can be divided into two broad categories:

- those which support routine functions of the organisation;
- those designed to support non-routine functions.

Routine functions are the activities of the organising team that occur on a regular basis and that constitute a large part of the day-to-day operations of the project team. They include procedures for financial transactions, communications, staffing and customer service. Booking systems and sales procedures, for example, are routine functions.

Non-routine functions, such as accidents and emergencies, occur infrequently, but still require procedures for dealing with them. These are covered under contingency planning on pages 429-431.

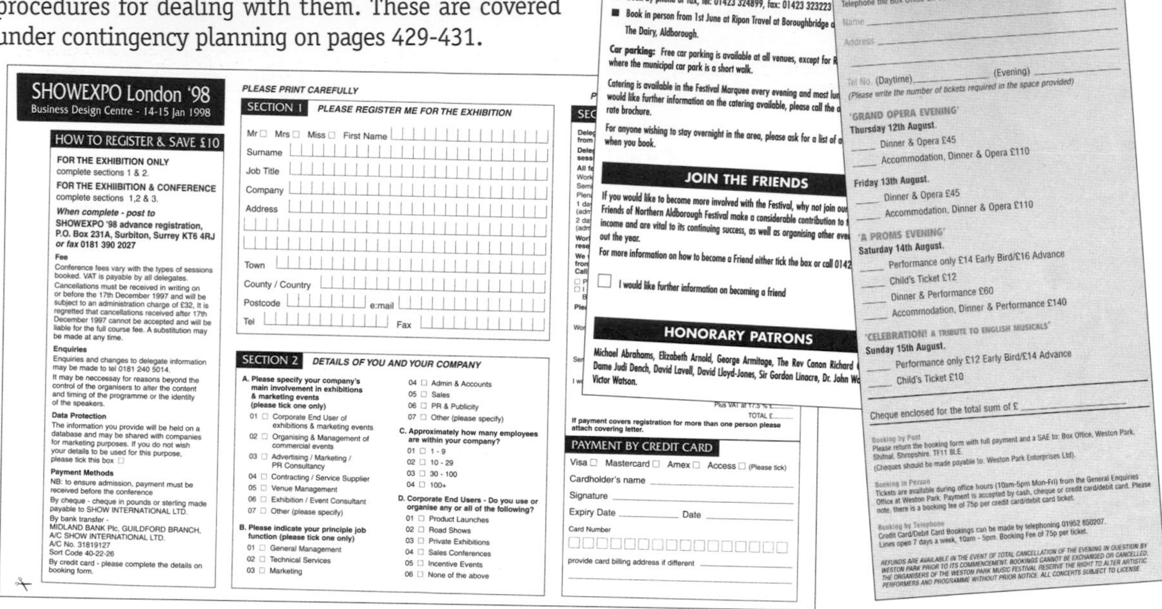
SHOWEXPO London '98
Business Design Centre - 14-15 Jan 1998

HOW TO REGISTER & SAVE £10

FOR THE EXHIBITION ONLY
complete sections 1 & 2.

FOR THE EXHIIBITION & CONFERENCE
complete sections 1,2 & 3.

When complete - post to
SHOWEXPO '98 advance registration, P.O. Box 231A, Surbiton, Surrey KT6 4RJ or fax 0181 390 2027

Fee
Conference fees vary with the types of sessions booked. VAT is payable by all delegates.
Cancellations must be received in writing on or before the 17th December 1997 and will be subject to an administration charge of £32. It is regretted that cancellations received after 17th December 1997 cannot be accepted and will be liable for the full course fee. A substitution may be made at any time.

Enquiries
Enquiries and changes to delegate information may be made to tel 0181 240 5014.
It may be neccessay for reasons beyond the control of the organisers to alter the content and timing of the programme or the identity of the speakers.

Data Protection
The information you provide will be held on a database and may be shared with companies for marketing purposes. If you do not wish your details to be used for this purpose, please tick this box ☐

Payment Methods
NB: to ensure admission, payment must be received before the conference
By cheque - cheque in pounds or sterling made payable to SHOW INTERNATIONAL LTD.
By bank transfer -
MIDLAND BANK Plc, GUILDFORD BRANCH, A/C SHOW INTERNATIONAL LTD.
A/C No. 31819127
Sort Code 40-22-26
By credit card - please complete the details on booking form.

PLEASE PRINT CAREFULLY

SECTION 1 PLEASE REGISTER ME FOR THE EXHIBITION

Mr ☐ Mrs ☐ Miss ☐ First Name
Surname
Job Title
Company
Address
Town
County / Country
Postcode e:mail
Tel Fax

SECTION 2 DETAILS OF YOU AND YOUR COMPANY

A. Please specify your company's main involvement in exhibitions & marketing events (please tick one only)
01 ☐ Corporate End User of exhibitions & marketing events
02 ☐ Organising & Management of commercial events
03 ☐ Advertising / Marketing / PR Consultancy
04 ☐ Contracting / Service Supplier
05 ☐ Venue Management
06 ☐ Exhibition / Event Consultant
07 ☐ Other (please specify)

B. Please indicate your principle job function (please tick one only)
01 ☐ General Management
02 ☐ Technical Services
03 ☐ Marketing
04 ☐ Admin & Accounts
05 ☐ Sales
06 ☐ PR & Publicity
07 ☐ Other (please specify)

C. Approximately how many employees are within your company?
01 ☐ 1 - 9
02 ☐ 10 - 29
03 ☐ 30 - 100
04 ☐ 100+

D. Corporate End Users - Do you use or organise any or all of the following?
01 ☐ Product Launches
02 ☐ Road Shows
03 ☐ Private Exhibitions
04 ☐ Sales Conferences
05 ☐ Incentive Events
06 ☐ None of the above

TOTAL £
If payment covers registration for more than one person please attach covering letter.

PAYMENT BY CREDIT CARD
Visa ☐ Mastercard ☐ Amex ☐ Access ☐ (Please tick)
Cardholder's name
Signature
Expiry Date Date
Card Number
provide card billing address if different

YOUR DETAILS

TICKETS ON SALE JUNE 1ST – BUT BOOK NOW BY POST
■ Festival Office, Aldborough Manor, Boroughbridge, York YO51 9EP
■ I enclose my cheque payable to The Northern Aldborough Festival for £..........
■ Please debit my credit card for £..........
Credit card no.
We regret that we can only accept Mastercard and Visa
Name.......... Expiry date..........
I enclose a stamped addressed envelope, my address is:..........
My phone number in case of difficulty..........
■ Book by phone or fax, tel: 01423 324899, fax: 01423 323223
■ Book in person from 1st June at Ripon Travel at Boroughbridge
The Dairy, Aldborough.
Car parking: Free car parking is available at all venues, except for
where the municipal car park is a short walk.
Catering is available in the Festival Marquee every evening and most
would like further information on the catering available, please call the
rate brochure.
For anyone wishing to stay overnight in the area, please ask for a list of
when you book.

JOIN THE FRIENDS
If you would like to become more involved with the Festival, why not join our
Friends of Northern Aldborough Festival make a considerable contribution to
income and are vital to its continuing success, as well as organising other
out the year.
For more information on how to become a Friend either tick the box or call
☐ I would like further information on becoming a friend

HONORARY PATRONS
Michael Abrahams, Elizabeth Arnold, George Armitage, The Rev Canon Richard
Dame Judi Dench, David Lavell, David Lloyd-Jones, Sir Gordon Linacre, Dr. John
Victor Watson.

BOOKING FORM
Telephone the Box Office on 01952 850207 or fill in the form below
Name
Address
Tel No. (Daytime) (Evening)
(Please write the number of tickets required in the space provided)

'GRAND OPERA EVENING'
Thursday 12th August.
____ Dinner & Opera £45
____ Accommodation, Dinner & Opera £110
Friday 13th August.
____ Dinner & Opera £45
____ Accommodation, Dinner & Opera £110

'A PROMS EVENING'
Saturday 14th August.
____ Performance only £14 Early Bird/£16 Advance
____ Child's Ticket £12
____ Dinner & Performance £60
____ Accommodation, Dinner & Performance £140

'CELEBRATION! A TRIBUTE TO ENGLISH MUSICALS'
Sunday 15th August.
____ Performance only £12 Early Bird/£14 Advance
____ Child's Ticket £10

Cheque enclosed for the total sum of £

Booking by Post
Please return the booking form with full payment and a SAE to: Box Office, Weston Park, Shifnal, Shropshire. TF11 8LE.
(Cheques should be made payable to: Weston Park Enterprises Ltd).

Booking in Person
Tickets are available during office hours (10am-5pm Mon-Fri) from the General Enquiries Office at Weston Park. Payment is accepted by cash, cheque or credit card/debit card. Please note, there is a booking fee of 75p per credit card/debit card ticket.

Booking by Telephone
Credit Card/Debit Card Bookings can be made by telephoning 01952 850207.
Lines open 7 days a week, 10am - 5pm. Booking Fee of 75p per ticket.

REFUNDS ARE AVAILABLE IN THE EVENT OF TOTAL CANCELLATION OF THE EVENING IN QUESTION BY WESTON PARK PRIOR TO ITS COMMENCEMENT. BOOKINGS CANNOT BE EXCHANGED OR CANCELLED. THE ORGANISERS OF THE WESTON PARK MUSIC FESTIVAL RESERVE THE RIGHT TO ALTER ARTISTIC PERFORMERS AND PROGRAMME WITHOUT PRIOR NOTICE. ALL CONCERTS SUBJECT TO LICENSE.

▲ These examples of booking forms illustrate different approaches which you might follow for your project

When deciding what to use for your team's systems, overall effectiveness can be judged as follows:

- Fitness for purpose: how well suited to your needs is the system?
- Value for money: will costs fit your budget?
- Accuracy: will it provide you with accurate records?
- Efficiency: will it take a minimum amount of time and effort to complete?
- Security: will information be kept confidential with no unauthorised access?
- Ease of use: whether paper-based or computer-based, is it easy to use?
- Users' opinions: consult everyone in the team over your choice.

Don't be afraid to modify and improve your systems if that helps the team, but make sure everyone is trained to use any new procedures or systems.

One administrative system you will have to invent for yourself is your personal log or diary, which records your involvement in the project. Whatever format you select, it has to cover all the actions or procedures undertaken by the team, from the start of the project to its completion, as outlined on pages 399-401.

Legal aspects

This section discusses many of the **legal aspects** of project scenarios, some of which will not apply to your chosen project. Legal aspects are laws or regulations which must be complied with in to ensure the health, safety and security of the staff and customers involved in the project. Unit 2 describes the main pieces of legislation that may influence your project.

Your team must ensure that any legal aspects of the project are fully investigated and acted upon. Your business plan will have to describe the measures (or actions) your team has taken in order to comply with those legal aspects. All organisations, irrespective of size or type of operation, must ensure the health, safety and security of their staff and customers at all times, in order to comply with the law. Failure to do so can have serious consequences. Inadequate procedures can result in loss of life, injury, prosecution, loss of income, loss of business, large claims for damages and, in extreme cases, complete closure of the business.

Figure 6.18 sets out the main benefits to organisations of effective health, safety and security policies and procedures.

Health and safety

The Health and Safety Executive (HSE) provides guidance and information to help organisations formulate and implement health and safety procedures, and also to meet their statutory duties. Figure 6.19 shows how these tiers of legislation and guidance apply.

Depending on the nature of your project, you may also need to consider other legislation such as the Data Protection Act or the Children's Act (see Figure 6.20)

Figure 6.18: Benefits of effective health, safety and security

The organisation:

- work is carried out within the law
- there are fewer accidents
- increased productivity
- compensation claims are reduced
- prosecution is eliminated
- company image and reputation is enhanced
- insurance premiums are lower
- fraud and theft can be reduced.

The environment:

- damage is reduced or prevented
- enhancement is encouraged
- wildlife or plants reinhabit
- more visitors may result.

The staff:

- morale and effectiveness can improve
- hazards and risk are reduced
- working conditions improve
- stress or threat level can be reduced
- awareness is increased of health, safety and security needs
- training needs are identified.

The customers:

- suppliers or workers on the premises are protected
- people with disabilities can have special provision
- a safe, secure environment is created for visitors
- standards of service may improve.

Figure 6.19: Tiers of legislation and guidance

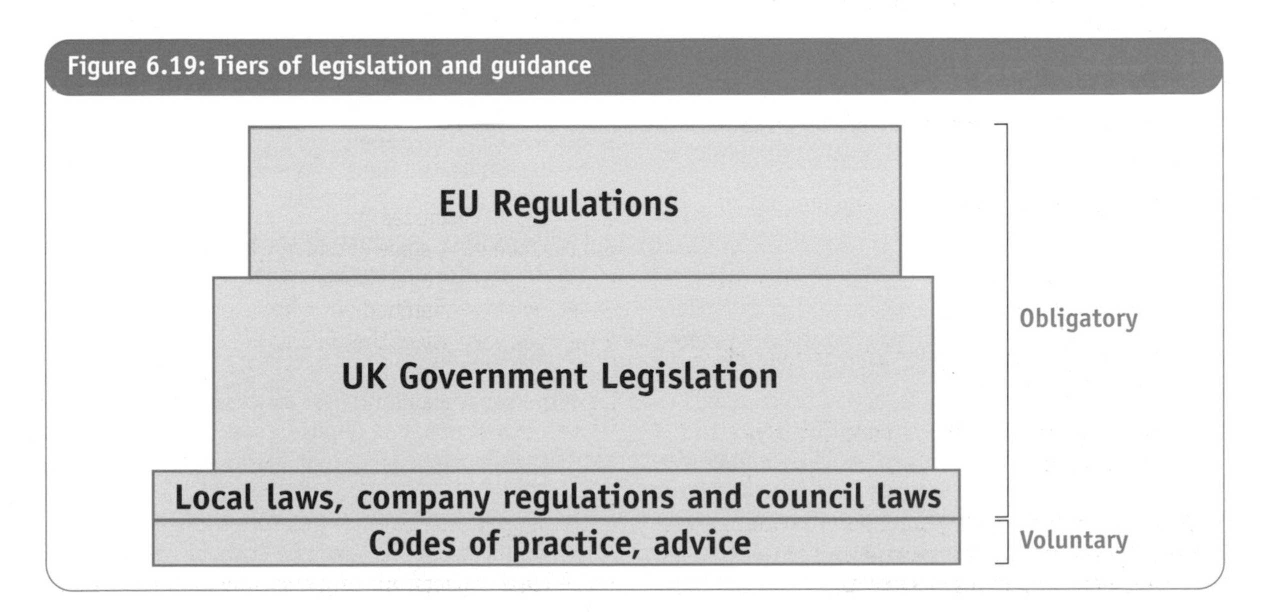

The obligatory health, safety and security legislation considered most widely applicable to leisure and recreation projects is shown in Figure 6.20. More detailed information about this legislation is provided in Unit 2 (pages 99-120).

Figure 6.20: Obligatory Legislation

EU regulations (to be followed by all member countries since 1992)

- Package travel directive
- Health and safety management
- Work equipment safety
- Manual handling of loads
- Personal protective clothing
- Display screen equipment

UK Government Acts (specific to the UK)

- Fire Precautions Act 1971
- Sale of Goods Act 1979
- Data Protection Act 1984
- Consumer Protection Act 1987
- Children's Act 1989
- Food Safety Act 1990
- Activity Centres (Young Persons' Safety) Act 1995.
- Occupiers Liability Act

Although you are not required to learn the contents of these Acts, you do need to be able to identify which parts of the key laws and regulations may apply to your project. The aims of health and safety law are to maintain minimum health and safety standards, to control the actions of employees and secure the health, safety and welfare of those working at or visiting premises or venues.

Under the legislation, actions taken to ensure health, safety and security for your project are covered under the principle of 'so far as is reasonably practicable'. In other words, the action taken needs to be balanced against the time, trouble, cost and physical difficulty of taking measures to avoid or reduce the problems. What the law requires here is what good management and common sense would lead employers to do anyway: that is, to look at what the dangers are and take sensible measures to tackle them. You must do the same! The onus is on organisers to assess health, safety and security risks and take measures to eliminate or control them. It is therefore important that the concepts of hazard and risk are clearly understood.

Risk assessment

Hazards are anything that can cause us harm in our everyday lives, such as chemical spillage, fumes, walking across a busy street, fire or undercooked food. **Risks** are the chances, however great or small, that someone will be harmed by a hazard. The chance or risk of a hazard harming us is obviously increased if we do not identify the hazard and take suitable measures to protect ourselves, such as wearing seat belts in motor vehicles, using protective clothing, or washing our hands after using the lavatory. Health and safety measures are precautions that we take to reduce the chance of accidents occurring, or to minimize the harm that an accident can cause.

Modern health, safety and security law in the UK and EU is based on the principle of **risk assessment**, which can be regarded as 'reasoned judgements about the risks and extent of these risks to people's health, safety and security, based on the application of information which leads to decisions on how risks should be managed'. The main requirement of employers is to carry out a risk assessment. Employers with five or more employees must record the significant findings of this risk assessment in a written statement. The five steps to risk assessment are shown in Unit 2 (pages 121-129).

Insurance

It is possible that your school or college will be insured to cover your activities for the project to some extent, but you should check what exactly is permitted. The following Department of Education guidelines for visits describe insurance needs very well.

> Section 147. Insurance policies are legal documents. They will impose conditions, limit the cover, and exclude certain people or activities. Insurance companies/travel firms can advise on particular types of insurance. However, the following are examples of cover which may be appropriate to many types of school visit (or project):
>
> - employer liability
> - public liability
> - personal accident cover for teachers, other adults, and pupils
> - costs of medical treatment
> - specialised risk activities (often excluded from standard policies) and the costs of repatriation for medical reasons when abroad

- damage to or loss of hired equipment (check the wording of the hire agreement)
- programmed and non-programmed activities
- transport and accommodation expenses in case of emergency
- compensation in case of emergency or delay
- compensation for loss of baggage and personal effects including money
- legal assistance in the recovery of claims
- failure or bankruptcy of the centre or travel company.

If your project involves making travel arrangements of any sort you may need to arrange travel insurance or activity insurance if you plan to provide activities where there is an element of risk, such as paintballing, skiing or go-karting.

ACTIVITY

Insurance

Appoint one person in your team to liaise with your tutor to assess what insurance cover your type of event should have. Find out about the insurance cover of your school or college and make recommendations where you find gaps, or make changes to avoid the difficulty of this aspect of planning. Assess what impact any additional insurance cover may have on your budget.

Identifying security hazards

In the leisure and recreation industry a great deal of investment is made to ensure the security of customers and their possessions. Security measures are necessary because if customers feel threatened or in danger due to security hazards, they will not use the products and services or visit the facilities and events provided. Security measures vary, depending on the organisation and environment, and may include use of elaborate entry systems, closed circuit television cameras (CCTV), and the deployment of specialist security personnel.

The security aspects of events can be complicated because they are one-off activities, which may involve the movement of large numbers of people. As with health and safety, the starting point for event organisers is to identify and evaluate security hazards and risks (a risk assessment). Security hazards and risk assessments are covered in detail in Unit 2, pages 131-142. Once an assessment of any security risk is completed, it is possible to consider the measures necessary to ensure security for both customers and staff.

The hazards which need to be identified depend on the scale of your project. The range of security hazards associated with a small local group going on a day trip, for example, is far smaller than that associated with the running of a large stadium, arena or attraction. Security hazards may involve:

- violence-for example against spectators, participants, VIPs or staff;
- theft-for example of information, cash, stock, equipment or property;
- fraud-for example by the sale of fake tickets;
- acts of terrorism and sabotage-for example bombs and kidnapping;
- damage-either accidental, deliberate or criminal.

Accidental damage is the security hazard you are most likely to face while running your project. Quite simply, the more activities there are going on and the more people there are involved, the greater is the probability of accidental damage. Staff or customers may drop equipment or misuse it, and people may be unfamiliar with how things operate or the surroundings in which they are working. Your team will have to try to anticipate where this type of damage is most likely to occur and either have someone on hand to ensure it doesn't happen, or propose measures such as clear instructions and warnings to help minimise the possibility. You should make sure that your institution's insurance covers you and any participants or spectators for the project you are going to undertake and any accidental damage which may occur.

To ensure security at your team project you should consider the following options:

- storing valuables in lockable containers or rooms
- security personnel patrolling vulnerable areas such as car parks
- using premises fitted with an alarm
- leaving lights on as a deterrent or to illuminate equipment and premises
- restricting access to certain areas.

ACTIVITY

Security risk assessment

Identify examples of the type of security hazards which might occur with the following projects and events.

- A three-day scout camp in the countryside.
- A weekend gathering of vintage cars in the car park of a large city-centre hotel.
- A group of students taking a trip to the Millennium Dome in London.

ACTIVITY

Risk assessment

As a group, produce a health, safety and security risk assessment on all the legal aspects of your project or event. You may need to look at Unit 2 (page121-142) to help you complete this activity. Include a copy of the risk assessment in your business plan and ensure everyone is familiar with its contents.

In this section we have looked at examples of security hazards and indicated how to identify those most likely to affect your business plan and operations. Your group should itemise all the hazards identified in order to evaluate them and propose measures to counteract them for inclusion in your business plan. You could use or adapt the format shown in Figure 6.21 to record your findings for all types of security hazards.

An evaluation of the security hazards identified must be undertaken to complete a risk assessment. The criteria and process for this are similar to those employed in the evaluation of health and safety hazards.

Figure 6.21: Security risk assessment record sheet

Security hazard identified	Who/what at risk	Probability of happening & importance	Measure to prevent
Violence	Staff or other customers	Low Important	Stewards on patrol
Theft	Cash/equipment	High Important	Locked till & lockable store
Fraud	Tickets	Low Low	Unique design
Damage	Exhibition stands	Low Low	Warning signs
	Cars	High High	Parking attendants
Other			

Figure 6.22: Examples of risk reduction measures for leisure and recreation projects

Violence

- Personal alarms and panic buttons
- Radios
- Staff training

Theft

- Alarms
- Sensors
- CCTV

Fraud

- Ultraviolet markers on tickets
- Swipe cards
- ID checks

Damage

- Patrols
- Security lighting
- Fencing
- Durable materials
- Clear signs
- Lockers
- Security guards
- CCTV

Contingency plans

Contingencies are those things which happen by chance, accident or design, but are unexpected. In many ways your risk assessment measures and procedures will cover your team for many types of contingency. This section will expand on that knowledge. Your team should expect some contingencies to occur and have some plans in place. Murphy's Law is often quoted at this point in planning: 'If something can go wrong it will!'

Effective contingency planning for emergencies is essential to ensure the health and safety of staff, participants and spectators. There have been some major disasters within the leisure and recreation industry in recent years, which have been due in part to the lack of effective contingency planning: the Hillsborough stadium tragedy and the Lyme Bay canoeing tragedy, for example.

Even the best-planned projects can suffer emergencies or disruptions of one kind or another. The erection of London's great millennium wheel was delayed, for example, because the calculations upon which the operation was based were incorrect and extra cables and safety checks were needed.

Contingency actions

If your project involves an event, then your project plan should include contingency actions to cope with anything that goes wrong. Formulating these plans is an important task for any team, as there can be serious consequences if contingency actions are not planned in advance.

There are three main types of disruption that can occur at an event. Foreseeable disruptions and unforeseen circumstances can range from the trivial and minor, which are dealt with quickly and easily, to the serious and major, which require dramatic action, or professional assistance. Foreseeable contingencies include things that project teams can usually predict, such as adverse weather, running short of something, lost property or late arrivals. Figure 6.22 shows some examples of the risk reduction measures.

Contingency plans for emergencies such as fire, accident and crowd control are also required. The unforeseen will test any team's abilities and resourcefulness. Things like major mechanical breakdowns, power cuts or acts of terrorism can lead to cancellation of events or a delay in the project. Your business plan should make reference to contingency plans that can be quickly put into action and

When preparing contingency plans, one starting point is for each person in the team to brainstorm all the possibilities for their area of responsibility. They can then present the most important ones at a team meeting for discussion and seek suggestions for solutions. Well-organised teams agree and write out the procedures to be undertaken should any emergencies or disruptions occur, so that the whole team knows them and can practice or rehearse them as necessary. Reactions need to be quick and positive to reassure the public that the organisers are in control.

The customers for your project might include quite a diverse range of people, and all of them will have to be considered as a likely source of contingencies. Equally, as organisers, you must not forget to consider your team itself. Some of the team may be in vulnerable positions or have hazardous responsibilities, such as collecting money, controlling access, dealing with complaints, co-ordinating activities or looking after VIPs. Each team member's role should be evaluated for likely contingencies, such as:

- equipment not working
- theft or loss of essential equipment
- dealing with damage or vandalism
- supplies not turning up.

The best preparation is to have good communications between team members and have professional support on hand should it be required. Training should also be undertaken to practise safety or security procedures agreed by the team or advised by the authorities, so that the time between any incident and response is minimal. The emergency procedures framework in the

CASE STUDY

Emergencies during school visits

If an emergency occurs on a school visit the main factors to consider include:

- establish the nature and extent of the emergency as quickly as possible
- ensure that all the group are safe and looked after
- if someone is hurt, establish the name of the casualties and get immediate medical attention for them
- ensure that all group members who need to know are aware of the incident and following agreed emergency procedures
- ensure that anyone taken to hospital is accompanied by an adult and that all others are safe and supervised
- notify the authorities if necessary and your emergency contact
- write down details of the incident and any casualties
- open up communications with individuals/parents and insurers if required
- don't speak to media or admit any liability
- complete an accident report as soon as possible.

ACTIVITY

Contingency action

1 Suggest some feasible contingency action for these scenarios.

- A small child becomes separated from her parents during a tour of a historic site.
- A tour bus breaks down in a safari park.
- A coach fails to appear at a school to pick up a football team.
- A power cut occurs, and there is no heating in the building you are using.
- A field you are using for parking turns into a bog after a torrential downpour.
- The caterer's van breaks down on the way to your venue.
- A key member of your team is off due to illness on a crucial planning day.

2 As a group, call a specific contingency planning meeting and keep notes of discussions. Consider aspects such as the following:

- all components of your business plan
- everyone's specific roles
- all tasks identified
- details of resources, materials, security and so on.

Discuss at length where the weaknesses are in your planning, weaknesses which might cause a contingency to be either a severe or moderate setback. Every time you identify a weakness devise a matching contingency measure.

case study opposite is recommended by the DfEE if an emergency occurs during a visit - which may well be a part of your project plans.

You cannot cover every contingency, but must try to anticipate potential problems. Some of it will of course be down to the luck of the day and good teamwork.

Review and evaluation

The last phase of planning is preparing for the final assessment of how it all went (**reviewing and evaluating**). This involves deciding if the objectives set by your team at the outset have been achieved. We have already highlighted the need to build evaluation into the plan as early as possible, so that outcomes can be measured. For the purposes of your assessment, every team member will have their input evaluated, since each role will be different and have different targets. Depending on the type of project and the nature of an individual team member's input, some of the following methods of evaluation may apply:

- video
- publicity reports
- photographs or slides
- witness statements or testimony
- questionnaires
- written records of meetings
- feedback from other team members
- tutor assessment
- customer complaints, compliments.

View the evaluation process as an essential element in improving both individual and team performance, as you can always learn from the strengths and weaknesses it reveals. Leisure and recreation organisations should continually monitor and evaluate their performance in order to improve service delivery.

We discussed earlier the need to set specific, measurable and realistic objectives and targets, in a form that could be evaluated after the project (see pages 407-409). Trying to build-in an evaluation process after the project or event is over is a poor approach to the management process. Your team will need to set objectives and then monitor progress and results at every stage of planning and implementation. You could use the checklist in Figure 6.23 to help you verify that all the necessary areas for evaluation have built-in **performance indicators** (ways of measuring performance). These headings will also form the basis for your evaluation report.

Figure 6.23: Project checklist of areas for evaluation

OBJECTIVES
❑
❑
❑

CUSTOMER NEEDS
❑
❑

MARKETING
❑
❑

USE OF RESOURCES
❑
❑

FINANCIAL
❑
❑

FINANCIAL TARGETS
❑
❑

STAFFING EFFECTIVENESS
❑
❑

EFFICIENCY OF SYSTEMS
❑
❑

TIMESCALES
❑
❑

HEALTH & SAFETY
❑
❑

SECURITY
❑

LEGAL ASPECTS
❑
❑

CONTINGENCIES
❑
❑

Gathering feedback

The process of **gathering feedback** (information on performance) should be done continuously, before, during and after the project, either formally through minuted meetings or informally through discussion or verbal feedback. Certainly, some assessment will be needed early in your planning; for example, with the meeting of deadlines, progress towards targets and suitability of people for roles. Other information, such as customer feedback, can be collected during the project, while some details, such as the profit made or take-up numbers, are likely to emerge after the project is over.

While collecting the data, it is important to make sure the information is:

- easily understood
- easy to collect and record
- helpful in the assessment of your event or team performances.

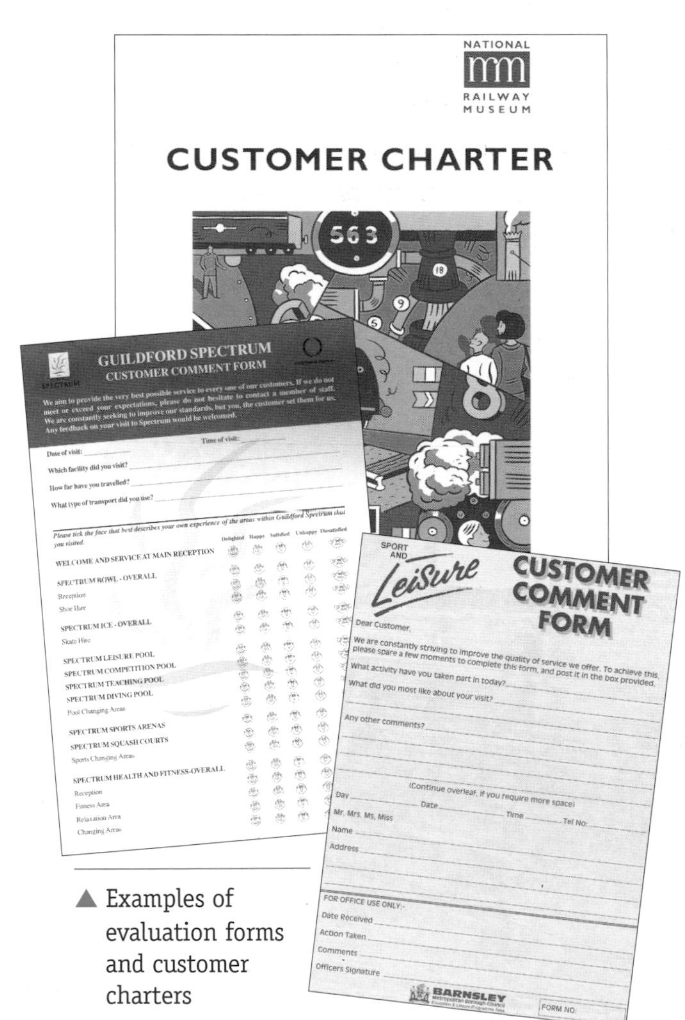

▲ Examples of evaluation forms and customer charters

Sources of feedback

You can use many sources of feedback when evaluating your team's performance. These might include customer interviews and questionnaires, sales records, visitor rates and usage figures, financial information and budget reports. For the staging of a very large event such as the London Marathon, feedback will also be sought from many other sources. This is because of the event's tremendous impact on the city each year: the influx of thousands of participants and visitors, traffic diversions, etc. A very close relationship is maintained through the exchange of feedback between the organisers and residents, police and emergency services, hotels and other businesses, and many departments of the city's councils. The organisers will keep records of the feedback from these sources each year as a basis for planning improvements for the next year. Although you won't be organising a project on such a large scale, you will have to use appropriate sources effectively to gather your feedback.

In general, feedback can be measured under one of the following headings.

- **Quantitative:** numbers or volumes; for example, tickets sold, profit made, levels of participation.
- **Qualitative:** by feature or superiority; for example, benefits, cleanliness, politeness.
- **Effectiveness:** for example, how successfully targets were met, almost met or surpassed.
- **Efficiency:** best use of resources; for example, people, budget, equipment.

Providing constructive feedback

Your group may well hold a team meeting to debrief and provide feedback on the outcomes of the project. It is most important to remember that any feedback should be given in a clear, constructive and sensitive manner. There is little likelihood of an individual or a team benefiting from inappropriately phrased feedback, for it is more likely to elicit a defensive or even aggressive response! The aim of giving feedback constructively is to enable people to reflect on it and learn from it in order to improve their performance next time. Your team needs to gather feedback from:

- team members
- customers
- your tutor.

It is important for personal feedback arrangements to be agreed beforehand. Here are some suggestions. Some possible formats are shown in Figure 6.24, and on

Figure 6.24: Sample feedback forms

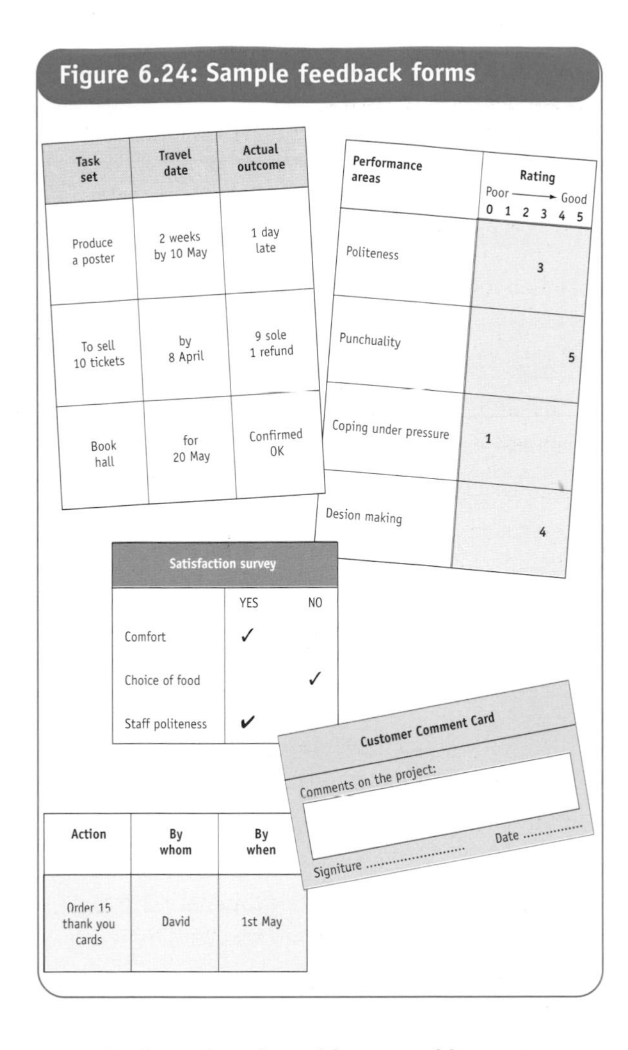

Task set	Travel date	Actual outcome
Produce a poster	2 weeks by 10 May	1 day late
To sell 10 tickets	by 8 April	9 sole 1 refund
Book hall	for 20 May	Confirmed OK

Performance areas	Rating Poor → Good 0 1 2 3 4 5
Politeness	3
Punchuality	5
Coping under pressure	1
Desion making	4

Satisfaction survey	YES	NO
Comfort	✓	
Choice of food		✓
Staff politeness	✓	

Customer Comment Card
Comments on the project:
Signiture .... Date ....

Action	By whom	By when
Order 15 thank you cards	David	1st May

page 431, in conjunction with personal logs.

Assessment by others can be in the form of:

- verbal feedback from colleagues given openly or in confidence
- grading or ratings on performance evaluation cards
- observational feedback using review sheets
- customer comments from questionnaires.

Evaluation data can be presented in many formats too, such as graphs, bar charts, pie charts, accounts showing financial performance, reports outlining actions taken, summaries of customer surveys, and statistical analysis (percentages, scores or ratios).

If your team has agreed on the types and methods of feedback at the planning stage, members will know which areas need attention and the materials and processes for collection can become a planned task.

Factors which affect performance

It is important during evaluation to identify those factors which affected the team's performance. For example:

- How good was teamwork and communications?
- How effective was project planning?
- How effective was team leadership?
- Did any factors prevent individuals from carrying out tasks?
- Did any constraints, such as lack of resources or adverse weather conditions, affect performance?

The checklist below provides a reminder of what to include in your team's project plan.

- Aims and objectives ❑
- Description of project ❑
- Project time-scales ❑
- Target customers ❑
- How it will be marketed ❑
- Physical resource needs ❑
- Human resource needs ❑
- Financial resources ❑
- Administrative systems ❑
- Legal aspects ❑
- Contingency plans ❑
- Evaluation plans ❑

BUILD YOUR LEARNING

Keywords and phrases

You should know the meaning of the words and phrases listed below. If you are unsure about any of them, go back through the last 27 pages to refresh your understanding.

- Aim
- Objectives
- SMART objectives
- Profitability
- Take-up
- Consumer interest
- Image
- Repeat business
- Community benefits
- Timing
- Time-scale
- Starting and finishing characteristics
- Deadlines
- Implementation schedule
- Timetables
- Critical path analysis
- Market research
- Target groups
- Resources
- Income
- Expenditure
- Budget
- Financial monitoring
- Break-even position
- Contingency fund
- Balance sheet
- Sponsorship
- Tasks
- Role
- Systems
- Legal aspects
- Hazards
- Risks
- Risk assessment
- Reviewing and evaluating
- Performance indicators
- Gathering feedback

End of section activity

Produce a business plan for your chosen project. The plan should be developed as a group, but presented individually. It should include:

- Objectives and time-scales for the project.
- Description of the project.
- Customer targets and marketing activities.
- Resource needs: physical, financial and human.
- Administration systems.
- Legal aspects of the project: health and safety, security and insurance.
- Contingency plans.
- Methods to be used to evaluate the project.

Effective teamwork

Teams of staff operate in the leisure and recreation industry in many different organisations, to deliver an enormous range of products and services to customers in all sectors of society. Examples of teams in a leisure and recreation context include the team of staff meeting and greeting customers at the Trafford retail and leisure centre in Manchester, staff at a hotel serving guests, and staff in a leisure centre attending to the needs of people using the pool, café or sports hall. We define a **team** as a group of people who work together in an effective way to achieve tasks or goals. It is the 'working together' aspect that you should remember as you prepare for your own project.

Whatever the nature and purpose of the team there are several attributes that it requires in order to be effective: it should work towards a common goal or objective, display enthusiasm and commitment, and communicate effectively.

Teams can develop **informally**, such as a social group, or **formally**, such as a working group put together for a specific task, with a **structure** (arrangement of its members) for leadership and accepted methods of communication. We will study in more detail the features of a formal team, as this will provide a model for your own project. The majority of people who work in a port or airport, for instance, form part of a formal team, each with their own functions: check-in, baggage handling, air crew and so on. Members of such teams know who is in charge and to whom they report by means of the team's structure - sometimes called a **hierarchy**.

Similar types of structure can be found in many other leisure and recreation contexts. For example, if you check into a hotel you will encounter the staff teams carrying out their regular duties: receptionist, waiter/waitresses, bar staff, chambermaids, porters, chef and manager. All these people work together, perhaps over a long period of time, to be an effective team.

Good **teamwork** doesn't just happen. It is a co-operative effort and something which needs working at. Achieving effective teamwork skills among a group of people requires careful consideration, as poor teamwork can ruin a project. The essentials of good teamwork come from:

- a clear purpose and objectives
- an effective structure and leadership
- sharing of roles and responsibilities
- making best use of skills and supporting each other.

The **purpose** of the team is to achieve the aims and objectives of the project. These aims and objectives should be very clear to everyone in your team, so that you all share this common purpose and work together to achieve success.

Figure 6.25: Example of a structure for a project team

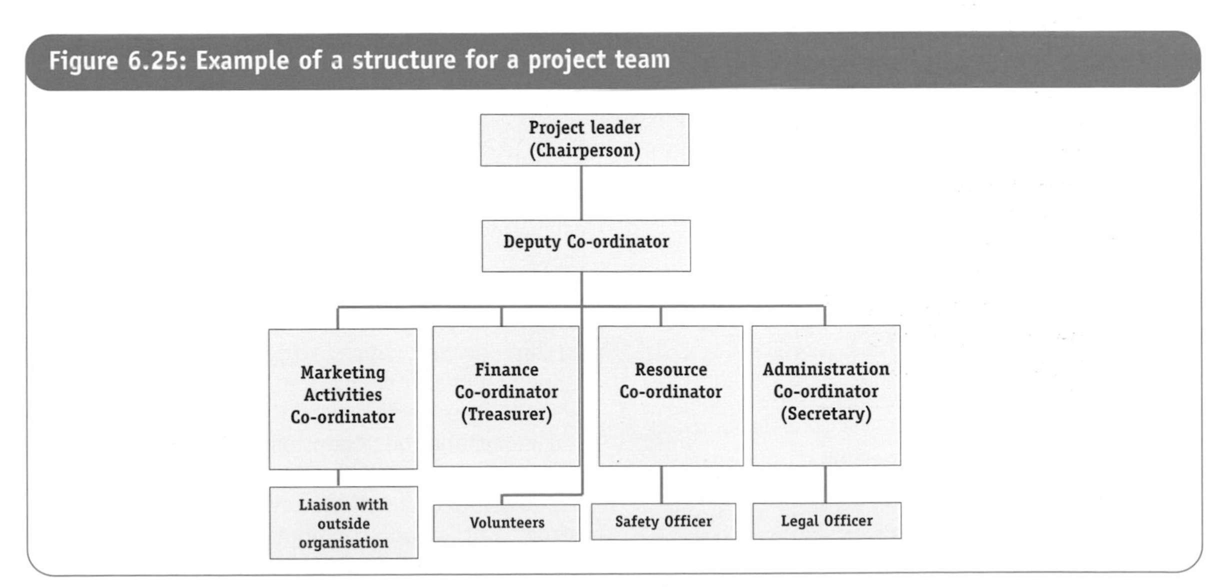

Team structure

Many leisure and recreation organisations create ad hoc teams to carry out short-term projects or special events. These teams are composed of members whose expertise is needed for that particular project only. Once the project is over, a team member may return to other 'organised' duties like marketing or finance, or would come to the end of their contract if he or she was employed on a temporary basis.

Members of an ad hoc team have much less time to get together and probably only a short time in which to deliver the project. However, they are also usually selected for their ability to get along with others, as well as having the right blend of skills and talents to complete the task on time. Your project involves setting up an ad hoc team, so a sound structure upon which to base your teamwork is a key requirement.

Committee structures

For most projects, a co-ordinator or leader oversees the whole process. The role of co-ordinating the project may, however, involve a small team with the right combination of skills and abilities. One form of team structure which may be suitable for your project is that of a committee, with people elected or nominated for certain roles. Normally this would be headed by a chairperson as team leader, with a treasurer in charge of finance and a secretary doing the administration. Some advantages of a committee structure are as follows:

- people are voted into positions
- they make decisions democratically
- they can form sub-committees to tackle certain areas, such as safety or marketing
- their meetings are minuted.

Disadvantages are that decision-making can be slow and the organisation of project tasks cumbersome.

Throughout your project you will need to record evidence of team meetings. This is probably best done by taking minutes of each meeting. An example of how to put together an agenda and keep minutes for a meeting is provided in Figure 6.26.

The **team leader** or **co-ordinator** normally has responsibilities for:

- liaison with outside organisations
- supervision of other team members
- making decisions on behalf of the team
- calling and running team meetings
- representing the project team at other meetings
- seeking advice or co-opting specialists and volunteers to help.

This represents a fairly formal structure such as the one depicted in Figure 6.25. Once the issue of leadership has been decided by the team, **lines of authority** (who is in charge of whom or what) can also be mapped out as shown in Figure 6.25.

This structure is usually subdivided into functions, or **areas of responsibility**, with subsections to cover more detailed areas, such as marketing or safety. The structure also represents the team's lines of communication for reporting progress or problems, as shown in Figure 6.25. All of this goes together to form an **organisational chart**. In larger project teams each function leader is likely to have a small team working for him or her which carries out allocated tasks. Individual team members in the structure know to whom to report, what authority they have in their area and understand the responsibilities appropriate to their role. Depending upon the type of project, the areas of responsibility or functions can be expanded to cover all needs, but good communication between team members and co-ordinators is vital.

Figure 6.26: Agenda and minutes

Agenda

1 Apologies
2 Welcome and introduction
3 Minutes of last meeting
4 Items arising (and not raised elsewhere)
Item (i) Update on venue and dates
Item (ii) Hospitality arrangements
Item (iii) Discussion of evening programme
Item (iv) Review of roles and responsibilities
5 Any other business (to be submitted at least two days before the meeting)
6 Date, time and place for next meeting

Minutes

Present:
Apologies:
Minutes from previous meeting:
Matters arising from the minutes:
Agenda items:
Any other business (AOB):
Date of next meeting:

You may find that your team starts out with a much less formal approach to the planning and running of the project, with no one acting as leader or co-ordinator and everyone responding to needs as they arise. However, this arrangement rarely occurs in the leisure and recreation industry for projects: more formal structures are the norm. Whatever team structure you decide on you need to include details in your business plan.

Ad hoc team members will also bring technical or operational talents and skills to solve a problem or tackle a project. In leisure and recreation this could be any of the following:

- computer skills, e.g. ability to use a spreadsheet or create good graphics
- mechanical knowledge, e.g. good at repairing equipment
- marketing knowledge, e.g. ability to design questionnaires
- communications, e.g. a confident announcer
- coaching ability, e.g. ability to work well with children
- technical ability, e.g. ability to demonstrate.

The selection of the team should reflect the expertise needed to carry out the project. The people brought together will also gain a sense of achievement, mutual support and friendship. As an example, preparations for the Commonwealth Games in Manchester illustrate how important teamwork will be in staging the games themselves, as shown in the case study below.

CASE STUDY

Commonwealth Games, Manchester 2002

There will be five centres involved in hosting the events on various sites, using a large range of teams to meet all the diverse needs. The games are primarily a sports event, but underlying it all is a huge commercial venture requiring £62 million to be successful. These are the teams preparing for the games:

- **Commonwealth Games Federation**
- **Commonwealth Games Council for England**
- **Manchester City Council (who are the major underwriters)**
- **Manchester Games Holding Company with its 'Manchester 2002 Ltd' operating company**
- **Sport England**
- **Sport UK**
- **Countries of the Commonwealth**
- **Sporting Bodies**
- **The competitors**
- **The sponsors**

Within each of the sections of the operating company 'Manchester 2002 Ltd' there are team directors for the following areas:

- **Sport**
- **IT**
- **Communications**
- **Logistics**
- **Special projects**

Manchester City Council has worked with Sport England since 1997 to plan and prepare for the games, and ensure that the venues are sustainable long after the games are over. Some £120 million has gone into development to help in this aim. The venues are organised into zones, overseen by smaller teams:

- **Play zones**
- **Training areas**
- **Changing rooms**
- **Parking**
- **The stadium (which will become Manchester City Football Club's new ground)**
- **The swimming pool (which will serve the community and three universities after the games)**
- **Sport City Eastlands (which will become a multi-play area after the games, for bowling, cycling, athletics, tennis and squash)**
- **Bolton Arena (the badminton centre near the Reebok stadium)**
- **Nynex Arena and G-Mex, hosting the gymnastics, judo and wrestling events**
- **Salford Keys, hosting the triathlon, marathon and walking events**

An overall venue manager has been seconded from Sport England to co-ordinate all the work at facilities, and each sports governing body has also seconded a manager to help with technical advice. Other teams work on such support services as:

- **Medical services**
- **Environmental health**
- **Disaster control**
- **Media liaison**

The network of teams has to co-ordinate and co-operate on every aspect of this important project.

ACTIVITY
Commonwealth Games

Form pairs and imagine you are in charge of one of the venues at the Manchester Commonwealth Games, such as the pool or velodrome. Try to create a list of resources and facilities you would have to provide to help the public enjoy the events.

Roles and responsilities

A **role** is the part or function a team member has to play in the project. The following guidelines provide help in allocating roles effectively.

- The definition of the role must be clear, so that a team member knows what is expected of him or her (a copy of the definition could be put into your personal log for reference).
- People need clear guidelines, leadership and co-ordination as a team. When allocating tasks to team members, it is important to ensure that they fully understand what is involved (i.e. what their responsibilities are) and have a chance to ask questions about their tasks.
- A person's role must be set out clearly in **task descriptions**. If this does not happen, the team member's perception or expectation of a particular role may differ from that of colleagues and the team co-ordinator or leader.
- If someone is uncomfortable or not suited to a role it can be a common cause of poor relations within or between teams. For example, one group may want to work as an ad hoc team with freedom of action, while another may prefer to organise in a structured way.
- Personal standards within a team can cause incompatible relations. For example, an untidy, unpunctual person or someone who does not pull their weight will not work well in a team which takes pride in punctuality, high-quality work and expects equal contributions from everyone.
- Difficulty may result if a person has several roles in an organisation which come into conflict. For example, a person who works in two or three teams may find decisions that he or she has to make in one team cause conflict with his or her role in another team or group.
- Bad feelings can arise if a team member hasn't been given enough work to do, or if a person thinks that they can handle more work, more challenges or more responsibility. **Delegation** (the passing on of work) to someone who feels like this is a good way of showing that his or her contribution to the team or organisation is valued.
- Role overload is when a person has too much work, or not enough time to do it in. Consequently the quality of his or her work suffers. Allocating more time for tasks or reducing the workload are the solutions to this problem.

If there is too much **role conflict**, overload or bad feelings then team members will suffer stress. Pressure to meet deadlines, sell tickets or fill seats is a common source of stress for a leisure and recreation project. Strain comes from tension, low morale, communication problems and the need to meet exacting or unrealistic targets or profits.

Once everyone is clear about responsibilities, these should be entered into the business plan, along with your team structure, functions and roles, so that they can guide each person.

ACTIVITY
Roles and responsibilities

On the basis of the structure that your team has agreed and the functions identified for the project, create areas of responsibility and identify suitable team members to perform the roles required to complete the tasks for those areas. Draw up job descriptions for each role and its tasks and put these into a file, so that anyone in the team can refer to them, should the need arise, during the project.

Team building

Whatever structure a team decides to adopt, all team members will have to get to know one another and work together. The following sequence describing the evolution of a group into an effective team sums up the necessary stages very succinctly.

Forming

At this stage there is very little evidence of teamwork, as people are simply getting to know each other. This may occur at the very beginning of your project when you brainstorm ideas and test the feasibility of options. It is often an uncertain time for people. At this stage it might help in the formation of the team if you can do something together, such as enjoying a night out or lunch together. Building confidence in each other is the key to completing this stage satisfactorily.

Storming

This is potentially the most difficult stage of team building, for each person is striving to attain a position in the team with which they feel comfortable. Stormy relationships can result if people vie for leadership or dominance, or if some people object to their role or appear lazy. Discussion is vital at this stage, so that everyone can have their say and decisions can be made and agreed by all the team. Once people are comfortable with their workload, have had their say or chance to object, and roles and tasks are mapped out clearly, things should settle down. One way to help your team pass through this stage is to set achievable aims and objectives and write out (minute) what has been agreed, so that if there is any future disagreement you can refer to them.

Norming

This is the stage where relationships settle down, work is underway and people are starting to pull together. Standards are set on performance which everyone tries to attain, such as meeting deadlines or completing tasks to a high standard. Some group pride and team identity emerge at this stage, and individual potential is beginning to show. You should expect to have your planning completed by this stage. In general, teams never leave enough time for planning all aspects, so make sure you make the most of this stage and 'plan till you drop!'

Performing

This is the most productive stage, often achieved by teams as they actually carry out their project, requiring the most energy and perseverance. A high-performance team should be able to achieve all its objectives and cope with any contingencies which present themselves. There will be no room for 'slackers' at this stage, so make sure everyone is really geared up to play their part. Respect and friendship are often established during this stage, which is also the best time to record personal performance in your log, gather feedback on levels of success and record evidence of key skills.

Maximising

This means making the most of the work done. During this stage everyone who contributed should be thanked and all information should be collated for submission. Once the project is over it is easy to relax too much, but your team needs to maximise the effort made to achieve good results and grades: then - and only then - can you afford to celebrate!

The following webstract shows how a well-known international team is presented to potential clients.

WEBSTRACT

LSO International

LSO International, a leisure and recreation management specialist company, really emphasises the personal approach of its staff team.

Hospitality: our mission. Staff will

- advise you in the choice of quality host personnel;
- be attentive to the aims of your event, and respect all shades of meaning, both cultural and professional;
- react and adapt to any modifications you introduce during your stay;
- be your partner at all times through the availability of our team.

Transport, logistics: our commitment

- from airport transfer up to the organisation of a cruise on a historic sailing vessel;
- guarantee unimpeachable quality of service, from both equipment and personnel;
- be present alongside you, to ensure strict co-ordination and perfect time-keeping.

Accommodation: our contribution

- detailed knowledge of the area used;
- our guarantee that your programme will run as planned.

The purpose of any kind of team is always to achieve some task or objective. To do this well it needs to have clear aims and objectives to follow, and a plan or procedures from which to work. A team will soon fall apart and waste its efforts if it does not have a plan and some agreed methods for working together.

The formation of effective teams is vital to the success of any leisure or recreation organisation, enabling the organisation to meet the challenging tasks and changing demands within the industry. There are also other benefits of teams which are often forgotten or taken for granted, for example teams can:

- provide a sense of achievement
- give help and support for members
- satisfy social and friendship needs
- meet personal needs through sharing.

An effective team leader and a well-structured team bring together all the talents of members to carry out jobs successfully, whether they are routine tasks or special events. The BT Global Challenge illustrates how important teamwork can be.

CASE STUDY

Sink or swim?

Sailing round the world must be one of the ultimate tests for anyone. For the amateurs who take part in the BT Global Challenge there are some tremendous leadership and team-building lessons to be learned during this tough yacht race. Volunteers for this ten-month 33,000-mile race first meet each other at the London Boat Show to discover who their crew mates will be and to which yacht they are allocated. The essence of the race is that you 'get who you get, and get on with it'. [You may have some choice of team mates, but this is a good maxim to remember.]

Crew have varying experience of sailing, so they are allocated to balance out their skills and experience and give each identical yacht the same chance to win. Any difference between the performance of each crew depends solely on leadership skills and the attention paid to teamwork and personal motivation.

The BT Global Challenge gives a host of challenges to test the best - elements of fear, life-threatening incidents, confinement, interpersonal problems, an unpredictable environment, elation, depression and many more.

Some teams immediately got down to the task of learning to sail their boat and the technical tasks; others spent some time getting to know each other and building team spirit, and understanding the leadership style of the professional skipper. The latter teams all finished in the top half of the race, showing the worth of this approach.

Right from the start it was important to set a strategy and target for each leg of the race which was believable and acceptable to everyone. The winning skipper of the 1996 race avoided telling his crew that they should go all out for victory. Instead, he emphasised that a consistently high performance would ensure that they did well and have a good chance of being successful. Several other skippers adopted this approach and finished in the top three every leg. Skippers who stated publicly that they were going all out to win did not do well.

Consistency was valued highly, along with effective job allocation, especially in the hazardous conditions in which they often found themselves. Crews who performed a range of tasks were never as effective when under pressure or in unfamiliar situations - tasks always took too long.

Giving people adequate information also proved to be essential. The more dynamic and complex the situation the greater the need for rapid communication. People knew what was happening - knowledge dispels fear and speeds up action. Often when the skipper was off watch (asleep below deck), the crew had complete control of the yacht and the tasks which were essential to keeping alive and racing across the oceans.

Apart from crashing walls of water and the fear of being washed overboard, there were other problems, such as the crew cracking under the pressure of relentless pounding and shortage of sleep. With such levels of stress people can often blame others for problems and not be very forgiving when disputes develop. Inevitably breakages occurred from human error, not just of equipment, but limbs as well. Lives were under constant threat in the southern ocean legs, survival was a matter of minutes, and depended totally on crew mates' speed of reaction if someone went overboard. It was therefore found essential that leadership and decision-making were carried out quickly. One skipper could pinpoint when niggles on the yacht had occurred simply by looking at the yacht log book to see when performance had been poorest!

A code of behaviour was needed among the crew. This brought out the idea that being a follower was as important as being a leader. This meant the crew were self-supporting on many occasions and did not always need the skipper to settle issues or provide motivation. Tolerance was at a premium, punctuality was next, followed by a willingness to apologise quickly for mistakes; saying sorry was in fact seen as a strength not a weakness. Gossip was the least tolerated aspect, idle chatter was outlawed. Yachts returning to Southampton with happy crews were those where the high-performance crews and teams were friends for life.

The highs and lows, the successes and failures, can all be related to the behaviour and skills of the crew and their skippers. These people will have harnessed energy, courage, determination and spirit to get through the worst the elements could throw at them.

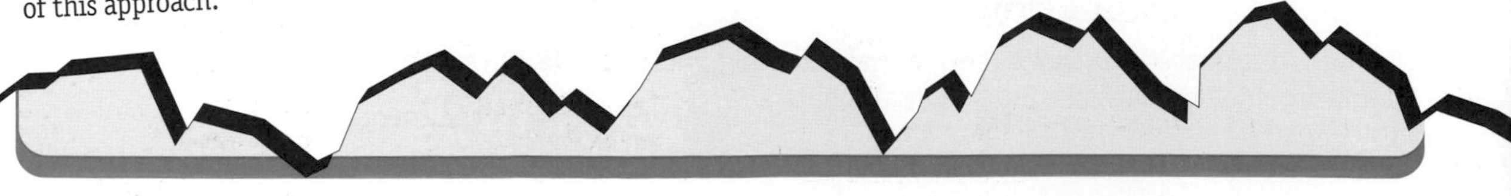

ACTIVITY

BT Global Challenge

Read through the BT Global Challenge case study to identify and discuss some key ideas that your team could adopt. Here are some to get you started:

- Dealing with personality clashes where value systems are different, or an autocratic style of leadership. This might mean exploring different spiritual/philosophical ideas on resolving conflict or prioritising, such as negotiating skills or a charitable aim for the project.
- How best to develop a teamwork style for your group and project and how you will manage your own role and responsibilities. This might mean exploring different ideas and motivations based on moral or ethical grounds, such as combating gender stereotypes, and how best to motivate a mixed team.

Group dynamics

Group dynamics is the process of interaction within and between teams and other individuals. A group will evolve into a team as it develops agreement among its members and with other groups or individuals. This process involves team members in the flow of interaction (dynamics), as shown in Figure 6.27.

Figure 6.27: Flow chart of group interactions

Accepting
↓
Communicating
↓
Co-operating
↓
Organising
↓
Responding
↓
Delivering
↓
Reviewing

At any stage of this interaction, conflict or problems can arise which may reduce the effectiveness of a group. For example, a group with too many people who want to lead or be at the 'centre of it all' may experience unhealthy competition, friction and personality clashes - so much so that the task or project may be forgotten for a while. Alternatively, no one may be willing to lead or co-ordinate, especially if a group is composed of people with no leadership skills.

ACTIVITY

Group Dynamics

Try this exercise to see how well your teamwork and communications operate to get you out of a difficult situation. Ask your team to stand in a circle. Each person should then reach out their right hand to hold the right hand of the person opposite them. Then each person should reach out their left hand to hold a different person's left hand. The challenge then is to unravel the hands without letting go and to recreate your circle as best you can.

Team effectiveness

We have looked at the structure and purpose of teams, along with roles and responsibilities and how all these things need to interact to make an effective team. In this section we shall investigate some of the factors which can influence a team's effectiveness, both positively and negatively. Figure 6.28 provides a list of these factors.

Figure 6.28: Factors affecting team performance

POSITIVE FACTORS	NEGATIVE FACTORS
Good working relationships	Poor group dynamics
Good leadership	Weak leadership
Adequate resources	Lack of resources
Clear roles and responsibilities	Confused roles and responsibilities
Sound but responsive structure	Inflexible structure
Good working environment	Poor working conditions
Clear procedures and processes	Poor or non-existent procedures
Regular feedback and evaluation	No feedback on performance

Communication

Groups and teams that do not communicate effectively are destined to fail. They will be unable to discuss issues or solve problems. Everyone in a team needs to have the ability to listen, thus enabling all points and opinions to be aired and understood. A team needs to establish **channels of communication** to ensure that vital information is reported in time, such as up-to-date minutes or accounts. This enables good decisions to be made quickly. Good communications are the glue that holds an operation together, particularly a project with many temporary arrangements that need to interlock.

Communication systems have two main functions. The first function is to make links with external organisations and individuals. Appropriate and relevant information should be communicated to all necessary people, such as customers, suppliers or the media: in fact, anyone who has an influence on the way the project will run. For example, you may need to put up signs to direct people to your project area, or issue regular progress reports to the press, or simply advertise tickets sales. Poor external communications - not ordering sufficient goods from suppliers, for example - will affect the ability of your team to operate effectively on the day.

The second main function of communication systems is to support the management and operation of an organisation. This largely serves an internal purpose: effective communication channels (ways of passing messages) between team members or staff on the project help to ensure that the project runs smoothly. For example, poor internal communication, such as failing to pass on a customer's request, may result in a double booking and therefore affect communication with customers on the day of the project.

The case study shows how reliable communications systems are vital to stadium management during a large event.

ACTIVITY

Communication Systems

List the systems which your group will need for the communication elements of your project. Some of these may be manual (paper-based) and some electronic, such as a database for example. Discuss the pros and cons of each, relative to your budget plans, abilities of the staff or team to use them, customer needs and availability of resources. Agree the internal and external communication procedures and systems you will use.

CASE STUDY

Communications at major events

The requirement for effective and reliable mobile communications at large stadia is the same for any large site where a major event is to be staged, such as the Ryder Cup or Ascot Races. Both require evermore complex solutions to achieve an acceptable outcome for organising teams. Historically, organisers have had to 'make do' until they get to the stage where the scale of the event means that they can no longer 'muddle through' with standard means and have to turn to radio communications. This brings with it many problems if the systems are new to organisers, such as poorly trained operatives; interference; too many people on the network; transmission control.

As all public events are under the jurisdiction of local authorities, the HSE and other relevant bodies, such as the police and the Radio Communications Agency, it is vital that the communications for the project are reliable and effective. Good communications can avert a disaster but, should communications break down, a major incident could be the result, so a contingency plan needs to be built in.

Twickenham, which is now one of the largest stadia in the country, has hundreds of radios in use on a match day, and pressure on the air waves is great, with the result that radio networks have to be set up to cover different functions at the game, such as stewards, parking attendants and security teams. Paging systems are also in use along with mobile phones, but with a large crowd the local cell sites get used up very rapidly.

It is often essential today to control communications for all large events in one central control room, thereby centralising emergency services, security functions and general crowd monitoring, as is often seen at major football stadia.

Source: *Leisure Manager*

Leadership styles

Finding the best **leadership style** for team effectiveness can be quite a challenge for someone who has not undertaken a leadership role before. Some teams may have dominant leaders who like to be 'the boss'. This is called an **autocratic style**, in which the leader is the only person making the decisions. This style is found most often in smaller team organisation.

Some teams have a **democratic style** of leadership that allows small committees or groups of people (teams) to make more of the decisions. Everyone elected has a role to play for the benefit of others and the success of the project. You are more likely to adopt this style for your project.

In between these extremes we find a mix of leadership styles dependent on the task or project involved. This is called a **contingency approach** or flexible style. Leaders select team members for specific jobs or tasks, in order to make full use of their skills and abilities. This is sometimes called a task culture, which also often suits project teams.

ACTIVITY

Leaderships styles

What leadership styles are being used in the following scenario?

A leisure and recreation student project team has recently elected its leader, who insists at every meeting that everyone should have their log books inspected. After several weeks, the leader allows a vote to be taken on this practice, due to the number of complaints from team members. As a result, the checking of log books is dropped.

In general terms, a project leader must have the ability to lead and delegate, co-ordinate and control, support and motivate. Above all, a project leader must be able to take an overview of proceedings and make decisions to smooth the progress of the team and the project. The contingency approach is best suited to these needs. Figure 6.29 is a chart of different **team types** created by **Belbin**, who argued that a range of different types is necessary to make a team work well. He believed that everyone has a dominant primary team type (some might also have a strong secondary team type) and that each team type has certain typical positive qualities and allowable weaknesses. Belbin claimed that each of us can be classified into one of eight different types.

On one hand, too many of some team types causes friction, such as more than one 'shaper' or too many 'plants'. On the other hand, a few 'team workers' and 'implementers' are always required as the core of the team, but perhaps only one 'resource investigator' and 'completer finisher'.

You might like to use some of Belbin's ideas to help select your team if you think any of your colleagues conform to his team types. Alternatively, after the project is over, you can use the chart to assess whether team members actually conformed to the type you thought they were.

ACTIVITY

Team Types

Analyse the different team types presented by Belbin and assess which of them is closest to your own. Your group should then discuss what you think your team types are, and assess how many of each type you have. Discuss if you have allocated the right people to tasks areas suited to their type. This exercise is normally done using a sophisticated assessment test, so your judgements will only be at face value. Nevertheless, it should make you think about people, their nature and the roles in which they will be most effective.

Personality clashes

A good team-working atmosphere is difficult to create, for it encompasses a variety of factors that may extend beyond the project. However, any condition that influences the growth, development or work of the team can be considered of importance. For example, if a person has an abrasive nature or is very quiet this might prevent him or her from getting along with others, and consequently prevent the team from being effective. If the team lacks cohesion it will definitely not perform effectively.

There is a concept known as **synergy**, which effectively means that the energy of the whole team applied to a task will be much greater than if just one or two work hard. As a consequence of team synergy, the end result is often that the team achieves a great deal more than it intended, perhaps exceeding all expectations. Synergy doesn't simply emerge: it needs effort and input from everyone:

- enthusiasm, even when things go wrong
- tolerance for others' views or ways of doing things
- perseverance in sticking to the task.

Team members' opinions of one another may also determine how well they work together. If they have low opinions of one another, attitudes become negative and conflict may occur. A positive atmosphere is the starting point for creating the best environment for teams to be effective.

Motivation is also a key factor, often seen as the responsibility of the leader, although this should not be the case. All team members should support each other, especially when someone is having an 'off day'. Motivation can take many forms. Intrinsic motivation comes from within ourselves, such as 'the will to win'. Extrinsic motivation come from outside ourselves, such as praise or reward from others.

Figure 6.29: Belbin's team types

Type	Symbol	Typical features	Positive qualities	Allowable weaknesses
Implementor	IM	Conservative, dutiful, predictable	Organising ability, practical common-sense, hard-working self-discipline	Lack of flexibility, unresponsiveness to unproven ideas
Coordinator	CO	Calm, self-confident, controlled	A capacity for treating and welcoming all potential contributors on their merits and without prejudice, a strong sense of objectives	No more than ordinary in terms of intellect or creative ability
Shaper	SH	Highly strung, outgoing, dynamic	Drive and a readiness to challenge inertia, ineffectiveness, complacency or self-deception	Proneness to provocation, irritation and impatience
Plant	PL	Individualistic, serious minded, unorthodox	Genius, imagination, intellect, knowledge	Up in the clouds, inclined to disregard practical details of protocol
Resource investigator	RI	Extrovert, enthusiastic, curious, communicative	A capacity for contracting people and exploring anything new, an ability to respond to challenge	Liable to lose interest once the initial fascination has passed
Monitor evaluator	ME	Sober, unemotional, prudent	Judgement, discretion, hard-headedness	Lacks inspiration or the ability to motivate others
Team worker	TW	Socially orientated, rather mild, sensitive	An ability to respond topeople and to situations,and to promote team spirit	Indecisiveness at moments of crisis
Complete finisher	CF	Painstaking, orderly, conscientious, anxious	A capacity for follow-through perfectionism	A tendency to worry about small things, a reluctance to 'let go'
Specialist	SP	Single-minded, self-starting and dedicated	Provides knowledge and skills in rare supply	Contributed on only a narrow front, dwells on technicalities, overlooks the 'big picture'

The working environment

For a team to be effective, the **working environment** in the facility or premises chosen for the project has to have certain desirable conditions. The working environment must be all of the following:

- Supportive, by encouraging staff to be innovative and trusting; this favours a democratic approach to leadership and involves staff in some decision-making.
- Based on clear goals and definite standards, with guidelines for teams to follow which are outlined in mission statements, charters or strategic plans.
- Allow people to measure their performance by evaluating objectives and outcomes using targets and feedback from senior staff and colleagues, such as appraisals and reports.
- Provide rewards and incentives for good performance, such as bonuses, or disincentives for poor performance, such as explanations and disciplinary measures.
- Provide opportunities for personal improvement, such as learning new skills.

The most effective organisations in the leisure and recreation industry spend a great deal of time trying to create these positive conditions for teams. You should try to follow their example on your project.

ACTIVITY

Effective teamwork

Look at the model created by John Adair, a renowned leadership analyst). Under each of the categories – Individual, Team and Task – list what each of them requires to help create effective teamwork and a successful task or project. Three examples are given to help you start.

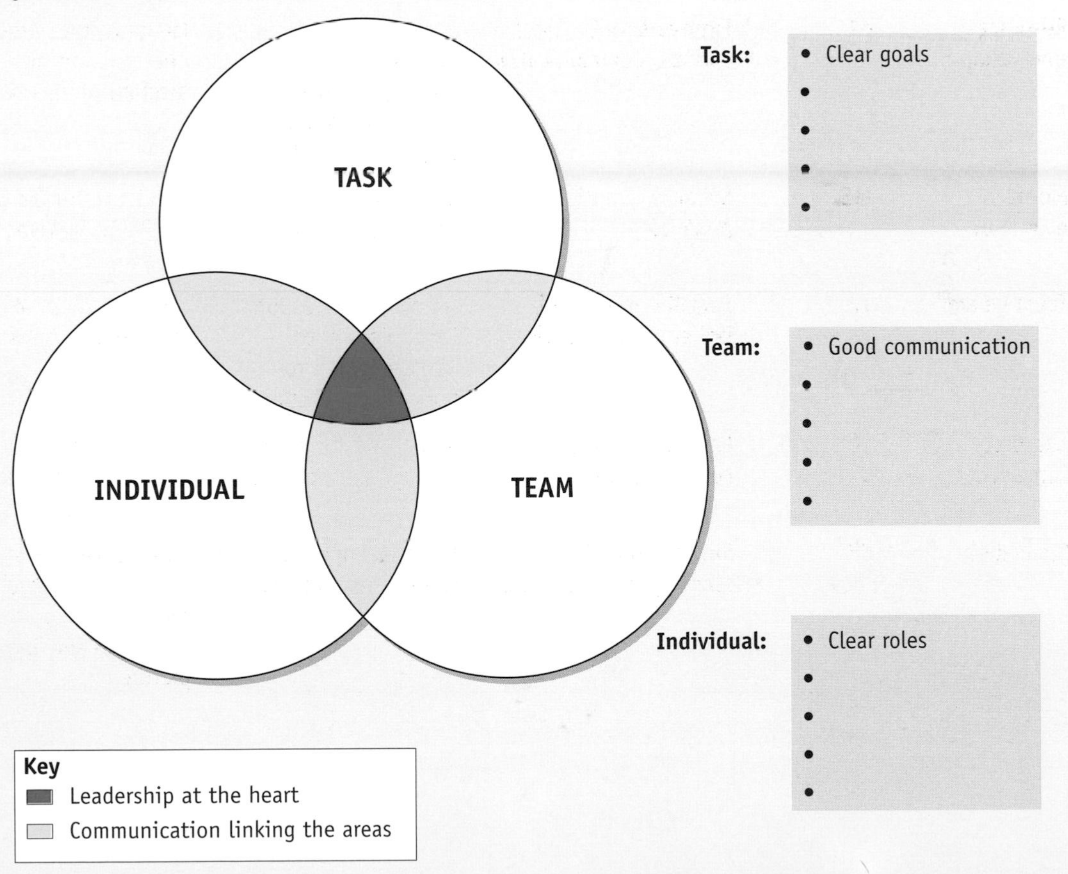

The final check

With an agreed structure in place, roles allocated, and an idea of what good teamwork and leadership entail, there only remains the painstaking but essential process of going over every detail in planning for the project. This enables everyone to make a final check (and note) of their exact responsibilities, tasks, contingency plans, use of resources and the desired outcome according to the targets agreed by the team.

Two methods used by leisure and recreation project teams that you might be able to adopt are a final meeting and a dress rehearsal.

A final team meeting can be called to which everyone brings their proposals, in order to discuss each stage in turn. The contributions of each person should help piece together the jigsaw puzzle of the plan. This can be a slow process, but it allows amendments to be made as necessary. It also means that any variations are dealt with by the team at the final planning stage rather than at the start of the project! Everyone sees the whole plan as it is brought together by the co-ordinator(s) into a workable format.

It is often possible to carry out a dress rehearsal of many of the practical aspects of an event/project. This provides tremendous feedback on a whole range of aspects important to the smooth running of the project, such as timings, shortages, resources used and communications. Rehearsals can lead to such useful changes as:

- adjustment of a deadline
- revision of a target
- the addition of a contingency plan
- redefining of a key factor
- increasing or decreasing a resource
- applying a new budget limit
- identifying other sources of feedback.

The benefit of the whole team working together to amend the plan is that everyone knows about any changes. It also means that agreement can be reached on the final operating version of the plan. This whole process is often called closing the loop, as shown in Figure 6.2 on page 399.

BUILD YOUR LEARNING

Keywords and phrases

You should know the meaning of the words and phrases listed below. If you are unsure about any of them, go back through the last 12 pages to refresh your understanding.

- Teamwork
- Formal
- Informal
- Structure
- Hierarchy
- Purpose
- Team leader/co-ordinator
- Lines of authority
- Organisational chart
- Areas of responsibility
- Role
- Task descriptions
- Role conflict
- Delegation
- Group dynamics
- Channels of communication
- Leadership styles
- Motivation
- Autocratic style
- Democratic style
- Contingency approach
- Belbin's team types
- Working environment
- Synergy

End of section activity

For each of the following scenarios make a recommendation as to how the project teams could improve their teamwork.

1 A student project team has had an argument about who should meet and greet two local celebrities who have agreed to appear at the start of the project. The group's leader insists that he should do so as he is the most important person. The woman in charge of marketing activities thinks that she should have this responsibility as it is part of her function. A third person thinks it should be her, as it was she who suggested the idea in the first place because her parents knew the celebrities. The group is having one of its regular team meetings, but is getting nowhere on this subject. How would you solve the problem?

2 A leisure centre team has decided to stage a promotional project for its town at a sports exhibition at London's Earl's Court. There is strong competition among staff to be on the stand at the exhibition. The manager of the centre decides that attendance should be based on merit, namely the attributes (skills and qualities) that staff on the stand need to have. She decides to ask everyone what they think these attributes should be. What do you think they should be? How would you proceed to select staff?

3 The staff at a theme park are asked to undertake an identical event on their site, every year, to raise money for charity. Each year there are always a good number of new staff or seasonal workers who are part of the team. This means that every year many of the preparations have to be gone over several times. What could you suggest to improve things?

Carrying out and evaluating the project

In order to carry out your project and its subsequent evaluation, you are expected to perform your agreed roles positively and work with the rest of the team to achieve agreed objectives. The following guidelines should act as a useful reminder.

- Perform the tasks allocated to you and your role(s) in the team plan, ensuring that everything you do helps the team achieve the project objective(s).
- Keep to agreed deadlines. If you fall behind with your contribution it will affect everyone else: team members and suppliers of goods or services.
- Know when to ask for help and advice. For example, as soon as you realise you're falling behind or are overloaded, report it to the rest of the team or your co-ordinator. This is where you will find the most help.
- At all times deal politely with customers, other members of your team and any other people involved with the project. Try to maintain this approach even when you are under pressure or things are not going as expected.
- Support other team members throughout the project. You may find that someone is particularly busy or under pressure. Any assistance is usually appreciated and demonstrates good teamwork.
- React quickly and confidently to any problems that arise. You may be the first in line when a problem occurs or someone needs assistance. Your team will have to obtain information on contingency procedures well before the actual day(s), to ensure that you have an effective sequence planned.

You can see from the Lakeside brochure page below how much emphasis is placed by employers on these types of skills, as they often form part of team-building courses for businesses.

Keeping to the team plan

Your team will have spent a lot of time preparing a plan, so it makes sense to follow it precisely. Any major deviation from the plan will have an effect and may even throw the whole project off course, with potentially disastrous results. Of course, a little flexibility should be allowed, but this should be anticipated through contingency planning or agreed in advance with the co-ordinator(s) to keep things under control.

Keeping to the team plan also means ensuring that all meetings are properly organised and minuted throughout the planning, running and evaluation phases, and that all team members record their personal or task objectives in a log book or diary, so that progress can be checked and any differences can be controlled. You should be able to find guidance on how to hold a proper meeting in your school or college library. Always have an agenda with numbered items of topics for

▼ Team-building courses

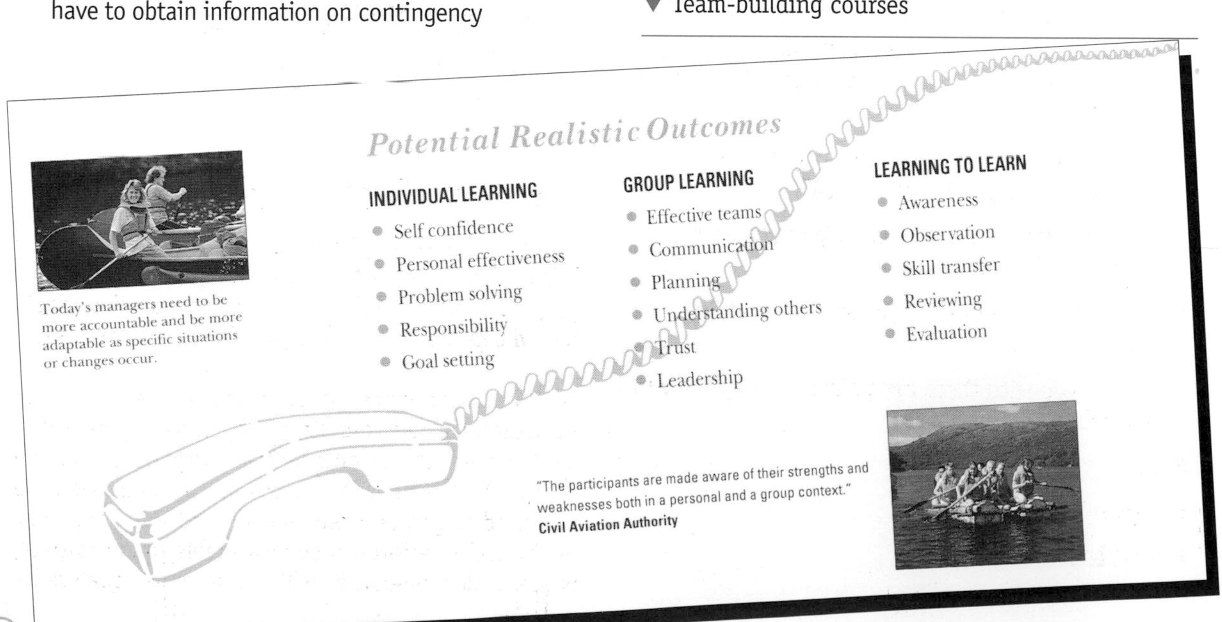

discussion, keep accurate minutes and conduct discussion through the chairperson. This will be another important source of evaluation. See Figure 6.26 on page 436 for an example of a format for an agenda and minutes.

Health, safety and security

One important factor worth reiterating at this stage is that you must never forget the need for team members to have due regard for the health, safety and security of:

- themselves
- colleagues
- customers
- facilities
- information
- the environment.

When collating evidence for your project log or diary, you may find it helpful to use a table like the one in the activity on page 428, in order to record the health, safety and security measures required for your project.

Here is a summary of key points you will need to keep constantly in mind.

- Try to complete the tasks you have been given 'as competently as possible'.
- Deal with all customers, colleagues and others involved with the project 'cooly, calmly and politely'. Here you can bring in all your customer care skills from other units.
- Have a 'positive attitude' to yourself and your responsibilities and 'support team mates' in the same way.
- Respond to changes or react to problems 'with confidence' using a proactive approach.
- 'Keep to any agreed deadlines' or 'give plenty of notice' to others if you cannot.
- 'Seek advice or get help if you are unsure at any stage.'
- To help you with these key points you might try to remember the Five Ps:

Proper
Planning
Promotes
Perfect
Performance

The planner produced by North Yorkshire County Council (Figure 6.30) shows how this kind of detail is extremely important when planning a residential visit.

Figure 6.30 Planning a residential visit

Be aware of **SKILLS** in planning inside and outside your group
Identify clear **STAFF ROLES** to get the best input
Encourage everyone to contribute to the **PLANNING**
Set some programme **OBJECTIVES** and timings
Always have a plan 'B' for **CONTINGENCIES** which may occur
Compile a list of essential **EQUIPMENT** for participants
Take out adequate **INSURANCE** for activities
Calculate the **GROSS COST** and set a price to cover it
Help yourself meet costs by **FUNDRAISING**
ADVERTISE early and by various means
Produce an **INFORMATION** sheet
Take **BOOKINGS** and personal details
Hold a **PRESENTATION** night
Stage a **FINAL BRIEFING** to check arrangements or changes
Collect all **MONIES** before departure
Gather **FEEDBACK** after the residential on its success
Balance the **ACCOUNTS**
Carry out some **POST-PROJECT** publicity
EVALUATE the objectives set

Evaluation of the project

Evaluation in this context means establishing the true value of your work and the part you played in the project: in other words, how you performed. You should regard this process as an essential element of the unit.

The performance of your project team will be measured against your stated objectives contained in the business plan. In order to evaluate performance and assess whether such objectives have been achieved you will need to gather a wide range of information. Some of this information will be measurable (quantitative), while other feedback will be a more qualitative judgement of performance. Consider the project under the following headings.

- Strengths, such as good teamwork, communications and meticulous planning which enabled your team to be successful.
- Weaknesses, such as poor leadership, no contingency plans or health and safety problems which prevented individuals from carrying out tasks.
- Constraints, such as inadequate resources or adverse weather conditions.

London and Continental Railways will use these types of criteria to assess who will be in charge of the £1 billion redevelopment of the King's Cross area, as you can see in the webstract below.

WEBSTRACT

King's Cross

17 pitch for £1bn King's Cross plan

By Malcolm Withers

The £1 billion development of the King's Cross area, Europe's biggest property regeneration project, has attracted 17 bidders, two-thirds of them British.

A short list of just three names is expected to be announced by developer London & Continental Railways (LCR) in the next two to three weeks with the winning partner - which could be a consortium - appointed in the New Year.

LCR is seeking a partner for the 130-acre site, now called King's Cross Central, and was advised by international property consultants Jones Lang LaSalle to approach 23 developers seen as big and financially sound enough to deal with the capital's largest-ever property project.

Seventeen were eventually approached to take the bidding process a stage further, including some of the blue-chips of the development world such as Land Securities (LSE: Land.L -news), British Land, MPEC (LSE: MEPC.L - news), St George and ING. It is also likely that a series of consortiums will be established to bid for the project which is based in the run-down area of King's Cross and St Pancras mainline stations.

The development is being masterminded by Stephen Jordan, managing director of LCR's property subsidiary. He has overseen much of the detail, including a meeting with Arsenal Football club directors.

Jordan told the Highbury club, which is looking for a new home, that if it wanted to build a new stadium it would have to approach one of the bidders for the whole project.

LCR is anxious for what it calls a 'people attractor', but such a venue must draw in visitors for seven days a week, not just alternate Saturdays. Property sources say that Arsenal may now link up with one of the development bidders for a combined exhibition centre and football ground. The London Chamber of Commerce is believed to be pushing hard for a new exhibition centre.

Arsenal may have been disappointed by Jordan's reaction but he is adamant there will be 'no cherry-picking of sites' and that there had to be an 'overall gain plan for the area'.

LCR is also anxious to avoid controversy at King's Cross about the development, which has in the past run into opposition from practically every local group.

LCR is now working closely with the local authorities Camden and Islington as well as English Heritage, King's Cross Partnership, Railtrack, rail operators using the two stations, London Underground and many other pressure groups.

Source: *uk.biz.yahoo.com*

Evaluation techniques

Right from the start, this unit highlighted the need to establish a project evaluation process, so that once planning was completed and the project underway you could set about evaluating the data you gathered. You should regard this process as an essential element of the unit, in order to judge your performance and level of success. Your teams **evaluation techniques** should:

- measure quantifiable activities, such as financial performance or attendance numbers
- classify information into similar categories, such as customer information or use of resources
- summarise data so that it is manageable, such as the effectiveness of team skills or the efficiency of systems present the findings clearly and objectively.
- present the finding clearly and objectively

Your team should work its way through each aspect of the business plan and implementation strategy, so that no potential source is left untapped. You should also discuss the relative advantages of a range of evaluation techniques in order to select those most appropriate. For example:

- a team debriefing session after the project, with the whole team present to report on areas of responsibility
- a team-member questionnaire
- feedback from your teacher
- customer feedback
- suppliers' or external organisations' input - what was done well or badly

Much of the information will help improve your personal skills, for you can use the feedback to increase strengths and overcome weaknesses. Many people fail to learn from their experiences and simply repeat their mistakes in other contexts and situations. You should be able to make use of the feedback given to improve your skills, knowledge and abilities.

You may wish to evaluate your personal outcomes against the skills listed by Young Enterprise in Figure 6.32 overleaf. Analysis might show where you could have done better by comparison.

Evaluation checklist

To meet the assessment criteria your team should be able to answer all of the questions shown in Figure 6.31 as part of your evaluation, and provide sufficient evidence to support its answers.

Figure 6.31 Evaluation checklist

		Yes	No
1	Did you meet all your objectives? If not, why not?	❑	❑
2	Were key deadlines met? If not, what caused them to be missed?	❑	❑
3	Did your planning prove effective? If not, what do you recommend should be done differently next time?	❑	❑
4	Was the project or event a success? If not, why not? If it was, what made it special?	❑	❑
5	What went well and what went badly? Can you identify the highs and lows and what caused them?	❑	❑
6	How well did the team work together? Was it some of the time, or all of the time, or never?	❑	❑
7	What did you gain from working in a team? (for example skills, or insight into others' behaviour).	❑	❑

Figure 6.32: Young Enterprise key skills and experience profile

These skills can be acquired through your experience in Young Enterprise.

Team working

- Take part in identifying the team's objectives.
- Agree each team member's task and report on own tasks.
- Work effectively with others to reach goals.
- Use own and colleagues' time effectively.
- Problem solving
- Identify and analyse problems.
- Choose solutions and implement procedures .

Communication

- Take active part in meetings and discussions.
- Negotiate with others effectively to agree objectives and procedures.
- Interact well with customers and colleagues.
- Produce clear concise written work using IT.
- Make presentations.

Marketing

- Create and carry out a market research plan.
- Identify customer target groups and develop the marketing mix.
- Choose strategies to sell to target groups.
- Maintain good public relations with suppliers and customers.

Operations

- Define resource, quality, legal requirements and health and safety requirements.
- Set up procedures to meet targets.
- Develop evaluation systems.
- Maintain systems to meet quality standards.
- Evaluate environmental impact.

Finance

- Identify financial resource needs and fund these from various sources.
- Use budgetary information and justify expenditure on projects.
- Record financial information using IT.
- Select strategies to improve financial performance.
- Carry out an audit.

Personnel and training

- Understand personnel requirements and set up systems to meet them.
- Identify training.
- Seek and make use of feedback to improve performance and motivation.
- Use self-assessment procedures and review personal objectives.
- Develop a personal record of achievement.

BUILD YOUR LEARNING

Keywords and phrases

You should know the meaning of the words and phrases listed below. If you are unsure about any of them, go back through the last five pages to refresh your understanding.

- Evaluation
- Evaluation techniques

End of section activity

1 Take part in running the project and produce a record of your involvement. You may be able to use the personal log book (explained on pages 399-401) as this record. Whatever format that you use to record your involvement, it should include:

- details of the tasks you were allocated.
- details of any problems that arose and how you reacted.
- details of any time deadlines you were given and whether you kept to them.

2 Evaluate your role in the project and the effectiveness of the team in achieving the project objectives. You may find it useful to base your evaluation on the checklist shown in Figure 6.31 on page 451. You will also need to gather feedback from a variety of sources to complete this task, including from:

- your own personal experiences
- other team members
- customers
- your teachers or supervisors.

3 Make valid recommendations for improvements to your own performance and that of the team, based on your critical evaluation of the project.

UNIT PORTFOLIO ASSESSMENTS

Units1,3,5 and 6 are assessed through your portfolio work. The grade for the assessments will be your grade for each unit. These pages are designed to help you review your work and to check whether you have covered the required tasks to the right standard. The assessment tasks show what your portfolio needs to contain. Your teacher can give you further advice on what you need to do for each task.

If you have completed all the end of section activities, you will already have done a great deal of the work for your portfolio. Sometimes you may need to reorganise or expand upon the work that you have done before it is ready to be submitted for your final assessment. The tables for each assessment show which activities from each unit can help you build your portfolio.

UNIT 1 PORTFOLIO ASSESSMENT

Assessment tasks

This assessment is in two parts. The first part (tasks 1 to 4) requires you to undertake an investigation into the UK leaisure and recreation industry covering:

- reasons for development of the industry since the 1960s
- its scale and significance to the UK economy
- its structure and key components
- the range of public, private and voluntary sector organisations within each component.

The second part of the assessment (tasks 5-7) involves an investigation into employment opportunities in the leisure and recreation industry. You will identify one job that interests you and produce your own CV.

The table below shows which activities from the unit can help you to build your portfolio.

Assessment tasks	
Task 1	Activities on pages 15, 18, 19, 25, 28
Task 2	Activities on pages 30,31,32
Task 3	Activities on pages 47,54,57,62,65
Task 4	Activities on pages 35, 36, 39, 41, 65
Task 5	Activities on pages 79
Task 6	Activities on pages 75, 77, 79
Task 7	Activities on pages 82, 87

Task 1.

Explain, giving suitable examples, the key factors that have promoted the rapid development of the industry since the 1960s. You should explain the impact of:

- increase in leisure time available for many individuals
- increase in disposable income
- improved mobility
- demographic changes
- changing fashions and trends
- technological developments

To achieve an A grade you will also need to show a thorough understanding of the reasons for the rapid growth of the industry and the factors that will affect its development in the future.

Task 2.

Describe the scale of the UK industry and its economic significance, using relevant data accurately in terms of:

- consumer spending in the UK on leisure and recreation products and services
- the number of people employed in the industry
- participation trends in the most popular leisure and recreation activities.

Task 3.

Summarise the present structure and the key components of the UK leisure and recreation industry, giving suitable examples of the main types of organisation, facilities, products and services within each component. You should cover the following key industry components:

- arts and entertainment
- sports and physical recreation
- heritage
- catering
- countryside recreation
- home-based leisure

You should also summarise the range of public, private and voluntary sector organisations for each component (except home-based leisure), giving suitable examples.

To achieve a grade A for tasks 2 and 3, you must also provide a clear demonstration of your ability to critically analyse information and data in order to draw valid conclusions about the scale and structure of the industry.

Task 4.
Evaluate the key characteristics of public, private and voluntary sector organisations to illustrate differences in their funding and business objectives.

Throughout your investigations for tasks 1 to 4, **to achieve a grade C**, your work must also show a logical and well structured analysis of the industry that effectively summarises key information and data, and an ability to use appropriate terminology.

To achieve a grade A your work must also show your ability to use a comprehensive range of information sources, showing how you have cross-checked the reliability of each source.

Task 5.
Summarise the range of employment opportunities available within the leisure and recreation industry.

Task 6.
Describe in detail one job that best matches your own aspirations, skills and abilities .

To achieve a grade C you also will need to provide additional information in order to critically evaluate why your chosen job best matches you personal circumstances. For example this information could involve contacting employers interviewing someone that works in your chosen area, obtaining a job description/person specification, or attending a careers event/exhibition.

Task 7.
Produce a curriculum vitae (CV) that is appropriate for seeking employment in your chosen job.

Key Skills

It may be possible to claim these key skills for this work depending on how you have completed the tasks and presented your work:

- Communication (C3.2, C3.3)
- Information Technology (IT3.2)
- Improving own learning and performance
- Working with others .

Your teacher will need to check your evidence against the key skills specification.

UNIT 3 PORTFOLIO ASSESSMENT

Assessment Tasks

You may be able to use the information contained in the football and tennis studies to help you complete this assessment (see pages 212-231). The table overleaf shows which activities from the unit can also help you build your portfolio.

You need to produce the results of an investigation into two sports of your choice that covers:

- the scale and economic importance of each sport
- the organisation and funding of each sport
- the importance of each sport for the mass media
- the ways in which the mass media have influenced each sport
- major trends in each sport

You should select sports for which you can access a wide range of relevant information and statistics.The result of your investigation can be presented in a number of ways including an oral presentation, a written report or a combination of these. Throughout your work you must demonstrate an ability to use terminology associated with the sports industry accurately.

UNIT 3 PORTFOLIO ASSESSMENT

Assessment tasks

Task 1	Activities on pages 193, 222 and 231
Task 2	Activities on pages 178, 186, 193, 205,222 and 231
Task 3	Activities on pages 170, 175, 222 and 231
Task 4	Activities on pages 197, 208, 209, 211, 222 and 231
Task 5	Activities on pages 175, 222 and 231
Task 6	Activities on pages 166,222 and 231

To achieve a grade C your work must be presented in a logical and well-structured format, and be based on a wide range of up to date and relevant information sources.

To achieve a grade A you will need to demonstrate an ability to use accurate, precise, reliable and sufficient data independently to support your investigation.

Task 1.
Briefly describe how your chosen sports are organised at local, regional, national and international levels. Support your description with diagrams showing organisational structures, if appropriate.

Task 2.
Explain the main sources of funding for your chosen sports and briefly describe how commercialisation has has affected them.

Task 3.
Explain the scale and economic importance of each sport in terms of the numbers employed, the number of participants and financial turnover. Support your explanantion with the use of appropriate statistics.

Task 4.
Describe the mass media coverage of each sport, and explain their importance to the media. You should also descirbe ways in which the mass media have influenced the sport. **To achieve an A grade** for this task you also need to provide an effective explanantion of the interrelationship between each sport and the media.

To achieve a grade C for tasks 3 and 4 you should compare and contrast the scale and economic importance of the two sports, and the ways in which the mass media have influenced them.

Task 5.
Describe at least one major trend occurring in each of your chose sports.

To achieve a grade C you should describe at least two trends for each sport and also interpret and explain the reasons for these trends.

To achieve an A grade you will need to demonstrate an ability to analyse data and draw valid conclusions about the trends in each sport

Task 6.
Explain how each of your chosen sports is affected by the sports industry as a whole.

Key Skills

While undertaking your investigation there may be opportunity to gather key skills evidence for:

- Application of number (Level 3, N3.1)
- Communication (Level 3, C3.2, C3.1b, C3.3)
- Information Technology (Level 3, IT3.1, IT3.3)
- Improving own learning and Performance (Level 3, LP3.1, LP3.2, LP3.3)
- Working with others (Level 3).

Your teacher will need to check your evidence against the key skills specification.

UNIT 5 PORTFOLIO ASSESSMENT

Assessment tasks

This assessment is in two parts. The first part requires you to produce a record for your involvement in a variety of customer service situations (tasks 1 and 2). These situations can be real, such as from a work placement or part-time job, or they could be simulated such as through role-plays.

In the second part you need to investigate the effectiveness of customer service delivery in two leisure and recreation organisations (tasks 3-5). The table opposite shows which activities from the unit can help you to build your portfolio.

Task 1.

Provide details of your dealings with at least four different types of customers in a variety of customer service and selling situations. This should include at least one situation for each of the following:

- face-to-face (to individuals and groups)
- on the telephone (to include making/receiving calls and taking accurate messages)
- in writing (to include replying in an appropriate format to a letter)
- handling a customer complaint

On each occassion you must show how you adapted your responses to meet customer requirements.

To achieve an E grade you must show:

- that you can provide accurate and appropriate information/ advice to customers
- your ability to use communication and selling skills appropriately, providing customers with the services they require, taking into account specific needs
- your ability to deal with customers on the telephone
- your ability to deal with customers in writing
- your ability to handle customer complaints effectively and sensitively

To achieve an C grade you will also need to demonstrate thorough product knowledge, that you understand the specific needs of different types of customer, and that you can adapt your responses by meeting these needs in an appropriate manner.

Assessment tasks	
Task 1	Activities on pages 344, 367, 374
Task 2	Activities on pages 344, 367, 374
Task 3	Activities on pages 329, 334, 345,351, 396
Task 4	Activities on pages 329, 334, 345,351, 396
Task 5	Activities on pages 334, 345,351, 396
Task 6	Activities on pages 334, 345,351, 396

To achieve an A grade you will also need to display excellent communication and selling skills in your dealings with different types of customers in a pressured work situation, and complete task 2.

Task 2.

Critically evaluate your performance in dealing with customers, suggesting actions on how you can improve. A proforma that you could use to record you performance is provided on page 460.

Task 3.

Explain the key customer service quality criteria in two leisure and recreation organisations or facilities, giving examples of the procedures and practices used by managers and staff to achieve them.

Task 4.

Using appropriate methods for measuring and monitoring, evaluate the effectiveness of the customer service delivery in each leisure and recreation organisation or facility.

Task 5.

To achieve an C grade you will also need to critically evaluate and compaare the effectiveness of customer service delivery in each organisation.

Task 6.
To achieve an A grade you will also need to suggest and justify appropriate actions to improve customer service delivery in each organisation.

Key Skills

It may be possible to claim these key skills for this work depending on how you have completed the tasks and presented your work:

- Communication (C3.1a, C3. 1b, C3.2)
- Improving own learning and performance (level 3)
- Working with others (level 3).

Your teacher will need to check your evidence against the key skills specification.

UNIT 6 PORTFOLIO ASSESSMENT

Assessment Tasks

The assessment involves planning, carrying out and evaluating a leisure and recreation related team project. The project could take the form of a sports tournament, a special event involving the local community, an educational visit or tour at a leisure and recreation facility, or a fundraising venture. You could incorporate the project into a school/college residential trip. Where resources or opportunities are limited the project can be implemented 'in-house', such as organising an open day for visitors to your school/college, entering a major competition or taking part in a local event such as a carnival or parade.

Whatever project you decide to do, you must ensure that it will enable you to meet the assessment criteria and provide a realistic experience in a leisure and recreation context. It must also be large enough to provide all members of your team with an opportunity to take on substantial responsibilities.

Task 1.
Produce a logical and coherent business plan for a leisure and recreation related project that covers all aspects listed below. The team project must be viable to run in terms of resources available, legal obligations and time. The plan should be developed as a group, but be presented individually. This should include:

- objectives and timescales for the project
- description of the project
- human, financial and physical resource needs.
- legal aspects of the project (health and safety, security and insurance)
- methods to be used to evaluate the project.

Task 2.
Effectively participate in running the team project. You will need to show an ability to use effective planning and communication skills throughout the project. You must also keep a record of your contribution, including:

- details of the tasks you were allocated
- details of any problems you encountered and how you dealt with them
- details of any time deadlines you were given and if you kept to them
- an evaluation of your role in the project

Your personal involvement may be recorded in a number of ways, such as a display, report, presentation or diary. You should keep records of team meetings, briefings or other relevant planning materials, such as marketing and contingency plans or financial projections.

To achieve grade C for tasks 1 and 2 you must make a significant contribution to planning and running the project, and show an ability to use initiative and creativity. All aspects of the project must be completed within an appropriate timescale.

To achieve grade A your work must also show independence in managing and running the project, and evidence of a high level of communication skills with team members and customers.

Task 3.
Evaluate your role in planning and running the project and the effectiveness of the team's performance throughout the project. You should base this on how effective the team was in achieving the project objectives.

Assessment tasks
Task 1 **Activities on pages 406, 407, 409, 422, 434**
Task 2 **Activities on page 453**
Task 3 **Activities on page 453**

The table above shows which activities in the unit can help you to build your portfolio.

To achieve grade C this evaluation should be a critical analysis of your own performance, and that of the team, while planning and running the project.

To achieve grade A you must also make valid recommendations for improvements to your own performance and that of the team, based on your critical evaluation of the project.

Key Skills

It may be possible to claim these key skills for this work depending on how you have completed the tasks and presented your work:

- Communication (3.1a, 3.1b, 3.3)
- Improving Own Learning and Performance (3.1, 3.2, 3.3)
- Problem Solving (3.1, 3.2, 3.3, 3.4)
- Working With Others (3.1, 3.2, 3.3)

Your teacher will need to check your evidence against the key skills specification.

PROFORMA

Describe the customer service situation and the types of customers	List the customer's need and key service quality criteria	Describe the communication methods used	List any necessary customer information recorded

What were the objectives of service delivery?	Personal evaluation of performance	Peer group group evaluation of performance	Tutor or work supervisor evaluation of performance
			Tutor/Supervisor signature .... Date ....

ANSWERS TO ACTIVITIES

Unit 1, page 45

Top 10 Film Hits

Rank	Film	Profit (£ m)
1	*Titanic* (1998)	68
2	*The Full Monty* (1997)	52
3	*Jurassic Park* (1993)	47
4	*Independence Day* (1996)	37
5	*Men in Black* (1997)	35
6	*Four Weddings and a Funeral* (1994)	27
7	*The Lost World: Jurassic Park* (1997)	25
8	*Ghost* (1990)	23
9	*The Lion King* (1995)	22
10	*Toy Story* (1995)	22

Top 10 Flop Films

Rank	Film	Loss (£m)
1	*Waterworld* (1995)	70
2	*Last Action Hero* (1993)	53
3	*The Avengers* (1998)	40
4	*Hudson Hawk* (1991)	37
5	*Raise the Titantic* (1980)	33
6	*Heaven's Gate* (1980)	28
7	*Revolution* (1980) 28	
8	*Ishtar* (1987)	27
9	*The Bonfire of the Vanities* (1990)	25
10	*Cleopatra* (1963)	14

Unit 1, page 55

1G, 2D, 3F, 4A 5B, 6C, 7J, 8K, 9L, 10H, 11I, 12E

Unit 3, page 159

Name	Sport	Worth (1998 £m)
Nick Faldo	Golf	41.0
Lennox Lewis	Boxing	38.0
Nigel Mansell	Motor racing	36.0
Damon Hill	Motor racing	36.0
Naseem Hammed	Boxing	19.5
Ian Woosnam	Golf	18.0
Alan Shearer	Football	17.5
Paul Gascoigne	Football	13.5
Colin Montgomerie	Golf	12.5
Linford Christie	Athletics	9.5

Unit 4, page 312

Is it legal?
Adjudication: Upheld
The advertisers insisted that the card worked and said it was gurarnteed for 12 months.
They said the card was intended to be used to receive Danish staellite channels, which they claimed was legal. They pointed out that the follow-up literature warned people that it was illegal to use the card to receive Sky channels. The Authority was concerned that the advertisers had described the card as a novelty, although they claimed that it worked and that they had failed to provide evidence for this. The Authority believed that using the card was likely to be illegal and considered that the advertisement encouraged readers to buy and use the card to break the law. It instructed the advertisers to withdraw the advertisement immediately and welcomed the Committee of Advertising Practice's decision to instruct its media members to check with the Copy Advice team before accepting fututre advertisements.

Is it decent?
Adjudication: Not upheld
The advertisers said they regretted the offence caused and, as a result, had decided not to repeat the advertisement. they pointed out that the advertisement had been approved by a chaplain who was on the Board of Directors. The Evening Standard said thay believd the advertisement reminded people of the Christmas message. the other publishers believed most of their readers would not be offended by the advertisement. The Authority noted that some people had been offended but concluded that this was not so serious or widespread that the advertisement broke the Codes.

Is it honest?
Adjudication: Upheld
The advertisers argued that the advertisement referred to a 'Founder Membership' scheme that gave members extra priviledge points over ordinary members and said this was made clear to members when they joined. They said it was wrong for new members to assume all recruiting for members would cease after the stated deadline. The Authority considered that the advertisement implied that all recruiting for members would cease after the ststed deadline and asked the advertisers, if they were to continue to advertise, to amend future

advertisements to make clear the nature of the scheme, and not to imply that only a limited number of new members could join it that were
not true.

Is it truthful?
Adjudication: Upheld
The advertisers said the quote was taken from a book published in 1982, when the author was a voluntary member of the League's Executive Committee; he was fully employed by the League when the book was reprinted, unchanged, in 1990. The advertisers provided documents and suggested that the complainants' publicly proclaimed neutral policy on fishing belied a strategy of political expediency. The Authority understood that the quote appeared only in 1,000 copies of the book and was changed in 1983; it considered the advertisement would be seen as representing the League's position, not that of the author, and it was wrong to use a quote over 14 years old to justify the league's present policy. The Authority considered that the advertisers' substantiation did not show that the league had an antiangling policy and asked the advertisers to avoid giving this impression in future advertisements.

Unit 5 page 332

1. Sometimes, but it depends on the situation and type of customer. For example, children or young adults at a sports club may prefer to be called by their first name. However, in most situations it is safer to address someone by their surname unless invited to use their first name.

2. Sometimes, again it depends on the situation. generally, if the customer is standing then so should you. However, there are situations, such as when welcoming a visitor to a health asnd fitness club, when it may be more appropriate to remain seated.

3. Never.

4. Never. You should always take the lead by approaching a customer and asking if you can be of assistance.

5. Always.

6. Never, it shows respect. However, if you know the customer's surname it is even better to address them as Mr/Mrs...

7. Never, it shows that you have lost control of the situation and is highly unprofessional.

8. Always, it is unprofessional and breaches confidentiality.

9. never, they expect excellent service every time. If you are so tired or unwell that you cannot do your job properly, you should not be at work!

10. Always.

11. Always

12 Sometimes, but what is important is that you always act as if the customer is right.

Unit 5, page 340

traffic circle - roundabout
divided highway - dual carriageway
freeway - motorway
sidewalk - pavement
second floor - first floor
faucet - tap
jelly - jam
check - bill/cheque
liquor store - off licence
chips - crisps
restroom - lavatory
ATM - cash point
pocket book - wallet
bandaid - plaster

Resource and internet directory

During your course, you will gather a wide range of information about leisure and recreation organisations, facilities, products, services and events. This textbook provides much of the information that you need to complete your coursework. However, you will need to use a range of information sources in order to complete your portfolio assessments successfully (see pages 454 to 460). This section provides you with a directory of information sources and websites that you may find useful throughout your course.

Information sources

Magazines, journals and periodicals

- *Leisure Management* (see also internet directory)
- *Attractions Management* (within Leisure Management)
- *Sports Management* (within *Leisure Management*)
- *Health Club Management*
- *Leisure Opportunities*
- *Leisure Marketing* (within *Leisure Opportunities*)
- *Caterer and Hotelkeeper*
- *Sports Illustrated*
- *Leisure Manager*
- *Leisure Week*

Government publications/research

The Office for National Statistics (ONS) is the government agency responsible for the presentation of government statistics and the 10-yearly population census. It provides a wide range of information on society, population, health, social trends, the labour market, business and the economy. Useful publications include:

- *Social Trends*
- *Annual Abstract of Statistics*
- *Family Spending Surveys*
- *General Household Surveys*

ONS also provides a useful booklet, *Statistics for Students*, to assist students with their research. See its website (www.ons.gov.uk) for further details.

Market research organisations

- Mintel (see also internet directory)
- Leisure Industries Research Centre (LIRC)
- Henley Centre for Forecasting
- Key Note (see also internet directory)
- Marketscape

Other sources of information

- Company reports of major leisure and recreation organisations
- Yellow Pages
- Thomson Directories
- Brochures and leaflets
- Travel guides
- Newspapers (sport, leisure, entertainments sections)
- Textbooks

Internet directory

Many organisations involved in leisure and recreation provide information on the worldwide web (www). Their websites provide up-to-date information that you can use for your coursework and assignments. When you use the internet, you will quickly find out that there is an enormous amount of information about leisure and recreation. To help you save time, you may find this list of websites useful. However, this list does not cover everything and you may need to search further for information on a particular topic, organisation or locality. Happy 'surfing'!

Arts Council

The Arts Council site provides information about the arts in the UK and their funding. Online regional arts pages provide information about the English Regional Arts Boards. Also has links to other arts related sites.

- Arts Council

http://www.artscouncil.org.uk
http://www.arts.org.uk

British Olympic Association (BOA)

http://www.olympics.org.uk

British Tourist Authority (BTA)

Extensive range of information about tourism in Britain including sports tourism, tourist destinations, environments to explore, places to stay, activities and attractions, travel information, tourist boards, interactive images and maps of Britain. The site also contains information about careers in the travel and tourism industry and qualifications.

- British Tourist Authority

http://www.visitbritain.com

Careers information in leisure and recreation

These websites provides information about jobs, type of work in the industry, qualifications needed and career choices.

http://www.careercompass.co.uk

http://www.ilam.co.uk
http://www.sprito.org.uk

Department of Culture, Media and Sport
This is the central UK government department responsible for government policy on the arts, sport and recreation, tourism, the National Lottery, libraries, museums and galleries and film.
Department for Culture, Media and Sport
http://www.culture.gov.uk

English Heritage
The 'Places to Visit' site provides information about historic houses, sites and monuments in England. This includes opening times, admission charges, group/school visits, visitor facilities, special events and concerts.
- English Heritage
http://www.english-heritage.org.uk

English and Regional Tourist Boards
The English Tourism Council shares the BTA site listed earlier. For further information about a particular region try the regional tourist boards. Examples include:

- English Tourism Council
http://www.englishtourism.org.uk
- Cumbria
http://www.cumbria-the-lake-district.co.uk
- Northumbria
http://www.northumbria-tourist-board.org.uk
- Yorkshire
http://www.ytb.org.uk
- East of England
http://www.eetb.org.uk
- West Country
http://www.wctb.co.uk
- South East England
http://www.se-eng-tourist-board.org.uk

Governing bodies of sport
There are a large number of governing bodies of sport that provide information about their sport on the net. The Sport England site's information gateway provides links to many of these governing body websites. Here is a selection.
- Athletics
http://www.ukathletics.org
- Football
http://www.the-fa.org
- Canoeing
http://www.bcu.org.uk
- Tennis
http://www.lta.org.uk
- Rugby Union
http://www.rfu.org.uk
- Hockey
http://www.hockeyonline.co.uk

Health and fitness clubs
There are hundreds of health and fitness clubs in the UK. Here are two examples. The Health Club Net site is a useful directory of clubs across the UK that includes details of their location and facilities.
- LivingWell Health Clubs
http://www.livingwell.co.uk
- Holmes Place Health Clubs
http://www.holmesplace.co.uk
- Health Club Net Directory
http://www.health-club.net

Health and safety
- Health and Safety Executive
http://www.hse.gov.uk

Holiday centres
- Butlin's
http://www.butlins.co.uk
- Centre Parcs
http://www.centreparcs.com
- Oasis
http://www. oasishols.co.uk

Industry lead bodies and associations
- Institute of leisure and amenity management (ILAM)
http://www.ilam.co.uk
- Institute of sport and recreation management (ISRM)
http://www.isrm.co.uk
- Sport, recreation and allied occupations industry training organisation (SPRITO)
http://www.sprito.org.uk
- Sprito education and employment zone
http://www.alive2000.com

Institute of Sports Sponsorship (ISS)

http://www.sports-sponsorship.co.uk

International Olympic Committee (IOC)

This site contains information about the winter and summer Olympics and provides links to the sites of all International Sports Federations and National Olympic Committees.

- International Olympic Committee

http://www.olympic.org

Leisure Opportunities

This site provides information about job vacancies in the sport and recreation/leisure industries.

- Leisure Opportunities

http://www.leisureopportunities.co.uk

Leisure Management

This site provides reports and job advertisements from the Leisure Management, Sports Management, Amenities Management and Health Club Management magazines.

- Leisure Management

http://www.leisuremedia.co.uk

Leisurehunt

This extensive database provides information about leisure and tourism facilities in localities throughout the UK, mainland Europe, North America, Canada and Australia. The search of localities within the UK will provide information about hotels, guest houses, hostels, campsites, farms and cottages, art galleries, museums, historic places, restaurants, parks and gardens, golf courses, leisure centres, swimming pools, airports, industrial heritage, libraries, wildlife attractions, racecourses, riding schools and tourist information centres.

- Leisurehunt

http://www.leisurehunt.com

Museums

There are many museums in the UK with websites. A good starting point is the '24 Hour Museum', which provides comprehensive information about a wide range of museums. You will find this site useful when researching museums in a chosen locality.

- 24 hour Museum

http://www.24hourmuseum.org.uk

- National Museum of Science and Industry

http://www.nmsi.ac.uk

This website has information on:
The Science Museum, London
The National Railway Museum, York
The National Museum of Photography, Film and Television

- Royal Armouries

http://www.armouries.org.uk

National Parks

Many National Parks in England and Wales have a website where you can access information about tourism in the Parks. This information may be useful when investigating countryside recreation. Here is a selection of National Park websites:

- Dartmoor National Park

http://www.dartmoor.npa.gov.uk

- Lake District

http://www.lake-district.gov.uk

- North Yorks Moors

http://www.northyorkmoors-npa.gov.uk

- Peak District

http://www.peakdistrict.org

- Pembrokeshire Coast

http://www.pembrokeshirecoast.org

National Coaching Foundation

This site contains details of products, courses, information sources and links to many sports related sites.

- National Coaching Foundation

http://www.ncf.org.uk

National Sports Medicine Institute of the UK

http://www.nsmi.org.uk

National Trust

This site provides information about more than 300 historic buildings and sites to visit. Every week the National Trust receives hundreds of enquiries about its work as the UK's largest land-owning conservation charity. As a major heritage organisation in the voluntary sector, the Trust provides an excellent case study for leisure and tourism students.

The Trust has a designated site for students aged 14+ **(http://www.nt-education.org).**
This provides information about the history of the National Trust, its funding, marketing, access to its properties for disabled visitors and a range of case studies about issues such as nature conservation and the impacts of tourism.

- National Trust

http://www.nationaltrust.org.uk

Northern Ireland Tourist Board

Information about tourism in Northern Ireland.

- Northern Ireland Tourist Board

http://www.ni-tourism.com

Rank Group

The Rank Group is one of the leading leisure, tourism and entertainment companies in the UK. The site provides information about the company and its many businesses which include Mecca Bingo, Grosvenor Casinos, Odeon Cinemas, Rank Entertainment, Tom Cobleigh, Haven, Warner, Butlin's, Oasis and Hard Rock Café.

- Rank Group

http://www.rank.com

Royal Mail

This website provides a range of useful information about customer service and direct mail marketing/promotional activities.

- Royal Mail

http://www.royalmail.co.uk

Sports councils

The sports council sites listed below provide extensive information about sport. The Sports Gateway, within Sport England's site, provides access to a wide range of sports organisations and contacts throughout England. You can also find links to organisations concerned with the promotion, development and administration of sport in England.

- Sport England

http://www.english.sports.gov.uk

- UK Sport

http://www.uksport.gov.uk

- Sport Scotland

http://www.ssc.org.uk

- Sports Council for Northern Ireland

http://www.sportni.org

- Sports Council for Wales

http://www.sports-council-wales.co.uk

Sports Industry Federation

The Federation represents a wide range of trade associations within the sports industry including manufacturers and retailers.

- Sports Industry Federation

http://www.sportlife.org.uk

Statistics and research

There is a wide range of research and statistics about leisure and recreation available, including:

- **http://www.staruk.org.uk**
- **http://www.Keynote.co.uk**

Free access to its executive summaries on-line.

- **http://www.Mintel.com**

Free access to report contents and introductions.

- **http://www.ons.gov.uk**

Information on the Office for National Statistics (ONS) website ranges from climate data to unemployment statistics. You can also search for statistical publications to find the subject you are interested in. The most frequently requested datasets and questions are also available on the Biz/ed website:

- **http://www.bized.ac.uk/dataserv/onsdata.htm**

StatBase is an extensive online information resource which can be accessed via the Government Statistical Service:

- **http://www.statistics.gov.uk**

Theme parks

There are many theme parks in the UK and the majority have websites. Here are four examples:

- Blackpool Pleasure Beach

http://www.bpbltd.com

- Alton Towers

http://www.alton-towers.co.uk

- Legoland, Windsor

http://www.lego.com/legoland/windsor

- Thorpe Park

http://www.thorpepark.co.uk

Virgin Group

Richard Branson's Virgin Group is one of the largest leisure and tourism operators in the UK. The site provides a company history, details of latest developments, career opportunities and information on the various Virgin businesses. These include Virgin Atlantic, Virgin Express, Virgin Trains, Virgin Holidays, Virgin Cinemas and Virgin Hotels.

- Virgin Group

http://www.virgin.com

Wales Tourist Board

Extensive information about tourism in Wales including holiday destinations, tours, places to stay and things to do. There is also information about the Rugby World Cup, 1999.

- Wales Tourist Board

http://www.tourism.wales.gov.uk

What's On

Britain's national performing arts information and ticketing service. At any one time, the database has information about more than 2,000 performances around the country. 'What's On' provides information about events in the UK, including theatre, opera, music, dance, ballet, and comedy.

- What's On

http://www.whatson.com

Yellow Pages

UK Web is a directory listing of websites in the UK. Organisations are grouped by category, such as travel and tourism, sports and leisure, entertainment and music, education and training.

- Yellow Pages

http://www.yell.co.uk

Index

Numbers in bold show the page on which the word is defined or used as a key word.